AFTER
CONVICTION

Ronald L. Goldfarb
and
Linda R. Singer

A TOUCHSTONE BOOK
PUBLISHED BY SIMON AND SCHUSTER

Acknowledgments

A grant from the Ford Foundation made writing this book possible. To it, and personally to Bill Pincus and Chris Edley, we repeat our immense thanks.

We wish to note the special contribution of Joanne Goldfarb, who along with designing our book's jacket, helped with many parts of our work and who, in particular, did much of the research along with the drawings which are reproduced in Chapter I.

We also wish to thank Dean Ralph Nash and Professor Richard Allen for making the facilities of the George Washington University Law School available to us.

Winifred Garcia typed the manuscript (and what seems like thousands of drafts) and kept our files—all with great competence, personal interest and good nature beyond the call of duty. We would also like to thank Gypsy da Silva for being our perfect editor.

We were assisted by several people who did research on particular points for us at different stages of our work during the past three years. In particular, our associate Sharon Shanoff is to be credited for research which we were able to include in Chapters II and VIII, and Stephen Booth helped accumulate data on federal programs which we were able to use in Chapter VIII.

We were counseled and helped by hundreds of informed and interested officials, experts, scholars, prisoners, ex-convicts—far too many to enumerate here. Several colleagues and friends reviewed portions of the manuscript and made helpful suggestions for improvements. We expect that they all know how grateful we are to them for their time and aid. However, we would be remiss not to say a special thanks to Norman

Carlson, the director of the Federal Bureau of Prisons, for being especially kind and helpful to two apparent critics and to Lloyd Hooker and Priscilla Doucette, the Bureau's able librarians, for their assistance.

Washington, D.C.

RONALD GOLDFARB and LINDA SINGER

Contents

INTRODUCTION

This book was first published in 1973. It was the product of years of earlier research, travel and experiences. We welcome the opportunity to revisit our text now, almost a decade after we began our original project.

Our book deals with the criminal justice system after the time of a defendant's conviction of a crime and continuing throughout the subsequent correctional processes. We cover a broad field including such diverse subjects as sentencing, probation, parole, clemency, prisons and community programs. For this reason, our book is long and thesaurus-like; it is the book we wished existed when we began our research. We are pleased because we have learned that it has been of use to professionals and students in the field.

Looking back, we are satisfied with our endeavor and comfortable with our conclusions. Nonetheless, the last five years have been marked by several trends that are worth noting. First, we will mention some of our perspectives on the correctional world and some conclusions we have drawn.

The American correction system is very American, does little correction, and is not very systematic.

It is very American in that both the contrasting systems of detention and probation were developed in this country; their evolution composes interesting episodes in this country's social history, which we will describe in chapters I and IV. For now, however, it should be noted that the resort to complete and prolonged detention as a system of punishment and the development of the system of probation or supervision in the community as an alternative to institutionalization are schemes that America created and exported to the world, and are now the key modern techniques of correction.

Our system is American in another respect. Social institutions tend to reflect the style and values of the societies of which they are a part. Certainly this is true of prisons; it was borne out by our visits to penal institutions abroad and to those in this country, as well. American prisons are vast, violent, dramatic, seething, and loaded with every conceivable problem; at the same time they contain great talent and resources, much as this country does.

So the system is quite American; whether it corrects is another question. Such personal reformation, rehabilitation or resocialization that may result from the present correction system occurs despite the system rather than because of it.

We profess to be correcting and reforming while following a senseless course. Real treatment is rare. Useful programs are unusual. The correction system interrupts the education and displaces the family connections of young offenders when it institutionalizes them, even though all informed studies have shown that most offenders are poorly educated and come from broken homes.

While statistics are incomplete and conclusions drawn from them are uncertain, no one disagrees that recidivism is very high. The best speculation places repeater rates between 50 and 80 percent. The average prisoner is back in society within three years, repeating crimes within a year.

As correctional expert Hans Mattick observed, "No business enterprise that turned out a product with a 30 to 50 percent failure rate could long remain in business, but our prisons and jails, with recidivism rates of that order, have been doing the public's business in that fashion for the past 150 years."

Does correction accomplish deterrence, then, if it does not accomplish rehabilitation? It is doubtful. The system has operated for two centuries with progressively worse results. One survey of prisoners disclosed that most inmates felt they had acted precipitously. They recalled having no thoughts prior to their crimes about the potential punishment that might be the consequence of their misconduct. A British survey of criminals reported recently that: "The men were detached and objective in their discussion of offenses, as if talking about some act of quite neutral morality. The consequences of being caught were unpleasant, but rarely was there any suggestion that the conduct was in itself reprehensible."

Professional criminals assume the risk of incarceration as an inherent and necessary chance of their business. Still others are so deranged or addicted or out of control that they would not be deterred even if they thought about such considerations as going to prison if caught. The people who are likely to be deterred from committing much serious crime do not require severe sentences to be deterred.

Those who argue that imprisonment at least deters crime for the period during which the criminals are imprisoned overlook the assaults, sexual attacks, thefts, property damage, arson and riots that are common in prisons. Furthermore, the vagaries of the system are such that many of the worst criminals never are caught, tried, convicted or sentenced to prison.

The system is not corrective in dealing with victims of crimes, either. In fact, for the most part the system ignores victims. Having abandoned antiquated systems of private law enforcement that did act against transgressors for the benefit of victims, our governmental system kept the vengeance but ignored the reparation. Victim compensation is in many cases the only, but certainly in all cases the clearest, most realistic and necessary aspect of criminal justice. It is hard to fathom why compensation and reparation are not key goals, at least, in cases of economic crimes. With unfortunately rare exceptions, they are no part of our system.

Is the American correction system really a system? What is generally referred to as "the correction system" is a composition of different parts of other systems that touch independently on the criminal justice process. Sentencing is a function of the courts; penal institutions are run by correctional officials; probation and parole offices usually operate as parts of both or as separate agencies; clemency usually is the province of the chief executive. Each frequently operates not only independently of the others but sometimes antagonistically as well.

The so-called "system" is composed of local, state and federal agencies. The resources, information, goals and philosophy of each collaborating agency frequently are parochial and inconsistent with its counterparts. The processes are similar only in that each operates with pathetic sameness upon the young and old criminal, the sick and the professional offender, the reformable and the inveterate convict, the repeater and the novice.

The philosophical aims of the system are so incompatible as to doom it from the start. How can the same process punish, deter, reform and rehabilitate? Does the system accomplish any of these purposes? When Sanford Bates, first director of the Federal Bureau of Prisons, was asked by President Franklin D. Roosevelt whether the goal of the federal prison system should be to reform the men incarcerated or to deter the general public, Bates answered, "Why not both?" That ideal notion causes the confounding crosscurrents of the correctional world.

What is more, the separate parts of the system operate without data or sufficient records to illuminate the efficiency or even the direction of the programs and institutions. Parole, to use one example, cannot be evaluated since there are no records to demonstrate its success or failure. We simply do not know what happens to individuals after they go off parole status—whether they do better than those who were released outright.

The most sovereign powers then, the severest social instruments that the state uses on its individuals, are ungoverned and in Professor Herbert Wechsler's words "unprincipled" and "anarchical."

Indeed, in the few isolated instances where data has been gathered to test any correctional hypotheses, there have been surprising discoveries that question the fundamental bases of the programs. For example, studies have shown that treatment programs do not treat, schemes for deterrence do not deter. We are persuaded that the most effective correction system is the one which uses the system least.

It is a paradox that, bad as our prisons are, our jails are far worse, even though the latter house men who have not yet had a trial (many of whom will never go to prison) and those who have been sentenced for comparatively minor crimes.

This chaotic and destructive process proceeds while enlightened correctional commentators call for a "continuum"—an integrated, coherent system to accomplish the perplexing job of correction. The whole post-conviction process should be unified and should draw upon various specialized experts in the community, as needed.

Ironically, along with the prisoners who are the system's consumers, no one knows better than the correctional establishment how bad the present system is. While conducting our research, we asked every correctional official the same question. How many of the people in your prison need to be there in order to protect people in free society from personal injury? Without exception they estimated that between 10 and 20 percent needed to be locked up. "If there is one thing that I am against in corrections," one official told us, "it is incarceration." The correction system is the only American social institution whose administrators do not believe in the institution they are administering.

By the late 1960's, then, most observers had concluded that the correctional system had failed, whether judged by standards of public safety, economics or humanity. In our view, the situation in the United States during the last decade was ripe for correctional reform. Riots all over the country—particularly the nightmare at Attica—riveted public and media attention to the problems of the prison system. A tangential result of the era of war protest and the drug culture was the introduction of the middle and upper classes to the inside of the criminal justice system. They did not like what they saw; and they said so publicly. In addition, their criticisms were repeated in high level, highly visible commission reports, books and studies about correction. The country was ready to move.

There were three possible directions for change: two that we have witnessed and a third that we would have preferred.

The first possibility was to do more of the same, only in longer draughts and more potent doses: longer sentences, less probation and parole, less use of community-based programs, no clemency, the renewal of capital punishment. Despite all the evidence that these techniques had failed in the past, this approach, whose advocates were led by former law-and-order President Richard Nixon, called for more reliance on old ways, in the guise of toughness.

This approach has simplistic and political appeal. Despite historic evidence to the contrary, it sounds tough and realistic to argue that if someone does something wrong we should lock him up and throw away the key. But the price we pay in money and public safety for our present correctional system is already high. Revving-up this system will only increase the costs without curing the problem.

A second direction for reform called for keeping but improving the present system, making what the convicts call "sweet joints." Advocates of this approach want to improve the system, but not to change it. They would send guards to college, build new "model" prisons, and attempt to alter the custodial atmosphere of institutions to a more social-service cast.

This is the rehabilitative model. It would replace simple imprisonment with treatment techniques based on such theories as behavior modification. This approach has impressed many reform-minded correctional officials, and demonstration projects are underway. The Government has loosened its purse strings to psychologists expressing an interest in penology. In our opinion, the rehabilitative model leads to a second, well-intentioned but fundamental and centuries-long error in correctional policy.

Reform could take a third direction. It would involve scrapping our old-fashioned correctional system and tearing down most of the prison walls. It would resist institutionalization, diverting offenders into varied and versatile community-based programs, and decriminalizing parts of the law relating to vice and victimless crimes. Wherever possible, it would exploit social welfare and health systems to deal with such groups as alcoholics, addicts, young offenders, and sick people in the community.

This system, which we prefer, would compensate the victims of crimes, and employ offenders and former offenders in the correctional process, it would rely as much as possible on contracts with private groups to carry out many correctional functions. Institutions would be few, reserved for the relative minority of hopeless and dangerous cases. The prisons we did not tear down would be redesigned, restaffed and reprogrammed according to more civilized standards.

This approach lacks political appeal and has few advocates. But it is the approach that we believe makes the most sense.

Before backing into the former approaches, it would have made sense to give the latter one a fair try. Yet, we seem to have ignored this possibility for real reform that could have occurred during the last five years and wavered between the tired and traditional conservative and liberal approaches.

Meanwhile, as theoreticians debated the direction our reforms might take, certain trends developed that are worth noting.

1. IMPRISONMENT

In the years since this book was written, decision-makers seem to have chosen to get tougher with offenders and have placed even greater reliance on imprisonment.

At the end of the 1960's, the use of imprisonment as the characteristic response to crime was on the wane. Despite a rising population and a rising crime rate, the number of people in state and federal prisons had decreased from a high of 220,000 in 1962 to a low of 188,000 in 1969. Prison populations continued to decline until 1973, when the National Advisory Commission on Criminal Justice Standards and Goals recommended that no new prisons be built for ten years owing to the reduced need for institutional confinement.

The downward trend of prison populations in the late 1960's began to be reversed in the early 1970's. By 1976, the population of state and federal prisons had risen to an all-time high of 250,000; it continues to increase. Virtually every prison in the country is overcrowded, with large numbers of prisoners doubled, tripled and quadrupled in tiny cells, packed into dreary dormitories, and even sleeping on the floor. Still more untried inmates (about 161,000 on any given day according to a recent census) back up in already cramped county and city jails.

In an effort to provide more space quickly, ingenious prison authorities have commissioned ships, tents, and trailers to house the overflow. The Law Enforcement Assistance Administration responded by purchasing a fleet of trailers to be made available for use as temporary prisons by state and local authorities. Hapless prison administrators call for new construction to relieve the inhuman overcrowding; outsiders opposed to the overuse of institutions warn that additional buildings would only encourage judges to sentence even greater numbers of defendants to prison.

There may be more than one explanation for this dramatic reversal of what had appeared to be a steady reduction in the prison population. The most obvious reason is that criminal justice officials are responding to the punitive climate that has overtaken the general public. Judges are imposing longer sentences; parole boards are reluctant to grant early release.

It is ironic, however, that the use of probation, at least in major cities, seems to be rising along with the use of imprisonment, perhaps as a response to overcrowded prisons. It is likely that at least some of the increasing volume of prisoners is attributable to improved police and prosecutory practices, which have resulted in greater numbers of convicted offenders to be sentenced.

A second explanation focuses on demographics. Although the country currently is experiencing a declining birthrate, the population most likely to be sentenced to prison is the fifteen- to twenty-nine-year-olds, particularly racial minorities and urban residents. This age group is at its peak and is expected to continue to grow until about 1990. Even then, the leveling off may depend on the fate of urban ghettoization. Thus, it can be expected that prison populations will continue to expand unless public policy is altered dramatically.

2. THE COURTS AND CORRECTIONAL REFORM

Chapter VII describes the relaxation by the courts of their traditional "hands-off" attitude toward the constitutional rights of convicted offenders. The active role in prison reform taken by the federal courts during the past ten years may have spurred more changes within the prisons than all the exhortations by reformers over the preceding two hundred years.

When the Supreme Court, led by Chief Justice Warren E. Burger, began to accept cases involving prisons and parole, it was hoped that the often-stated interest of the Chief Justice in correctional reform would be reflected in decisions of the Court. Yet, early decisions by the Burger Court affirming prisoners' rights to religious freedom, access to law libraries, and detailed procedural protections during parole and probation revocation proceedings soon gave way to Court rulings sanctioning blanket prohibitions of interviews with prisoners by the news media, a series of cases rejecting or minimizing due process protections when prisoners are disciplined or transferred to more punitive facilities, and the imposition of renewed procedural obstacles to the access of state prisoners to federal courts. The earlier, short-lived movement by the federal courts away from the historic judicial "hands-off" doctrine appears to have come full circle.

Part of the explanation for the renewed deference to the discretion of correctional administrators may be attributed to the changed personnel of the Supreme Court. However, some systemic developments also are relevant. By the end of 1975, prisoners' suits accounted for one-sixth of all filings in federal courts—the largest single category of federal civil litigation. Coupled with what many judges consider to be a flood of complaints, there appears to be growing disillusionment on the part of both judges and lawyers with the courts as the primary means to deal with prisoners' grievances. The time required to pursue an issue through the courts, the enormous sums of money involved in seeking judicial redress and the difficulties of enforcing favorable judgments inside the closed setting of prisons all have combined to temper early enthusiasm over the courts as primary agents of correctional reform.

Administrative grievance procedures, on the other hand, have been gaining acceptance among correctional administrators as less expensive and more responsive to their needs than litigation. Inmates, for their part, are willing to submit their complaints through administrative grievance mechanisms where the procedures include three crucial elements: participation by inmates themselves in resolving grievances; appeal to some person or agency independent of the department of corrections; and responses to problems within relatively brief, enforceable time limits.[1]

Beginning in 1972, the California Youth Authority, and the New York and South Carolina Departments of Corrections have developed procedures that enable inmates to appear before grievance committees composed of other inmates and institutional staff members and to appeal decisions to advisory arbitration by volunteers from the general community. When inmates at Attica went on strike in July, 1976, officials attributed much of the success of peaceful settlement to the efforts of the inmate-staff grievance committee. Other states, including Minnesota and Connecticut, have established independent correctional ombudsmen answerable to the governor or the legislature; others still continue to rely on totally internal procedures or inmate councils as their sole means of resolving complaints.

1. See J. M. Keating, Jr., V. A. McArthur, M. K. Lewis. K. G. Sebelius and L. R. Singer, *Grievance Mechanisms in Correctional Institutions* (1975).

3. REHABILITATION

Since the 1790's, when prisons first were built in the United States, correctional reformers have hoped to find a cure for crime by curing criminals. As time went on, the quest for rehabilitation described in Chapter I, became less religious (enforced penitence) and more pseudo-scientific (enforced treatment). A "medical model" of correction became fashionable in the 1960's. The idea was that professionals, with sufficient flexibility and expertise, could cure criminals. The corollary to this idea was that these experts must be given unfettered discretion to prescribe particular kinds of treatment for particular kinds of criminals and to control the length of prison terms.

While there were sceptics in the early 1960's, it was not until the end of the decade that most professionals in the field reached the conclusion expressed throughout this book, that prisons could not rehabilitate. Then, in 1974, Robert Martinson, a sociologist, compiled and published a review of all research studies of correctional programs that had been conducted to date.[2] The review concluded that, whether because of ineffective programs or inadequate research, there was no proof that any program of coerced rehabilitation, conducted in prison or in the community, made a demonstrable difference in the likelihood that offenders would commit future crimes.

Martinson's conclusions, supported by most of the other sociologists and criminologists who have reviewed the data, had several important implications for correctional programming. The pretensions of treatment professionals to superior expertise, and their consequent justification of unfettered discretion to treat offenders, were seriously undermined. So too was the rationale for compelling the participation of offenders in rehabilitative programs. If it could not be demonstrated that such programs actually succeeded in rehabilitating those who took part, there was little basis on which to refute the arguments against coerced participation, which are based on considerations of personal privacy and autonomy. And the philosophical justification of the indeterminate sentence, which permits administrators to release prisoners when they appear to have been rehabilitated, ceased to exist.

On the other hand, many of the professionals in the system became demoralized by their apparent inability to change offender's behavior and wondered whether the new data would provide an excuse to decrease the system's already skimpy level of services. Such programs, although imperfect, generally are not harmful and represent a benign attempt to provide services to people whose lives we control.

4. REDUCING DISCRETION

Partly as a result of the general disenchantment with the claims and the excesses of rehabilitation, much scholarly attention is being focused on the

2. Robert Martinson, *The Public Interest*, 22, Spring, 1974, "What Works?—Questions and Answers About Prison Reform."

inequality and unpredictability of the criminal justice system. As we discussed at some length in chapters III and V, both the sentencing of defendants and the release of prisoners on parole frequently depend more on who an offender is than on the seriousness of the crime he or she has committed. Such disparate treatment is justified on the basis that middle-class criminals are punished more than poor criminals by conviction and loss of reputation, and that the middle-class offender has reformative resources in the community not available to the poor.

Thus the report by the blue-ribbon Committee for the Study of Incarceration, published in 1976, recommended the imposition of legislatively prescribed, determinate sentences based on the seriousness of the crime committed, termed the offender's "deserts."[3] This philosophy has had a significant influence. For example, both California and Maine recently abolished indeterminate sentences and the discretionary authority of parole boards to release prisoners. In devising new flat-time sentences (subject to slight reduction or increase by a judge only on the basis of aggravating or mitigating circumstances associated with the crime or on the basis of the offender's prior criminal record), the California Legislature selected the average time in prison currently being served for the crime in question.

These and similar developments will have a salutary effect on reducing some of the inequities in the operation of the correctional system. The danger is that the welcome focus on equality may have deflected reformers' attention from the costly, draconian overuse of imprisonment in the United States. Although it may be evenhanded to send all convicted criminals, rich and poor alike, to prison, we cannot be satisfied with a principle of equal evil.

Watergate is a classic example. Many critics seized on Watergate as the perfect example of the double standard of criminal justice and called for harsher sentencing of Watergate defendants. We share this concern over a double standard. Yet, we also think that the system gains nothing by being equally cruel to Watergate and other white-collar defendants as it is to poor and minority defendants who have committed street crimes.

Watergate might have been used to set an example in the treatment of white-collar criminals that could have been expanded to cover other criminals. Tough, substantial sentencing in the community, working for significant periods on public service projects, would make sense for Watergate defendants, white-collar defendants, indeed all defendants.

We fear that the revision of criminal codes to prescribe a narrower range of penalties will not produce the fundamental reforms that we believe are needed unless it is coupled with a legislative prohibition on the use of imprisonment for most crimes and the mandating of alternative sanctions. This is the approach taken by the American Bar Association—Institute for Judicial Administration Joint Commission on Juvenile Justice Standards. In its proposed *Standards on Dispositions,* the Commission recommends a

3. Andrew von Hirsch, "Doing Justice: The Choice of Punishments" (1976).

variety of sanctions for juvenile crime, almost all of which can be carried out in the community. A juvenile's removal from home is authorized only in cases of serious or repeated criminal behavior.

Liberal critics persistently have provided the counterpoint to hardliners' efforts to increase the use of imprisonment. If those critics, disillusioned by the failure of the correctional system to change offenders' behavior, fail to challenge the severity of the system itself as well as the unfairness with which it is administered, there is unlikely to be any fundamental reform.

5. ALTERNATIVES TO IMPRISONMENT

While there has been much talk about the use of alternative punishments, more humane and less costly than imprisonment, the American correction system continues to provide little choice between the total custody provided by imprisonment and the minimal incursion on liberty provided by probation. In view of the meager resources allocated to probation and the large caseloads and multiple responsibilities assigned to probation officers, we are deluding ourselves if we think that this one widely used alternative to imprisonment provides either meaningful services or supervision that is anything more than cursory.

There has been a greatly increased use of pretrial diversion since this book was written. Such programs, referred to in Chapter II, commonly require the participation of people who have been arrested in programs in lieu of trial and imprisonment. In some cases, particularly those involving alcoholics and drug addicts, minor offenders, who otherwise would have gone to jail, are being diverted to treatment programs. It appears, however, that much of the clientele of diversion programs consists of juvenile status offenders, whose "offenses" would not be illegal for adults, or of people whose cases otherwise would have been dismissed. In other words, the programs may not be alternatives to formal processing through the criminal justice system but may be bringing more people into the system who otherwise would have been filtered out.

During the next decade, we hope that there will be greater impetus toward the development of alternative sentences. Prison populations are up drastically at the same time that state and local budgets generally are being cut. The costs of constructing new prisons, which range from $30,000 to $50,000 a bed, frequently are prohibitive. At the same time, a few courts have ruled that crowding prisoners into less than a prescribed minimum of space violates the Eighth Amendment's constitutional prohibition of cruel and unusual punishments.

Models of alternative programs for convicted offenders already exist and are described throughout this book, particularly in chapters IV and VIII. The most important program, in our opinion, is restitution to victims of crime. Dealing with the problems of victims should be at the top of any sensible agenda for reform. It also lends itself to constructive sentencing practices. In addition to restitution, alternatives include the payment of fines to the state, the performance of services for the benefit of the commu-

nity at large, intensive supervision in the community, and the use of different forms of intermittent forms of confinement, including work release and
day custody. The challenge lies in expanding such alternatives from the
exception to the norm and in making them subject to standards of rational-
ity, fairness and consistency.

I

The Sources of Our System

The general practice of imprisonment as punishment for the commission of crime is less than two centuries old. "Few realize that America gave to the world the modern prison system," Barnes and Teeters reported in their book *New Horizons in Criminology*. "Fewer still know that it was chiefly the product of humanity." Fewer still, it might now be added, have questioned how such humanity could have been so misused, or noted such a paradox as that which attributes so gross and failing an institution as our prison system to the reform efforts of well-intentioned and good men.

Of course, men have been detained against their will at all times in history; cannibals even kept their victims to fatten for future feasts. From primitive to medieval times, men progressed modestly in their means of punishing their fellow men. Vengeance through retaliatory blood feuds or compensation between the private parties involved were the personal means of responding to crimes. But as the state assumed the collective responsibility for enforcing criminal law, ceremonial murder gave way to ingenious public tortures. Techniques such as burning and drowning were replaced by more moderate ones such as mutilating and branding. Humiliation was a part of each technique; hard labor was required by law to be "publicly and disgracefully imposed" upon prisoners.

In Europe, until a century and a half ago, and in England, from whose common law our legal system derived, capital punishment was decreed for hundreds of crimes, and when capital punishment was not resorted to, corporal punishment was the alternative; hands and other

19

appropriate appendages were lopped off. Offenders were pilloried and subjected to public degradation. In some situations, the property of the convict was confiscated and he was banished from the country to labor in frightful prison colonies.

A few isolated prisons existed in early history, particularly in ecclesiastical dominions. In the sixteenth century, with the fall of feudalism and the rise of vagrants and roving outlaws in England and on the Continent, came the workhouses (in England called Bridewells), in which large groups of paupers were housed indefinitely and without care in large dormitories. Some of these places eventually developed cells and required hard labor.

The early prisons were, in the words of Yale historian George Wilson Pierson, "simply boarding-houses reserved for the safe lodging of the impecunious and the unfortunate: places where debtors and those awaiting trial could be confined. . . ." These workhouses, modeled after a species that flowered on the Continent in the mid-sixteenth century, especially in Holland, were reserved for the poor, the idle, "ne'er-do-wells, lunatics, disobedient children, and lepers," left over after the collapse of feudalism. The detention facilities were terrible places—overcrowded, dark, dirty, models of idleness and vice, without ventilation and with the scantiest of facilities. In some, inmates were made to pay for the privilege of their incarceration. If they could not afford the fee, they were imprisoned indefinitely. The unfortunate clientele of these establishments were thrown together, treated oppressively and lived in degrading debauchery, profligacy and squalor.

There were a few isolated, historical predecessors of our present prison system. Pope Clement XI in 1704, for example, founded in Rome St. Michele, a papal prison for incorrigible youngsters, and Hippolyte Vilain XIII erected a house of correction in Ghent, Belgium, in the early 1770s. The famous English reformer John Howard reported them in his late-eighteenth-century tracts. Howard succeeded in getting the British Parliament to approve a planned penitentiary system, and a few cell houses were actually built, notably those in Sussex (1775), Norfolk (1785) and Millbank (1821). There were similarities between the characteristics of penal prisons and the Church confinements—monasticism, meager subsistence, sexual abstinence and the contemplation of past transgressions.

Confinement historically was essentially an intermediate step in the punishment process. In America today it has become the chief end of the correction system. The first prisons were built to hold people until their trials or executions, or at times for the confinement of debtors and religious or political offenders. The imprisonment decreed by courts was reserved for special situations. Prisons were places of temporary housing to await the actual punishment decreed.

Our criminal justice system still employs fines, capital punishment and probation as alternative sentencing techniques. Corporal punishment is rarely condoned, as it still is in some societies and as it once was in ours.[1] Essentially, our correction system is built around imprisonment. The story of the development in this country (and the spread elsewhere) of the prison system is a chapter of American history that portrays the dismal failure of a benign dream.

In our early colonial period, the harsh criminal codes and sentencing practices of the Continent and Stuart England prevailed. Criminals in the colonies were killed, flogged, mutilated, branded, put in stocks, lashed. Criminals were released after their physical punishment—and executed men, needless to say, required no penal confinement.

Reform-minded observers late in the seventeenth century and early in the eighteenth, particularly the American Quakers in Pennsylvania, deplored prevailing conditions and pressed for more enlightened practices. Prisons run by the state as agencies of punishment were a result of their reaction against the profanities and laxities of earlier penal systems and their opposition to corporal and capital punishment. In 1682, at the initiation of William Penn, one who himself had been an inmate in the Tower of London, a law was passed making hard labor in a house of correction the chief form of punishing most crimes.

Enlightened Rationalist notions of the times sought social progress through purging superstitious convictions and applying more humane treatment to the sick, the poor and other infirm as well as prisoners. English, French, Italian and American writers such as Bentham, Voltaire, Montesquieu, Beccaria, Livingston and Jefferson criticized the crudeness of the prevailing criminal system at this time. These forces came together in Philadelphia, the country's cultural center, during the late eighteenth century.

---

1. Delaware Code Annotated, Section 3908, provides: "The punishment of whipping shall be inflicted publicly by strokes on the bare back well laid on." The statute goes so far as to decree that in one county the whipping shall be done by the Board of Trustees of the county workhouse, while in two other counties it shall be done by the warden of the jail. A case in 1963, *Balser v. State*, 195 A.2d 757, held that a sentence of twenty lashes for robbery did not constitute cruel and unusual punishment.

Indeed, the present system of imprisonment generally could be questioned as (a) condoning some corporal punishment, and (b) being a form of corporal and psychological punishment in itself.

When in 1794 Pennsylvania abolished capital punishment for most crimes, the purpose for prisons and the theory of punishment changed. The need for reform was manifest: What to do with convicted criminals if they are not to be killed or maimed? How to resocialize an errant man? According to one prison chronicler, the moment of the conception of the American prison system can be pinpointed:

> Pennsylvania had replaced execution and corporal punishment with hard labor performed in public odium. Prisoners dug ditches or swept the streets while chained to a heavy iron ball and dressed in harlequin suits. Dr. Benjamin Rush, an eminent physician and a signer of the Declaration of Independence, opposed this so-called reform. On March 9, 1787, he read a paper on the subject before a small gathering in the home of Benjamin Franklin. *That date can serve as well as any for the beginning of the movement that produced the American prison system.*
>
> Dr. Rush proposed imprisonment instead of public degradation as the penalty for crime. He proposed that criminals be classified and segregated, that they be put to work, since work was the road to regeneration, that their sentences should be indeterminate and geared to their progress toward regeneration.
>
> The Rush group became the Pennsylvania Prison Society. Among its members were many Quakers.[2] [Italics added.]

The Quakers and the Philadelphia Society for the Alleviation of the Miseries of the Public Prisons led by Dr. Rush, Caleb Lownes, John Connelly and Robert Vaux, brought about the major change which began the first penitentiary system. Their goal was to take the publicity, venality and cruelty out of the criminal process and to end the debauchery and evil waste characteristic of local jails. Their moral and religious scruples were violated by the brutality of the criminal justice system and the waste of human life implicit in the colonies' adopted schemes.

> While the principal recommendation made by Dr. Rush, namely the treatment of offenders not according to the crimes committed but rather according to the problems underlying the crimes, was not put into effect until approximately 150 years later, the more obvious recommendation that "doing time" should replace capital and corporal punishment was in 1790 written into American penal philosophy for all time.[3]

2. Martin, *Break Down the Walls: American Prisons: Present, Past and Future* (1953).
3. Gill, "Correctional Philosophy and Architecture," 36 A.I.A. *Journal* 67 (1961).

The Quakers decided that the best way to reform criminals was to lock them in cells and keep them alone—in total and unrelieved solitude —day and night. The use of solitary cells as a means of repentance was an extreme adoption of John Howard's very reasonable urgings of partial segregation; it also was previewed in the religious writings of the seventeenth-century Florentine churchman Filippo Franci and the French scholar and Benedictine monk Jean Mabillon, who had suggested, almost in complete anticipation of the Pennsylvania system:

> Penitents might be secluded in cells . . . and there employed in various sorts of labor. To each cell might be joined a little garden, where at appointed hours they might take an airing and cultivate the garden. They might, while assisting in public worship, be placed in separate stalls.[4]

The ideal of the Quakers' notion was that out of this enforced solitariness, prisoners would have no alternative but to consider their acts, repent and reform themselves. Part of their theory was that to bring this about convicts had to be kept from contaminating one another and be forced to remain alone and idle. They would, it was thought, emerge penitent and chaste. Solitary confinement, one report noted, helped the prisoner "fill the zodiac of his time, which would otherwise be spent in unavailing complaint. Shut out from a tumultuous world, and separated from those equally guilty with himself, he can indulge his remorse unseen and find ample opportunity for reflection and reformation."[5]

Out of their hopeful and high-minded but misplaced intentions was to develop the Pennsylvania solitary, cellular system of penitentiaries. The very word "penitentiary" comes from the heart of the Quaker idea of the criminal's need for penitence and repentance. Indeed, Dr. Rush had insisted that the word "prison" not be used as it was associated with places of promiscuity and debauchery.

The first Quaker version of the cell block was built in Philadelphia in 1790 within the existing three-story stone Walnut Street Jail (erected as a general jail in 1773 but converted in 1790 to a state prison). Penitentiary House, the "cradle" of the modern penitentiary, as one scholar called it, sat in the middle of the famous old jail; it was reserved for the solitary confinement of sentenced, hardened criminals. The plain brick

4. DeFord, *Stone Walls* 46 (1962).
5. Report of the Inspectors of the Western Penitentiary, 1854, Legislative Documents 271.

building, forty feet by twenty-five feet, housed eight cells on each floor. Each separate outside cell in the blocks (separated by a corridor) was small, dark (six feet wide, eight feet long and nine feet high), with a small attached yard leading from the cells on the ground floor. Until 1835, when it was abandoned, it served as the first experiment for a new and evolving system.

The sentenced inmates were kept alone and indolent in tiny cells with small, grated windows so high atop the outside wall of the cell that they "could perceive neither heaven nor earth"; they existed without conveniences or communication of any kind. Inmates were given work to do alone in their cell, and eventually together in small groups. Food was spare; the accommodations in the rooms of whitewashed plaster were austere and grim. A lead pipe in the corner of each cell was the privy. There was no socialization or even communication. The walls were so thick as to muffle any attempt at conversation between cells. The sex, drinking and idleness that earlier characterized the common jail were eliminated. Recreation was unknown. The men were preached to regularly.

A crude attempt was made to classify prisoners so that women, vagrants, capital offenders and debtors were not intermingled. The prison population reflected the society of the day. Many were servants who stole from their masters, oppressed seamen who jumped ship, runaway slaves, the poor and impotent. The solitary system of confinement could be considered an advance only relative to the excesses it replaced.

The Walnut Street Jail failed after an experiment that lasted from 1790 to 1835. Escapes, riots, administrative and financial problems collapsed this historic landmark institution which so widely and profoundly influenced prison architecture and administration. The sponsors had hoped to serve the public, help their fellow man and uplift the unfortunate. They were not to be deterred in their zeal and drew upon their experiences here to transfer their reforms in a bigger and better way.

The first complete penitentiary institutions with the program and plan of the Pennsylvania reformers were the Western Penitentiary on the Ohio River on the outskirts of Pittsburgh and Cherry Hill, the Eastern Penitentiary in Philadelphia, both formidable bastilles. The overcrowding and financial strain on the Walnut Street Jail and the difficulties transporting men from far distances led to the planning of a more systemic approach to the initial penitentiary plan.

St. Michele featured tiers of outside cells on each side of an interior corridor that was used as a workshop. Ghent had eight wings composed of inside double-tiered cell blocks (like the later Auburn prison), each radiating around a central rotunda. The late-eighteenth-century prisons in Norfolk and Sussex included solitary confinement in single cells, hard labor and segregation of sexes. But until John Haviland designed the Philadelphia prison and redid the penitentiary in Pittsburgh there was no organized system of prisons anywhere. These two penitentiaries in Pennsylvania emerged in 1829 and 1836 to house the first planned sovereign system of penitentiaries in the world.

At Western, $60,000 was appropriated in 1826 to build an institution on eight acres of land in the center of the city for solitary confinement of sentenced criminals. The first building, a circular one, contained outside cell blocks of five tiers each with service corridors between. Cells were eight feet long, six feet wide and ten feet high, somewhat smaller than the $100,000 Eastern Penitentiary constructed a few years later in Philadelphia whose 250 original cells were eleven feet nine inches long by seven feet six inches wide by sixteen feet high and whose principal characteristic also was solitary confinement with no labor. Ten years later a second Western penitentiary was built on the style of the new Auburn, New York, penitentiary, which followed but changed the Philadelphia form.

At each penitentiary, a walled yard was provided behind each cell on the ground floors where solitary exercise was permitted. At Western the institution was surrounded by an octagonal wall, at Eastern by a rectangular one. "The fear lest even one prisoner escape played a large role in early prison construction . . ." a 1949 Federal Bureau of Prisons handbook reported. The idea was to construct each cell so as to make it "safe from escape by the most desperate and ingenious prisoners within the walls." The model prisons were durable, secure and sternly administered.

Each cell was itself a complete prison unto its occupant. At no time did the inmates leave their cells to work, eat or do anything else except to "exercise" in their own small, attached courts. Solitary labor was to be the key to moral regeneration within prison walls.

Service came from holes in the walls from the inside corridors. Entry to the cells was from the courts. There were no doors to the corridors until years later when they were added to allow prisoners to hear sermons delivered from the central rotunda. The men had a Bible as companion and saw only their keeper and on Sunday the clergy. The floors were stone, the walls whitewashed. Heat and light systems were crude and inadequate. Initially, the men did not work. Soon, solitary labor in the cells was required. Later, some were given work outside.

At Eastern, seven such cell blocks (more were added later), each with thirty-eight cells (all but one were one-story), were placed around a central observation rotunda like spokes, and the whole wheellike arrangement of cell blocks was enclosed by a thirty-foot-high, very thick rectangular wall with guard towers at the corners. The cells were along the outside walls of the blocks, and inside corridors ran between. The radiating idea came from the early prisons at Ghent and the cellular idea from the ecclesiastical prisons in Rome and later used in England for some jails, mental hospitals and houses of correction.

The atmosphere was like a medieval fortress. It incorporated no imaginative plan, nor did it create a reformative atmosphere.

Charles Dickens on a visit to Eastern Penitentiary described the scene:

> . . . the dull repose and quiet that prevails is awful. Occasionally, there is a drowsy sound from some lone weaver's shuttle, or shoemaker's last, but it is stifled by the thick walls and heavy dungeon door, and only serves to make the general stillness more profound. Over the head and face of every prisoner who comes into this melancholy house, a black hood is drawn; and in this dark shroud, an emblem of the curtain dropped between him and the living world, he is led to the cell from which he never again comes forth, until his whole term of imprisonment has expired. He never hears of wife and children; home or friends; the life or death of any single creature. He sees the prison officers, but with that exception he never looks upon a human countenance, or hears a human voice. He is a man buried alive; to be dug out in the slow round of years; and in the meantime dead to everything but torturing anxieties and horrible despair.[6]

One noted archivist thought this edifice was an artistic masterpiece:

> The idea that a prison building could have the qualities of a work of art is a somewhat arresting paradox. However, without pressing the point too far we may say that this prison comes nearer to being a work of art than any other building of its

6. Dickens, *American Notes,* 155, 156.

kind, and makes the examination of its unusual structure worth while and the story of its creator, John Haviland, worth retelling.[7]

The two institutions began what was to develop as the continuing and critical flaw in correctional design: the creation of expensive, perpetual buildings inimical to the very programs they were designed to administer and precluding any change of vision in the future.

At about the same time, in New York State a public outcry emerged against barbarous forms of punishment and a call for a more humanitarian system for treating criminals. A Quaker merchant from Philadelphia who had moved to New York, Thomas Eddy, led the reform movement against capital punishment and for an imprisonment system. In 1796, in reaction to vocal opinion, Governor John Jay urged the state legislature to provide for institutions to detain and reform criminals such as those being tried in Philadelphia. New York reformers relied heavily on the Pennsylvania experiences. Prisons were authorized for New York City and Albany, New York.

In November 1797 the Newgate Prison was opened in New York City, in which convicts were confined in groups of ten or twenty at night in apartment-like spaces and made to work together from dawn to dark. This scheme seemed to create nothing more than a school for crime. By 1808, according to a history of Auburn State Prison, ". . . the courts were sending such large numbers of men to the prison that it was necessary for the Governor to exercise his pardoning power to make room for new commitments. In 1809 the number of pardons and commitments were equal, and it was then that the suggestion was made for a new prison in the interior of the state."[8] The prison anticipated for Albany was never built, and instead the legislature in 1815 provided for a second institution in Auburn, New York. This action has been attributed to a local political payoff, sought for the economic growth that could be anticipated in the area surrounding a large penal institution.[9]

In 1816, Auburn Prison was established in the center of the city of Auburn not far from the Erie Canal along the Owasco River on a fourteen-acre rectangular piece of land enclosed by a high gray limestone

7. Gardner, "A Philadelphia Masterpiece: Haviland's Prison," *The Metropolitan Museum of Art Bulletin*, XIV 103–8 (1955).
8. *Auburn State Prison: Its History, Purpose, Makeup and Program* 6, a publication of the New York State Department of Correction.
9. Lewis, *From Newgate to Dannemora* 54 (1965).

wall. It followed the same plan as the Walnut Street Jail and Newgate, with multioccupancy cells and dormitories. The first inmates were received in 1817. According to the history of the prison: "Originally, the prison consisted of a main building and a south wing which contained sixty-one double cells as well as twenty-eight apartments, each of which accommodated from ten to twenty inmates. This phase of the prison was completed in the year 1818."

However, the influence of the widely heralded Pennsylvania experience prompted orders to William Brittin, the architect, to design a second wing for solitary confinement. And, within a few years (1821), a new wing was erected at the Auburn Prison which immediately became a model for American prisons.

This prototype cell block created a fashion that eventually was adopted around the world. It was designed to keep the prisoners from mingling in the large workrooms during the day and in the large chambers at night. While influenced by the Pennsylvania prison concepts, it was in part a reaction against a growing dissatisfaction with the Philadelphia plan's advertised failures. Designed to encourage long and rigorous daytime labor and to adopt the silent seclusion in solitary cells of the Pennsylvania system at night, it replaced solitude with silence, introspection with labor. The physical plant was equally as awesome as the Pennsylvania prisons. The solitary cells were tiny. The floors were of oak planks on brick arches. The external walls were of stone, two and a half feet thick. The middle wall between the banks of cells was two feet thick, the partition walls between the cells one foot thick. In the walls were large grated windows. The cell doors were of oak planks bound together with iron. The gallery outside the cells was three feet wide.

The multistory building that housed the men in inside cell blocks became known as the Auburn prototype. The cells could be smaller than those in the Pennsylvania system (they were seven feet long, three and one half feet wide and seven feet high), as work was done in groups outside the cells, which were used at Auburn only for sleeping. The cell blocks were placed inside the walls, back to back, piled in five tiers, with a corridor all around them. The walls and roof of the building composed the outer shell. Heat, light and ventilation systems were crude. The system was cheaper to construct than the Pennsylvania model since there were fewer openings on the outside walls, and back-to-back mechanical services could be provided between the cells. This plan also was more efficient for conducting congregate industrial labor and more secure since inside cells are more easily guarded and more open to view. The small corridor space between the prison's walls and the inside cells provided an additional distance to discourage flight and tunneling escapes.

In 1821 the New York legislature devised a threefold grading or classification system for Auburn inmates. One was composed of the most hardened and vicious criminals, who were kept in solitary confinement all the time. Another class were those considered reformable. They were allowed congregate work in association with one another during the day and were kept in seclusion at night. The middle group, classified somewhere between the other two in incorrigibility, alternately were kept in solitary confinement or were provided with work as a reward.

As with those prisoners in solitary confinement in the Pennsylvania system, there was an unexpected and drastic reaction to this form of imprisonment. Of the first group of eighty-three hardened prisoners in solitary confinement, five died and others went insane. The system was abandoned, but the style of prison architecture remained.

By 1823, the "Auburn system" had evolved. It included separate confinement of prisoners in silence locked in tiny individual cells at night, and congregate employment in shops, fields or quarries during the day, also in silence. Reflecting capitalistic notions arising from the industrial revolution that prisons should be self-supporting, and religious conceptions about solitariness and self-revelation, the men were supposed to have had the benefits of labor and meditation. The motivating idea was to assure maximum industrial production and prevention of contamination and plotting. The men were provided industry but kept in a state of submission devoid of any human intercourse that could corrupt them. A strictly enforced rule of silence was imposed when they worked.

Prisoners had no contact with the outside world, and inside they were marched in and out of their cells in lock step with downcast eyes or hoods over their heads. Even the pews in the church were single walled-off cubicles. One rationale offered to justify this total seclusion of prisoners was that before this development ex-prisoners were known to have blackmailed each other after leaving prisons. Others attribute these practices to a calculated program of humiliation based on ridiculous-looking striped outfits, zoolike living quarters and treatment like outcasts.

According to histories of the times, "Prison life and its punishment was organized to be full of dread and terror" in order for the prisoner to be able to obtain salvation. Repressive rules, undeviating routine and cruel punishments, especially flogging, were applied to maintain tight control, the latter an aspect of life that was not so characteristic of the Pennsylvania system. The inmates were made to spend their non-working hours living ascetically under militaristic regimen and silently reflecting on "the errors of their lives." They were dressed in the classic striped outfits that have been used to picture prisoners, and their hair was cropped. Their food allowance was parsimonious. Their handling was brutal and degrading. They could not even recline on their mats or hammocks at night until specifically granted permission. The whole arrangement was designed to be one of efficiency, silence and gloom. Fear of riot and escape had led to the building of the now standard wall around the already super-secure fortress.

American reformers saw this not as an experience of inhuman hardship but as a great penological advance. In 1826, a Boston society interested in prisons described the details of the Auburn system with an adulation that is now hard to fathom:

> At Auburn, we have a more beautiful example still, of what may be done by proper discipline, in a Prison well constructed. . . . The unremitted industry, the entire subordination, and subdued feeling among the convicts, has probably no parallel among any equal number of convicts. In their solitary cells, they spend the night with no other book than the Bible, and at sunrise they proceed in military order, under the eye of the turnkey, in solid columns, with the lock march to the workshops thence in the same order at the hour of breakfast, to the common hall, where they partake of their wholesome and frugal meal in silence. Not even a whisper might be heard through the whole apartment.
>
> Convicts are seated in a single file, at narrow tables with their backs toward the center, so that there can be no interchange of signs. If one has more food than he wants, he raises his left hand, and if another has less, he raises his right, and the waiter changes it. When they have done eating, at the ringing of a bell, of the softest sound, they rise from the table, form in solid columns, and return under the eyes of the turnkeys to the workshops.
>
> From one end of the shops to the other, it is the testimony of many witnesses that they have passed more than three hundred convicts without seeing one leave his work, or turn his head to gaze at them. There is the most perfect attention to

business from morning till night interrupted only by the time necessary to dine—and never by the fact that the whole body of prisoners have done their tasks and the time is now their own, and they can do as they please.

At the close of the day, a little before sunset, the work is all laid aside, at once, and the convicts return in military order, to the silent cells where they partake of their frugal meal, which they are permitted to take from the kitchen, where it is furnished for them, as they returned from the shop. After supper, they can, if they choose, read the scripture, undisturbed, and can reflect in silence on the error of their lives. They must not disturb their fellow prisoners by even a whisper. The feelings which the convicts exhibit to their religious teacher are generally subdued feelings. . . . The men attend to their business from the rising to the setting of the sun, and spend the night in solitude.[10]

The Auburn system was copied in most American states; the Auburn prison reported that its plan "found many imitators and influenced prison architecture for nearly a century. What could with propriety be done for criminals that is not done at Auburn? Here is exhibited what Europe and America have long been waiting to see, a prison which may be a model of imitation."

The Pennsylvania system, on the other hand, has been emulated in only a few states but widely abroad, especially in England, Europe and South America. In 1913, it was abandoned in Pennsylvania. In part, the difference in vogue was probably due to an American tendency to emphasize economy and efficiency even at the expense of humanity, and the raves of visiting foreign officials for the "reformative" qualities of the Pennsylvania system as opposed to the too vigorous emphasis on order in the Auburn system.

Jeremy Bentham designed the Panoptican Plan for prisons. It derived from a plan for an inspection house meant to supervise industry which Bentham designed in 1791 when he and his brother conducted a business in Russia. The Panoptican is a circular structure with cells around the circumference. All cells are outside cells like the Pennsylvania plan, and the inside circular corridor is used for servicing. A guard was stationed in the center and he was able to view all prisoners at all times. In fact, the observations run in the other direction. The guards

10. New York State Department of Correction, *Auburn State Prison: Its History, Purpose, Makeup and Program* 10.

cannot possibly watch hundreds of men stacked in cells in this round hive, but the prisoners are able to measure the controls this system administers over them.

Bentham was enthusiastic and proud of his idea. In his little treatise *The Panoptican* he wrote, "Morals reformed—health preserved—industry invigorated—instruction diffused—public burthens lightened—Economy seated as it were upon a rock—the Gordian knot of the Poor-Laws not cut but untied—all by a simple idea in Architecture!"

Bentham's ideas for prison reform extended beyond architecture. He went into great detail regarding construction of cells, passageways, heating arrangements and care for prisoners. He recommended that prisoners be served unlimited quantities of the cheapest foods and be given the cheapest clothing consistent with health and comfort. He prescribed minute rules of cleanliness and recommended prisoners be given adequate exercise and ventilation, educational instruction and religious services.

Though Bentham's idea received consideration at the time, it was never widely adopted. Politics prevented its construction in England; a few Panopticans were built in the United States (the one in Joliet, Illinois, is still in use); three remain standing and in use in the Netherlands. They are essentially an architectural aberration, dinosaurs of the penal world.

Almost all prisons in the world now follow one of the two prototypical cell-block designs evolving from the Pennsylvania and Auburn plans. There have been other variations on the Pennsylvania and Auburn themes, but they were not significant. One prison in Maine was constructed with dungeonlike cells built underground with ground-level gratings covering the meager holes. As one student of prisons has said, after describing a Flemish workhouse built in Ghent late in the eighteenth century that used professional staff and a classification system, "The prison system has had few new ideas since."

Every prison can be designated either as an outside cell block of the Pennsylvania variety or an inside cell block of the Auburn variety, the two styles identified by the situation of the individual cells in relation to the outside wall of the cell house or block.

If one of the walls of the cell itself composes the outside wall of the building, it is called the outside-type, or Pennsylvania-variety, cell. Here, the service corridor for the cell block runs down the middle of the building between two rows of cells. The far walls of each of the facing cells compose a part of the outside wall of the building.

In the inside, Auburn-variety, cell the individual cells form an island within the walls of the building. The cells do not use the outside wall as part of the wall of the cell itself; they run instead in two rows back to back within the cell house with a service corridor wrapped around them. The outside wall makes a shell for the building and composes the far side of the corridor opposite the cells.

Where the cell blocks are piled in tiers one on top of another, the area of space beyond the corridors between the cells in the Pennsylvania system and around the cells in the Auburn system form rotundas. Frequently, there is a skylight over this open-spaced area providing light and air. The rotunda, while it makes clandestine communications across corridors more difficult, adds to the din of noise that typifies prisons.

The two forms of individual cell blocks are collectively situated in one of four classic patterns or arrangements. Where there is more than one cell block, as is usually the case, the cell blocks themselves are assembled, one to the other, in one of the forms described below.

In the lateral formation, two cell blocks run in a horizontal line, end to end. A small, separate administration area is situated between them. The cell houses usually contain 300 feet of interior space, the size of a narrow football field. Since the cell houses themselves are so easily patrolable due to this aspect, they are often built without a wall around the institution. The clear, basic concept of this lateral style is frequently altered by additions and changes so that the formation may take on the visual aspect of a square, an L or a T shape, composed of arrangements of several lateral formations.

In the radial formation the cell blocks are arranged as if they were individual spokes in a wheel. They all point to and connect with a central control area which, while it does not allow complete observation as does the observation tower in the Panoptican, does allow control of all intercourse between the separate cell blocks. Frequently, the whole radial formation of cell blocks is further protected by a square or rectangular outside wall circumscribing the grounds.

The telephone-pole formation is composed of a series of lateral-type cell houses, connected by a long corridor bisecting the separate cell houses at right angles and extending from an administration building nearby. The corridor runs perpendicular to each of the individual cell houses and connects each of them with another and with the administration building. One distinct aspect of this formation is that it allows variations on the amounts of security within one institution. For example,

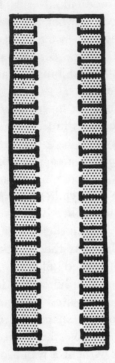

A. Prototypical outside cell block

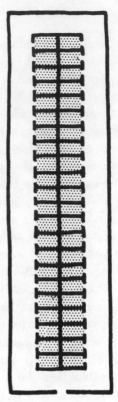

B. Prototypical inside cell block

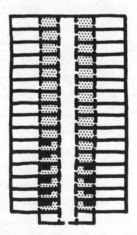

C. Eastern Penitentiary, Cherry Hill, Pa.
   Architect: Haviland, 1829
   Cell: 7'6" x 11'9" x 16'   Yard: 8' x 20'

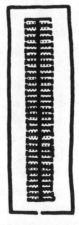

D. Auburn Prison, Auburn, N.Y.
   Architect: Britten, 1821
   (abandoned 1824)
   Cell: 3'6" x 7' x 7'

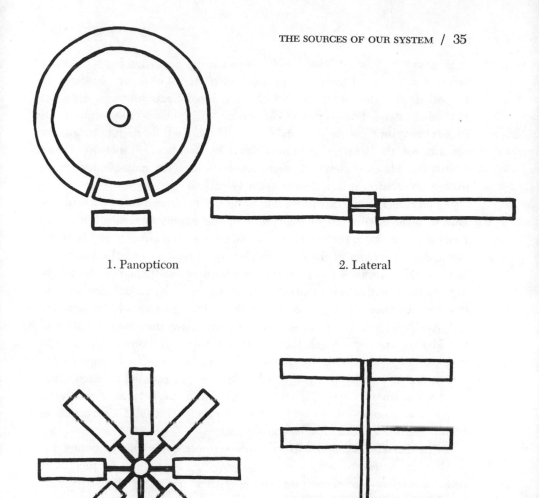

1. Panopticon

2. Lateral

3. Radial

4. Telephone pole

Each prison will have either outside cell blocks (the Pennsylvania system) as in A and C, or inside cell blocks (the Auburn system) as in B and D. In addition, the cell blocks (whether they follow design A or B) will be arranged in one of four classic patterns shown in drawings 1 through 4.

each of the individual lateral cell blocks can be governed by a different form of security without that particular strictness or lenience affecting the others. Furthermore, each of the cell blocks can follow a different individual style. That is, some can be of the Pennsylvania variety and others can adopt the Auburn style. This telephone-pole design, originally devised for the Fresnes Prison in 1898 by architect Francisque-Henri Boussin, has been widely followed and is considered a major influence on maximum-security prison design in the twentieth century.

The rare Panoptican formation is one circular cell house. An observation tower is situated in the center of the gaping space in the round room. By definition, the cells are outside cells with a circular inside corridor around the front of the cells which is used for service. The back wall of each cell composes a part of the circular outer-wall shell of the building. As the circular cell blocks (or, in this case, cell circles) are stacked one atop another, the whole center of the building forms a huge rotunda.

Another form of prison which does not share the characteristics of the above varieties we call the supermarket or warehouse type of cell-block arrangement. This species is no more than one vast room within which are several inside-type cell blocks running parallel to each other as in a supermarket row. This was the nature of the notorious institution at Alcatraz, and it can be seen in the Maryland House of Correction in Jessup, Maryland, and in some county jails.

The Pennsylvania and New York systems came to symbolize the worldwide American influence on correction. The zealous Pennsylvania reformers spared no pains in advertising their programs. From the Old World came reformers, writers and officials to see this great advance in penology developing in the new country. Compared to what they had seen, and limited by the conservatism of those times, they were impressed. Prison buildings all over the world still reflect this imported vogue in design and construction.

When Alexis de Tocqueville and Gustave de Beaumont, wealthy young French scions of aristocratic families, made their famous tour of the United States in 1831, one of their first visits was to the new prison at Sing Sing. Built in 1825 in a stone quarry close to the Hudson River, by convicts from Auburn to handle Newgate's overflow, this ominous walled, fifty-five-acre complex at first contained a sixty-cell cell block of five tiers, with cells seven feet by three feet by six and one half feet with no plumbing and the most inadequate ventilation. Lest there be any mistake about the philosophy behind this institution, Elam Lynds, its first warden, remarked: "Reformation of the criminal could not possibly be effected until the spirit of the criminal was broken."[11] It was fashioned after the Auburn model under the guidance of Lynds; the construction was done by the inmates. A Bureau of Prisons publication wrote, Sing Sing ". . . provided the model for the long, dark cell corridors which were the curse of prison construction for the following century."[12]

Nevertheless, the impact on the two men of the new and evolving American penitentiary system—after all, they were traveling to study social and political institutions of the new republic—moved them to write a book on prison reform for France. The new prisons they saw in Pennsylvania and New York were symbolic of an important change which had just taken place in American penology and which would develop around the world.

The motives of the eighteenth- and nineteenth-century American Quaker reformers were humane. Their basic idea seemed generous and benign at the time, but instead of communing with God and becoming purified, the men they imprisoned went insane, committed suicide or died due to the extreme conditions. As Thomas Mott Osborne, one of our foremost prison administrators, has said, in attempting to reform men by forcing them to think right by locking them in a solitary cell with a Bible, the Quakers "showed a touching faith in human nature, although precious little knowledge of it."

The *American Notes* of Charles Dickens record his reaction to the supposed reforms of the Pennsylvania penitentiary plan:

> . . . The system here is rigid, strict, and hopeless solitary confinement. I believe it, in its effects, to be cruel and wrong.
>
> In its intention, I am well convinced that it is kind, humane, and meant for reformation; but I am persuaded that those who devised this system of prison discipline, and those benevolent gentlemen who carry it into execution, do not know what it is they are doing. I believe that very few men are capable of estimating the immense amount of torture and agony which this dreadful punishment, prolonged for years, inflicts upon the sufferers; and, in guessing at it myself, and in reasoning from what I have seen written upon their faces, and what to my certain knowledge they feel within, I am only the more convinced that

11. New York State Department of Correction, *Sing Sing Prison: Its History, Purpose, Makeup and Program* (1968).
12. Federal Annex of Prisons, *Handbook of Correctional Institution Design and Construction* 32 (1949).

there is a depth of terrible endurance in it which none but the sufferers themselves can fathom, and which no man has a right to inflict upon his fellow-creature. I hold this slow and daily tampering with the mysteries of the brain to be immeasurably worse than any torture of the body; and because its ghastly signs and tokens are not so palpable to the eye and sense of touch as scars upon the flesh, because its wounds are not upon the surface, and it extorts few cries that human ears can hear, therefore I the more denounce it, as a secret punishment which slumbering humanity is not roused up to stay.

The cultural foundation of our prison system was analyzed and explained in the following way by one scholar:

The American prison system of the 20th century is a product of two major cultural beliefs of the 18th and 19th centuries, in western society; of the 18th century classical doctrine of the rational basis of the behavior of man, as determined by enlightened self-interest; and of the 19th century doctrine of progress, i.e., that man could achieve the millennium through a combination of a materialistic philosophy and a religious ethic, specifically the philosophy of productivity through the factory system, assisted by individual enterprise and enlightened self-interest, hard work and frugality; and the religious ethic of the Christian-Hebraic theology, particularly as expounded in the Protestant doctrine of good works as the foundation of faith.[13]

Men locked in cells—in circles like the Panoptican, with corridors between the tiers, or with corridors around tiers, or any other variation on this theme—without regard to the differences of the deeds or needs of the inmates is presently the standard prison institution. Physical environments intrinsically affect human behavior within space. Therefore, architectural planning must consider the working purpose and anticipate the varied uses of a proposed building. Otherwise, the theoretical goals of a building may be hindered or even precluded instead of being augmented by the design. Knowledge about the users or clients therefore is necessary in conceiving and programming an institutional structure.

This architectural axiom finds no clearer example than the penitentiary which was initially designed as a special environment to aid the

13. Shulman, "A Social Science Approach to American Correctional Practice," speech to the Conference on Specialized Education Planning for Personnel in Correction, May 21, 1963.

reformative process and to displace cruel punishment as the end of the correction system. One wonders today how architects and planners ever could have dreamed that the resulting array of American prisons could ever do more than securely contain and punish men. Surely more of the other services and needs of penitentiaries—such as versatile, inexpensive facilities for housing, education, training or uplifting troubled men—are prohibited in the typical prison form.

Furthermore, the lasting nature of buildings and the economic investment in their construction in effect freezes the vision and values and commitments of one moment for centuries, inhibiting evolution and change. In so evasive and so adaptive a field as behavior modification, which is the primary goal of prisons, this problem is acute. The secure and militaristic architecture of the penitentiary not only does not create an atmosphere of personal reformation; it makes attempts to do so difficult if not impossible.

The durability and inflexibility of these monstrous institutions define and limit the programs that go on within. The buildings create such barriers to meaningful reform that however correctional policies may evolve, the prisons are not crucibles for new programs or approaches. The remote fortress prisons, as John Conrad, a practicing expert in the field, recently pointed out, are so expensive to replace that they survive in spite of obsolescence and deterioration. "They impose by their structure the constraints of the early nineteenth century on the correctional practice of today. New ideas get smothered by the system; new facilities supplement the old but do not supplant them," he says. Furthermore, this kind of institution creates an atmosphere hostile to any purpose other than security and propagates a staff attitude dedicated to "counting and locking inmates."[14]

However prison administrators may have attempted to be guided by changing theories of human nature and social policy, the prisons themselves make most reformative efforts impracticable. By the mid-nineteenth century, for example, reformers had become disillusioned with the theories and the results of penitentiary movements. As Zebulon Brockway wrote in 1912:

> The Auburn system . . . achieved admirable financial results, the greatest productive results from employment of the prison-

14. Introduction to American Academy of Political and Social Science, special issue, *The Future of Corrections* xi (1969).

ers' labor; but in public protection from crimes by deterrence, or the reclamation of prisoners, the Auburn was no better than the Pennsylvania system. . . .

[T]here exists not within our human ken any reliable standard of retributive requital. Equally, the deterrent principle was inconsistent, and its inadequacy had long been observed. Evangelism would not do. . . . [T]he religious instrumentality in prisons had not so generally effected a change of moral character and behavior with prisoners as to commend evangelism for the central guiding principle. Nor had the combined influence of punishment, moral maxims, precepts, and personal persuasion, with the intended introspection, been so effective as to warrant reliance upon such means wielded directly upon the minds of prisoners.[15]

From the growing faith that education would change human character came the belief that prisons no longer should be used to ostracize their inmates but to educate and reshape them into useful and productive citizens. According to Brockway, a career prison administrator who, as superintendent of the Elmira Reformatory, would be the first prison official to put the new theories into operation:

The effect of education is reformatory, for it tends to dissipate poverty by imparting intelligence sufficient to conduct ordinary affairs, and puts into the mind, necessarily, habits of punctuality, method, and perseverance. By education the whole man is toned up, and not only are the habits improved, but the quality of the mind itself; so that its strength and activity render possibly nicely discriminating moral perceptions, whose tendency is to better impulses and acts. If culture, then, has a refining influence, it is only necessary to carry it far enough, in combination always with due religious agencies, to cultivate the criminal out of his criminality, and to constitute him a reformed man.

Brockway was confident that the exalted task "of forming and reforming character" was within the realm of the new prison science.

Relying on British criminologists who advocated prison reform, Enoch Wines, secretary of the New York Prison Association, and Theodore Dwight, the first dean of the Columbia Law School, reported to the New

15. Brockway, *Fifty Years of Prison Service* 166, 173 (1912; reprinted in 1969).

York legislature that reform of the criminal, the ultimate aim of prison policy, could be achieved only "by placing the prisoner's fate, as far as possible, in his own hands, by enabling him, through industry and good conduct, to raise himself, step by step, to a position of less restraint; while idleness and bad conduct, on the other hand, keep him in a state of coercion and restraint."[16]

If the purpose of prisons was to reform rather than punish, should it not follow that the length of a prisoner's sentence should depend on his progress toward a cure? In 1870, when the National Prison Association, an organization of corrections professionals and the forerunner of today's American Correctional Association, met in Cincinnati, Brockway delivered a paper urging that all prison sentences be indeterminate. This was a principle the tenacious reformer had proposed earlier, unsuccessfully, to the Michigan legislature when he was superintendent of the Detroit House of Correction:

> No man, be he judge, lawyer, or layman, can determine beforehand the date when imprisonment shall work reformation in any case, and it is an outrage upon society to return to the privileges of citizenship those who have proved themselves dangerous and bad by the commission of crime until a cure is wrought and reformation reached. . . .
> *They shall either be cured, or kept under such continued restraint as gives guarantee of safety from further depradations.*[17]
> [Italics added.]

The high-sounding Declaration of Principles, prepared primarily by Brockway and adopted by the convention to guide future correctional policy, stressed reformation rather than vindictive suffering as the purpose of imprisonment. The delegates adopted the principle of indeterminate sentencing and advocated social training and rewards for good conduct in order to impress upon prisoners a recognition that their destiny was in their own hands.

The first institution to embody these new ideas was the Elmira Reformatory, opened in 1876, which dealt with young men, primarily first

16. Wines, *The State of Prisons and of Child-Saving Institutions in the Civilized World* (1880).
17. Brockway, "The Ideal of a True Prison System for a State," paper delivered before the National Prison Congress held in Cincinnati in 1870, reprinted in Brockway, *Fifty Years of Prison Service* 389, 391, 400.

offenders, between the ages of sixteen and thirty, who were transferred from Auburn. With Brockway as its first superintendent and the new indeterminate-sentence law enacted by the New York legislature in 1877, the reformatory took custody of "thousands of men . . . directly for the public protection but also for the purpose of forming and reforming of their characters. . . ." It applied a system of rewards which behavioral psychologists later would urge upon prison administrators.

While their theory of practice was a great change, in prison architecture the reformers had few new ideas. As late as 1910 Brockway suggested in "The American Reformatory Prison System" that, with the exception of a few modifications to ensure "suitable modern sanitary appliances" and an "abundance of natural and artificial light," reformatories be constructed according to the Auburn plan, with perhaps 10 percent of the cells (for the "intractable" prisoners) built on the Pennsylvania model. Apparently he saw no connection between an institution's architecture and its rehabilitative purpose. Elmira was housed in a "turreted, gray-lined, massive building," Gothic and cathedralesque, that looked like a fortress. The barred cells and locked corridors of the penitentiary, its custodial officers (augmented by a few underpaid and overworked instructors), the vestigial allegiance to strict discipline, regimentation and routine—all were carried over into the reformatory. But, in a perversion of the popular architectural cliché, function was to follow form. Reformatories became, in one observer's words, "swallowed up by the prisons."

Efforts at behavior modification became even more difficult when the institution, built originally to house five hundred prisoners, was filled to double or even triple capacity. Six years after the reformatory opened, Brockway lamented that he must house two prisoners to a cell and that the program of uplift and self-improvement could not be effective under the overcrowded conditions.

There were other problems in the reformatory program. The mark system of accumulating points for promotion to higher grades and eventual release was the incentive to reform. But even Brockway recognized the difficulty of measuring the critical difference between changes in attitude and superficial outward conformity to prison rules:

> The best behaved prisoner is often the worst citizen; men of whose reform there is absolutely no hope in many cases, will grade out early by the best mark system that can be devised, if conduct in prison is the test; while some, whose reformation is

already obtained, cannot possibly keep a clean record. The true
basis of classification of prisoners is *character*, not conduct.[18]

These problems, still with reform-minded prison officials, were compounded by an almost classic administrative problem. The prison staff
found the reformative system too demanding and adopted a superficial
scheme that re-emphasized the traditional penitentiary virtues. The tendency was to put everyone who behaved himself into the first grade,
leaving a few in second grade and only those under punishment in the
third grade. The traditional emphasis on being a "good prisoner" still
prevailed.

Even more basic than the difficulty of gauging prisoners' progress
was a problem inherent in the reformers' concept of institutional socialization: What was to be done with the prisoners who were not sufficiently
motivated by the rewards of the mark system to change their ways?
Brockway concluded that, in order to avoid a "relaxation of requirements
and consequent institutional disintegration," he would have to resort to
"more coercive measures to maintain the established standards" in the
face of recalcitrant inmates. Despite criticism, which he dismissed as "the
product of . . . sentimentalism, and of mendaciousness," he enforced his
standards by the use of a spiked paddle—never, he assured, to punish or
subdue prisoners but "to effect some change in the channels of the mental
activities."

As with the penitentiaries earlier, the repressive features of reformatories predominated. A committee of the Pennsylvania Prison Society
visited the Pennsylvania Industrial School, an institution for younger
boys patterned after Elmira, and reported on the method of handling
boys who did not respond to treatment:

> We were taken to the cells reserved for the punishment of
> the disobedient and difficult to manage. Perhaps there are twelve
> or fourteen in all—one half of these are very nearly dark, the
> other half have some light. These cells are bare of furniture and
> are dismal indeed. In some of these the boy enduring punish-
> ment is allowed to walk freely. In the case of others, he is hand-
> cuffed and chained to the wall, in which position he stands, his
> hands fastened at a level with his waist, and he is able to move
> a few steps, and in an uncomfortable way to rest himself upon
> the edge of his commode. The boy thus punished is allowed but

18. *Ibid.*, 397, 406.

scant food, during the time thus spent. The length of time spent
in these dark cells depends upon the offense or disobedience of
the boy. We felt great care should be observed as to the condition of boys placed in these cells and as to the time they are kept
in them.[19]

Still, at least in name, the reformatory movement spread. In 1893,
General Rolliff Brinkerhoff, chairman of the National Conference of Charities and Corrections, predicted that by the end of the opening decade of
the twentieth century the Elmira system (graded prisons and classified
prisoners) would dominate in every state. By 1900, twelve states had
built reformatories or, more usually, attempted to convert existing
maximum-security prisons to reformatories by statute or administrative
fiat. That the changes were often hollow is demonstrated by the fact that
Kentucky merely changed the name of its bastionlike prison at Frankfort
from penitentiary to reformatory. Six more states would build reformatories in the early years of the twentieth century.

European observers were enthusiastic about the reformatory movement, thinking it a humane effort at rehabilitating youthful offenders.
When Sir Evelyn Ruggles-Brise returned to England after studying American reformatories he began to experiment with special programs for
young prisoners aged sixteen to twenty-one. Eventually, this group was
moved to the old Convict Prison at Borstal. The resulting borstal system
was destined to have a far greater impact on corrections than the American reformatory movement that partially inspired it. The Attorney General's Survey of Release Procedures in 1940 noted, "As reformatories were
accepted as part of the prison system after 1900, it became the thing to
talk about reformation through trade training in prison industries even
though a prison could claim to teach nothing but the 'habits of industry.'"

In 1916, the District of Columbia made a change in the architecture
of reformatories, constructing its new reformatory for carefully selected
felons at Lorton, Virginia, with dormitories instead of cell blocks and without a prison wall. During the next decade, this pattern was followed in
Massachusetts, New Jersey and New York. Each of these new institutions made some attempt to introduce sociological and psychological concepts (such as case-by-case counseling) to the diagnosis and treatment
of the inmates sentenced there.

This, then, is the source of our prison system—a well-intended reformist

19. Teeters, *They Were in Prison* 174–75 (1937).

plan which has failed for almost two centuries by any decent, sensible standard. Yet the progeny of prison forms survive and continue to proliferate all over the world. The dream has become a nightmare. It is hard to understand how civilized men of good intentions could assume the prison system ever could make sense. It seems such an incredible logic that could presume that on one day the average man incarcerated (more often a check bouncer or car thief or tax evader than a vicious murderer) is so dangerous that he needs to be locked in a cage that could hold a wild lion, but on the next day he can go free, having served his sentence—and be expected to emerge a normal, adjusted citizen. As preposterous as this notion is, it is the basic scheme underlying the prison system.

America has devised the architecture of confinement and invested in the policy of massive and crude restraint. And in caging men to keep them from chain gangs, gallows and "vile pits," we condemned them to over a century of despair. Prisons have composed what one of America's foremost prison administrators, Richard McGee, has called a long and painful chapter in the history of man. As one critic has said: "Prison history is a history of ideals and errors."[20]

20. The remark is attributed to Karl Krohne in the Introduction to Teeters and Shearer, *The Prison at Philadelphia, Cherry Hill* (Columbia University Press, 1957).

II

The Institutions of Correction

From these historical antecedents and based on the architectural forms described in Chapter I, a vast series of prison constellations have proliferated around the United States and abroad. There are over 400 American prisons and more than 4,000 jails at the present time. With a few notable exceptions, they comprise the grim progeny of a misplaced dream of reform. We describe them next in basic categories which we define as: adult prisons, juvenile institutions, military facilities, jails, classification centers and special medical and treatment institutions.

Adult Institutions

In the United States, more than 214,000 adult offenders are confined daily in federal and state prisons.[1] In addition, untold thousands are serving from a few days to several weeks or months in a variety of local lockups and jails. The 1967 President's Commission on Law Enforcement and Administration of Justice estimated that on an average day in 1965 nearly 363,000 adults were serving sentences in federal, state or local correctional institutions, excluding police lockups.[2] More than 20,000 of them are in federal institutions, including nearly 1,000 youthful offenders, 4,000

1. Galvin and Karacki, *Manpower and Training in Correctional Institutions,* report of Joint Commission on Correctional Manpower and Training 15 (1969).
2. The President's Commission on Law Enforcement and Administration of Justice, Task Force Report: *Corrections* 1 and n. 2 (1967).

young adults and 750 (a figure comprising less than 3% of the total population) women. Approximately three-fifths of that total are serving sentences for felonies, two-fifths for less serious offenses, misdemeanors and petty offenses.

These prisoners are confined in about 5,000 city and county jails, about 400 federal and state prisons and innumerable local lockups, workhouses, camps, farms, ranches and detention facilities. They are guarded, fed and treated by nearly 54,000 full-time and 2,000 part-time employees, according to the 1967 Joint Commission on Correctional Manpower and Training, and a total of more than 71,000 personnel, according to the crime commission (whose figures include local as well as federal and state institutions). Only 4 percent of the federal and state employees (probably fewer of the local employees) are vocational or academic teachers, 3 percent are involved in health services and less than 6 percent are psychologists, social workers or counselors. The other 87 percent of America's correctional personnel perform only custodial or administrative functions.[3]

Prisons account for the greatest bulk of the correctional budget. The crime commission estimated that, of the approximately $1 billion spent on corrections in the United States in 1965, excluding new construction, $435 million (or an average annual cost of $1,966 per offender) were spent to operate federal and state institutions for adult offenders. With the additional over $300 million it cost to operate city and county jails, the amount spent on adult institutions constituted more than half of the total correctional spending. Yet only 28 percent of all offenders under supervision were in adult institutions. Less than half of the funds went to community programs or to juvenile corrections, which together accounted for the other 72 percent of the correctional population.[4] In addition to the costs of operating institutions, state and local governments surveyed for the crime commission in 1965 estimated that they would spend a total of over $1 billion on capital improvements before 1975.

TYPES OF PRISONS

According to a survey of prisons in 1965 by the National Council on Crime and Delinquency, the 398 state correctional institutions (including

3. Galvin and Karacki, *Manpower and Training in Correctional Institutions*, report of Joint Commission on Correctional Manpower and Training 15 (1969).
4. The President's Commission on Law Enforcement and Administration of Justice, Task Force Report: *Corrections* 1, 5 (1967); Criminal Justice Information and Statistics Service, *1970 National Jail Census* (Series SC-1, 1971).

forty satellite units of larger state prisons, generally farms or camps) could be classified as follows: 170 prisons, penitentiaries or major correctional institutions; seventy-six ranches, camps or farms; seventy-two road camps; eight facilities for the ill, the psychotic or the defective; seven reception centers; and ten unclassified.[5]

Another survey, conducted two years later by the Joint Commission on Correctional Manpower and Training, including federal as well as state institutions, identified a total of 249 prisons for adults operated by fifty states, the District of Columbia and the Federal Bureau of Prisons.[6] The commission's study employed a different classification scheme, dividing institutions into "work-oriented" prisons, which housed 70 percent of the inmates, "special-function" institutions, such as prison hospitals and reception centers, 7 percent, and "rehabilitation-oriented" for the rest.

Of the total number of prisons the commission classified, only the thirty-one prisons for women and fifty-eight for men (housing only about one-fifth of all adult male prisoners), were deemed primarily rehabilitation-oriented. These institutions usually have developed rehabilitative programs such as vocational and educational training, casework and counseling services and medical and psychiatric care. All but sixteen of the rehabilitative institutions are restricted to men under thirty-one years of age and thus can be considered the progeny of Zebulon Brockway's reformatory. The commission considered these rehabilitation-oriented facilities "far superior" to the typical mass prisons. Concentrated primarily in the Midwest and Northeast and in the federal system, they

> . . . provide fairly extensive programs of treatment and training for younger male offenders or, as the case may be, for male offenders who, regardless of age, have been classified as "hopeful and tractable."
>
> On the average [these institutions] are smaller, newer, more open, and more "humanely" designed. Comparatively few are walled or use group cells for confining inmates. In fact some are attractively designed on a campus model and provide open dormitories and "honor room" housing. Several are fully open institutions, having no fence or guard towers and operating essentially on an honor system to prevent escapes.

5. National Council on Crime and Delinquency, *Correction in the United States* 192 (1966).
6. Galvin and Karacki, *Manpower and Training in Correctional Institutions,* report of Joint Commission on Correctional Manpower and Training 15 (1969). This figure excludes the nine state-operated jails that were included in the commission's survey.

Except for the few in special facilities, all the other prison inmates are in prisons that place the chief emphasis on the operation of prison agriculture or industry, on work designed more to defray the cost of maintaining the institution than to provide rehabilitation services. With only 61 percent of total staff and 48 percent of the non-custodial personnel of American prisons, these generally large, maximum-security prisons "resemble dreary walled fortresses, studded by armed guard towers and sealed shut by massive steel doors." According to the Joint Commission, as a class of institution, prisons represent correction's closest and strongest tie with the past and the main locus of the field's inertia; yet they have survived for almost two centuries.

Of seventy-seven institutions categorized as maximum-security, work-oriented prisons by the Joint Commission survey, twelve were built before 1850, thirty-three between 1850 and 1899 and only thirty-two since 1900. According to the National Council on Crime and Delinquency, sixty-eight prisons in the United States have been in use since the nineteenth century, and twenty-five of these are more than one hundred years old.

The 2.8 percent of the adult prison population who are women (4 percent, according to Elizabeth B. Koontz, director of the Women's Bureau of the N.S. Department of Labor) are housed in thirty-one separate women's prisons and, in twenty-one states, in special sections of large, multipurpose prisons. (Two states send their female prisoners to women's institutions in adjacent states, and two more board women prisoners in facilities operated by the Federal Bureau of Prisons.) Originally, all states kept women housed in special sections of traditional prisons or jails. In 1873, Indiana opened a separate women's prison, but in the next forty years only three other states (Massachusetts, 1877; New York, 1901; and New Jersey, 1913) and the District of Columbia did likewise. In the last three decades there has been a trend toward separate institutions for women, with two-thirds of the existing institutions built since 1930 and one-fifth since 1950. Women's prisons tend to be smaller than men's, with an average population of 190 in 1967, as compared to an average of more than 800 for all prisons.[7]

The Joint Commission survey classified all separate women's institutions as rehabilitation-oriented. In contrast to the "walled fortresses" which predominate for male offenders, women's institutions often feature a campus layout with landscaping, small dormitories or cottages and

7. *Ibid.*, 24–25.

unobtrusive security measures. Women's facilities are better staffed than men's—thirteen inmates per full-time treatment and training staff member (educational, health and other special service personnel) as compared to a ratio of thirty-one inmates per staff for all other prisons.

Over 8,900 offenders, or 4 percent of all adult federal and state prisoners in early 1967, were confined in prison camps or road force units, generally performing labor for highway and conservation departments. (A few counties also operated camps.) The first prison camps existed before 1900, but the greatest growth in these camps came after World War II as a way of dealing with burgeoning prison populations and financial costs. Most prison camps tend to be small, with a population of between twenty-five and seventy-five inmates; very few house more than 300. In the Southeastern states, road crews tend to receive a heterogeneous group of offenders, with little prior screening; consequently, these camps are more secure physically than those in other regions, which receive only those prisoners considered suitable for minimal supervision and restraint.

Camps have a lower staff-to-inmate ratio than other institutions, and most have no full-time training or treatment personnel. Thus the primary value of these camps is their small size and more relaxed atmosphere than is the case with the usual prison. The flexibility of camp buildings, many of which were designed for other purposes or were built to last only a short time, and the use of movable trailers in a few states enable camp inmates to be taken to where work needs to be done, instead of limiting them to work that can be done within prison walls.

In addition to work-oriented and rehabilitation-oriented institutions for men, women's prisons and camps, the Joint Commission survey identified twenty-four special institutions, which include medical prisons, reception centers and pre-release centers.[8]

Institutions for Juveniles

Every state has some special correctional institutions for children. The ages of eligibility for these institutions varies. In some jurisdictions the common-law rule that a child under the age of seven is presumed incapable of committing a crime operates to set the minimum age limit for commitment to an institution; in other places, statutes set an age limit of between eight and twelve years; some states have no lower limit. Sim-

8. *Ibid.*, 18.

ilar diversity exists with respect to the maximum age for treatment as a juvenile. Statutes define the upper age limit for juvenile institutions anywhere from sixteen to twenty-one years.

In addition to special institutions for juveniles, ten states have made special provisions for housing youthful offenders, people between the ages of eighteen and twenty-three, in separate institutions. Five of these states have youth authorities with jurisdiction over children and youthful offenders up to the age of twenty-five. In these states, the sentencing judge generally decides whether to commit a youthful offender who is too old to be treated as a juvenile to a youth institution or to an adult prison. In addition, fifty-eight prisons in the United States house young adults, generally under thirty or thirty-five years old.

Institutions for juveniles are used to contain and rehabilitate children found by courts to be "delinquent." Statutory definitions of delinquency vary, but they generally include a broad range of conduct from using vulgar language to committing murder. Consequently, a child may be labeled delinquent and sent to an institution for behavior that is illegal only for children—truancy, incorrigibility, drinking, associating with criminals and refusing to obey parents—or for behavior that is not illegal but simply shows the child to be "in danger of leading an immoral life." The concepts employed to define delinquency are so vague that, as some critics have observed, "to many they may appear to describe the normal behavior of the little-inhibited and non-neurotic child. . . . There is no doubt that much of what is officially defined by law as delinquent represents no more than the perennial nonconformity of youth."[9] Even with these broad categories of delinquency, many of the children in juvenile institutions have never been found delinquent but only "dependent" or "neglected." Some are mentally retarded; many are emotionally disturbed. Although officials generally recognize that these children do not belong in correctional institutions, frequently there is no place else for them to go. With questionable generosity, juvenile correctional institutions are the only agencies that will always make room for another child. Furthermore, a child placed in a special facility for dependent and neglected children and found troublesome or difficult to handle by staff members may be transferred to an institution for juvenile delinquents without the necessity of a further court hearing.

In addition to the formal institutions for children committed by the

9. Morris and Hawkins, *The Honest Politician's Guide to Crime Control* 148–49 (1970); Tappan, *Juvenile Delinquency* 3–31 (1949).

courts, countless other facilities are used to provide temporary care for children in secure custody pending court disposition. This function is performed either by detention homes (sometimes called "juvenile halls") or by local jails.

THE HISTORY OF INSTITUTIONS FOR JUVENILES

Before 1825 there were no separate correctional institutions for children in the United States. In European cities, after Pope Clement XI started St. Michele in 1704, there evolved several reform schools for juvenile delinquents, usually provided by religious or charitable organizations in conjunction with orphans' homes. In 1727 a separate institution was opened in New Orleans for homeless children who previously had been kept in almshouses, but children convicted of criminal offenses continued to be sent to adult prisons and jails.

Separate facilities for juvenile offenders came with the growth of American cities. By 1816 many homeless children were wandering about New York City. As part of a general investigation of the condition of these children, the Society for the Prevention of Pauperism discovered that seventy-five young New York City boys were being sent to prison each year. The society's report prompted a newly formed Society for the Reformation of Juvenile Delinquents to solicit private contributions and a small subsidy from the state legislature for a "House of Refuge," which was opened in 1825. After 1830 the institution was operated solely with public funds. A similar facility was opened in Boston in 1828 as part of an adult jail, and thereafter another was opened in Philadelphia.

The purpose of these early facilities for young offenders was simply to remove the children from the "wretched jails and prisons of the day [which] were, especially for the young, nothing but nurseries of crime." By mid-nineteenth century, twenty cities had established separate houses of refuge for children. These institutions sometimes indentured children to private employers, who were supposed to give them a home and training in a trade.

Beginning in the late 1840s, three states (Massachusetts, New York and Maine) opened "training schools" or "schools of industry" for boys. Eight other states had done so by 1870. The schools were supposed to reform delinquent youths by teaching them correct behavior and the rudiments of a trade. Although they frequently aped the architecture and repressive discipline of contemporary prisons, none of the schools employed the silent system. The training schools all attempted to provide their inmates with some elementary education, and several of the schools instituted supervised games.

In the latter part of the nineteenth century, social reformers became increasingly alarmed by the conditions in which children were living in city slums. The "child-saving" movement, which included efforts to control child labor and an attack on infant mortality as well as increased concern for the training and care of homeless and misbehaving youth, culminated in the establishment of special courts to deal with the problems of children. The concept guiding the development of the juvenile court—namely, that, in the words of an early juvenile-court judge, "a child that broke the law was to be dealt with by the State as a wise parent would deal with a wayward child"[10]—has had far-reaching implications for the treatment of children who have difficulties with their families or with the law. The purpose of the new courts was to apply every possible resource to solving children's problems: to investigate a child's background, diagnose his problems and prescribe treatment. Since the courts presumably would act in the best interests of the children who were brought before them, there was to be no need for lawyers or adversary proceedings to prove the commission of a crime.

The institutions envisioned by the reformers most active in the juvenile court movement were supposed to replace the inadequate homes of slum children with wholesome living in small cottages:

> . . . the inmates are classified and limited numbers are placed in modest, but well built cottages, which are free from anything like the usual prison appliances and furnished with all the necessaries and comforts of a well-ordered home, presided over by a Christian gentleman and lady, who, as husband and wife, hold the relation of father and mother toward the youth of the household.[11]

Since, according to one training-school superintendent, it was impossible to reform children among "the crowded, slum-life of a noisy, disorderly settlement where 70% of the population is of foreign parentage," the children were to be "taken away from evil association and temptations, away from the moral and physical filth and contagion, out of the gas light and sewer gas; away out into woods and fields, free from temptation and con-

10. Mack, "The Juvenile Court," 23 *Harvard Law Review* 104 (1909).
11. Howe, *The Family System,* Proceedings of the National Conference of Charities and Correction 210 (1880).

tagion; out into the sunlight and the starlight and the pure, sweet air of the meadows."[12]

Once removed from the atmosphere of the city, the children would be taught the morals of the middle class and the rudiments of a trade. Unfortunately, the rural location of the training schools generally meant that the children would be taught to do farm work, already outdated at the end of the nineteenth century, and old-fashioned crafts that no longer were practiced in the cities to which the children would return. Added to these drawbacks was the remoteness of the institutions from the children's families and meaningful personal relationships.

Throughout their history, juvenile courts have dealt in euphemisms— a conviction is either a "finding of involvement" or of "jurisdiction"; a sentence is a "disposition"; an offender is a "ward." And the services for children that were to justify the great latitude given juvenile courts in most cases have failed to materialize. In many cases, the juvenile court has become the vehicle for using what are essentially criminal sanctions to deal with a range of child-welfare problems; at that the court has avoided the constitutional protections that apply to adults accused of crime and applied precipitous procedures rationalized on hollow paternalistic motives. In fact, as former Justice Abe Fortas recognized, in speaking for the Supreme Court, "there may be ground for concern that the child receives the worst of both worlds: That he gets neither the protections accorded to adults nor the solicitous care and regenerative treatment postulated for children."[13]

The experience of the juvenile court in the United States is another example in the history of corrections of a dream of reform gone bad. After stating that the juvenile court had not succeeded "in rehabilitating delinquent youth, in reducing or even stemming the tide of juvenile criminality, or in bringing justice and compassion to the child offender," a report of the 1967 President's crime commission noted: "To say that juvenile courts have failed to achieve their goals is to say no more than what is true of criminal courts in the United States. But failure is most striking when hopes are highest."

In the past few years, most notably in the landmark case *In re Gault,*[14]

---

12. Remarks of Nelson McLain in Proceedings of the Illinois Conference of Charities (1901), in 17th Biennial Report of the Board of State Commissioners of Public Charities 232 (1902).
13. *Kent v. United States,* 383 U.S. 541, 555–56 (1966).
14. 387 U.S. 1(1967). *See also In re Winship,* 397 U.S. 358(1970); *but see McKeiver v. Pennsylvania,* 9 *Criminal Law Reporter* 3234 (U.S. Supreme Court, June 21, 1971).

the Supreme Court has begun to reverse this trend by extending the procedural constitutional protections given juveniles, and, at least until recently, it seemed likely that eventually the entire range of due-process rights would be applied to juvenile-court hearings. Although the enhanced protections given to children in court, hopefully coupled with a narrowing of the range of conduct for which the courts may intervene, should result in fewer commitments to juvenile institutions, these reforms bear only indirectly on the quality of the institutions themselves.

Institutions for Delinquent Children

The large training school, far removed from population centers and staffed predominantly by custodial personnel, remains the typical institution to which juveniles found delinquent are committed. In 1968, the date of the last national survey, approximately 54,000 children were living in public (federal, state and local) institutions for delinquent children in the United States. Of these youths, 44,593 were in federal or state institutions; the rest were in city or county facilities.[15] In addition, an unknown number of children were in private facilities such as military schools or schools for emotionally disturbed children. In thirty-one states, juvenile courts sometimes commit delinquent children to these private institutions, some of which are subsidized from public funds, but private institutions generally have long waiting lists and are prohibitively expensive for children whose parents are not wealthy.

In 1968 there were approximately 322 public institutions for delinquent children, of which three were federal, 235 state and eighty-four county or city. The average population of the federal and state institutions was approximately 184 children. These children were under the care of 21,397 employees, one for each two children. However, only 5,535 of these employees (or one for every eight children) were involved in providing health, educational or other non-custodial services.

Of the 322 public institutions for juveniles, 229 were training schools, thirteen were reception and diagnostic centers and eighty were forestry camps. Of 205 training schools that responded to a survey by the Department of Health, Education and Welfare, eighty-seven, or 42 percent, were built to house fewer than 150 children, and 188 (58 percent) had capacities

15. Galvin and Karacki, *Manpower and Training in Correctional Institutions*, staff report of Joint Commission on Correctional Manpower and Training 30 (1969). The Joint Commission's survey was made in early 1967.

of 150 or more. Of this latter group, forty-seven had capacities of 300 or more children. Another survey disclosed that early in 1967 two-thirds of all children in state juvenile institutions were confined in large facilities with an average resident population of 383 children. According to the HEW survey, approximately 35 percent of the institutions were housing more children than their stated capacities and thus reported being "overcrowded."[16]

Of the 243 federal and state institutions, a survey made for the Joint Commission on Correctional Manpower and Training classified at least 143 as "multi-purpose institutions" which house juveniles of different ages and with different problems. These institutions, which house an average of 263 children per institution, included children who committed serious crimes, children who were emotionally disturbed, children who were mentally retarded and children who simply had no place else to go. The other 100 institutions include ten reception and diagnostic centers, where children are put for short periods for testing and diagnosis, fifty-eight forestry camps, four security institutions that house children considered to be particularly aggressive or prone to escape (in most states these children are housed in a special part of a multipurpose institution) and twenty-eight small institutions that range from group homes to halfway houses.

Although juvenile institutions generally have not separated children according to their age or their needs, they have separated them according to their sex. In 1967 there were only twenty-one coeducational institutions for juveniles. Nine of these were in small states where they were the only institutions. Two were in one Southern state where, while sexes were mixed, white and black children were separated.

Although there have been heart-rending tales of children who have been kept in remote institutions for many years, the average amount of time spent in institutions for children perforce is much shorter than that spent in adult prisons. In 1968, 55 percent of the public institutions for delinquents kept children for an average of eight months or less, 20 percent for an average of nine months to one year and 25 percent for an average of one year or more. For training schools alone the average length of stay in 1967 was approximately ten months. However, these figures varied greatly among states, and at least eight institutions reported keeping children for an average period of two years or more.

16. U.S. Department of Health, Education and Welfare, Office of Juvenile Delinquency and Youth Development, *Statistics on Public Institutions for Delinquent Children: 1968* 2 (1970).

In 1968 public institutions for delinquent children spent an estimated $227.2 million. Of this total, 93 percent was allocated to current operations and 7 percent to capital improvements. The average annual operating expense per child was $4,516. However, this figure represents enormous variations among states, from $1,263 per child in South Carolina to $9,499 in Hawaii. Most states are planning to build new institutions for delinquent children or to make their already large institutions even larger. In 1965 only eight states had no plans for new construction of children's institutions. The construction already under way or authorized by state legislatures was expected to increase the present capacity of institutions for delinquent youth by more than 42 percent by 1975.[17]

DETENTION HOMES

Aside from the children committed to institutions by juvenile courts, many more children are locked up before courts even hear their cases. Juvenile-court laws allow children to be detained prior to their court dispositions when the judge or the arresting official determines that it will be in the child's best interests. Generally this means that children from poor families are put in institutions for their own good, while those from prosperous homes are released. In 1965, more than 409,000 children, approximately two-thirds of all juveniles arrested, were detained in jails or detention homes for an average period of twelve days. Approximately three-quarters of these children were held in 242 detention homes for children. The rest—over 100,000 a year—were locked up in local jails or police lockups.

Nine states have laws that forbid placing children in jail at all. In nineteen states juveniles are permitted to be jailed as long as they are segregated from adults. But, as a recent report of the Youth Development and Delinquency Prevention Administration of the U.S. Department of Health, Education and Welfare recognized, "with few exceptions, individual counties do not have a sufficient number of detention cases to justify maintaining a detention service." Consequently, 93 percent of the country's juvenile-court jurisdictions, which serve 44 percent of the population, have no special facilities to detain children. When children are jailed, officials generally try to separate them from the adult population, but overcrowding frequently makes separation impossible. Even when they are separated, children, who may be held only because they are

17. National Council on Crime and Delinquency, *Correction in the United States* 78–79 (1966).

suffering from child abuse or are needed as state's witnesses, are locked in cells with nothing to do and no supervision. Children as young as three years old have been kept in jail because there was nowhere else to put them. Only three states claim that they never use jails to hold children. Of the jails where children are housed, the HEW study reports that fewer than 20 percent have been rated by the Federal Bureau of Prisons as suitable by minimum standards of decency for adult federal prisoners.

The purpose of providing separate detention facilities for children, as stated close to forty years ago, was "to keep the child from the evils of jail . . . [and to care for him] as a wise father would care for his children."[18] Yet a recent federal report, written to urge states to accept responsibility for providing regional detention facilities, noted that makeshift detention homes often are "virtually child jails . . . [consisting] of a barred room in a county court house, or home for the aged, or in other institutions." Even specially constructed detention homes were criticized by the report for glaring deficiencies:

(a) the programs are so inadequate that they are little better than jails, failing to meet their objectives of offsetting the potentially damaging effects of confinement and beginning the process of rehabilitation;
(b) these detention homes are staffed and programmed in such a way that they are unable to care for the seriously delinquent children for whom they were intended, with the result that these youngsters are still being held in jail;
(c) mildly delinquent children and neglected children are being detained unnecessarily, and harmfully, in close association with sophisticated delinquents; or
(d) because of indiscriminate use, detention homes are often dangerously overcrowded to the degree that an adequate program is practically impossible to achieve.[19]

Children kept in detention homes pending court disposition rarely are given anything to do. Less than one half the detention homes in the United States have school programs, and only twelve offer remedial education. Fewer than half the detention facilities have recreation programs or the services of psychiatric counselors or social workers. Although one

18. Wagner, *Juvenile Detention in the United States* (1933).
19. Downey, *State Responsibility for Juvenile Detention Care* 2, U.S. Department of Health, Education and Welfare, Youth Development and Delinquency Prevention Administration (1970).

of the reasons often advanced for detaining children prior to court disposition is to enable court authorities to observe their behavior, half the
juvenile detention homes offer no diagnostic services for detained
children.

Responding to evidence of such inadequacies, a District of Columbia
court recently ruled that the city's Receiving Home violated the statutory
requirement of "custody, care, and discipline as nearly as possible equivalent to that which should have been given [a child] by his parents."[20]
The court refused to release the occupants of the detention home from
custody, but ruled that it would cease ordering the detention of juveniles
if a new facility was not built within two years.

Problems of Training Schools

Despite the recent proliferation of smaller institutions and group
homes for juveniles, the large, congregate training school remains the
typical institution for delinquent youth. Frequently surrounded by high
walls, guarded by armed officers and possessing such features of a modern
prison as locked rooms and solitary-confinement cells, these large multi-
purpose institutions are primitive, overcrowded and oppressive. Youths
committed to training schools continue to be subjected to oversized living
units, inadequate and occasionally sadistic staff, lack of programming,
primitive academic and vocational training, isolated location, emphasis on
custodial security and insulation from legal protection.

The "cottages" in which institutions typically house their children fail
even to approximate the family atmosphere for which they originally were
created. Of the 1,344 living units under state-run juvenile institutions only
24 percent have a capacity of twenty or fewer children. In 68 percent the
capacity is from twenty-one to fifty; in 8 percent, fifty or more boys are
housed in a single group. Due to faulty design, shortages of staff and
inadequate supervision, there have been serious physical and sexual
assaults among children in these living units.

Some of the people who work in institutions for juveniles are dedicated to helping children. Some have received formal training for their
jobs; others are simply "emotional rejects." (One institutional superintendent said, "The boys we get have failed in society. But the people we
hire have, too.") A recent report by Howard James, a prize-winning re-

20. In the Matter of Savoy, No. 70–4808, Juvenile Court of the District of Columbia,
October 13, 1970.

porter for the *Christian Science Monitor*, categorized the typical institutional employee as occasionally sadistic and frequently untrained, uneducated and not fit to be around children.

A few institutions practice flagrant brutality against the children confined there. Recent investigative reporting and Congressional testimony have provided a growing literature of corruption, sadism and despair. James discovered that in three states, flogging of children was a common occurrence. Another critic reports having seen children chained to the head and foot of a cot spring when employees found them difficult to control.[21] At some institutions heavy use is made of tranquilizing and antidepressant drugs on troublesome children with neither adequate medical care nor psychiatric treatment. Many institutions use solitary confinement freely, particularly for children who are emotionally disturbed or who are chronic escape risks. A federal court recently issued a temporary injunction against further isolation of a fourteen-year-old girl who had been confined for two weeks in her pajamas in a "strip room" with no view of the outside, no furniture but a wooden bench and no medication or reading material. After considering the views of several experts in the field of adolescent psychology concerning the psychological destructiveness of such prolonged isolation, the court ruled that it constituted cruel and unusual punishment forbidden by the Eighth Amendment.[22]

Institutions for delinquent children, where children with problems that cry out for treatment are mistreated or left untreated, are no places where a person with any choice would send someone he loves. Milton G. Rector, executive director of the National Council on Crime and Delinquency, testified to a Senate committee:

> The loneliness and isolation, the disinterest and emotional neglect, and the still too often administered brutality experienced by our youth in detention homes, jails and institutions somewhere in practically every state of this nation are basic causes of the mounting juvenile delinquency and crime rates. . . . [M]any of these youngsters are dependent and neglected children—when they are first subjected to such dehumanizing treatment by the "protection" of the juvenile court.

21. Alper, "The Training School: Step-Child of Public Education," 33 *Federal Probation* 24, 25, December 1969.
22. *Lollis v. New York State Department of Social Services,* 322 F. Supp. 473 (S.D.N.Y. 1970).

Although brutality exists in institutions for children, the predominant atmosphere is not one of torture but of idleness. Shortage of facilities, staff and imagination mean that outside of the few hours a day spent by some children in school, the institutionalized child's time is spent performing menial tasks such as making beds, polishing floors or working in laundries or fields. Many institutions do not have sufficient staff to supervise children for outdoor recreation. Some children watch television; others do nothing at all.

Many of the children in juvenile institutions are young enough to be required by law to be in school. Frequently, in fact, they have been placed in institutions because of their truancy. Yet a report by the Citizens' Committee for Children of New York charged that many of the children in correctional institutions do not receive even the minimal educational services to which they are entitled by law. In at least one jurisdiction, juveniles committed to institutions do not receive credit in the public schools for the work they do in institutional classrooms.

Except for the experimental programs appearing at a few institutions for youthful offenders, vocational training programs in juvenile institutions are virtually non-existent. Even more serious than the lack of training is the fact that, in the name of vocational education, juveniles have been farmed out to private employers to work as unpaid domestics or factory hands. As one experienced observer points out, the most menial maintenance jobs, which can include washing the superintendent's car or mowing his lawn, are justified euphemistically as training in good work habits:

> It is easy for the institution to describe the children's activities as "educational" when, in fact, they are not. Many children in institutions do grubby, unpleasant, boring work, which does not educate or train them. . . . The children are a cheap and indispensable source of labor necessary to maintain the institution.[23]

Institutions for juveniles, originally built in rural areas out of an allegiance to the supposed virtues of country living, almost always are located far from population centers. Their location, together with the bastionlike design of their buildings, their security practices and the administrators' prevalent fear of angering local residents by permitting youths to escape, have combined to insulate the institutions from public view. Not only

23. Forer, *No One Will Listen* 160 (1970).

are the institutions free from public scrutiny, they are isolated from public help. Visits to children by their families are extremely difficult; enrichment of institutional programs by contact with the people and resources of the community is almost impossible. Because the institutions are removed from population centers, they must duplicate expensive services, such as schools, hospitals and mental health clinics, that already exist in the community.

Some of the problems of juvenile institutions may be the inevitable results of attempting to handle difficult and sometimes seriously disturbed children in a closed setting. Without strict controls, older and stronger children terrorize smaller and less aggressive children. The difficulties of managing children in large institutions frequently cause staff members to emphasize conformity to institutional regulations rather than preparation for re-entering the community. According to Howard James' report in the *Christian Science Monitor,* "It is clear that children understand the institutional game. Dozens of youths interviewed told me that they were just 'doing time,' and that if they followed the rules they would do 'easy time.' "

Just as in the adult prison setting, efforts to treat juveniles in institutions generally are superimposed on a pre-existing custodial structure. Programs are introduced piecemeal, often with little new staff to implement them, and the custodial and treatment goals of the institution frequently conflict. For this very reason, even when training schools have modern physical facilities and well-trained staffs, they may have no better success than their overcrowded, inadequately supervised counterparts.

At one new institution for youthful offenders a psychiatrist told us that he and his colleagues constantly were undercut by custodial officials "who do not understand that behavior reflects problems." As he pointed out to us, the therapists can be working on a boy only to have a custodial officer say something like "How can you be so dumb as to . . ."—and thus, again his words—"blow the whole thing?" This problem is simply part of the fundamental inherent inconsistency of all correctional schemes where goals of rehabilitation are attempted within the framework of punishment.

But despite the benevolent purpose of an institution supposedly securing for a child custody, care and discipline equivalent to that which should have been given by his parents, there have been virtually no legal challenges to the treatment of juveniles in training schools. Each year approximately five hundred children are transferred from training schools to adult prisons and reformatories without benefit of a court hearing,

on the ground that they are unmanageable.[24] Children regularly are denied even the elemental rights that recently have been secured to adult
prisoners through court orders. Most institutions have not made provision
for a child to be visited by a lawyer. Enlightened correctional authorities
and knowledgeable attorneys agree that the failure of children to challenge the conditions of their confinement cannot be ascribed to satisfaction with their lot but to their lack of sophistication and to the feeling
that experts and officials alike will take the conventional view that what
is done to children is for their own good and thus not subject to challenge. As children routinely begin to receive legal representation in juvenile and appeals courts in connection with their commitment to institutions, this situation can be expected to change.[25]

Some New Directions

Some interesting new programs have been devised for juveniles.
Some of the common features receiving new emphasis include classification of delinquents into different categories and assignment to different
programs and staff members according to special needs; efforts to confine
children in small institutions or to divide large institutions into smaller
units; experimentation with different methods of motivating youths to
accept responsibility for themselves and others by using systems of rewards; increased interaction between institutions and the families and
communities of their residents; and the use of offenders in their own
correction and to assist in the correction of others.

One widespread innovation is the use of small conservation camps
for older delinquent boys. The camps are modeled on the Civilian Con
servation Corps programs of the New Deal. Most are situated in state
facilities or parks, where conservation and fire-fighting projects are supervised by state conservation service personnel. The camps generally do
not provide formal academic or vocational training. Their purpose is to
remove delinquent boys from their environments for a few months
and expose them to sympathetic adults and physical activities in a
healthy, rural environment. While for some such an experience can be
very invigorating, for many others these camps have little relation to the

24. Department of Health, Education and Welfare, Children's Bureau, *Delinquent
Children in Penal Institutions* (1964).
25. For example, the Youth Law Center in San Francisco, which recently was opened
with a grant from the U.S. Office of Economic Opportunity to represent juveniles with
legal problems, has begun to challenge the procedures under which decisions are made
regarding juveniles in state institutions. *See* Complaint, *Taylor v. Breed*, Civ. Action
No. C-70 15220 JC, N.D. Calif., filed July 16, 1970, at 4-6; San Francisco *Chronicle*,
August 5, 1970, at 2W.

problems that caused their delinquency or to the communities to which they must return.

Another innovation, involving commitment of delinquent children to separate reception and diagnostic centers for a period of study before they are assigned to other programs, is becoming increasingly common. Thirteen states now have separate reception and diagnostic centers for juveniles, and others perform this classification function within existing training schools. The purpose of these centers is to determine the child's educational, emotional and social problems before he is assigned to regular institutional programs. In some states, such as California, the diagnostic studies are highly developed and may include psychiatric examinations as well as academic tests and investigations into social history. As a result of thorough diagnosis, youths are sent to different kinds of institutions or to forestry camps, and some are released directly to parole supervision. In other states, where fewer alternative programs are available, classification workers may be faced with the problem of having diagnosed the difficulties when there are no resources to treat them or having classified children who nonetheless must be committed to the same institutions and the same programs.

Another newer and less frequent aspect of classification further divides youths within an institution into various treatment "typologies," based on their maturity level and special needs. Staff members also are classified according to their ability to work with different types of youths. According to their typologies, the youths are assigned to living units and counselors and treatment goals tailored to their special needs. This method of classification, developed originally as part of the California Youth Authority's Community Treatment Project, is now in use in several California institutions, and a slightly different adaptation has been introduced by the Federal Bureau of Prisons at the Robert F. Kennedy Youth Center in Morgantown, West Virginia. A further adaptation of this method of classification was instituted recently at a California training school to match students with teachers in an effort to increase compatibility and educational achievement.

Education is one area in which some juvenile institutions seem to be making significant progress. Using federal funds available under the Elementary and Secondary School Act of 1965, training schools in Ohio, Illinois and California have set up elaborately equipped reading laboratories, small classrooms, programmed instruction and other means of individualizing education for children who need remedial instruction. These methods allow children to progress at their own pace and to bring their academic skills up to (or above) grade level without waiting for the passage of the conventional school year. Although teachers are enthusiastic, there is as yet little evaluative information on their success in using these methods.

An imaginative experiment in using the principles of behavioral psychology to motivate delinquents to learn took place at the National Training School in Washington, D.C., from 1965 to 1967. In the first phase of the project, entitled Contingencies Applicable for Special Education (CASE I), fifteen students, among the worst educational problems at the institution, spent three and one half hours each day in a specially designed environment, which included individual study booths and group classrooms, a social lounge and a small store. The students were paid in points, convertible into money, for completing educational tasks. The points could be spent on admittance to the lounge, refreshments, special study facilities and, later, purchases from a mail-order catalogue. Students were not required to learn but were motivated to spend more and more time on educational activity. The students' academic achievement advanced an average of one and a half school years in slightly more than four months.

In the second phase, the experiment was expanded to include the entire day of thirty students. A much greater variety of privileges was used, such as private sleeping rooms and showers, the right to wear personal rather than institutional clothing, a choice of foods at mealtime and furloughs outside the institution. The ability to purchase these privileges together with the status attached to earning points caused the students to seek increasing amounts of study time and course work. In addition, the freedom to choose, within limits, the ways to spend their points was considered beneficial. As the originator of the CASE project wrote:

> By establishing a welfare state within a correctional institution, the participating inmate does not learn to deal with the problems and requirements of a competitive democratic society which is based upon relatively free choice and remuneration for work produced. . . . When an inmate is finally released into the free society and he has not really learned how to deal with the freedom of choice as to a means for sustenance, he resorts to the limited choices that were available to him before: the welfare agency, the Army, and antisocial activities. . . .[26]

26. *See* Cohen "Educational Therapy: The Design of Learning Environments" 3 *Research in Psychotherapy* 21, 45 (1968).

When the National Training School was closed and the Robert F. Kennedy Youth Center (one of five in the federal system) opened, elements of the CASE project were incorporated into the institutional program. Each youth (sixteen-to-nineteen-year-olds) at Morgantown earns points for meeting the individual goals set by him in consultation with the staff members who comprise his treatment team. Points may be earned in all areas of institutional life (academic, vocational, work, cottage life and recreation). This feature expands the CASE project, which attempted only to manipulate a youth's academic performance. All of the achievements for which points may be earned are no longer concrete and measurable, and some may involve subjective judgments on the part of the staff.

Points are convertible into money that is used to pay for the students' rent, laundry and the use of some recreational facilities. As students (as they are called) accumulate points, they move through the three levels of trainee, apprentice and honor class. Each level is entitled to progressively better living quarters, clothing and greater freedom to leave the institution. Boys at the higher levels earn greater rates of pay. Saving a portion of their funds is required of trainees and apprentices but not of honor residents. Savings earn interest and may be withdrawn only when a youth is paroled or released at the end of his sentence.

The complex of facilities at Morgantown is very attractive physically. The barbershop, hospital and dining rooms are all cheerful-looking places. A positive feature of the facility is that it not only does not appear to the rest of the community as an ominous refuge but in fact draws the community in. The local university uses the swimming pool; a theater group uses the theater; local people, including a number of women, are employed as much as possible. But when we commented to one of the officials that coming to the camp might seem like one big reward to an offender, he replied, "Not a one would stay if he had a choice; they are all here against their will."

SMALL GROUP INSTITUTIONS: HIGHFIELDS

One very interesting innovation in juvenile institutions that would provide the model for much that was to come was developed in New Jersey. A proposal was made in 1949 by a committee of New Jersey judges for legislation to allow the state trial courts to impose short, fixed-term reformatory sentences of from three to six months. The New Jersey

Department of Institutions and Agencies responded with an alternative proposal that a small special institution for the short-term treatment of a limited number of selected delinquent boys be established on an experimental basis. With the help of private-foundation funding, in July 1950 the first boy was admitted to what has become well known as Highfields but which is officially referred to as the New Jersey Experimental Project for the Treatment of Youthful Offenders.

The philosophy of the project is that an informal setting with small groups composed of boys who have intimate contact with one another and with the professional and non-professional staff will be a significant factor in aiding rehabilitation. Highfields, then, is a real alternative to the typical correctional institution. Neither large nor complex nor formally bureaucratic, Highfields functions in a fourteen-room stone house on 390 acres in a relatively isolated, wooded hilltop between Hopewell and Princeton, New Jersey, on an estate that was the former home of General and Mrs. Charles Lindbergh. In addition to its physical attractiveness and accessibility to local towns, the estate is near enough to the New Jersey Neuro-Psychiatric Institute to make it feasible for the boys to work there. There are four dormitories on the estate used as sleeping rooms for the boys, in addition to a dining room, office, kitchen, a three-car garage which serves as a combination winter recreation room and workshop.

The originators of the program designed a method of rehabilitation which involves four major factors. The first is the provision of an informal and intimate living situation for a short period, an average of four months in a small group of about twenty boys in a non-custodial, residential center. The physical situation at Highfields augments this purpose, as does the fact that the staff consists solely of a director who is also a therapist and administrator and a few assistants who serve similar functions.

As therapist, the director leads the guided group-interaction sessions. There also is a work supervisor who is responsible for supervising the boys at work at the hospital nearby and taking them to town on their Saturday evenings off. Probably the most intimate contact is with the cottage supervisors, who interact with the boys more frequently than any of the other employees. The supervisors are a married couple with no professional training or experience in correctional work. The male supervisor is responsible for the maintenance and upkeep of the building and grounds and supervises the boys' work around the house. (When a boy has disobeyed one of the few rules he is usually assigned to "work in the pit," which involves digging a hole in the woods behind the main house where refuse is buried.) His wife serves mainly as cook and house mother. She prepares the meals with the help of the one boy who acts as KP—a rotating job. The kitchen also serves as an informal meeting place, and it is common to see the boys chatting with the cottage supervisor as she prepares meals.

In addition there is a secretary and an intern who is a graduate student in sociology and remains in residence for one year. The aim of the internship is to provide training in the techniques of guided group interaction and an opportunity to gain an intimate knowledge of delinquent boys through close contact with them.

As part of the idea of keeping the program informal there are few rules and regulations and no security provisions at Highfields. The two major rules are that boys are not permitted to leave the property unless accompanied by an adult, and they are not permitted to talk to female patients at the state hospital where they work.

The second major factor is providing the boys with the experience of a regular routine of work under supervision. The boys have a structured day in which they depart Highfields for the Neuro-Psychiatric Institute at 7:30 A.M. and return at 5:00. They work usually as farm laborers for the state hospital, for which they receive 50 cents each day. The work program has been set up to approximate as nearly as possible a work situation a boy might find in the community. He must cooperate with his peers as well as maintain acceptable relationships with his work supervisor and other adults at the state hospital. He can be suspended or fired. In that case he would return to Highfields and be assigned to duties there. The idea behind this plan is that the boy is the key to his own fate and must learn to live with his problems in his environment.

As part of their process of "normalization" boys are provided a wide range of contacts with the community. In addition to the work situation, they are allowed to decide for themselves when each inmate has earned his three-day furlough. During their stay at the project all boys get two or more furloughs from Friday morning to Sunday evening to visit their families and contact their probation officers. They leave the project alone or in the company of other boys who are also on furlough and return without official help.

There are also trips to nearby towns to attend movies and church. There are no restrictions on the number of visits a boy may receive or on the persons who may visit him. There is no type of censorship of mail, movies, newspapers, magazines.

The most notable rehabilitation technique is the evening sessions of guided group interaction designed to give the boys insight into the motivations for their conduct and to provide incentive to change their attitudes. Each new inmate is assigned to a small group consisting of eight to ten inmates. These groups meet three times a week for forty-five minutes after dinner. The subject matter discussed in the group sessions is not as important as the sharing of ideas and feelings and the exposure of the inmate to a group counseling experience. As one young man said to us: "The program is the key."

The fourth factor is the least formal one, the continuation of the group discussions outside the guided group-interaction sessions. Because of the informal setting at Highfields the boys are free to continue discussions in the rooms, at work or at recreation. It is hoped that these continuing discussions will help the boys to change their attitudes and values. Much emphasis is placed on the importance of the peer group as a rehabilitative factor. We found these youngsters very attractive, vital, interested.

For the most part the boys sent to Highfields are probation failures selected by the juvenile-court judges throughout the state of New Jersey. The boys must be between sixteen and eighteen years old. This age group is chosen because in New Jersey the compulsory school age is sixteen years and the upper age in juvenile court is eighteen. Since there is no school program at Highfields, boys younger than sixteen are not considered. The boys all have been in trouble, are at the stage where institutionalization would be a next step; and while they are sent here because they have promise, they know it is a last chance for them.

Boys who have had previous commitment to a state correctional institution are not considered. As a result, there are few blacks at Highfields, fewer than ten each year. The reason for this requirement is that the relatively short period of residence in the Highfields program requires that boys respond to the program in terms of their personal problems from the beginning, and it is believed that institutionalized boys would tend to react in terms of their prior experiences in a training school. Admission to Highfields also is limited to boys who bear no severe handicaps, either physical, intellectual or psychological. The results of the selection are that many of the boys have been involved in property offenses and usually these offenses were committed with other delinquents. Since the judges consider Highfields as a third alternative to incarceration or probation, a boy can be returned to court for another disposition if he does not complete the period at Highfields or if he fails there. All the boys are returned to the supervision of the probation department after release.

A five-year evaluation of Highfields was attempted recently using a group of inmates at Annandale, a traditional reformatory with long-term institutional custodial care, as the control group. Questionnaires were filled out by the two groups on entry and after leaving. The conclusions were that more than 77 percent of the Highfields boys who completed treatment had been successful in that they were still in the free community and had committed no new offenses or violated rules of probation as opposed to only 20 percent of the Annandale boys. The research attempted to determine how much change in attitude had taken place during residence and treatment, but the results were unclear.

The short period of rehabilitation (four months as opposed to over a year in other institutions) is important as a rehabilitative tool. It is additionally significant because Highfields is less expensive per boy treated than is the conventional facility (it costs one-third as much as the traditional program). This financial saving combined with the higher success rate at Highfields makes it a very hopeful alternative to the more popular but less effective correctional institution for juveniles.

OTHER SPECIAL INSTITUTIONS

The Highfields approach and philosophy have been adopted in several communities. A Ford Foundation grant in 1961 enabled Essex County, New Jersey, to establish Essexfields, a group rehabilitation center situated in Newark which was closed in the late 1960s when the grant expired. Although the boys at Essexfields followed the Highfields plan by working in a supervised setting during the day and participating in guided group-interaction sessions at night, Essexfields was not a residential unit and the boys returned to their homes in the evenings and on weekends. By providing the services on a non-residential basis, Essexfields was able to operate on a much lower budget than Highfields. The program is about to resume operation under a federal grant.

Other Highfields-type residential centers in New Jersey include centers at Oxford and Farmingdale for boys and a center for girls at Turrell.

The New York State Division for Youth, an independent agency established in 1960 to develop experimental programs to combat juvenile delinquency, operates a variety of small facilities for juveniles. Youths may be housed in homes or apartment houses, placed in non-residential

THE INSTITUTIONS OF CORRECTION / 71

programs similar to Essexfields, or sent to forestry camps for short stays and then transferred to urban facilities. The Division for Youth has established START centers (Short Term Adolescent Residential Treatment) at Middletown, Brentwood and Staten Island. While living at these centers the boys work at the nearby state hospitals. There is, in addition, a START center for girls at Armenia. The girls work at Wassaic State Hospital, often playing card games with patients and styling hair. Thus work as a rehabilitation tool for delinquent girls may be operating to help the patients at mental hospitals.

A five-year rehabilitation program known as Pinehills was established in Provo, Utah, under a Ford Foundation grant in 1959. Designed to emulate Highfields, this temporary program departed from the model only by providing no regular work except on Saturdays and offering its services on a non-residential basis.

Outside of New Jersey and New York, the only residential group center of the Highfields type is Southfields, a facility operated by Jefferson County (Louisville), Kentucky. Southfields opened in 1961 under a Ford Foundation grant designed to determine whether Highfields could be duplicated under different conditions and in a different part of the country. Studies undertaken in four successive years indicate that it could. Recidivism statistics for boys released from Southfields were found to be similar to those of boys released from Highfields or placed on probation in Jefferson County and lower than those of boys sent to Kentucky Village, the large state juvenile institution. An evaluation concluded, "All evidence indicates that the Highfields method for rehabilitating male juvenile delinquents between sixteen and eighteen years of age is highly successful and can be replicated in a community and penal system far different from the one in which it originated."[27]

Some states and communities have established group homes for delinquent children who may be kept in the community but, for a variety of reasons, cannot live with their own families. Some of these homes simply provide a clean, secure and pleasant place to live, with mature, sensitive adults acting as group "parents." Others attempt to provide counseling services and a fairly structured program to work toward returning youngsters to their homes as quickly as possible.

One of the latter group is Fairfax House, a county facility in a middle-class suburb of Virginia, which attempts to deal with the entire

27. Miller, "Southfields—Evaluation of a Short-Term Inpatient Treatment Center for Delinquents," 16 *Crime and Delinquency* 305 (1970).

families of problem children. Parents are seen in individual and group-therapy sessions with other families several times a week. No parent has refused to attend these meetings, and other children from the same families also attend. Fathers serve as evening recreation counselors and mothers occasionally as cooks. Frequent home visits, some over the weekends, are encouraged as soon as staff members feel the youths can handle them. Efforts are made to prevent the family from adjusting to a new life without the difficult child and to enable parents and children to learn to understand each other.

A study prepared by a group of correctional experts and architectural planners recently proposed creation of youth correctional centers located in the high-delinquency areas from which their clients come. The centers would house in a setting that emphasizes group responsibility for the entire program, youthful offenders who currently are sentenced to conventional institutions. A unique feature of the plan is its emphasis on community involvement by providing for community meeting space and recreational facilities in the center and community participation in various aspects of the program. The first facility to be patterned on this model, the Youth Crime Control Project, was opened recently in the District of Columbia.

These small, flexible facilities, close to the communities they serve, are one hopeful change in the treatment of juvenile offenders. But it would be a mistake to think that they are typical of juvenile institutions. Despite the favorable attention they have received, a recent survey disclosed that in 1967 only 8 percent of all juveniles confined in New Jersey state facilities, which make the greatest use of these institutions, and less than 1 percent of all confined juveniles in the nation were in this type of institution.[28]

GROUP METHODS IN LARGE TRAINING SCHOOLS

A few states are attempting to bring at least some of the benefits of small institutions into large congregate facilities. When Paul Keve, the former Commissioner of Corrections of Minnesota, visited Highfields, he wondered whether the group process used there might be adapted to a large training school. Later, following a rash of runaways in the State Training School for Boys at Red Wing, Minnesota, the 250 youths there

28. See Galvin and Karacki, *Manpower Training in Correctional Institutions,* report of Joint Commission on Correctional Manpower and Training 32 (1969).

were divided into groups of ten each, which were assigned as units to cottages and academic and vocational classes, and a program modeled after the Highfields idea and directed by a former member of the Highfields staff was introduced.

Under the new program, each member of a group was encouraged to help the other members solve their problems and to accept responsibility for the behavior of the entire group. Behavior that formerly would have called for disciplinary action by the staff was considered a "problem" that must be dealt with by the group. Each boy participates in the decisions that are made about the others in his group, including the decision of when a boy is ready to go home. The staff of the institution presents the inmates' recommendations to the parole board, which has followed them in the majority of cases. Although it is too early to measure the effects of the experiment on the recidivism rates of boys released from Red Wing, the number of runaways has been sharply reduced, and both youths and employees report a marked improvement in morale at the institution. A few of the more sophisticated delinquents have become so involved in the program that they have been hired as group leaders after their release.

Other efforts to integrate small group methods into large institutions have been undertaken by the California Youth Authority. For example, the Youth Authority's James Marshall Program, which houses forty-eight boys for a stay of ninety days each, uses group methods. The Marshall Program began in 1964 as one approach to the problem of overcrowding in California Youth Authority institutions. If delinquent boys could participate in a special program to prepare them for release to the community in ninety days—approximately one-fourth of the Youth Authority's median institutional stay—population pressures on other institutions could be relieved. In addition, the program hoped to test the theory that delinquents could be enlisted to help one another to change.

The Marshall Program was structured around large and small group meetings in which the boys would discuss their problems and attitudes. The goal of the program is to help each boy learn to accept responsibility for his own actions and to resolve his problems in non-delinquent ways. Other innovations made by the program were the organization of staff members into treatment teams headed by a common supervisor to replace the usual organization according to professional specialty (such as education or counseling) and a concerted effort to bridge the gap between the boys' experiences in the institution and on parole.

The program accepts only boys from neighboring counties whose parents agree to participate in the program, in order to permit furloughs and family counseling. In addition, after a boy is interviewed by a Marshall staff member and several residents, and the goals of the program are explained to him, he must volunteer for the program. Most do, if only to get the benefits of the shorter term. Since the objective of the program is to reverse the usual institutional experience, in which all important decisions are made by staff members, and the inmates gain one another's approval by thwarting the goals set by those in authority, all residents of the Marshall "community"—residents and staff alike—meet daily to discuss the problems of group living.

These meetings are supplemented by smaller group sessions, where more attention is given to individual difficulties. The small groups are responsible for disciplining their members (generally through loss of privileges when they fail to abide by the rules of the community). Thus, "instead of being made to account to adults—the resident finds he must now account to himself and his peers, as well as staff, working in the framework of a community."

Because of the residents' short length of stay, there is no attempt to provide a formal academic program. Instead, an educational psychologist conducts sessions devoted to practical problems related to success in school or employment or living in the free community. Special tutoring by college students is provided, and there are frequent outside speakers, some of them former delinquents.

All residents participate in the half-day work program. Many of the jobs are on paint or maintenance crews, but they are handled in an unusual way. Boys who work well may be promoted to more interesting jobs, some of which "pay" in extra hours added to passes. To get one of these jobs a boy must fill out an application form and have a personal interview. On the other hand, a boy who does not perform his job adequately may be fired by the maintenance supervisors. (Occasionally entire crews are fired.) When this happens, the boy must discuss the difficulty with his group and attempt to find another job on his own. If he cannot find a job, he may be dropped from the program.

A central feature of the program is the use of gradually lengthening furloughs to help the youths and their families readjust to one another. When boys return from their furloughs, they are encouraged to discuss their experiences and confront family problems. Parents who return to the institution with their sons to attend parents' meetings are encouraged to share with one another and with the institution's staff the problems and successes they encountered during their sons' visits and to prepare for their return home.

The Marshall Program differs from other special institutions in that all sentences are uniform. The only sanctions for failure to cooperate are denials of furloughs or transfer to another institution. Staff members feel that these, plus the pressure brought by the other boys, are sufficient to motivate residents to change and avoid the prolonged anxieties inherent in the indeterminate sentence. Since decisions about furloughs and special privileges are made frequently, there is no time for boys to "coast."

From what we were told by residents and staff members and from what we witnessed ourselves, the Marshall Program seems to succeed in helping boys to confront their own problems and to develop strong, constructive relationships with one another during their stay. The residents were talkative, enthusiastic and involved in their program; they appeared able to deal successfully with the usual problems of group living.

Whether this improvement carries over into the boy's return to the community or has any lasting effect is less certain. There is as yet little participation by parole agents in the program and no continuation of group activities once the boys leave the institution. As a special feature, the option is open to Marshall graduates in danger of failing on parole to return to the institution on a thirty-day "guest" basis.

A comparison of boys released from Marshall and a control group released after considerably longer (and more expensive) stays in other institutions made fifteen months after release showed that Marshall graduates in general performed as well as the control group. However, certain types of boys—those who were older and more "sociable"—performed considerably more successfully during and after the Marshall Program.

The Marshall Program is serving as the model for several planned county probation programs, where it will be used in a non-residential setting. In addition, the Youth Authority hopes to implement the program in its community parole offices.

Other Innovations in Large Institutions for Juveniles

Building on the hypothesis that shorter terms in institutions have no adverse effects on the success of releasees, another California institution, the Fred C. Nelles School for Boys, has established two experimental cottages for boys who live in the general area of the institution. The length of stay for all the boys is reduced, and the money saved is used to bring parole agents and others from the community into the institution to conduct special activities related to the residents' early release.

At two other California institutions, the O. H. Close and the Karl Holton Schools for Boys, an ambitious research project, partially funded by a grant from the National Institute of Mental Health, is under way to attempt to integrate all the program elements of two large institutions into different strategies for changing behavior. The institutions, in Stockton, are built adjacent to each other and look almost identical. Each accepts four hundred boys who are assigned to one institution or the other at random. Both classify their residents into living units of fifty boys each according to a boy's personality type and level of maturity. Each living unit is the responsibility of a treatment team, made up of teachers, counselors and social workers, assigned according to their ability to work with different types of delinquents. The staff teams hold frequent meetings with individual residents and with the entire group. Some residence halls rely on self-government; others, with less mature youths, are more structured.

Up to this point, the program is similar to the Marshall Program, adapted to large institutions where boys generally spend from nine months to one year. The longer stay means that greater emphasis can be put on education. Both institutions use newly developed methods of programmed instruction that enable youths to tackle subjects according to their interests and speed of learning. In addition, the two institutions are engaged in comparing the efficacies of two "treatment frameworks" —transactional analysis and behavior modification.

At Close, where transactional analysis is used, the emphasis is on helping boys to understand the feelings in themselves that led them to make the "self-destructive" decisions that got them into trouble. Transactional analysis is a simplified version of Freudian psychology, adapted from the work of Eric Berne. Its general principles are taught to residents as well as staff members. On entering the institution, the boys fill out questionnaires to indicate what they wish was different about themselves. Staff members later help them work out contracts to work to change some of these characteristics.

One element of the program at Close, not part of the research project but worthy of note in its own right, is the Student Aide Program.

Financed by a federal grant under Title I of the Elementary and Secondary Education Act of 1965, the program trains older Youth Authority wards as new careerists in the field of youth work. The aides, all of whom are at least eighteen, are chosen from the inmates of an institution for older delinquents. They must have at least two and one half years of high-school credits. Youths who committed certain serious felonies are excluded. After a two-month selection period, they are transferred to Close, where they undergo six months of training in educational tutoring, recreational planning and supervision and youth counseling. Meanwhile, they are expected to work toward their high-school diplomas.

Aides take responsibility for many duties normally assigned to regular staff members. They are treated as junior staff members but sometimes find that they are more successful than those with more experience in communicating with the younger residents of the institutions. (One reported proudly, "They talk to us when the regular staff can't reach them.") When they leave Close most aides go on to college. Some accept jobs in Youth Authority institutions. The only factor marring the program to date was that California law precluded probation and parole departments from hiring anyone with a felony record as a case worker. However, legislation recently was enacted to eliminate this disqualification in some cases.

At Holton, the program is similar to the one at Morgantown, where greater emphasis is placed on objectively measurable achievements than on attitudinal change. Boys contract to complete certain concrete educational tasks and to improve their observable behavior in residence halls and on jobs around the institution. When they complete contracts, they are "paid" in points. Accumulation of a set number of points brings special privileges around the institution and, eventually, referral to the Youth Authority Board for parole consideration. Although the boys earn points at different paces, there are supposed to be no failures.

At the end of the three-year research project, graduates from the two institutions will be compared in an effort to discover which method is more effective. In the meantime, both have their critics. Behavioral modification is criticized for adopting the theory that "every child has his price, and if he is paid off, he will do whatever the staff wants him to to."[29] Some of the youths at Close told us that with transactional analysis it is easy to "con" staff members into believing that genuine change has

29. James, *Children in Trouble* 139 (1970).

taken place. ("The clever ones can 'front' it.") On the other hand, many residents of both institutions reported that they were making progress, that staff members were sympathetic and that their institutional experience would help them to be successful in the community.

Critics have questioned whether children being held in institutions involuntarily should be used as guinea pigs to test different treatment theories. Our observations were that these youths were benefitting from the experiment. Whether because of their special training in the different theories or because of the competition between the two institutions, staff members seemed committed and enthusiastic about the possibilities for helping the residents avoid delinquent behavior. In any event, the differences between programs such as this and the bleak, Dickensian, all-too-typical institutions mentioned earlier are like night and day.

THE ROLE OF INSTITUTIONS FOR JUVENILES

It has been questioned whether sending urban youngsters far away to a bucolic atmosphere is a realistic form of treatment. It may be that institutions never can cope with the problems of juvenile delinquency because of their lack of involvement with problems that cause children to get into trouble in the first place. As one official of the Robert F. Kennedy Youth Center in Morgantown, West Virginia, told us, "You can't help a boy's stress if he is away from it." Most of the offenders are there for property offenses, mostly (70 percent when we were there) for car theft. It struck us that the pinups in the rooms were cars, leaving little question where these boys' thoughts were.

Even more than with adults the problems of children are inextricably tied to the problems of their families and their communities. Marguerite Warren, one of the founders of California's Community Treatment Project, says, "You may deal with twenty percent of the problem if a kid is sent off to an institution in the hills. But maybe the rest of the problem is in Oakland, and Oakland is not being treated while the kid is in the hills." Research related to that program has shown that most types of delinquents can be treated more successfully in the community than in juvenile institutions. Dr. Douglas Skelton, a Georgia psychiatrist, suggested to us that criminal careers generally start at eleven or twelve. "We can't help kids because we get them too late. The patterns are unbreakable by the time they get to institutions." In Massachusetts the director of the Youth Services Department is attempting to close all the state's juvenile institutions and return all children to their home communities or to private agencies.

On the other hand, correctional institutions may be able to coordinate the services of a variety of professionals and guarantee the attendance of recalcitrant youths in training and counseling programs in a way that is difficult if not impossible in the free community. The most promising recent innovations aim at preserving these advantages in smaller institutions, close to the communities they serve, with programs that seek to use short terms of confinement to motivate youths to change their behavior in ways that will carry over after their release to the community. In all but the most difficult cases, the limited advantages of institutions may be able to be preserved, and most of their disadvantages avoided, by non-residential programs in which youths return to their homes each night.

With young offenders, especially, the key question always should be whether alternatives to the official institutions exist. Middle-class parents are able to divert their children from the juvenile-court system. Aided by their financial position and the power to deal with their community and officials, middle-class parents are able to provide rational alternatives to institutionalization when their children run afoul of authority. Because this approach is informal and individualized, there is no data available to document the exact number of children who never become a "juvenile delinquent statistic." No one doubts that the technique is fundamentally wise and relatively successful.

How does this middle-class strategy work? The parent, faced with a juvenile problem, turns to private community resources. He asks advice from the family doctor, minister, social worker or psychologist. The creativity of the individual adviser will determine how the parent proceeds. He may send the child to a military academy or private school specializing in discipline or dealing with children who are difficult to teach. Restitution may be offered.

Camps and boys' ranches are other frequently used alternatives. Private psychiatric clinics and day hospitals also provide a place for the child who has become a problem. Sometimes the child is sent out of town to a relative for a period or, in the case of pregnant daughters, to another city to arrange for abortion or adoption.

The juvenile-court movement, insofar as it created false promises of curing all the problems of youth through use of compulsory judicial power, has had dangerous and far-reaching results. It is clear that the awesome power of the courts never should be used to require penal treatment of problem children who have done nothing to endanger the safety of the public. Nor should youths be committed to institutions with anything less than the procedural protections given adults charged with crimes.

There does appear to be a place for special programs devoted to the correctional needs of youth, most of whom presumably have greater potential for positive change than adults. For many of these youths, early diversion from the criminal justice system and exposure to all available, helpful community resources may well offer the last chance to be rescued from the cycle of crime and imprisonment.

Military Institutions

Over 15,000 military prisoners presently are confined in a variety of military penal institutions. Statutory authority for the development of military prisons provides only for "the establishment of such military correctional facilities as are necessary for the confinement of offenders."[30]

In addition, the statute provides that the Secretary of each military branch should provide regulations to guide the officers in command of the various facilities. The policy expressed in these regulations stresses the importance of rehabilitation aimed at returning the prisoner to active duty after his sentence has been completed. If restoration to duty is not possible, the rehabilitation program is supposed to attempt to train inmates to cope with civilian life after discharge. While some military prisoners are confined for committing crimes for which they would have been incarcerated in civilian institutions had their offense been committed when they were civilians, the vast majority (85 to 90 percent)

30. Army Regulation 190-1 defines the objectives of confinement as follows:
> Return to military duty the maximum possible number of military prisoners whose sentences do not include a punitive discharge as morally responsible and well trained soldiers with improved attitudes and motivation toward their obligation to self, the United States Army, and the Nation.
> Return to civil life or restore to duty, as appropriate, the maximum possible number of military prisoners whose sentences include a punitive discharge as morally responsible and well trained individuals with improved attitudes and motivations who are capable of assuming responsibilities associated with their return to civil life or military duty.
> Promptly identify and expeditiously release from Army confinement facilities, through separation from the service or through transfer to the Federal correctional system, military prisoners who will not respond or are incapable of effectively responding to Army correctional treatment, retraining or discipline.

of military prisoners have been confined for relatively short terms (six months or less) for unauthorized absence, a strictly military offense.

Military prisoners who are considered restorable to active duty are transferred to a retraining facility. If the sentenced prisoner is not restorable and has at least six months' confinement time left to serve, he will be committed to a disciplinary barracks. Generally, prisoners are discharged upon release from the disciplinary barracks. Military prisoners who have been convicted of crimes "attended by aggravated or reprehensible circumstances" such as murder or rape and whose sentences include dismissal or punitive discharge as well as more than one-year confinement may be transferred to a federal correctional institution. A very small number of transfers to federal institutions occurs each year.

The Army, the largest branch of the military service, has the largest number of military prisoners. Approximately 11,000 men are confined to Army institutions.

The Installation Confinement Facilities, or stockades, confine approximately 7,000 men. At last count at the end of 1969, there were almost 6,000 prisoners in the twenty-four Army stockades in the continental United States; and there were over 1,000 prisoners in nine overseas stockades. In addition to the stockades, the Army operates a disciplinary barracks at Fort Leavenworth, Kansas, housing approximately 1,200 prisoners and the Correctional Training Facility at Fort Riley, Kansas, with a capacity of 2,400 prisoners.

The Navy has a total of thirty-three institutions, including thirty-two facilities at naval bases and a maximum-security facility at Portsmouth, New Hampshire. The Coast Guard has no institutions; its prisoners are incarcerated in naval institutions.

The Marine Corps tends to provide the guard force for the Navy correctional institutions, although it does have thirteen of its own on-base correctional facilities. Maximum-security Marine Corps prisoners are sent to the naval institution at Portsmouth.

The thirty-two correctional centers at Navy bases vary in size from a capacity of 308 at Great Lakes to six at the Naval Air Station at Glynco, Georgia. The twelve Marine facilities also vary in size from 600 at Camp Pendleton, California, to nine at Yuma, Arizona. In 1969 the total number of Navy and Marine Corps prisoners in correctional centers varied between 3,300 and 4,000. In addition, the Naval Disciplinary Command at Portsmouth has a capacity of 1,200 prisoners.

The Navy also confines men in its forty-six brigs, thirteen of which are used exclusively by the Marine Corps. Every large ship has a brig, which is usually composed of six single-occupancy cells and is used just for temporary confinement, usually less than two weeks. The brigs can be used at sea or in port, and while the cells are single-occupancy, they often have two or three men in them.

The Air Force, the smallest of the services, also has the smallest number of prisoners, less than 500 worldwide, according to officials we interviewed. The Air Force has the best reputation in the services regarding the operation of its prisons. Its largest institution is the Prisoner Retraining Program at Lowry Air Force Base, Colorado, with a capacity of 180. The remainder of the Air Force prisoners are maintained in forty-one correctional facilities, each of which contains fewer than six prisoners, and eighty detention cells providing overnight detention. Generally, the detention cells are located in the base security office and provide short-term detention until a prisoner can be transferred to one of the forty-one base correctional facilities.

Three types of facilities are provided for military offenders. These facilities include installation confinement, disciplinary barracks and retraining programs. The largest number of military prisoners are confined in facilities at the local military installations. In the Army these confinement facilities are known as stockades. The Army has thirty-three and the Navy has thirty-two stockade-type facilities. The Marine Corps has established twelve installation confinement facilities. The Air Force has forty-one facilities at local bases.

The physical design of the stockades varies greatly, from wood and metal units with no interior plumbing in Vietnam at the Long Binh stockade to the brownstone buildings at the Fort Riley stockade originally constructed in 1889 to be used by the Cavalry as barracks and stables. A report recently published by the Special Civilian Committee for the Study of the U.S. Army Confinement System[31] was highly critical of the physical plant of the Army stockades. It concluded that most of the permanent stockade buildings are poorly designed with many features inconsistent with modern correctional standards.

Another major problem in the operation of installation confinement facilities reportedly is the severe inadequacies of the personnel due to immaturity, lack of training and experience, and turnover. Dramatic ex-

31. Report of the Special Civilian Committee for the Study of the U.S. Army Confinement System (Ad Hoc), Department of the Army 131 (May 1970)—hereinafter referred to as the Committee Report.

amples were described in Robert Sherrill's *Military Justice Is to Justice as Military Music Is to Music*, including several incidents where prisoners were killed for "attempting escape" from work detail by trigger-happy guards.

The U.S. Disciplinary Barracks located at Fort Leavenworth, Kansas, was originally built in 1873, when it was called the United States Military Prison. It is the oldest federal prison, predating the U.S. penitentiaries in Leavenworth and Atlanta. Historically the institution has been used twice as a prison for civilian offenders, in 1895 and again in 1929. On the latter date the transfer took place following a major riot at the federal penitentiary at Leavenworth, which was seriously overcrowded, and the Disciplinary Barracks had empty dormitories.

The Navy operates a similar facility known as the Naval Disciplinary Command at Portsmouth, New Hampshire. This facility contains minimum-security prisoners as well as those requiring maximum security. Unlike the present program at Fort Leavenworth, the Portsmouth facility provides a restoration program with an estimated success rate of 75 percent of prisoners restored to active duty.

Since the goal of the Disciplinary Barracks is to rehabilitate military prisoners for restoration to duty or return to civilian life, and the Army facility at Fort Riley now has the function of returning men to duty, the Fort Leavenworth program is primarily concerned with training and treatment for life outside the military. The program includes academic and vocational training, on-the-job training on work assignments as well as individual counseling, religious activities and indoor and outdoor recreation. High-school courses and junior-college courses are made available to the prisoners as well as a farm, greenhouse and vocational-training shops such as appliance repair, barbering and upholstering, etc. The Army committee in its report stated that it was "favorably impressed by the administration and operation of the Disciplinary Barracks, the competency and attitude of its officers and cadre and the efforts being made to promote the rehabilitation of its inmates."

The Army, Navy and Air Force also operate retraining programs designed to restore military offenders to active duty as competent and well-motivated soldiers.

Aside from the U.S. military prisoners imprisoned in a variety of military correctional institutions, occasionally situations exist wherein U.S. military personnel are incarcerated in non-military correctional facilities. Included in this category of non-military facilities would be federal prisons, local civilian jails and prisons and foreign correctional institutions.[32]

Jails

Jails compose a vast unseen part of the proverbial correctional ice-berg. As a place of detention for persons accused of crime but not yet tried and punished, jails are institutions with historic roots. When the American innovation of confinement as the primary means of punishment and reform became the widely accepted form of sentence, jails continued to perform their traditional function of pretrial detention. In addition, however, the accessibility of local jails suggested that they also be used for the confinement of minor offenders whose sentences were too short to warrant transportation to state or federal prisons or for a few prisoners who were used to perform the housekeeping chores necessary to main-tain the unsentenced prisoners. This dual role of jails, as places of tem-porary detention, and as short-term correctional institutions, has con-tinued to the present.

While there are about 400 prisons in the United States, a survey con-ducted for the President's Crime Commission estimated that there are just under 3,500 local jails. That figure, which derives from the number of counties in the United States, omits the city jails and workhouses that do not hold prisoners for the counties. Since almost all jails are under varied local controls and most keep inadequate records and have no duty to report to a central authority, no one knows exactly the total number of jails that exist in the United States.

A recent survey of jails in Illinois found that there are 160 jails in that state (excluding police lockups), of which the Crime Commission survey presumably included only 102 (the number of Illinois counties).[33] If this undercounting of more than 50 percent of the jails were true of other states, one might extrapolate from the Crime Commission's figures and arrive at an estimated total of at least 5,250 jails in the United States.

A survey of American jails done for the Law Enforcement Assistance Administration by the Census Bureau was published in 1971. It canvassed

32. *O'Callahan v. Parker*, 395 U.S. 258 (1969); *see also* The Uniform Code of Mili-tary Justice, 10 U.S.C. 814, which provides: "(a) . . . a member of the armed forces accused of an offense against civil authority may be delivered upon request to the civil authority for trial." *Wilson v. Girard*, 354 U.S. 524 (1957), upholds these Status of Forces agreements as binding waivers of U.S. jurisdiction to host countries where military men commit local crimes.
33. Mattick and Sweet, *Illinois Jails—Challenge and Opportunity for the 1970's* i (1969).

every municipality having over 1,000 population according to the 1960 census. Inquiries were made and responses received regarding all jails that confined inmates forty-eight hours or more. An advance report showed that as of March 15, 1970, there were 4,037 such locally administered jails holding a total of 160,863 people, including 153,063 adults and 7,800 juveniles. According to the report:

> About 52 percent of these inmates were confined for reasons other than being convicted of a crime. Thirty-five percent were arraigned and awaiting trial and the remaining 17 percent were being held for other authorities or were not yet arraigned. The Nation's jails employed 33,729 persons, including 28,053 full-time employees and 5,676 part-time employees, or 28,915 full-time equivalent employees.[34]

In addition, almost every police precinct station has a lockup where people may be held after an arrest, usually for a few hours to a few days. (Although there are no statistics on the number of police precincts in the country, the International Association of Chiefs of Police reports that there are approximately 40,000 police departments, some of which are divided into as many as twenty or thirty precincts.) The number of people going through police lockups in a year may be in the hundreds of thousands.

Not only are there many more jails than prisons in the country; jails touch the lives of many more citizens than prisons do. Again, there are no reliable statistics. According to the Crime Commission survey, more than one million convicted offenders, mostly misdemeanants, served sentences in jails in 1965. The average daily population then serving sentences was 141,303.[35] Although some of these people undoubtedly served more than one jail term in a year and thus were counted more than once, the figure still represents a gross underestimate of the entire sentenced population, since this survey excluded prisoners serving sentences in facilities where convicted offenders could not serve sentences of at least thirty days. Add to this an unknown number of pretrial defendants (who generally comprise more than half of the population of most jails) and people put in jail for violations of motor-vehicle laws and other civil offenses, and United States jails probably hold from three to four million people—per-

34. Criminal Justice Information and Statistics Service, 1970 National Jail Census (Series SC-1, 1971).
35. National Council on Crime and Delinquency, *Correction in the United States* 140 (1966).

haps fifteen times the number handled by all state and federal prisons—
a year. Many of these people never go to prison, and the jail is the only
part of the system with which they have contact. Others get their initial
reception into the correction system in jail.

Jails are the repository for a wide range of problems of health and
welfare, as well as of criminal justice. Alcoholics fill half of many jails;
narcotics addicts, who have special, non-penal problems are thrown into
jails at random; men detained pretrial for lack of money for bail compose a large percentage of jail inmates; short-termers, some in jail because they cannot pay a fine, men on work release, youngsters and first
offenders who could be reached and corrected, inveterate criminals who
ought to be segregated, mentally ill individuals, and social delinquents
like alimony dodgers—all compose parts of this often nightmarish melange.

Of the prisoners sentenced to jail for commission of a crime, a 1967
survey of one city jail and three large county workhouses in Massachusetts revealed that more than half were there for drunkenness. Other common sentences, in order of frequency, were for non-support, motor-vehicle
violations, larceny, breaking and entering and assault and battery.[36]

According to a recent survey, the maximum sentence that may be
served in jail is twelve months in thirty states; the range in other states is
from less than six months to life. About half the jails studied admit felons,
some of whom are serving short jail terms as a pre-condition of their probation.[37] Many, perhaps most, of the petty offenders are in jail because the
services they need are unavailable in the community. According to the
National Council on Crime and Delinquency:

> The problem is that the courts handling minor offenders are
> themselves minor courts that do not have diagnostic and pro-
> bation services. Consequently, the easiest and sometimes the
> only way to clear the crowded courtroom of the "nuisance cases,"
> persons who have no friends and no money, is to order them off
> to the county jail or workhouse for a few days.[38]

36. Powers, *The Basic Structure of the Administration of Criminal Justice in Massachusetts* 95 (Massachusetts Correctional Association, 5th ed., 1968).
37. National Council on Crime and Delinquency, *Correction in the United States* 141
(1966). Even in states where there is a one- or two-year maximum, the legal limits
may be circumvented through the use of consecutive sentences. In a recent ten-
year period, the felon population of the San Francisco County jails tripled, growing
from 715 in 1956–57 to 2,457 in 1966–67. The Advisory Committee for Adult Detention, City and County of San Francisco, *San Francisco Adult Detention Facilities*
18 (March 1968).
38. National Council on Crime and Delinquency, *Correction in the United States* 154
(1966).

It is both ironic and perverse that the first contact of the young and the first offender with a correctional institution is so often the worst. A former director of the Federal Bureau of Prisons commented that "one of the outstanding riddles of our American penal system is why persons who commit minor offenses or who have not yet been convicted are so much more badly treated than all the inmates of our state prisons."[39] The few published surveys of local jails, together with our own visits to a variety of large city and small rural jails, document conditions of filth, dilapidation, brutality and total lack of hygiene, medical care or any type of constructive program that are far worse than those at most prisons for convicted, confirmed criminals. Recent widespread jail riots are indications of the increasingly open and violent hostility of inmates toward their treatment.

It is difficult to determine the costs of operating jails since most jails keep incomplete records and their budgets often are merged with those of the larger city or county governments. However, the jails surveyed for the Crime Commission (again excluding those that do not hold sentenced prisoners for thirty days or more) reported spending an average of $2.87 per day, or $1,046 per year (excluding capital costs) on each sentenced inmate. This figure compares with an average annual operating budget of $1,966 spent by state and federal prisons on each prisoner and $3,613 spent by institutions for juveniles.

Staffing patterns show similar disparities. In 1965, over 19,000 people were employed in the jails surveyed for the Crime Commission, of whom only 500, less than 3 percent, performed any sort of rehabilitative functions. There was one social worker for each 850 inmates, one psychologist for each 4,300 and one academic teacher for each 1,300. Some of these professionals worked in jails only part time, and most were concentrated in the large institutions. Two-thirds of the jails surveyed reported having no rehabilitative programs at all. (If institutions receiving no prisoners with sentences greater than thirty days were included, the proportion of jails with no programs doubtless would be considerably higher.) The few programs reported included work release (11 percent), educational classes (10 percent), alcoholics' meetings (7 percent) and group counseling (9 percent).[40]

---

39. Bates, *Prisons and Beyond* 38 (1936).
40. National Council on Crime and Delinquency, *Correction in the United States* 142, 147 (1966); the President's Commission on Law Enforcement and Administration of Justice, Task Force Report: *Correction* 75 (1967).

Although many of the jails we visited were dingy and filthy, most inmates are not given even housekeeping chores to keep them busy. The Illinois Jail Survey found that in only 3 percent of city jails and 14 percent of county jails were inmates given any sort of work to do. "In general, only the small minority of inmates who are designated as 'trusties' are allowed to do more than clean their own cell areas. Even inmates who are remanded to jails in lieu of paying fines are more accurately described as 'laying out' rather than 'working out' their fines. . . ." The inmates simply fester, corrupt one another and, as more than one jailer told us, "figure out ways to break out of here."

Of the jails surveyed for the Crime Commission, only 24 percent were less than ten years old, 11 percent ten to twenty-four years old, 30 percent twenty-five to fifty years old and 35 percent more than fifty years old. Built to hold the most dangerous offenders prior to trial, the jails impose maximum security on all their inmates. This security may be necessary for a few prisoners, but it is unnecessarily expensive and restrictive for the great majority who are simply awaiting trial or serving short sentences for minor crimes.

Jails are administered almost exclusively by local governments, although states have taken over administrative responsibility for jails in Delaware, Connecticut and Alaska. Fewer than half the states set any standards for local jails, and even fewer than that (nineteen by last count) inspect to determine whether their standards are being met. Even where inspection uncovers deficiencies, the only way to enforce changes is to close the jails—a politically unlikely solution. Only six states provide subsidies for local improvement of jails.[41]

The Federal Bureau of Prisons, which runs only two jails (the Federal Detention Headquarters in New York City and the Federal Detention Center, Florence, Arizona), contracts with local authorities to hold between 3,500 and 4,000 unsentenced federal prisoners each day in eight hundred local jails. The Bureau has twelve inspectors whose job it is to evaluate the jails. When the inspectors consider a jail unsuitable for federal prisoners, the Bureau's only remedy is to revoke its contract and send its prisoners elsewhere. Consequently, the inspectors take into account the needs of the local courts and the available alternatives when rating 825 jails as acceptable.

Since there is neither national nor regional and sparse statewide cen-

41. The President's Commission on Law Enforcement and Administration of Justice, Task Force Report: *Correction* 80 (1967).

tral administration of American jails, there is no way to distribute their population. Most big-city jails and some county jails are chronically over-crowded, with as many as four inmates housed in six-by-nine-foot cells, sleeping on the floor and confined to their cells or a narrow adjoining cor-ridor for meals and "recreation." Others, generally in rural areas, are often half empty. Since some jails have from only one to ten sentenced pris-oners in custody, rules requiring separation of prisoners by age or sex may mean that they are kept in solitary confinement. In this type of system, any attempt to classify prisoners according to their special needs is foreclosed.

All but a few of the largest jails are administered by law-enforcement personnel, generally sheriffs, as part of their responsibility for confining defendants prior to trial and escorting them to and from court. Jail ad-ministration is only one of several functions performed by a sheriff. He generally lacks knowledge of or commitment to correctional programs. Even when a sheriff instigates programs, frequent changes in officials and jail personnel following each election may make them short-lived. In some rural counties, the jailer is on duty twenty-four hours a day, seven days a week. He sometimes has other functions, such as cleaning the courthouse, and in some places his profit still may depend on the fee sys-tem, under which he keeps any money he saves from the allotment for the inmates' food and upkeep and pays any excess out of his own pocket.

From our experience, the absence of programming in jails seems to derive less from a lack of resources (although the absence of any space other than cells and narrow corridors in most jails presents very serious obstacles) than from a lack of imagination. Most jailers prefer to exclude outsiders from jails, citing the troublesome problems of guarding extra people and searching visitors for contraband. The easiest course is to keep inmates locked in their cells, where they can be guarded with the least amount of effort. Even at well-staffed jails, employees state that all their time is taken up with checking inmates in and out for court appear-ances and receiving and discharging prisoners.

But a few resourceful jail administrators have used existing com-munity resources, such as other government agencies, community volun-teers and funding available under federal manpower or educational acts. These outside resources enable a few jails to provide short educational and vocational-training courses for inmates, occasionally in the community on a partial release basis, professional medical care, mental health and employment counseling, well-stocked libraries and contact with community groups.[42] Many of these programs are organized on an *ad hoc* basis by an interested official and may be discontinued when he is replaced by a new administration. Several California counties have gone further and established jail honor camps and farms for sentenced inmates who can be kept safely with a minimum of security.[43]

A few counties are exploring the possibility of cooperating to build regional detention centers that will be administered by regional correctional authorities. Some cities, notably Philadelphia and Los Angeles, recently have built metropolitan detention centers. While these new facilities are infinitely more cheerful and spacious than their predecessors, with windows, skylights, doors or security screens in place of bars, courtyards and recreation areas, they continue to be concerned primarily with pretrial detention and transportation of inmates and have little to offer either the sentenced offender or the man awaiting trial.

Jails have no part to play in rehabilitating the convicted offender. They should be reserved for the very small proportion of persons accused of crime who cannot be released pending trial. Although some jail facilities still might be used as reception and diagnostic centers for screening, classifying and counseling offenders who will serve their sentences elsewhere, no one should be sentenced to serve time in the present standard jail. The present jail population should be broken down into its different components and assigned to other facilities or community programs designed to deal with the special needs of each group. In some cases, alternatives to jail already exist in the community. A greater use of suspended sentences, probation, fines or restitution, special programs for alcoholics and drug addicts, group homes, halfway houses and work-release centers would return jails to their original function as places of temporary detention and permit minor offenders to be handled more appropriately in the community.

42. *See, e.g.,* Case, "Incentives in a County Prison," *The Prison Journal,* Spring-Summer 1967, at 4; Case, "Citizen Participation: An Experiment in Prison-Community Relations," *Federal Probation,* December 1966, at 18; Erwin, "Cook County Jail's Short-term Education Program," *American Journal of Correction,* March–April 1970, at 14; Westchester Citizens Committee of the National Council of Crime and Delinquency, Report on the Pilot Project for Women, Westchester County Jail (1965); Institute for the Study of Crime and Delinquency, Model Community Correctional Program, Report III: *Crime and Its Correction in San Joaquin County* 246–95 (1969); National Council on Crime and Delinquency, *Correction in the United States* 148–150 (1966).
43. *See, e.g.,* The Advisory Committee for Adult Detention, City and County of San Francisco, *San Francisco Adult Detention Facilities* 261–72 (March 1968); Institute for the Study of Crime and Delinquency, Model Community Correctional Program, Report III: *Crime and Its Correction in San Joaquin County* 246 (1969).

Classifications

Classification is a relatively recent correctional innovation. As obvious and necessary a technique as it might seem, until a few decades ago there was no significant separation of prisoners or individualization of their imprisonment experience. With the relatively modern talk about "making the punishment fit the criminal" as well as the crime has come the evolution of the classification function in American correction. Now the federal government uses classification throughout its system, and about two dozen states have classification programs.

There are certain obvious categories of classification to which most systems give at least some recognition at present—young and old offenders, male and female offenders, sane and insane offenders, local and federal offenders—and they usually end up in different institutions, due at least to those characteristics. Some states go further and purport to have treatment-oriented institutions designed not only to segregate types but also to serve the special needs of individual prisoners.

At least in the better correctional rhetoric and writing on the subject, it is now presumed that the correction of criminal behavior requires multiple and tailored forms of controls and programs based on the individual's social history. Of course, this approach takes a certain philosophical commitment as well as a significant economic ability. But about the need to avoid crude and mass incarceration there can be no question. A handbook distributed in 1947 by the American Prison Association that serves as the basic instruction on classification states.

> Whether classification is provided for by legislation or not, it is absolutely necessary that there be legal authority within the central department for the transfer of inmates from one institution to another.

A crucial element which is reflected in these developing reception centers is that once a man is convicted in court for committing a crime, the decision as to the place and method of treatment should be made by correctional specialists.

There are, the handbook points out, three types of classification systems in the United States: 1) the classification clinic or bureau (used in a few states) within individual institutions which serves as a professional diagnostic unit; 2) the integrated classification system (most commonly used) where professional and administrative personnel of the institution work as a committee to recommend programs for individual prisoners; and 3) the reception center where all offenders within a jurisdiction spend a short time in a central receiving institution for observation, classification and eventual transfer. In thirteen states, juveniles are sent to separate reception and diagnostic centers before being assigned to training schools, camps or special institutions; several other states perform the classification function within juvenile training schools. According to the handbook:

> The purposes of a period of reception are threefold: first, to segregate new prisoners from the general population long enough to ascertain whether or not they are suffering from any communicable diseases; second, to provide opportunity for the staff to become acquainted with the inmate through personal contact during the initial examinations and interviews; and third, to acquaint the inmate through an orientation program with the policies, regulations and training opportunities of the institutions.[44]

Assuming a special central institution exists within a jurisdiction to serve a classification purpose and that appropriate personnel can be found to operate it, the inmate is sent there for a brief period, usually for two or three months. Here he is indoctrinated into the system, given medical treatment and a battery of psychological and vocational aptitude tests, interviewed by caseworkers, chaplains and training officers, and generally phased into the system.

We visited the Georgia Diagnostic and Classification Center, a new $8 million facility in Jackson, Georgia. Every convicted felon comes here first to be classified and assigned to the state's different institutions. After describing and showing us this diverse, well-equipped and professionally staffed institution, the warden reported that before it was built in 1968 the whole state processing, interviewing and evaluating function, now conducted in forty to fifty days in this new institution, was supplied to the Correction Department by a one-page fact sheet prepared by a probation officer and an FBI rap sheet.

The classification (and reclassification) function, however, does not

44. The American Prison Association, *Handbook on Classification in Correctional Institutions* 16 (1947, rev. ed. 1965).

end with diagnosis or even the recommendation and assignment to a so-called "treatment program" but should provide the basis for a continuum of attention which follows the inmate through his correctional career. For example, the classification report can serve an important function regarding the subsequent decision to put a prisoner on work release or for later parole disposition of the inmate.

Some places include the inmate in the decision about assignment. An ideal classification system will tailor prisoners' assignments to the appropriate physical environment as well as the most appropriate programs and personnel. Both obviously are relevant to his treatment. So too are the custodial officers, who, along with the specialists—in most places even more than the others—hold the key to prisoners' treatment.

Under the federal system, geography precludes centralizing the classification function in one place. The whole process is overseen administratively by the Federal Bureau of Prisons in Washington. The process operates in two steps. At the first step, after sentence many convicts initially are assigned to an institution by the local U.S. marshal, whose discretion is limited by a manual dictating who should go where and in what circumstances. His basic considerations are the convict's age, prior criminal record, duration of sentence and the nature of his offense. Of course, the limited variety of institutions often precludes much discretion. Each marshal for each federal judicial district has such a guide manual. However, juvenile, youth, young adult and female offenders and other special cases are assigned initially by the federal bureau's classification officials. Some statutes require that special cases be sent to the bureau for limited assignments for special purposes. We were told by bureau officials that in 40 percent of the cases initial assignment is made by the marshals.

The second step is the continuing classification process which goes on in institutions once a convict is incarcerated. Each institution has case workers and other staff members who, in teams of three or five, review all cases, recommend programs and occasionally recommend the transfer of men to other, more appropriate institutions (for example, to be nearer home or because a particular program is available). They function with general freedom and autonomy, although they too are limited by the inherent limitations of their system's institutions. Again, while the Federal Bureau of Prisons must approve certain special transfers, most of the actual reclassification is done at the local level by the wardens and their classification teams.

How central a technique classification can be within a prison system became apparent in our visit to the Borstal Allocation Center at Wormwood Scrubs in London. Two of the four wings of this old prison building in a dilapidated outskirt of London are used to house young offenders who have been given prison sentences and young offenders who have been sentenced and are awaiting assignment to borstals. The latter group stays at Scrubs for allocation only. The procedure these youngsters go through is an interesting one.

Borstal boys range in age from fifteen to twenty-one. They have been sentenced by courts to terms between six months and three years. All such young offenders from all over England are first sent to Wormwood Scrubs for interviews and assignment to a particular borstal. A special staff thoroughly interviews and tests all the boys and, without delay, recommends to an allocation board the most appropriate borstal for that particular boy. Borstals may be open or closed institutions; each stresses different vocational facilities; and they are located geographically all over the country. They vary in size and there are twenty in all.

On his ninth day at Scrubs, after having been screened by all the officials, the boy appears before the allocation board and is assigned to a particular borstal. The allocation board is composed of professionals from various disciplines—a correctional governor, a social worker, a psychologist, a vocational-guidance officer, an educational specialist, sometimes where appropriate a medical officer—and a custodial officer as the clerk. Seventy private specialists from London are on call for appropriate individual cases.

In discussing each case, the allocation board assesses whether the boy can adjust to an open institution or whether he should be sent to a closed one for his welfare, as well as public safety; what kinds of vocational skills the youth has and which institution can best further them; whether the boy should be in a rural or agrarian setting; how far the appropriate institution is from the boy's home or from those people who are most likely to visit him; and other questions of this nature.

In each boy's file was a full report discussing his problem, police record, medical report and all other pertinent data. The boys had been interviewed by agents of the allocation staff constantly since their arrival. One day a week the board makes assignments. Thereafter, within a few weeks from their arrival, the boys leave Wormwood Scrubs for the borstals chosen for them.

Before the individual under consideration enters the board room, each person around the table representing a different discipline and expertise comments about the boy, notes his special agency's recommendation for assignment and describes the reasons for it. After each person has reported, a consensus is reached—it is usually unanimous—about where he should go. The basis for the decision always is what seems best for the rehabilitation of that individual so far as space and facilities are available. The board prefers open borstals if it is possible and almost always assigns a boy to an open borstal if it is his first time and where his offense is relatively minor.

When a decision is made by the board, the young man is called in. He is treated kindly and told briefly but clearly not only what the board members tentatively have decided but the reasons for their decision. They ask his opinion. In most cases, he agrees; but sometimes he does not, and occasionally he will persuade the board to change its decision. For example, while we were in attendance at one classification meeting we witnessed a frank discussion between the board and one boy about whether he should go to an open borstal for boys of higher intelligence. The board wanted the boy to go there for programmatic reasons, but at the same time had legitimate fears that he might flee. They discussed this fear with the boy and in fact at one point found themselves urging the boy to assume the responsibility to go there, however hesitant he was himself about his ability to adjust.

While most American jurisdictions and institutions still do not have significant classification features and those that do have them are frequently inadequate, there can be no doubt that the evolution of this type of procedure—in institutions or, preferably, in the community—is critical to correctional reform.

The necessity of extending classification activities to the large majority of institutions in the United States which still lack such services is obvious. The failure of mass treatment methods to provide a solution to the problem of criminal behavior can no longer be ignored. Prisons cannot continue to operate indefinitely with a failure rate of sixty or seventy percent. No longer can the prison properly be regarded solely as a place for punishment.

Institutions for Treatment

Some institutions in the United States and abroad have experimented with programs that go beyond custody and the provision of minimal medical care and attempt to use incarceration as the framework within which to "treat" criminals and thereby to effect their socialization. The initial idea behind all prisons was to provide a reformative alternative to the simple punishments of earlier systems. In this section, however, we will deal with special penal institutions that recognize the inadequacy of ordinary prisons to do much beyond containing and punishing and that attempt to do something more constructive. These innovations too were intended as a positive step in the direction of reforming the strictly punitive correction system by seeking to use the imprisonment experience as an opportunity to change prisoners and socialize them. However dangerous some of the techniques used to do this may be, the ideal and intention of treatment has been to be helpful and curative, more redemptive and less punitive than conventional imprisonment.

Theoretically, the notion of treatment is eminently sensible and logical. In practice, however, the experiment to date can only be called inconclusive. While some observers already consider these special institutions *avant-garde* successes, others view them as frightening and meddlesome cures tending to be worse than the old, standard alternatives. As W. R. Outerbridge, a Canadian expert, has commented, "During recent decades . . . a fascinating anomaly has developed in the field of corrections. On the one hand, behavioral scientists with a 'treatment' orientation have been gaining more and more authority in the administration of correctional programmes; on the other, research has been establishing with greater and greater precision the ineffectiveness of the methods which they espouse."

These special institutions devised for treatment instead of punishment are called by some "therapeutic communities," in the fashion of the famous English hospitals at Henderson and Dingleton founded and run by Dr. Maxwell Jones. In the novel *One Flew Over the Cuckoo's Nest* by Ken Kesey a patient describes the therapeutic community in his mental institution:

> I've heard that theory of the Therapeutic Community enough times to repeat it forwards and backwards—how a guy has to learn to get along in a group before he'll be able to function in a normal society; how the group can help the guy by showing him where he's out of place; how society is what decides who's sane and who isn't, so you got to measure up. All that stuff. Every time we get a new patient on the ward the doctor goes into the theory with both feet; it's pretty near the only

time he takes things over and runs the meeting. He tells how the goal of the Therapeutic Community is a democratic ward, run completely by the patients and their votes, working toward making worth-while citizens to turn back Outside onto the street. Any little gripe, any grievance, anything you want changed, he says, should be brought up before the group and discussed instead of letting it fester inside of you. Also you should feel at ease in your surroundings to the extent you can freely discuss emotional problems in front of patients and staff. Talk, he says, discuss, confess. And if you hear a friend say something during the course of your everyday conversation, then list it in the log book for the staff to see. It's not, as the movies call it, "squealing," it's helping your fellow. Bring these old sins into the open where they can be washed by the sight of all. And participate in Group Discussion. Help yourself and your friends probe into the secrets of the subconscious. There should be no need for secrets among friends.

Our intention, he usually ends by saying, is to make this as much like your own democratic, free neighborhoods as possible —a little world Inside that is a made-to-scale prototype of the big world Outside that you will one day be taking your place in again.[45]

If not an example of a true therapeutic community, certainly a step in that direction has been provided by a few attempts at involving inmates in self-government in prisons. The late Thomas Mott Osborne is credited with the first noble attempt at this when he was the warden at Sing Sing. But that was long ago and its success was very short-lived.

Since then inmate participation in the institutional decisions that govern their lives has been unremarkable in this country. Recently an interesting experiment took place at the Washington State Penitentiary, a large (over 1,000 men) maximum-security prison in the countryside near Walla Walla. There the warden and the state prison director modeled a prisoners' self-government program upon experiments they had noted in Denmark and Holland. The institution is governed by a constitution that was drawn up by the inmates and that provides for a resident governmental council of eleven convicts elected for six-month terms. The council has written and unwritten many of the prevailing intramural rules (no gambling, narcotics or alcohol; unlimited mail privileges). Inmates may grow beards and long

45. Kesey, *One Flew Over the Cuckoo's Nest* 47 (1962).

hair and wear clothes of their choice. Inmate council members attend disciplinary sessions and may defend respondents and protest decisions. Furloughs of up to thirty days may be granted and even lifers are invited home by staff for dinner.

The long-range results of this program are impossible to evaluate at this premature stage, but the notion of building responsibility, allowing some self-government and avoiding many of the unnecessary but typical and provocative prison regulations certainly seems laudatory.

Common features exist in most of the prevailing special-treatment institutions: inmates usually are serving indefinite sentences; psychiatric, medical and paramedical personnel are in relative abundance and hold critical powers; the facilities are comparatively new and less unpleasant than their prison counterparts; there is some plan guiding the program for the inmate's stay and determining when he may be released; frequently there is a continuation of services after release; inmates usually are given some participatory role in the treatment of one another and in the affairs of the institution.

PATUXENT

The most remarkable of these places in the United States is the Patuxent Institution in Patuxent, Maryland, created in the early 1950s to deal with the state's most serious, repeat offenders "until cured, if curable, or for life, if not curable."[46] The Department of Correction, the state's attorney, the defendant, his attorney or the court may request that a person be examined to determine if he is a defective delinquent at any time after he has been sentenced for a crime, as long as he is still incarcerated. He must have been convicted and sentenced in a Maryland court for: (1) a felony; (2) a misdemeanor punishable by imprisonment in the penitentiary; (3) a crime of violence; (4) a sex crime involving physical force, disparity of age, or a sexual act of an uncontrolled or repetitive nature; (5) two or more convictions in Maryland of offenses punishable by imprisonment.

To avoid the use of the terms "psychopath" and "sociopath," which have no universally accepted meaning, the drafters of the statute created the new legal designation "defective delinquent"—"an individual who, by the demonstration of persistent aggravated antisocial or criminal behavior,

46. Judge Joseph N. Ulman, *A Judge Takes the Stand* (1933).

evidences a propensity toward criminal activity and who is found to have either such intellectual deficiency or emotional unbalance, or both, as to clearly demonstrate an actual danger to society so as to require such confinement and treatment, when appropriate, as may make it reasonably safe for society to terminate the confinement and treatment." Such a person must be deficient intellectually or emotionally, have some history of antisocial behavior and have been convicted and sentenced for a crime.

When an examination is requested, the court has the discretion whether or not to order it. If it does, the prisoner is then transferred to the Patuxent Institution for diagnosis. He remains there until the statutory procedures have been completed, even if his sentence should expire in the interim. On the basis of physical, psychiatric and psychological examinations, personal interviews and any other reports which other institutions have made about the defendant, the Patuxent staff within six months must agree on a diagnosis and make its recommendations to the court. In addition, whenever the request for examination is made by someone other than the defendant or his attorney, the defendant is entitled to be examined at state expense by an alternate private psychiatrist of his own choice.

In about 35 percent of the cases the Patuxent staff has ruled that the defendant was not a defective delinquent. The defendant in such a case is returned to a conventional prison. If, on the other hand, the examiners recommend confinement for defective delinquency, the court must inform the defendant that there will be a hearing and assure him counsel. In preparing for the hearing, defense attorneys have access to all institutional records and reports that bear on the case. The hearing, with a jury if the defendant or the state requests, determines whether the recommendations of the Patuxent staff should be followed and the defendant sentenced as a defective delinquent. The defendant may summon witnesses, present evidence and use all the procedures for discovery of relevant facts that are available in civil cases. Because the proceeding, which has been compared to one to commit the mentally ill, is not considered to involve criminal sanctions, the judge or jury need not be convinced of the defendant's status "beyond a reasonable doubt." In more than 80 percent of the hearings, the court or jury has followed Patuxent's recommendation that the defendant is a defective delinquent. Defendants may appeal from such conclusions only with the permission of the appellate court. A finding of defective delinquency suspends the original criminal sentence, and the defendant is assigned to Patuxent for an indeterminate period.

Each person so confined may petition the court for reconsideration of his status after he has been at Patuxent for two years or after two-thirds of his original sentence has expired, whichever is longer. He may request a jury. Such initial rehearings have resulted in the release of 44 percent of those who have requested them. Thereafter, an inmate may petition the court for release once every three years. Second and subsequent rehearings have resulted in the release of slightly more than half of those who have requested them. Prisoners released by court orders are not paroled but are immediately freed from all legal ties to the institution. This possibility of court-ordered release avoids to some extent the problem of most states' indeterminate sentences for sociopathic offenders or involuntary commitments of the mentally ill, where the possibility of release depends entirely on obtaining the favorable recommendation of one or more psychiatrists. An alternative way to be released is by the Institutional Board of Review, established by the statute, as discussed in Chapter V.

To date, both Maryland and federal courts have found the defective-delinquent statute constitutional. In the opinion of a United States court of appeals, the statute provides a "humanitarian and progressive approach," of which "no person who has deplored the inadequacies of conventional penological practices can complain." However, in 1964 the court felt that the statute was "so serious a departure from traditional concepts of justice" that it deserved "a critical analysis on the broadest of terms after a careful factual development of its present operation." Consequently, the court asked both the federal district court and the Maryland court of appeals to consider "whether the proposed objectives of the Act are sufficiently implemented in its actual administration to support its categorization as a civil procedure and justify the elimination of conventional criminal procedural safeguards."[47]

After considering the legislative history of the statute and expert testimony about the operation of Patuxent, both courts concluded that the statute is constitutional;[48] specifically, that it provides a precise enough definition of "defective delinquent"; that the wording and history of the statute somehow indicated that its purpose was not penal but civil and regulatory, thus avoiding constitutional objections such as double jeopardy; that it provides at least as many procedural safeguards to the accused as do similar statutes of other states already held constitutional; that there is no constitutional ban on including individuals whose crimes in-

47. *Sas v. Maryland,* 334 F.2d 506 (4th Cir. 1964).
48. *Sas v. Maryland,* 195 F.Supp. 389 (D.Md. 1969); *Director, Patuxent Institution v. Daniels,* No. 520 (Court of Appeals, 1966).

volved only a danger to property and not personal violence; and, finally, that Patuxent in fact furnishes treatment for the treatable defective delinquents who are sent there.

On appeal from the federal decision, the appeals court ruled that, at least at this stage of the experiment, Patuxent's implementation of the statute is constitutional. The court rejected the contention that Patuxent is in fact a penal institution and held that the diagnostic and treatment purposes of the statute would be subverted if procedural protections, such as the assistance of counsel and freedom from compulsory self-incrimination, were required. A minority opinion would have required the state to make counsel available to defendants being examined for possible defective delinquency and to prove that a defendant is a defective delinquent by "clear and convincing" evidence rather than by a mere preponderance of the evidence. All the judges agreed that the decision did not represent a final adjudication of all constitutional questions involved in the administration of the statute, particularly "if later experience should show serious unfairness in the administration of the act."[49]

The Supreme Court has granted *certiorari* in two cases to consider several constitutional issues raised by Patuxent's procedures, including the question of whether an inmate may refuse to participate in any diagnostic questioning in order to protect himself from the possibility of compulsory self-incrimination.[50]

Other states have laws prescribing specialized treatment and indefinite commitment of certain offenders. Many of the laws deal only with sexual offenders, and the full range of procedural safeguards provided in Maryland generally are not available. The most significant difference, however, is that Maryland is the only state which has designed and erected an institution expressly for the diagnosis, confinement and treatment of defective delinquents. Professor Samuel Fahr points out, "The brute fact is that, while legislatures have rushed to pass these sexual psychopath laws, they have generally been unwilling to take the really wrenching steps of appropriating the money to carry them out."

The institution, opened in January 1955, currently contains a multi-sectioned building for the custody of inmates, a diagnostic center, a kitchen-dining room, a gymnasium-theater, a hospital, vocational shops and a school area. An academic building is under construction. Built to

---

49. *Tippett v. Maryland*, 436 F.2d 1153 (4th Cir. 1971).
50. *McNeil v. Director*, No. 71-5144; *Murel v. Baltimore City Criminal Court*, No. 70-5276, 10 *Criminal Law Reporter* 4115 (1972).

hold 600 inmates, the current population is between 485 and 500.

The statute provides for a psychiatrist as chief administrator of Patuxent in place of the usual warden. The director's role emphasizes the hospital rather than prison atmosphere. Staff members refer to the inmates as "patients." Some research personnel are there to aid the therapeutic activities. Of the approximately sixty psychiatrists in the country who are said to devote their full time to correction, twelve are at Patuxent. Rejecting the peripheral role that most institutions give to psychiatry, Patuxent gives it a central role. In addition, the institution has ten psychologists and fourteen social workers.

Staff members consider their diagnostic function of prime importance. They relate stories of men diagnosed by them as defective delinquents but released by sympathetic judges or juries only to commit further violent crimes.

Once inmates have been diagnosed and committed, they remain for an average of four and one half years. Virtually no one leaves in less than two years. Approximately 20 percent are serving beyond their original sentences, and two men have been in the institution since it opened. The relatively short duration of most sentences has proved contrary to the expectation of those who drafted the statute. Early predictions were that most inmates were incurable and would remain in the institution for life. However, of those leaving the institution more than half are released by judges or juries against the recommendation of the Patuxent staff.

In most cases, inmates come to Patuxent with long histories of criminal activities, after having spent unsuccessfully a large part of their lives in correctional institutions. The defective-delinquency law adds to the restraint of confinement the motivation of the indeterminate sentence. Inmates can no longer serve out their sentences secure in the knowledge that they will be released at the end of a set period, which may have no relation to their "correction." Most have come to recognize that the only way to get out of Patuxent through institutional channels is to convince the professional staff that they have gained an understanding of their personal problems and made some progress toward solving them.

A side effect of the need to demonstrate constructive change may be that the men mouth phrases of self-awareness that many cannot really understand. Inmates who appear before the Board of Review recite that they have grown more "mature"; when we visited to observe, one proudly reported that his therapy had taught him to "rationalize." Another said, "My moral character isn't so good, but I've been working on it." Staff members believe, however, that whether the men think they are "conning" them is secondary; what is important is that they are motivated to strive for change in their attitudes and behavior.

The indeterminate sentence is credited with providing the impetus necessary to overcome inmates' initial reluctance to attend the weekly group-therapy sessions: "After a while it became clear to all inmates that those who got out were the ones who had been in therapy and who had at least managed to convince the professional staff that in some way they had benefitted from it." Group therapy, adopted because of the need to economize with the time of the professional staff, has come to be preferred by staff members to individual treatment. Individual therapy involves a relationship that is too intense for many of the inmates, who are extremely hesitant to form close personal ties, particularly with staff members. Inmates are less reticent to talk to a group of six or seven fellow men, although even this has proved too small a group for some. In addition, the presence of other inmates makes it more difficult for the patient to fabricate stories about what is going on in the institution for the benefit of the therapist.

Many of the groups are specially formed from patients who are likely to benefit from the same kind of treatment—for example, sex offenders, blacks, particularly aggressive men or inmates of superior intelligence. (The large number of men with drinking problems attend institutional meetings of Alcoholics Anonymous in addition to the therapy sessions.) Retarded inmates (those with IQs below 79), who comprise at least one-quarter of Patuxent's committed population, present special problems for psychotherapy. At first they were not included in the groups. Most of them are now receiving therapy in groups that concentrate on solving everyday problems rather than on developing an individual's psychological insight.

According to staff members these weekly sessions, no matter how productive, were not by themselves sufficient to cause the inmates' patterns of behavior to change. The staff therefore determined to reinforce what was learned in the sessions by organizing the entire institution to serve therapeutic purposes. In order to provide continuing incentive, the institution was structured according to a graded tier system based on the behaviorist hypothesis that rewarding socially desirable behavior increases its frequency. The institution is divided into four tier levels, distinguished primarily by the number of privileges permitted the inmates of each level: increased physical comforts in cells and recreation areas;

freedom of movement within the institution; decreased custodial supervision; types of jobs; the availability of different hours of lights-out at
night; and the variety of commissary items that may be purchased.

When an inmate has been diagnosed by the staff as a defective delinquent, he is transferred from the receiving tier to the first level. He lives
in an ordinary prison cell, exercises in a bleak recreation yard and works
on a sanitation crew. Thirty days later, regardless of whether his judicial
hearing has been held, he becomes eligible for promotion to the second
level. This promotion involves a move from the diagnostic building across
the yard to the building where the three upper tiers are housed. Inmates
place great value on promotion to a higher level. A demotion, given for
failure to show sufficient motivation as well as for serious disciplinary infractions, is viewed as a serious personal loss.

Vocational training is available only to men who have reached the
third level. An inmate generally must be on the third or fourth level to
be granted leave or parole. Summer picnics are held for the families of
fourth-level residents, who also are given the freedom to paint and
decorate their cells. The fourth-level recreation room, with its comfortable chairs, magazines and pool table, adjoins the less elaborate third-
level facility, so that third-level inmates may see the rewards that await
their efforts. Thus the tier system gives each inmate tangible signs of
where he stands in the institutional structure and of how far he has
progressed.

Conventional prison practice is not to reinforce good behavior with
rewards but to control inmates by punishing their misbehavior. (Recent
disclosures made in the course of litigation revealed that even at Patuxent
the most recalcitrant inmates are punished in much the same way as in
the typical prison.) Patuxent's shift to a system of rewards was not accomplished without difficulty. When the institution first opened, it was under
the administrative control of the Department of Correction. Work was
assigned according to institutional needs. The department segregated inmates' housing and meals according to race, type of crime committed and
length of sentence. Security officers emphasized authoritarian and punitive
attitudes. Disciplinary methods generally consisted of confinement in seclusion on bread-and-water diets. The officers' view of the inmates as people
of little worth conflicted with what the inmates were learning in therapy,
and much of each therapy session had to be spent in attempting to resolve
these conflicts.

At the urging of a governor-appointed commission in 1960, the institution was granted autonomy. The professional staff took over responsibility for training security officers, transferred disciplinary authority to teams of professional and custodial personnel and arranged split work shifts to allow inmates sufficient time for therapy, education and vocational training.

The great majority of Patuxent's population has had very little formal schooling and possesses no employment skills. The institution runs a school which offers primary through high-school education. Researchers who tested a large number of inmates diagnosed communications problems in 50 percent of the population; they currently are conducting speech therapy groups for inmates. Vocational training is provided. The institution maintains its own placement service and has a backlog of job offers for parolees. The explanation of Patuxent's attraction to employers seems to lie in the quality of the training the institution provides and the continuing readiness of personnel to deal with any problems its former inmates may encounter on their jobs.

To integrate the various rehabilitative efforts and create the feeling of a smaller institution, inmates are divided into units of ninety men. Each unit contains three housing groups. Six professionals are assigned to each unit and seem to know every man in the unit. The professionals meet once a week with each unit to discuss the week's events. Staff members have found that some of the men who are reticent to speak in group-therapy sessions had fewer inhibitions when meeting in the larger, more impersonal housing groups.

The six professionals assigned to each unit comprise a Classification Committee. Determination of job assignments and promotions and demotions among tiers are made on the basis of personal contacts with the inmates and monthly progress reports by the professionals involved in their treatment. Committee members frequently disagree about the action to be taken on some inmates, and we observed several dispositions made by closely divided votes. Inmates do not attend the meetings, but they are advised of the reason for each disposition. The Classification Committee also makes recommendations to the Institutional Board of Review.

When the Board of Review recommends an inmate's release after intensive interviewing, he is supervised on parole by the institution's Social Service Department, aided by the entire professional staff. A social worker becomes acquainted with the inmate and his family before he is paroled and determines whether the parolee would benefit from the services of the halfway house or the apartment building which Patuxent runs in Baltimore for men who lack family ties. Parolees are seen weekly in an outpatient clinic by the same professionals who treated them in the institution, a practice which helps the transition from the institution to the outside.

Of 217 inmates paroled by the Board of Review, ninety-seven were returned to the institution, thirty-six for violation of the conditions of parole and sixty-one for the commission of new offenses. Some, finding that they could not cope with problems on the outside, came back voluntarily.

No definitive figures comparing the experiences of inmates released from Patuxent with those of releasees from conventional correctional institutions are available.[51] Perhaps no valid recidivism comparisons can be made, since Patuxent's population is not typical of correctional populations in general. Economically, the annual cost of maintaining and treating an inmate at Patuxent, with its employee–inmate ratio of 1 : 1.4 (with professional staff it is 1 : 35), is currently estimated at $7,000—at least twice the cost at a conventional prison.

Although a Maryland judge recently stated that confinement of defective delinquents at Patuxent, rather than in the state's penal institutions, has enabled such institutions to develop more effective programs for the conventional male prison population (women are not allowed at Patuxent), there is no evidence that the ordinary prisoner in Maryland has been benefitted in any way by the existence of the specialized institution.

Patuxent does seem to be helping some of the offenders referred to it. Solving some of the problems of men who have represented such serious threats to society must be considered one measure of success. It was the optimistic opinion of a National Conference of State Trial Judges committee in 1966 that the institution ". . . represents the most enlightened and forward-looking approach existing anywhere in the United States to the solution of the problem of the sociopathic offender."

In its fifteen years of experience, Patuxent has provided at least the most interesting experiment, if not a demonstrably successful one, in treating what may be the most difficult and dangerous category of American convicts. Yet, given the limited over-all resources available for corrections, it remains questionable whether this money and effort might better be spent on programs for young or first offenders, where the possibility

51. However, preliminary data furnished to the federal courts indicated that the recidivism rate of offenders released from Patuxent was lower than the average for U.S. prisons. *Tippett v. Maryland*, 436 F.2d 1153, 1157 (4th Cir. 1971).

for real correction is so much greater.

While the theoretical arguments concerning the wisdom and the constitutionality of Patuxent's program continued in medical and correctional circles and in the federal courts, a state court recently challenged the institution's theoretical justification on pragmatic grounds; in doing so, the court exploded some of the myths surrounding treatment at Patuxent.[52]

A two-judge state court ruled in favor of inmates who challenged the treatment given recalcitrant inmates who refused diagnosis and treatment, as well as the insulation of the entire institution from contacts with the outside world through restrictions on visiting and mail. The court found that inmates were placed in solitary confinement as "negative re-enforcers" for periods of up to thirty days without adequate light, ventilation, exercise or sanitation. In fact, some of the conditions were far worse than those proscribed by the American Correctional Association for prisons, not treatment centers. Such practices, the court held, are "contrary to the rehabilitation of the inmates and serve no therapeutic value of any kind"; in fact, they are contrary to the Eighth Amendment's ban on cruel and unusual punishment.

Concluding that the institution had "neither promulgated nor published any written rules for the conduct of the patients, rules governing the conduct of the custodial staff, or procedural rudiments necessary to govern disciplinary hearings," and that "the current unstructured and uncontrolled processes result in decisions that are unfounded, inconsistent and unrelated to any of the professed goals of the institution," the court ordered the implementation of due-process protections of notice and hearing before any solitary confinement can be imposed by the Patuxent staff. Extensive changes in institutional practices relating to admission of the press, censorship and mail, and the diet given inmates of the Moslem faith also were ordered.

In addition, the court went beyond the issues the inmates had raised and dealt with some of Patuxent's basic claims as a "total treatment facility." The court noted that newly employed correctional personnel were trained for their treatment-oriented or rehabilitative roles not by the medical staff but by the senior shift officer. According to the court:

> Such training includes indoctrination of past and present policies
> handed down by top ranking officers and the professional staff,
> as well as those traditional rules and regulations established by

52. *McCray v. Maryland*, Misc. Pet. 4363 (Circuit Court for Montgomery County, Md., Nov. 11, 1971).

the custodial staff, based upon individual experiences over a number of years—all related to the general "lock and key," "watch out for this one" approach.

The court strongly recommended that Patuxent hire additional medical personnel and institute a comprehensive treatment program designed to deal with narcotic addiction. The court was particularly concerned with the lack of treatment and the "overall lack of concern on the part of the staff" with the plight of recalcitrant inmates who refused to cooperate in the rehabilitative effort:

A person cannot receive a life sentence by civil rules on the theory of treatment and then not be treated because he may be so emotionally unstable that he refuses help. . . . Treatment in its broadest sense must be applied to this group of recalcitrant patients. The court finds little, if any, effort is, in fact, made in this direction. . . .

The court concluded that "the maintenance of prisoners in cells in a prisonlike setting with the offering of group therapy and limited rehabilitative vocation training is not a total rehabilitative effort. Treatment in the Patuxent Institution should be immediately accelerated without regard to strict budgetary limitations imposed by the state."

There are a few other American institutions that make a stab at treatment of the "sociopathic," or mentally ill, criminal—Vacaville, California; Springfield in the federal system; Bridgewater, Massachusetts; Dannemora, New York. All of these have been called a cheap version of Patuxent by some, an Orwellian nightmare by others.

Abroad, experiments toward creating treatment-oriented institutions, if not therapeutic communities, have had some notoriety at Herstedvester and Horsens in Denmark, at Grendon Underwood in England, at the Psychiatric Observation Clinic and its satellite treatment centers in the Netherlands. A new institution, for which members of the Patuxent staff have served as consultants, is being planned in Montreal.

We had heard and read impressive praise of the foreign institutions which had reputations for innovative work in establishing treatment-oriented prison environments. After visiting Patuxent, we went to see the most notable ones: Herstedvester and Horsens; Grendon Underwood; the Psychiatric Observation Clinic and the Van den Hoeven Clinic in Utrecht; the Pompeii Clinic in Nijmegen, Groot Batelaar, and a relatively new and slightly different institution for young offenders, De Corridor, all in the Netherlands.

HERSTEDVESTER

The Detention Center at Herstedvester, about a half-hour train ride outside Copenhagen, began its work on March 30, 1935. We visited the small, spare group of yellow, relatively modern buildings surrounded by a white wall and situated amidst a group of greenhouses and orchards and met with some of the staff and its famous, long-time director, Dr. Georg Sturup. The buildings are open all day and locked at night; the rooms are open all the time. The rooms are orderly and personally decorated; the atmosphere is relatively relaxed, neat and amenable. Rooms are in small units with a common social and dining room. The focus of the staff on treatment rather than security was evidenced by one nurse's remark to me as she showed me around: "How do you resocialize within a wall?"

The institution was designed to serve the criminal described by the 1930 Danish Penal Code as not susceptible to punishment because of the "defective development, or impairment or disturbance of his mental faculties but in need of detention in order to protect society." Prior to the experiment at Herstedvester these criminals were termed "partially responsible offenders" and were given shorter sentences than normal offenders.

The issue of "susceptibility to punishment" is a judicial decision made by the court, usually based on a psychiatric report. The psychiatric review of a case, which may be proposed by either the prosecution or the defense, is made by the public psychiatrist or a local medical officer. The review usually takes more than a month and contains a detailed case history, the findings of a physical examination and a psychiatric examination based on many hours of interviewing. If the court wishes, the report may be sent to the Danish Medico-Legal Council, an independent medical board headed by the professor of forensic medicine at the University of Copenhagen, for another review. Three psychiatrists experienced in legal problems review all the material placed before the court and present their psychiatric views in a joint summary. Informed by these reports, the court then decides the offender's fitness for punishment.

If it is decided that special treatment is necessary, there is a wide choice of measures available, ranging from appointment of a supervisor to placement in a hospital or special detention center such as Herstedvester. Persons sent to Herstedvester are given an indeterminate sentence; the court decides when parole should be granted (some are released after several months) based on the institution's recommendation. The institution is trusted by the courts and its recommendations usually are followed.

According to royal decree, the goal of Herstedvester is to detain those persons who would pose a threat to society if they were free and yet provide treatment that is individually designed to prepare these people for eventual return to free life. A psychiatrist always has been employed as the full-time superintendent, and each inmate has his own therapist—a psychologist or psychiatrist. "Treatment within adequate security is the answer," Dr. Sturup says. "We don't cure; we only control." Reflecting the modesty of his pretensions and the realistic limits of his goals, Dr. Sturup told us: "It is not bad if a man wants to commit another crime after he is released, just so he does not do it." However, he added, "crime is not a destiny any more than it is a disease; but treatment can help."

Psychotic and mental defectives are not accepted at Herstedvester but are cared for in special mental hospitals. Since 1951, women who would qualify for Herstedvester treatment have been sent to a section of the Women's Prison at Sorserød. Those inmates who are detained at Herstedvester have been described as "people who irrespective of their will and desire are driven by impulses of thought and conduct which impel them to antisocial conduct." They also have been described as people who "consider themselves as outcasts and find it easier to develop relationships with people who are also outcasts." The institution also takes problem inmates from the country's other institutions to ease tensions at those places and to try to treat these difficult clients.

In his book *Treating the Untreatable* Dr. Sturup uses the phrase "emotionally disturbed, chronic criminals" to describe his inmates and states that as a group they are not welcome in prisons because they are troublesome and recalcitrant; nor are they welcome in hospitals because they are neither clearly psychotic nor mentally defective."[53] Most of the inmates have been men between the ages of twenty and thirty-five. Approximately 60 percent of the inmates at Herstedvester are there for property offenses, 25 to 30 percent for sexual offenses and slightly more than 10 percent for aggressive offenses (including arson).

Rather than adhering to a particular philosophy of treatment, the professional orientation at Herstedvester is selective, intuitively using whatever approach is thought to be the most valuable in any given situation. In describing the treatment program that has developed at Herstedvester, Dr. Sturup uses the terms "situational approach" and "therapeutic climate," meaning that the program is based on collaboration between

53. Sturup, *Treating the Untreatable: Chronic Criminals at Herstedvester* 7 (1968).

the inmate and all those who deal with him in the institution: therapists (psychiatrists and psychologists), social workers, teachers and guards. The idea is that to create a therapeutic climate in which all of the staff and inmates contribute in the treatment plan, the psychotherapist must fit into this climate by working closely with the ward officers and others who have frequent direct contact with the inmate.

The treatment process includes not only psychotherapy but a kind of group therapy carried out by all who interact with the inmate in the institution, including persons with varied training and backgrounds. Treatment at Herstedvester may be anything that attempts to improve the individual inmate's chance for living a crime-free life in society.

Unlike mental hospitals which emphasize the lessening of daily stress and strain, Herstedvester attempts to place as much social strain on each inmate as he can stand so that he can learn to expand his own limits. Therefore he is forced to face those situations and feelings that he had difficulty coping with in the past.

All inmates are required to work unless they are physically unable to do so. Since an inmate must be able to keep a job as well as obtain one upon release, the institution attempts to train him in work habits and techniques. Workshops exist for such employment as printing, bookbinding, furniture making, market gardening. Maintenance work in the institution also is available. All of the work is in areas that do not cause conflict with labor unions. Detainees are paid either by the day or by the piece, bonuses being added for work on Sundays and after hours. One-third of the inmate's modest income must be saved for the parole period; one-third may be spent for new clothes and a third may be used for other personal purchases.

Herstedvester uses three full-time and seventeen part-time teachers. The courses vary from basic reading, writing and arithmetic to acting and playwriting. One teacher interested in drama has stimulated an "extemporaneous theater" in which the inmates enact a situation such as adapting to employment after parole, escaping and the like and present the play to an audience of inmates and staff. Afterward there is discussion of the theme of the play with audience and actors participating. This form of theater differs from psychodrama in that there are three or four rehearsals prior to the performance, thus eliminating the risk that some of the actors spontaneously might "act out" too strongly.

Monthly leave under supervision is considered one of the most important treatment tools. After twelve months of good behavior an inmate can become eligible for six-hour leaves. Those who have attempted to escape or have returned to Herstedvester must wait a minimum of two years, while those who have committed homicide, arson or dangerous sexual or property crimes must wait three years before leave can be granted.

The purpose of the leave is to give the inmate some realistic contact with outside life, to evaluate his chances for the future and to maintain contacts with relatives and friends. The institution believes that the granting of leave is an important therapeutic aid because it shows confidence in the inmate.

The escort is a uniformed officer (guard) who is selected by the inmate. It is the duty of the escort to have the inmate under direct surveillance so that sexual contacts are not committed. The first six leaves must take place during the day, but the later leaves may extend to 9:00 P.M. Inmates may write an unlimited number of letters, which are not censored; and they all may have one outside contact whom they can see without limitations.

Since the staff considers crime an interpersonal problem, the group approach is combined with individual therapeutical interviews. The therapist usually selects members for the group he is conducting. No special therapeutic technique is advocated; each therapist is encouraged to use the technique that best suits him and his group.

It is felt that group therapy gives the detainees a chance to give vent publicly to inner feelings that have been bothering them and to discuss their misunderstandings and mistakes; that criticism coming mainly from fellow inmates is easier to accept; that acceptable norms are internalized through the teamwork with other group members; that participants feel a sense of belonging to a group with socially acceptable goals and norms; and that this gives the criminal, who has suffered many defeats, a chance to talk over his difficulties with people who have had similar experiences.

Therapeutic techniques used include exploration of an emotion-laden situation to help the inmate see his problems in a new light. Hypnosis and narcoanalysis have been used to help speed up treatment. LSD has been used occasionally to reduce aggressive tendencies. Another technique used is "anamnestic analysis," which is a method aimed at the patient's emotional and intellectual reliving of earlier interpersonal conflicts on the basis of his attitude toward present interpersonal situations. The aim of this method is to acquaint the inmate with his patterns of reaction to difficult situations and thus to help him see the possibility for change.

One controversial practice used at Herstedvester is voluntary castration. It is not used to punish sex or other offenders. It is used only when the inmate asks for it and the staff thinks it might help that particular individual's treatment. During the period 1935 through 1957, more than 50 percent of the non-castrated sexual and other aggressive offenders at Herstedvester served sentences of over four years. Castrated sexual offenders, on the other hand, have spent an increasingly shorter amount of time at the institution.

Established in 1944, Kastanienborg is a transitional halfway house to which inmates may be transferred three to six months before parole. Parolees who get into trouble but do not need institutionalization at Herstedvester can live at Kastanienborg, as can parolees who have lost their jobs or are looking for jobs. Farm work is performed by the residents and, while they have more freedom than at Herstedvester, no inmate can leave the boundaries of the farm unless escorted by a staff member. Community visits are without limitation and attendance at local churches and movie theaters is permitted.

Dr. Sturup emphasizes that recidivism rates (about 40 percent) do not tell the whole story of the work at Herstedvester, he feels the gain in knowledge of how to help chronic criminals is important. He believes that there has been some "success" if the criminal gains insight into his behavior even if he cannot control it. Of course, the fact that many of the "chronic criminals" were able to receive enough help at Herstedvester so that they could live without committing criminal acts after release is even more significant. The key is, according to Dr. Sturup, to get the man to know his problem when he is released; this is done by making him work through his problem while he is incarcerated.

A sense of Dr. Sturup's balance can be seen in his final remarks to us. "Inmates must trust our judgment. They know if we are foolish and not worth listening to. One way to show them we are foolish is to overdo our powers. For example, while custody is important to prevent escape, we should be sure not to overdo what is sensible by going too far with it."

HORSENS

To fill the overflow of cases coming to Herstedvester, a new institution was created in 1951 in a century-old prison in the rural, western province of Jutland, Denmark. Horsens Detention Center now is a complex of neat and tidy buildings sitting on a hill in a small town. One hundred and seventy-five inmates there are tended by over 250 in staff headed by five psychiatrists. The director, Dr. Jan Sachs, is a former colleague of Dr. Sturup at Herstedvester, with whom he presently maintains a friendly competition.

The institution itself is a redone, old Pennsylvania-type prison designed for security reasons alone; it had no regard for features of treatment. However, the security of the institution is viewed by the administrators as a necessary aspect of their treatment program. Detention is viewed not only as a means to protect society temporarily but also to provide the detachment needed to treat the prisoners in a long-term way. Horsens does demonstrate nevertheless how much can be done by simple redecoration of a grim old facility. It provides, in its director's words, "a suitable atmosphere of friendliness, humaneness, and a reasonable degree of comfort."

Horsens converted its design from a grim old bastille to a tidy, human environment with a very simple plan. First, the big central rotunda space running the entire height of the building was floored over on each level. Next, doors were installed to replace the clanging bars used to cage cells in most prisons of this variety. A paint job added colors that softened the over-all scene. Then each floor was divided in the center by a small room which houses a guard for that division.

Aside from toning down and quieting the general atmosphere, this division also reflects the common Scandinavian notion that a prison must not be too big or crowded if it is to be effective and positive. Each wing at Horsens houses only fifteen men. The walls are painted blue and white and the whole place is maintained immaculately.

Since the prison is secured and circled with a high wall (prison administrators in Scandinavian countries and some here as well dislike these walls), some relative freedom of movement may be allowed within the building. Units have community sitting rooms where the men may, in their free time, mix, play cards or watch television. They are locked in their rooms at 9:30 for the night. The men may eat alone in their rooms or together in small dining spaces in each unit.

The men are sent to Horsens on indeterminate sentences. The reason for this, the staff suggested, is that "prisoners cannot understand the punishment of imprisonment." They are treated kindly and given considerable privacy and a modest dose of the amenities of life—pleasant personally decorated rooms, some simple forms of entertainment, work and hobbies, an opportunity eventually to work in open conditions outside the walls and, toward the end of their stay, short furloughs.

Nonetheless, the specially trained staff wears uniforms and maintains security on the theory that the certainty of authority and identity are necessary. Orderliness, respect and discipline between staff and inmates is strived for. However, the approach is non-moralistic: The staff seeks to treat the prisoner's problems. All the daily incidents of life at the institution are deemed the stuff of treatment. The staff meets regularly to discuss them, and their daily dealings with the inmates are carefully calculated to make them feel this active interest. We attended the daily staff meeting and found the attention and concern of the staff remarkable.

Treatment includes narcoanalysis to provide a "short cut to the deeper-lying levels of consciousness," to get at "repressed emotional material" and to develop better relationships between the inmates and their treaters, and muscular relaxation sessions combined with psychotherapy.

At the end of a man's sentence he may be sent to a satellite farm institution, Amstrup, where he can work in an open institution and gradually ease his way back to liberty. This flat farmland has houses with thatched roofs and lies near a fjord-like bay in a very pleasant rural and rustic environment.

The institution also provides after-care for former inmates and sometimes brings men back for short periods from their conditional release. In addition, 10 percent of the inmates released from Horsens receive pensions on the theory that this takes away some of their stresses and is both a therapeutically and economically sound measure.

While the Horsens staff makes recommendations, the ultimate decision for release is with the court, which usually keeps men several years longer than the doctors think is necessary. The professionals at Horsens thought that short, determinate sentences with supportive after-care in the community would be the ideal practice. The doctors felt that for them to be able to do anything for an inmate they must have him for a year; after that very little that they can do will matter. They told us that "a man can get released too late, but not too soon."

While the Horsens staff agree with their counterparts at Herstedvester that it is impossible to prove the effect of treatment statistically, they have a stronger opinion about the medical cause of and treatment for criminal behavior. The theory of this institution is that criminal behavior is caused by mental disturbances. Unlike the rationale at Herstedvester, crime is considered a psychic phenomenon requiring treatment of a psychiatric kind. For example, the Horsens staff told us that a high percentage of their inmates had chromosome abnormalities, while those at Herstedvester told us that it was rare there.

GRENDON UNDERWOOD

Grendon is a psychiatric prison situated in a remote, rural setting several hours north of London. It sits behind a small, open men's prison, Spring Hall; and though it was designed before World War II, it did not come into being until 1962. About 200 inmates are sent here for psychiatric treatment or for investigation from the other prison establishments in England that do not have facilities or staff to deal with psychopaths. ("We take 'em from Dartmoor to Durham," one of the officials there told us.)

The institution operates in what was described to us as maximum security and minimum supervision. This seemed to mean that the buildings are surrounded by walls and fences but that the men can walk freely along the locked inside corridors. Rooms are unlocked all day, though the buildings are locked. The goal is forty men to a wing (there are dormitories and individual cells) along with two professional therapists.

Prisoners may remain at Grendon for periods from eighteen months to life, but nine out of ten times, we were told, they eventually are released. The governor is a doctor, and there are numerous psychiatrists and psychologists and other civilian employees on the staff. They do a lot of testing, psychological treatment, plastic surgery (mostly to remove tattoos), along with the usual dose of work and athletics. There are several self-contained wings each housing fifty men, some with dormitories and others with cells. Each man gets at least six or seven hours a week of individual medical treatment along with group therapy and inmate committee meetings.

The staff-inmate ratio is comparatively high. Administrators claim a 40 percent success rate, based on reconviction figures, within three years, although they told us, "We've helped more than we can prove." There was a relative ease in the relationships between staff and inmates, we noticed, and we were told there are fewer petty restrictions than exist in most typical prisons. One official made this revealing remark when we asked how they dealt with minor misconduct: "We could put them on report, but that's not what we're here for."

Nonetheless, we found the place awesome-looking and depressing. Officials there agreed with our impression that the institution was not designed appropriately for its intended purpose. The architects and the program administrators never got together. However, the staff's feeling that it had developed a special culture within the institution ("Inmates are not bashed about as they are in other places") was not evident to us. We felt the place had an aimless drift and a depressing physical aspect. We failed to see, as others have, that it was better than the monotonous and meaningless emphasis on purposeless confinement which is the most that nearly all other prisons aspire to. Its theoretical posture, its physical newness and the nature of its staff all would indicate that the institution would be sensible and progressive; yet to us it did not seem to come off.

UTRECHT, THE NETHERLANDS

In the Netherlands there is another variation on special penal institutions. Individuals convicted for committing a crime and deemed responsible go to prison; those deemed not competent are sent to psychiatric hospitals; but those deemed partially incompetent are sent for indeterminate sentences to treatment institutions. About 550 individuals are in such treatment institutions out of a total of about 2,500 in the whole Dutch prison system. These people usually have been convicted of severe aggressive, sexual or repeated crimes.

In an old building in the center of Utrecht, originally designed to hold Dutch prisoners of war under the Nazi occupation during World War II, there presently is housed what is known as the Psychiatric Observation Clinic and the Selection Center.

When a judge considers that a defendant is of diminished responsibility, as described by the Dutch statute, he is sent for a six- to eight-week period to the Psychiatric Observation Clinic. After going through a testing and interviewing process a recommendation is made to the court suggesting that the individual be either punished or treated. If the judge decides that the recommended treatment course should be followed, the adjacent Selection Center recommends which particular treatment institution would be most appropriate for the individual. The judge ultimately decides whether a person should go to one of these institutions and which one would be best for him.

To some extent, however, the nature of the treatment institution in effect defines or predetermines the length of the sentence. For example, if a man is sent to a particular open institution, it is unlikely that he will be there over two years unless new problems evolve.

All of the individuals who are sent to treatment institutions have, we were told, similar social histories which typically include chromosome imbalances, family disorders and early frustrations. The majority of them are considered sociopathic individuals with life histories that, in the words of a Dutch psychiatrist, have "seriously hampered a normal development of . . . social stability and morality."

These individuals are sent to one of several treatment centers around the country, each run under different conditions of openness, each with special facilities and operational practices unique to it. Some of these institutions are run by the Government; but several are run by private and religious organizations, such as the established churches and the Salvation Army, to whom service contracts are issued by the Prison Department of the Ministry of Justice. These private agencies administer the institutions; the Government pays the bill.

We visited several privately run Government-subsidized treatment institutions, including Groot Batelaar, a small open institution in the country housed in an old complex of buildings that once functioned as a farm estate; a new modern facility called the Pompeii Clinic, which was recently built in the outskirts of a suburban area in Nijmegen in the center of the country; and the Van den Hoeven Clinic, which is an old building lost in the busy urban center of Utrecht.

In each of these places the staff was composed of well-meaning, professional people with whom there was an opportunity for considerable inmate participation in the conduct of internal institutional affairs. The places were, physically, not at all in the image of traditional prisons; they were all residential with minimal accouterments of custodial equipment or personnel. The intensity of the controls varied in each of the places, but the overriding style and tenor of each of them was similar. The staff at these institutions all specifically made the point that ". . . Our institution is not a prison. It is a clinic, which treats psychically disturbed delinquents, a psychiatric hospital." We were told that the people sent to asylums like these under this special law usually had deeply ingrained behavior problems for which prolonged and intensive treatment was deemed to be required, although the chances that this treatment would provide a cure were uncertain. For all the assertion of goals, the really hard and serious cases are not solved, and the rather minor ones are overblown to ends that are at best questionable. Cases seem to mushroom into much more intensive and prolonged episodes than appeared necessary to us. This creates a situation, we felt, where the patient fears the cure worse than the disease; and the social utility of the cure is dubious as well.

For example, at the Pompeii Clinic one of the officials told us about the case of a man who exposed himself commonly and who eventually was sent there for treatment. The clinic kept him for over two years, no doubt seriously attempting to do him some good, more so than any prison even would have purported to. Yet after he was released he was soon apprehended again for the same offense. The official admitted to us that it made more sense simply to have this person serve out his short, fixed sentence since the treatment did him little good at great expense to the state and perhaps to the individual's inordinate personal sacrifice. In all cases the indefinite sentences and the big-brotherish control over the prisoners gave a pervasive impression of gamesmanship between the participants and a frightening absolute control over human destiny.

Another case history described to us at the same institution involved a girl who had committed a series of petty larcenies at the place she worked in order to throw parties for her friends. Because her offense could have been viewed as psychiatrically motivated (that is, she was insecure and needed to buy friendship and warm personal relationships), she was made to go through a prolonged treatment process whose value to her at best could only be said to have been questionable.

These kinds of illustrations came up constantly in our interviews with officials at these institutions. Attempts at treatment for relatively minor offenses, however logically, reasonably and sensibly motivated, became exaggerated beyond what the situation seemed to have called for. As one inmate at such an institution told us: "I hate the helpful society; I am suspicious of those white, always asking persons."

The director of one of the treatment institutions described the Dutch feeling about the spirit of these places and at the same time suggested their danger:

> We continue to trust that everyone who comes to us has sufficient opportunities to live his life otherwise than he has lived it hitherto. We believe that each patient in himself, though often very timidly and hardly noticeably, continues to long for and to strive for a greater development of himself. In a certain sense we persecute him with our hope that we can help him in that laborious process. Thus, in that sense we are very democratic.

A different variation of these special institutions began recently. At a recent Benelux conference the need to segregate juvenile offenders from more inveterate criminals and to treat them in special institutions was discussed. As a result, De Corridor was evolved by a psychologist and a sociologist who worked for the Dutch Prison Department; they later became the first two directors of that new institution.

In the center of the country in the province of Zeeland stands an enclave of low, modern brick, handsomely situated and tastefully appointed buildings named De Corridor, both because it is situated on what was the road to liberation followed by British and American troops in World War II and because it symbolizes the notion which motivates the institution. To this physically attractive place young offenders are sent for short, definite sentences. They must agree to come, but they do not work their way out as their counterparts on indeterminate sentences do.

As its innovator-director, Dr. Nicholas Pieck, said to us, it is felt that to deal with intractable young offenders successfully, "the starting point must be in conflict." He is realistic about his institution, pointing out to us that the experience there is simply a choice between lesser evils although they seek to provide positive contact between the boys and the institution. He holds a non-romantic view of the institutional experience. ("Make no mistake about this being homey. These young men are here for serious business.") When we asked about the lack of therapeutic treatment, he said that they preferred to "permit the mask" to remain on a man and not go too deep into his mind and personality. Instead, the accent is on group work, all contact being social and non-medical. They do not attempt deep psychological plunges into men. Rather group action is stressed in every phase of the institution's life, government of the small dormitories, athletic and work projects, social activities.

The place and the people there were appealing. The director himself was modest in his claims but we thought realistic in his judgments. The place had a pleasant air. Each group of young inmates had two leaders who were young, athletic types whom the inmates seemed to admire and respect.

The idea behind De Corridor is to avoid the negative risks of the ugly prison experience as well as the unplumbed risks of the so-called treatment experience. The place, while pleasant, is not a cozy home but rather "a corridor to go through temporarily," as Dr. Pieck described it to us. The boys work half a day and partake in athletics half a day. Groups meet every day. The over-all atmosphere was relevant to the users of the institution. There was open space, some animals roaming free, a small forest in which they did commando exercises, a "pop" church. The boys we saw there and spoke with seemed happier and more attractive than their counterparts in other places. They seemed vibrant, enthusiastic, some even smiling.

The results Dr. Pieck seeks seem realistic. The episode at De Corridor does not provide an exhibit of the criminal life as a status experience as ordinary prisons do; it is not a deeply stigmatizing experience for the persons going through it; it minimizes the opportunity for the young offenders to develop hostilities to justice and life and society as a result of the experience; and, finally, it provides a situation in which harmfully unrealistic masks and images of the inmates can be removed voluntarily by life together with the group.

The experience at De Corridor, coming at the end of our visits to all these special, so-called "treatment" institutions, became especially meaningful and enlightening to us. The fundamental question was raised about the very *raison* of treatment institutions and the means to seek appropriate correctional goals of rehabilitation.

We have fundamental questions about the operation of prison institutions for treatment. What are the responsibility and controls that officials and institutions ought to have over their wards? Traditional ideas about the role of the prison over the prisoner have been that anything could be done to an inmate who is a total subject of the state. The progress from punishment-oriented prisons to treatment oriented institutions involves a change from an emphasis on physical punishment to forms of enforced personality modification. The Quakers wanted to force prisoners to change through revelatory religious experiences by means of isolation and solitude. Now the psychiatrists and their collaborating scientists want to do the same thing under the benign label of "treatment."

The essential difference between these two approaches appears to be a move from the auspices of religion to those of psychiatry, although both are essentially inexact and frequently unsuccessful in modifying human behavior. Both are willing to aid the process with a heavy dose of imprisonment and deprivation to aid the "therapy." The danger is in how much power society is willing to give the therapists without better proof of their theories.

We have concluded that the only power society should have in enforcing individuals to modify their behavior is to require individuals to pay for their past wrongs and to act according to the law. Both the religionists' ideas of imprisonment and penitence and the scientists' ideas of analysis and treatment make the man his own prison; both act with the well-meaning motive of eventually making him happy, whole and social. But neither has ever been subject to appropriate controls; under neither system has the prisoner been protected from the excesses of the government administering the programs. The legal establishment seems willing always to defer in respect to the religionists and in deference to the scientists, each of which groups frequently wants to use the prisoner, in one case as a penitent to proselytize, and in the other as a patient as a means for tranquil experimentation.

A better idea may be to use institutions to teach controls of antisocial behavior rather than trying to alter men's minds or souls. The latter approach is equivalent to making artificial people, and, when combined with imprisonment, may be viewed as a psychiatric form of gradual, capital punishment.

It can be argued that the only valid institution is one which makes the prison experience less personal and does not purport to alter either the psyches or souls of its subjects. The prison experience is finite; it creates an impersonal, artificial new world which usually is worse than the one it replaced.

If the correctional route is sufficiently brief and creative, it has possibilities for success. It does not predicate itself on hypocritical rationales of reform, nor is it based on inconsistent philosophies of punishment and rehabilitation. It is a non-romantic experience which is the lesser of alternate evils. Contacts are social, not therapeutic. The experience is long enough to encourage self-enlightenment. It is not long enough to result in adaptation or institutionalization. It is not an imposition of values or personality, which is always a questionable way to teach; rather it is an opportunity for voluntary growth.

The first prisons were considered departures from traditional schemes of punishment. Their intent was to replace punishment with rehabilitative treatment, first in the form of prolonged reflective solitary confinement and later in the form of confinement combined with some labor.

However, yesterday's progressive treatment became today's arduous ordeal. In the latter part of the intervening two hundred years since the creation of the penitentiary system, some critics of the prisons thought these institutions should serve more than what had developed into essentially a punitive and custodial function. The work of some professionals who were treating patients at non-penal therapeutic institutions prompted some correctional officials to attempt to adapt these new medical and psychiatric techniques to the problems of correction. In theory this made good sense; in practice it has been an imperfect and disturbing experiment.

Few prison institutions in this country even purport to be motivated primarily to treating prisoners' problems. Of those that do, the evidence that they do is at best unclear; and, except in a few special places such as Highfields, New Jersey, the operations of these institutions raise more serious questions than they appear to answer. The best evidence is that all prisons create more behavioral problems than they cure. Finally, there is the problem of highly specialized and professional tasks being assimilated and carried out by inadequately trained correctional personnel who, however well intended, may not be doing their patient-inmates any good and might well be doing some of them considerable harm.

Hovering over all considerations about the efficacy and wisdom of penal institutions for treatment is the elusive question of proof. Simply stated, how do we ever really know how effective such techniques are? Evidence is scarce and inconclusive. The results of those few available attempts at measuring treatment programs can be interpreted differently. As one skeptical Finnish criminologist told us: "Good intentions are not useful correctional tools; more evidence is needed to prove the value of treatment in prisons." Another critic, Sol Rubin, of the National Council on Crime and Delinquency, noted that "bad things had been done and are being done under the guise of treatment," things that are not humanitarian and that invade civil rights.

The best answer that advocates of treatment could advance to cynics is that available evidence certainly does not show that treatment techniques are worse than those prevailing at standard prisons for punishment. As one observer aptly commented: "Is it the public policy to punish offenders, especially young offenders, beyond the fact of imprisonment itself? If not, does humane and respectful treatment, not as therapy but as civilized conduct, require a special justification?"[54]

Indeed, that atmosphere, that attitude, that sense of relationship and that measure of individualization of the prison experience which flows from an institutional existence which is at least treatment-conscious is, especially in comparison with the primitive and militaristic atmosphere of

54. Selznick, Foreword to *C-Unit, Search for Community in Prison* ix (1968).
55. Quoted by Selznick, *ibid.*, at ix.

traditional prisons, a salutary change of direction. Treatment adds "a civ-ilizing influence on correctional systems." The English psychologist Pauline Morris says:

> The most that can be expected of the newer policies of relaxed discipline, increased opportunity for group discussion, encour-aging a sense of responsibility and similar "reformative" meas-ures, is that they should restore the balance and help to avoid destroying the man's own sense of personal worth whilst he is in prison. It is a mistake to think that in our present state of peno-logical theory we know of any way of "reforming" prisoners, but if we are able to avoid some of the staff/inmate conflicts and make prison life more reasonable and civilised for both, then something, at least, has been achieved.[55]

III

Sentencing—The Beginning of the System

Sentencing is the beginning and end of any system of criminal justice. It is the time when, the trial over and guilt established, the judge must decide what to do with a convicted criminal. Sentencing requires a judge to exercise Solomon-like powers of wisdom, insight and prediction. The best of systems and the best of men are likely to find such responsibilities awesome and confounding; here the fate of an individual, the public image of the legal system and the values of society are in the balance.

Up to this point, the criminal justice process is preoccupied with catching and convicting criminals. When this is accomplished, public interest in the criminal justice system wanes. Yet this last stage in the criminal law system, after an individual has been identified, adjudged criminal and subjected to sanction by the state, is of crucial importance. The criminal justice system has no end without a working system of correction.

Public attention to the criminal justice process is focused on determination of guilt through criminal trials. Despite the publicity that surrounds a handful of sensational jury trials, however, the vast majority of criminal defendants in this country—from 70 percent in some jurisdictions to 90 percent in others—plead guilty. For them the only issue at stake is the choice of an appropriate sentence.

Sentencing defines the limits within which correction operates. It determines whether programs may be conducted in the community or must be confined to institutions, whether institutions may be small and flexible, designed to house offenders for short periods, or whether huge and super-secure institutions must be built to hold prisoners for years. The nature of the facilities and the personnel required to administer the system are also predetermined by sentencing. Long-term prisoners require specific employees, places and related resources; non-custodial functions aimed at rehabilitating prisoners held for shorter periods and in less secure custody can be dealt with differently.

Available Sentences

The available programs and facilities also impose limits on potential sentences. The sentences currently imposed on convicted criminals fall into five general categories: suspended sentences, probation, fines, capital punishment and imprisonment.

When execution of sentence is suspended, the judge imposes some penalty, generally a fine or imprisonment, and allows the defendant to avoid it. The judge retains the power to reimpose the sentence at some future time. Occasionally, a judge suspends imposition of any sentence but still retains the power to set sentence at a later date if conditions warrant. Historically, the judicial power to suspend sentence preceded the development of probation and will be dealt with in the next chapter as an antecedent to probation. Today, the suspended sentence is used most frequently with supervision by a probation officer. Judges sometimes do suspend sentences on condition that the defendant, usually a first offender, stay out of trouble or make restitution for his crime.

Probation is simply a suspended sentence coupled with a list of conditions, one of which is supervision in the community by a probation officer. A sentence to probation is generally for a definite term of years. It may be revoked if the offender fails to conform to its terms. Legislatures frequently preclude the use of probation for serious crimes or for offenders with criminal records. The uses of probation, as well as its limitations, will be dealt with in detail in the next chapter.

FINES

The original purpose of fines was to help feudal overlords defray the expense of trials. Today fines seem to be imposed routinely to dispose of the cases of minor offenders, whether or not the defendants gained financially from their crimes. According to one commentator:

Too much reliance is placed on fines as a method of punishing antisocial behavior. The statutes authorize countless fines almost indiscriminately for widely different offenses. Judges use this authorization automatically for certain crimes without considering whether it does any good. The fact is, fines serve almost no function other than satisfying the community's desire for revenge against the criminal.[1]

A sentence to pay a fine frequently is stated with its alternative: pay or go to jail. Some pay; many go to jail.

In the federal system and in forty-seven states a person who cannot or will not pay a fine may be imprisoned. In some states there was formerly no limit on the length of time that could be served for non-payment. Non-payment of fines has become a major cause of imprisonment. For example, the District of Columbia Crime Commission found that of 1,183 convicted misdemeanants included in a sample, 222 (19 percent) were fined. Of these, 105 (47 percent) were imprisoned for non-payment. A study of the Philadelphia County Jail showed that 60 percent of the inmates had been committed for non-payment of fines.[2] Over 26,000 prisoners were in New York City jails in 1960 for failure to pay fines.

In 1966, the New York Court of Appeals held that a statute permitting courts to imprison a defendant for one day for each dollar of his unpaid fine unconstitutionally imposed cruel and unusual punishment where the defendant was indigent and his incarceration for non-payment resulted in imprisonment beyond the maximum term authorized for the crime.[3]

A District of Columbia court reviewing the sentence of an indigent jaywalker to a $150 fine or sixty days in jail invalidated the prison sentence because it exceeded the ten-day maximum provided for the offense and ruled- that "in every case in which the defendant is indigent, a sentence of imprisonment in default of payment of a fine which exceeds the maximum term of imprisonment which could be imposed under the substantive statute as an original sentence is an invalid exercise of the court's discretion for the reason that its only conceivable purpose is to impose a longer term of punishment than is permitted by law."[4]

1. Barrett, "The Role of Fines in the Administration of Criminal Justice in Massachusetts," 48 *Massachusetts Law Quarterly* 435.
2. The President's Commission on Law Enforcement and Administration of Justice, Task Force Report: *The Courts* 18 (1967).
3. *People v. Saffore*, 18 N.Y.2d 101, 218 N.E.2d 686 (1966).
4. *Sawyer v. District of Columbia*, 238 A.2d 314, 318 (D.C. Mun. App. 1968).

The Supreme Court, in a 1970 decision, agreed.[5] The Court invalidated the imprisonment of an indigent for 101 days beyond the maximum sentence provided by law, to "work off" an unpaid fine and court costs at the rate of five dollars a day. In the opinion of Chief Justice Burger, the Court ruled that "when the aggregate imprisonment exceeds the maximum period fixed by the statute and results directly from an involuntary nonpayment of a fine or court costs we are confronted with an impermissible discrimination which rests on ability to pay" and consequently violates the equal-protection clause of the Fourteenth Amendment. The Court limited its holding to cases where an indigent defendant is imprisoned for a period beyond the statutory maximum for the offense. However, its reasoning—that a defendant's choice of paying a fine or serving a prison term that is greater than the maximum for the offense is illusory if he is indigent—seemed to apply equally to the case where an indigent defendant is given the "choice" of paying a fine or serving a jail term within the statutory ceiling.

Less than a year later, the Court took the logical next step. Preston Tate, an indigent, had been convicted in the Corporation Court in Houston, Texas, of nine traffic offenses and fined $425. Unable to pay the fine, he was sentenced to the municipal prison farm for eighty-five days to work off his fine at the rate of $5 per day. The Texas courts upheld this practice, even though Texas law provided only for fines for this offense and not for imprisonment, though it did require people unable to pay their fines to work them off in jail.

The Court called it an unconstitutional discrimination to subject someone to imprisonment solely because of his indigency. Standards of imprisonment, the Court held, must fall equally on all defendants irrespective of their economic conditions. Quoting one of its earlier decisions, the Supreme Court declared that the equal-protection clause of the Fourteenth Amendment "requires that the statutory ceiling placed on imprisonment for any substantive offense be the same for all defendants irrespective of their economic status."[6]

In addition to the unconstitutionality of a practice that amounts to imprisonment for debt, the jailing of indigents for non-payment of fines is self-defeating. The state must undergo the expense of keeping an offender in jail when a judge already has determined imprisonment unnecessary. At the same time the defendant is prevented from earning the

5. *Williams v. Illinois,* 399 U.S. 235 (1970).
6. *Tate v. Short,* 401 U.S. 395 (1971).

money to pay his fine. The state ends up by supporting the defendant and often his family (through welfare payments) as well.

If jailing for non-payment of fines is unacceptable, what is to be done with those defendants who cannot—or will not—pay fines? Many jurisdictions have no probation services for misdemeanants. As the Crime Commission recognized:

> The fact that our society has not devised suitable alternative punishments gives rise to a vexing dilemma in the use of fines. For so long as jail is the routine alternative to a fine, those unable to pay will be punished more severely than those of greater means. Putting all offenders in jail is a wholly unacceptable alternative, as is relieving those unable to pay a fine of all penalties.[7]

The lack of the basic services necessary to deal with minor offenders does not justify the routine use of fines and jail. Programs in which offenders could work off fines would be inexpensive to administer and seem to make more sense than jail.

Two approaches have been suggested to broaden the alternatives of a court wishing to impose a fine. The first is the development of more flexible collection methods. In California, New York, Michigan and Pennsylvania, judges may authorize payment of fines at periodic intervals.[8] In addition to authorizing installment payments, the American Law Institute's Model Penal Code would permit courts to allow additional time for payment if necessary or to change the terms of payment.[9] The use of civil attachment and execution to collect unpaid fines might be helpful in some cases.

The second approach is more basic. The District of Columbia Crime Commission recommended that fines be imposed only on those defendants who are likely to be able to pay them:

> If a fine is to be imposed, it should be set in light of the offender's ability to pay and this information should specifically appear in the presentence report. If the offender cannot pay a fine all at once, periodic installment payments should be estab-

7. The President's Commission on Law Enforcement and Administration of Justice, Task Force Report: *The Courts* 18 (1967).
8. California Penal Code §1205 (1966 Supp.) (misdemeanors); N.Y. Code Crim. Proc. §470-d(1)(b), as amended, N.Y. Sess. Laws 1967, c.681, §61 (all fines); Mich. Stats. Ann. §28-1075 (1959); Pa. Stat. Ann. tit. 19, §§953-56 (1964).
9. Model Penal Code §§302.1(1), 302.2(2); *see also* A.B.A. Minimum Standards for Criminal Justice, Sentencing Alternatives and Procedures §2.7(b), pp. 117-23 (approved draft, 1968).

lished. If it appears that he will not be able to pay a fine under any circumstances, the court should impose a sentence of either imprisonment or probation, whichever is appropriate in the case, and not offer an offender a false option unrelated to his character or his offense.[10]

A New York law provides that:

In any case where the defendant is unable to pay a fine imposed by the court, the defendant may at any time apply to the court for resentence. In such case, if the court is satisfied that the defendant is unable to pay the fine, the court must . . . revoke the entire sentence imposed and . . . may impose any sentence it originally could have imposed except that the amount of any fine imposed shall not be in excess of the amount the defendant is able to pay.[11]

A recently enacted Maryland statute contains similar provisions and, in addition, sets maximum periods of imprisonment for non-payment of fines (one-third the maximum or ninety days, whichever is less; no more than fifteen days if the offense itself was not subject to punishment by imprisonment; in any case no more than one day for each ten dollars of the unpaid fine).

A new Delaware statute has the greatest potential for eliminating imprisonment for non-payment of fines. It provides that a person sentenced to a fine who is unable or unwilling to pay may be ordered to report to the Commissioner of the Department of Correction for work on public-works projects to discharge the fine. A defendant may be assigned to state, county or municipal agencies or to private employers (for standard compensation). Wages not required for his support are withheld until the fine has been discharged. Only if he fails to comply with the work order may the defendant be held in civil contempt of court or imprisoned for less than thirty days for violation of a probation condition. When first enacted, this provision was reported to have reduced the adult prison population in Delaware by 105 inmates in less than five weeks.[12]

Courts generally have some leeway in setting fines for a particular offense. But it is not clear whether their decisions are made according to the severity of the crime or the defendant's ability to pay. Any fine may

10. Report of the President's Commission on Crime in the District of Columbia 394 (1966).
11. N.Y. Code Crim. Proc. §470-d(3), as amended, N.Y. Sess. Laws 1967, c.681, §61.
12. Md. Ann. Code, art. 38, §4 (1970); 57 Laws of Del., Ch. 198 (1970).

impose a greater burden on a poor defendant than a rich one. A judge at least should inquire into the defendant's resources before deciding how much to fine him.

The laws of Switzerland, Finland, Cuba, Sweden and Mexico explicitly determine the amount of fines according to the means of the offender. This method seems to be the most suited to equalizing the effects of fines on different defendants.

Where terms of payment can be arranged, fines represent a simple, cheap and effective form of punishment. A recent study of chronic drunkenness offenders showed that in five out of six cases there were longer periods of time between arrests when offenders were given fines instead of jail or suspended sentences. More appropriate than fines for the large group of offenders who cannot pay, however, would be some system of work release, with or without partial confinement, that would enable the offenders to earn money or to repair some of the damage caused by their crimes.

Victim Compensation

The routine use of fines as a penalty for crime has obscured the original purpose for which money payments were exacted from offenders. In primitive and early European cultures, where no central authority existed to determine guilt or punishment, families or tribal groups were responsible for punishing offenders. The basis of the criminal law was the requirement that the offender or his family make reparation to the victim or his family. Thus punishment and compensation had common origins. The victim and his family were compensated for a crime by means of blood feuds or personal revenge against the offender and his family.

As cultures attained greater economic development, material goods or payments of money replaced physical revenge. Under the Code of Hammurabi, the criminal was obligated to make reparation to his victim in order to serve alternate purposes of vengeance and compensation:

> If a man has committed robbery and is caught, that man shall be put to death.
> If a robber is not caught, the man who has been robbed shall formally declare whatever he had lost before a god, and the city and the mayor in whose territory or district the robbery has been committed shall replace whatever he has lost for him.
> If [the victim's] life [is lost], the city or the mayor shall pay one maneh of silver to his kinsfolk.

Systems of pecuniary compensation by offenders to their victims existed in early Hebrew, Arabic, Greek, Germanic and Anglo-Saxon cultures. Early German law provided even for murder to be compensated, by payment to the victim's nearest relative. In England an elaborate system of money payments was developed as reparation for various injuries.

Gradually, however, social groups larger than the family or tribe began to take responsibility for punishing criminals. As the state's responsibility increased, the king claimed a payment from the offender for the state's participation in bringing the criminal to justice and for the injury done to the public peace. Thus one part of the compensation went to the victim and one part to the sovereign. In the twelfth century in England, the victim's share of the reparations began to decrease while the king's share increased. Eventually the king took the entire payment.

The victim's right to receive compensation had been transformed into the state's right to collect a fine. The criminal's obligation to pay damages became separated from the criminal law and developed into the civil law of torts, in which the state plays a neutral role. Modern concerns about crime have focused more on the relation of society to the criminal who has threatened it than on society's obligations to the victims of crimes or on the victim's rights against the criminal. Thus the offender's punishment is measured by his supposed moral guilt and the injury to the peace of society, not by the more concrete harm to the personal or property interests of the victim.

Restitution sometimes is made a condition of probation.[13] In the area of property crimes, restitution to the victims probably is made more often than official records indicate. In some cases the victims, whose interest is primarily in recovering their property, agree to refuse to prosecute a thief if he returns what he has stolen. In other cases, insurance companies, which cover the losses from many property crimes, may fail to report a crime or to urge prosecution if restitution is made. Even after a case is brought to trial, an attempt to make restitution, while not technically a defense, may move a court or jury to be lenient in its verdict or sentence.[14]

Such extra-judicial methods rarely have been used with crimes of per-

13. *See, e.g., Harrell v. United States*, 181 F.2d 981 (9th Cir. 1950); *State v. Scherr*, 9 Wis.2d 418, 101 N.W.2d 77 (1960); *State v. Barnett*, 110 Vt. 221, 3 A.2d 521 (1939).
14. *See, e.g., Schafer v. Fenton*, 104 Ariz. 160, 449 P.2d 939 (1969); A.L.I. Model Penal Code §7.01(2) (proposed official draft, 1962) (restitution to be accorded weight in favor of withholding sentence of imprisonment); *cf. People v. Harpole*, 97 Ill. App. 2d 28, 239 N.E.2d 471 (1968).

sonal violence. In these cases, as well as in the majority of cases of property crimes, where the criminal is not caught or no longer has the goods, the victim has no remedy. His theoretical right of action against the criminal in the civil courts is practically worthless.

The Minister of Justice of Queensland, Australia, remarked to Parliament in 1968:

> I feel obliged to point out that no scheme to provide public compensation would ever have been necessary if the wrong-doers who committed acts of violence had all been persons of substance. . . . Unhappily, those who seem to be involved in crimes of violence all too often turn out to be men of straw, without means. . . . [T]he victim of an act of violence sued in the civil court if his assailant was worth suing, and if not, he got no recompense, save by private act of charity or from the satisfaction of seeing his assailant committed to prison.

Not only does the offender, when he is identifiable at all, frequently turn out to be judgment-proof; the victim himself may lack the sophistication or the resources necessary to initiate legal proceedings. For whatever reason, a survey of Canadian victims of crime disclosed that only 1.8 percent of those responding had collected anything from the offenders who were responsible for their losses.[15]

Although a state or municipality may be negligent in failing to protect a citizen from criminal acts, the doctrine of sovereign immunity insulates this negligence from being actionable in court. Occasionally private laws have been passed to aid particular victims, usually, however, the victim must absorb the expense himself (in many cases without the aid of private insurance) or rely on inadequate and demeaning doles from public welfare or private charity. "In the end," according to former Supreme Court Justice Arthur J. Goldberg, "the victim sustains the burden of medical expenses, lost wages, and related expenses. Ultimately, of course, society pays the cost in terms of lost jobs, unemployment compensation, welfare, and a dangerous feeling of insecurity."[16]

Swedish legislation requires convicted criminals to make reparation payments to the victims of assaults and to the dependents of murdered victims. A proposed Delaware statute would have given a judge who is

15. Linden, "The Report of the Osgoode Hall Study on Compensation for Victims of Crime" 20 (1968).
16. Preface, "Symposium on Governmental Compensation for Victims of Violence," 43 *Southern California Law Review* 1, 2 (1970).

imposing a fine discretion to hold a hearing to determine the defendant's gain or the victim's tangible loss from the crime and to remit any money collected from the defendant to the victim. But for victims to be compensated in most cases, the ultimate responsibility for making restitution must belong to the state.

A renewed interest in government compensation for victims of crime was kindled by a 1957 article in *The Observer* written by Margery Fry. In this article, Miss Fry, an English magistrate and social reformer who earlier emphasized the desirability of restitution by the criminal, presented the two rationales for acceptance of the Government's responsibility for compensation to crime victims. These reasons that continue to be used to justify the adoption of indemnity schemes—namely, that the risks of crime, which are inevitable in modern society, should be distributed evenly throughout the population, or that the state has a duty to protect its citizens from violence and a collateral obligation to indemnify them when it fails to do so. In an earlier book, *Arms of the Law*, Fry had written:

> In our modern systems of collective responsibility for sickness and injury, we have evolved a machinery for assuring compensation which could well be extended to injuries criminally caused, affording equal benefits to the man whose enemy pushed the ladder from under him at home. . . . The logical way of providing for criminally inflicted injuries would be to tax every adult citizen . . . to cover a risk to which each is exposed.
> . . . The State which forbids our going armed in self-defence cannot disown all responsibility for its occasional failure to protect.

Two years later, an official White Paper supported Miss Fry's proposal, stating that the Government, which has the duty to protect the victim from antisocial behavior and the resources to indemnify him when it fails to do so, should assume the obligation to compensate victims of crime. A Working Party subsequently was constituted to study the subject. Although it disagreed with the hypothesis that the state is legally obligated to indemnify victims, it recognized a moral obligation to provide compensation:

> . . . we do not believe that the State has an absolute duty to protect every citizen all the time against other citizens: there

is a distinction between compensation for the consequences of civil riot, which the force of law and order may be expected to prevent, and compensation for injury by individual acts of personal violence, which can never be entirely prevented. . . . [T]he most [the State] has done is to create an assumption that it will provide a general condition of civil peace.

The public does, however, feel a sense of responsibility for and sympathy with the innocent victim, and it is right that this feeling should find practical expression in the provision of compensation on behalf of the community.[17]

This recommendation culminated in the adoption of the English Compensation for Victims of Crimes of Violence Scheme in 1964. But the first jurisdiction to enact legislation providing for victim compensation was New Zealand in 1963. According to members of the Government, the incumbent National Party, which recently had abolished capital punishment and was sponsoring legislation to establish halfway houses, proposed victim compensation "as a palliative to blunt opposition to these penal reforms, as well as to respond to the public's general concern about crime." The legislation, characterized as a rational extension of existing social legislation rather than a recognition of some right of victims to state indemnity, followed the administrative model used for workmen's compensation. Other Commonwealth jurisdictions—namely Great Britain, Saskatchewan, Newfoundland, Alberta, Ontario, New South Wales and Queensland—have adopted legislation embodying the theory that the state has the ultimate responsibility for compensating victims of crimes causing personal injury. Most of these Governments have established administrative tribunals to determine awards. No criminal need be convicted of a crime for his victim to receive compensation from the Government. In the first six and one half years of its existence, the British Criminal Injuries Compensation Board has considered almost 30,000 claims and paid out £7,900,000 in compensation.[18]

Several proposals modeled on the scheme used by the Commonwealth Governments have been introduced in Congress. Most would provide federal compensation only for crimes committed in the limited areas of federal police power and responsibility. Similar legislation would

17. Compensation for Victims of Crimes of Violence, Law Reform Committee, Cmnd. No. 1406, at 7 (1961); see also British Section of the International Commission of Jurists, Justice—Compensation for Victims of Crimes of Violence (1962).
18. Harrison, "Criminal Injuries Compensation in Britain," 57 American Bar Association Journal 476 (1971).

apply to the District of Columbia. A bill introduced recently by Senator Mike Mansfield to establish a three-member Federal Violent Crimes Compensation Commission with power to make awards of up to $25,000 to victims or their estates also would provide technical assistance and block grants to establish similar programs in the states.[19]

California, in 1965, became the first United States jurisdiction to enact a program to compensate victims of crime. It was followed by New York, Hawaii, Maryland, Massachusetts and Nevada.[20] All the victim-compensation schemes created so far provide for indemnity for personal injuries from violent crimes. Loss of property is not covered. Although it has been assumed that most victims of property crimes are—or could be—protected by insurance, it is not clear that this is so. Many of the victims of property crimes are residents and merchants in marginal neighborhoods for whom insurance is unobtainable or prohibitively expensive. And since unofficial restitution for property offenses has worked in some cases, it seems odd to overlook this area when devising an official scheme. In fact, a few local jurisdictions have passed legislation assuming liability to compensate property owners for damage incurred in urban riots.

No one has argued that the Constitution requires a state to compensate victims of crime. But Arthur Goldberg sees a connection between recent "equal protection" decisions of the Supreme Court and state responsibility for indemnity:

> [T]he victim of crime has, in a fundamental sense, been denied the "protection" of the laws, and . . . society should assume some responsibility for making him whole. What the equal protection clause of the Constitution does not command it may still inspire.

Another scholar suggests that American society, by accustoming children to violent behavior and excluding certain groups from responsible channels of political communication, bears direct responsibility for violent criminal behavior.[21] A third sees the problem in terms of social responsibility for injury by forces that society attempts to control:

19. S.4567, 91st Cong., 2d Sess. (1970).
20. Cal. Gov't Code §§13960-66 (West Supp. 1968), *formerly* Cal. Stat. Ch. 1549, §2 (1965). N.Y. Exec. Law §§620-35 (McKinney Supp. 1969); Hawaii Rev. Laws Ch. 351 (1968); Criminal Injuries Compensation Act, Md. Ann. Code art. 26A, §§1-17 (Supp. 1968); Mass. Gen. Laws Ch. 258A, §§1-7 (1968); Nevada Revised Statute Ch. 217 (1970).
21. Wolfgang, "Social Responsibility for Violent Behavior," 43 *Southern California Law Review* 5 (1970).

Although great sympathy may be extended to victims of natural forces, accidents, and negligence, there is little society can do to prevent such injuries. It is certainly desirable to consider, as New Zealand has, the adequacy of the remedies available to persons receiving injuries from any source, but as long as the resources of society are limited, it would seem appropriate to devote primary allocation to persons injured by forces which society has undertaken to control. Inaction or less than successful action to prevent crime obligates society to insure that the victim is adequately recompensed.[22]

Despite the emphasis of theorists on a social obligation to indemnify victims, the existing statutes are based on the assumption that there is no such obligation, and any compensation is a "privilege" extended by the state "as a matter of grace."[23] The New York statute does consider the state's duty to compensate victims as a "matter of moral responsibility." All the statutes put maximum limits on the amount of any award and require that payments be made only from a specially appropriated fund. Perhaps more significantly, all the states except Massachusetts and Hawaii require an applicant for compensation to pass a financial-need test. Such a need test is not found in the compensation systems of the Commonwealth countries.

For reasons of economy, California's first law made the state's Welfare Department responsible for administering the program. It also required that the victim show a "need" for "aid." Consequently, payments to victims were not made to satisfy a right to compensation or to spread the risk of loss from crime. Rather, they were part of the state's welfare laws and in effect required the victim to sign a pauper's oath. Awards were tied to an elaborate formula based on an applicant's income and property holdings. Before it would grant an award, the Welfare Department conducted a sweeping inquiry of the applicant's social as well as his economic background. In 1967, the California legislature transferred administration of the victim-compensation program to the State Board of Control. But the "need" test remains. Before an award can be granted, the state's attorney general must conduct an investigation and submit a report on the applicant's financial condition.[24]

22. Lamborn, "Remedies for the Victims of Crimes," 43 *Southern California Law Review* 22, 24 (1970). A report by the Commission of Inquiry, "Royal Compensation for Personal Injury in New Zealand" (1967), proposed a unified, comprehensive system to provide benefits to all injured persons regardless of the cause of injury.
23. Criminal Injuries Compensation Act, Md. Ann. Code Art. 26A, §1 (Supp. 1968).
24. Cal. Gov't Code §13963 (West Supp. 1969).

The New York and Maryland statutes continued the welfare aspects of the California law. In Maryland, for example, although the legislative purpose of the new Criminal Injuries Compensation Act was to recognize "that many innocent persons suffer personal physical injury or death as a result of criminal acts or in their efforts to prevent crime or apprehend persons committing or attempting to commit crimes," and, consequently, to have the state provide "aid, care and support . . . as a matter of moral responsibility, for such victims of crime," the statute directs the newly created Criminal Injuries Compensation Board to deny any request for aid if it finds that "the claimant will not suffer serious financial hardship, as a result of the loss of earnings or support and the out-of-pocket expenses incurred as a result of the injury, if not granted financial assistance. . . . In determining such serious financial hardship, the Board . . . shall consider all of the financial resources of the claimant."[25]

After a year's experience with the New York statute, the New York Crime Victims Compensation Board amended its rules to provide that a board member, "in his discretion, may make an award in order to maintain the claimant and family at approximately their normal standard of living, and where the expenses or loss of earnings, or support, would lower this standard, the Board Member may, in his discretion, determine this to be serious financial hardship."

The Australian compensation programs allow the victim to intervene in the criminal trial to claim compensation. Payment of the amount awarded is made by the Government. Combining the determinations of guilt and compensation is efficient in cases where a defendant actually is brought to trial; however, situations may arise where equity for the victim can prejudice justice for the defendant, or vice versa. In addition, tying the victim's claim for compensation to the defendant's criminal trial almost inevitably creates long delays in payment.

Some of the problems of combined trials can be seen under current practice in cases where restitution is ordered. In most jurisdictions where existing legislation gives courts discretion to impose restitution as a condition of probation, statutes limit the compensation that may be ordered to the harm proximately caused by the crimes of which the probationer was convicted.[26] Thus in one case an appellate court reversed a judge's order that a defendant, convicted of assault and battery on a store owner

25. Md. Ann. Code art. 28, §1 (1968); Md. Ann. Code art. 28, §12(f) (1968).
26. E.g., 18 U.S.C. §3561 (1964); Mich. Stat. Ann. §28.1133 (1954); N.Y. Penal Code §6510 (McKinney 1967); Wis. Stat. Ann. §57.01 (1957).

who refused to honor his Diner's Club credit card, pay the Diner's Club the money owed on the card. The court's opinion expressed an unwillingness to make the courts collection agencies for debts only remotely related to the criminal charge.[27]

The following year, however, the same court affirmed the action of a trial court increasing its order of restitution by a defendant convicted of theft growing out of a breach of contract to perform construction work, from $821 to $8,600. The increase was based on a memorandum by the defendant's probation officer, submitted eight months after the original sentencing, which stated that the victims had suffered greater losses than originally known and that in addition there had been similar "crimes," of which the defendant had never been charged or convicted, whose victims also should be compensated.[28] In addition to its harshness, this type of order gives the defendant no hearing on the question of his liability for the additional debts and puts criminal courts in the role of collecting obligations only tenuously related to an adjudicated crime. (The court in this case expressed the opinion that the rehabilitative value of the probation condition involved "belies the remoteness" of the injury from the conduct for which the defendant had been convicted.) These problems would be solved by a requirement of a direct relationship between the defendant's conduct and the victim's loss.

In Massachusetts claims for compensation must be brought in a district court, before a judge who has not heard the criminal case involved. Although this procedure assures the victim of the usual procedural safeguards of a civil trial, including, presumably, the right to appeal an adverse judgment, it involves the usual delay of court proceedings. Attorney's fees are provided. The other state statutes provide for administrative determinations of compensation, generally before one member of an administrative board, with an appeal to the full board. Judicial review is either unavailable or limited to determining the board's jurisdiction.

None of the statutes requires that the person responsible for the injury be charged or, if charged, be judged criminally responsible. (Thus the perpetrator may be a juvenile or insane.) All schemes require prompt reporting of the crime to the police and allow a relatively short period for filing claims. Although some statutes disqualify a member of the offender's family from receiving compensation, most simply reduce the amount

27. *People v. Williams*, 247 Cal. App.2d 394, 55 *California Reporter* 550 (1966). *See also U.S. v. Taylor*, 305 F.2d 183 (4th Cir. 1962) (order of restitution limited to actual loss caused by offense of which defendant was convicted).
28. *People v. Miller*, 256 Cal. App.2d 348, 64 *California Reporter* 20 (1967).

of compensation where the victim is found to be partially responsible for the crime. The statutes also provide for indemnity to private citizens injured in the course of preventing a crime, apprehending a criminal or rescuing a person in danger, presumably without the requirement of proving financial need.[29]

Only a small proportion of the victims of violent crime have made use of any of the compensation programs, even where they have existed for several years and entail no requirement of financial need. During the first year and a half of the oldest program's operation in New Zealand, fifty-seven awards were made for a total amount of $24,227.20. (However, a majority of the awards were made in the last year and a half.) According to an observer, the program has not been publicized sufficiently, and there are no public reports of its proceedings. A similar criticism has been made of the program in New South Wales, where only five people applied for compensation in the program's first ten months. In Massachusetts, thirty-five claims were filed in district courts in the program's first year and two cases were closed.

In New York, 196 claims were accepted the first year of its program. After a publicity campaign, 519 claims and 1,307 "inquiries" were received the second year. (The great majority of the claims—311—were for assault, although there were ninety-two murder claims.) According to the Crime Victims Compensation Board, "the public is not as yet well informed."[30] Our experience indicates that this is so. When one of us mentioned the availability of compensation on a New York television show recently, we received several letters from victims and their relatives, who claimed that they had never heard of the program and asked to be referred to the appropriate agency.

The Maryland Criminal Injuries Compensation Board, which publicized its scheme through radio and television broadcasts and distributed brochures to police stations and attorneys, received approximately 250 applications in its first year, of which approximately thirty-five, totaling $328,000, were granted. According to the secretary to the board, removal of the need test could mean that the state would pay out more in compensation to victims than to injured workers under workmen's compensation, since the state has more crimes than work-related accidents.

29. See, e.g., 26A Md. Ann. Code §10 (1968) (judicial review only on application of Attorney General); Mass. Gen. Laws Ch. 258A, §3 (1968); Hawaii Rev. Laws Ch. 351-31 (1968); Cal. Gov't Code §13970 (West Supp. 1968).
30. State of New York, 1968 Second Annual Report of the Crime Victims Compensation Board 7–10 (1969).

In all the schemes recently proposed or enacted, the Government has a right to sue the offender for reimbursement when it has made a payment to his victim. In addition, the Maryland program is financed in part by a special fine levied on all persons convicted of non-traffic offenses as part of their court costs. Approximately $300,000 was collected in this way in the first year of the Maryland program. The Maryland board undertook no suits against the responsible offenders, although one was contemplated and two awards had taken into consideration orders of restitution made by criminal courts as conditions of probation. The California statute provides that a defendant convicted of a violent crime that results in the injury or death of a California resident shall, in addition to any other penalties, be ordered to pay a fine to an Indemnity Fund for state compensation of victims.[31]

Despite these provisions for fines, none of the schemes has integrated governmental efforts to compensate victims with additional efforts to rehabilitate criminals. The indemnity procedure is conducted apart from the correctional process. Even if the state must pay when the criminal cannot, some reparation to the victim might well be considered part of an offender's expiation for his crime. The requirement that an offender perform services directly for his victim where that is possible, and for the community at large where it is not, should help to increase his own self-respect and his awareness of the consequences of his crime. At the same time, reparation by the offender could help to reinforce the victim's feeling of vindication and society's sense of justice.

Restitution, either through money payments or through performing services directly for the victim or for the public through public-works projects, can most easily be performed in the community. Thus this form of community correctional program, which can be justified on so many other grounds, also gives the offender a better chance of working for the benefit of the people he has harmed than confinement in a remote institution. Someone who has damaged property might be required to repair it; this method of restitution is particularly appropriate for vandals or participants in a riot. In California, juveniles who violate the Fish and Game Code may be required to do day work in a park or conservation area.

Even in a prison setting, constructive efforts to perform services for the community are not impossible. For example, inmates of Maryland's Patuxent Institution make recordings for the blind. A drama group at the District of Columbia's Lorton Reformatory performs skits dealing with

31. Cal. Gov't Code §13964 (West Supp. 1968).

drug abuse in local schools and churches in an effort to deter young people from crime.

Efforts to reconcile offenders and their victims were common in primitive societies. For different reasons and through different methods, such efforts again should become part of society's response to crime.

CAPITAL PUNISHMENT AND IMPRISONMENT

Physical and capital punishments are rarely used today. Corporal punishment, as such, is authorized in only one state (Delaware) in this country.[32] The use of the death penalty to punish people convicted of murder, rape and other crimes involving serious threats to the physical safety of persons is on the decline. Although all but thirteen states have laws authorizing capital punishment, there was only one execution in 1966, two in 1967 and none since. Capital punishment, always a profoundly engaging issue, is of little statistical significance (although close to 700 people currently are in death rows throughout the nation). The death penalty recently has been subject to a variety of constitutional challenges that may well end it in this country completely. The California Supreme Court recently declared that capital punishment violates state constitutional prohibitions against cruel or unusual punishments. The court found both "execution itself" and "the dehumanizing effects of the lengthy imprisonment prior to execution" to be "impermissibly cruel," only "rarely imposed or implemented" in the United States, "unnecessary to any legitimate goal of the state and . . . incompatible with the dignity of man and the judicial process." (The United States Supreme Court currently has this question under consideration.)[33]

Of all the possible sentences that American courts adjudicate for crimes, the most characteristic penalty in the last century and a half is imprisonment. Although close to half of all people convicted of crimes are now sentenced to probation, incarcerating people in prison cells, as described in the preceding chapter, remains the most widely used form of punishment in the United States. It is almost the exclusive means of pun-

32. *See State v. Cannon*, 55 Del. 587, 190A 2d 514 (1963), *rev'd on other grounds*, 55 Del. 597, 196A 20 399 (1963).
33. *People v. Anderson*, Calif. Sup. Ct., decided Feb. 18, 1972. *See Witherspoon v. Illinois*, 391 U.S. 510 (1968); *United States v. Jackson*, 390 U.S. 570 (1968); *Rudolph v. Alabama*, 375 U.S. 889 (1963) (opinion of Goldberg, J., Douglas, Jr., and Brennan, J., dissenting from denial of *certiorari*). *Cf. State v. Funicello*, 10 *Criminal Law Reporter* 2304 (New Jersey Sup. Ct., Jan. 17, 1972).

ishing serious crimes. Offenders found guilty of petty offenses or misdemeanors usually are sent to local jails for days, months or one year. Those
convicted of felonies are sentenced to state or federal prisons for periods
ranging from one year to life.

Sentencing Procedure

Except in capital cases, the trial judge has the exclusive responsibility
for sentencing in a majority of the jurisdictions in this country. The
sentencing judge has been called "one of the most powerful and autonomous officials of our government. No other judicial act of such importance is committed to the single discretion of one man."[34]

This judge makes the choice among the different penalties provided
by law in almost all cases. He alone must choose among the different types
of sentences prescribed and, if the sentence is to prison, he also must determine the length of time to be served. In making these decisions, he generally is given wide latitude and is under little control. For example, a defendant who violates the federal bank-robbery statute[35] may be sentenced
to prison for a period from one day to twenty years. There is no indication
in the statute or anywhere else of the criteria a judge should use in choosing an appropriate sentence within that wide range.

Since he has little information or assistance in coming to this difficult
decision, the judge generally postpones sentencing for a short period
after a criminal trial. Some agency, usually the probation department, prepares a presentence report for him that contains some basic information
about the defendant.

Men convicted of minor offenses, and possibly the ones most likely
to be reformable, frequently are sentenced immediately after they are
found guilty or, in the great majority of cases, when they plead guilty.
Counsel, when available, may request a presentence investigation, but
the delay necessary for its preparation can require a defendant to spend
a period of time in jail (or to raise bail). If his offense can only bring a
short sentence, he seldom will consider the price worthwhile.

34. Low, Comment on the Sentencing System, draft prepared for the National Commission on Reform of Federal Criminal Laws 168 (Oct. 11, 1968).
35. 18 U.S.C. §2113 (1964).

In the municipal court of Los Angeles, for example, from 200 to 250 charges of drunkenness are handled each day. A group of lawyers who studied the operation of the Los Angeles trial courts in 1956 described the system as follows:

> The bailiffs bring in the defendants from the jail in groups of about 20. The men stand in two lines behind a three-foot high horizontal bar which separates the defendants from the rest of the courtroom. After the defendants have filed into the court the judges repeat the following rubric: "You men are all charged with being publicly drunk. Do any of you plead not guilty?" (The judge pauses about five seconds to see if there are any "not guilty" pleas.) "All guilty, answer to your name as it is called."[36]

The entire sentencing procedure for a misdemeanant in this court takes from one to two minutes. No transcript is made of the proceedings.

Most misdemeanants are sentenced to ten days to one year in jail. A few of them without prior criminal records may get suspended sentences or, occasionally, probation. Some are given the alternative of a fine or imprisonment—thirty dollars or thirty days.[37]

The sentencing of more serious offenders generally is done with greater deliberation. Many judges take their responsibilities in this area very seriously. As one surmised:

> If the hundreds of American judges who sit on criminal cases were polled as to what was the most trying facet of their jobs, the vast majority would almost certainly answer "sentencing."

36. Research Report to the Survey of Metropolitan Trial Courts—Los Angeles Area (1956).
37. During a two-week period in 1965, one judge in the District of Columbia Court of General Sessions sentenced 105 defendants as follows:
   65 (62 percent) to jail, for an average of 239.5 days;
   17 (16 percent) to pay a fine or go to jail;
   10 (9 percent) to suspended sentences;
   13 (12 percent) to one year on probation.
Three other judges sentenced as follows:

	Judge A	Judge B	Judge C
Jail	65 percent (average time: 108 days)	65 percent (average time: 87 days)	81 percent (average time: 147 days)
Fine or jail	25 percent	11 percent	11 percent
Suspended sentence	13 percent	11 percent	6 percent
Probation	0	11 percent	2 percent

Subin, *Criminal Justice in a Metropolitan Court* 88–89 (1966).

In no other judicial function is the judge more alone; no other act of his carries greater potentialities for good or evil than the determination of how society will treat its transgressors.[38]

In thirteen states the jury, subject to review by the judge, sets the sentence in some or all non-capital cases. Both the 1967 President's Crime Commission and the 1968 American Bar Association's Advisory Committee on Sentencing and Review urged that jury sentencing be abolished. Chief among the arguments advanced for doing away with sentencing by juries is that the average citizen has neither the knowledge nor the experience required for such difficult decisions:

> . . . a proper sentencing decision calls on an expertise which a jury cannot possibly be expected to bring with it to the trial, nor develop for the one occasion on which it will be used. The day is long past when sentencing turned solely on the degree of moral approbation which the offense commanded. An enlightened sentencing decision today calls for a sophisticated and informed judgment which takes into account a vast range of additional factors, from the likelihood that the defendant will commit other crimes to the types of programs and facilities which may induce a change in the pattern of activity which led to the offense.[39]

Yet judges are not trained in correctional theories but in rules of evidence and courtroom procedures. While they, more than the general public, are oriented to the adversary process of determining guilt, few are prepared for the peculiarly discretionary faculties needed to impose sentences that give effect to the contradictory correctional goals—at once, to punish, deter and reform. It has been estimated that judges spend as much time on the 10 percent of defendants who stand trial as on the remainder who plead guilty. Though some courts are willing to devote unlimited time to trials in order to see that justice prevails, most devote little time and effort to the vitally important task of assessing penalty.

Criminal arrests and trials are carefully circumscribed by a network of procedural safeguards designed to protect the defendant. Any depar-

38. Irving A. Kaufman, "Sentencing: The Judge's Problem," 24 *Federal Probation* 3 (March 1960).
39. American Bar Association Project on Minimum Standards for Criminal Justice, Standards Relating to Sentencing Alternatives and Procedures (approved draft, 1968), 46–47.

ture allows the defendant to appeal his conviction. But when the time comes for sentencing, the defendant loses his power to insist that the police, the prosecutor and even the judge abide by these carefully drawn rules. This change in a defendant's legal status once his guilt is pronounced was described by the Illinois Supreme Court:

> Any person indicted stands before the bar of justice clothed with a presumption of innocence and, as such, is tenderly regarded by the law. Every safeguard is thrown about him. . . . After a plea of guilty . . . instead of being clothed with a presumption of innocence they are naked criminals, hoping for mercy but entitled only to justice.[40]

INFORMATION AVAILABLE TO THE JUDGE

A judge sentencing a defendant who has pleaded guilty to a minor crime generally knows nothing about the defendant except the charge to which he pleaded and, in most cases, his criminal record. The sentencing judge in a felony case, on the other hand, commonly uses information from three sources: his observation of the defendant at trial; the presentence report prepared by the probation department; and information supplied by the defendant or his attorney.

Some trial judges have stated that their unique opportunity to observe the defendant during the stress and intensity of his trial allows them to base their sentences on personal familiarity with the defendant's character. On the other hand, a federal trial judge in California has questioned whether a trial judge's opportunity to observe the defendant at trial provides insights and a sound basis to fashion an appropriate sentence. Judge Stanley Weigel points out that the observations of a judge who presides over a long trial are subject to three important limitations: (1) in many cases he is limited to visual observation because the defendant does not testify; (2) the great majority of defendants plead guilty and the judge's personal confrontation with the defendant is brief, perhaps only ten or fifteen minutes at the time of sentencing; and (3) the defendant at trial understandably is under great stress and in many cases he may fail to present a reliable picture of himself.

> But whether the observation be literally and exclusively visual or is supplemented by a trial judge's assessment of a defendant's

40. *People v. Riley*, 376 Ill. 364, 368, 33 N.E.2d 872, 875, *cert. denied*, 313 U.S. 586 (1941).

testimony and demeanor on the witness stand, is it really reliable as the controlling criterion, for example, as to whether defendant should be imprisoned for 2 years or for 20? Who among us would really want to have that vital determination turn upon one man's assessment of our personality under such unusual and difficult circumstances? . . . So far as justice in sentencing turns upon appraisal of the personal traits of a defendant, I doubt if there be a worse time to make that evaluation than when the always anxious, often frightened, human being stands before us to learn the particular fate we are about to make his.[41]

In the experience of Judge Tim Murphy of the District of Columbia Superior Court, "the only defendants who express themselves well at sentence are cons with long records."

Federal judges primarily rely for information relevant to sentencing decisions not on their own observations but on the written presentence reports prepared by "completely trusted and independent probation officers." Statutes or court rules in about one-quarter of the states make presentence reports mandatory for certain classes of offenses, generally those punishable by imprisonment for more than a year. In the rest of the states and in the federal system the trial judge has discretion to request a presentence report. In some of these latter jurisdictions probation may not be granted unless there has been a presentence investigation.

Little information is available describing the extent to which presentence reports are used in the states where they are not mandatory. In the federal courts some kind of presentence investigations were made in 88 percent of the felony convictions in 1963. Few misdemeanor courts have the probation services to prepare reports. Even those that do have them rarely use them. For example, in Detroit presentence investigations were ordered in 400 out of more than 12,000 misdemeanor convictions in 1965. Yet there is some evidence that the mere fact that a presentence report is completed on a misdemeanant will reduce his chances of being sentenced to jail. A survey of court dispositions in San Joaquin County, California, found that in the one month when the Probation Department conducted full presentence investigations, 16 percent of the misdemeanants investigated were given jail sentences, 36 percent were put on probation and 48 percent given suspended sentences. In a "typical" month, without the re-

---

41. *Appellate Review of Sentences*, Hearings on S.2722 Before the Subcommittee on Improvements in Judicial Machinery of the Senate Committee on the Judiciary, 89th Cong., 2d Sess. 75–76 (1966).

ports, nearly 32 percent were sent to jail, less than 1 percent were put on probation and 68 percent received suspended sentences.[42]

The information gathered in the typical probation report is limited chiefly to interviews with defendants and perusal of facts in criminal records. In addition, officers sometimes telephone a defendant's employer to see if the defendant will be able to return to his job if he is put on probation. Relatives may be contacted to verify a defendant's "community roots." Probation officers' recommendations, rather than suggesting special facilities or rehabilitative plans, usually are limited to the question of whether a defendant should be put on probation. Even in this limited area, they rarely are enlightening.

Even if all the faults associated with presentence investigations, which will be discussed more fully in the next chapter, could be remedied, the reports would not produce enough information to enable judges to make an intelligent choice among sentencing alternatives. The investigations do not reflect the current state of behavioral-science notions of diagnosis. They are not conducted by professional psychiatrists or psychologists. The investigators do not observe their subjects long enough to be able to make diagnoses. Paradoxically, while the critical time to discover the particular problems of a criminal probably is after he has committed his first offense (usually a misdemeanor), there is presently virtually no effort being made to perform adequate investigations in misdemeanor cases.

Federal judges have available diagnostic facilities to administer psychological, social and physical examinations to defendants before they impose final sentence.[43] A judge who uses the facilities initially sets the maximum term authorized for the offense. The defendant is sent to a federal prison that has psychological and psychiatric services. Within three months a report is prepared and sent to the sentencing judge containing a social history, the results of psychological and psychiatric examinations and a recommended sentence, together with a correctional program keyed to the facilities available at a particular institution. After reviewing these findings and recommendations, the judge may affirm or reduce the original sentence, or put the offender on probation. Norman Carlson, director of the Bureau of Prisons, estimates that the judges who decide to

42. The President's Commission on Law Enforcement and Administration of Justice, Task Force Report: *The Courts* 18 (1967); Institute for the Study of Crime and Delinquency, Model Community Correctional Program, Report III: *Crime and Its Correction in San Joaquin County* 341-42 (1969).
43. 18 U.S.C. §§4208(b), (c), 4252, 5010(e), (1964).

commit offenders to diagnostic facilities follow the recommendations of the facilities' staff in the great majority of cases.

Yet few judges have taken advantage of these commitments.[44] Former Attorney General Ramsey Clark noted that only 442 diagnostic commitments were ordered in 1965. This figure represented 3 percent of the total number of commitments to institutions and 1.5 percent of all sentences in that year.[45] In fiscal 1968 there was an increase of 200 cases in diagnostic commitments.

California currently has an institutional diagnostic center. The violation rate for those put on probation after evaluation at the diagnostic center has been encouragingly low. In addition, some judges feel that the ninety days' incarceration at the center may have a salutary effect on the probation performance of first offenders.

In addition to the diagnostic commitments, the California Department of Correction operates two Reception Guidance Centers to receive offenders already sentenced to prison and to determine the institutions and programs to which they should be assigned. Although statutes[10] direct the staff at the centers to request the sentencing judge to reconsider his decision and place the offender on probation when further evaluation makes such disposition appear reasonable, sentencing judges may—and frequently do—ignore such requests.

Despite the success with institutional diagnosis, there is a need for diagnostic centers operating in the community on an "outpatient" basis. Institutionalization, even for ninety days, makes no sense for many people, particularly first offenders. And it is the first offenders who may be the most in need of diagnostic study.

In addition to information gathered by official presentence investigations or diagnostic studies, judges sometimes learn about a defendant from other sources. Although a federal court of appeals overturned a sentence because the trial judge had relied on a presentence report containing information about evidence that had been obtained as a result of an illegal search and seizure,[47] a federal district judge recently refused to reduce an unusually severe sentence admittedly based on an illegally wiretapped conversation, which revealed that the defendant, convicted of tax

44. See Leach v. United States, 334 F.2d 945 (D.C.Cir. 1964).
45. Letter to Senator Joseph D. Tydings from Deputy Attorney General Ramsey Clark, March 23, 1966, Appellate Review of Sentences, Hearings on S.2722 Before the Subcommittee on Improvements in Judicial Machinery of the Senate Committee on the Judiciary, 89th Cong., 2d Sess. 130, 131 (1966).
46. Cal. Penal Code §1203.03 (1966 Supp.).
47. Verdugo v. United States, 402 F.2d 599 (9th Cir. 1968). See Chap. IV.

evasion, was a big-time "criminal figure." The judge was aware of the information since he had presided at the hearing on the defendant's successful motion to suppress the evidence at trial. In the court's opinion, the enforcement of the Fourth Amendment exclusionary rule to discourage unlawful police activity did not require that illegally seized evidence be excluded from sentencing, as long as the evidence was not obtained solely for the purpose of enhancing the sentence. This test appears specious and extremely difficult to apply, since it generally is impossible to prove such a motive. In addition, the judge emphasized the desirability of receiving as much data as possible concerning the defendant's background, including hearsay evidence and evidence obtained illegally.[48]

As well as the information gathered from his observations of the defendant, presentence reports and possible extraneous evidence, a judge's sentencing may be influenced by whatever the defendant or his attorney says at the sentencing hearing. The Supreme Court has never held that a defendant is constitutionally entitled to a sentencing hearing, although it recently implied that he is by ruling he is entitled to be represented by an attorney at sentencing.[49]

The defendant is required to be a witness to his sentencing, if not a participant in the process. The general rule in this country has always been that an offender has the right to be physically present at sentencing. If a felony offender absconds, it is assumed that he cannot lawfully be sentenced until he is brought before the court.

The defendant's role at the sentencing hearing is ritualized and frequently meaningless. Contrary to the traditional democratic philosophy that a person should be given the opportunity to participate in determinations affecting his liberty, the defendant can rarely feel that he has participated in making the decision that may affect the way he will spend the next years of his life.

Tied to the right to be present at sentencing is the ancient English common-law concept of allocution—the defendant's right to make a statement in mitigation of his offense. It has been recorded that before imposing sentence on one of his subjects, Henry II could be moved by an earnest plea directed to the mercy of the King rather than to the merits of

48. *United States v. Schipani,* 315 F.Supp. 253 (E.D.N.Y., June 4, 1970).
49. *See Mempa v. Rhay,* 389 U.S. 128 (1967). If there is a right to counsel at sentencing, a right to be present with counsel at some sort of hearing seems implied. *See* Cohen, *The Legal Challenge to Corrections* 19 (1969). *Cf.* Matter of Raoul P., #11020 (First Judicial Dept., App. Div., New York, Dec. 14, 1966); *In re* Mikelsen, 226 Cal. App.2d 467, 38 *Cal. Rptr.* 106 (1964) (statutory requirements of dispositional hearings in juvenile cases).

the case. The practice has been continued under the Federal Rules of Criminal Procedure (Rule 32), which provide that the court, before imposing sentence, shall

> afford counsel an opportunity to speak on behalf of the defendant and shall address the defendant personally and ask him if he wishes to make a statement in his own behalf and to present any information in mitigation of punishment.

One admittedly unusual case[50] demonstrates both the persistence of the idea of the appropriateness of a plea for mercy at the sentencing hearing and the influence of the individual predilections of judges on the range of sentencing. A federal district judge sentenced a defendant who had been convicted of robbery to five to fifteen years in prison. In the course of the sentencing hearing, the judge stated his reasons for imposing such a severe sentence:

> Now the Court didn't believe your story on the stand, the Court believes you deliberately lied in this case. If you had pleaded guilty to this offense I might have been more lenient.
>
> And he got on the stand and he lied about it. The other boy at least pleaded guilty after he heard the government's evidence —threw the sponge in, so to speak—because he knew he didn't have a chance.
>
> Now in view of his attitude and in view of the fact that he lied on the stand, in the Court's opinion, the jury didn't believe him, I didn't believe him; the evidence in this case as I said is overwhelming.

The defendant then submitted a letter he had received from his attorney. The letter referred to a visit the lawyer had made to the judge's law clerk. The clerk had stated to the lawyer that "there was only one way to get a light sentence from Judge —— and that was to confess that you did the robbery, to apologize four or five times and to say that you were willing to turn over a new leaf. . . . [I]f he comes here and says he did it and that he was sorry, the judge will give him a very light sentence. If you or he say anything else the judge will probably throw the book at you."

50. *Scott v. United States*, No. 20, 954 (D.C. Circuit, Feb. 13, 1969).

The judge read the letter and confirmed its contents:

> I have said more than one time, I have said it in open court, it is a strange thing to me that a defendant who comes up after getting the benefit of good representation, trial before jury, the evidence being overwhelming as it is in this case, I hope sometime I hear some defendant say, "Judge, I am sorry, I am sorry for what I did." That is what I have in mind.

The court of appeals sent the case back to the trial judge for resentencing. In the opinion of the reviewing court, efforts by a trial judge to impel a defendant to confess at his allocution would violate his Fifth Amendment right not to incriminate himself and would prejudice his right to appeal the conviction. The appeals court pointed out that "the peculiar pressures placed upon a defendant threatened with jail and the stigma of conviction make his willingness to deny the crime an unpromising test of his prospects for rehabilitation if guilty."

The peculiar fact about this case is that the considerations thought important by the sentencing judge were discussed so openly. It is impossible to estimate the number of other defendants who are given lenient or heavy sentences because of judges' individual notions about their demeanor at allocution.[51]

In addition to its being the most meaningful part of the criminal justice process—or possibly because of it—the sentencing decision is the least visible part of the trial and correction system.

> The defendant and his counsel rarely see the sentencing decision take shape and even more rarely feel that they have participated in its formulation. . . . The prosecutor and defense counsel make their arguments and the judge decides. One frequently does not know what influenced the judge and how he went about making up his mind. . . . One often gets the impression that the judge had his mind made up before argument and that counsel played no meaningful role in influencing the final result.[52]

51. For this reason, when the same trial judge, this time without comment, gave the defendant the same sentence on resentencing him, the defendant claimed that in order to insure appellate review of improper sentencing criteria, sentencing judges must be required to state their reasons for imposing a sentence. *Cf. North Carolina v. Pearce*, 395 U.S. 711 (1969). Brief for Appellant, *Scott v. United States*, No. 23,057 (1969). The second appeal was mooted by the defendant's death.
52. Enker, "Perspectives on Plea Bargaining," in the President's Commission on Law Enforcement and Administration of Justice, Task Force Report: *The Courts* 115 (1967).

In 1967, the Supreme Court directly held that the right to counsel applies at sentencing.[53] Furthermore, a federal court of appeals has ruled that a prosecutor may not convey any information or discuss any matter concerning a case with the sentencing judge unless the defendant's attorney is present, since "at a minimum, to permit only tardy rebuttal of a prosecutor's statement, not accurately transcribed, is a substantial impairment of the right to the effective assistance of counsel to challenge the state's presentation."[54]

However, the attorney frequently does little more than the defendant: he pleads with the judge for leniency, makes general references to the defendant's family responsibilities, his job and his penitent attitude. Thus it is somewhat ironic to find a case where an appellate court orders a defendant resentenced because the trial judge approached the sentencing hearing with a "closed mind." This happened in one case, in which before the judge had heard the defendant or his lawyer he announced that he considered the case "perfect" for imposition of the maximum penalty and added that if the Public Defender had tried to say anything good on the defendant's behalf, "I was going to stop him." The Supreme Court of Delaware reversed, holding that due process requires the sentencing judge to have "an open mind at least to the extent of receiving all information bearing on the question of mitigation."[55]

Participation by the defendant's attorney is particularly insignificant when the judge relies on a presentence investigation in which he has had no part and about which he may have no knowledge. Disclosure of presentence reports is left to the discretion of the trial judge in most states and under the federal system under Federal Rule of Criminal Procedure 32(c)(2). The most recent federal court of appeals ruling on the subject upheld the absolute discretion of the sentencing judge to deny defendants access to their presentence reports.[56]

Courts denying disclosure justify the constitutionality of their refusal to permit inspection of the presentence report by citing the Supreme Court's 1949 decision in *Williams v. New York*.[57] The jury found the de-

53. *Mempa v. Rhay*, 389 U.S. 128 (1967). In *Townsend v. Burke*, 334 U.S. 736 (1948), the Court had ruled that the absence of counsel during sentencing on a guilty plea, coupled with the use of false information about the defendant's criminal record, deprived the defendant of due process of law.
54. *Haller v. Robbins*, 409 F.2d 857, 860 (1st Cir. 1969).
55. *Osburn v. State*, 224 A.2d 52, 53 (Dela. 1966). *See also Wyatt v. Ropke*, 407 S.W.2d 411 (Ky. 1966).
56. *United States v. Dockery*, 447 F.2d 1178 (D.C. Cir. 1971).
57. 337 U.S. 241 (1949); *see, e.g., United States v. Fischer*, 381 F.2d 509 (2d Cir. 1967), *cert. denied*, 390 U.S. 973 (1968); *United States v. Conway*, 296 F. Supp. 1284 (1969).

fendant guilty of first-degree murder and recommended life imprisonment. The judge nevertheless imposed the death sentence, relying in part
on a presentence report that cited the defendant's involvement in "thirty
other burglaries" of which he had not been convicted, referred to his
"morbid sexuality" and described him as a "menace to society." The defendant did not challenge the accuracy of the report, and its disclosure
never was at issue. His appeal to the Supreme Court raised the question
of whether the use of a presentence report prepared outside of court and
outside of the presence of the defendant and the court's refusal to disclose the contents of the report to the defendant violated his right to due
process and confrontation of the witnesses against him. The Court disregarded the issue of disclosure and justified the use of the report by reference to "the modern philosophy of penology that the punishment should
fit the offender and not merely the crime":

> We must recognize that most of the information now relied on
> by judges to guide them in the intelligent imposition of sen-
> tences would be unavailable if information were restricted to that
> given in open court by witnesses subject to cross-examination.
> And the modern probation report draws on information con-
> cerning every aspect of a defendant's life. The type and extent
> of this information make totally impractical if not impossible
> open court testimony with cross-examination. Such a procedure
> would endlessly delay criminal administration in a retrial of col-
> lateral issues.[58]

Proponents of disclosure argue that while courts have discretion to
determine sentences within the range of penalties permitted by the appropriate statute, there is a special need to assure fairness to the offender
when that range is as wide as it is today. Complete reliance on an administrative agency to provide full and accurate information to the court,
without an opportunity for the defendant to refute or qualify the content
of the report, is a questionable and unprecedented legal procedure. This
is particularly so since experience shows that judges follow probation officers' recommendations in most cases and that the report may be used to
determine not only a defendant's sentence but his prison program and
parole date as well. These reports contain emotionally toned value judgments, prejudicial epithets and diagnostic terms loosely and inaccurately

58. 337 U.S. at 247.

used. They also may contain prejudicial factual errors.[59] It has also been argued that giving defendants access to these reports helps them understand their sentences. Some of the authoritativeness of the judicial setting can be counteracted by revealing what the court knows about the defendant.

Those who continue to favor the confidential report contend, on the other hand, that the Supreme Court has clearly established a distinction between the rights of a defendant during trial and after conviction. The protection of due process of law before conviction is not considered . . . to apply to the procedures used at sentencing. The matter is no longer an action at law but a social problem. These assumptions have been undermined in recent years by a long series of cases involving prisoners' rights. And where juveniles are involved in sentencing, the Supreme Court recently recognized the importance of full access to the child's "social records."[60]

The standard bogey used to justify non-disclosure is that families, employers and community agencies would be unwilling to cooperate without guarantees of secrecy. Thus essential sources of information would be cut off, crippling probation investigations.[61] Some case workers feel that an offender's treatment might be handicapped by the sudden disclosure of much painful material, such as an evaluation of his defense devices. One spokesman has argued that if it became known that the federal courts disclosed confidential information, probation officers would lose their status in the community as highly respected professionals.

Paul Keve, former State Commissioner of Correction, an author and himself once a probation officer who argued against disclosure, later concluded that making presentence reports public is the only way to ensure that the probation officer's recommendations are based on his own observations and not on hearsay or loosely drawn moral judgments. Disclosure should result in reports that are more thoroughly prepared and consequently more useful. In fact, except in rare cases, the officer not only should be willing to disclose the contents of the report; he actually should share in its preparation with the defendant.

The Model Penal Code proposes that courts advise defendants or their counsel of the factual contents and conclusions of the presentence

---

59. *See, e.g., State v. Killian*, 91 Ariz. 140, 370 P.2d 287 (1962); *State v. Pohlabel*, 61 N.J. Super. 242, 160 A.2d 647 (App. Div. 1960).
60. *Kent v. United States*, 383 U.S. 541, 562 (1966).
61. *See, e.g., Parker v. United States*, 388 F.2d 931, 933–4 (4th Cir. 1968).

investigation and afford a fair opportunity for rebuttal. Neither delivery of the report itself nor revelation of the sources of confidential information would be required. This compromise recommendation has not been widely accepted. Critics claim that the defendant is already aware of the factual material contained in the report.

The federal district court in Maryland has adopted a compromise in which reports are prepared in two parts: (1) the body of the report, setting out the facts, and (2) a shorter portion, containing the recommendation of the probation officer. The recommendation is kept confidential, but the defendant's lawyer is invited to read the judge's copy of the factual portion and to comment on any material it contains before sentence is imposed. The probation officer may request that certain information in the body of the report be withheld from the defendant. According to one judge, "These instances have not been as frequent as one would suppose, and have usually been handled quite satisfactorily by the judge explaining the situation frankly to the defendant's lawyer."[62]

The Advisory Committee on Sentencing and Review of the American Bar Association Project on Minimum Standards for Criminal Justice has recommended that the substance of all derogatory information which has not otherwise been disclosed in open court be called to the attention of the defendant, his attorney and others acting on his behalf. With one dissent, the committee members determined that the simplest, fairest method of implementing this principle is to permit the parties to inspect the report. In extraordinary cases, after stating his reasons, a judge could except from disclosure information that might seriously disrupt a program of rehabilitation or that was obtained on a premise of confidentiality, as long as the information is not relevant to a proper sentence. The court's action in refusing to disclose any information should be subject to appellate review. The committee majority concluded that the need to protect sources of information should be given no more weight at the sentencing stage than it would be at the stage of determining guilt. "Long since exploded is the theory that a defendant who has been convicted of crime no longer has any rights, or that any sentence less than the maximum is the result of an act of grace."[63]

Statutes in California, Alabama, Minnesota, Connecticut, Kansas and Nevada now give the defendant or his attorney the right to examine the

62. Roszel C. Thompson, "Confidentiality of the Presentence Report: A Middle Position," 28 *Federal Probation* 3, 8–10 (March 1964).
63. American Bar Association Project on Minimum Standards Relating to Sentencing Alternatives and Procedures 221 (tentative draft, 1967).

presentence report. In Ohio and Virginia the probation officer makes his report in open court and is subject to cross-examination by the defense.[64] In several other states, court decisions have made disclosure mandatory. In a recent New Jersey case, for example, a first offender, convicted of knowingly purchasing a stolen car, received an extended prison term on the basis of a presentence report that claimed he was the "contact" for a stolen-vehicle ring and had made several other similar purchases for which he had not been tried. The New Jersey Supreme Court concluded that defendants could not be represented effectively at their sentencing by an attorney who was ignorant of the bases on which sentence was to be imposed:

> It is indeed difficult to see how there can be meaningful representation by counsel at sentencing time when there is no disclosure to him of the presentence materials on which the sentence is being based.
> Counsel for the defendant was in the dark and his participation in the sentencing hearing was largely meaningless. He based his stand on the open record of the trial whereas the judge based his sentence on the closed presentence report. Surely this type of hearing with its cross bases does not fit within any rational concept of the sound administration of justice.[65]

For the assistance of counsel to be effective at sentencing, the defendant's attorney must be provided full access to presentence reports used by the judge. The Supreme Court has recognized the importance of disclosure in the context of juvenile cases, although not in adult criminal trials.[66] One of the primary functions of counsel at sentencing could be to rebut incorrect items and supply information that is missing from the reports. As it is, the use of *ex parte* presentence investigation reports whose contents are unknown to the offender has removed much of the

---

64. Cal. Penal Code §1203 (1966 Supp.); 42 Ala. Code §23; Minn. Criminal Code of 1963, §609.115(4); Gen. Stats. of Conn. §54-109 (1968); 21 Kan. Stats. Ann. §§4604-4605 (1970); Nev. Rev. Stats. §176.15(d) (1967).
65. *State v. Kunz,* 55 N.J. 128, 259 A.2d 895 (1969). *Cf.* United States *ex rel. Brown v. Rundle,* 417 F.2d 282 (3d Cir. 1969) (cross-examination of probation officer who prepared report permitted in "special and extraordinary circumstances").
66. *See Kent v. United States,* 383 U.S. 541, 562 (1966):
> With respect to access to the social records of the child, we deem it obvious that since these are to be considered by the juvenile court in making its decision to waive, they must be made available to the child's counsel.

Cf. State v. Gattling, 95 N.J. Super. 103, 230 A.2d 157, 161–62 (1967) (sentencing judge may not rely on outside facts recorded neither in trial transcript nor in presentence report).

adversary character of the sentencing hearing. One need not believe that the adversary system is the only or the best means for reaching rational decisions to conclude that it is the fairest and most balanced way to estimate a just sentence in a criminal case.

RESPONSIBILITY OF THE DEFENSE ATTORNEY

Even where the defense attorney has access to all the facts on which sentencing will be based, his responsibility is not clear. Is it his duty to identify the sources of the defendant's problems and suggest a correctional program that is relevant to these problems? Or is his function simply to argue for the most lenient sentence possible, focusing only on the short-term interests of the defendant, leaving protection of the public interest to the prosecutor and probation officer? At present, defense counsel, perhaps in part because of legitimate skepticism over the availability of meaningful correctional programs, seem to regard their duty almost exclusively in terms of obtaining their clients as lenient sentences as possible.

Some commentators, both lawyers and probation officers, have suggested that the defense attorney should go beyond disputing the contents of the presentence report prepared by the probation staff and work with the probation officer while he conducts the investigation. At this stage he can legitimately attempt to influence the content of the report and its recommendations.

The Offender Rehabilitation Project in the District of Columbia attempts to enlarge the limited role of the defense attorney at sentencing by providing attorneys, primarily Public Defenders, with their own presentence reports, which wherever possible recommend realistic alternatives to imprisonment. The project, which began in 1966, was the first major, systematic effort in this country to help attorneys develop community-based rehabilitation programs for their clients at the presentence stage. It was established to provide the "auxiliary services" necessary if attorneys were to fulfill the expanded role at sentencing that various studies were beginning to suggest:

> When the presentence report is not disclosed, the only way in which counsel can ensure that the sentencing decision is based on adequate facts is to gather and present information to the court himself. . . . When counsel believes that probation would

be an appropriate disposition for his client, he should be prepared to suggest a positive program of rehabilitation. He should explore possibilities for employment, family services, educational improvement, and perhaps mental health services and attempt to make specific and realistic arrangements for the defendant's return to the community.[67]

At its inception, the three main purposes of the project were to provide attorneys with "defendant studies" to use at sentencing, to develop rehabilitative plans to facilitate probation and to help obtain community services for defendants and their families. In effect, the project was to become the defense counsel's alternative to the probation office.

Of the 226 defendants referred to the project in its first year of operation, defense attorneys requested full studies in only eighty-eight cases. In the other 138 cases, the attorneys decided that no alternatives to imprisonment were feasible and requested only assistance with specific services, such as employment, a loan or housing. Judges frequently indicated their reliance on the defendant studies and followed their recommendations in a majority of the cases for which the studies were submitted. (The defense attorney had the alternatives of submitting the full report or of deciding not to use any of it.) However, some judges have indicated privately that they feared that some unfavorable information about defendants was being withheld.

Of the eighty-eight studies, forty-five recommended probation only. Of these cases, thirty-five defendants received probation. In fourteen other cases, although probation was the primary recommendation, alternative dispositions also were recommended. Of these, four received probation and eight received the alternative disposition recommended. The project also recommended several innovative dispositions, including two split sentences (jail and probation) and four sentences involving work release. The court agreed to the latter recommendations in only one such case.

Several differences appeared between the defendant studies and the presentence reports prepared by the probation office. First, probation officers did not see defendants as often or as early in the criminal process as did members of the project staff. In addition, the relationship of the project to the defendants' lawyers enabled the project staff to establish

67. The President's Commission on Law Enforcement and Administration of Justice, Task Force Report: *The Courts* 19–20 (1967).

closer relationships with defendants than the probation officers. Second, the project staff spent a larger proportion of its time interviewing friends, relatives and others who knew the defendants better than the probation officers did. Thus project workers felt that they developed greater insight into defendants' social relationships.

On the other hand, the project lacked access to previous presentence reports on defendants with records, as well as other official documents concerning previous court and institutional experiences. However, the project staff prepared its studies and developed its programs through the use of community resources and agencies wherever possible. (In its first three years, the project contacted at least 137 community agencies in the Washington metropolitan area, as well as many private employers.) The probation officers rarely, if ever, used these resources. The most significant difference was that the reports prepared by probation officers rarely included rehabilitative plans, the distinctive feature of the defendant studies.

At first lawyers did not refer defendants to the project until one or two months before sentencing. It became increasingly clear, however, that project members should be brought into the case as early as possible after the defendant was assigned counsel. Early referral was necessary for a thorough study of a defendant's background. In addition, the sooner the project staff began to work on a case, the better the chance to get a defendant who was not being held in jail into a job, a training program or some kind of therapy before the time for sentencing.

Two additional benefits sometimes resulted from early referral to the project. Project staff members sometimes could help to alleviate the impact on the defendant's family of his arrest, particularly where the family was deprived of his earning power by pretrial imprisonment. In addition, an early development of background material and a plan for rehabilitation could be relevant for discussion between the defense lawyer and the prosecutor even before trial. On occasion, this information convinced the prosecutor to divert a case out of the criminal system for solution through other community resources.

The idea of an early referral and recourse to social services is the basis of two other projects sponsored by the Manpower Administration of the United States Department of Labor. The Manhattan Court Employment Project in New York and Project Crossroads in the District of Columbia offer selected arrestees job training and counseling immediately after arrest. If they adjust successfully the criminal charges against them are dropped. These two programs have provided the models for several "pre-trial diversion" projects now operating in several cities.

An evaluation of the Offender Rehabilitation Project discovered that, when compared with a control group of similar defendants, defendants served by the project were less likely to be convicted (52 percent of the experimental group as opposed to 63 percent of the control group in General Sessions Court; 58 percent of the experimental group as opposed to 88 percent of the control group in District Court); those convicted were less likely to be sentenced to prison (42 percent of the total experimental group as opposed to 65 percent of the control group); and those imprisoned were sentenced for shorter periods of time (an average of thirty-seven months for the experimental group as compared to forty-eight months for the control group). And even though more defendants in the experimental group were free in the community they had fewer rearrests.[68] The Offender Rehabilitation Project recently became institutionalized as part of the District of Columbia Public Defender Service.

However sensible the idea of the Offender Rehabilitation Project, it is unfortunate that defense efforts must be devoted to collecting information that the probation department already has in its possession. Professor Fred Cohen has criticized the idea of a separate agency to provide defense lawyers with their own pre-sentence investigations and rehabilitative plans:

> This proposed solution . . . merely highlights the sad reality that the narrow scope of the debate over disclosure has served to obscure the larger issue of the proper role and function of counsel and the probation staff in shaping an appropriate disposition. Disclosure is only one aspect of that issue and, indeed, is better stated as the *mutual* sharing of information relevant to sentencing.

On the other hand, a conscientious defense attorney might not risk jeopardizing a favorable disposition by permitting the defendant to provide possibly incriminating information before sentencing. Whether it is ever considered appropriate for the information that is furnished the judge at sentencing to be produced through a joint effort depends on whether the sentencing hearing is conceived of as a continuation of the adversary process of the criminal trial.

68. Institute of Criminal Law and Procedure, *Rehabilitative Planning Service for the Criminal Defense* x-xi (1970).

The Legislative Role in Sentencing

On the basis of whatever information is available to him, the judge pronounces sentence. In doing this, he must stay within the confines of those sanctions that have been authorized by the legislature for the defendant's offense. For all crimes the legislature provides statutory limits that include a maximum and, for many, a minimum sentence.

Congress and the legislatures of each state have arrived independently at a myriad abstract decisions concerning the structure of sentencing laws: that a particular offense should carry a statutory maximum sentence of five, ten or twenty-five years; that sentences should be definite or indeterminate; that statutory minimum sentences should be set; that probation or parole should be available for certain types of offenders.

Different legislatures make different choices. The variations among these choices seem more the result of chance than the reflection of any unique interests of the different states. The following statutory sentences have been cited as an example of the marked disparity among jurisdictions:

> The longest term for burglary with explosives in Louisiana is less than the shortest term in Mississippi and the minimum in the latter state is five times the minimum in the former. The minimum penalty for armed burglary is one year in ten states, five years in twelve, and death in two. Whereas the minimum penalty for unarmed burglary is one year in eight states, it is a life sentence in one state. . . . For rape, minima vary from one year in six states to death in four.[69]

Within any one jurisdiction, the sentencing structure may make little more sense. Sentences have been adopted as new crimes have been legislated or changed as the public has become sensitive to some new (real or imagined) danger. There has been little concern for the relationship of each change in the law to other parts of the jurisdiction's criminal code.

As a result of such patchwork legislation, the differences in penalties for various crimes within any one jurisdiction are chaotic and lack rational bases.[70] For example, in Colorado, due to the inclusion of separate

69. Taft, *Criminology* 327 (1950), quoted in Cohen, *The Legal Challenge to Correction* 16 (1969).
70. *See* American Bar Association Project on Minimum Standards for Criminal Justice, *Standards Relating to Sentencing Alternatives and Procedures* 49–50 (approved draft, 1968).

provisions in the penal code at different times, a person convicted of first-degree murder must serve ten years before he first becomes eligible for parole; one who is convicted of a lesser degree of murder must serve fifteen. Destruction of a house with fire is punishable by a maximum of twenty years; destruction of the same house with explosives by a maximum of ten. Stealing a dog could warrant a sentence of ten years; killing the same dog would bring a sentence of six months and a $500 fine.

Penal statutes do not relate to one another or to an over-all scheme. In Iowa, where no complete revision of the criminal code has occurred since 1860, the same maximum sentences apply to larceny of domestic animals and kidnapping of persons. On the other hand, burning an isolated empty dwelling may lead to a twenty-year sentence, while burning a church or a school carries a ten-year maximum.

The federal criminal statutes are in no better order. Myrl Alexander, former director of the Bureau of Prisons, has commented that "the Federal Criminal Code . . . is so inconsistent in its penalty structure as to be almost incoherent." For example, armed robbery of a bank is punishable by a fine, probation or a prison term of up to twenty-five years. But for armed robbery of a post office the judge must choose between probation or twenty-five years in prison. One who "harbors or conceals" any person after he has been convicted of an offense is subject to a maximum term of five years. One who "harbors or conceals" any prisoner who has escaped from the custody of the Attorney General can be punished only by a three-year maximum. Whoever commits the crime of robbery by stealing "any kind or description of property belonging to the United States" is punishable by a maximum term of fifteen years. However, if he commits the same crime by robbing any custodian "of any . . . property of the United States," he is subject to a ten-year maximum.[71]

In addition to the irrational relationships among penalties for different offenses, the sentencing distinctions among offenses are legion. In Wisconsin, for example, there are sixteen possible statutory maximum terms of imprisonment for the first conviction of a felony: two, three, four, five, six, seven, eight, ten, fourteen, twenty, twenty-five, thirty-five and forty years and life imprisonment. The Oregon Penal Code contains 1,413 criminal statutes, with 466 different types and lengths of sentences.

71. Alexander, "A Hopeful View of the Sentencing Process," 3 *American Criminal Law Quarterly* 189, 190 (1965). 18 U.S.C. §2113(d); 18 U.S.C. §2114; 18 U.S.C. §1071; 18 U.S.C. §1072; 18 U.S.C. §2112; 18 U.S.C. §2114; see Low, Preliminary Memorandum on Sentencing Structure, in Working Papers of the National Commission on Reform of Federal Criminal Laws 1246–50 (1970).

It is extremely doubtful that any legislature has at present enough information about crimes and criminals to make such fine distinctions.

Several states have attempted to rationalize their criminal laws by undertaking complete revisions. New York and Minnesota have completed new penal codes. California, Texas and the United States Congress are in the process of revisions. These codes all follow the general pattern of grouping offenses into broad categories (for example, five grades of felony in New York) for the purpose of limiting the number of permissible sentences. Thus, sentencing judges will be directed to follow one scheme of penalties for each group of crimes.

The history of sentencing legislation in this country has proceeded from a system of fixed sanctions for each type of offense to one of greater flexibility aimed at allowing the individualization of penalties. The first state legislatures severely restricted judicial discretion in sentencing, frequently providing only a single penalty for each offense. The antecedents of this system of "definite sentences" were both American and European: the colonial Americans' general distrust of high-handed, autocratic judges and the attacks by eighteenth-century European philosophers, such as Beccaria and Bentham, on the arbitrary punishments that had been imposed by undemocratic judges, particularly on the poor.

The rigidity of this early system was tempered in three principal ways. First, the legislatures themselves drew distinctions between the diverse types of misbehavior that were susceptible to being characterized as a single offense and among the many possible motivations and the individual characteristics of the offenders. Distinctions among offenses were accomplished by creating various "degrees" of each crime, depending on the culpability of the offender (murder, manslaughter and negligent homicide) or the seriousness of the harm (grand larceny, petit larceny). Some distinctions among offenders were drawn legislatively, such as specifying greater penalties for offenders with previous criminal records.

Second, since legislatures could not tailor sentences to fit offenders in advance, they gradually gave judges more flexibility to adjust penalties. Courts were given ranges between maximum and minimum sentences from which they could choose a particular penalty. For many crimes, alternative forms of punishment such as imprisonment, probation or fines were provided.

This process of giving increased discretion to the sentencing judge has gone further in the United States than abroad. The spread between maximum and minimum sentences generally is greater in the United States. In addition, many foreign criminal codes contain more or less elaborate standards for determining sentences. For example, the French and Italian codes enumerate aggravating and mitigating circumstances which should increase or decrease the applicable penalties for each crime. Some foreign codes even attempt to rate the importance of the correctional goals of retribution, deterrence and rehabilitation.

American legislatures, on the other hand, have not provided objective statutory criteria to guide judges in the exercise of their sentencing discretion. Consequently, the sentencing judge is left without guidance in his choice among the frequently contradictory goals of correction.

As a result of the absence of statutory sentencing criteria, judges have no idea what sort of defendant a legislature had in mind for the minimum or the maximum sentences it has authorized. An illustration of the possible results of such an approach occurred recently at a federal sentencing institute. The judges present were asked to consider the appropriate sentence for an unarmed, unaggravated bank robbery. (The statute provided for a sentence of from one day to twenty years' imprisonment.) Most of the judges agreed that eight years would be a reasonable sentence; some considered five years sufficient. But one judge objected on the ground that since Congress had set twenty years as the maximum sentence for the offense, the judges in his district would begin with the assumption that twenty years was the appropriate sentence and reduce it as mitigating factors appeared. (Interestingly, he did not consider it equally rational under this theory to begin with the minimum sentence and raise it as aggravating circumstances warranted.) Through this process, he arrived at a sentence of fifteen years, nearly double that of the other judges.

The characteristic of wide-ranged sentencing authority makes sense from the standpoint of encouraging individualized sentences; it is criticized as offering no guide to judges and no protection for defendants. One scholar has questioned whether criminal statutes that permit judges to make sentencing choices between a broad range of alternatives with no indication of what criteria are to guide the choices might be subject to attack as unconstitutionally vague.[72]

State courts in the nineteenth century were hesitant to uphold such

72. *Appellate Review of Sentences,* Hearings on S.2722 Before the Subcommittee on Improvements in Judicial Machinery of the Senate Committee on the Judiciary, 89th Cong., 2d Sess. 89 (1966) (statement of Professor Gerhard O. W. Mueller).

statutes. We are much more accustomed to them today. Nonetheless, the United States Supreme Court recently held unconstitutionally vague a statute that permitted the jury to impose court costs on an acquitted criminal defendant because of its failure to provide any guidance as to when costs were to be imposed and when not.[73] The majority added that the distribution of varying punishments based only on the reprehensibility of the offender (rather than the seriousness of his crime or some additional factors that could be determined objectively) certainly would violate the due process clause of the Constitution. A concurring opinion argued that much of the majority's reasoning casts doubt on the constitutionality of statutes which leave sentencing to the unguided discretion of a jury. Perhaps the point could be taken one step further: What of the unguided discretion of a judge?

The Model Sentencing Act, drafted in 1963 by the National Council on Crime and Delinquency's Advisory Council of Judges, attempted to establish guides for judicial discretion by stating clear statutory preferences for various types of sentences in different cases:

> This act shall be liberally construed to the end that persons convicted of crime shall be dealt with in accordance with their individual characteristics, circumstances, needs, and potentialities as revealed by case studies; that dangerous offenders shall be correctively treated in custody for long terms as needed; and that other offenders shall be dealt with by probation, suspended sentence, or fine whenever such disposition appears practicable and not detrimental to the needs of public safety and the welfare of the offender, or shall be committed for a limited period.

According to the draftsmen of the act, "The Model Sentencing Act diminishes the major source of disparity—sentencing according to the particular offense. Under it the dangerous offender may be committed to a lengthy term; the nondangerous defendant may not." The Sentencing Chapters of the Proposed Revision of the Federal Criminal Laws, as well as recent state penal-code revisions, contain similar criteria to aid courts in deciding when to impose fines, probation and concurrent or consecutive sentences. Such general statements of legislative criteria for sentencing decisions seem to represent the current trend.

Once degrees of crimes had been established and judges were given

73. *Giaccio v. Pennsylvania*, U.S. (1966).

choices within broad ranges, the third step in making sentencing more flexible came with the development of non-judicial methods of conditional release from prison—parole and good-time laws. As a consequence of these devices, an offender sentenced by a court to a fixed term of imprisonment for a felony actually does not know how much time he will have to serve before he is released by prison or parole authorities whose power over prisoners supersedes the court's sentencing power. To this extent there are no more absolutely "definite" sentences.

The most common categories to classify sentencing structures, however, are still the terms "definite" and "indeterminate." This dichotomy is confusing, since all felony sentences in fact involve some indeterminacy. Parole authorities almost always are given some measure of discretion to release a prisoner before the end of his sentence.

The term "indeterminate sentence" has at least four generally accepted meanings. Originally, it referred only to completely open-ended sentences that called for an offender to be released only when he was cured. It is now used for offenders found to be "sexual psychopaths," in lieu of the fixed sentence normally provided for the offense of which they were found guilty. Typically, indeterminate sentences may be imposed on sexual offenders regardless of the seriousness of their offenses.[74]

The most obvious form of indeterminate sentencing in general use occurs in California, Hawaii and Washington. The sentencing judge is directed by the criminal statute to commit offenders for the maximum term provided by statute. However, the precise period actually to be served is left to the later discretion of the parole board.

Another variant of the indeterminate sentence is found in Alaska and Illinois, where the trial judge selects a minimum and a maximum term, and the parole authorities are free to exercise discretion within this range.

Under still another variation, the Florida legislature has fixed a six-month minimum sentence to apply in all non-capital cases no matter what maximum the trial judge imposes. In Minnesota, judges are pre-

---

74. *See, e.g.,* Cal. Welfare and Institutions Code §§5500–22 (1966); Colo. Rev. Stat. Ann. §39–19–1 (1963) ("indeterminate term having a minimum of one day and a maximum of his natural life"); Kan. Gen. Stat. Ann. §§62–1534–1537 (1964); Mass. Gen. Laws Ann. §§4–5 (1966 Supp.); Ore. Rev. Stat. §137.111 (1965); Pa. Stat. Ann. tit. 19 §1166 (1964); Ala. Code tit. 15, §436 (1965 Supp.), §440 (1959) (discharge "only after he shall have fully recovered from such psychopathy"); D.C. Code Ann. §§22–3504–3509 (1961) (discharge "when the Superintendent of Saint Elizabeths Hospital finds that he has sufficiently recovered so as not to be dangerous to other persons"); Mich. Stat. Ann. §§28.967(3), 28.967(7) (1954) (discharged when "recovered . . . to a degree that he will not be a menace to others").

cluded from imposing any minimum, except where the maximum is a life sentence. The parole board has discretion up to the maximum.

The "definite" sentence. found in most Southern states, actually is but a further variation of indeterminacy. The judge sentences the defendant for a fixed period of time. However, statutes provide that he is eligible for parole either at any time or after the expiration of a certain portion of the sentence. Thus, the parole authorities again have discretion over the actual time served.[75]

A more detailed classification of sentencing structures follows.[76] It should be noted that many jurisdictions use different arrangements for different offenses and that the sentencing judge sometimes is given a choice of alternative types of sentencing.

(1) Both maximum and minimum terms are fixed by the court within limits set by statute for each offense. Parole eligibility occurs at completion of the minimum term (sometimes minus time for good behavior).[77]

(2) The same system is used as in (1), but the minimum sentence may not exceed a certain fraction of the maximum. The fraction is one-fourth in Montana and North Carolina, one-third in the District of Columbia and Alaska, one-half in Pennsylvania and one-half the statutory maximum (as opposed to the maximum actually imposed by the judge) in New York and Maine.

(3) The maximum is fixed by the court, within statutory limits, but the minimum is fixed by statute. The minimum is sometimes a stated fraction of the sentence, sometimes a specific period and sometimes a fraction or a given number of years, whichever is less.[78]

---

75. Cal. Penal Code §§1168, 3041 (1966 Supp.); Hawaii Rev. Laws §258-52 (1965 Supp.); Wash. Rev. Code Ann. §§9.95.010, 9.95.040 (1961); Alaska Stat. §33.15.230 (1962); Ill. Ann. Stat. C. 38, §1-7(e) (Smith-Hurd 1966 Supp.); Fla. Stat. Ann. §921.18 (1966 Supp.); Minn. Stat. Ann. §609.11, 609.12(1) (1964); see N.C. Gen. Stat. §148-58 (1964); Va. Code Ann. §53-251 (1967).

76. This classification is based on the compilation in Glaser, Cohen and O'Leary, *The Sentencing and Parole Process* 10-15 (U.S. Dept. of Health, Education and Welfare, Office of Juvenile Delinquency and Youth Development, 1966).

77. Used almost exclusively in New Hampshire, Vermont, Massachusetts, New Jersey, Kentucky, Georgia, Arizona, Colorado and Wyoming. Used for most offenses in Illinois, Nebraska, North Carolina and South Carolina and as an option in Arkansas and the federal system.

78. Used exclusively or almost exclusively in Mississippi, Louisiana, Oklahoma, Texas, Rhode Island and the federal system (parole eligibility occurs at one-third of sentence), Alabama (parole eligibility at one-third of sentence, or ten years, whichever is shorter), Virginia (parole eligibility at one-fourth of sentence or twelve years, whichever is shorter), Delaware (parole eligibility at one-half of sentence), Florida (six-month minimum), Connecticut (one-year minimum), Wisconsin (one-half of sentence or two years, whichever is less), and Tennessee (minimum varies with offense). Used for some offenses in Arkansas, Idaho, Illinois and South Carolina (one-third), North Carolina (one-fourth) and Indiana (one year).

(4) The maximum term for each offense is fixed by statute, the minimum by the sentencing judge. This system is used only in Hawaii and Michigan. In Michigan, the court sets a minimum at the time of the trial. In Hawaii, an offender sentenced to prison automatically receives the statutory maximum sentence for his offense. He is sent to prison, where he receives a parole-board hearing within three months. The parole board recommends a minimum sentence to the court, which then makes the final decision.

(5) The maximum and minimum sentences for each offense are fixed by law. Once a defendant is convicted of a particular type and degree of crime, the sentence follows automatically and indiscriminately. The court plays no part in fixing the sentence.[79]

(6) The maximum term for each offense is fixed by statute. The minimum term is set by the parole board at an early hearing. Although the court may recommend a specific period of imprisonment, its recommendation does not bind the board.[80]

(7) There is no minimum sentence. Thus the parole board may release an offender at any time. The maximum is determined by the trial court.[81]

(8) The minimum sentence, the maximum period before the first parole and the maximum sentence all are fixed by statute. Thus, under the Federal Youth Correction Act,[82] which was patterned on the British borstal sentencing structure, offenders under twenty-six may receive a six-year "indeterminate" sentence, from which they are eligible for parole after sixty days and from which they must be paroled at least once before four years. This guarantees that all first releases are by parole.

(9) Some laws prescribe that a person may be kept under correctional supervision until he reaches a certain age (usually twenty-one but sometimes twenty-five). He may be paroled at any time. This sentencing structure is used for juveniles adjudged delinquent, although in theory they are neither convicted nor sentenced.

SOME SPECIAL CONSIDERATIONS REGARDING INDETERMINACY

The indeterminate sentence, in all its forms, was introduced as a reform for young offenders in the 1870s. Although originally hailed as a

79. Used exclusively or predominantly in Ohio, West Virginia, Indiana, Kansas, North Dakota, South Dakota, New Mexico and Nevada; used in some cases in Maryland and South Carolina.
80. Used in California, Washington, Utah and Iowa. Optional in the federal system. Used in Maryland for females and for some males under twenty-six.
81. Used exclusively in Oregon, Missouri and Minnesota and predominantly in Idaho.
82. 18 U.S.C. §§5005–26.

way to motivate prisoners to reform and to reward their efforts in this direction, the purpose of indeterminacy frequently has been interpreted as making it possible to keep offenders imprisoned until they have convinced a parole board that they no longer threaten the safety of the community. With this criterion of release, it is not surprising that states with the most indeterminacy in their sentencing structures also have the longest sentences. In addition, prisoners serving indeterminate sentences must undergo protracted periods of uncertainty regarding the length of their imprisonment, during which they frequently feel that there is little they can do to influence the decision regarding their release. Finally, the ability of his keepers to add to a prisoner's sentence can constitute a powerful negative threat to him as long as his keepers can influence the date of his release.

For these reasons, the indeterminate sentence recently has been subjected to a great deal of criticism from those, such as former California Correction Director Richard McGee, who once advocated its use. In addition, California prisoners have gone to court to challenge the indeterminate sentence on equal-protection and due-process grounds. Thus far, they have had no success. Both state and federal courts have ruled that a prisoner has no legal right to have his sentence set at less than the maximum provided for the offense and that, regardless of his prior record, his conduct in prison, his adherence to prescribed programs, or the sentences given his codefendants, the paroling authority has complete discretion to determine and redetermine the time he must spend in prison.[83]

However, in *Hester v. Craven,* a recent federal case, a small inroad was made into this theory. The court attempted to distinguish between the revocation of parole, which had previously been ruled not to require due-process protections, and the redetermination of a sentence occurring automatically on the parole revocation (in this case changing the time to be served from five years to life). In the case of a redetermination of sentence, the court held that when the facts on which the redetermination depends (generally the violation of parole conditions) occur outside of prison, a hearing must be held at which the parolee is given the opportunity to confront and cross-examine the witnesses against him. (The issue of legal representation at such a hearing was not raised.) According to the court, "While the petitioner did not have a right to have his sen-

83. *E.g., Bennett v. California,* 406 F.2d 36 (9th Cir. 1969); *Sturm v. California Adult Authority,* 395 F.2d 446 (9th Cir. 1967); *In re* Schoengarth, 66 Adv. Cal. 228, 57 *Cal. Rptr.* 600, 425 P.2d 200 (1967); *Azeria v. California Adult Authority,* 193 Cal. App.2d 1, 13 *Cal. Rptr.* 839 (1961).

tence determined at less than life, he does have the right, once it is so determined, to have his sentence terminate on that date absent some change which justifies redetermination. . . . [W]here a new 'finding of fact' . . . must be made procedural due process requires that the defendant be given a right to confront and cross-examine witnesses against him."[84]

In some states women sentenced to prison are covered by special statutes making their terms indeterminate within certain limits. Indeterminate sentencing is also a feature of the juvenile-court legislation and of the youthful-offender statutes in California, New York, Minnesota, Illinois, Massachusetts and the federal system. Modeled after the American Law Institute's Model Youth Correction Authority Act in 1939, these statutes attempt to provide special treatment for young offenders, usually between sixteen and twenty-three years old, who are above juvenile-court age but considered too young to be subjected to the punitive features of the adult prison system. Common to the youthful-offender legislation was an effort to eliminate all minimum sentences (an upper age limit generally determines the maximum) and to transfer decisions regarding the length of sentence, assignment to institutions and release on parole to central administrative boards.

Although all these special schemes originated in a desire to temper the rigidity of the criminal law for certain classes of offenders, they frequently have not had that effect. Often the same criteria that govern adult sentencing by courts are applied to youth sentencing by boards. Although there are indeed no minimum sentences, some boards make a practice of granting "continuances," or "set-offs," of a year or more, during which they will not review an offender's case to determine if he is ready for release. Continuances generally depend on the seriousness of the offense for which a youth was convicted rather than on his particular history or needs. For example, we witnessed the initial hearing of a California youth who had been convicted of selling drugs. Although he was married, had a child, had committed no prior offenses and his presentence report had recommended a four- or five-month sentence to county jail, the board continued his case for a year because of the "need to deter the sale of narcotics."

Just as the use of minimum sentences limits the possibilities for correctional programs, the use of continuances requires programs for youthful offenders to have a longer duration than they otherwise might. (The average length of stay in many institutions for youthful offenders is nine

84. *Hester v. Craven*, 322 F. Supp. 1256 (C.D. Cal. 1971).

months when continuances are not given.) Continuances also remove the motivation that comes from knowing that one will be released as soon as he has reached certain educational or vocational goals.

In some cases, women and youthful offenders sentenced under special statutes are sent to the same institutions as people sentenced under regular criminal statutes. They receive no special treatment, yet frequently serve longer terms than they would have if they had not been given indeterminate sentences. Women in Connecticut and Pennsylvania[85] recently succeeded in overturning statutes that allowed them to be imprisoned for longer terms than the maximum provided for the offense of which they were convicted. According to the federal court that invalidated the Connecticut statute:

> The state seeks to justify [the statute] by noting that it is one among a number of provisions . . . dealing with "Humane and Reformatory Agencies and Institutions" as distinguished from the "Penal Institutions" . . . and that it is, therefore, "part of the integral whole which constitutes the State's attempt to provide for women and juveniles a special protection and every reformative and rehabilitative opportunity." . . . This purports to be a way of concealing the abrasive nature of imprisonment under the charming image of an educational institution. But this should not blind one to the fact that the institution is still a place of imprisonment. . . .
>
> Even assuming . . . that there is a difference in the quality of treatment and conditions of incarceration at the Farm, these facts are not enough to justify a longer period of imprisonment for adult women as opposed to adult men. . . . The state has failed to carry its burden in support of the proposition that a greater period of imprisonment is necessary for the deterrence of women than for men.

Legislation regarding juveniles generally allows them to be kept in state custody until they become twenty-one, regardless of their age or the nature of their offense. In the *Gault* case, Gerald Gault was sentenced to spend up to six years at the Arizona State Industrial School for Boys for an offense carrying a maximum criminal penalty for adults of a $5 to $50 fine or imprisonment for not more than two months.

85. United States *ex rel. Robinson v. York*, 281 F. Supp. 8 (1968); *Commonwealth v. Daniel*, 430 Pa. 642, 243 A.2d 400 (1968).

A sixteen-year-old committed under Pennsylvania juvenile-court law until the age of twenty-one for assault, a misdemeanor carrying a maximum penalty for adults of a $1,000 fine and two years in prison, claimed that the longer sentence deprived him of equal protection of the laws. The Pennsylvania Supreme Court recently upheld the contention:

> There is no disguising the fact that had this boy been tried as an adult he could not have been committed to Camp Hill for a maximum period of five years. Does the Constitution of the United States permit this discrimination in treatment by reason of the mere fortuity that this boy was tried in Juvenile Court instead of in adult court? We believe that the Constitution forbids such invidious discrimination.

> Under the Equal Protection Clause of the Fourteenth Amendment to the United States Constitution a state may make distinctions only upon the basis of reasonable classifications. If the Commonwealth wishes to make individuals guilty of similar conduct eligible for maximum sentences of varying lengths it must demonstrate that the distinctions which it makes are based on some relevant and reasonable classification. . . .
> It is our view that there can be no constitutionally valid distinction between a juvenile and an adult offender which justifies making one of them subject to longer maximum commitment in the same institution for the same conduct.[86]

The court went on to say, however, that a longer maximum commitment for a juvenile might be permissible, but "it must be clear that the longer commitment will result in the juvenile's receiving appropriate rehabilitative care and not just in his being deprived of his liberty for a longer time." Two judges disagreed, since in their opinion it is impossible for the sentencing court to determine "whether a certain period of commitment will result in appropriate rehabilitative care or deprivation of liberty. Use of this approach will require courts to guess what the defendant will be doing and what will be done for him during the period of commitment, and it is being unrealistic to expect that courts can make such a determination in a meaningful way."

Recent amendments to the Colorado Children's Code limit the maximum term of juvenile probation to two years without a violation and of

86. *In re* Wilson, 264 A.2d 614 (Pa. 1970).

commitment to an institution to two years unless the Department of Institutions petitions the committing court to extend the term for an additional two years. Similar legislation has been enacted in Connecticut. Even under these statutes, it is still possible for a child to be incarcerated longer than an adult for the same offense.[87]

MANDATORY SENTENCES

Many legislatures have precluded judicial discretion in sentencing for certain offenses and for recidivist offenders by making prison commitments and, frequently, minimum terms mandatory.

The most pervasive mandatory sentence is the legislatively prescribed minimum term. Offenses that have a maximum term of life imprisonment generally have a fixed minimum. These minimum terms range from seven years to thirty, with most states requiring ten or fifteen years.

Some statutes deny certain offenders eligibility for probation or parole. The federal narcotics statute mandates a five- and, in some cases, a ten- and twenty-year prison term without parole. It also precludes sentencing to probation.

In California, where parole authorities normally are given complete discretion over minimum terms, the legislature has imposed mandatory minimum sentences for many offenses. For example, anyone who possesses marijuana or who attacks a policeman must be sentenced to state prison. Assault with a deadly weapon requires that a minimum of five years always be served in state prison.[88]

The model sentencing codes that have been developed recently by the American Law Institute, the National Council on Crime and Delinquency and the American Bar Association adopt the principle that it is inappropriate for the legislature to prescribe minimum terms that courts must impose regardless of the circumstances.

As for judicially imposed minimum terms that must be served before an offender is eligible for parole, the Model Sentencing Act, drafted by the National Council on Crime and Delinquency flatly states that there should be immediate parole eligibility in every case. The American Bar Association has recommended that there should be no minimum sentence

87. Colo. Rev. Stat. 22–3–18(2)(b) and 22–3–14(3)(a) (1963, as amended); Conn. Public Acts 664 (1969).
88. Nev. Rev. Stat. §213.120(2) (1963); Me. Rev. Stat. Ann. tit. 34, §1672(3) (1966 supp.); Int. Rev. Code of 1954, §7237; see P.L. No. 89–793, 89th Cong., 2d Sess. §501 (Nov. 8, 1966); e.g., Cal. Penal Code §§3043, 3044, 3046 (1966 Supp.).

unless the sentencing judge acts affirmatively to impose one. Where the judge feels that confinement for a minimum term is necessary in order to protect the public from further criminal conduct by the defendant, he can impose a minimum of one-third the maximum.

Sentencing deals with the criminal as well as the crime—in mitigation and in aggravation of the criminal act. In most states harsh sentences are required not only for particular offenses but for offenders who commit several crimes.

Legislation in at least twenty-one states provides mandatory terms for the repeat offender. In at least twenty-three states life sentences are authorized or required for offenders who have been convicted of three or four offenses. (The offenses concerned are usually felonies. However, Washington State requires a life sentence for the fifth conviction of petit larceny, Nevada for the sixth.[89]) In addition, the recidivist may have his eligibility for parole denied outright or postponed by high minimum terms. Yet the few empirical surveys that have been made tend to show that the number of previous convictions is a totally unreliable guide to the dangerousness of an offender.[90]

Habitual-offender legislation has resulted in sentences which are far more stringent than those generally imposed for the same offenses. For example, one offender just over juvenile-court age committed three felonies during a three-month period. He was sentenced to mandatory life imprisonment without parole. A burglar was given ninety-nine years for his second offense; the first burglary had occurred five years before. A thirty-dollar forgery won a third offender ten to eleven years. His previous crime was petit larceny, a misdemeanor.[91]

Two states' recent statutory revisions have replaced the automatic imposition of high sentences and denial of parole by making extended terms available, but not mandatory, for persistent offenders. The Minnesota statute allows the sentencing court to impose an extended term where it finds, in addition to the commission of prior felonies, that "the defendant is disposed to the commission of violence and that an extended term of imprisonment is required for his rehabilitation or for the public

89. Wash. Rev. Code Ann. §9.92.090 (1961); Nev. Rev. Stat. §207.010 (1965).
90. *See* Tappan, "Habitual Offender Laws and Sentencing Practices in Relation to Organized Crime," in Ploscowe (ed.), *Organized Crime and Law Enforcement* (1952); Note, "Court Treatment of General Recidivist Statutes," 48 *Columbia Law Review* 238 (1948); Brown, "The Treatment of the Recidivist in the United States," 23 *Canadian Bar Review* 640 (1945).
91. *Canupp v. State*, 197 Tenn. 56, 270 S.W.2d 356 (1954); *Joseph v. Texas*, 367 S.W.2d 330 (Tex. Crim. App. 1963); *State v. Sedlacek*, 178 Neb. 322, 133 N.W.2d 380 (1965).

safety." The maximum term imposed may in no event be greater than forty years and cannot exceed the maximum available for the present offense multiplied by the number of prior felony convictions within the past ten years. Enhanced terms may not be given for misdemeanors, since "by their very nature, misdemeanors and gross misdemeanors do not involve acts of violence, dangerous to the public and calling for extended periods of confinement of the perpetrator." The statute is unique in its requirement that for an extended term to be adjudged, a defendant's criminal acts must have involved violence. Since the Minnesota statute also provides immediate eligibility for parole for all but life sentences,[92] the court lacks authority to impose a minimum term.

The revisers of the New York Penal Law rejected any system under which a sentence would depend on any formal findings regarding character. They did not want to make necessary a full hearing or disclosure of any confidential information in the probation report. The New York statute authorizes imposition of sentences with a minimum of fifteen to twenty-five years and a maximum of life imprisonment when the sentencing court "is of the opinion that the history and character of the defendant and the nature and circumstances of his criminal conduct indicate that extended incarceration and lifetime supervision will best serve the public interest."[93] This standard has been criticized as overly vague and as allowing sentences far out of proportion to the ordinary sentences provided for the crimes of which a defendant has been convicted.

Congress recently enacted two laws that provide extended penalties for repeat offenders. On a person's second conviction of any non-moving traffic offense, the District of Columbia Court Reform and Criminal Procedure Act of 1970[94] permits the court to impose a fine or prison term that is one and one half times the maximum statutory penalty; on his third conviction, the sentence may be triple the usual maximum. The Organized Crime Control Act of 1970,[95] which applies nationally, creates a category of "dangerous special offenders" who, after notice and a special hearing held subsequent to a trial or guilty plea, may be sentenced to prison for a term not to exceed twenty-five years and "not disproportionate in severity to the maximum term otherwise authorized by law for such felony." In order to be sentenced under these provisions, the court must find "by a preponderance of the information" (including the pre-sentence report,

92. Minn. Stat. Ann §§609.12, 609.155, 609.16 (1964).
93. N.Y. Penal Law §70.10 (1967).
94. 22 D.C. Code, §907 (1970).
95. 18 U.S.C., §3575 (1970).

which must be made available for inspection by the defendant in all but exceptional cases): (1) that a felony defendant has been convicted of two previous offenses; (2) that he committed the present offense "as part of a pattern of conduct which was criminal under applicable laws of any jurisdiction, which constituted a substantial source of his income, and in which he manifested special skill or expertise," or as an active participant in a criminal conspiracy; and (3) that "a period of confinement longer than that provided for such felony is required for the protection of the public from further criminal conduct."

The Model Sentencing Act would reserve long prison sentences for the dangerous offender, shown to be "suffering from a severe personality disorder indicating a propensity toward criminal activity," or the professional racketeer. Under the Model Penal Code a court may impose an extended term only if it finds that lengthy imprisonment is necessary for the protection of the public from a persistent offender, a professional criminal, a "dangerous, mentally abnormal person," or a multiple offender whose criminality is so extensive that an extended term is warranted. An American Bar Association proposal confines itself to noting that the extended term is meant for the "professional criminal" and the "persistent felony offender." Unlike the New York statute, however, elaborate procedural safeguards are provided under the ABA's proposal.

Mandatory sentences seek to assure potential offenders and the general public that people caught committing specific crimes or repeated crimes face the certainty of severe punishment. However, various observers have pointed out that this certainty is illusory. Numerous discretionary devices exist, ranging from reduction of the charge by the prosecutor or refusal by the judge to accept a guilty plea to a charge carrying a harsh mandatory sentence, to refusal by juries to convict of such offenses. Such devices may cause a defendant to be convicted of an offense that could not possibly have occurred under the circumstances of the case in order to permit imposition of a more realistic sentence. According to a survey by the American Bar Foundation of criminal justice in Michigan:

> [A]rmed robbery is so often downgraded that the Michigan parole board tends to treat a conviction of unarmed robbery as *prima facie* proof that the defendant had a weapon. And the frequency of altering nighttime burglary to breaking and entering in the daytime led one prosecutor to remark: "You'd think all our burglaries occur at high noon."

In Detroit, judges' opposition to the mandatory twenty-year minimum sentence for sale of narcotics was so great that they almost always instructed defense counsel and prosecutors to negotiate for a reduction of the charge to possession or use. During the first four years after the mandatory penalty was enacted, there were only twelve convictions for the sale of narcotics out of 476 defendants originally charged with the crime. The fact that participants in the criminal justice system seem to have developed accommodations to avoid the injustice of the mandatory sentence rule is compelling proof of its unacceptability.

The Rationales for Long Prison Sentences

According to the most recent statistics available, more than half the adult felony offenders sentenced to state prisons in 1960 were committed for maximum terms of five years or more; almost one-third were sentenced to terms of at least ten years.

A few examples: seven consecutive life sentences imposed on a boy for a series of offenses committed at the same time;[96] a case in which one defendant received consecutive sentences totaling 170 years, 110 of which were suspended;[97] the cumulation of fourteen counts of narcotics violations to result in a fifty-two-year sentence for a fifty-one-year-old defendant;[98] and the forty years given a twenty-year-old man who had robbed a bank in order to get enough money to convince his divorced wife and children to come back to him but shortly thereafter had become remorseful and turned himself in.[99]

In European countries, sentences greater than five years are rare. For example, in Sweden in 1964 only eight commitments out of 11,227 were for terms of more than ten years and only thirty-eight were for more than four years. In England, sentences of from twenty to thirty years "are now entirely exceptional . . . and are generally disapproved."

Sentences are commonly justified as necessary for three purposes: to protect the public from criminals, to rehabilitate the criminals and to deter people from committing crimes.

96. *State v. Oberst,* 127 Kan. 412, 273 Pac. 490 (1929).
97. *State v. Smaldone,* 216 F.2d 891 (10th Cir. 1954), *rev'd per curiam,* 348 U.S. 961 (1955).
98. *Smith v. United States,* 273 F.2d 462 (10th Cir. 1959).
99. *See* R. F. Kennedy, "Justice Is Found in the Hearts and Minds of Free Men," 30 F.D.R. 401, 425 (1961).

Are long prison sentences necessary to protect the public? We have asked every experienced, practicing prison official we know how many of the inmates currently held in confinement really need to be incarcerated in order to protect the public from personal injury. All agree that only a small minority of all the present inmates in American prisons—most estimated between 10 and 15 percent—could be considered to be so dangerous. The American Bar Association's Advisory Committee on Sentencing and Review recently concluded that long prison sentences are unnecessary to public protection in close to 90 percent of the cases of criminals now sent to prison.

However clear it may be that there is a need to imprison some dangerous criminals until they no longer threaten the safety of others, for the largest percentage of offenders, institutional commitments, particularly for long periods, can cause more problems than they solve. In the words of the 1967 President's Crime Commission:

> For a great many offenders . . . correction does not correct. Indeed, experts are increasingly coming to feel that conditions under which many offenders are handled, particularly in institutions, are often a positive detriment to rehabilitation. . . .
>
> Institutions tend to isolate offenders from society, both physically and psychologically, cutting them off from schools, jobs, families, and other supportive influences and increasing the probability that the label of criminal will be indelibly impressed upon them.[100]

Do long prison terms give the public more protection than shorter terms? While far from conclusive, there is some persuasive, objective evidence that the answer is no.

When in 1963, as a result of the famous *Gideon* case, the Supreme Court overturned the convictions of defendants who had not been provided with attorneys at their trials, the state of Florida was compelled to release more than one thousand inmates from its prisons. A researcher from the state's Division of Correction conducted a study to determine if such a sudden, arbitrary release of prisoners would result in an unusual increase in crime. The researcher matched pairs of recently released inmates on the basis of their individual characteristics. One member of each pair had been released at the expiration of his sentence; the other was

100. The President's Commission on Law Enforcement and Administration of Justice, *The Challenge of Crime in a Free Society* 11, 159, 165 (1967).

released abruptly at some point during his prison term as a result of the Supreme Court decision. Of the 110 inmates in the first group, 25.4 percent committed another crime within approximately two years. Of the second group only 13.6 percent committed further crimes within the same time period. The researcher concluded that such a large difference in recidivism between the two groups could occur by chance less than once in twenty times.[101]

The American Bar Association noted that the findings of the Florida study, taken to their logical conclusion, could support a shocking proposition:

> Baldly stated . . . if we, today, turned loose all of the inmates of our prisons without regard to the length of their sentences and, with some exceptions, without regard to their previous offenses we might *reduce* the recidivism rate over what it would be if we kept each prisoner incarcerated until his sentence expired. . . . At the very least the study underscores the need for reexamination of the purposes and consequences of present sentencing practices.[102]

A similar study recently launched in Israel will compare the behavior of prisoners released by the wholesale General Amnesty of 1967 during the six-day war with that of prisoners released at the end of their regular terms.

If the administrators of our correction system and the small but increasing amounts of evidence are to be believed, long prison terms are unnecessary for public protection in the overwhelming majority of cases. No better, more scientific or more rational evidence is presently available.

Do the long sentences, then, rehabilitate the prisoners who serve them? President Nixon campaigned for election by charging, as part of his "get tough" law-enforcement program, that the country is operating "a crime university" graduating more than 200,000 hardened criminals a year. The President, no sentimentalist in the crime business, said that it is hard enough to catch and convict a criminal without bearing the added burden of finding him "a worse menace to society upon his release" from

101. See *Gideon v. Wainwright*, 372 U.S. 355 (1963); Eichmann, *Impact of the Gideon Decision Upon Crime and Sentencing in Florida: A Study of Recidivism and Socio-Cultural Change* 71–73 (1966).
102. American Bar Association Project on Minimum Standards for Criminal Justice, *Standards Relating to Sentencing Alternatives and Procedures* 59 (approved draft, 1968).

prison, and called for steps to "break the vicious cycle that snares a first offender into a lifetime of crime."

This opinion echoed others that already had been expressed by professionals in the correctional field:

We can take a minor property offender and help him to develop into a more serious offender by unnecessary and long incarceration as surely as if we have conducted vocational training in hate, violence, selfishness, abnormal sex relations, and criminal techniques.[103]

We ran a contest by mail in all the federal prisons asking the inmates for their comments about the correctional system in which they were the silent consumers. One common observation was reflected in these responses: "During my stay in the county jail waiting to be tried and sent here to Leavenworth, I have learned how to mix nitroglycerine and how to peel a safe, and what weapons I could use to commit a robbery." Another convict wrote: "I have been rehabilitated so many times in the last 27 years that I now know how to pick locks, open safes (not 'crack' them), sort junk from real jewelry, fence stolen goods, put in a fix with the local politician and draw up a writ. I have arrived! I am what you call a 'subject' of the system. I have learned my lessons well, and instead of being a doctor, engineer, or a tug-boat captain, I am a burglar doing a bum rap for bank robbery." One prisoner from Atlanta warned, "Despair and frustration is at the end of each sentence and we are all planning who to rob when we get out, not only for the money but for revenge. Another blow at society, that's about all we crave. I would rather be me in here scheming than you out there just waiting for your turn as victim."

Some evidence of the detrimental effect of long prison sentences may be seen in data provided by the California Department of Correction regarding the relation between the time served in prison and a releasee's success on parole. Prisoners who had been paroled after serving sentences for robbery or burglary convictions were paired according to their individual characteristics such as age, prior criminal record, ethnic group and the area where they spent the time on parole. One member of each pair had served more than the state's average time in prison for his offense; the other had served less. A comparison of the subsequent criminal

103. California Youth and Adult Correction Agency, *The Organization of State Correctional Services and the Control and Treatment of Crime and Delinquency* 152 (1967).

histories of the two groups showed that the longer prison sentences consistently produced higher rates of crimes committed on release.

The median time served by first-degree robbers paroled in 1965 was forty-five months. Of this group, 139 matched pairs were selected. After two years 13 percent of those who had served less than the median time had been returned to prison for conviction of a new felony. Of those who had served more than the median time, 23 percent had been returned with a new felony commitment.

A more recent and exhaustive study was undertaken by the California legislature to determine the relationship between the length of time served in prison and the success of releasees on parole. The study disclosed that the performance of groups of prisoners on parole could be predicted accurately by using the Base Expectancy Scores developed by the Department of Correction. These scores, discussed more fully in Chapter V, are arrived at by assigning points to various characteristics, such as number and type of prior arrests, use of alcohol or narcotics, employment, previous commitments and use of aliases, which have been found useful in predicting parole outcome. The present study showed that the scores, comprised exclusively of factors that were known at the time of imprisonment, were the best predictors of performance on parole. The amount of time served in prison had *no* relationship to performance after release.[104] Commenting on the finding that time served is unrelated to parole outcome, one correction professional said, "If this conclusion is accepted, and I do not see how we can upset it, it follows that when prisoners are confined for three years when two years would do, the parole board intuitions have imposed an enormous amount of needless distress at a huge economic cost."[105]

The median time served by second-degree burglars released to parole in 1965 was twenty-four months. From this group, 240 pairs were selected. After two years, 16 percent of those who had served less than the median time had been returned to prison for conviction of a new felony. Of those who had served more than the median time, 25 percent had been returned with new felony commitments.

Do long sentences deter the sentenced or others from committing crimes? Obviously those who are sentenced are not deterred. Crime in

104. Public Systems, Inc., *A Study of the Characteristics and Recidivism Experience of California Prisoners*, Appendix to California Assembly, Parole Board Reform in California (1970).
105. Conrad, "Decisions and Discretion—A Critique of the Indeterminate Sentence" 17 (unpublished, 1970).

prison is common. Furthermore, most offenders will leave prison only to commit another crime and go back through the "revolving door" of the jail. But long sentences are commonly justified as necessary for showing the public that anyone caught committing certain crimes will suffer grave penalties. For example, the judges who attended a recent federal institute on sentencing agreed that "except in unusual circumstances, a sentence of at least eight years is needed in bank robbery with a gun, or other weapon, so that there may become a general recognition by the community that a major period of confinement will be involved."[106]

A governor's committee to recommend changes in the treatment of offenders in New York noted that consideration of the needs of individual offenders may have to be sacrificed in certain cases in order to assure the public that those who commit certain crimes, such as forcible rape, will in fact be punished.[107]

There is no relation between the sentencing practices in various states and the amount of reported crime in those states. The median time served in the fifty states runs from nine months in New Hampshire to thirty-nine months in Hawaii. High and low crime rates are found in states with both low and high sentences. And within the same state, although there are large variations among the sentencing practices of different counties, these variations appear to be completely unrelated to crime rates, felony arrest rates or rates of violation of probation. If the variant practices serve any function it would seem to be in reflecting local values and thus sublimating local needs.

Should we make an example of those criminals who are caught and sentenced? It should be remembered that very few criminals actually go to prison. In fact, our correctional apparatus has very little quantitative impact on the mass of offenders and offenses.

In California, for example, according to the state's Bureau of Criminal Statistics, 56,942 crimes of personal violence were reported to police in 1966. Of the reported violent offenses, 51 percent were cleared by arrest or other methods. Only 4,397 adults were convicted for these crimes. Of this group, 1,672—representing only 2 percent of the number of offenses reported—were committed to state prisons. In the same year, 362,025 felony property crimes were reported. Only 21 percent of these

106. Recommendations and Concluding Remarks, United States Court of Appeals for the 4th and 5th Circuits, Institute on Sentencing (Atlanta, Georgia, Oct. 1967), 45 F.R.D. 149, 197, 198.
107. Preliminary Report of the Governor's Special Committee on Criminal Offenders 11, 40, 102 (1968).

offenses were cleared by arrest or other methods, and 11,207 adults were convicted. Of those convicted, 2,037 were sentenced to state prisons—0.5 percent of the number of offenses reported.

And reported offenses comprise, according to the best estimates, less than half of the crimes actually committed. The 1967 President's Crime Commission estimated that only from one-tenth to one-third of all crimes committed are even reported to the police in the first place.

Rather than the most dangerous criminals, the prison population may represent the least skillful. We may be punishing the incompetents and rewarding the ingenious—and, in doing so, unwittingly contributing to the creation of a professional criminal class. Perhaps our sentencing practices reflect the fear that if so few criminals are actually caught, convicted and sentenced to prison, only the image of a potentially terrifying sanction will deter potential criminals.

Do long prison sentences really serve a symbolic function? In fact, the general public has extremely little knowledge of the specific penalties available for various crimes.

In a recent research project, a cross-section of Californians were questioned about their knowledge of the existing penalties. The responses showed that most people had little knowledge of what would happen to them if ever they were convicted of a crime. Most of them underestimated the severity of the penalties currently provided for different crimes, although a quarter of the group stated that penalties should be increased in order to lessen the crime rate. When questioned about recent legislative action increasing penalties for certain crimes, about one-half of the respondents had no idea whether the penalties had been changed or in which direction.

There was some evidence that the more delinquent a group of respondents was, the more knowledge it had about criminal penalties. The less delinquent group seemed to be controlled by "internal sanctions," such as feelings of personal guilt, family attitudes and the opinions of other people. The more delinquent groups were concerned with avoiding detection. While the fear of arrest, conviction and imprisonment did seem to loom large with the more delinquent respondents, there was no evidence that the fear of length of incarceration affected decisions to refrain from crime:

> The understanding of the motivation for criminal actions does
> not involve a balance sheet of penalty versus gain. Rather people

engage in crime and learn of the penalties not as deterrents but only as factors of a criminal career faced *after* the fact.[108]

The theory behind antiquated English common law which provided public capital punishment for hundreds of crimes (including picking pockets) was that the example would deter. Yet it has been recorded that while the hangings were going on and the crowds large and attentive, pickpockets commonly plied their trade among the spectators at these outings. Even today, the use of capital punishment for murder persists, despite evidence that executions have no demonstrable effect on the rate of homicides.

Legislative efforts to increase penalties for particularly abhorrent crimes actually seem to have little or no effect on crime rates. In 1966 the Pennsylvania legislature reacted to a particularly atrocious case of multiple rape by amending its penal code to make mandatory a fifteen-year minimum sentence for any rape involving injury. A criminologist from the University of Pennsylvania analyzed police records for 1965 and 1966 in an effort to determine the effect of the increased penalties on the gravity and frequency of reported rapes. The investigation concluded that the legislative changes had produced no noticeable change:

> Philadelphia found no relief from forcible and attempted rape either during the examination leading up to the imposition of strong penalties for these offenses or after the imposition itself. This holds true with respect to both the frequency and intensity of these crimes. We are therefore bound to conclude that Pennsylvania's new deterrent strategy against rape was a failure as far as Philadelphia is concerned. The inefficacy of the new legislation should create much disappointment among those in Philadelphia who had taken for granted the deterrent impact of increased penalties.[109]

In 1961 the California legislature removed the sentence of twelve months in a county jail as an optional penalty for the possession of marijuana and required that all defendants convicted of possession serve from one to ten years in a state prison. Penalties also were increased for possess-

108. California Legislature, Assembly Committee on Criminal Procedure, *Deterrent Effects of Criminal Sanctions* 16 (1968).
109. Schwartz, "The Effect in Philadelphia of Pennsylvania's Increased Penalties for Rape and Attempted Rape," 59 *Journal of Criminal Law, Criminology and Police Science* 509 (1968).

ing marijuana after a prior conviction and for selling the drug. In 1961, 3,500 persons were arrested for marijuana offenses. In 1968, despite the increased penalties, approximately 56,800 persons were arrested for the same offenses.[110]

The question of the appropriate severity of sentences should not be confused with the general necessity of inflicting some sort of criminal sanction. While the proposition is unprovable, some criminals may be deterred from further antisocial conduct by the experience of conviction and punishment. Since we have no idea of what the crime rate would be if we did not punish criminals at all, we cannot say that punishment has no deterrent effect. The fear of being publicly declared a criminal may sufficiently reinforce the morality of the law-abiding. A British survey of young male prisoners discovered that once they had been labeled as criminals and sentenced to prison, the inmates saw little risk in committing further crimes. College students, on the other hand, reacted strongly to the threat of censure.[111]

In the limited area of parking violations, an increase in the severity and certainty of punishment has been shown capable of reducing the number of violations.[112] We have little knowledge about the types of punishment that deter different types of offenders and the crimes where deterrence is effective. One researcher has suggested that the legal system punishes most severely the people who commit offenses such as murder, which are least able to be deterred, and punishes the least severely those who commit offenses such as antitrust violations and other corporate crimes, that can be deterred most effectively.

The severity of possible punishments may be less significant as a deterrent than a criminal's fear of being punished at all. According to some California correction officials, "potential criminals do seem to calculate the chances of being apprehended more than the punishment of the offense if caught . . . loss of freedom in any degree, isolation from families and community, no matter how many treatment services are provided is substantial punishment."[113] If this is so, one can question that

110. California State Assembly, *Preliminary Report on the Costs and Effects of the California Criminal Justice System and Recommendations for Legislation to Increase Support of Local Police and Correction Programs* 86 (1969).
111. Rettig, "Ethical Risk Sensitivity in Male Prisoners," 4 *British Journal of Criminology* 582 (1964).
112. Chambliss, "The Deterrent Influence of Punishment," 12 *Crime and Delinquency* 70 (1966).
113. California Youth and Adult Correction Agency, The Organization of State Correctional Services in the Control and Treatment of Crime and Delinquency 155 (1967).

priority which elevates confinement at the expense of rehabilitation. In the hope of deterring crime through long periods of imprisonment we continue to spend millions of dollars that might be better spent on detecting and apprehending criminals. In 1967, California spent almost as much money on state prisons, with 12,500 new admissions in one year, as the state and local police did to deal with the 476,000 felonies that were reported in the state that year.

In an effort to save money and to "indicate to the offender that rehabilitation is a part of criminal justice," the Ohio legislature passed a "Shock Treatment Law,"[114] which permits the sentencing judge to hold a special hearing after a prisoner has served from thirty to sixty days of his sentence. As of June 30, 1970, 1,343 convicted felons had been placed on probation as a result of these hearings. Only 120 of these had been returned to prison for violating the terms of their probation. According to the chief of Ohio's Adult Parole Authority, the idea behind the law is to "shock the offender into realizing that by violating the law he can be punished and deprived of his freedom."

Plea Bargaining

The possibility of severe mandatory sentences increases the bargaining power of the prosecutor, who can reduce the charge to one carrying a much lower sentence in return for a guilty plea. According to one study:

> Defendants with a number of prior felony convictions are potentially susceptible to long sentences or separate convictions as habitual criminals. It is not an uncommon practice for prosecutors to mention this to recidivistic defendants, and there is little doubt that this exerts a strong pressure on them to "cooperate" with the state by pleading guilty.[115]

The guilty plea is undoubtedly the most frequent method of conviction in all jurisdictions. Defendants agree to plead guilty in return for the prosecutor's promise to reduce the charge or seek a lenient sentence for the original charge.

Plea bargaining is motivated on the part of the defendant by his de-

---

114. 29 Page's Ohio Rev. Code 2947.061 (Supp. 1970).
115. Newman, *Conviction—The Determination of Guilt or Innocence Without Trial* 58 n.3 (1966).

sire to get as light a sentence as possible and on the part of the prosecutor by his need to move cases quickly through the overworked criminal justice system. It is commonly observed by judges and others that if all those who are accused of crime were to refuse to plead guilty on any given day, the entire system of criminal justice would break down.

Although plea bargaining is not visible to the public, it is tacitly recognized by all the participants in the criminal justice system. After a bargain has been made between the prosecutor and the defense, the judge typically asks the accused whether any promises or threats have been made to induce his plea. The answer, invariably, is "No, Your Honor."[116] Nonetheless, as Professor Fred Cohen has noted, "only the most naïve can believe that a significant number of these guilty pleas result from pangs of conscience, indicate the first step toward repentance, or show a willingness to assume responsibility for one's conduct. Guilty pleas, by and large, are the result of bargaining sessions where the plea is offered in return for charging and sentencing concessions."[117]

One unfortunate result of plea bargaining may be a sentence bearing no relation to the needs of the defendant or the protection of the public, and a man subjected to correctional supervision with little information about him or his crime.

The judge is not supposed to participate in the process of plea bargaining because of the likelihood that his participation will overawe the defendant or compromise his impartiality. However, prosecutors would lose much of their bargaining power if they could not assure defendants that judges will be lenient with them if they plead guilty. Thus, it is not uncommon for a judge to "ratify" an agreement already reached between defendant and prosecutor.[118] To this extent, the judge has diluted his sentencing discretion by deferring to the prosecutor.

Some judges have gone further and imposed their own sanctions on defendants who insist on a trial. One blunt judge sentenced a convicted defendant to three years in jail, adding that

> Had there been a plea of guilty in this case probably probation
> might have been considered under certain terms, but you are all
> well aware of the standing policy here that once a defendant

116. *See, e.g.,* United States *ex rel. McGrath v. LaVallee,* 319 F.2d 308, 310–11 (2d Cir. 1963).
117. Cohen, *The Legal Challenge to Correction* 17 (1969).
118. *See* United States *ex rel. Posa v. Follette,* 395 F.2d 721, 725–26 (2d Cir. 1968); *see generally Scott v. United States,* No. 20,954 (D.C. Circuit, Feb. 13, 1969).

stands trial that element of grace is removed from the consideration of the Court in the imposition of sentence.[119]

There is evidence that as a rule judges sentence defendants who demand a trial more severely than those who plead guilty. At least one
federal court of appeals has gone so far as to take "judicial notice of the
fact that trial courts quite generally impose a lighter sentence on pleas of
guilty than in cases where the accused pleaded not guilty but has been
found guilty by a jury."[120] In 1970, the Supreme Court ruled that there is
no constitutional bar to accepting a guilty plea from a defendant who is
unwilling to admit participation in the crime, but who agrees to accept a
prison sentence out of fear of the death penalty.[121]

An advisory committee of the American Bar Association suggested
that it is proper for the court to grant charge and sentence concessions to
defendants who enter a plea of guilty when the interest of the public in
the effective administration of criminal justice would thereby be served.
Adopting the ABA's recommendation, the District of Columbia Superior
Court has announced an experiment to bring the practice of plea bargaining into the open and give defendants some protection from bad bargains.
Prosecutors and defense attorneys will sign forms on which the prosecution, in return for a guilty plea, agrees to withdraw some charges and to
recommend certain maximum sentences on others. A judge not wishing to
impose the sentence recommended will permit the defendant to withdraw
his plea.

The Supreme Court has endorsed the practice of plea bargaining and
begun to impose requirements to ensure that bargains, once made, are
kept by the state. In the recent case of *Santobello v. New York*[122] Chief
Justice Burger stated for the Court:

> The disposition of criminal charges by agreement between the
> prosecutor and the accused sometimes loosely called "plea bar-
> gaining" is an essential component of the administration of
> justice. Properly administered it is to be encouraged. . . . It
> leads to prompt and largely final disposition of most criminal
> cases, it avoids much of the corrosive impact of enforced idleness
> during pre-trial confinement for those who are denied release
> pending trial; it protects the public from those accused persons

119. *United States v. Wiley*, 267 F.2d 453, 455 (7th Cir. 1960).
120. *Dewey v. United States*, 286 F.2d 124, 128 (8th Cir. 1959).
121. *North Carolina v. Alford*, 400 U.S. 25 (1970).
122. No. 70–98 (Dec. 2, 1971).

who are prone to continue criminal conduct even while on pre-trial release; and by shortening the time between charge and disposition it enhances whatever may be the rehabilitative prospects of the guilty when they are ultimately imprisoned.

The Court ruled that a defendant who had pleaded guilty to a lesser charge on the prosecutor's supposed agreement to make no recommendation as to the sentence must be permitted either to withdraw his plea or to be resentenced by a different judge when a new prosecutor, apparently unaware of the bargain, recommended the maximum sentence. This was so despite the judge's statement that he was not influenced by the recommendation. (The choice between the two possible remedies was to be left to the trial court.)

One commentator has suggested that defendants at least be given copies of their presentence reports before they plead so that they can assess the risk of the judge's departing from the bargain. Such a procedure would require that presentence investigations, which presently are conducted only after a finding of guilt, be conducted before the defendant even enters a plea. The recommendation can be justified in view of the large number of defendants who forgo trial.[123] The Vera Foundation's Bronx Sentencing Project recently began making available information concerning defendant's social histories and predictions of possible sentences to be used as the bases of plea-bargaining sessions.

Power of the Sentencing Judge

Despite the legislative imposition of mandatory sentences for certain crimes and despite the prosecutional role in sentencing through negotiated pleas, the last word in most cases belongs to the trial judge. When he looks upon the defendant after having read a presentence report and listened to the defendant's pleas for mercy, the decision of probation or imprisonment, county jail or state prison, one year or ten, belongs to him. In the last hundred years, the sentencing alternatives available to the trial judge have increased. But there has been no corresponding requirement that the judge explain his choice of sentence to the defendant, to the correctional personnel who must treat him (often with no knowledge of why he received the particular sentence) or even to other judges.

123. Note, "Procedural Due Process at Judicial Sentencing for Felony," 81 *Harvard Law Review* 821, 830 (1968).

A comparison with the practice in other countries underscores the uniqueness of the sentencing power of American judges. Observers of comparative sentencing techniques have noted that we are the only country in the free world where a single judge may, without being subjected to any review of his determination on the merits, decide absolutely the minimum period of time during which a convicted offender must remain in prison.[124]

In several other countries, not only do the legislatures provide some criteria for the sentencing judges but a number of judges participate in sentencing for serious crimes. In Germany, for example, sentencing for serious offenses is done by three professional and several lay judges. In Italy, two professional and six "popular judges" participate. The amount of punishment for serious crimes is determined by three judges in France and in Japan.

Judges in European countries are required to explain in detail their reasons for choosing a particular sentence. And the supreme courts in Europe have forbidden judges to use clichés such as the "gravity of the offense" or the "record of the perpetrator."

Still another respect in which the American system is unique is in the complete immunity from appellate review of the trial court's sentencing decision. Even in other common-law countries—England, Canada, Pakistan and India—defendants may appeal from sentences they consider too harsh. In addition, Commonwealth countries allow the government or the injured party to appeal matters of sentence. As Professor B. J. George of the University of Michigan has written, "Certainly the fact that every other leading system of the free world, including the English, abandoned the position of non-reviewability of sentence at least 50 years ago ought to impose some kind of close scrutiny on our basic assumptions."

American appellate courts have declared themselves powerless without specific statutory authorization (which has been given only in seventeen jurisdictions) to modify sentences that are imposed within prescribed statutory limits.[125] Most courts follow the chauvinistic view enunciated by one state court regarding appellate review of a trial court's sentence:

124. B. J. George, Jr., "Comparative Sentencing Techniques," 23 *Federal Probation* 27 (March 1959).
125. *See, e.g., Gore v. United States*, 357 U.S. 386, 393 (1958); *Blockburger v. United States*, 284 U.S. 299, 305 (1932); *Leach v. United States*, 334 F.2d 945, 951 (D.C. Cir. 1964); *State v. Wright*, 261 N.C. 356, 134 S.E.2d 624 (1964); *Mason v. State*, 375 S.W.2d 916 (Tex. Crim. App. 1964); *Michell v. State*, 154 So.2d 701 (Fla. App. 1963).

If the punishment is grossly and inordinately disproportionate to the offense so that sentence is evidently dictated not by a sense of public duty, but by passion, prejudice, ill-will or any other unworthy motive, the judgment ought to be reversed, and the cause remanded for a more just sentence. But no such instance of judicial misconduct has ever occurred in our good old State, and we trust that the day may never come when it will be witnessed.[126]

If such "misconduct" ever did occur, the lack of a requirement that judges state their reasons for choosing a sentence almost certainly would preclude an appellate court from recognizing it. Even where local court rules require trial courts to give reasons for imposing prison sentences, they are easily circumvented. For example, this justification was given for a sentence imposed recently: "Although this is the defendant's first arrest, incarceration is deemed necessary."[127]

Strangely enough, this refusal to review sentencing decisions is not the general rule with regard to the dispositions made by juvenile courts. Although some courts of appeals apply to juvenile cases the same self-abnegating rule they have developed in reviewing adult sentences, several do not. Since juvenile court cases were originally considered to be non-criminal, some courts have reviewed them under the same standards that apply in civil cases.[128]

One appellate court, believing that "considerations of expediency, the satisfaction of public indignation, or example are contrary to the whole spirit of the juvenile act," ruled that "the good of the State requires a child to be removed from a community only when his delinquency is such that he has become a danger to society either because of his own conduct or his influence upon others." The court reversed the commitment to state training school of a sixteen-year-old boy whose "immoral" conduct admittedly had brought him within the jurisdiction of the juvenile court:

. . . drastic remedies should not be invoked where we can have

---

126. *Mitchell v. State,* 82 Md. 527, 534, 34 Atl. 246, 247–48 (1896).
127. *State v. Kunz,* 55 N.J. 128, 259 A.2d 895, 896 (1969).
128. *Cf. In re* Lewis, 11 N.J. 217, 224, 94 A.2d 328, 332 (1953) (court has no power to modify disposition within statutory·limits) with *State v. Myers,* 22 N.W.2d 199 (N.D. 1946), citing N.D.R.C. 27–1632 (1943): "Any order made by this [juvenile] court may be reviewed or appealed in the manner provided for the review of civil cases."

reasonable hope that lesser ones will have an equal if not a complete success. . . .

After a full consideration of the evidence we have concluded that it is not for Frank's best interest to commit him to the State Training School. We think that he has demonstrated traits of character that entitle him to another chance to show he can accommodate himself to the normal healthy life society requires of a sixteen-year-old boy.[129]

Several years later the same court ruled that where a reasonable alternative to institutional confinement of a pregnant seventeen-year-old girl was available, the juvenile court had abused its discretion by committing her to a state industrial school.[130]

In a Maryland case, two young civil-rights demonstrators were found delinquent and sent to state training school. On review, the court of appeals held that, although the behavior of the juveniles, which had amounted to criminal trespass and disorderly conduct, justified the finding of delinquency, it was "not so fundamentally wrong as to require permanent treatment, as distinguished from temporary custodial care."[131] The court ordered the juvenile court to reconsider its disposition in light of a state statute[132] which provided that a case against a juvenile should be dismissed if the "judge determines that the child is not within the jurisdiction of the court or that the child is not in need of care or treatment."

Since lawyers only recently have been appointed to defend juveniles, juvenile dispositions rarely have been appealed. However, statutes governing juvenile courts frequently contain clauses that direct the judge to provide care and guidance preferably in the child's own home or to secure for a child removed from his home the kind of care that most closely approximates parental supervision. Virtually every commitment of a child to an institution could be challenged as inconsistent with these provisions. According to former Denver juvenile court judge Ted Rubin:

A lawyer can properly ask why a child was placed away from home when the purpose clause states he shall receive care and guidance preferably in his own home. What services have been provided to reasonably prove that the statutory preference

129. *State v. Myers*, 22 N.W.2d 199, 201–202 (N.D. 1946).
130. *In re* Braun, 145 N.W.2d 482 (N.D. 1966).
131. *In re* Cromwell, 232 Md. 409, 194 A.2d 88, 90 (1963).
132. Md. Code, Art. 26, §61 (1957).

should be discarded? And can anyone say that all the private and public facilities into which court children are placed . . . can provide the . . . requirement of "custody, care and discipline as nearly as possible equivalent to that which should have been given by his parents"?

The Supreme Court held recently that on resentencing a defendant whose first sentence was overturned on appeal a trial court may impose a more severe punishment than the original sentence. To ensure that the second sentence is not motivated by a desire to punish the defendant for his appeal, however, the judge must state reasons for the increased sentence, "based upon objective information concerning identifiable conduct on the part of the defendant occurring after the time of the original sentencing proceeding."[133] In other cases where appellate courts, while not willing to modify sentences, will examine the criteria used in sentencing,[134] it is impossible for the appellate court to know what considerations actually influenced the sentence. As the Supreme Court recognized in the context of a juvenile court's waiver of its jurisdiction:

Meaningful review requires that the reviewing court should review. It should not be remitted to assumptions. It must have before it a statement of reasons motivating [the decision]. . . .[135]

In support of their position, opponents of appellate review of sentences generally cite the increased workload of appellate courts that would result. They do not find it anomalous that while all other decisions made by trial judges in both civil and criminal cases are subject to appellate review, criminal sentences alone are immune. As an American Bar Association advisory committee has recognized, "To say, as we do, that we care more for the integrity of the hearsay rule than for the difference between one and twenty years is hardly revealing of a sound system of values."[136]

While an appellate court judge before his appointment to the Supreme Court, Justice Potter Stewart noted the difference in the protection afforded the defendant before and after his guilt is determined:

133. *North Carolina v. Pearce*, 395 U.S. 711, 726 (1969).
134. *E.g., Townsend v. Burke*, 334 U.S. 736 (1948); *Verdugo v. United States*, 402 F.2d 599 (9th Cir. 1968); *Coleman v. United States*, 357 F.2d 563 (D.C. Cir. 1965).
135. *Kent v. United States*, 383 U.S. 541, 561 (1966).
136. American Bar Association Project on Minimum Standards for Criminal Justice, Standards Relating to Appellate Review of Sentences 27 (approved draft, 1968).

Justice is measured in many ways, but to a convicted criminal its surest measure lies in the fairness of the sentence he receives. . . . It is an anomaly that a judicial system which has developed so scrupulous a concern for the protection of a criminal defendant throughout every other stage of the proceedings against him should have so neglected this important dimension of fundamental justice.[137]

In an indirect way, some criminal sentences are reviewed by appellate courts. Lawyers for defendants who actually are concerned with what they consider a disproportionately severe sentence find other technical grounds upon which to base their appeals, and appellate courts frequently reverse on technical grounds for the same reason. The effect, according to one judge who has worked for reform of sentencing procedures, is to

multiply appeals involving less significant features of the trial. These are desperately seized upon and are really only thinly veiled appeals from sentences. This has a deleterious effect on the whole appellate process.

When judges sense that injustice has been done, they strain to magnify minor defects in a search for reversible error. . . . [S]uch considerations sometimes tip the scales and result in a very technical ruling on a question of law, when what is uppermost in everybody's mind is not the trial itself but the appropriateness of the sentence.[138]

Along with legal and policy questions that have been raised about American sentencing practices, there also have been constitutional questions. Appeals to the constitutional prohibition against cruel and unusual punishments, contained in the Eighth Amendment, generally have been of no avail.[139]

One early Supreme Court decision overturned as cruel and unusual the punishment of prolonged imprisonment, chaining and the imposition of "painful as well as hard labor" adjudged against an American national

---

137. *Shepard v. United States*, 257 F.2d 293, 294 (6th Cir. 1958).
138. *Appellate Review of Sentences*, Hearings on S.2722 Before the Subcommittee on Improvements in Judicial Machinery of the Senate Committee on the Judiciary, 89th Cong., 2d Sess. 25 (1966) (statement of Judge Simon E. Sobeloff).
139. *See, e.g., Reid v. State*, 200 Md. 89, 92, 88 A.2d 478, 479 (1952):
   It is not cruel and unusual punishment if it is within the statutory limits prescribed for the crime of which the accused is found guilty, and the trial court alone has the right to determine the penalty within these limits.

in the Philippines.[140] However, one commentator recently surmised that it was the peculiar form of the punishment, rather than its severity, that incurred the court's displeasure:

> The opinion breathes righteous indignation at the description of practices that are, as it reiterates, unknown in this country. It was plainly not the length of the imprisonment alone, considered in relation to the gravity of the offense, that determined the result. Rather, it was the combination of an excessive but conventional mode of punishment with a good deal of laid-on unpleasantness offensive for its novelty as well as its severity that supported the characterization of Weems' punishment as cruel and unusual.[141]

Since that decision, the Supreme Court has failed to condemn a single form of corporal punishment, sterilization of criminals,[142] such brutal treatment of prisoners as chaining and mutilation,[143] the loss on conviction of a license to practice a trade or profession,[144] or any of the various methods by which the death penalty is imposed.[145]

In 1963, three Supreme Court Justices dissented from the Court's refusal to consider a state case that upheld the death penalty for rape.[146] Writing for the minority, former Justice Goldberg urged *certiorari* to consider whether the cruel and unusual punishment clause permits imposition of the death penalty on a convicted rapist who has neither taken nor endangered human life. A unanimous federal court of appeals panel agreed recently and overturned the imposition of a death penalty for a rape in which the victim's life was neither taken nor endangered.[147] The court pointed to the growing disinclination to authorize or impose capital punishment for rape and to the anomaly in the selection of the death penalty for a rapist who does not endanger his victim's life, when the large number of rapists sentenced to prison is considered.

140. *Weems v. United States,* 217 U.S. 349 (1910).
141. Packer, "Making the Punishment Fit the Crime," 77 *Harvard Law Review* 1071, 1075 (1964).
142. *See In re* Andrada, 380 U.S. 953 (1965); *Skinner v. Oklahoma ex rel.* Williamson, 316 U.S. 535 (1941).
143. *See Sweeney v. Woodall,* 344 U.S. 86 (1952); *Dye v. Johnson,* 338 U.S. 864, rehearing denied, 338 U.S. 896 (1949).
144. *See Barsky v. Board of Regents,* 347 U.S. 442 (1953).
145. *See McElvaine v. Brush,* 142 U.S. 155 (1891); *Ex parte* Medley, 134 U.S. 160 (1889); *Wilkerson v. Utah,* 99 U.S. 130 (1878).
146. *Rudolph v. Alabama,* 375 U.S. 889 (1963).
147. *Ralph v. Warden, Maryland Penitentiary,* 438 F.2d 786 (4th Cir. 1970), *rehearing denied* (1971).

Relying in part on the Supreme Court minority's opinion, the Court of Appeals of Kentucky concluded that, since "incorrigibility is inconsistent with youth," the sentence of life imprisonment without possibility of parole, given to two fourteen-year-old youths convicted of raping an elderly woman, "shocks the general conscience of society today and is intolerable to fundamental fairness." The sentence was ruled inconsistent with the ban on cruel and unusual punishment in the state constitution.[148]

The Supreme Court recently agreed to consider the constitutionality of the death penalty. In the meantime, the California Supreme Court outlawed the use of any capital punishment in that state as violative of the state constitution's "cruel and unusual" ban.

The effect of a system that allows a lone trial judge to sentence offenders, with no need to explain his choices or face challenges on constitutional grounds, is that judges may choose sentences with no particular justification or for reasons based on their own emotional proclivities. Some judges treat certain crimes as particularly horrendous and regularly give the maximum sentences available in every case of narcotics or rape or whatever particular crime especially offends them. Others base their sentences on their personal notions of morality.

At the recent sentencing of a man convicted of involuntary manslaughter for shooting his girl friend's husband, the rural Virginia judge told the defendant he had shown "moral decadence." In sentencing the defendant, the judge declared: "You are not a criminal in the habitual sense. You've been a constructive, progressive, useful member of society . . . but you stepped into the gutter to satisfy some kind of sex drive." According to the judge, the presentence report showed the defendant's spiritual life to be lacking. He criticized him for church attendance so "spasmodic" that the church's rector did not know him personally. The judge suggested that the defendant use his prison term to "try to get your spiritual house in order. . . . The full value of life lies in the relationship between God and man."

Researchers from the staff of the President's Crime Commission who spent one week observing the operations of the Recorder's Court in Detroit reported that they had seen one judge offer a man convicted of begging and arrested with six cents on his person an alternative between paying a thirty-dollar fine or spending sixty days in the house of correction. The same judge was told by a bailiff that he would have to speak loudly because a vagrancy defendant was almost deaf. The judge re-

148. *Workman v. Commonwealth*, 429 S.W.2d 374, 378 (Ky. 1968).

sponded immediately, "Well, he'll hear this! Seventy days in the house of correction!" The defendant had made no plea. He discovered his fate through a slip of paper handed to him by a police officer.

A former director of the Bureau of Prisons has criticized the way some sentencing judges use their great power:

> That some judges are arbitrary and even sadistic in their sentencing practices is notoriously a matter of record. By reason of senility or a virtually pathological emotional complex some judges summarily impose the maximum on defendants convicted of certain types of crimes or all types of crimes. One judge's disposition along this line was a major factor in bringing about a sitdown strike at Connecticut's Wethersfield Prison in 1956. . . .
> I know of one judge who continued to sit on the bench and sentence defendants to prison while he was undergoing shock treatments for a mental illness.[149]

However reflective of general practices these extreme examples may be, however conscientious and judicious other judges may be, nonetheless the absence of statutory sentencing criteria or written judicial opinions to serve as precedents and standards, coupled with the lack of scientific knowledge available to aid judges in making their sentencing choices, virtually guarantee that offenders of similar backgrounds will receive vastly different sentences for the same crimes. This is one of the most common complaints made to us by prisoners all over the United States: extraordinary and provocatively disparate sentences of similar men for similar crimes. The director of the federal Bureau of Prisons has stated that unreasonable sentencing disparities present one of the greatest hindrances to rehabilitation that plague prison staff members.

The following cases have been described by Court of Appeals Judge Simon E. Sobeloff:

> . . . one . . . man was convicted of fraudulently cashing a check for $58.40. He was out of work at the time, his wife was ill and he needed the money for rent, food, and doctors' bills, so he yielded to temptation. This man had no prior record.
> At about the same time another defendant also fraudulently cashed a check, also for a small amount, $35.20. He too was out

---

149. Bennett, "The Sentence—Its Relation to Crime and Rehabilitation," in *Of Prisons and Justice*, S.Doc. No. 70, 88th Cong., 2d Sess. 307, 311 (1964).

of work and in desperate financial condition, and yielded to the temptation under precisely similar circumstances. His only criminal record consisted of a drunk charge and a nonsupport charge.

Now, what happened to these two men in these two cases that are so alike as two peas in a pod? One judge gave the first man 15 years in prison; in the second another judge imposed a penalty of 30 days.[150]

In many jurisdictions, the well-known proclivities of different trial judges on the same court have made "judge-shopping" the most important task of the defense lawyers. Unwarranted sentencing disparity also has a damaging effect on the ideal of the even-handed administration of justice. As former Attorney General Robert W. Jackson recognized almost thirty years ago, "It is obviously repugnant to one's sense of justice that the judgment meted out to an offender should be dependent in large part on a purely fortuitous circumstance; namely, the personality of the particular judge before whom the case happens to come for disposition."

Sentencing disparity may be based not only on which judge a defendant gets; it may sometimes depend on his own race. Although one study concluded that most major differences in the treatment of racial and ethnic groups occur earlier in the criminal justice process than either verdict or sentencing, other surveys have found consistent differences in the length of sentence, the choice of imprisonment and imposition of the death penalty that could only be explained by the race of the defendants.[151] For example, discrepancies occur in the case of executions. According to the federal Bureau of Prisons, of the 3,857 persons executed in the United States since 1930, 53.5 percent were black, 45.4 percent white and 1.1 percent members of other minority groups.

Disparity in sentencing harms not only the ideal of justice; it interferes with the practical task of rehabilitating criminals. While it is too much to expect that prisoners will consider their punishment to be in their own best interest, at least they should be made to feel that they have been dealt with fairly.

---

150. Appellate Review of Sentences, Hearings on S.2722 Before the Subcommittee on Improvements in Judicial Machinery of the Senate Committee on the Judiciary, 89th Cong., 2d Sess. 25 (1966).
151. Lemert and Rosberg, *The Administration of Justice to Minority Groups in Los Angeles County* (1948); Bullock, "Significance of the Racial Factor in the Length of Prison Sentences," 52 *Journal of Criminal Law, Criminology and Police Science* 411 (1961); Garfinkel, "Research Note on Inter- and Intra-Racial Homicides," 27 *Social Forces* 369 (1949); Johnson, "The Negro and Crime," 217 *Annals of the American Academy of Political and Social Science* 93 (1941).

Aids to Sentencing

Many judges are fully aware of the importance of their sentencing decisions. Some have made efforts to visit prisons to see what happens to the offenders they sentence. (One member of the American Bar Association's Advisory Committee on Sentencing has said that if he could have his way he would sentence all new judges, and some old ones from time to time, to thirty days in prison.) And they have attended federal and state sentencing institutes to study new developments in correction and try to develop a consensus on appropriate sentences for the more common cases. A joint resolution introduced in the Maryland House of Delegates would require state judges to meet periodically to discuss sentencing procedures and to visit the state's prisons. A similar policy recently was instituted in New York by order of the Chief Justice of the Court of Appeals.

A committee of the American Bar Association recommended that regular sentencing institutes be held for new judges (before they begin to serve) and that they include other participants in the sentencing process such as prosecutors and defense attorneys. The National College of State Trial Judges has held several such institutes; they include police, correctional officials, attorneys, private citizens and prisoners as well as judges. Psychodrama, role reversals and other group methods are used to help the various participants in the criminal justice system understand one another and some of the implications of decisions made in parts of the fractionalized system. Sentencing judges are processed into prisons as arriving inmates, work at prison labor and eat prison food. Said one, "I'll look at the man across from me for sentencing far differently after this." Repetition of these innovative techniques in every state would do much to expose judges, as well as other criminal justice officials, to the results of their decisions.

Appellate review may provide an additional aid to rational (or at least consistent) sentencing decisions. Professor B. J. George, Jr., has termed review the "first salvo in reducing the stronghold of the judge who believes that he is divinely ordained in passing sentence." In the seventeen American jurisdictions where it is available, review of sentences has been said to cause both trial and appellate judges to give greater consideration to the justifications for particular sentences. And the opinions written to explain modifications of excessive sentences may provide a body of judicial precedent to guide trial judges.

States allowing appellate review of sentences have followed two basic patterns. Most of the jurisdictions have given the review power to the regular courts of appeals.[152] New York has varied this pattern by allowing only the intermediate appellate courts and not the highest court of appeals to review the propriety of sentences.[153]

The other approach, followed in Massachusetts, Connecticut, Maryland and Maine, provides a specially created court, staffed by experienced sitting trial judges, to review the duration of sentences. Other questions about the sentence, such as the sufficiency and accuracy of the information on which it was based, are reviewed by the regular appellate courts.[154]

Appellate review of sentencing decisions can serve to moderate sentences that are obviously excessive or motivated by the unduly strong feelings of a particular judge toward certain crimes. The process tends to make the sentencing process more fair. In some cases, however, it must be admitted that appellate review may do no more than substitute one guess of the right disposition for another. As one former prosecutor has noted:

> . . . where, as in criminal sentences, there is no objective standard set up, where the rule really is a rule of discretion, but with a large footnote in bold print that you hope this discretion will be sensibly exercised, then I really don't see that there is a clear framework from which the appellate function can proceed. I don't think there you are dealing with the question whether a judge was right or wrong—you are dealing with a question whether he was sensible.[155]

A study of Arizona's thirty years of appellate review of criminal sentencing concluded that

> . . . the impact of review upon trial court sentencing has been minimal. . . .
>
> Despite the incorporation into the formal legal framework of an authorization for appellate supervision of the sentencing process, the participants in the process (the appellate judges as

152. *E.g.,* Ill. Ann. Stat. C. 38, §§121–3(a), (b), 121–8(b) (Smith-Hurd 1964).
153. *See People v. Minjac Corp.* 4 N.Y.2d 320, 151 N.E.2d 180 (1958).
154. *See State v. Meleganich,* 25 Conn. Supp. 3, 195 A.2d 439 (1963); *Commonwealth v. Conroy,* 333 Mass. 751, 133 N.E.2d 246 (1956).
155. *Appellate Review of Sentences,* Hearings on S.2722 Before the Subcommittee on Improvements in Judicial Machinery of the Senate Committee on the Judiciary, 89th Cong., 2d Sess. 110 (1966) (statement of David C. Acheson).

well as the trial bench and the bar) rejected the underlying assumption of the proposal: (a) that scientific sentencing was possible; (b) that a body of relatively precise rules for the conduct of sentencing could be developed; and (c) that the appellate judiciary was the appropriate agency to supervise reform of the sentencing process. Given this failure of the participants to accept the underlying assumptions, the attempt to achieve reform by revision of the legal framework was destined to fail from the beginning.[156]

Some judges within a fairly small geographical area have attempted to work together to moderate their initial sentencing decisions. In New Jersey, state judges decided to avoid disparity (and, apparently, leniency) in sentencing bookmakers by having one judge in each county sentence in gambling cases whether or not he tried the case.[157]

In the federal districts in eastern Michigan and northern Illinois and in Portland, Oregon, panels of three trial judges meet each week to discuss the sentences each of them must impose. In the District of Columbia, where the judges decided that their mounting criminal caseload precluded a general use of sentencing councils, advisory councils composed of district judges were used in the cases that resulted from the April 1968 riots.[158]

Before the weekly conference held by the operating sentencing councils, each judge reads the presentence reports for all the cases to be discussed and works out a recommended sentence, together with the considerations that led him to choose it, for each case. The recommendations are discussed at the meeting and a consensus usually is reached. The sentencing judge, who participates in the council, may accept or reject the recommendation or change it after he hears the defendant's arguments and any additional information presented at the sentencing hearing. In the first five months of operation, the Michigan council changed the sentencing judge's initial recommendation of the appropriate sentence in slightly more than 40 percent of the cases it considered.

The way in which sentencing councils operate has been criticized for failing to give the participating judges the benefit of whatever information

156. Dix, "Judicial Review of Sentences: Implications for Individual Disposition," 1969 *Law and the Social Order* 369, 404–05; *see also* Note, "Appellate Review of Primary Sentencing Decisions: A Connecticut Case Study," 69 *Yale Law Journal* 1453 (1960).
157. *See State v. DeStasio*, 49 N.J. 247, 229 A.2d 636, *cert. denied*, 389 U.S. 830 (1967).
158. *See Scott v. United States*, No. 20, 954, F.2d (D.C. Circuit, Feb. 13, 1969).

is developed at the sentencing hearing. In addition, the sentencing judge presides at the hearing after he has met with the council and made up his mind about the appropriate sentence. A possible solution would be to hold the council after the hearing. This would require a separate proceeding for the imposition of sentence.

Alternatives to Judicial Sentencing

The prevailing opinion still is that, whatever the shortcomings of judicial sentencing, the legal training of judges and their relative insulation from public pressures make them the most appropriate people to make sentencing decisions. According to Federal Judge Irving Kaufman:

> I believe that the sentencing responsibility should remain where it has traditionally rested—with the judge. Of all public officials, he is the best insulated from public and political pressures. Certainly the judge is not an expert sociologist or criminologist, but he need not be. He is an expert in making difficult decisions on the basis of the best information available, and this is exactly what is called for in sentencing.[159]

This faith in the virtues of the bench is supported by some correction experts. One, the now deceased Paul Tappan wrote:

> . . . seasoned judges are much less inclined to express improper subjective motives in their sentencing decisions than are other authorities. Legal training and more particularly the tradition of the bench emphasizes forcefully the requirement of impartiality and the necessity of weighing conflicting interests and of repressing emotional reactions. In this respect the attitudes and practices of the judiciary are in striking contrast with administrators' preoccupation with immediate problems and *ad hoc* solutions. . . . Perhaps there is no other professional training and experience that places such value upon objectivity in harmonizing conflicting interests. It is precisely this sort of preparation that is needed for the sound implementation of the state's correctional objectives in sentencing.[160]

159. Kaufman, "Sentencing: The Judge's Problem," 24 *Federal Probation* 9 (1960).
160. Tappan, *Crime, Justice and Correction* 454 (1960).

Some observers are skeptical about this assumption and feel that basic changes are needed in sentencing procedures. In the opinion of Professor B. J. George, Jr., at the time of sentencing no judge can estimate accurately the minimum or maximum period of correctional supervision necessary for effective rehabilitation. "If rehabilitation is a process and not an event, its achievement can be ascertained only after a period of time has elapsed."

Thus Professor George would have no minimum sentences imposed, and he would define the maximum sentences by statutes. The sentencing judge would choose only between prison and probation, as is currently the practice in California and Washington for most crimes. At regular intervals a board of parole, which would include judges as well as other members, would review the prisoner's status. A prisoner could be transferred to community supervision or released outright at any time. An appellate parole board, composed only of judges, would handle appeals from decisions of the parole board.

In New York, a Governor's Special Committee on Criminal Offenders recently recommended that judges continue to sentence convicted criminals. However, it recommended that the sentencing decision be limited to deciding whether the protection of the public or deterrence of other potential criminals require the use of mandatory imprisonment. In doubtful cases, this decision could be deferred for three months while an offender was observed under supervision by behavioral scientists and a report on his behavior given to the judge. In all other cases, the question of whether to supervise an offender in an institution or in the community, and the length of time (within the statutory maximum) for which supervision is required, would be an administrative decision made by professionals in the department of correction.

A bill repeatedly introduced in the Maryland House of Delegates without success would do away entirely with judicial sentencing in cases involving convictions for violent crimes, replacing it with sentencing by "Sentencing Boards." Each board would consist of one expert in each of the fields of criminology, law, psychology and sociology and one member from another field. Presumably, since Maryland already provides for appellate review of sentences, the decisions of the "Sentencing Boards" also would be subject to judicial review.

The whole question of sentencing is a ponderous one: this can be seen in its critical relationship to all that follows in the correctional process as well as in the perplexing nature of each of its many aspects. Indeed, fundamental questions are raised about the very desirability of resting these powers in judges alone, about the appropriateness of the adversary system, about the absence of guidelines and controls. Until these questions are resolved, all phases of the correctional process that follow will be limited because it is so inextricably tied to the profound and pervasive judicial power of sentencing.

IV

Probation—An Alternative to the Prison System

One August day in 1841 a prosperous, middle-aged bootmaker named John Augustus had business before the Boston Police Court. According to his autobiography,[1] as Augustus was awaiting his turn, an officer led in "a ragged and wretched looking man, who took his seat on the bench allotted to prisoners." A few moments later the clerk read a complaint charging the man with being a "common drunkard." The defendant's guilt was quickly established. But before the judge passed sentence, Augustus approached the prisoner's bench and spoke briefly with the defendant. "Although his appearance and his looks precluded a belief in the minds of others that he would ever become a *man* again," something in the man's face or his words moved the bootmaker to conclude that "he was not yet past all hope of reformation. . . . He told me that if he could be saved from the House of Correction, he never again would taste intoxicating liquors; there was such an earnestness in that tone and a look expressive of firm resolve, that I determined to aid him; I bailed him, by permission of the Court."

Thus began the career of the man who would later be described as the world's first probation officer. Augustus persuaded the court to release the defendant into his custody. He took his charge home with him, fed him and found him a job. As a result of the timely intervention, the man who had been saved from prison "signed the pledge and became a sober man." Three weeks later Augustus returned to the courtroom with his charge.

1. John Augustus, *A Report of the Labors of John Augustus, for the last ten years, in Aid of the Unfortunate* (1852); reprinted as *John Augustus, First Probation Officer* (1939).

The man's appearance was so altered that "no one, not even the scrutinizing officers, could have believed that he was the same person who less than a month before, had stood trembling on the prisoner's stand." The judge was pleased with the obvious improvement in the defendant. Instead of sending him to prison, he fined him one cent. Years later, Augustus noted, "The man continued industrious and sober, and without doubt has been by this treatment, saved from a drunkard's grave."

What made a prosperous businessman who had never before come into contact with the criminal law take an interest in rehabilitating an offender? Augustus was an avid follower of the temperance movement, which was striving "to liberate the wretched inebriate from the prison of his own destructive vice, and to loose the bonds which [hold] him captive, by removing from him the pernicious influences by which he had been surrounded, and by causing him to feel that he was still a man." Augustus was firmly convinced that alcoholics needed specialized medical treatment in place of punishment. Foreshadowing a movement that has not yet reached fruition, he advocated the establishment of a state asylum expressly devoted to the cure of those "who are now locked up in jails and houses of correction, and lost to their families, to society and to themselves." (The legislative committee to which Augustus and others who shared his interest had addressed a request for such an asylum denied it on the ground that it must be left to private charity.)

Augustus was so encouraged by the progress of his first charge that he accepted responsibility for seventeen more alcoholics that year. In each case he insisted that the offender promise to give up drinking. As far as he could tell, "they have sacredly kept the pledge which they were then induced to take."

Once Augustus started attending court regularly to bail out alcoholics, he began to be troubled by obvious inequities in the administration of justice. In 1843 he expanded the scope of his efforts to include a wide range of offenses, as well as female and juvenile offenders. The untrained bootmaker became a one-man probation department, exercising what were, in effect, social-work techniques and admirable administrative skills. When he undertook the responsibility for offenders, Augustus would agree to "note their general conduct" and to "see that they were sent to school or supplied with some honest employment." Where required, he made complete progress reports to the court and maintained a careful register of all cases he handled. He urged without success that courts and correctional institutions do likewise.

During the eighteen years preceding his death in 1859, Augustus "bailed on probation" from the police and municipal courts of Boston 1,946 offenders. His proportion of successes was reputed to be high. Of the nearly two thousand offenders for whom he became responsible, only ten absconded before their term of probation had expired. But Augustus did not choose to measure his achievements in terms of statistics. "Suppose one out of ten was reclaimed, would not that be well worth the time, labor and money that is expended on the whole? Do we not read that he who turns one sinner from the error of his ways, shall save a soul from death, and hide a multitude of sins?"

Augustus' phenomenal success rate may have been influenced by his selectivity. Despite the large number of offenders he rescued, Augustus did not extend aid to all who wished to be bailed. He concentrated on first offenders and minor recidivists, "whose hearts were not wholly depraved. . . . It should not be supposed that I assumed such obligations merely at the solicitation of the unfortunate. . . . Great care was observed, of course, to ascertain whether the prisoners were promising subjects for probation, and to this end it was necessary to take into consideration the previous character of the person, his age and the influences by which he would in the future be likely to be surrounded. . . ."

Augustus was convinced that all but the most hardened criminals stood a better chance of reformation on probation than in institutions. Prisons, established to punish infractions of the law, had a corrupting influence. "Almost invariably all who are sent to the House of Correction . . . at the expiration of their term of imprisonment, return to their former mode of life." He stoutly maintained that "the object of the law is to reform criminals and to prevent crime and not to punish maliciously, or from a spirit of revenge." In response to police officials who accused a chronic alcoholic of failing to provide for his family, Augustus retorted:

> For the best of all reasons, probably . . . he has been locked up in jail and in the House of Correction, he has been hunted by the laws and every infirmity of his nature punished. You have tried the experiment fully and now see before you a living witness of the folly of attempting to force a man into a reformation.

Augustus—and his supporters among the local residents—also recognized that keeping offenders in the community was much less expensive than supporting a large prison population:

It will readily be seen . . . that a large sum has been saved, by so many intemperate persons having become useful citizens, instead of being shut up in prison at the public charge. To those towns in the county which occasionally receive large bills for the support of drunkards in the House of Correction in South Boston, this point is not unworthy of notice.

It is only in the last few years that some pioneering state legislatures have begun to recognize the financial benefits of using probation as the chief correctional tool.

Augustus' efforts were carried on in the face of opposition from several quarters. On the one hand were those who thought he was coddling criminals and allowing rogues to escape into the community. On the other were those who enshrined courtroom ritual and urged the exclusion of all but "professionals" from the judicial process. To such philosophical motivations for opposing Augustus' efforts was added an economic one. Since the police were paid seventy-five cents for every offender put in jail, they lost money every time Augustus succeeded in having someone released to his custody.

Augustus provided the seeds from which our system of probation has grown. Probation was first formally established in the United States. The system, since emulated by other countries, is considered America's contribution to progressive penology. Today over one half of all convicted offenders in the United States are placed on probation. In 1965 approximately 459,140 adults and 224,948 juveniles were on probation, while 475,042 adults and 123,256 juveniles were in institutions or on parole.[2] Under probation, sentences are suspended and defendants continue to live in their communities under conditions imposed by the court and supervised by probation officers.

Augustus provided probation with its characteristic feature: the personal services of a probation officer (a title that was not applied to Agustus himself but was used by his successors) who views his work with offenders as assistance rather than punishment. He was building, however, on methods of humanizing criminal justice that had developed under the English common law.

A hundred years before Augustus, Blackstone, in his *Commentaries on the Laws of England,* had criticized the uniformity and severity of

2. The President's Commission on Law Enforcement and Administration of Justice, Task Force Report: *Correction* 27 n.1 (1967).

criminal punishment: "It is, it must be owned, much easier to extirpate than to amend mankind. Yet that magistrate must be esteemed both a weak and a cruel surgeon who cuts off every limb, which through ignorance or indolence he will not attempt to cure." Actually, common-law courts in England and the United States had developed a variety of devices to mitigate the harshness of prescribed penalties. All were based on the court's power to suspend sentences for specific purposes and definite periods of time. The devices, known as the benefit of clergy, judicial reprieve, recognizance, release on bail and the filing of indictments, partook of many of the characteristics we now associate with probation.

The benefit of clergy originated in a thirteenth-century compromise between the English king and the Church. The compromise required members of the clergy and, later, anyone who could read to submit to the jurisdiction of the King's Court but allowed them to escape the death penalty. Consequently, according to some observers, the ignorant were doomed to die for offenses for which only a slight punishment was inflicted on those who had received some education and were therefore less excusable.

The judicial reprieve, commonly used by early English judges who were not satisfied that a defendant should have been convicted, temporarily suspended the imposition or execution of a sentence to permit the defendant to apply to the Crown for a pardon. The practice, instituted at a time when there were no retrials or appeals, generally allowed a defendant to remain at liberty until the final disposition of his case. Neither supervision nor any conditions were imposed on his behavior during suspension.

With the establishment of settlements in America, English courts began to grant reprieves to prisoners who were under sentence of death on the condition that they accept deportation. While the reprieve was conceived of as only a temporary suspension of sentence, its use sometimes resulted in the termination of prosecution or subsequent court action. American courts later interpreted the practice as an inherent common-law power to suspend sentences indefinitely.

The now distinct practices of post-conviction release on probation and pretrial release on bail have common antecedents in the release on recognizance. The practice of "binding over for good behavior" suspected criminals, which developed in England in the fourteenth century as a means of preventing crime, was later extended to persons who had been convicted of misdemeanors, as a means of avoiding punishment. Used as a pretrial device, the recognizance involved a stipulation, sworn to under court order by a suspect or an accused person who had not yet been convicted, that he would "keep the peace" and "be of good behavior." The court generally required a bond, with or without sureties. The person who stood surety might return the offender to court for further action if the suspect failed to comply with the conditions of his release.

By the beginning of the nineteenth century, recognizance was employed in England for young and petty offenders, both before trial and as a conditional disposition following conviction. Later the English Criminal Law Consolidation Act of 1861 specifically authorized employment of the practice with persons convicted of any non-capital felony.

The use of recognizance and release on bail is revealed in court records of seventeenth-century colonial Massachusetts. At this time the devices still were performing the dual function of pretrial release and release after conviction. A description appears in the 1830 opinion of Judge Oxenbridge Thacher of the Municipal Court of Boston in the case of *Commonwealth v. Chase:*

> It has sometimes been practiced in this Court, in cases of peculiar interest, and in the hope that the party would avoid the commission of any offense afterwards, to discharge him on a recognizance. . . . The effect is that no sentence will ever be pronounced against him, if he shall behave himself well afterwards, and avoid any further violation of the law.[3]

If the defendant was later indicted for another offense, suspension was revoked and sentence imposed on the original conviction.

In 1836 the Massachusetts legislature sanctioned the use of recognizance after trial. Magistrates were authorized by statute to discharge petty offenders under recognizance "in such sum as the magistrate or court shall direct, with sufficient sureties for [their] good behavior for a term not less than six months, nor more than two years, paying the costs of prosecution, or such part thereof as the magistrate or court shall direct." According to the state commissioners who had formulated the law, an offender who could find a sponsor willing to stand surety for him would have a powerful motive to improve his behavior. On the other hand, "if his character and habits are such that no one will consent to be sponsor for him, it must forcibly impress on his mind, the value of good

3. Woodman (ed.), *Reports of Criminal Cases Tried in the Municipal Court of the City of Boston before Peter Oxenbridge Thacher, Judge of that Court from 1823 to 1843,* 269–70 (1845).

character, while it deprives him of all ground of just complaint of the severity of the law, or the magistrate."

Another practice peculiar to Massachusetts in the nineteenth century allowed a court, with the consent of both the defendant and the prosecutor, to suspend imposition of sentence after a criminal conviction by "filing" the indictment. The device was employed when a court recognized extenuating circumstances or when a case with a similar legal question was awaiting action on appeal. It did not constitute a final judgment, and the court could take further action at any time. But on proof that a defendant had been staying out of trouble, a judge might continue his case indefinitely.

Through the use of recognizance and the filing of indictments, petty offenders were spared the corrupting influence of imprisonment. At least in theory, offenders were impelled to obey the law by fear of punishment and concern for their sureties, and their sponsors exercised some supervision over their conduct. As they developed, recognizance and related devices came to contain the features basic to modern probation: dealing with offenders outside of institutions, the object of rehabilitation, and the element of supervision (although not by an official agent of the court).

The principle of probation thus evolved through judicial experimentation motivated by the humanitarian, missionary and temperance movements of the early nineteenth century. The practice eventually became so well established that it was endorsed by the Massachusetts legislature. From Massachusetts the system spread all over the country.

The first probation laws were intended to regulate the courts' exercise of the power of temporary release. They did not create the authority to suspend sentence indefinitely. Thus the question remained whether a court had the power to suspend sentence not merely as a temporary stay for specified purposes but as the final disposition of a case. This power was necessary if judges were to be able to sentence defendants to probation.

Indefinite suspensions had become common due to the failure of the courts or the interested parties to take further action. The belief thus arose in some states that indefinite suspension of sentence was a traditional judicial prerogative created by the common law. Appellate courts in several jurisdictions found that lower courts possessed such power,[4]

4. *E.g.*, People *ex rel. Forsyth v. Court of Sessions*, 141 N.Y. 288, 36 N.E. 386 (1894); *Gehrmann v. Osborne*, 79 N.J. Eg. 430, 82 Atl. 424 (1912); Commonwealth *ex rel. Nuber v. Keeper*, 6 Pa. Super 420 (1898).

while others held that the practice constituted a usurpation of the power of clemency that was vested exclusively in the executive.[5]

In 1916 a challenge to the power of indefinite suspension of sentences reached the United States Supreme Court. Attorney General T. W. Gregory had been campaigning against such suspensions, ordering all United States attorneys to insist that federal courts had no power to issue them. Gregory's conservative position on the proper range of judicial power was expressed by his assistant:

> Let judges confine themselves to their true function of administering rather than thwarting the law; . . . If the guilt is established, let the judge impose the punishment decreed by law . . . so that the court when so acting may be enforcing the law and not flying into the very teeth of it.[6]

The Attorney General found a test case in the Northern District of Ohio, where Judge John M. Willits had suspended, during good behavior, execution of the minimum sentence for a young man who had pleaded guilty to embezzling money from the bank where he was employed. The defendant had no prior criminal record and had made full restitution. He was employed and supporting a wife and mother. The bank's officials did not desire to prosecute. Although the offender was particularly appealing and deserving of special consideration, the United States attorney moved that the order of suspension be vacated as beyond the powers of the court. Judge Willits overruled the motion. Responding to the position of the Attorney General, he argued that "otherwise than for this crime, his disposition, character and habits have so strongly commended him to his friends, acquaintances and persons of his faith, that they are unanimous in the belief that the exposure and humiliation of his conviction are a sufficient punishment, and that he can be saved to the good of society if nothing further is done with him."[7]

The prosecution appealed to the United States Supreme Court, which unanimously granted the Government's petition. Holding that federal courts possessed no inherent power to suspend sentences permanently, the Supreme Court ruled that, without legislation by Congress, the sus-

5. *Spencer v. State*, 125 Tennessee 64, 140 S.W. 597 (1911); *Brabandt v. Commonwealth*, 157 Kentucky 180, 162 S.W. 786 (1914); *Neal v. State*, 104 Georgia 509, 30 S.E. 858 (1898).
6. Letter from William Wallace, Jr., to W. Snowden Marshall, March 25, 1915, quoted in Chute and Bell, *Crime, Courts and Probation* 94 (1956).
7. Statement of Judge John M. Willits, filed October 14, 1915, *Ex parte United States*, 242 U.S. 27 (1916).

pended sentence could no longer be used as a final disposition. The ruling was disputed by evidence submitted by lawyers' groups from different parts of the country to the effect that release on probation had become a common and useful practice:

> . . . it helps to reform, it helps to deter, and it helps to educate those against whom criminal process is directed. As a modern and valuable idea it has arisen out of practice and customs, not out of statutes or pieces of paper. It is serving the community well today.[8]

The Willits case did not affect probationary practices in those states whose legislatures had already authorized the use of recognizance and suspended sentences. By the turn of the century, legislation providing for the release on probation of selected offenders had been passed in Massachusetts, Maryland, Missouri, Vermont and Rhode Island. Although not all the laws provided explicitly for supervision of released offenders, supervision by officers appointed for that purpose evolved in each of the five states. By 1910, nineteen states had passed laws that provided for the probation of adults and children. Ironically, the Willits case unwittingly provided the impetus for other states and the federal government to fashion laws which conferred upon American courts the powers that the common law had not given them.

Probation was given additional impetus by the creation of juvenile courts. The movement for specialized courts to handle young offenders took hold in the United States at the turn of the century. Illinois enacted the first juvenile-court act in 1899, and by 1910 thirty-seven states and the District of Columbia had passed similar laws. Juvenile courts generally were provided with salaried probation officers. The program of juvenile probation gained ground much faster than the parallel plans for adult or general probation. Thirty states introduced probation through juvenile-court laws. Introduction of adult probation was slower in those jurisdictions which enacted juvenile-court legislation providing for probation exclusively in those courts. In 1940 seven jurisdictions had failed to provide for adult probation; only one of these had not yet established children's courts.

Despite the impetus provided by the Willits case, federal probation was not established until 1925. One reason for the delay was the opposition of Prohibitionists in Congress, some of whom believed that proba-

8. Brief in Support of the Practice in the First Circuit, *Ex parte United States*, 242 U.S. 27 (1916).

tion would allow the release of too many Volstead Act violators. Support for the federal probation law was organized by Charles L. Chute, executive director of the National Probation Association (now the National Council on Crime and Delinquency). Most judges and United States attorneys supported the proposal, but a few and the Attorney General nonetheless continued to oppose probation in principle. One judge argued that the use of probation in the United States was responsible for a crime rate higher than that of countries where "a man is either at liberty after a trial and acquitted, or with a discolored ring around his neck dead within thirty days after he has sent someone into eternity without the sanction of the law." A memorandum from a staff member advised Attorney General Harry M. Daugherty to adopt a firm stand against the use of probation, characterizing it as "part of a wave of maudlin rot of misplaced sympathy for criminals that is going over the country."[9]

In spite of the opposition, Congress sanctioned the use of probation by the federal courts. With the passage of enabling legislation in Mississippi in 1956, all states finally had authorized some scheme for adult and juvenile probation.

Probation today represents the most enlightened method we have devised for working with most offenders. People allowed to remain in the community are not forced to sever family, social or employment ties. They are spared the degrading, and frequently corrupting, experience of imprisonment. And, under proper supervision, they may be helped to avoid commission of further crimes. However, while the probation system may represent our greatest advance in correctional theory, it is handicapped by a number of serious problems: organizational chaos; restrictive and uninformed methods of selection for probation; the imposition of unrealistic conditions on probationers; and reliance for supervision on too few probation officers with too little training. These problems must be solved if the system is to realize its potential as the primary technique for rehabilitating offenders.

The Administration of Probation Services

The organization of probation administration varies among states and often within states. According to the President's Crime Commission,

9. Letter to Charles L. Chute from John F. McGee, U.S. District Judge, Minnesota, December 19, 1923, quoted in Chute and Bell, *Crime, Courts and Probation* 106 (1956).

"Probation in the United States is administered by hundreds of different agencies operating under a different law in each state and under widely varying philosophies. . . . In one city, a single state or local agency might be responsible for handling all three kinds of probation cases; in another, three separate agencies may be operating, each responsible for a different type of probationer."[10] In Wisconsin, for example, there is a state probation and parole system with responsibility for all areas except Milwaukee County. County probation officers, employees of the local courts, handle probation services in Milwaukee. In a recent report, the Governor's Special Committee on Criminal Offenders in the State of New York spent virtually its entire chapter on probation attempting to bring some order to the administrative chaos created by the existence of sixty-nine separate probation departments.

The organization of services involves two controversial questions: whether control of probation administration should be centralized in a state administration or diffused among various localities and whether probation should be controlled by the courts or by an executive department of correction.

LOCAL VERSUS STATE ADMINISTRATION

Juvenile probation services, which developed as part of the nineteenth-century juvenile-court movement, rooted in the idea of local charity and good works, continue to be administered locally in thirty-five jurisdictions. Services for adults, on the other hand, were grafted onto the statewide parole services already in existence in most states. Consequently, in thirty-seven jurisdictions the administration of adult probation is a state function.

Both California and New York, our most populous states, retain local administration of all probation services. Advocates of local administration point out that local programs typically develop better support from local citizenry and agencies, since they are more open to participation by outside groups. Also, smaller operations tend to be more flexible and less bound by bureaucratic rigidity. Finally, combining all probation services in the larger states could result in cumbersome operations which might place a tremendous burden on administration.

10. The President's Commission on Law Enforcement and Administration of Justice, Task Force Report: *Correction* 28 (1967).

On the other hand, local administration frequently results in underfinanced, fragmented and overlapping services. The New York study noted much duplication of effort by the state's probation departments. In addition, it was impossible to evaluate the performance of so many separate departments. A 1964 probation study in California had to confine itself to an examination of services in fifteen counties selected from the total of fifty-eight.

Organization in small units has resulted in a dearth of the resources necessary for in-service training of probation officers. Except for a few large cities, such as Los Angeles and Minneapolis, state and federal agencies generally have been responsible for research and innovation. The Governor's Special Committee on Criminal Offenders in the State of New York was "unable to find published studies conducted in New York State that evaluate the effectiveness of any treatment method used in probation through acceptable research techniques. Nor are we likely to have any body of meaningful research so long as our system remains fragmented."[11] The standard and sophisticated methods of record-keeping essential to research into various techniques of dealing with offenders have yet to be developed.

The federal system, on the other hand, has used its central staff organization to spread ideas among the various offices. The Administrative Office of the United States Courts contains a Probation Division which publishes a quarterly journal (not confined to matters related to federal probation) and sponsors week-long training sessions for probation officers. Such practices as the deferred prosecution plan (which saves juveniles from the stigma of a court record on condition that they complete probation satisfactorily), pre-commitment counseling, pre-release counseling and special office hours for probationers who are employed, were begun as experiments in a few federal field offices and are now used extensively in many offices.

In 1963 the Administrative Office of the United States Courts adopted a system of reporting which for the first time accounted for all persons responsible to the Federal Probation System. The reports include information about all persons under supervision and probationers and parolees who have been removed from supervision, distinguishing among those who have successfully completed the period of probation, those whose probation was revoked due to a major violation of the conditions of probation and those whose supervision was terminated because of a minor in-

11. *Preliminary Report of the New York Governor's Committee* 195 (1968).

fraction. Referring to the reports, former Chief Justice Earl Warren commented in an address to the American Law Association in 1964 that

> . . . they amount to a major breakthrough in the barrier of official ignorance as to what kind of people are processed through the federal criminal courts and what actually happens to those released on probation under varying terms, to those who are incarcerated in institutions for varying periods and to those who are placed on parole or conditional release under varying conditions.

In California, where there is a strong tradition of local government, local administration of probation services has been retained, but an effort has been made to achieve some of the benefits of centralization by developing a statewide research center in Sacramento. In addition, the state legislature has recognized the role of adequate probation services in keeping down the population of state correctional institutions.

JUDICIAL VERSUS EXECUTIVE ADMINISTRATION

In addition to the question of local versus centralized administration, there is a controversy over whether probation services should be administered by the judiciary or by executive departments. At present, only five states include both juvenile and adult probation in their departments of correction. In thirty states, adult probation is combined with parole in a separate administration. Adult probation is locally administered by the courts in thirteen states, juvenile probation in thirty-two states.

Federal probation services are administered independently by the individual district courts, with research, statistical and training services provided by the Administrative Office of the United States Courts. This delegation of responsibility has created some inconsistencies in the federal system, with wide variations among districts in the proportion of cases using pre-sentence investigations and in the proportion of defendants placed on probation.[12]

The Department of Justice has proposed that probation administration be integrated with parole and institutional administration within that department. Advocates of the merger point out that the allocation

---

12. *See* Olney, "The Federal Probation System in 1963: Where We Stand," 27 *Federal Probation* 3, 4 (September 1963).

of probation functions to the Administrative Office in 1939 was an historical accident. They argue that integration of services would produce expanded research programs, uniform and presumably higher standards of professional competence among probation officers and an organization better able to obtain financial support from Congress. Opponents, who include most probation officers and trial judges, fear that judges might not be willing to rely on informational reports furnished by personnel not subject to their supervision. (For this reason the New York Governor's Committee recommended the retention of judicial control of presentence investigations.) In addition, the Chief and Assistant Chief of Probation for the federal courts have expressed opposition to placing control of the probation officer's investigative functions in the same department that prosecutes cases. In none of the states with a unified system of correction is the prosecutive agency part of the system.

Officials in the states retaining judicial control of probation departments have criticized the operation of the system. In all but two California counties, for example, probation officers are the only county officials who are neither appointed by the Board of Supervisors nor elected. Local judges have not taken the lead in obtaining additional resources for probation. Nor have boards of supervisors been willing to allocate sufficient resources, since probation is not considered their responsibility.

The responsibility for probation departments increases the administrative duties of local judges, causing collateral problems for the county. In addition, there is no continuity of responsibility for probation. The judges who appoint probation officers may change every year, and each probation department may have duties to perform for several courts. According to correctional expert Robert Montilla, former deputy director of the District of Columbia Department of Corrections and former director of the Model Community Correctional Project in Stockton, California, "It is an illusion that the Probation Department works for the courts; it works for no one."

A possible solution would be to separate the investigative and supervisory roles of probation officers, leaving only the investigators to work for the courts. The efficiency of a probation department may be enhanced by the division of its two chief labors—investigation and supervision. The practice of dividing the department into specialized staffs to carry out these separate functions has been tried in Oakland, Chicago, Cincinnati, Los Angeles, Newark and New York City. These departments have found the separation more efficient and expert.

Ninety-five percent of the federal offices, on the other hand, assign probationers to the officer who conducted the presentence investigation in order to facilitate "continuity of service" to the probationer. Advocates of this system feel that the treatment process begins during the presentence investigation, when relationships are being formed and the probation officer acquires an understanding of the defendant and his problems. To separate the probation officer's two functions is seen as artificial, since "common skills are required for both tasks and . . . much of the insights and information obtained by the investigating officer concerning an offender may be lost in the process of transmitting it to a supervising officer. . . . Rapport should be built from the beginning . . . and . . . transfer to another officer may be damaging to the casework process."[13]

Critics claim that the impartial and objective investigator who reports to the court cannot, and perhaps should not, attempt to establish a close relationship with the defendant and that the treatment process should start when the defendant is placed on probation. The officer who prepared the pre-sentence report may have a stake in corroborating his first, perhaps erroneous, impressions of the probationer. In more practical terms, the pressure of court deadlines for investigations often means that supervision, which has been described as "that residue left over when all other duties and responsibilities are carried out," is neglected. One experienced former probation officer, questioning why probation had become so enmeshed in the process of court investigation, which "is not probation in a literal sense and certainly is not what John Augustus had in mind when he suggested that the unfortunate creatures in the toils of the law be referred to him rather than to the less tender mercies of the Boston gaol keepers," suggests that the obligation to perform pre-sentence investigations often has served as a convenient excuse for "our failure to provide adequate and appropriate supervision."[14]

Selection for Probation

The earliest laws stipulated no restrictions on the use of probation. According to Romilly's *Observations on the Criminal Laws of England*, they followed "the common-sense reasoning that the court should have

13. Tappan, *Crime, Justice and Correction* 552 (1960).
14. Smith, "A Breakthrough in Probation Service," 21 *Youth Authority Quarterly* 24, 25–26 (Winter 1968).

the discretion to determine each case on its merits, that the individual and not the crime was being treated, and that the past criminal record, while important in appraising character, was not always the determining factor in deciding disposition of the case." Later, state legislators imposed restrictions tied to specific offenses, the number of previous convictions or the offender's age.

Although the use of probation in juvenile cases is rarely restricted by statute, all but fifteen states restrict the use of probation in adult felony cases. Some statutes contain a long list of exempt crimes. However, there is little agreement among states as to which specific offenses, other than murder and rape, will preclude probation. Some states categorically deny probation to recidivists.

In states whose legislatures impose few or no restraints on the discretion of the courts, judicial discretion does not seem to have been abused. The Attorney General's Survey of Release Procedures, published in 1939, concluded that the offense for which probation is granted has no significant relationship to the offender's outcome on probation and that, "in light of these findings, there seems to be no particular justification for the statutory provisions excluding persons convicted of certain offenses from probation."[15]

More recent experience has confirmed the survey's conclusion. The federal statistics on the commission of new offenses by persons on probation in 1966 show that the proportion of violations remained approximately the same regardless of how frequently different courts used probation.[16] One researcher has stated that "there is, at present, no statistical evidence to suggest that a reasonable increase in the rate of probation will produce a compensating increase in the rate of recidivism."[17]

In California, the proportion of adults granted probation after a criminal conviction in a superior court increased by 31 percent between 1961 and 1967. Yet the rates of violation of the terms of probation by all probationers remained constant during this period.[18]

As part of a well-known demonstration project, Saginaw County, Michigan, increased the number and qualifications of its probation staff. At

15. 2 *Attorney General's Survey of Release Procedures* 400 (1939).
16. *Annual Report of the Director of the Administrative Office of the U.S. Courts* 161 (1967).
17. Davis, "A Study of Adult Probation Violation Rates by Means of the Cohort Approach," 55 *Journal of Criminal Law, Criminology and Police Science* 70, 84 (1964).
18. California State Assembly, *Preliminary Report on the Costs and Effects of the California Criminal Justice System and Recommendations for Legislation to Increase Support of Local Police and Correction Programs* 79 (1969).

the same time the court began to use probation much more liberally. The result of the experiment was that the rate of probation violations was actually reduced by almost one half.

In California, the Community Treatment Project established by the Youth Authority has experimented with intensive treatment in the community for youths who have been sentenced to institutions by the courts. The success rate of the project participants as a group, as measured by tests purporting to assess their behavior and attitudes, has been significantly higher than that of their counterparts sent to institutions. In addition, researchers working with the project have been able to divide the participants into nine homogeneous groups according to type of personality (such as "asocial aggressive," "immature conformist" and "neurotic acting-out"). Of these groups, three clearly are more successful in a community program than in an institution; one can do well in either; three probably are better off in the community; and one seems to do better in an institution.

Kenyon Scudder, a prison official with previous experience as a probation officer, two decades ago urged greater use of probation for first offenders:

> Our courts could safely double the number now granted probation . . . and thus capitalize on the normal reaction of contrition which follows almost every conviction. In this way many more promising first offenders would be able to make restitution 'for the wrongs they have done, at the same time support their families and avoid the lasting stigma of a prison term.[19]

In addition to the restrictions imposed by state legislatures, the use of probation is limited by the lack of facilities in some parts, generally the rural counties, of certain states. For example, services for juveniles are available in every county in only thirty-one states. In one state only two counties have probation services. A child placed on probation in other counties is presumed to be adjusting satisfactorily until he is brought back to court on a new charge. Recent testimony before a Senate subcommittee revealed that, although a juvenile probation department in Texas is considered to exist anywhere that at least one worker is paid by a county to devote part of his time to work with juveniles, only seventy-two counties out of 254 meet even this criterion.[20]

Probation services require greater resources than most counties can

19. Scudder, *Prisoners Are People* (1952).
20. Testimony by John Corcoros, Texas Director, National Council on Crime and Delinquency, before the Subcommittee on Juvenile Delinquency of the Senate Committee on the Judiciary, 92d Cong., 1st Sess., May 3, 1971.

afford without state aid. In 1965, the California legislature authorized the payment of subsidies to the counties for each offender placed on probation instead of being sent to a state institution. (Some county officials previously had urged local judges to sentence offenders to state prison rather than probation so that the cost would be borne by fifty-eight counties rather than one.) Between July 1966, when the Probation Subsidy Program went into effect, and early 1971, the state paid approximately $43.4 million to the counties for improvement of services to probationers.[21] Participating counties were able to provide special supervision for three to five of the probationers for every new case not committed to a state institution.

No detailed information has yet been made available on the counties' success with their new treatment resources. In fact, a frequently heard criticism of the program is that although counties' proposals for special supervision must be approved by the director of the state Youth Authority before funds are released, there are no provisions for state inspection of county programs financed by the subsidy for the purpose of enforcing minimum standards or for research and evaluation by some central agency.

The most dramatic change caused by probation subsidies has been in the types of sentences imposed by the courts. In 1965 more than 23 percent of defendants convicted in superior courts were sent to state prison; in 1969 less than 10 percent went to prison. The proportion of defendants put on probation by superior courts was 51 percent in 1965; by 1969 it had risen to 66 percent. Since July 1966 approximately eleven thousand people have been diverted from the state correctional system (both adult prisons and Youth Authority institutions) by the program. According to Allen F. Breed, director of the Youth Authority, the decline in the number of juveniles and youthful offenders sent to state institutions has been so great since 1965 that one institution has been shut down and another will close shortly.

Even with its payments to the counties, the state has saved approximately $15.6 million in the first four years of the program's operation. (It currently costs an average of $2,827 per year to support each adult offender in state prison and an average of $6,378 per year to keep a youth in an institution.) Added to the savings in operating costs were an estimated $216 million saved from projected capital construction costs.[22]

21. R. Smith, "A Quiet Revolution: Probation Subsidy," U.S. Department of Health, Education and Welfare, *Delinquency Prevention Reporter* 3, 5 (May 1971).
22. *Ibid.*

Even jurisdictions with strong probation services employ probation infrequently in misdemeanor cases. Eleven states, none of them highly urbanized, have no probation services at all for misdemeanants. New York City uses probation for less than 2 percent of its lesser offenses; Los Angeles County for less than 9 percent. "Apparently," according to the last President's Crime Commission, "judges in such jurisdictions choose to concentrate probation resources on a small proportion of offenders where they are most needed, using fines or suspended sentences in other cases."[23]

But it is still not clear that probation is being used where it could do the most good. In a survey of the District of Columbia correctional agencies, the American Correctional Association concluded that many misdemeanants who could have benefitted by probation were sentenced to prison, while, paradoxically, most of those who were recommended for probation did not appear in need of any supervision at all. "The Probation Director is proud of his low (5 per cent) revocation record, but this seems to reflect not so much good supervision as the fact that clients selected for probation were not in need of supervision. . . . There are many individuals who may become involved with the law due to a situational circumstance; for these there often is no need for either incarceration or supervision in the community. No one should be placed on probation or kept on probation longer than is necessary to accomplish the purpose for which the probation sentence was imposed."[24] Unfortunately, many state laws, as well as the federal law, do not permit the imposition of suspended sentences without provision for supervision of the offender by a probation officer.

A recent study attempted to determine the effectiveness of probation in reducing recidivism among sixteen- and seventeen-year-old delinquent boys in New Jersey as compared to short-term residential treatment and commitment to a state reformatory.[25] Unlike California's Community Treatment Project, however, the boys were not assigned to the different programs on a random basis, and probation received the "best risks." Nonetheless, the recidivism rate of the boys who completed probation without a revocation (72 percent of those originally assigned) was substantially lower than that of any other program, even when boys from different pro-

23. The President's Commission on Law Enforcement and Administration of Justice, Task Force Report: *Correction* 75, 76, Table 6 (1967).
24. American Correctional Association, *The Organization and Effectiveness of the Correctional Agencies* 693 (1966).
25. Scarpitti and Stephenson, "A Study of Probation Effectiveness," 59 *Journal of Criminal Law, Criminology and Police Science* 361 (1968).

grams were matched on the basis of various characteristics. However, the boys who failed on probation continued to commit crimes after their release. The study concluded that, "if probation is extended greatly, failure and recidivism rates will grow markedly, unless, of course, there is some monumental change in treatment techniques." Considering the current levels of probation supervision and services, a slightly different conclusion might be that the majority of the boys would have done as well if their sentences simply had been suspended, while the others needed greater efforts than currently are being employed.

Despite its limitations, probation is used for more than half of all convicted offenders. Their success on probation depends at least in part on two features: effective decision-making regarding who should receive probation and the availability of adequate probational programs in the community.

CRITERIA FOR SELECTION

Of all the methods of correction presently in general use, probation has the greatest potential for rehabilitating offenders. As at least one state (California) correctional authority has come to recognize, the circumstances leading to delinquency and criminal behavior are the product of life in the community, and the resolution of these problems must be found in the community. Local treatment keeps an offender close to his family and his job. It enables him to work with his problems under some supervision in the environment where he must learn to live eventually. And supervision in the community is much less expensive than imprisonment. While the average state spends about $3,400 a year (excluding capital investment) to keep a youth in a state training school, it spends only one-tenth of that amount to keep him on probation. During 1967 the cost of keeping one offender on probation in the federal system was $285, less than one-tenth of the $3,100 spent on a year's confinement in federal prison.[26] For all but the most dangerous offenders, probation should be the treatment of choice.

The detrimental effect of correctional institutions makes it crucial for legislatures and courts to lay down a legal principle that offenders should be imprisoned only when confinement is shown to be essential

26. *Annual Report of the Director of the Administrative Office of the U.S. Courts* 162 (1967).

to public safety. Although this principle never has been applied to the sentencing of adult prisoners, one state court ruled that in the case of juveniles "the good of the State requires a child to be removed from a community only when his delinquency is such that he has become a danger to society either because of his conduct or his influence upon others."[27] The court reversed a lower-court decision committing a juvenile to a state training school. "Certainly if we can have reasonable hope that other measures will suffice, we should not resort to a commitment to the Training School. In this case we have that hope."

The American Law Institute set forth in its 1962 Model Penal Code a set of criteria for courts considering probation:

(1) The Court may deal with a person who has been convicted of a crime without imposing sentence of imprisonment if, having regard to the nature and circumstances of the crime and to the history and character of the defendant, it deems that his imprisonment is unnecessary for protection of the public, on one or more of the following grounds:

(a) The defendant does not have a history of prior delinquency or criminal activity, or having such a history, has led a law abiding life for a substantial period of time before the commission of the present crime;

(b) The defendant did not contemplate that his criminal conduct would cause or threaten serious harm;

(c) The defendant's criminal conduct neither caused nor threatened serious harm;

(d) The defendant's criminal conduct was the result of circumstances unlikely to recur;

(e) The defendant acted under the stress of a strong provocation;

(f) The victim of the defendant's criminal conduct consented to its commission or was largely instrumental in its perpetration;

(g) The imprisonment of the defendant would entail excessive hardship because of his advanced age or physical condition;

(h) The character and attitudes of the defendant indicate that he is unlikely to commit another crime.

(2) When a person who has been convicted of a crime is not sentenced to imprisonment, the court shall place him on

27. *State v. Myers*, 22 N.W.2d 199, 201 (N.D. 1946).

probation if he is in need of supervision, guidance or direction that is feasible for the probation service to provide.

The more recent American Bar Association's Advisory Committee on Sentencing and Review took a different position concluding that the starting point for every sentence should be probation or some other sentence not involving commitment or confinement, thus reversing "the automatic response of many in the criminal justice system that imprisonment is the best sentence for crime unless particular reasons exist for 'mitigating' the sentence." The presumption in favor of probation should be rebutted only by specific reasons (namely, public protection, a need for correctional treatment that can best be provided in an institution or an offense whose seriousness would be "unduly depreciate[d]" by a sentence to probation) calling for a sentence to an institution.[28]

The National Commission on Reform of Federal Criminal Laws agrees that dispositions short of imprisonment should be used unless the facts of a particular case require imprisonment. The judge should start his thinking with probation in mind and be moved from that sentence only if a particular reason appears from his study of the case.

An idea that has gained some currency is that probation should be the mandatory sentence for all property crimes, at least for first offenders. It should be noted, however, that since property offenders repeat their crimes more frequently than violent offenders, their failure rate on probation probably could be expected to be higher.

THE PRE-SENTENCE INVESTIGATION

The pre-sentence investigation is designed to assist the court in determining the appropriate sentence. The investigative report also reduces duplication of services by being available to other agencies: the probation officer for development of treatment plans when the defendant is placed on probation; the correctional department for classification and planning of treatment when the defendant is committed to an institution; and the parole officer in preparing for the prisoner's release. The format and contents of federal pre-sentence reports were recently ad-

28. American Bar Association Project on Minimum Standards for Criminal Justice, *Standards Relating to Probation,* 1–2 (tentative draft 1970); American Bar Association Project on Minimum Standards for Criminal Justice, *Standards Relating to Sentencing Alternatives and Procedures* §§2.2, 2.3(e), 2.4(c) and 2.5(c) (approved draft 1968).

justed in order to supply information essential to the Bureau of Prisons and the Board of Parole. On the other hand, the problem of duplication of investigative efforts in the states, among counties and among different states, remains unsolved. A New York study has recommended establishment of a unified information service that would use photostatic devices to transmit data on individuals to different agencies throughout the state.[29]

Pre-sentence reports prepared for the federal courts are supposed to include the offender's prior criminal history, his co-defendants, the complainant's attitude, the defendant's personal development, circumstances in his neighborhood and community, a recommended sentence and a suggested program for the offender if he is granted probation. The detail and quality of pre-sentence investigations vary widely. A chief United States probation officer confessed:

> Too many of what we call investigations could not possibly be labeled systematic inquiries, particularly when we interview the defendant and *maybe* just one or two other persons and then proceed to write up a voluminous report. Many of what we produce are not investigations in any sense of the word, but more correctly are merely pre-sentence interviews. Short cuts and careless haste in conducting an investigation are almost a guarantee that the report will contain many data that are downright erroneous and that it will not reflect the defendant's true social and personal problems.[30]

A recent study pinpointed major weaknesses in the investigations of misdemeanants in one city: failure to verify information secured from the defendant, lack of contact with members of the defendant's family and little interpretation of factual data. Statements about the present offense were obtained from the arresting officer and the defendant, but in only twenty-eight of the 130 cases reviewed was there a statement by the complaining witness. No attempt was made to resolve any conflicts in the statements of the defendant and the arresting officer or even to point out that conflicts existed. There was no discussion of mitigating and aggravating circumstances, such as provocation by the complainant. Where the present offense was part of a repetitive pattern, the fact was not revealed. Previous arrest records were furnished but without any attempt

29. See *Preliminary Report of the Governor's Special Committee on Criminal Offenders* 189 (1968).
30. Zeigler, "Pre-sentence and Pre-parole Investigation," *National Probation Association Yearbook* 155 (1946), cited in Tappan, *Crime, Justice and Correction* 556 (1960).

to find the substance of the charges or to include the defendant's version of what had happened. The only family background provided was the ages, occupations and addresses of the defendant's immediate family. Instead of a complete picture of the defendant's history of employment, only his present employment was verified.[31]

In a two-week period in one court in the District of Columbia, probation officers completed questionnaires concerning seventeen pre-sentence investigations. Of the seventeen, only three defendants were recommended for probation. The investigators' reasons were less than enlightening: one had a "satisfactory background"; another was a "first offender, good background"; and the third was a "steady worker," with "no significant record" and "nothing of an antisocial nature in his background." If those reports recommending probation were terse and obscure, those recommending against it were more subjective and arbitrary. Of the fourteen not recommended for probation in this group, for example, seven had "prior records," two had additional charges lodged against them during the period of the investigation, three were "uncooperative" and two were heavy drinkers, one with a history of "aggressive, assaultive behavior" and the other with an "unstable and dishonest past work history."[32]

One critical defense lawyer commented that probation officers put a premium on "middle-class values," such as neatness, promptness, education and steady employment. He cited the psychological advantage of a neatly dressed defendant who can go to the probation office for his interview over the defendant who is jailed before trial and must have the officer come to see him. And he criticized the inclusion of typical subjective evaluations such as "the subject seemed evasive—refused to cooperate."[33]

An appellate court in New Jersey has taken the unusual, and perhaps unprecedented, step of reviewing the quality of a pre-sentence report. The court agreed with the defendant's complaint that he was denied the benefit of a pre-sentence report required by statute because the writing

31. American Correctional Association, *The Organization and Effectiveness of the Correctional Agencies* 691–92 (1966).
32. Subin, *Criminal Justice in a Metropolitan Court* 105–106 (1966).
33. Wald, "Poverty and Criminal Justice," in the President's Commission on Law Enforcement and Administration of Justice, Task Force Report: *The Courts* 148 n.78 (1967) (interview with Richard Arens).
For whatever reasons, defendants who spend the pretrial period in jail receive prison sentences more often than defendants who are released prior to trial. Jailed first offenders have been shown to be half again as likely to be sentenced to prison as repeaters who can make bail. Rankin, "The Effect of Pre-Trial Detention," 39 *New York University Law Review* 641 (1964).

submitted was inadequate and biased. The report at issue contained the following: "details of the offense," obtained from the prosecutor's file; a cryptic description of the defendant's prior criminal record; a family history limited to the names, ages, religion and residence of his father, mother and sister; the defendant's statement that he was never married; the fact that he had attended school only through the eighth grade; records of employment and military service; his stated religion; and a notation that in his leisure time the defendant admitted to drinking too much. The court found "strong indications in the record suggesting that if defendant had been fairly interviewed by a probation department representative in whom he had some confidence, and the entire background of the occurrence disclosed, the degree of his offense might well have been tempered and his punishment proportionately lightened."[34] The rigorous insistence upon thorough and fair pre-sentence evaluations reflected in this unusual case, while not common, ought to be.

Judges also may begin to police the way in which probation officers obtain the material used in pre-sentence reports. A federal appeals court recently held that, since "the use of illegally seized evidence at sentencing would provide a substantial incentive for unconstitutional searches and seizures," such evidence should be disregarded by the sentencing judge.[35] The court reversed the defendant's fifteen-year sentence for sale of narcotics, since the pre-sentence report had included, and the judge considered, a reference to heroin and large sums of money that had been seized illegally from the defendant's home. A concurring opinion cast doubt on the use of hearsay in pre-sentence reports and suggested a right to examine the probation officer on the sources of his information.

One method of curing some of the defects in investigation would be to give the defendant or his counsel the right to inspect the pre-sentence report and an opportunity to rebut its contents. This change in the usual practice of secrecy, justified in Chapter III on several grounds, also should serve to improve the quality of reports by making probation officers accountable for their contents.

A controversial innovation used for a time in the then District of Columbia Court of General Sessions was a screening process to see which cases warranted full investigation. On conviction, the judge scanned the police statement of the facts and used it, together with any evidence

34. *State v. Leckis*, 79 N.J. Super. 479, 486–87, 192 A.2d 161, 165 (1962); *cf. State v. Gattling*, 95 N.J. Super. 103, 230 A.2d 157, 161–62 (1967).
35. *Verdugo v. United States*, 402 F.2d 599, 613 (9th Cir. 1968).

which had been adduced at trial, to decide whether to sentence immediately, request a full pre-sentence report or request a preliminary screening report by the probation department. In cases where the judge chose the third option, the defendant was taken to the cell behind the courtroom and interviewed by the director or deputy director of probation. A typical screening lasted from five to ten minutes and attempted to elicit facts regarding the defendant's prior arrest record, his roots in the community and his employment status. On the basis of these three items of information, the officer decided whether to recommend a full pre-sentence investigation or to indicate to the court that the defendant did not require a full investigation.

A study of this procedure by the American Correctional Association found, however, that the interview elicited little information not already available to the court. In more than five out of six cases screened in 1965, the probation department reported that the defendant was not worthy of further investigation. The study criticized the procedure for being slipshod and for pre-empting the discretion of the court:

> It logically follows, if one has faith in the Probation Department, that if they deem a defendant unworthy of a presentence investigation, he is by inference not worthy of a suspended sentence. At such a point, the Probation Department appears to have moved into the area of preempting the judicial discretion of the court. The contents of the interview are not made available to the court, which is furnished only a terse statement regarding the person screened. No records are kept of these interviews, so neither the Probation Department nor any outside source can review and analyze the criteria used in forming conclusions. In general, the screening process is little more than a hurried and inadequate interview, with the recommendation to the court based largely upon hunch.[36]

In an effort to provide some information to the courts about minor offenders without requiring them to remain in institutions, the Bronx Sentencing Project of the Vera Foundation in New York has developed a shortened report for use with misdemeanants. The report, based on information gathered from a defendant and then verified, can be prepared in one day by a relatively untrained interviewer. It focuses on an offend-

36. American Correctional Association, *The Organization and Effectiveness of the Correctional Agencies* 696–98 (1966).

er's roots in the community, prior offense, present charge and evidence of narcotics use, without any effort to explore his deep motivations, and bases its recommendations on an objective point scale. The theory behind the short report is that it is critical to return a probationer to the community as quickly as possible, so that his job will not be lost or his family and social ties broken. At present, an offender awaiting a full presentence report may have to remain in jail for weeks (or post an expensive bond) while the report is prepared. The development of computerized information systems would facilitate the investigative process.

Actually, according to one recent study, most of the data collected during pre-sentence investigations plays no part in determining the probation officer's sentencing recommendation to the court.

> This leads to speculation as to how much presentence investigation time is utilized to gather information which may be of very minor significance in making a recommendation. . . . It also raises the question of whether probation officers, once they have "decided" on a recommendation for a specific case early in the presentence investigation, conduct the balance of their investigation in search of further information which justifies the previously made decision, rather than seeking information which might lead to a modification or rejection of that decision.[37]

Once a short report has convinced the judge that an offender should be put on probation, professionally staffed community diagnostic centers could take over and perform more extensive diagnoses while the probationer lives at home and works in the community.

Supervision of Probationers

Supervision distinguishes probation from the suspended sentence. The probationer remains legally subject to the jurisdiction of the court. The court may fix the length of the probation term, receive progress reports from the probation officer, impose conditions requiring the probationer to come to court when the officer alleges violation of some condition, and most critically, continue or revoke probation once a violation is established and impose a new sentence if probation is revoked.

37. Lohman, Wahl and Carter, *Decision-Making and the Probation Officer: The Presentence Report Recommendation* (1966).

Although supervision is the responsibility of the court which granted probation, the responsibility may be transferred to a different court when the probationer changes his residence. The Federal Probation Act[38] and several state acts specifically provide for transfer of such supervisory jurisdiction to any other federal district or to another court district within a state. The Interstate Compact for the Supervision of Parolees and Probationers, adopted by all fifty states and supplemented by the administrative practices agreed on by compact administrators, provides for the transfer of jurisdiction among states.

Where a term of probation is not stated, the length of the maximum sentence for the offense sets the term. Since the probationer is not serving a sentence of commitment, the probation statute may authorize or specify a probation term longer than the maximum sentence for a given offense.[39]

Judges are criticized for keeping offenders on probation for an unnecessarily long time. The first few months are considered the critical period of probation. After that, it is generally agreed that a probation officer's time could be better spent elsewhere. From the point of view of the probationer who has successfully completed the early months of probation, the restrictions thereafter imposed may be onerous, reducing his opportunities for employment and mobility. Either the probation officer or the sentencing judge should, on his own or upon request, review cases periodically to determine whether a probationer is ready to be released. Most federal offices use early termination of probation as an incentive to probationers and a means toward more efficient use of the officers' time.

On the other hand, longer periods of probation than normal for a particular crime sometimes are considered desirable in the case of misdemeanants. A probation period of thirty, sixty or ninety days may be too short to give a probation department an opportunity to help an offender.

38. 18 U.S.C. §3653:
    Whenever during the period of his probation, a probationer . . . goes from the district in which he is being supervised to another district, jurisdiction over him may be transferred, in the discretion of the court, from the court for the district from which he goes to the court for the other district, with the concurrence of the latter court. Thereupon the court for the district to which jurisdiction is transferred shall have all power with respect to the probationer that was previously possessed by the court for the district from which the transfer is made, except that the period of probation shall not be changed without the consent of the sentencing court. This process under the same conditions may be repeated whenever during the period of his probation the probationer goes from the district in which he is being supervised to another district.

39. E.g., Mich. Comp. Laws §771.2 (two-year probation terms for misdemeanors, five years for felonies).

Many probation acts authorize extension of the term of probation by the court after it is first fixed. Any extension must occur within the original period or be subject to the argument of double jeopardy.[40]

CONDITIONS OF PROBATION

When it grants probation, a court generally specifies conditions which the probationer must meet. Some courts have ruled that a judge may not delegate his power to impose conditions to a probation department.[41] However, some juvenile courts require probationers to cooperate with the probation officer, in effect leaving the setting of rules to the discretion of the officer responsible for the case. This practice was criticized by the President's Crime Commission because it invites abuses, causes self-defeating conflicts by making one official simultaneously rule-maker, enforcer and helper and sometimes results in a failure to define clearly the rules each probationer must follow.

Conditions must be communicated to the defendant in writing. In some jurisdictions, the defendant is merely asked to sign a standard list of conditions. A better practice is used in the federal system, where the probation officer sees the defendant immediately after sentencing and explains each condition.

Individualized treatment may require that special conditions be imposed for certain offenders. Some courts follow the procedure of having the probation officer who conducts the presentence investigation recommend conditions, then discuss the recommendations with the prospective probationer and his counsel.

A universal requirement of probation is that the probationer report periodically to the officer assigned to supervise the case. In addition, the following standard conditions are imposed in most states: lawful behavior, restitution or payment of fines, and, occasionally, a jail term prior to probation.

The condition of lawful behavior requires a probationer to do more than avoid additional criminal convictions. For example a judge in Maryland recently revoked the probation of a man who had been acquitted of a second offense, on the basis of the alleged—but unproved—offense. The

---

40. Rubin, *The Law of Criminal Correction* 194–95 (1963); *contra, People v. Marks,* 340 Mich. 495, 65 N.W.2d 698 (1954).
41. *E.g., People v. Good,* 287 Mich. 110, 282 N.W. 920 (1930).

revocation proceeding itself frequently falls far short of the procedural requirements of a criminal trial.

The payment of fines and restitution to victims of the probationer's crime are common conditions. Probation officers frequently have the responsibility to see that the money is collected; fifty-eight federal probation offices recently reported that over 20 percent of their probationers are paying fines, and seventy-eight offices reported that over 20 percent are making restitution. Restitution, although it gives some aid to the victim, is not considered a sentence but part of the defendant's rehabilitation.

The central problem of any monetary condition is proportioning the rate of payment to the offender's ability to pay, so that the probationer is not prevented from meeting his family obligations and re-establishing himself in the community, or, worse yet, destined for jail for failure to meet financial terms of probation. An installment plan may aid the offender in making payments, but in many cases only partial restitution is possible. One workable approach is for the probation officer to include in his presentence report for court approval an analysis of the defendant's financial situation, the estimated amount of restitution and a recommended plan for payment.

A particularly controversial "condition" followed in some courts is that of routinely imposing a brief jail term prior to the probation period. This practice is authorized by statute in California and Michigan and in the federal system. A Michigan statute gives courts discretion to sentence youthful offenders to up to a year in a "probation camp" as part of the probation term. A study of probation practices in California reported that over 46 percent of all adult probationers in the state serve time in a county jail as a condition of probation. Rarely do the jails offer any treatment, training, education or placement services for these people.[42]

Proponents of the practice argue that it gives the offender "a taste of jail" which tends to deter him from further criminal activities. In the case of misdemeanants, for whom the vast majority of jurisdictions provide no parole, probation may take the place of a parole from jail.

The National Commission on Reform of Federal Criminal Laws has recommended that judges continue to be permitted to sentence offenders up to six months in jail, to be followed by probation. The reason for such a

42. Mich. Stat. Ann. §28.1133 (Supp. 1970); 18 U.S.C. §3651 (1964); California Board of Correction, *Probation Study* 21 (1965).

provision is to permit parole supervision following short-term commitments to local facilities. The idea of such short-term commitment is to provide a shock and to make the offender more amenable to the subsequent supervision on probation. The commission has no illusions that offenders will be rehabilitated during their short jail terms.

Critics, such as the President's Crime Commission, feel that short-term detention prior to probation should be used extremely sparingly, as it is a questionable deterrent which "may complicate reintegration by causing an offender to lose his job and otherwise [disrupt] his community ties. . . . [T]he indiscriminate use of incarceration in a class of cases that presumably includes many offenders not likely to repeat their acts and amenable to other corrective methods is unwise." Other critics claim that "the irrational practice of some judges of ordering probation *after* some period spent in jail surely betrays a fundamental misunderstanding of the purpose of probation. Probation is an alternative to jail, not a supplement."[43] A sentence cannot be termed true "probation" if it is preceded by a term in jail.

Courts seem to impose certain conditions less for the deterrence of crime than for the offender's moral instruction: forbidding use of an automobile; restrictions on travel; abstention from the use of intoxicants—even from visiting establishments where liquor is served; prohibiting contacts with ex-convicts and other disreputable persons and places; requiring attendance at church; and even marrying the mother of the probationer's unborn child. The failure of legislatures and higher courts to develop workable limitations on the discretion of trial courts has enabled judges to impose their own moral standards on probationers. Judges have no special qualifications in this area, and their standards may bear no reasonable relation to the purposes of probation.

Some probation conditions involve serious constitutional questions. For example, some courts have put political or civil-rights demonstrators on probation on condition that they refrain from participating in further demonstrations. Although it can be argued that this condition is preferable to imprisonment, where all demonstrations are usually forbidden, if the condition is designed to proscribe participation in lawful protests, it violates the First Amendment.

---

43. The President's Commission on Law Enforcement and Administration of Justice, Task Force Report: *Correction* 30 (1967); Mattick and Aikman, "The Cloacal Region of American Correction" 381 *The Annals of the American Academy of Political and Social Science* 109, 111 (January 1969).

A defendant convicted of refusing to file income- or withholding-tax returns because of his opposition, described by the court as "fanatical," to federal income-tax laws, recently challenged the conditions of his probation. The trial court had forbidden him to speak, write or circulate materials questioning the constitutionality of the tax laws or the Federal Reserve system. According to the court of appeals:

> To muzzle the appellant to this extent is on its face a violation of his First Amendment freedom of expression. This is not to say that one on probation has the rights of citizens who are not on probation. He forfeits much of his freedom of action and even freedom of expression to the extent necessary to successful rehabilitation and protection of the public programs.

The court invalidated the condition "to the extent that it prohibits the expression of opinions as to invalidity or unconstitutionality of the laws in question," but upheld it "insofar as it prohibits public speeches designed to urge or encourage others to violate the laws."[44]

A more difficult question arises when a probationer is required to allow what normally would be considered unreasonable visiting rights, searches and seizures. A divided California Supreme Court recently ruled that a defendant put on probation after a conviction of possession of marijuana, on condition that he submit at any time to a warrantless search by police, voluntarily waived all Fourth Amendment protections.[45] The dissenters argued persuasively that

> . . . such a total denial of Fourth Amendment rights is [not] necessary or even desirable in rehabilitating a criminal offender. First, the proper level of surveillance and interference with personal rights is in part dictated by the gravity of the crime committee . . .
>
> Even if possession of marijuana be deemed as dangerous as possession of more dangerous drugs, the proper authority for determining whether a probationer or parolee is obeying the terms of his conditional release is the probation or parole officer . . .
>
> There is also good reason to believe that such all-encompassing waivers of constitutional rights are not conducive to effective rehabilitation. Treatment of the probationer like a prisoner— stripped of all controls over others' knowledge of him because he

44. *Porth v. United States,* 10 *Criminal Law Reporter* 2244 (10th Cir., Dec. 13, 1971).
45. *People v. Mason,* 10 *Criminal Law Reporter* 2029 (Calif. Sup. Ct., Sept. 22, 1971).

is not deemed to have sufficient internal controls or knowledge of himself—simply weakens the will of the prisoner to behave responsibly because he thinks it right.

This problem is discussed further in Chapter V.

Although appellate review of conditions of probation is rare, a California court of appeals reversed the order revoking probation of a twenty-year-old unmarried woman who had violated a condition that she "not . . . become pregnant without being married." On sentencing the defendant for a robbery conviction, the trial judge had warned her, "You are going to prison unless you are married first. You have already had too many of those." When the woman, who already had two children, again became pregnant, the judge ordered her imprisoned, saying, "It appears to me this woman is irresponsible; she is foisting obligations upon others, and one of the objectives of probation is to teach and encourage responsibility in all phases, including the economics of life and being able to support the dependents who will naturally flow from this sort of conduct. . . ."

The appellate court, in reversing the revocation of probation, expressed its disapproval of the use of probation conditions to impose controls unrelated to the public safety:

[A] court cannot use its awesome power in imposing conditions of probation to vindicate the public interest in reducing the welfare rolls by applying unreasonable conditions of probation. The interest of the public in saving money for the taxpayers is by no means the same thing as the public interest in the reformation and rehabilitation of offenders.

The court relied on the sensible general rule—that a "condition of probation which (1) has no relationship to the crime of which the offender was convicted, (2) relates to conduct which is not in itself criminal and (3) requires or forbids conduct which is not reasonably related to future criminality does not serve the statutory ends of probation and is invalid."[46]

The American Bar Association's Advisory Committee on Sentencing and Review recommends in its *Standards Relating to Probation* that conditions be imposed by the courts on an individual basis, that they be reason-

46. Cal. Pen. Code §1203.1; *People v. Dominguez*, 64 *Cal. Rptr.* 290, 292–94 (Court of Appeal, Second District, 1967); *see also In re* Bushman, 83 *Cal. Rptr.* 375, 463 P.2d 727 (1970); *People v. Higgins*, 22 Mich. App. 479, 177 N.W.2d 716 (1970).

ably related to the probationer's rehabilitation and that they be no more restrictive than necessary to prevent further violations of the law:

(a) It should be a condition of every sentence to probation that the probationer lead a law-abiding life during the period of his probation. No other conditions should be required by statute; but the sentencing court should be authorized to prescribe additional conditions to fit the circumstances of each case. Development of standard conditions as a guide to sentencing courts is appropriate so long as such conditions are not routinely imposed.

(b) Conditions imposed by the court should be designed to assist the probationer in leading a law-abiding life. They should be reasonably related to his rehabilitation and not unduly restrictive of his liberty or incompatible with his freedom of religion. They should not be so vague or ambiguous as to give no real guidance.

(c) Conditions may appropriately deal with matters such as the following:

(i) cooperating with a program of supervision;

(ii) meeting family responsibilities;

(iii) maintaining steady employment or engaging or refraining from engaging in a specific employment or occupation;

(iv) pursuing prescribed educational or vocational training;

(v) undergoing available medical or psychiatric treatment;

(vi) maintaining residence in a prescribed area or in a special facility established for or available to persons on probation;

(vii) refraining from consorting with certain types of people or frequenting certain types of places;

(viii) making restitution of the fruits of the crime or reparation for loss or damage caused thereby.

A widely respected study of probation violation rates concluded that revocation rates increase as more conditions are imposed:

. . . [P]robation with no special conditions had a revocation rate of 19.0 percent, probation with one condition had a revocation rate of 24.9 percent, probation with two conditions had a revocation rate of 39.2 percent, and probation with three conditions had a revocation rate of 47.0 percent. Still another combination of conditions produced the following rates: jail only as a condition of probation had a revocation rate of 24.9 percent, fine or restitution only as a condition had a revocation rate of 26.9 percent, and jail with fine or restitution as a condition had a revocation rate of 40.5 percent.[47]

The relative difference in the rate of revocations according to the conditions imposed remained even when the experiences of probationers convicted of similar offenses were compared.

REVOCATION OF PROBATION

Probationers who violate probation conditions may be taken to court. Probation statutes do not require that every violation be brought to the court's attention, and probation officers have discretion in recommending revocation. There are great disparities among judges and probation officers as to what constitutes a basis for revocation. Some judges and probation officers insist that convictions of new offenses should be the only basis for revocation. Others believe that violations of other conditions justify revocation, particularly when the violations are committed by an indifferent probationer who is unwilling to cooperate with the probation office and the court. Still other judges contend that the circumstances of the violation, the general attitude and outlook of the probationer, his adjustment with his family, in the community and on the job, and his efforts to comply with the conditions also should be considered before revocation is recommended.

Once an officer has decided to call a violation to the attention of a court, the probationer may be summoned by notice, arrest or warrant, according to the circumstances and the requirements of the particular statute. If the court does not proceed at once, it may detain the probationer or release him pending the hearing and may fix bail.

In most states courts are required to conduct hearings on alleged violations.[48] In about half the states and in the federal system, statutes

47. Davis, "A Study of Adult Probation Violation Rates by Means of the Cohort Approach," 55 *Journal of Criminal Law, Criminology and Police Science* 70, 81 (1964).
48. Several courts have read into state probation statutes provisions for notice and hearing—e.g., *Baine v. Beckstead,* 10 Utah 2d 4, 347 P.2d 554 (1959). Hearings have not been required in at least seven jurisdictions: Iowa, Missouri and Oklahoma (by statute); Arizona, California, District of Columbia and South Dakota (by judicial decision). Sklar, "Law and Practice in Probation and Parole Revocation Hearings," 55 *Journal of Criminal Law, Criminology and Police Science* 175 (1964).

require these hearings to be preceded by notice of the charge. There is no right to a jury trial. No general right to counsel had been applied to revocation hearings. However, in *Mempa v. Rhay*,[49] the Supreme Court determined that a state probationer was constitutionally entitled to counsel at the revocation proceeding, "whether it be labeled a revocation of probation or a deferred sentencing." Subsequent cases seeking to limit the decision have read it to require counsel only where the revoking authority also determined the original sentence.[50] A recent federal decision held that counsel, either retained or appointed, is required in all cases to contest issues of fact related to the violation of probation conditions and develop other information bearing on the proper exercise of the court's discretion to revoke or to continue probation. However, the court also ruled that, while a hearing is necessary in every case, it might be administrative rather than judicial where sentence already has been imposed.[51]

The *Mempa* case makes no specific reference to the right to a hearing in a probation revocation proceeding. However, the right to counsel necessarily implies the right to a hearing if counsel is to have any function. Thus *Mempa* seems to have overruled an earlier dictum by Justice Cardozo that there is no constitutional right to a hearing when probation is revoked.[52] A better view would require a hearing and representation by counsel in all probation proceedings. Whatever the technical classification of such a proceeding, its import warrants the protection of constitutional safeguards.

Once a violation has been established, the court has discretion to continue or revoke probation. Where probation is revoked, the court's sentencing power depends on whether it originally suspended the imposition or the execution of sentence. If the former, it may impose any sentence it might have imposed originally; if the latter, it cannot set a penalty greater than the original sentence.

Sometimes probation is revoked on the basis of a new crime for which the probationer has not been tried. This dubious practice was questioned during the oral argument before the Supreme Court in *Mempa v. Rhay*:

49. 389 U.S. 128, 137 (1967).
50. *E.g., Rose v. Haskins*, 388 F.2d 91, 97 (6th Cir.), *cert. denied*, 392 U.S. 946 (1968); *Skidgell v. State*, 264 A.2d 8 (Me. 1970). *John v. State*, 160 N.W.2d 37, 43–44 (N.D. 1968).
51. *Gunsolus v. Gagnon*, 10 *Criminal Law Reporter* 2282 (7th Cir., Dec. 28, 1971); *see also Hahn v. Burke*, 430 F.2d 100 (7th Cir. 1970).
52. *Escoe v. Zerbst*, 295 U.S. 490, 492–93 (1935).

Mr. Justice Fortas asked if it was true that [a petitioner] had never actually been tried in connection with the criminal charges that led to revocation of his probation, and thus to his imprisonment. This was true, replied [counsel for the petitioner]. Mr. Justice Fortas then commented that this must make for efficient administration of justice. "Very efficient administration," replied [the attorney].

In its *Standards Relating to Probation*, the American Bar Association's Advisory Committee on Sentencing and Review suggests that a revocation proceeding based solely on the commission of another crime ordinarily should not be initiated until the charge has been disposed of. However, in order to accommodate the pressure that might exist to revoke probation in order to prevent the defendant from being at large pending disposition of the new charge, the committee would give the court discretion to detain the probationer without bail on showing of probable cause that he had committed another crime.

In general, the committee proposes the following procedural protections to govern the revocation of probation:

(a) The court should not revoke probation without an open court proceeding attended by the following incidents:

(i) a prior written notice of the alleged violation;

(ii) representation by retained or appointed counsel; and

(iii) where the violation is contested, establishment of the violation by the government by a preponderance of the evidence.

Sentence should be imposed following a revocation according to the same procedures as are applicable to original sentencing proceedings.

(b) The government is entitled to be represented by counsel in a contested revocation proceeding.

(c) As in the case of all other proceedings in open court, a record of the revocation proceeding should be made and preserved in such a manner that it can be transcribed as needed.

(d) An order revoking probation should be appealable after the offender has been resentenced.

A recently enacted Oklahoma law requires that a suspended sentence (with or without probation) may not be revoked without competent evidence presented to the court at a hearing, at which the defendant has the right to be represented by counsel, to present evidence in his own behalf and to confront the witnesses against him. An order of revocation is appealable, although bail may not be allowed pending appeal if either the reason for which the suspended sentence was imposed or for its revocation was the commission of a felony.[53]

When a court revokes probation, it generally imposes a sentence of imprisonment. A fine might sometimes be preferable; particularly where the violation does not consist of commission of a new crime, monetary punishment may constitute a sufficient sanction. And, although the violation may be established, the judge may conclude that continued probation, possibly for an extended period or under more—conceivably less—stringent conditions, with an unrealistic or particularly onerous condition dropped, is preferable to incarceration.

Probation Officers' Caseloads

The success of the whole probation process depends on the quality of supervision by probation officers. However, a recent study of probation in one state concluded that if "supervision is what probation is all about . . . —and most authorities agree that it is—then probation in a large number of those counties studied by this project is about nothing."[54] A committee of the American Bar Association agrees:

> Too often a sentencing judge is faced with the Hobson's choice of a sentence to an overcrowded prison that is almost a guarantee that the defendant will emerge a more dangerous man than when he entered or a sentence to an essentially unsupervised probation that is little more than a release of the defendant without sanction, as well as without incentive to avoid the commission of a new offense.[55]

If a probationer is thought to need supervision, he will require a probation officer with time to devote to him. The President's Crime Commission

53. 22 Okla. Stat. Supp. §991b (1969).
54. California Board of Correction, *Probation Study* 34 (1965).
55. American Bar Association Project on Minimum Standards for Criminal Justice, *Standards Relating to Probation* 2 (tentative draft 1970).

concluded that a desirable caseload average for supervision of juveniles and adult felons by a probation official is thirty-five cases at a time. The National Council on Crime and Delinquency says that where officers perform the dual functions of supervising offenders and conducting presentence investigations, the limit should be thirty-five cases for supervision and six for investigation and that officers doing only supervisory work should handle no more than fifty cases at a time.

Compared to these figures, the statistics collected for the Crime Commission demonstrate the gap between desirable and actual staffing levels. These statistics show that two-thirds of the juveniles under supervision in 1965 were supervised in caseloads of between sixty and 100; more than 10 percent (largely in high-crime, urban areas) were in caseloads over 100. For adults the situation was worse: over two-thirds of the felons and over three-quarters of the misdemeanants were "supervised" by officers who had caseloads of more than 100 offenders.

The California probation study pointed out that the time required to supervise each of the average California probation officer's cases for each month is equivalent to three and one half months of work. "The absurdity of the overload carried in some departments is demonstrated by our finding that one department had officers carrying a median supervision caseload of 288 cases in addition to completing a median of fourteen court investigations per month. Needless to say, probation officers of this department had not seen a probationer out of the office or jail for many years."

Caseloads too large to allow the probation officer any time to supervise individual cases may endanger the safety of the public, preclude any meaningful efforts toward rehabilitating offenders and cause probationers to lose respect for the entire system of justice.

One way to reduce caseloads would be to assign to supervision only those probationers who appear to require it, leaving others to simple suspended sentences. Thus a recently adopted New York statute, as well as proposals being advanced in Michigan and in Congress, allow conditional release with or without supervision. Supervision thus becomes a condition of probation which may or may not be imposed in a given case.

The probation department attached to the juvenile court in Seattle, Washington, uses a unique device for caseload management which it calls its Review Load. About 800 cases that appear to need no help, or for which help can be arranged outside the department, are assigned to one person with the expectation that he will give practically no supervision. This device enables the other officers, who handle more difficult cases, to restrict caseloads to about forty each.

Some countries, notably Australia, Japan, Sweden and Denmark, have compensated partially for a shortage of trained probation staff by making extensive use of volunteers. Under the direction of paid probation officers, volunteers supervise offenders and provide supplementary services, such as shelter, clothing or employment. The use of volunteers has been more successful in small towns and rural areas than in large cities. Some European observers predict that the role of volunteers will dwindle if more people with professional training become available and as more specialized techniques are developed.

In Holland probation and parole functions are handled by the same agency. This work is extensive: while 2,600 people are in prisons in Holland (about 1,200 in pretrial detention and about 1,400 serving sentences), over 17,000 are on probation and about 600 have been conditionally released from prison. Probation and parole functions are conducted by private agencies completely subsidized by the government. These agencies are the Salvation Army, the Roman Catholic Church, the Protestant Church, the Neutral Dutch Society of Reclassering and the Meijers Society (which handles mostly cases with psychiatric problems) along with some state agencies as well. These private agencies run some of the correctional institutions as well as carrying out probation supervision and the after-care of prisoners. Individuals may choose which private agency they wish to work with, and the government pays them all. This scheme seems to be competitive, reflective of the private-enterprise stress of the society in general, and, according to our brief observations, to work well.

Probation offices in the United States have used volunteers since 1960, when a program was begun in the Municipal Court of Royal Oak, Michigan. The first large city to use volunteers in probation was Denver, Colorado, where volunteers have counseled misdemeanants since 1966. At present nearly 1,000 volunteers in Denver have agreed to spend three evenings in training, followed by at least one hour per week with a youthful offender. (Judges involved in the program have concluded that it works best when they assign probationers to volunteers on a one-to-one basis.) In Los Angeles over 950 volunteers spend an average of eighteen hours each month with over 2,000 probationers. In Cedar Falls, Iowa, college students serve as probation officers for juvenile offenders. The purpose of the program is to allow youths who all their lives have seen failure to come in contact with people who have had success. In Memphis, Tennessee, Project First Offender assigns all first-offender probationers to volunteers to be supervised on a one-to-one basis. In Grand Rapids, Michigan, one district judge assigns first offenders to ministers of their own choosing, who serve as their probation officers.

Preliminary evaluations of the Royal Oak and Denver projects show fewer failures among probationers who have had volunteer counselors in addition to paid probation officers than among those supervised solely by the paid officers. In 1969, an estimated 300 to 400 courts were using volunteers. Two federally financed centers, the Boulder, Colorado, Juvenile Delinquency Project and Project Misdemeanant, have been established to provide consulting services and communication among the volunteers. An extensive literature has developed for volunteers, including a "Volunteer Courts Newsletter," published six times a year. However, there has been little systematic evaluation of the impact of volunteers on probation services.

All the volunteer projects rely chiefly on people with middle-class professional backgrounds. In other places, probation offices have begun to employ paid workers, frequently ex-offenders, who come from the same neighborhoods and have backgrounds similar to those of the probationers. Generally hired as "community workers" or "probation aides," the new careerists work under the supervision of professional probation officers. Although they have been praised for their ability to communicate effectively with probationers and their families and show the potential success to be found in non-criminal careers, paraprofessionals have yet to win complete acceptance from the professionals or to be given an opportunity to win promotion to full probation-officer status.

Despite the obvious need to reduce officers' caseloads, there is no ultimate magic in any particular number of probationers assigned to each officer. The San Francisco Project, conducted by the School of Criminology at the University of California in cooperation with the United States Probation Office in the Northern District of California, attempted to determine the optimum size of probation caseloads. Individuals were assigned at random to four types of caseloads: minimum supervision, in which probationers were required to submit written reports once a month and were provided with whatever assistance they requested themselves; "ideal" caseloads, in which officers with the academic and vocational backgrounds suggested by various authorities on probation had caseloads of less than fifty and saw each probationer at least twice a month; intensive caseloads, in which officers had caseloads of twenty-five and saw each probationer at least once a week; and "normal" caseloads, reflecting the current situation in the federal system, in which officers had caseloads of ninety to 100 and saw each probationer approximately once every six weeks.

After two years, a preliminary examination of the minimum, ideal and intensive caseloads showed that despite substantial differences in the amount and intensity of supervision (the ideal cases received about six times as much attention as the minimum-supervision cases, and the intensive cases received about fourteen times the attention of the minimum-supervision cases), there was no significant difference in the rates of violation of probation conditions. All the violation rates were well below those recorded for federal offenders under "normal" levels of supervision.[56] Thus, although the competition generated by the officers' participation in special supervision programs may have done something to improve the level of supervision, the size of caseloads in itself did not affect the outcome of supervision.

Since the random assignment of offenders to different caseloads seemed to eliminate the type of probationer as a variable, the project next assigned probationers to caseloads of different sizes and supervision intensity according to the likelihood of their successful completion of probation. Offenders were classified by age (younger probationers have higher violation rates), prior criminal record, current offense and psychological stability. The offenders with the greatest anticipated difficulty were assigned to caseloads where they would receive the most supervision. This part of the San Francisco Project operated for too short a time to permit any meaningful evaluation of the results.[57] However, similar experiments with parole caseloads, discussed in Chapter V, indicate that differential supervision possibly may be used successfully. And the second phase of the San Francisco Project did demonstrate that 300 selected offenders could be handled by one officer, thus freeing other officers to concentrate on offenders appearing to need more intensive services. The question of whether probation supervision actually makes a difference in the incidence of crime among probationers remains unanswered empirically.

56. Robert M. Carter, "The San Francisco Project: Implications and Models for Correctional Supervision Caseloads," address to the American Congress of Correction, Miami, Florida, August 21–23, 1967.
57. Lohman, Wahl, Carter and Wilkins, *Classification Criteria for Establishing Caseload Models* (1967); Robison, Wilkins, Carter and Wahl, *The San Francisco Project —Final Report* 73 (1969).

Probation and parole offices in Seattle and Tacoma, Washington, instituted "minimum-service caseloads" for some offenders in 1968, thereby reducing the size of caseloads for others. After one year, only 15 percent of the offenders assigned to minimum-service caseloads had violated probation or parole conditions.[58] However, the absence of control groups precluded analysis of the reasons for the apparent success of the specialized caseloads. Interestingly, although most Washington probation and parole officers favored the idea of minimum-supervision caseloads, they were unenthusiastic about the prospect of being assigned to supervise them.

Other plans for classifying probationers have been suggested. The District of Columbia Crime Commission recommended in 1966 that until caseloads could be reduced to acceptable levels, probationers should be classified into categories for high-, medium- and low-risk offenders. "Special emphasis should be given to intensive services for youthful offenders, who are usually the most resentful of authority and most likely to become involved in situations that need immediate services. Experimentation with new techniques for treating these offenders necessitates small specialized caseloads supervised by the most capable staff members." A study conducted by the federal probation office in Sacramento, California, showed that it is possible to classify probationers into caseloads of various risk levels by using a modified method of base expectancy scoring, currently employed to predict success on parole.[59] Federal probation offices in several districts currently are experimenting with the use of large minimum-supervision caseloads for probationers identified as low-risk. In the District of Oregon, those thought to be the best risks are monitored by clerical employees, who bring them to the attention of probation officers only if problems arise.

Since studies of the outcome of both probation and parole have consistently revealed that most difficulties occur within the first year or two of probation, reducing supervision during the latter portion of probation terms and, correspondingly, intensifying early supervision seems to make sense.

58. Carter and Dightman, "A Description and Evaluation of the Minimum Service Caseloads in the Division of Probation and Parole," 2 State of Washington, Department of Institutions, *Research Report* 15 (November 1969).
59. *Report of the President's Commission on Crime in the District of Columbia* 402 (1966); Nicholson, "Use of Prediction in Caseload Management," 32 *Federal Probation* 54 (Dec. 1968).

The Training of Probation Officers

A task force studying probation in one state concluded that the reduction of officers' workloads would not improve their performance without additional training for recruits and for officers already on the job. As one officer told the task force:

> There is a lack of training in this department. Many of our officers feel that they do not know enough about what they are supposed to do. . . . If our workloads were to be reduced, were to become reasonable, our lack—or specifically, my lack—of skill would be apparent and it would be obvious that I need additional training. . . . Our new probation officers are assigned a full caseload with little or no training. What training we do have emphasizes departmental policy and procedures. . . .[60]

Another observer warned that additional training is essential if probation departments "are not to be guilty of turning loose, on seriously disturbed people, staff who don't know what they're doing and who—with reduced caseloads—can make bad situations infinitely worse."

Probation supervisors who actually have experienced working with the reduced caseloads made possible by the California probation subsidy program emphasize that now "that we have escaped from a condition in which high caseloads served as an excuse for all ills . . . staff training can no longer be viewed as a nice adjunct to the Department; it is an absolute prerequisite if one ever lets the genie of low caseloads out of the bottle."

In one county, probation officers operating in a subsidized Intensive Supervision Unit discovered that it was extremely difficult to determine what their function should be. Once they had agreed on certain basic principles of treatment, they discovered that their implementation required information about the probationers that they never had collected. In another county, the officers quickly recognized that routine office visits and referral of probationers to other private and public agencies for help did not seem to achieve the meaningful changes in behavior expected in a specialized treatment unit and that the officers themselves were ill equipped to fill the role of "treators." A third agency hired an outside consultant to devise a training program for probation supervisors. His

60. California Board of Correction, *Probation Study* 30–33 (1965).

conclusion after examining the department: "You are supervising people who are not trained to do a job which isn't defined."[61]

For probation to work, those who supervise probationers must be professionally competent. No longer may missionary zeal be considered an adequate substitute for thorough training. Yet no pre-service professional training programs currently are available, and none but the largest metropolitan areas has the facilities, personnel and budgets to carry out effective in-service training programs.

In England, by comparison, university training for some prospective probation officers is paid for by the Home Office, which also provides specialized courses, including three months' preparation in a probation office under the supervision of a tutor and an additional three months in a residential program devoted to the study of human behavior. No special educational qualifications are required; in fact, the most successful trainee in a recent class was a retired butcher. In-service courses in fields such as criminology, matrimonial counseling and methods of supervision also are offered.

METHODS OF SUPERVISION

The requirement that probationers report regularly to the probation office is solidly entrenched. This emphasis on regular reporting was not part of the work of John Augustus. Paul Keve has traced it to the rapid growth of juvenile probation in the early part of this century:

The many men and women who entered the new probation field . . . took a simple, directive approach to the task of getting each young charge to behave. They developed the system of having the probationer report on regular schedule to the probation office, there to be questioned, admonished, advised, scolded or praised as the circumstances required. It was a highly satisfying system for probation personnel—so much so that it became solidly entrenched in probation practice and has often been a deterrent to the improvement of probation and parole methods. It was satisfying because of its simplicity. It made minimum demands upon the officer's resourcefulness and it had a specific kind of visibility that enabled the officer to prove the volume of

61. Orrock, "The Decline of Alienation," 21 Youth Authority Quarterly 12, 13 (Winter 1968).

his work in terms of the number of office visits per day and per probationer. It offered the comfortable illusion that the "discipline" of having to report to the probation office once a week was good for the child and would somehow encourage the exercise of discipline in other aspects of his living.[62]

The most common pattern of supervision is a monthly meeting between the probationer and his supervising officer. Most officers schedule occasional home visits. The shortcomings of the reporting system in an office which has a shortage of caseworkers (as most offices do) and a badly planned work week were detailed in a survey of one probation department made several years ago by the American Correctional Association:

> In better than 90 percent of the cases, new placements on probation were required to report on a monthly basis. Because there are no night reporting hours, and as the officer works every sixth Saturday on a monthly reporting basis, it is possible for a probationer to complete an entire year on probation supervision without ever being seen by his probation officer. In fact, one of the probation officers has been excused from taking his reports on Saturday and his probationers, who work a nine-to-five day, actually are never seen by him except at such time as they can get off during the day or when they lose their jobs.
>
> A printed form is given probationers on which they indicate their gross earnings during the month, their present address, the use made of their earnings, whether they have been arrested during the month, and whether they "have any problems." The majority of probationers report at the office on Saturday morning to make their monthly report. Even if their probation officer is working that day, the best they can do is to hand in their completed form and get a new blank form, which they must return the following month. The chronological recordings in the supervision cases reviewed reflected only the date that this form was submitted and its contents. If information of any greater depth and import was secured from probationers who were fortunate enough to have true contacts with their officers, it was not reflected in the chronological summaries.
>
> In fiscal year 1965 there were 1,148 persons placed on probation. During the same period only 633 visits were made to

62. Keve, *Imaginative Programming in Probation and Parole* 3–4 (1967).

probationers' homes. This is an average of less than one-half visit per case per year.[63]

A variant of the reporting process, particularly useful with heavy workloads, is group counseling. Several probationers meet periodically in the evening to discuss common problems with a supervisor. Groups may be formed according to specialized needs, concentrating on such problems as family relationships, employment and alcoholism. While this technique affords a probation department the opportunity to supervise more clients for longer periods of time at the same time as it affords the participants the benefits flowing from open analysis of shared problems, group counseling is used infrequently. Only one office of the 175 federal offices responding to a recent survey indicated that it regularly held group counseling sessions. No corresponding figures are available for state probation offices.

In Santa Clara County, California, over sixty juvenile probationers meet twice weekly in nine "encounter groups" conducted by other trained, paid probationers. Official probation workers do not participate in the groups, but they do serve as consultants to the young leaders. According to the program supervisor, "attendance and enthusiasm for this program has been astounding. Youth in [other] treatment programs who were classified as being too hostile and unamenable for treatment verbally expressed their anxiousness to participate in the sessions, and parents have remarked about the positive attitude change of their children— intrafamily communication has increased appreciably. A noticeable concern of youths for their peers rather than only self-concern is becoming more prevalent, and this concern for one another appears to be promoting a decrease in difficulties in the community."[64]

Obviously, the better a probation officer knows the neighborhood in which a probationer lives, the more effective he can be. However, most probation offices are now located in courthouses far from the areas of caseload density. Relocation of offices into neighborhood headquarters would allow staff members to become better acquainted with community resources, to divert offenders requiring minimal supervision to non-correctional channels and to interact regularly with offenders needing organized correctional programs. Neighborhood probation

63. *Report of the President's Commission on Crime in the District of Columbia* 404 (1966).
64. James, "The Student Aide Program: The Correctional Consumer as Rehabilitator," in *Second Progress Report of the Special Supervision Unit of the County of Santa Clara Juvenile Probation Department* (1968).

services could well be housed with other community agencies, closer to the services which these agencies provide. In Baltimore, where the probation and parole departments were recently moved into community centers, workers have discovered that they can provide their clients with a fuller range of services in less time than before.

The New York committee studying the treatment of offenders recommended that probation and parole supervision be handled by treatment teams composed of therapists, vocational counselors, indigenous neighborhood workers and investigators (for surveillance). "To have the caseworker —even the worker with an M.S.W.—as the vortex of treatment planning is to entrust the function of detecting symptoms of psychosis, neurosis and brain damage, of evaluating vocational and educational deficits, of determining levels of maturity and of inadequacy, and of evaluating degree of identification with delinquent subcultures, etc., in the hand of one individual."[65] Under the proposed system, a treatment plan for each offender placed on probation would be formulated by regional panels of correctional authorities, approved by a state board of corrections and implemented by the treatment teams, which would work out of regional centers.

Adequate probation services frequently require that the officer provide probationers with more than surveillance and counseling. Offenders may be more in need of practical help, sometimes on nearly a daily basis. Finding a probationer a job, getting him readmitted to school, helping him find a place to live or establish his eligibility for welfare or medical care may in some cases be the most valuable service an officer can perform.

Another view is that the provision by correctional agencies of services, such as education, job placement, psychotherapy and even police work, which could be purchased in the community gives existing community services an excuse to slough off serving offenders and denies the versatility and variety of assistance given by the community to others who have problems to the group which needs the assistance the most. Consequently, a recent design of a "Model Community Correctional Program" was conceived of as a "service delivery system," based on the concept that "the correctional system should not provide or duplicate services that are available within the community."[66]

65. *Preliminary Report of the New York Governor's Special Committee on Criminal Offenders* 247–49 (1968).
66. Institute for the Study of Crime and Delinquency, Model Community Correctional Program, Report II: *Community Organization for Correctional Services* 73 (1969) (original in italics).

Non-correctional social agencies generally have resisted work with probationers. Offenders do not seek help for their problems voluntarily. They often try to evade agency workers, keep them at a safe distance and conceal their thoughts so that the workers do not get to know them too well. In addition, social agencies may feel uncomfortable working within a court setting, believing that courts lack understanding of the behavioral sciences and do not have a proper appreciation of their work.

Federal probation officers generally make frequent use of public employment agencies and, although not so frequent, some use of alcoholic-treatment agencies. Occasional use is made of family counseling services and of psychiatric clinics. Private employment agencies are used infrequently. The agencies used by one probation department studied recently were restricted to the public psychiatric clinic and employment service; no use was made of private agencies. In some California counties judges have sentenced offenders to state prison so that they may receive the psychiatric or psychological counseling that is unavailable to probationers.

A modest former director of a large probation department has noted that "The probation or parole officer may be doing his best work when he gets someone else to do his work for him."[67] The juvenile-court probation department in Seattle, Washington, at one time had one staff person assigned full time to escort clients personally to other agencies and help them get started there. It is crucial that probation officers enlist the aid of the full range of community services—medical, legal, educational, vocational and domestic—in aiding probationers.

David Fogel, a former probation officer and now Commissioner of Corrections for Minnesota, once said to us: "You know, when John Augustus started probation he really had a great idea; we ought to try it some time."

In the course of our visits to European countries, even those most enlightened in their approach to correctional institutions, we were surprised to find that many have no probation services at all; a judge has only the alternatives of imprisonment or a suspended sentence with no supervision. In other countries probation is a recent innovation, heavily dependent on the example set by American practices.

Yet in the United States probation frequently amounts to little more than counting heads. Augustus' use of probation to "advise, assist and

67. Keve, *Imaginative Programming in Probation and Parole* 7 (1967).

befriend" has been lost in a vast bureaucratic sea of checklists and reports. We have devoted neither the resources nor the imagination that are necessary to make the institution work.

A revitalized probation system could be the means of using both public services and private organizations to help reconcile the offender and his community. With greatly reduced caseloads, there could be almost a one-to-one relationship between probation officer and client where necessary. (For every two or three offenders kept out of prison a state could afford to hire an additional probation worker.) This relationship could be supplemented by a full range of community programs. (Of course, in many cases probationers need no special treatment and are best off when left alone. Forcing treatment on those who do not need or want it can be as self-defeating as failing to help those who do.)

In some areas special programs have been developed for probationers, primarily juveniles, that center on particular tasks or activities. Some of these programs, such as summer or weekend camps, are partially residential. In others juveniles on probation spend their after-school hours in community centers engaged in a mixture of educational, recreational, creative and physical activities. These programs generally are more expensive to operate than the standard probation caseloads. (According to Paul Keve, a juvenile program currently being tried in Minnesota, using caseloads of twelve to fifteen and a storefront community center, costs three times the amount of regular probation but only one half the cost of an institution.) There has been little systematic research to evaluate these special programs. But administrators are convinced that they are worthwhile, not only because of the social, educational or cultural experience involved but because juvenile probationers are given an opportunity to develop meaningful relationships with adults who care about them.

An unplanned but potentially exciting by-product of the group programs, particularly of those that involve neighborhood activities, is the participation of parents and friends of the probationers. As one example, the Los Angeles County Probation Department has instituted a special Family Treatment Program in which the entire families of delinquent children meet with probation officers—and with other families in a similar situation—over a six-week period. One experienced observer has expressed the hope that this participation by "unlabeled" clients represents a trend that will eventually cause probation workers to focus their efforts on community rehabilitation work, as well as on individuals found delinquent.

Other experimental programs aim at high-risk probationers or those who already have failed on probation. New York's Division for Youth, which operates small, intensive but open programs, primarily in urban areas, for fifteen- to eighteen-year-olds, accepts 75 percent of its people as a condition of their probation. (Most of the remaining 25 percent are referred to the program by social agencies and commit themselves voluntarily.) Of the probationers, some are recommended to the program by the sentencing judge, but most are assigned after they have violated other conditions of probation.

In addition to the intensive group counseling and individual help offered, one striking difference between the New York program and traditional probation is the division's readiness to allow a youth to stay in the program if he breaks a rule or even if he commits a new crime. These youths are expected to get into trouble, and the idea of the program, wherever possible, is to keep them in open facilities in the community where they will have a real choice of behavior and to work with them until they are able to make the proper choice.

"Halfway Probation" programs, in which selected adult felony offenders are sentenced directly to an open residential center where they will live while working or attending school in the community, represent a sensible compromise between probation and imprisonment. The idea is being used in the Probationed Offenders Rehabilitation and Training Program in Olmsted County, Minnesota, and in the "work release centers" operated by the Department of Correction in the District of Columbia.

Even the most exotic probation programs are less expensive than imprisonment. Consequently, the Justice Department's Law Enforcement Assistance Administration has announced that it will concentrate its resources on them over the next several years as the most cost-effective way to invest in correctional programs. According to Associate LEAA Administrator Richard W. Velde, in a speech to the American Correctional Association, "If the personnel that probation ought to have were made available, and the necessary supplementary resources, probation ought to cost perhaps $1,000 a client, or possibly more. This would still be much cheaper than an institutional disposition, and considering the potential resources of the typical community, the opportunities for effecting the rehabilitation of the client would be much enhanced."

V

Parole—Moving Back to Society

Parole is the practice of conditionally releasing adult prisoners after they have served part of their sentence in an institution. It was first used as a military practice, whereby armies freed captured soldiers on condition that they stay out of combat. Parole as it is now known had no place in a system that used imprisonment primarily for detaining defendants before trial; but when confinement became the principal means of punishment, parole evolved as a method of early release from prison.

Our modern system of parole has evolved from several previous measures, including the use of conditional pardons, indentures and tickets of leave for criminals who were transported from England to the British colonies. In order to meet the demand for labor in the American colonies, the English government used a 1597 law that authorized the banishment "beyond the seas" of "rogues." In 1617 the Privy Council passed an order granting reprieves and stays of execution to persons convicted of robbery and strong enough to be employed in the colonies. From lists of felons recommended by the courts, the king selected those to be pardoned and shipped to Virginia at the government's expense.

Once in Virginia, the offenders were auctioned to the highest bidders as indentured servants. This practice later caused Jeremy Bentham to remark that under the transportation system bondage was added to banishment.

The system of indenture, which originally had no connection with prisoners, required each apprentice to sign an agreement with his new master. Some of the rules of conduct imposed on all apprentices, although unrelated to the fact that some of them were former prisoners, have persisted as conditions of parole. At first, the British government exercised no control over prisoners once they had been pardoned and indentured. However, since many evaded transportation or returned to England, the pardons were amended shortly after the middle of the seventeenth century to include specific conditions, such as a ban on returning to England and provision for revocation of the pardon on violation of the conditions.

The American Revolution ended the transportation of criminals by the English government to its American colonies. But English judges continued to impose sentences of transportation to other countries such as Australia to relieve the overcrowding of detention facilities. Unlike the pardoned offenders who became indentured servants in the American colonies, those who were shipped to Australia remained prisoners under governmental supervision. The prisoners worked either for the government or for settlers. This led to another variation of what were to be the precursors of modern parole—the ticket of leave.

In 1790 a special British enabling act gave governors of the penal settlements power to discharge and grant land to prisoners who had shown good conduct and work records. The governors developed a form of conditional pardon known as the "ticket of leave," which freed a prisoner from governmental supervision during good behavior as long as he supported himself in a lawful occupation in a specific district.

Gradually the governors adopted a policy requiring prisoners to serve certain portions of their sentences before being granted tickets of leave. In 1821 a formal scale, the forerunner of current sentencing requirements, was established: Prisoners serving seven-year terms were eligible for tickets of leave after four years, those with fourteen-year terms after six and those with life sentences after eight.

But these comparable historic devices are not the clearest sources of our present parole system. Captain Alexander Maconochie, governor of the penal colony of Norfolk Island off Australia from 1840 to 1844, has been called the "father" of parole. Although he did not originate the ticket-of-leave system, he incorporated it into a new prison regime. Maconochie voiced the criticisms of definite prison terms that eventually would lead to the imposition of various types of indeterminate sentences:

> I think that time sentences are the root of very nearly all the demoralization which exists in prisons. A man under a time sentence thinks only how he is to cheat that time, and while it

away; he evades labour, because he has no desire to please the officers under whom he is placed, because they cannot serve him essentially; they cannot in any way promote his liberation.[1]

Maconochie devised a system of rewards that many behavioral psychologists of today would applaud. This system allowed prisoners to shorten the terms that had to be served before a ticket of leave would be granted. A certain number of marks was charged against each prisoner according to the term for which he had been sentenced. Through good conduct and satisfactory work, a prisoner earned marks with which he could shorten his term of confinement. If he preferred, he could use some of the marks to buy extra food and supplies. Misbehavior was punished by the forfeiting of marks.

In order to prepare prisoners gradually for release, Maconochie set up a graded system through which prisoners moved according to the number of marks they had accumulated. The stages of custody included strict imprisonment, followed by work on chain gangs, then a period of freedom within a narrow geographical area and finally a ticket of leave that enabled the prisoner greater freedom of movement until he attained a complete discharge.

Maconochie's ideas were considered too lenient by Australian colonists, who protested the use of their land as a "dumping ground for criminals." He was replaced as governor and returned to England—a fate often reserved for reform-minded prison officials. The colonists' opposition finally forced an ending of the transportation of criminals to Australia in 1867.

Prison administrators have come to accept Maconochie's theories. His idea of giving wages for convict labor and charging special privileges and supplies against those wages is still considered a promising innovation. His system of progressive moves from strict custody to freedom is the forerunner of the behaviorist "graded tier" system, which is in use at the Patuxent Institution in Maryland, and of less structured systems at a few small, innovative institutions for juveniles and youthful offenders.

The English built on the Australian experience with conditional release of prisoners on tickets of leave. The English Penal Servitude Act of 1853 allowed tickets of leave for prisoners who had served specified portions of their sentences. The tickets could be revoked at any time:

1. Quoted by Sheldon G. Glueck in his Foreword to Barry, *Alexander Maconochie of Norfolk Island* (1958).

[If the holder] associates with notoriously bad characters, leads an idle or dissolute life, or has no visible means of obtaining an honest livelihood, etc., it will be assumed that he is about to relapse into crime, and he will be at once apprehended and recommitted to prison under the original sentence.

However, there was no attempt to provide for supervision of offenders released on tickets of leave in order to determine whether they were abiding by the conditions of release.

Although the ticket-of-leave system gained acceptance in England, Maconochie's idea of requiring prisoners to earn their early release was not implemented. An English prison reformer writing in 1864 noted that prison administrators failed to use the prospect of early release as an incentive to rehabilitation:

We cannot find that the release of the convict is ever deferred beyond the earliest date on which it can be granted except in the case of positively bad conduct and then . . . only for short periods. This is . . . an entire abandonment of . . . the looking to hope as the principal means of exercising influence on the number of convicts. The remission of sentence ceases to be an object of hope as soon as it comes to be regarded as a matter of certainty and of right and offers no motive for industry and active exertion to do well when it is to be obtained by mere passive abstinence from gross breach of prison rules.[2]

A series of prison riots in 1862, together with public complaints about the incidence of serious crime, led to the appointment of a Royal Commission to study the condition of the prisons and abuses in the ticket-of-leave system. The commission's report criticized the lack of preparation of prisoners for release and the total lack of supervision once they were freed. As a result of the report, the police were given responsibility for checking on ticket-of-leave men. The system was abrasive, since offenders claimed that the police were their enemies, who harassed them and informed their employers of their criminal status.

Supervision of released prisoners by the police had proved successful in Ireland, where Sir William Crofton had built on Maconochie's idea that a prisoner's experience in prison and on ticket of leave was part of

2. Mary Carpenter, *Our Convicts* 165–66 (1864).

the same program. Under Crofton's system each prisoner spent about nine months in solitary confinement, eating a reduced diet and working at monotonous tasks. Then his privileges were increased, he was moved to different quarters and he began to earn marks for good conduct and achievement in industry and education. In the third stage, prisoners lived in small groups where they worked with very little supervision.

After provisions had been made for employment and police supervision, prisoners were discharged on tickets of leave. The conditions of release were stated broadly. In addition to the requirement that he obey all laws, a releasee could not "habitually associate with notoriously bad characters, such as reported thieves and prostitutes," or "lead an idle or dissolute life, without means of obtaining an honest livelihood." Releasees in rural areas were required to report monthly to the police. Those who lived in Dublin reported to a special civilian inspector who helped releasees find jobs, visited their homes every two weeks, verified their employment and cooperated with the police when there was suspicion of improper activities.

In both England and Ireland after 1864, private citizens interested in furnishing released prisoners with material and moral support came to recognize that the prisoners would not go to their police supervisors. Thus supervision of releasees by the police was replaced gradually by supervision by full-time paid agents of Prisoners' Aid Societies. The societies, established in the nineteenth century by citizens who were interested in aiding offenders recently released from prison, were financed by private contributions, matched by government funds. Their agents had the duties of visiting local prisoners on a weekly basis; visiting local employers of labor in order to secure their cooperation; visiting the prisoner at jail and, when necessary, providing board and lodging; visiting both the unemployed and the employed on a regular and constant basis.

The "Irish System" developed greater public acceptance than its English counterpart. Four conditions contributed to the program's success: It was a prison system that aimed at reforming criminals; it provided a period of transition for prisoners between confinement and conditional freedom; there was strict supervision during the ticket-of-leave period; and a community attitude developed receptive to the assimilation of offenders (perhaps due to the efforts of the Prisoners' Aid Societies). Crofton's successes were widely publicized in the United States, where critics of American prison programs came to view his program as a model for reform.

Conditional pardon and reduction of sentences for "good time" became part of American penal practice in the nineteenth century and preceded the adoption of parole in the United States. Governors in many states were considered to have the power to pardon offenders they deemed worthy. In some states the constitution or legislation provided that the governor might attach conditions to a pardon.[3] Before the establishment of parole, conditional pardons were the only form of conditional early release from prison.

Commutation laws ("good-time laws") were designed to aid prison discipline by providing an incentive for good behavior. These laws, passed by New York in 1817 and by forty-four states before the turn of the century, allowed early release to inmates who behaved well in prison. Those offenders whose terms were shortened simply were released early with no conditions or supervision. Commutation statutes were applied (and still are) perfunctorily, so that earning good time became automatic. Thus discipline was exercised by withholding good-time credit for gross misconduct instead of by using early release as a reward.

Although parole is now possible where prisoners are serving fixed terms, its early development was associated with the use of indeterminate sentences. The idea of nineteenth-century reformers was that no prisoner would be paroled until he had been changed so thoroughly that he might safely be permitted to resume his place in society.

New York enacted an indeterminate sentencing statute for juveniles in 1824. The first application of indeterminate sentencing to adults coincided with the first American use of parole. Both systems were instituted at the New York State Reformatory at Elmira in 1876.

The law governing the reformatory, drafted by its first superintendent, Zebulon Brockway, provided for the following features: indeterminate sentences (not to exceed the statutory penalty for the crime involved); a marking system patterned on the Irish experience that allowed prisoners to earn increased privileges and early release; and early release on parole for offenders who maintained good conduct for at least one year and could show a suitable plan for employment. Paroled offenders were not prepared for release by an intermediate period of reduced supervision. Nor were they supervised after release by agents of the state. Because the American proponents of a parole system disliked the idea of police surveillance of any individual, they replaced the Irish use of police supervision with a requirement that releasees report

3. *E.g.*, Rhode Island Constitutional Amendments Art. II (1854).

monthly to "guardians" of their own choosing. This token supervision continued for only six months; it was believed that a longer period would discourage the parolee.

Once the Elmira system had been established, parole legislation spread more rapidly through the United States than indeterminate sentences. Some system of parole existed in twenty states by 1900 and in forty-four states, the federal system and Hawaii by 1922. At first used primarily for young and first offenders, who were released with little supervision, eligibility for parole was gradually enlarged and supervision by professional agents was added. Today, every state and the federal system uses parole as one form of release.

All methods of parole currently existing in the United States include the following features: some administrative discretion concerning the time of release from prison; the imposition of conditions on the release; some supervision during the period of parole; and the power of an administrative agency to revoke parole and return the offender to an institution. None of the states' systems has included an adequate effort to prepare prisoners for release while they are incarcerated or to help them to adjust to freedom while they are on parole.

Only a small portion of all convicted offenders is ever placed on parole. Misdemeanants sentenced to jail rarely are released on parole. Well over 90 percent are simply released when their sentences expire.[4] Figures on felons released from prisons, collected by the 1967 Crime Commission, indicate that the inmates placed on parole in different jurisdictions vary from 9 percent of all state-prison releases in one state (South Carolina) to 98 percent in two others (New Hampshire and Washington). In the United States as a whole, slightly more than 60 percent of adult felons are released on parole. The extent to which parole, or after-care, is used for juveniles remains unclear.

The last Crime Commission found no relation between the proportion of prisoners released on parole in a state and the average institutional time served for felonies in that state. In 1960, the five states where prisoners served the longest sentences were Hawaii, Pennsylvania, Illinois, New York and Indiana. The percentages released by parole in those states in the same year were, respectively, 99, 89, 47, 87, and 88. The states with the shortest sentences were New Hampshire, Maine, South

4. Information from a sample of 212 local jails showed that 62 percent had no procedure for parole. In the others, only 8 percent of the inmates were released on parole. The President's Commission on Law Enforcement and the Administration of Justice, Task Force Report: *Correction* 60 (1967).

Dakota, Montana and Vermont. In these states, 98, 92, 49, 90 and 5 percent of adult felons were released through parole.[5]

Whether through parole or through expiration of sentence, more than 90 percent of all prisoners eventually are released. As political winds change, a short-sighted way to reassure the public about its security is to decrease the number of paroles granted. The question of whether to release prisoners by means of parole is in reality a question of whether to release them with or without supervision and assistance. Because the granting of parole has been considered a reward, those prisoners who are considered the worst prospects for rehabilitation are released with the least assistance and the least supervision. The idea behind parole is to release convicts from imprisonment with some help in readjusting to the free community and refraining from further crime.

The Paroling Authority

In several states the decision on whether to parole offenders originally was made by the governor. In 1939, the Attorney General's Survey of Release Procedures indicated that in sixteen states the governor remained the only paroling authority. Other states established administrative boards to make decisions related to parole. All states now have a parole authority separate from the governor, although in four states the parole board's power is limited to recommending dispositions to the governor. In the others, the board's disposition is final.

The composition of parole boards follows similar basic lines. In twenty-five states, members devote only part of their time to their parole-board duties; in the other half the job is full time. In four states parole-board membership is automatically given to people who hold certain public offices: in most other states boards are composed of political appointees. In Michigan, Wisconsin, Maine, California, Florida and New Jersey candidates to be considered for appointment must possess certain qualifications, such as a college degree or some experience in the correction field. The governors of thirty-nine states appoint parole-board members; in the other states members are appointed by other state officials or are automatically members because of their positions. In forty-four states the members serve terms of six years or less.[6]

5. The President's Commission on Law Enforcement and the Administration of Justice, Task Force Report: *Correction* 62 (1967).
6. *Ibid.*, 65–67.

Most critics agree on certain reforms: every jurisdiction should have a full-time releasing authority and political appointments should be eliminated. The District of Columbia Crime Commission concluded in 1966, "Measuring human behavior is a most complicated, inexact science, and it seems incongruous that in dealing with such an involved, complicated problem, the Government of our Nation's Capital [sic] would be satisfied with the services of people on a part-time basis."

A few states have established some qualifications for members of parole boards. One state requires candidates to pass an examination in penology and criminal law. The President's Crime Commission suggested that appointments be made from lists of candidates submitted by qualified groups, such as legal or correctional associations.

A more controversial and perhaps less easily resolved question than the appointment and tenure of parole-board members is the place of the paroling authority within a correction system. This question involves the issue of how to assure coordination while preserving the principle of separation of powers of different branches of government. At present, the dominant organizational pattern in the area of adult parole is to place the power to release inmates with an autonomous parole board. In the juvenile field, on the other hand, most releasing decisions are made directly by staff members from the institutions.

There are several rationales for independent parole boards. Removing releasing decisions from institutional control reduces—although it does not eliminate—the danger that these decisions will give undue weight to institutional adjustment or infraction of petty rules. The existence of independent parole boards is supposed to prevent staff members from releasing troublesome inmates because of threats of retaliation or a desire to get them out of the institution or, conversely, from forcing them to serve long sentences as punishment for their independence. Some authorities also have referred to the danger that institutional administrators will use the releasing power for irrelevant goals such as controlling the size of the prison population. Since parole authorities are not responsible for running prison institutions, they are not receptive to pressures of overcrowding and operating costs.

On the negative side, the existence of autonomous parole boards may lead to conflicts between correction authorities and people with different orientations and allegiances. Parole boards respond to public pressures. Whenever there is an outcry over rising crime waves, the boards are criticized for releasing prisoners on parole. Board members come to recognize that they can avoid criticism by keeping offenders in prison as long as possible.

Members of one parole board, when questioned about their restraint in granting prisoners paroles, responded that they felt they had to be extremely careful in releasing prisoners. "If they become involved in further violations of law, their misconduct would be prominently reported by news media, with the result that the Board of Parole would continually be on the defensive and, in fact, could be abolished if the number of rearrests of parolees proved to be too high."[7] The logical extension of this point of view may well be, as John Conrad, a correctional expert, recently remarked, that "the parole board can assure zero recidivism of parolees by paroling no one." However, Conrad goes on to emphasize that, although "we can speculate on how many crimes the public is spared by longer retention of all offenders in custody," the reality is that "nearly all prisoners must some day be released. Protracting all terms will only defer the return to criminality; there is no reason at all to believe that such a policy will prevent it."[8]

Fragmentation of decision-making may mean that institutional staffs and parole boards are working at cross-purposes. Board members may have little concern with prison programs or with staff members' recommendations concerning the optimal time for release. Partial-release programs further complicate the situation. An inmate may be allowed to go into the community on work-release or weekend furlough without incident. Nonetheless, the parole board may decide not to parole him, basing its decision on the ground that the "community" would not accept his release. Some correction departments have attempted to work with parole boards by placing prisoners on work release, sometimes even housing them in community correctional centers, approximately six months prior to the date of minimum parole eligibility, with the understanding that a good record on work release will increase a prisoner's chances for parole.

Members of the federal Parole Board report that most of the board's refusals to follow the recommendations of staff at the institutions are due to the uncorroborable, subjective judgments of board members that these prisoners cannot safely be returned to the community.[9] Many prisoners

7. American Correctional Association, *The Organization and Effectiveness of the Correctional Agencies* 720 (1966).
8. Conrad, "Decisions and Discretion—A Critique of the Indeterminate Sentence" 11–12 (unpublished, 1970).
9. Memorandum for the National Commission on Reform of Federal Criminal Laws re: Suggested Modifications of the Paroling Authority 8 (Feb. 7, 1969).

have told us that they would prefer to have the releasing decision made by institutional personnel who know them personally rather than by outside parole boards. "All they have is paper."

Obviously, the willingness of the community into which a man is released to receive an offender can have a profound effect upon his success on parole. But by giving vent to general community prejudices, rather than attempting to substantiate or modify those prejudices and prepare offenders to cope with them, parole boards serve neither the offenders nor the community.

Coordination between institutional staffs and releasing authorities may be achieved best by making the releasing authorities part of centralized correctional agencies. In Wisconsin, Michigan and Ohio the parole board is part of the department of correction, with members appointed by that department. In Illinois, Massachusetts, Ohio, California and Minnesota, youth authorities with control over the entire correctional system also control release from institutions. In California, for example, the director of the Youth Authority is both the administrator of the department, with responsibility for institutional, parole and prevention programs, and chairman of the Youth Authority Board, which makes the decision to assign wards to institutions and put them on parole. A legislative committee has recommended that the California Adult Authority adopt the same system.

In adult departments as well, a compromise between autonomous and departmental parole boards has been attempted in Alaska, Tennessee and Maine by having the director of correction serve as chairman of the parole board, composed of members appointed by the governor. However, since the director has so many other responsibilities in these situations, the President's Crime Commission considered it preferable that he appoint someone else to serve as parole-board chairman. This is done in Minnesota.

It seems reasonable for the agency most closely responsible for the success of correctional programs to control the transfer of offenders from the status of institutionalization to conditional release to full freedom. Still, participation of qualified citizens from outside the agency adds perspective to correctional decisions and sometimes prompts officials to question their assumptions. One way to assure both these features is to include some community representation, including representation by ex-offenders who have experienced the system from a different vantage point, in parole decision-making. Another is to make the agency with over-all responsibility for correction a reviewing board with the power to consider appeals from decisions of an independent parole board.

A third possibility is to delegate to professional parole staff members the function of making actual decisions, according to policy guidelines established by parole-board members. The parole board would be responsible for setting standards and reviewing decisions that are appealed. In most places, these functions could be performed by a part-time board, which might be able to attract the services of prestigious, talented and committed members of the community who cannot serve on a full-time board.

A different type of release procedure is used by the Patuxent Institution in Maryland. The statute providing for indeterminate sentences for offenders found to be "defective delinquents" established an "institutional Board of Review" to act as the releasing authority. The board is composed of four psychiatrists from the institution (a majority of the board's membership), one professor of constitutional law from the state university, one attorney and one professor of sociology from a nearby college or university.

The board is required to review at least once each year the status of each person confined as a defective delinquent. (Patuxent inmates have the right to petition the sentencing court for outright release once every three years.) The board may authorize him to leave the institution daily on work release, on weekends or holidays or on parole, attaching any conditions it deems wise. Thus, continuing decisions concerning partial-release programs, parole and unconditional release are the responsibility of the same authority. If the board concludes that a person is ready to be released unconditionally, it must report to the court which initially committed him. The court may approve outright release, conditional release, or it may order the return of the inmate to a conventional prison for the unexpired portion of his original sentence.

In a correction system which includes several distinct institutions, the use of institutional boards of review modeled on Patuxent's might cause a lack of consistency in the releasing policies of different institutions. However, provision for appeals from the boards to a court or to a non-judicial reviewing authority might produce some generally applicable standards.

One report suggested that local panels of correctional authorities recommend dispositions for the consideration of a central board, which would make the final decisions. In addition to deciding when to change offenders from institutional custody to field supervision, the panels and the board would have the responsibility for inmates' assignments to institutional programs or other treatment techniques. On release, the panels would recommend plans for field supervision. Under this plan, the correctional process is viewed as a continuum, with one agency controlling all of an offender's treatment, whether he is on probation, in an institution or on parole. Despite the plan's stress on local panels, it provides for inmates who are incarcerated for long periods of time to be interviewed periodically by personnel from outside the institution. In such cases representatives of the central board would visit the institutions, conduct personal interviews and report back to the central board.[10]

A New Jersey legislative committee appointed to survey the state's criminal justice system made a similar, though less detailed, recommendation that convicted offenders be handled in a continuum by a single department:

> We recommend a major reform in the system: All convicted offenders, adult, juvenile, male, female, long-term, short-term, should be held or supervised under the custody of the Commissioner of Criminal Justice. With great administrative flexibility he could develop a wide range of different facilities to meet individual needs of programs best for the offender and they could be moved between them as desirable.[11]

Actually, this system already exists to some extent in the states using the youth authority model for juvenile and youthful offenders. In California, for example, a Youth Authority Board, consisting of eight members appointed by the governor and a chairman who is also the director of the Youth Authority, is responsible for assigning wards to institutional and parole programs (probation is a county rather than a state function), directing transfers and furloughs, granting and revoking parole and reassigning wards to new programs and recommending new commitments or unconditional release to the committing court. In addition, the board exercises a general policy-making function over Youth Authority programs.

The Youth Authority Board hears cases in two-member panels, which may include hearing examiners as well as board members. Difficult decisions sometimes are referred to regional, three-member panels or to the

10. *Preliminary Report of the New York Governor's Special Committee on Criminal Offenders* 227 (1968).
11. *Report of Joint Legislative Committee to Study Crime and the System of Criminal Justice in New Jersey* 15–16 (1968).

full board. All decisions concerning wards who have committed certain specified offenses, generally those that involve violence, are made by the full board or regional panels.

One difference between this organizational pattern and that of Patuxent, discussed above, is that other than the chairman, professional staff members are not a part of the Youth Authority Board. All board members are supposed to represent the broad and changing spectrum of community sentiment toward offenders. Consequently, there is a dichotomy between the board's emphasis on community reaction toward certain offenses and the concern of professional staff members (for example, social workers in Youth Authority institutions) with the needs of a particular ward.

Where a serious offense is involved, the board may refuse to follow a staff recommendation that a ward be released on parole despite its agreement that the ward has nothing further to gain from an institutional program. With some offenses, this policy is formalized, and a ward is given a year's "continuance" at his initial hearing before the board. This means that, regardless of staff recommendations, the board usually will decline to review the case until after a year. In effect, it is equivalent to the minimum period of parole eligibility for adults. Continuances (known as "set-offs") also are used by paroling authorities dealing with youths sentenced under the Federal Youth Correction Act. A continuance limits the number of programs to which a ward can be assigned and often frustrates the purpose of various innovations. For example, where a behavioral modification approach to institutional programming provides that when inmates earn a specified number of points through good conduct and school or other work they will be referred to the board of parole for release, the existence of a continuance prevents the inmate subject to it from earning this reward.

In the federal system, the United States Board of Parole currently consists of eight members appointed by the President and ratified by the Senate. Members serve overlapping six-year terms.[12] Until 1948, members were appointed by the Attorney General. In that year, Congressional hearings disclosed that Parole Board members and the Attorney General himself had submitted to pressures to release former members of the "Capone gang" after they had served minimum sentences.

The Board of Parole is now considered independent of the Justice Department and the Bureau of Prisons, although it remains part of the Justice Department. A recent consultant's report to the Administrative Conference

12. See 18 U.S.C. §4201; 18 U.S.C. §5005.

of the United States recommended that the Parole Board be removed from the Justice Department, the number of members from any one party be limited, and the terms of members be lengthened in an effort to avoid political influence. These changes are incorporated in a bill now pending in Congress.[13]

The board is divided into adult and youth divisions. Individual members regularly travel to all the federal prisons to interview prisoners. However, hearing examiners are used to conduct approximately two-thirds of the interviews. The board currently conducts approximately 12,000 interviews each year. The traveling board member or examiner recommends a disposition to a two-member panel of the board, which makes the final decision. In selected cases, the entire board votes on whether an inmate should be paroled. A poll taken in the early 1960s revealed that in 90 percent of the cases the hearing member's recommendation to grant or deny parole was followed by a majority of the Parole Board.

The federal Parole Board also is responsible for the supervision of people on parole. Actually, the field supervision is performed by federal probation officers. Probation officers are appointed by district judges and perform their probation functions under the judge's direction. However, when they function as parole officers, they report to the Parole Board. This dual system of administrative responsibility is peculiar to the federal system.[14]

The American Correctional Association recommends that parole boards should not have administrative responsibilities for parole and probation services. "A full-time Board, divorced from the responsibility of administering its own parole staff, can devote its entire energies to the making of sound decisions."[15]

A staff proposal to the National Commission on Reform of Federal Criminal Laws (not adopted by the commission) suggested two major changes in the administration of parole. First, it recommended that the Bureau of Prisons retain responsibility over an offender through the period of parole. The proposal recognized the desirability of integrating closely related correctional functions. The Bureau of Prisons already is responsible for preparing the inmate for parole and for making decisions in connection with partial-release programs, such as work release.

13. Johnson, Federal Parole Procedures 50–53 (1971). H.R. 13118 §4201 (92d Cong., 2d Sess., 1972).
14. See U.S.C. §3655.
15. American Correctional Association, *The Organization and Effectiveness of the Correctional Agencies* 717 (1966).

No particular reason, save the inertia of the present system, can be seen for separating these two closely related functions. It is those who have worked with the prisoner in the Bureau who should be in the best position to estimate his chances of success on parole and to plan from the earlier stages a continuous program which leads up to his complete discharge from supervision.[16]

Second, since the Bureau of Prisons would then make the initial decision on whether to parole an inmate, the present Board of Parole would become an appellate tribunal, with the power to review the denial or the revocation of parole by the bureau. This structure would retain an element of separation between the custodial and the releasing functions. In addition, it would provide an appellate process which, in the opinion of the author of the proposal, would make the present insulation of parole decisions from review by the courts more palatable.

A former chairman of the United States Board of Parole, Walter Dunbar, has suggested that the board should consist of the director of a proposed United States Correction Service and two to four other members, all appointed by the President. An expanded staff of hearing examiners assigned to geographical regions should grant and revoke paroles according to criteria set by the board and subject to review by the board. The board would set the general policies governing supervision of parolees, but the parole supervision staff in the field would report to the director of the correctional service.

Although Dunbar's proposals did not represent a radical departure from the existing parole structure, they were opposed vehemently by six of the Parole Board's eight members. The opposing members feared concentration of too much power in a director of correction. In addition, they predicted that the pressures of his other duties would prevent him from fulfilling his responsibilities as a member of the paroling authority.

The members objected to reducing the size of the board. They preferred a ten-member board, with one member assigned to coordinate releasing functions and field supervision in each of the federal judicial circuits. They also objected to placing all initial decisions in the hands of hearing officers, who would apply the criteria set by the board. "Any application of such rigid criteria would result in a stereotype approach, culminating in almost a complete exclusion of independent judgment in

16. Low, "Comment on the Sentencing System: Part C," in Working Papers of the National Commission on Reform of Federal Criminal Laws 1289, 1298 (1970).

decision-making." (Since the board does not seem to have developed any standard criteria for granting or denying parole, this reluctance to delegate may be understandable.) The board members did think that funds to enable them to make greater use of more hearing examiners at their discretion would be helpful. Finally, with additional funds for parole supervision, the board members felt "that the Federal Board is perfectly capable of administering, as well as supervising, its own parole field services."[17]

George J. Reed, who replaced Dunbar as chairman of the board, immediately announced that the Board of Parole would become an appellate body, to review the initial recommendations of parole hearing examiners. All hearings would be conducted by the examiners, who would be directed to provide the Parole Board with verbatim transcripts of the hearings, as well as with written reports of their reasons for granting or denying parole. This procedure would mark a change from the present system, under which the board frequently grants parole after conferring by telephone with the board member or hearing examiner who conducted the hearing. As yet, this change has not been implemented.

This basic pattern, with hearing examiners or panels to travel to institutions and make the initial decisions relating to parole and a central board to establish criteria and hear appeals (and perhaps also to hear cases of unusual public concern), has been gaining influential support. Its adoption is recommended in a report to the Joint Commission on Correctional Manpower and Training and by a committee of the California legislature, whose recent report concluded that "considering the number of offenders involved and the complexity of making wise decisions, Adult Authority members should devote their time to basic policy formulation and evaluation and the supervision of those doing the day-to-day parole decision-making. In this context, considerably greater attention must be paid to the skills and backgrounds of those appointed to the Authority."[18]

Louis B. Schwartz, executive director of the National Commission on Reform of Federal Criminal Laws, concluded a critique on the commission's work by remarking:

> We should move from the concept of "sentence to imprisonment" to a concept of "sentence to social control." In practice, this would mean that the prison authorities would have considerable

17. Memorandum for the National Commission on Reform of Federal Criminal Laws re: Suggested Modifications of the Paroling Authority 11 (February 7, 1969).
18. California Assembly, Report of the Select Committee on the Administration of Justice, *Parole Board Reform in California* 15 (1970).

discretion with regard to the amount of freedom to be allowed prisoners, varying from maximum security through intermediate degrees of freedom, limited home visits, and to the virtually complete but conditional freedom we know as parole. In such a scheme, the parole board would assume a purely appellate function, hearing appeals from prisoners dissatisfied with the correctional authority's refusal to grant "parole."

The Releasing Decision

The eligibility of an inmate for parole depends on two objective criteria: requirements set by statutes and the sentence imposed by the court or initially established by the paroling authority.

In most places statutes provide that prisoners with short sentences will not be considered for parole. For example, in federal jurisdictions, people sentenced for less than 180 days are not eligible for parole; in New York the minimum sentence for parole consideration is ninety days.

In some places eligible inmates must apply for consideration by the parole board. A survey in the District of Columbia, where consideration for parole was not automatic, revealed that only 50 to 60 percent of all eligible inmates (75 to 85 percent of the eligible felons) apply for parole. Those who did not apply for consideration supposedly knew of their right and had signed a statement foregoing it. Nevertheless, the District of Columbia Crime Commission recommended that a parole hearing automatically follow parole eligibility and that the hearing be used in appropriate cases to determine why certain inmates do not want to be paroled.[19]

In some states the legislature prohibits parole for certain offenses or, more often, requires that minimum sentences be served for certain crimes before parole can be considered. In three states even a juvenile must serve a fixed minimum term (as high as eighteen months in one state, twelve in another) before he can be paroled. The paroling authority thus cannot make allowances for unusual cases.

In the few states that use indeterminate sentencing, the paroling authority has greater latitude. In California, for example, an offender may be sentenced for a period of not less than six months nor more than fourteen years. Here, the parole authority has great flexibility to adjudicate a minimum or a very onerous sentence. Consequently, the lack of

19. *Report of the President's Commission on Crime in the District of Columbia* 441–42 (1966).

criteria governing sentences is as crucial to the parole board as to the sentencing judge.

The applicable federal statute provides that when a court imposes a sentence for more than one year, it may designate a minimum term at the end of which the prisoner shall become eligible for parole. The term may be less than but shall not be more than one-third of the maximum sentence imposed by the court. In the alternative, the court may fix only a maximum sentence. In that case the court may specify that the prisoner may become eligible for parole at such time as the board of parole may determine.[20]

Where the court imposes a minimum sentence, the parole board ordinarily conducts a hearing with the prisoner in the institution during or before the quarter in which the minimum term date occurs. Following the hearing the board decides to grant or deny parole. In the event the decision is to deny parole, the board sets the period after which it will hear the case again.

Where the court imposes a maximum sentence only and specifies that the board of parole may determine the parole eligibility date, the board conducts an "initial hearing" in the institution prior to determination of the parole eligibility date. The "initial hearing" usually is held within ninety days of the prisoner's incarceration. Except in highly unusual circumstances, the board will not parole a prisoner in the absence of at least one personal hearing.

Following the initial hearing the board takes one of three possible actions: (a) it may grant parole effective on a set date; (b) it may deny parole; (c) it may continue the case to a later date for reconsideration. The "continuance date" may be set at any time prior to the mandatory release date or the minimum expiration date. During the quarter in which the "continuance date" occurs, the board reviews the case on the basis of a personal hearing or an institutional progress report. At that time the board either grants or denies parole. In the event of a denial, the board conducts further reviews from time to time. Most prisoners are reconsidered at least annually on the basis of a progress report.[21]

20. 18 U.S.C. §4208(a).
21. When the court has imposed a sentence and specified that the board is to determine the eligibility date, and has also imposed a definite-term sentence under the general criminal law and orders them to run consecutively, the Board, except where it directs otherwise, will consider the prisoner eligible for parole on the aggregated sentence after service of one-third of the definite term. In those instances where the Board directs otherwise, the eligibility date will be set not later than one-third of the maximum of the aggregated terms. Rules of the United States Board of Parole 11 (July 1, 1965).

A report to the National Commission on Reform of Federal Criminal Laws by Professor Peter Low recommended that a prisoner sentenced to an indefinite term, with no minimum sentence specified, be eligible for release on parole at any time. A minimum term, no longer than one-third of the maximum, would be specified only in exceptional cases where the sentencing judge had taken affirmative steps to include it. In such cases it is contemplated that the judge would use all available information and state his reasons for imposing a minimum sentence. (The reasons generally would involve protection of the public from a dangerous criminal.) Appellate review would be available.

Under that plan, all felony sentences would have both a prison component and a parole component. The prison sentence would state the maximum time for which an offender may be retained in prison before his first parole. The parole sentence would serve to guarantee that every offender serve some time on parole before he is completely released from supervision. No matter at what point during his prison sentence an inmate was paroled, the time he must serve under supervision without a violation before being entitled to complete discharge would be governed by the parole component of the sentence. Thus, the length of time on parole would be stated independently rather than, as at present, a period dependent on the readiness of the parole board to release a prisoner to the community.

The proposed system would change the present anomalous situation where the offender who is a good risk and consequently is now released earlier in his term serves a very long time on parole. On the other hand, the offender who is released late in his term and who thus is presumably a poorer risk serves only a short time on parole. And an offender who is kept until his sentence has expired and who thus is presumed the worst risk serves no time on parole at all.

An offender who violated parole under this scheme might be returned to prison for his entire remaining sentence, minus the time served on parole without violation. Under the present law, all the time spent on parole is lost if the parolee is returned to prison for a violation.

The proposed federal statutes recommended by the commission report set up criteria to govern release on parole. The revelant criteria depend on the different stages in the service of a prison sentence. In cases where no minimum term was imposed, except in the most unusual circumstances, prisoners would not be paroled during the first year of their sentence. Thereafter, or after the expiration of any minimum term, a prisoner would be presumptively entitled to parole unless there were affirmative reasons for keeping him in prison. The proposed statute states four reasons for retention: (1) substantial risk that he will not conform to reasonable ·conditions of parole, including a condition that he not violate the law; (2) his release at the time in question would unduly depreciate the seriousness of his crime or promote disrespect for law; (3) his release would adversely affect institutional discipline; or (4) continuation in his rehabilitative program would substantially enhance his chances of leading a law-abiding life after release at a later date.

Prisoners who have served five years or two-thirds of the prison component of their sentence, whichever is longer, would be paroled unless there appears a great likelihood that they will engage in additional criminal conduct on parole. Thus, as more time was served, the validity of the reasons for retention would lose its force. Unless there was fear that the prisoner would endanger the public, there would be no reason for keeping him in an institution.

A defendant who completed service of the prison component of his sentence without having been paroled would be required to be released on parole. The proposal eliminates the "good-time" provisions of the current statutes, which are seen as historical remnants of pre-parole days. According to the commission report, the sentences offered in its proposal do not need good-time reductions in order to make them civilized. In view of the proposed possibilities for parole, that feature would be unnecessary as an inducement to prison discipline. Finally, the questions of forfeiture and reinstatement of good time seem to present administrative headaches which outweigh any potential benefits.[22]

Based on an empirical study that showed a lack of any relationship between the amount of time served in prison and eventual success or failure on parole, a bill introduced before the California legislature and endorsed by a Select Committee on the Administration of Justice would direct paroling authorities to release on parole every state prisoner who had served his minimum statutory sentence, unless the prisoner comes within one of the following provisions:

(a) The nature of the offense and the circumstances surrounding its commission were substantially more serious than

22. Low, "Comment on the Sentencing System: Part C," in Working Papers of the National Commission on Reform of Federal Criminal Laws 1289 (1970). Many of these provisions were included in H.R. 13118 (92d Cong., 2d Sess., 1972). However, the bill does not abolish statutory good time and, in fact, provides that it may be earned during the period spent on parole.

usual and indicate a need for continued imprisonment.

(b) He has a history of excessive criminality and has earned a substantial portion of his livelihood over an extended period of years by engaging in criminal activities.

(c) There is a substantial danger that he would, if released, inflict serious bodily injury on others.

(d) He has been previously granted parole for the offense and has been returned to prison for a violation of the parole.

(e) He is serving two or more sentences and has not served the minimum term on all such sentences.

(f) Another provision of law requires that the person be imprisoned for a longer term before he may be granted parole.

When denying parole, the parole board would be required to state its reasons in writing.

PAROLE PREDICTION

Releasing authorities generally depend on case workers in the prison institutions for information about inmates. These staff members have large caseloads. (The ratio of case workers to inmates in 1965 was 1 to 53 for juveniles and 1 to 253 for adults.) The case workers depend for their information on brief interviews with the prisoner, meager institutional records and letters from community officials. They rarely use information that could be gathered from parole staff, professionals working in the institutions or other criminal justice agencies, such as the police and probation services. Social workers in the prisons have been criticized on the one hand for writing reports for parole boards that are so filled with jargon that board members cannot get a picture of the individual aspects of a case, and on the other hand for failing to include their own evaluation of each offender and his prospects.

There is no empirical evidence to support the assertion that professional correctional workers, even when supplied with full case histories, can assess the probability of prisoners' success on parole. An associate superintendent of a California prison, with many years of correctional experience, recently was asked to interview 283 inmates just before their release on parole and predict their success on parole. Neither from the interviews alone nor from the interviews augmented by psychiatric case histories of the men interviewed could the superintendent make predictions with any significant relationship to the actual outcome of the cases.

In an experiment to determine whether the training and experience of parole officers gave them a special competence for prediction, the same case histories of parolees from a state prison were given to ten experienced parole officers and ten laymen with no particular education or experience in working with offenders. The participants were asked to predict the probable success on parole of each subject. The two types of participants turned out not to differ significantly in their predictive efficiency. The two groups correctly identified slightly more than half of the potential parole violators but less than half of the non-violators. (The results for non-violators would have been better had the predictors made random choices.) There was no relationship between a participant's feeling of confidence in a particular prediction he had made and the likelihood that his prediction was accurate.[23]

More accurate than the foregoing illustrations of attempts to predict behavior on parole through the clinical method are the procedures that have been developed for assigning offenders to risk categories according to characteristics previously found to be associated with continued criminal behavior. Attempts to use such prediction tables date from the 1920s, when Professor S. B. Warner compared the characteristics of 300 parole successes, 300 violators and 80 prisoners at the Massachusetts State Reformatory who had not been paroled, in an effort to determine whether the criteria used by the parole board in deciding which prisoners to release had any relation to the prisoners' actual outcome on parole. Warner concluded that the board's criteria had no foundation, placing the blame for its failure to develop more meaningful determinants "upon the present undeveloped state of the science of criminology rather than upon either the Board of Parole or the Department of Correction."[24]

The first attempt to predict statistically the probable success on parole of various groups of prisoners was made by Professor Ernest W. Burgess of the University of Chicago in 1928. When Burgess divided each factor, such as type of offense and previous work record, into categories (for example, offenses into larceny, sex offenses and murder), he discovered that certain categories had higher violation rates than others. "Do not these striking differences," Burgess asked, "which correspond with

23. Savides, "A Parole Success Prediction Study," and Gottfredson, "Comparing and Combining Subjective and Objective Parole Predictions," in California Department of Correction, *Research Newsletter* (Sept.-Dec. 1961); Hakeem, "Prediction of Parole Outcome from Summaries of Case Histories," 52 *Journal of Criminal Law, Criminology and Police Science* 145 (1961).
24. Warner, "Factors Determining Parole from the Massachusetts Reformatory," 14 *Journal of Criminal Law, Criminology and Police Science* 172-207 (1923).

what we already know about the conditions that mould the life of the person, suggest that they be taken more seriously? These factors have, of course, been considered, but in a common-sense way so that some one or two of them have been emphasized out of all proportion to their significance."[25] Consequently, Burgess gave each potential parolee one point for each factor that, on the basis of the past examination of categories, appeared to be favorable. On the basis of the favorable points received, Burgess assigned "Expectancy Rates of Violation." He did not, however, follow the actual careers of the prisoners whose success he had predicted in order to test the reliability of his findings.

Burgess' method was introduced into Illinois prisons in 1933. Since then, a "prediction report" has been prepared for each inmate eligible for parole. This report states that the inmate is in a class out of which a certain percentage may be expected to violate parole. The parole board uses the report along with other data (interviews and tests) in reaching its decisions.

The base expectancy scales in use in a few states today are based on the model that Burgess developed. A base expectancy is a statement of the expected rate of parole violation for a given group of prisoners, based on past experience with groups having similar characteristics. Several characteristics have been found particularly helpful in predicting parole outcome: past criminal record; type of offense (offenders against persons are better risks on parole than offenders against property); the age of the offender (the probability of parole violation tends to decrease with age); history of opiate use or alcoholic problems where there is a tendency to violate parole; and measures of "social maturity" derived from personality testing.

The statistical methods of predicting outcome on parole have been criticized for three basic shortcomings. First, there have been few follow-up studies of predictions to test their accuracy. In addition, only a small number of comparisons have been made among the various predictive measures that have been used. And it has been difficult to apply predictor items found useful in one jurisdiction to prisoners in another jurisdiction.[26]

25. Bruce, Burgess and Harno, *The Working of the Indeterminate Sentencing Law and the Parole System in Illinois* 246 (1928).
26. For example, the history of opiate use may be a helpful predictor in a jurisdiction where a high proportion of the prison population has used drugs, while it would have little value in a jurisdiction where only a small proportion has used them. *See* Gottfredson, "Assessment and Prediction Methods in Crime and Delinquency," the President's Commission on Law Enforcement and Administration of Justice, Task Force Report: *Juvenile Delinquency*, Appendix K, 174 (1967).

Despite these criticisms, however, a recent study of the parole performance of prisoners released from California prisons determined that the prisoners' base expectancy scores could be used to predict their returns to prison for new felony convictions with 86 percent accuracy and their return to prison for any reason (such as violation of a parole condition) with 95 percent accuracy. The base expectancy score was the best discriminator of "success" or "failure" on parole.

Even if statistical prediction tables were perfected, it is doubtful that parole boards would make full use of them. The boards currently have such tables available to them, together with evidence that the tables are more reliable indicators of success on parole than the board members' own intuitions. Yet a fairly recent survey showed that, of forty-eight states responding to a questionnaire, parole boards in forty-four never made use of parole prediction tables for any purpose. Nor did federal, New York City, Puerto Rican, Canadian or District of Columbia paroling authorities.[27] Parole boards seem to believe that more justice is done when an individual gets a "personalized" prediction than when he is assigned to a risk category on the basis of characteristics over which he has no control.[28] Yet a recent study could discern no measurable difference in characteristics of California prisoners released after serving short prison terms and those released by the same parole board after long terms.[29]

A federal prisoner recently told us that discriminatory granting of paroles is the "greatest source of bitterness in the entire system" and that "this manhandling of the parole system has defeated the only source of hope the system has." He suggested legislation to fix definite terms after which parole is mandatory to replace the present system of "unqualified

27. Evjen, "Current Thinking on Parole Prediction Tables," 8 *Crime and Delinquency* 215 (1962). The only states that ever had used statistical prediction methods were Illinois, Ohio, California and Minnesota. The Colorado Parole Board planned to do so. However, the chairman of the federal Board of Parole recently announced that the board would rely more heavily on statistical methods of prediction, and researchers have inaugurated a federal prediction project.
28. Dershowitz, "The Concept of Legal Responsibility and Its Relationship to Psychological and Sociological Knowledge" (consultant's paper prepared for the President's Commission on the Causes and Prevention of Violence, 1969).
"Attitudes which help to explain the lag by parole boards in the use of prediction tables may be summarized roughly under five heads: (1) sensitivity to public opinion, (2) desire to encourage constructive use of prison time, (3) a firm belief in the uniqueness of each case, (4) frustration of intelligent selection for parole because of legal or traditional restrictions, and (5) reactions to the prediction devices themselves." Waynes, "Why Do Parole Boards Lag in the Use of Prediction Sources?" *The Pacific Sociological Review* 73 (1958).
29. Public Systems, Inc., "A Study of the Characteristics and Recidivism Experience of California Prisoners," Appendix to California Assembly, *Parole Board Reform in California* 22 (1970).

people playing with a man like a cat playing with a mouse." Such a change actually has been recommended to Congress by the National Commission on Reform of Federal Criminal Laws.[30]

PAROLE PROCEDURES

As long as parole boards continue to decide the fate of would-be parolees on an individual rather than statistical basis, some procedural checks on the complete discretion of board members are necessary. For example, if applicants for parole are told that they will be paroled as soon as they have proved themselves worthy of release, they need to be given reasons why they are not now considered worthy and an idea of what steps to take to become worthy, as well as the means of challenging the board's decision.

One reason for the continued existence of independent paroling authorities is that their decisions are supposedly fairer than those of institutional staffs. Unquestionably, it is important that prisoners should perceive that the decisions concerning them are well reasoned and based on sufficient information. Yet most parole boards operate in a private setting. In several states the boards hold no hearings for prisoners but make decisions solely on the basis of written reports.

Parole boards in effect exercise a discretion very much like that of the sentencing judge. In some jurisdictions, in fact, the parole board has even more control over the sentence than the judge, fixing both a minimum and maximum sentence. Yet, as Sol Rubin, a lawyer long critical of parole procedures, recently pointed out, "in the face of similar responsibilities a marked contrast prevails in the procedures used by parole boards and judges. Whereas the sentencing procedure must be surrounded by a fair amount of due process of law, the parole hearing is entirely devoid of either substantive or procedural due process requirements." There are no announced criteria for granting or denying parole. Parole boards do not hold hearings but "interviews." If the presence of an attorney is permitted at all, his role is restricted to that of a supplicant rather than an advocate. The prisoner or his attorney has no right to examine the reports of probation officers or prison personnel on which the board bases its decision. If parole is denied, he need not be given reasons and he has no appeal.

While some parole boards summon prisoners after a hearing to discuss their decision, others rely on letters or institutional staff members to relay

30. National Commission on Reform of Federal Criminal Laws, Study Draft of a New Federal Criminal Code §3201(2) (1970).

the message. Even where reasons for denying parole are given to prisoners in person, they frequently amount to little more than a paraphrasing of the law to the effect that the inmate does not currently represent a good risk. The New Jersey Supreme Court recently struck down a state parole-board rule that forbade the board to inform a prisoner of the reasons for denying him parole.[31]

Parole boards must become more sensitive to the effects of their decisions. Paul Keve, a former correctional administrator, suggests that boards should permit prospective parolees to be present during their deliberations. "As far as the prisoner knows, they are flipping a coin. There are often nice things said about him, and concern shown. The prisoner only knows the questions the board members asked him, which may have no relation to the real reasons for their decision."

Attorneys for a group of federal prisoners recently filed a class action seeking to force the United States Board of Parole to inform prospective parolees of the factors it considers in passing on applications for parole, to apprise an applicant or his representative of the information about him that has been conveyed to the board, to provide an opportunity for a response to the information prior to the parole hearing and, when an application for parole is denied, to provide a statement of the reasons for the denial and an explanation of the changes in behavior that are expected if the applicant is to win parole at his next hearing. Judge William B. Bryant of the District of Columbia District Court denied the Parole Board's motion to dismiss the complaint, noting he had failed to become convinced that "the processes or lack thereof by which the United States Board of Parole exercises its enormous powers, albeit with a broad discretion, are utterly closed to judicial scrutiny."[32]

Subsequent to this decision, the Parole Board announced that it would begin to provide written reasons for its denials of parole by means of a checklist. The degree of specificity that the reasons will contain is still unknown. When the plaintiffs attempted to take the deposition of the chairman of the Parole Board concerning the board's policies and practices, he resisted on the ground that the board is immune from judicial review. The court's order requiring him to appear and answer questions has been appealed by the Justice Department.

The anomalous disparity between the protections afforded an offender at the sentencing and parole decisions may be explained partially

31. *Monks v. State Parole Board*, 58 N.J. 238, 277 A.2d 193 (1971).
32. *Childs v. United States Board of Parole*, Civil Action No. 1616–70 (D.D.C. Aug. 19, 1971).

by the tenacious legal fiction that imprisonment and parole are merely different forms of custody. A typical state statute governing the status of a parolee provides that "a prisoner on parole is in the legal custody of the department of mental hygiene and correction, and under the control of the commission." As interpreted by the courts, this language puts the parolee in substantially the same position as a prison "trusty," who may "be allowed temporarily to leave the confines of the institution, but who is obviously, while enjoying that privilege, still within the legal custody and under the control of the head of that institution. It would hardly be contended that such a prisoner would be entitled to any hearing because of a determination by the head of the institution that he was no longer entitled to privileges which he had previously been accorded as a trusty. Nor could it reasonably be contended that any court should be required to review such a determination. . . ."[33]

In 1963 the Supreme Court gave a perhaps unintended boost to the continuing custody fiction when it ruled that since "in fact, as well as in theory, the custody and control of the Parole Board involve significant restraints on petitioner's liberty because of his conviction and sentence, which are in addition to those imposed by the State upon the public generally," the Virginia Parole Board had sufficient "custody" of a parolee to enable him to challenge the legality of his original conviction by petitioning a federal court for a writ of *habeas corpus.*[34] The Court's opinion emphasized the flexibility of *habeas corpus,* which it considered capable of doing more than reaching "behind prison walls and iron bars." In recognizing the restraints imposed by the conditions of parole, it is doubtful that the Court intended to circumscribe the protections surrounding the granting and revocation of parole while it enlarged the protections afforded by *habeas corpus.*

A federal court of appeals, faced with a challenge to a regulation prohibiting the attendance of retained counsel at parole hearings, ruled (over a strong dissent) that a prisoner is not entitled to due process of law when he is considered for parole. Its reasons: the parole board is not the prisoner's adversary; the prisoner has no present interest that qualifies for protection; and extension of due-process rights would create an administrative burden on the parole system.

---

33. Ohio Rev. Code §2965.01(E) *In re* Varner, 166 Ohio St. 340, 346–47, 142 N.E.2d 846, 850 (1957). *See also* 18 U.S.C. §4203.
34. *Jones v. Cunningham,* 371 U.S. 236, 242 (1963). 28 U.S.C. §2241 gives federal district courts jurisdiction to grant a writ of habeas corpus "to a prisoner . . . *in custody* in violation of the Constitution of the United States." (Italics added.)

A federal court of appeals recently dismissed a complaint by a California prisoner that he had been denied parole because of his refusal to divulge information on the criminal activities of fellow prisoners. He claimed that the California Adult Authority had violated his constitutional right to the equal protection of the laws by paroling a co-defendant with the same six- to ten-year sentence after three and one half years, while, after seven and one half years, he still remained in custody. Relying on the fiction of "continuing custody," the court dismissed the claim without a hearing:

> Parole is a form of custody. . . . Thus, the gist of the complaint is that the authorities have refused to transfer him from one form of custody to another. This is not sufficient to state a claim under the Civil Rights Act, because it does not allege a violation of a right secured by the Constitution or statutes of the United States.[35]

A dissenting opinion charged that, in refusing to take into account the obvious differences in the degrees of liberty afforded by imprisonment and parole, the court was being "ignorant as judges of what we know as men." The dissenting judge insisted that

> [T]he parolee's status has far more in common with liberty than with imprisonment. When the State grants, denies, or revokes parole it takes action which directly and significantly affects the personal freedom of the accused, and the State violates the Fourteenth Amendment whenever that action is arbitrary, basically unfair, or invidiously discriminatory. . . . No one would contend that officers of the State could grant, deny, or revoke parole on the basis of the accused's color or religion, for example, without offending the Constitution and exposing themselves to liability under the Civil Rights Act.

At present, the majority opinion remains the prevailing view. Other courts have been unwilling to hear claims by black prisoners that denial of their parole was motivated solely by their race, since white prisoners with worse records had been granted parole.[36] However, recent cases

35. *Padilla v. Lynch,* 398 F.2d 481, 482 (9th Cir. 1968). *See also Sturm v. California Adult Authority,* 395 F.2d 446 (9th Cir. 1967).
36. *Peterson v. Rivers,* 350 F.2d 457 (D.C. Cir. 1964); *Richardson v. Rivers,* 335 F.2d 996 (D.C. Cir. 1964).

discussed in Chapter VII, which require certain procedural protections when a prisoner's eligibility for parole is postponed under a system of definite sentences, or when a prisoner is transferred from one institution to another that is substantially more restrictive, should foreshadow a change in the restrictive interpretation of parole as "continuing custody."

The New York Court of Appeals recently considered whether a parole board must afford the usual due-process rights to an evidentiary hearing, the assistance of counsel and cross-examination of adverse witnesses when considering whether to put a prisoner on parole.[37] A prisoner complained that, although he was a first offender, with an excellent prison record and substantial ties in the community, the New York Board of Parole had refused to release him as "a poor parole risk." (This was the only "reason" given by the board.) The court refused to review the merits of the prisoner's claim, ruling that "so long as the Board violates no positive statutory requirement, its discretion is absolute and beyond review in the courts." Nor would it require an adversary hearing or the presence of counsel. The court construed the legislative requirement that the board "personally examine" the prospective parolee as giving the board complete discretion as to the nature and extent of the "examination."[38]

The issue of whether to allow—or provide—attorneys at parole hearings is admittedly difficult. Although some parole-board members have stated that they are skeptical of the contribution to be made by counsel, a better view is that there is a need for someone from outside the system "wholly identified with the parole applicant and by his presence exercising a continuing challenge on behalf of the individual client."[39] At the very least, prisoners should be allowed to retain attorneys to appear before parole boards on their behalf. But allowing retained counsel inevitably raises the question of whether participation of legal counsel is so vital to parole proceedings that lawyers should be provided for all prisoners who cannot afford them. Other possibilities include representation by law students, ex-offenders or conceivably even correctional personnel operating in conjunction with lawyers.

H.R. 13118, introduced in Congress in February 1972, would require the U.S. Parole Board to provide prisoners for whom parole is being considered with several significant procedural protections: written notice of

37. *Briguglio v. New York State Board of Parole*, 24 N.Y.2d 21, 298 N.Y.S.2d 704, 246 N.E.2d 50 (1969).
38. *Cf. Berry v. Attica Prison Bd.*, 59 Misc. 2d 392, 299 N.Y.S.2d 82 (1969).
39. Cohen, *The Legal Challenge to Correction: Implications for Manpower and Training* 37 (1969).

the time and place of the hearing; copies of all non-confidential documents to be used by the board in reaching a decision (here the exceptions could cause serious problems); representation by retained or appointed attorneys, or, if the prisoner wishes, by any "qualified" person of his choice; the opportunity to testify on his own behalf; a full record of the hearing; and, within two weeks of the hearing, a written statement of the board's decision and the reasons for it.

It is crucial for parole boards (or state legislatures) to develop standards for granting or denying parole. A mere listing of "factors . . . considered," such as the list provided by the U.S. Parole Board in its 1971 Regulations, including "family and marital; intelligence and education; employment and military experience; leisure time; religion; and physical and emotional health," is far too cryptic to provide the necessary guidance. Only when the paroling decision is made according to objective criteria known to the prisoners will prospective parolees—and their attorneys—be able to participate meaningfully in the deliberations, by arguing that the criteria in fact have been met.

Supervision of Parolees

The paroling authorities' decisions to release are governed partially by the resources available for supervision in the community. As the 1967 President's Crime Commission remarked, "Releasing authorities face one sort of question in considering parole for an offender who will be supervised in a small caseload by a trained parole officer working intensively with the offender and community agencies. The questions are very different in considering release to a parole officer who is so overburdened that he can give no more than token supervision."

The average parolee is supervised by an officer who is responsible for sixty-eight offenders, as well as for investigating release plans and developing future employment opportunities for inmates still in prison. In thirty states the officer also must conduct presentence investigations for the courts. Although parole caseloads do not appear as overwhelming as those of probation officers (in the jurisdictions where the two functions are separate), they are twice the average size most frequently recommended by current experts.

The Crime Commission recommended that parole offices make use of paid, subprofessional aides to perform certain tasks such as collecting and verifying information about offenders. These workers, drawn from the neighborhoods served by the office, could establish effective communication with the releasees and serve as examples to them of the opportunity for achievement. As an added feature, many of the parole aides should be ex-offenders. In addition to the empathy for the parolee's situation that may be possible only in a person who has endured the same experience, the useful employment of ex-offenders by parole agencies can provide a model to private employers and other government agencies. In the District of Columbia, this suggestion has been carried one step further: fifty parolees are being supervised by BonaBond, a private organization of ex-offenders. Their performance is being compared with that of fifty parolees supervised by the regular parole staff; to date the BonaBond-supervised parolees have done slightly better than their counterparts.

The state parole agency in Texas uses citizen volunteers under the supervision of parole officers. The volunteers contact parolees on their release, help arrange jobs for them or get them into school. Thereafter they are available for counseling.

In Connecticut a private agency, the Connecticut Prison Association, provides parole sponsors for prison inmates without families or with special problems. The sponsor is assigned at least six months before the inmate's parole date and visits the prison once or twice a month. The hope is that a good enough relationship between the inmate and the sponsor will develop so the inmate will want to continue to see the sponsor after his parole. At the end of 1965 there were about 100 people actively working as sponsors, each assigned to one prisoner or parolee. There has been no systematic evaluation of the program, but participants feel that at the least it has been effective in producing greater community awareness and support for correctional programs.

A survey of parole facilities in the District of Columbia made several years ago disclosed that offenders released from prison by operation of good-time laws were assigned to parole officers with caseloads averaging eighty. Inmates released on parole, on the other hand, were supervised in caseloads averaging forty-four. Thus, the good-time releasees, who never had applied for parole or who had been denied parole and presumably were worse risks than the parolees, were receiving the least supervision, and the prisoners who were retained in prison until their full sentences had expired—presumably the worst risks of all—received no supervision or parole services at all.[40] This practice raises the fundamental

40. American Correctional Association, *The Organization and Effectiveness of the Correctional Agencies* 709 (1966).

question, discussed elsewhere, of where limited correctional resources should be spent. Does it make more sense to concentrate on the best or on the poorest risks?

The District of Columbia survey disclosed that within the parole supervision units the number of contacts a parolee had with his parole officer varied with the time he had been on parole. For the first six weeks after an individual was released from prison, his parole officer saw him once a week at his home or job. Thereafter he was seen once every two weeks. When he had been on parole with a good record for six months to a year, he was seen only once a month.

This pattern may be contrasted with that of probation, where the monthly contact, generally in the case worker's office, remains the same. Of course, when caseloads are high, the availability of parole services is limited by the agents' need to handle emergencies.

Several studies conducted in California, including the federal San Francisco Project, discussed in Chapter IV, and earlier efforts by the California Youth Authority and the Department of Correction, showed that merely reducing parole caseloads made no difference in the performances of parolees. A modest increase in services made no difference to high-risk cases, and low-risk cases succeeded in either case.[41]

Consequently, in an effort to provide a more sophisticated approach, the California Department of Correction developed a Parole Work Unit Program. The program, in operation since 1965, is based on the idea of providing different amounts of supervision at different stages and for different types of offenders. Cases are classified according to presumed needs for supervision. Officers' allotments of cases are weighed according to the amount of time required to supervise each case and the time required for office duties, training and maintaining contacts with the prisons and community agencies.

"Special supervision" (three hours per month) is used for a minimum of six months for about half the parolees—offenders in need of close supervision because of histories of aggressive behavior, use of narcotics or special responsiveness to supervision in small caseloads. "Regular supervision" (one and four-fifths hours per month) is provided for parolees whose backgrounds do not indicate that they pose a major threat to the community, although their predicted success on parole may

41. Johnson, "The 'Failure' of a Parole Research Project," 18 *California Youth Authority Quarterly* 35 (1965); California Department of Correction, Special Intensive Parole Unit Reports, Phases I-IV (1953–64).

be low (for example, the alcoholic or the check borrower), and releasees who have made a satisfactory adjustment under special supervision. "Conditional supervision" (three-fifths of an hour per month) is used almost entirely for parolees who have successfully completed a period of regular supervision.

In December 1965 a follow-up study was conducted of all parolees assigned to Conventional and Work Unit supervision during the initial three months of the program's operation (February, March and April of 1965). The findings showed no significant differences in the success of parolees in Work Unit and Conventional supervision caseloads. According to the study, parole agents were emphasizing increased contact with parolees and greater awareness of their behavior. However, less attention was given to mobilizing community resources for those subjects experiencing problems of adjustment. In fact, Work Unit agents were detecting minor parole violations that ordinarily might not have been uncovered. In their efforts to take some type of action, agents were considering other forms of intervention that might provide more effective and economical means of treatment and long-term control.

Following the study, administrative efforts, including special meetings with regional administrators and Work Unit supervisors, encouraged maximum use of available community services, such as health and counseling agencies. Community resources were more widely used and special programs to handle alcoholics without a return to prison were implemented. Greater emphasis was placed on key decisions by parole officers (whether to recommend revocation of parole for a technical violation of parole conditions), particularly where alternative community-based programs were available and no serious risk to the community was apparent.

Subsequent evaluations showed a reduction in the rates of return to prison of parolees supervised on both Conventional and Work Unit caseloads. The department attributed the over-all improvement to the sense of competition that developed between Work Unit and Conventional Unit offices. Nevertheless, the performance of parolees in Work Unit caseloads, in terms of both avoiding crime and getting and keeping jobs, was significantly greater than that of parolees in conventional caseloads.[42]

42. A one-year follow-up showed 19.6 percent of Work Unit parolees and 23 percent of those in conventional supervision returned to prison. California Department of Correction, "The Parole Work Unit Program: An Evaluative Report" i (1967). A follow-up after two years showed 33.9 percent of the Work Unit parolees and 38.4 percent of the conventional supervision group back in prison. California Dept. of Correction, "The Work Unit Parole Program" 14 (1968).

While parolees in the Work Unit group were returned to prison because of new felony convictions in fewer cases than their counterparts in conventional caseloads, the Work Unit parolees showed a greater number of technical violations than the conventional group. The most logical explanation of this disparity is that the parole agents in the Work Unit program had more time to devote to discovering technical violations.

The New York Governor's Special Committee on Offenders has recommended that the same treatment teams be used for parole as for probation. The use of such teams, augmented by aides and neighborhood workers, might make it easier to mobilize community health and social agencies to serve offenders. Funds could be made available to probation and parole agencies to enable them to purchase community services, such as psychiatric counseling or vocational training.

The New York Division for Youth, a state agency established in 1960 to conduct experimental programs for juvenile delinquents, recently has opened aftercare offices in several high-crime areas of large cities. The offices are staffed by "aftercare teams." Each team consists of a supervisor (who must have an advanced degree in social work), two parole officers and two paraprofessional case aides. One of these is an adult "community aide," often an ex-offender, who is responsible for developing community resources to deal with the youths' problems. The other is a "youth aide," who must have been released for at least one year from a Division for Youth program, and who frequently conducts group meetings for the parolees in the program. An entire team is responsible for the success of each of the parolees assigned to it.

For a man who has been locked up in an institution, perhaps for many years, re-entry into the community presents special problems. The parole period forces an abrupt change in the inmate's life. The psychological effects of this change, sometimes termed "gate fever," have been described as follows:

> With minimal preparation the offender moves from a subservient, deprived, and highly structured institutional life into a world that bombards him with stimuli, presents complicated problems requiring immediate solution, and expects him to assume responsibilities to which he has long been unused. All the roles he must assume after release are problematical; they differ from those to which he has been accustomed for some time, and are complicated by the fact that he is now a parolee as well as a son, husband, workman, or student. The expectations,

norms, and cues appropriate to an institutional inmate, learned under threat of severe sanctions, have little pertinence for behavior in the free world. This abrupt introduction to the tasks of status-passage constitutes a crisis for the individual, inducing major disorientation and requiring strenuous adaptive maneuvers by the individual himself and others who play significant roles in his adjustment.[43]

Evidence of the difficulty of the jail-to-street transition is provided by the fact that parole violations tend to occur relatively soon after release from an institution. Nearly half of these parole violations occur during the first six months and over 60 percent within the first year. At the very least, the releasee must find a job, and he must somehow support himself until he receives his first wages.

Many parole boards require an inmate to have a job before they will release him. If labor were scarce, this requirement would not be onerous. Today, unless an inmate has participated in one of the very few prison vocational training programs run by private companies guaranteeing trainees jobs on release, the requirement can be extremely difficult and demoralizing. Prisoners may take any job at all, with no thought to future employment possibilities. Consequently, in some states inmates fulfilling certain conditions, such as having a stable home situation and possessing a marketable employment skill, may be released without a prearranged job. Parole violation rates of these releasees are reported to be no higher than those of inmates who were required to find a job before release.[44] In Maryland, where employment continues to be required for parole, special legislation allows prisoners to leave the institutions for prearranged job interviews (although not for general job-hunting).

Gratuities given prisoners on release are minimal in most states and not enough to support most releasees. In some states the assistance is scarcely enough to get the prisoner home, let alone sufficient to see him through his transition period and to the point where he is earning a living. The payment of wages for work (and perhaps schooling) done in prison, coupled with some compulsory savings of earnings, could provide releasees with enough cash to get settled and support themselves until they have found the right job and begun to earn wages.

A related problem is the usual inability of people with felony rec-

43. Studt, *The Reentry of the Offender into the Community* 3 (1967).
44. Stanton, "Is It Safe to Parole Inmates Without Jobs?" 12 *Crime and Delinquency* 147 (1966).

ords to obtain charge accounts or buy on credit, regardless of their income or employment record. In order to meet this problem, the residents of Brooke House, a private halfway house in Boston, Massachusetts, organized a Federal Credit Union—the first ever to be run by ex-convicts. A credit union requires some "common bond" between its members (in this case, residence at Brooke House) on the theory that this gives the members more information about applicants for loans and that borrowers are more likely to repay loans borrowed from their friends. Shareholders who purchase shares for five dollars each are eligible to apply for credit-union loans. All residents are urged to borrow some small amount of money during their residence at Brooke House in order to establish a record of repayment. Members may then use the union as a credit reference.

THE STATUS OF PAROLEES

The conditions under which parolees are released are broadly defined by statutes and set by parole boards. Parole conditions frequently seek to control all facets of the releasee's behavior, including some areas of his life and conduct totally unrelated to his true reformation.[45] Typical conditions may involve church attendance, abstinence from alcohol or extramarital sexual relations, remaining in a certain geographical area and keeping free of associations with other parolees. Other conditions recently adopted in some areas require frequent urine samples to enable the detection of narcotics and a waiver of the parolee's constitutional protections against search and seizure. A typical statement of the parole conditions imposed automatically on parolees in one state reads as follows:

(a) Upon his release, a paroled person must proceed directly to the place to which he has been paroled and within a period of 24 hours must make his arrival report. At the time he reports to the proper area office or to the proper parole officer he must have in his possession the money he received at the time of his release, except the funds expended for necessary travel, food and shelter.

(b) He must not leave the State . . . or the community

45. In *Mansell v. Turner*, 14 Utah 2d 352, 354–55, 384 P.2d 394, 396 (1963), a concurring judge argued that there should be a relation between the condition (banishment from Utah) and the parolee's rehabilitation or society's protection. The majority rejected such a "bold view," since a prisoner not wishing to comply with a condition need only reject parole.

to which he has been paroled without the written permission of his parole officer.

(c) He must carry out the instructions of his parole officer, report as directed and permit the parole officer to visit him at his residence and place of employment. The parolee must not change his residence or employment without first securing the permission of his parole officer. The parolee understands that he is still in the custody of the superintendent or warden of the institution from which he is being paroled. He hereby consents to any search of his person, his residence, or of any property or premises under his control which the Board of Parole or any of its representatives may see fit to make at any time in their discretion.

(d) He must make every effort to maintain gainful employment and, if for any reason he loses his position, he must immediately report this fact to his parole officer and he must cooperate with his parole officer in the officer's efforts to obtain employment for him. He must conduct himself as a good citizen, must not associate with evil companions or individuals having criminal records. He must abstain from wrong-doing, lead an honest, upright and industrious life, support his dependents, if any, and assume toward them all legal and moral obligations. His behavior must not be a menace to the safety of his family or to any individual or group of individuals.

(e) He must avoid the excessive use of intoxicating beverages and abstain completely if so directed by his parole officer.

(f) He must not live as man and wife with anyone to whom he is not legally married, and must not have sex relations with anyone not his lawful spouse. He must obtain written permission from his parole officer before he applies for a license to marry.

(g) Immediately after his release on parole he must surrender any motor vehicle license which he had in his possession at the time of his conviction and sentence. While on parole he must not apply for a motor vehicle license, or own or operate a motor vehicle without permission of his parole officer. If, while on parole, a parolee purchases a motor vehicle without a valid license, it will be considered a violation of parole. A valid license will be deemed to be one issued subsequent to release on parole after permission has been obtained.

(h) If a parolee carries firearms of any nature, it will be considered a violation of parole.

(i) A paroled person must not carry from the institution from which he is released, or send to any penal institution . . . any written or verbal message, or any object or property of any kind whatsoever, unless specific permission to do so has been obtained from the warden, superintendent, or other duly authorized officers of both the institution from which he is released and the institution to which the message, object, or property is to be delivered, and he must not correspond with inmates of correctional institutions without the written permission of his parole officer. . . .

(m) As the right of franchise is revoked when a person is sentenced to a State prison, a person released on parole . . . must not register as a voter and must not vote in any primary, special or general election.

(n) No parolee can accept employment in any capacity where liquor is made or sold without the written approval of the State Liquor Authority permitting such employment.

(o) Before being released on parole a parolee must agree in writing that if he is arrested in another State while on parole, he will waive extradition and will not resist being returned by the Board of Parole to the State of New York.

(p) In addition to these general rules of parole which all prisoners released on parole must adhere to, the Board of Parole has the authority in any case to impose additional or special conditions of parole.[46]

The National Commission on Reform of Federal Criminal Laws has recommended that, in addition to the explicit condition of refraining from committing further crimes, the United States Board of Parole have the power to require a parolee to

(a) work faithfully at a suitable employment or faithfully pursue a course of study or of vocational training that will equip him for suitable employment;

(b) undergo available medical or psychiatric treatment and remain in a specified institution if required for that purpose;

(c) attend or reside in a facility established for the instruction, recreation or residence of persons on probation or parole;

(d) support his dependents and meet other family responsibilities;

(e) refrain from possessing a firearm, destructive device or

46. 9 N.Y.C.R.R. §155.15.

other dangerous weapon unless granted written permission by the Board or the parole officer;

(f) report to a parole officer at reasonable times as directed by the Board or the parole officer;

(g) permit the parole officer to visit him at reasonable times at his home or elsewhere;

(h) remain within the geographical limits fixed by the Board, unless granted written permission to leave by the Board or the parole officer;

(i) answer all reasonable inquiries by the parole officer and promptly notify the parole officer of any change in address or employment;

(j) satisfy other conditions reasonably related to his rehabilitation.

A bill introduced in Congress by Congressman Robert Kastenmeier is less specific but potentially more useful in preventing the imposition of unreasonable or overly restrictive conditions. It requires the parole board, in imposing conditions of parole, to consider the following:

(1) There should be a reasonable relationship between the conditions imposed and the prisoner's previous conduct and present situation.

(2) The conditions should provide for the minimum deprivation of liberty, freedom of conscience and freedom of association.

(3) The conditions should be sufficiently specific to serve as a guide to supervision and conduct.

(4) The conditions should be such that compliance is possible, given the emotional, physical and economic resources of the offender.

The provision, allowing conditions "reasonably related" to the parolee's past conduct and present situation could serve to eliminate many of the moralistic, unreasonable, boiler-plate conditions now imposed automatically as part of parole, as long as the board and the courts insisted on a clearly demonstrated connection between the conditions imposed and the criminal conduct sought to be prevented. One Maryland parolee who was an extraordinary musician told us that he was not allowed to work as a professional guitarist in a nightclub because the parole board disapproved of the environment; he was forced to take a job as a laborer to attain his release.

Some sort of reasonableness standard may have lain behind the Supreme Court's recent—and highly unusual—reversal of a decision of the United States Parole Board to revoke parole because of the parolee's association with other ex-convicts as part of his employment. Basing its decision on the board's failure to follow its own regulation requiring "satisfactory evidence" of a parole violation to justify an arrest warrant, the Court stated:

> We do not believe that the parole condition restricting association was intended to apply to incidental contacts between ex-convicts in the course of work on a legitimate job for a common employer. Nor is such occupational association, standing alone, satisfactory evidence of nonbusiness association violative of the parole restriction. To so assume would be to render a parolee vulnerable to imprisonment whenever his employer, willing to hire ex-convicts, hires more than one.[47]

In another unusual decision a federal court granted summary judgment to a parolee, a convicted atomic spy and acknowledged Communist sympathizer, invalidating the refusal of the United States Board of Parole to permit him to participate in peace demonstrations and to address meetings of an allegedly Communist organization. The board had justified its refusal to grant permission on the basis that these activities would not be in the public interest or conducive to the parolee's rehabilitation, considering his offense. The court rejected these justifications as naïve and chimerical and forbade the parole board to interfere with the parolee's exercise of First Amendment rights, except where necessary to safeguard against "specific, concretely described and highly likely dangers of misconduct by plaintiff himself." A similar decision invalidated the condition that a California parolee obtain permission from his parole officer prior to giving any public speech. The condition was disapproved on the dual bases that the inevitable scrutiny of the proposed content of speeches abridged First Amendment rights and that the condition was unrelated to any valid rehabilitative end.[48]

One unusual and potentially controversial requirement that could some day become a condition of parole is the wearing of some sort of tracking device. One such device, consisting of two small units (each

47. *Arciniega v. Freeman*, 404 U.S. 4 (1971) (*per curiam*).
48. *Sobell v. Reed*, 327 F. Supp. 1294 (S.D.N.Y. 1971); *Hyland v. Procunier*, 311 F. Supp. 749 (N.D. Cal. 1970).

the size of a thick paperback book) that contain batteries and a radio transmitter, has been developed by Dr. Ralph K. Schwitzgebel, a psychologist and law student. The tracker, currently being tested with volunteer parolees in Cambridge, Massachusetts, emits radio signals that pinpoint his geographical location. In addition, it may be possible to monitor such physiological facts as the wearer's pulse rate or his consumption of alcohol.

According to one study, the use of electronic tracking might enable more thorough supervision of parolees and consequently allow a larger number of convicted offenders to be supervised in the community rather than in prison:

> Requiring the wearing of a tracking device as a condition of parole or probation would permit parole officers to know whether their charges were obeying conditions of release. It would deter the tracked person's former criminal associates from reenlisting him in their activities. If he obeyed the law, it would protect him from the tendency of the police to fasten on ex-convicts as suspects. Most important of all, tracking would make it possible to extend the relatively free and therapeutic experience of parole to convicts who would otherwise have to be imprisoned until their terms expired.
>
> On the other hand, tracking—entirely apart from its possible offensiveness to human dignity—might in practice impede parole therapy. The parolee or probationer might experience anxiety or fail to develop self-confidence as a result of excessive surveillance. He might curtail proper as well as improper activities. If third persons became aware that their conversations with him were being recorded by parole officers, he might find it impossible to get a job and might undergo social isolation. Despite these drawbacks, however, tracking may be more effective than imprisonment.[49]

The concept of tracking raises several basic questions of policy and constitutionality. If tracking is to be employed, the issues of privacy, freedom of choice, unreasonable search and seizure and compulsory self-incrimination will have to be met. However, the same general guideline that has been suggested for judging existing conditions of parole—namely,

49. Note, "Anthropotelemetry: Dr. Schwitzgebel's Machine," 80 *Harvard Law Review* 403, 406 (1966).

whether the condition imposed is reasonably related to the parolee's crime—could prove useful here. In some cases constant surveillance, limited to relevant data (for example, alcoholic consumption), might be a preferable alternative to imprisonment.

Traditional legal theory assumes that because a state is not required constitutionally to provide for parole, when it does there are no constitutional restrictions on the conditions it may place on a parolee's status.[50] Consequently, the breach of any one of these frequently picayune rules can lead to the revocation of parole and return to prison. Implicit in the "continuing custody" idea of parole is the acceptance of the possibility that parole may be revoked summarily without the need to prove violation of a valid condition.

This same myth of "continuing custody" has been used to dilute a parolee's Fourth Amendment protection from unreasonable search and seizure. In ruling on the admissibility of evidence seized from parolees by their parole officers without a search warrant or the usual requirement of probable cause for a search, courts have made no distinction based on the parolee's actual waiver of his Fourth Amendment rights or on the relationship of the parolee's prior offense to the necessity of frequent searches.

The generally accepted view, stated by the California courts in 1964,[51] is that the standards relating to probable cause for search or arrest "have little relevance as between correctional authorities and paroled prisoners. The parolee, although physically outside the walls, is still a prisoner; his apprehension, although outwardly resembling arrest, is simply a return to physical custody. . . . For the purpose of maintaining the restraints and social safeguards accompanying the parolee's status, the authorities may subject him, his home and his effects to such constant or occasional inspection or search as may seem advisable to them."

Other courts have made slight inroads into this view. One federal court of appeals recently questioned a district court's ruling that

---

50. See e.g., *Ughbanks v. Armstrong,* 208 U.S. 481 (1908); *Rose v. Haskins,* 388 F.2d 91, 93 (6th Cir. 1968). *But see* State *ex rel. Joyce v. Strassheim,* 242 Ill. 359, 90 N.E. 118, 121 (1909):

> But we do not regard his parole as a mere act of grace and favor by the board of pardons. . . . We cannot believe that the legislature understood that the board, in establishing rules for parole . . . or exercising the discretion confided to them, would be merely dispensing favors to those whom they might choose to release . . . or that the rearrest . . . should be considered merely a withdrawal of a favor bestowed upon him.

51. *People v. Hernandez,* 229 Cal. App. 2d 143, 40 *Cal. Rptr.* 100 (1964), *cert. denied,* 381 U.S. 953 (1965).

> [a]ny search by a parole officer in good faith to determine
> whether a paroled prisoner is complying with the conditions of
> his release would . . . be reasonable. . . .

> [a] search by a parole officer of the person, residence, or effects
> of a parolee is not in violation of the Fourth Amendment because
> done without a warrant, without consent, and without probable
> cause.

According to the appellate court, "It is possible that this formulation is too broad. A parolee is said to be entitled to some quantum of Fourth Amendment protection against 'unreasonable searches and seizures.' . . . However, a search which would be 'unreasonable' if an ordinary citizen were involved, might be reasonable if directed against a parolee. It would be unrealistic to ignore the fact that parolees, as a class, pose a greater threat of criminal activity than do ordinary citizens."[52] The court upheld the search at issue as incident to a valid arrest for violation of the parole condition forbidding association with a known criminal.

In a recent opinion by a federal court of appeals, three judges ruled unanimously that the Fourth Amendment exclusionary rule does not apply to parole revocation hearings; consequently, parole could be revoked on the basis of evidence that a parolee had been carrying a pistol obtained from him as a result of an illegal search by New York City policemen:

> A parole revocation proceeding is not an adversarial pro-
> ceeding. . . . A parole revocation proceeding is concerned not
> only with protecting society, but also, and most importantly,
> with rehabilitating and restoring to useful lives those placed in
> the custody of the Parole Board. To apply the exclusionary rule
> to parole revocation proceedings would tend to obstruct the pa-
> role system in accomplishing its remedial purposes.[53]

A concurring opinion suggested that the parole board prescribe submission to whatever searches it considered reasonable as a condition of parole. Another concurrence expressed a preference for searches of parolees by parole officers rather than policemen, but cited the shortage of parole

52. United States *ex rel. Randazzo v. Follette,* 282 F. Supp. 10, 13, 15 (S.D.N.Y. 1968), *aff'd,* 418 F.2d 1319, 1322 n. 7 (2d Cir. 1969). *Cf. United States v. Lewis,* 274 F. Supp. 184 (S.D.N.Y. 1967).
53. United States *ex rel. Sperling v. Fitzpatrick,* 326 F.2d 1161 (2d Cir. 1970). *See also In re* Martinez, 83 *Cal. Rptr.* 382, 463 P.2d 734, 1 Cal. 3d 641 (1970).

manpower to conduct surveillance as the reason for allowing continued searches by the police. The ruling of this case limiting the reach of the Fourth Amendment in parole should be reconsidered in light of that in *Sobell v. Reed* and *Hyland v. Procunier*, which extend the benefits of the First Amendment to parolees.

A state court recently broke with existing precedents to hold that evidence seized in a search of a parolee's premises by a parole officer without a warrant could not be used in a subsequent and independent criminal action.[54] To permit the evidence to be used in such a way, the court reasoned, when the same rules do not apply to defendants not on parole might constitute a denial to parolees of equal protection of the law, in violation of the Fourteenth Amendment.

These possibilities of constant surveillance mean that during a period when the parolee must make an incredibly difficult readjustment, he is always aware that a single misstep might send him back to prison. The parole experience is filled with a sense of constant jeopardy. Every decisior he makes involves the possibility of risking his liberty.

A study of the effects of the parole experience on sixteen adult parolees in Berkeley, California in 1966 concluded that although Berkeley has an unusually progressive parole organization, the conditions under which parolees are required to operate diminish their chances of adjusting successfully. The group found that parolees studied were subject to the following pressures:

> The parolee was in general defined both by the parole agency and by relevant persons in the community as a person to be distrusted. He was often cast in the role of a problematic person, and admitted to normal social positions, such as employee or student, only hesitantly or as a special favor. He often felt "treated like a child." Most parolees lacked those evidences of accreditation on which all of us depend when presenting ourselves in a new community, such as acceptable identification, references, clothing appropriate for various occasions, a telephone where he could be reached, explanations about the recent past.

> The parolee often lacked the resources needed to cushion the strains of the early release period, such as adequate funds, supplies for personal grooming, a watch, comfortable shoes, easy ac-

54. *State v. Cullison,* 173 N.W.2d 533 (Iowa 1970).

cess to transportation. If the parolee relied on family members to supply these necessities, he might find himself heavily obligated to persons for whom his presence was already a source of strain. The standards of behavior applied to him immediately after release were more strict than those required of non-parolees, and there was little tolerance for the trial and error behavior characteristic of difficult transitional periods.

. . . Rules were usually presented as absolutes with little guidance about the modifications of behavior that might be permissible under various kinds of circumstances. Parole agents made decisions affecting the parolee without explaining the reasons; more than one parolee spent anxious hours trying to figure out the rationale for decisions made about him. Parole agents varied in the kinds of instructions they gave in such matters as informing employers of the parolee status, what permission was needed to cross jurisdictional lines within a metropolitan area, or under what conditions association with other parolees was illegitimate. . . .

The parolee often found it difficult to establish warm, tension-free relationships with anyone. Parole agents sometimes intruded in family or employer relationships in a way that changed relationships for the worse. No one gave attention to the parolee's common complaint about empty leisure time and his lack of ways to fill time outside of work. Fear of social rejection restrained many parolees from approaching old friends or seeking new ones; the rule against association interjected an element of danger into relationships with other persons who had shared his institutional experience.[55]

How many of the best adjusted people could succeed in such circumstances? As for the sixteen parolees under observation, the study concluded that, in the majority of the cases, where personal inadequacies and lack of resources combined to produce problems, the general tendency of the parole system was to intensify strain unless counteracted by the exceptionally able management of an individual parole agent.

55. Studt, *The Reentry of the Offender into the Community* 809 (1967). *Cf.* Milligan, "California's Parole Rules," 15 *Crime and Delinquency* 275 (1969): "If a parolee cannot live successfully under these restrictions, to confer total freedom upon him immediately upon release from prison will not bring about any greater conformity to society's standards."

The releasees' perceptions of authority make the situation even more difficult. While it is not simple for agents of the system to work with offenders who are involuntarily in prison, according to observers, the difficulty is aggravated after they have been released. The experience of imprisonment alienates its captives; it makes inmates fearful and resentful of authority.

No one has tried systematically to discover what needs the offenders themselves think they have, or what kind of help they would like to receive. In fact, it is likely and natural that they would prefer to be free from any interference by correctional officials after their formal release from institutions. As one observer reported, "In many ways, offenders accept the punishment philosophy and are extremely ritualistic. They believe that once they have 'paid their debt to society' they should be free from omnipresent supervision."[56]

Until the laws and administrative practices that establish parolees as persons without rights are changed and the parolee given greater responsibility for his own decisions, programs to help parolees' adjustment can only be artificial and palliative. A few successful efforts to ease the transition have been made, however.

There has been some progress in making the transition less abrupt. The establishment of furloughs from prison, work-release programs and community-based pre-release guidance centers in the areas to which the parolees eventually will return all represent sensible efforts to ease at least the long-term prisoner back into the community. In addition, some parole departments for juveniles have established "intensive parole units," which include agents with small caseloads and neighborhood centers, similar to some privately run programs, where parolees meet daily for counseling and work or recreation.

Pre-release classes in prisons, on the other hand, have shown few tangible results. According to one study, prison personnel are much more concerned with the standards of programs to orient incoming inmates to prison than with those of programs designed to prepare them for release. Although administrators have described a few pre-release programs enthusiastically, claiming their benefits to be practical if intangible, researchers have denied that there is any real evidence of their success in reducing recidivism after release. One study used questionnaires to test inmates who took four different pre-release courses in California prisons. The results showed that the prisoners' attitudes toward such things as

56. Empey, *Alternatives to Incarceration* 68 (1967).

budgeting money and working with parole officers had been changed very little by the pre-release instruction.[57]

More positive results are expected from the programs that go beyond pre-release instruction to include tangible help to prospective parolees. For example, when we visited a reception-guidance center operated by the California Youth Authority, we observed a thirty-day parole preparation program for wards who had been assigned directly to parole following their stay at the reception-guidance center. Not only are the wards introduced to their parole agents and told, along with their families, what is expected of them on parole; they actually are taken by staff members to re-enroll in school, enter a training program or find a job. In addition, they are placed in a foster home, where necessary, and given whatever other kinds of help the program's staff can arrange.

Releasees from Maryland's Patuxent Institution are seen in an outpatient clinic by the same professionals who treated them in the institution. The men are thus given continuing help in making the transition from the institution to the outside, and the problem of forming new relationships with parole supervisors during a difficult period is avoided. Staff members see each parolee once a week. This expansive kind of assistance is very unusual in the United States, although it is common in some of the smaller countries in Europe.

The Youth Services Division of the District of Columbia Department of Correction assigns each inmate a classification and parole officer in the institution. The same officer is responsible for giving assistance and supervision to his young men when they are transferred to a halfway house or released on parole. According to former Director of Youth Services Alan M. Schuman, the idea behind this continuing responsibility is to provide continuity for the offenders in the program and to broaden the perspectives of staff members to include the entire correctional process.

Such a system is possible in the District of Columbia, a single city, and in Maryland because the state is not very large and has only one big city. In most places, only institutions that are located close to the offenders' homes might be organized to offer such continuity.

A few agencies, particularly those that are responsible for youthful

57. Glaser, *The Effectiveness of a Prison and Parole System* 406–407 (1964); Clark, "The Texas Prerelease Program," 30 *Federal Probation* 53 (1966); Catalino, "A Prerelease Program for Juveniles in a Medium-Security Institution," 31 *Federal Probation* 41 (1967); Boller, "Preparing Prisoners for Their Return to the Community," 30 *Federal Probation* 43 (1966); Holt and Renteria, "Prerelease Program Evaluation: Some Implications of Negative Findings," 33 *Federal Probation* 40 (1968).

offenders, have attempted to use parole agents to keep youngsters in contact with their families and communities even when they are sent to distant institutions. For example, parole officers may visit the families of youths admitted to institutions to acquaint them with the planned programs and to evaluate family and community problems. The agent may have to find a foster home or other alternative living arrangements. Whenever possible, parole agents visit their clients in the institutions to develop plans for parole.

Where prospective parolees live in the same general area as the institution, more continuity is possible. As part of a short-term institutional program for juvenile offenders, some parole agents from the Los Angeles area spend one day each week at the Fred C. Nelles School working with groups of boys whom they eventually will supervise on parole. In return for this cooperation, administrators permit the agents to return parolees who are having difficulty in the community for short stays in the institution.

In addition to the problem of discontinuity between institutional and parole personnel, there is little coordination between institutional and parole programs. In the few institutions experimenting with innovative programming, there has been little success in extending the programs into the community. For example, parole officers have yet to be trained in the behavior modification or transactional analysis models currently in use in a few juvenile institutions.

The answer ultimately seems to lie in using only small institutions located close to the communities where people will return on parole and employing essentially the same personnel in the institutions and in the community. In the interim, there should be at least some effort to train parole agents in whatever rehabilitative techniques are being used with their prospective parolees.

The Revocation of Parole

The rate of parole revocations is often used as a measurement of the success of various programs tried in prisons. By the use of base expectancy tables, researchers can compare the actual parole performance of certain groups of prisoners exposed to conventional or experimental treatment programs with their expected performance based on the statistical prediction tables. One obvious assumption in these evaluations is that successful completion of parole depends on an offender's ability to adjust to free society. A key test—a corroborable and relevant one—is whether a released prisoner commits further crimes. Unless a parolee commits a new crime, however, his parole officer has discretion in dealing with technical violations of parole conditions. And since revocation presently depends largely on the recommendation of the parole officer, the way in which a particular officer reacts to certain conduct is crucial.

In 1965 researchers collected data from the 318 parole officers and supervisors of the Parole and Community Services Division of the California Department of Correction. The subjects all were part of the same department, were governed by the same rules and had to deal with the same parole board. All participants were given summaries of ten actual case histories of parolees who had been involved in some incident that could precipitate a revocation of parole. In each case the subjects were asked to decide what they would have done if they were handling the case—whether they would have recommended return to prison or continuation on parole.

The responses document the great variability among parole agents on case recommendations and the disparity in subjective judgments in the parole area. Responses ranged from one agent who chose to continue nine of the ten cases on parole to five other agents who chose to return all ten to prison. About half the agents chose to return either six or seven of the cases to prison. But even those who continued the same number of cases on parole frequently disagreed about which of the cases to continue. Interestingly, the lower the position of each officer in the parole-agency hierarchy, the more ready was he to return a parolee to prison. Apparently, experience breeds faith—if not in the prisoners on parole at least in the judgments of the parole officers of their own abilities and the sense of the system.

Differences seemed to localize in general areas. Recommendations varied not only among parole officers but also among parole offices. In one office the average number of cases continued on parole was 1.62 and in another it was 4.62. Within general areas, views seem to spread from the top down. The number of cases continued by the agents in an office showed a definite correlation with the number continued by the office supervisor and with the agents' assessment of their supervisor's orientation. A majority of the agents agreed that it mattered to them whether their recommendations were accepted and that violation reports were sometimes prepared on the basis of what the parole board could be expected to "buy."[58] This factor makes it difficult for agents to explain their actions to parolees.

In addition to the differing judgment of parole agents, considerations affecting the rate of revocations are the size of parole officers' caseloads and the degree of surveillance provided. Programs with smaller caseloads or more diligent agents conceivably could show higher rates of failure than conventional programs.

The variation among parole officers in their readiness to recommend parole revocation makes it especially crucial that parole boards exercise an independent judgment regarding whether a violation occurred and the appropriate disposition of the offender. Recently, the proceedings surrounding parole revocation, in which parole is terminated and a term of imprisonment imposed or reinstated, have been the subject of a great deal of litigation. In eight jurisdictions parole may be revoked without any hearing; the Supreme Court currently is considering the constitutionality of the practice. Only one state guarantees the right to appointed counsel; in many jurisdictions even retained counsel may not appear on the parolee's behalf.

Even in states where parole boards have made some effort to introduce elements of due process of law into parole revocation hearings, there is no real opportunity for the parolee to refute the charges against him or to participate in the board's decision. One procedure we observed in a juvenile system provides that the parolee must be informed of the charges against him and advised that he may present additional information to the board. However, in many cases board members appeared to have decided to revoke parole before the youths even entered the room; one was told, "We are going to have to revoke your parole," before he was given a chance to speak. The parolees were young, often inarticulate and sometimes frightened. None was represented. None made much of a statement. The bulk of the hearings consisted of lectures, delivered in kindly, almost fatherly tones, which attempted to justify the board's action and impress the boy with the seriousness of his offense.

Three approaches have been used to deny parolees' claims to fair hearings and legal representation when parole revocation is at issue. The first is that the granting of parole is merely an act of grace on the part of the executive that may be withdrawn at any time.[59] A second fictional and

58. Robison and Takagi, "Case Decisions in a State Parole System" (Research Report No. 31, Research Division, California Department of Correction, November 1968).
59. "Conditional liberty is not a constitutionally compelled aspect of criminal law, but exists because of the beneficence of the state." *Hiatt v. Compagna*, 178 F.2d 42 (5th Cir. 1949). *See also Ughbanks v. Armstrong*, 208 U.S. 481 (1908); *Poole v. Stevens*, 190 F. Supp. 938 (E.D.Mich. 1960).

legalistic rationale characterizes parole as a contract between the sovereign and the prisoner, in which the prisoner agrees to certain conditions, one of which is revocation without notice or hearing, in return for early release.[60] Under the third fiction, the parolee is deemed to remain in the custody of the prison warden or parole board. The revocation is merely a change in the form of custody and thus requires no special protection.[61]

Federal parolees first received some protection from the most flagrant procedural abuses in 1963, when the Circuit Court of Appeals for the District of Columbia[62] decided the case of *Hyser v. Reed.*[63] Prisoners whose parole had been revoked claimed that the parole board's revocation procedures were illegal. They argued that their statutory right[64] to an "opportunity to appear before the Board," as well as their right to counsel under the Sixth Amendment and the Fifth Amendment guarantee of due process of law, should assure them: (1) appointed counsel for indigents; (2) specification of charges; (3) confrontation and cross-examination of the board's informants; (4) the right to examine confidential reports of the board; (5) compulsory process to obtain witnesses; and (6) a hearing held in the district where the alleged violation occurred.

The court construed the statutory language to require only that: (1) the arrest warrant reveal with reasonable specificity the reasons why revocation is sought; and (2) the preliminary interview be conducted as close as possible to the place of the alleged violation; (3) as promptly as is convenient after the arrest.

60. *E.g., Wilson v. State,* 240 S.W. 2nd 774 (Texas Crim. App. 1951).
61. *E.g., McCoy v. Harris,* 108 Utah 407, 160 P.2d 721 (1945).
62. A prisoner confined in any federal penitentiary may petition the District Court for the District of Columbia for a declaratory judgment to determine the validity of his parole revocation, and it is within the province of the court to order his release if it finds that the board abused its discretion. A prisoner may thus circumvent a particular district court where prevailing authority may deny him relief. *E.g., Howell v. Hiatt,* 199 F.2d 584, 585 (5th Cir. 1952): ". . . any remedy appellant has against the Parole Board lies in the jurisdiction of the District of Columbia and not in the district where he is held as a prisoner of the warden." Previously, the procedure for appeal from a determination by the parole board was to petition the district court nearest the prison in which the parolee was reincarcerated for a writ of *habeas corpus.* Now it appears that whether or not a court of appeals for a given circuit has ruled specifically that it will disallow appeals from adverse decisions on petitions for *habeas corpus,* the District of Columbia courts will take jurisdiction of suits for mandamus or declaratory judgment against the U.S. Board of Parole. *But see* United States *ex rel. DeFillio v. Fitzpatrick,* 378 F.2d 85, 87 (2d Cir. 1967); *Beatty v. Kearny,* 357 F.2d 667 (5th Cir. 1966).
In *Hunly v. Reed,* 288 F.2d 844 (D.C. Cir. 1961), the District of Columbia court justified the jurisdiction of the District of Columbia courts of suits against the parole board under the provisions of the Administrative Procedure Act, 5 U.S.C., §1009 (1958), that location of an administrative agency in the District of Columbia satisfies the requirements of venue. (It is generally held that the rest of the Administrative Procedure Act is inapplicable to parole revocation hearings.)
63. 318 F.2d 225 (D.C. Cir.), *cert. denied* 375 U.S. 957 (1963).
64. 18 U.S.C. 4207.

The court refused, however, to apply the asserted constitutional protections. The majority opinion, written by the present Chief Justice Warren E. Burger, reasoned that the "parole revocation process is neither a 'criminal prosecution' nor an adversary proceeding in the usual sense of the term. The primary issue before the Board is: Has the parolee violated a condition of his parole? Even if this determination is adverse to the parolee, the Board has discretion to continue his parole notwithstanding a violation." The court's opinion classified the hearing as administrative and pointed out that the law does not require that an interested party in an administrative or regulatory proceeding be entitled to free counsel if he cannot afford one. "Congress has not authorized the Parole Board to appoint counsel for indigent parolees appearing before it and . . . Congress has not empowered the federal courts to make such appointments."

In line with its characterization of the proceedings as administrative and not as criminal trials, the court considered the scope of judicial review to be extremely circumscribed:

> Once the violation is established or admitted, the exercise of discretion in determining whether or not parole should be revoked, represents a very high form of expert regulatory and administrative judgment, and the expert appraisal of the Parole Board in this area can be regarded as almost unreviewable.

Since *Hyser* was decided, the assumptions on which it was based have been eroded. The assumption of "expert regulatory and administrative judgment" has been challenged by a widely respected expert on administrative law; the legal theory that constitutional rights can depend on the labeling of a proceeding as "criminal" or "administrative" has been rejected by the Supreme Court.[65] Reacting to such changes, as well as to case law in other jurisdictions, a panel of the court that decided *Hyser* recently served notice that the precedent should be reviewed by the entire court.[66]

Following the same line of reasoning as that of the *Hyser* court, a federal district court ruled recently that neither the Fifth nor the Eighth Amendment nor the Federal Bail Reform Act of 1966 requires that a parolee apprehended for an alleged violation of a condition of his parole be given a bail hearing.[67] Since by federal statute the parolee remains "in the legal custody and under the control of the Attorney General," the parolee

65. Davis, *Discretionary Justice* (1969). *Goldberg v. Kelley,* 397 U.S. 254 (1970).
66. *Baker v. Sard,* No. 22757 (D.C. Cir., Feb. 16, 1972).
67. 18 U.S.C. §4203; *Marchand v. Director, U.S. Probation Office,* 296 F. Supp. 532 (D.Mass. 1969).

may be arrested and detained in a federal institution until he has been given a revocation hearing.

When the facts that form the basis of the parole violation also are, or may be, the subject of additional criminal charges, serious questions of double jeopardy and the right to remain silent arise. Courts consistently have refused to invalidate parole revocation on either of these bases, on the theory that revocation hearings are non-criminal in nature. Some courts have ruled, however, that any self-incriminatory statements made by parolees at these hearings may not be used against them in a criminal trial.[68]

Since the Supreme Court decided *Mempa v. Rhay*,[69] a decision holding that in order for probation to be revoked and a new sentence imposed an offender must be given counsel, some courts have tried to distinguish between the revocation of probation and the revocation of parole.[70] One federal court of appeals ruled recently that, despite *Mempa*, state legislatures continued to have the power to give parole boards freedom to send parolees back to prison. Disregarding the recent enlargement of offenders' rights even while they remain in prison, the court adhered to the traditional view of parole revocation, refusing to require either a hearing or representation by counsel:

> The Parole Commission may declare a prisoner, who has been paroled, a violator when *in its judgment* he has violated the conditions of his parole. . . . The Constitutional rights of Rose, which he claims were violated, apply *prior* to conviction. They are not applicable to a convicted felon whose convictions and sentences are valid and unassailable, and whose sentences have not been served. A state prisoner does not have a constitutional right to a hearing on a state parole revocation. . . .
>
> Involved here is not judicial power, but state prison discipline administered by the state parole board.[71]

In dissent, one judge urged that parole is an integral part of the criminal justice system:

68. *Melson v. Sard*, 402 F.2d 653 (D.C. Cir. 1968); United States *ex rel. Carioscia v. Meisner*, No. 70C 906 (N.D. Ill., Sept. 10, 1971); *cf. Clutchette v. Procunier*, 328 F. Supp. 767 (N.D. Cal. 1971).
69. 389 U.S. 128 (1967).
70. *E.g., Hutchinson v. Patterson*, 267 F. Supp. 433, 434–35 (D.Colo. 1967); *Johnson v. Wainwright*, 208 So.2d 505 (Fla. App. 1968); *Earnest v. Willingham*, 406 F.2d 681 10th Cir. 1969); *but see Murray v. Page*, 429 F.2d 1359 (10th Cir. 1970).
71. *Rose v. Haskins*, 388 F.2d 91, 95, 97 (6th Cir.), *cert. denied*, 392 U.S. 946 (1968); *accord, Williams v. Patterson*, 389 F.2d 374 (10th Cir. 1968).

By taking this narrow conceptual approach, these courts ignore the essential identity of the position of persons whether they are paroled, put on probation, or conditionally pardoned. Each has been found guilty of a crime; each has been deemed worthy of rehabilitation; and each has been given a status that is considerably more desirable than that of a prisoner. When revocation is threatened, they all have the same interest in maintaining that status.

Although he conceded that a parole board has broad discretion in deciding whether to grant or deny parole, once freedom has been granted, the board's discretion is limited to determining whether a specified condition of release has been violated. This determination may not be made constitutionally without a hearing:

. . . the Petitioner's parole was revoked because he was *accused* of committing a felony, but he was given no opportunity to rebut that accusation. Under these circumstances, the least due process requires is a hearing where the accused can explain his position on the accusation.

Other courts continue to reject the notion that a hearing is constitutionally required for revocation of parole.[72]

While requiring a hearing, a federal appeals court recently adopted the unusual—and probably impractical—position of resolving to determine on a case-by-case basis whether the denial of appointed counsel to an indigent parolee served to deny him due process of law. The court refused to adopt the proposition that counsel is required in every case of parole revocation.[73]

One inroad into the theory of complete parole-board discretion to prescribe revocation procedures was made when still another federal court of appeals ruled that, while counsel is not constitutionally required for revocation of parole, the "opportunity to appear" granted by the same federal statute construed in *Hyser v. Reed,* had been interpreted by the United States Parole Board to permit prisoners to retain counsel. Since the board permitted those prisoners who could afford it to be represented by attorneys, it must appoint lawyers for those prisoners who could not:

---

72. *Morrisey v. Brewer,* 443 F.2d 943 (8th Cir. 1971); *Baxter v. Commonwealth,* 9 *Criminal Law Reporter* 2085 (Mass. Sup. Ct., Apr. 5, 1971).
73. *Bearden v. South Carolina,* 443 F.2d 1090 (4th Cir. 1971).

[W]here liberty is at stake a State (or a federal agency) may not grant to one even a non-constitutional, statutory right such as here involved and deny it to another because of poverty. . . .

[T]he Board is required to provide substantially the same type hearing for one violator as another. So long as the Board allows retained counsel at revocation hearings it must provide such for those financially unable to hire one.[74]

The Maryland Court of Appeals ruled in 1957 that a parolee must be permitted to be represented by retained counsel at a revocation hearing.[75] The Supreme Court of Pennsylvania recently went further, holding that appointed counsel must be provided where necessary, since counsel is required to determine the constitutional validity of the hearing that determines on which side of prison walls a man will reside.[76] A few other courts, distinguishing between the procedures necessary to grant and revoke parole, have done likewise.[77]

Some lower courts in New York have recognized that once all the legal niceties have been disposed of, parole revocation and probation revocation both involve the same question of whether an individual shall continue at liberty or be imprisoned, and the right to counsel applies to both.[78] Early in 1970, the New York Court of Appeals agreed:

74. *Earnest v. Willingham*, 406 F.2d 681, 683–84 (10th Cir. 1969). The court now requires appointment of counsel only when the parolee denies the violation. *See Earnest v. Moseley*, 426 F.2d 466 (10th Cir. 1970). *Cf. Alverez v. Turner*, 422 F.2d 214 (10th Cir. 1970). *See also Warren v. Michigan Parole Board*, 179 N.W.2d 664 (Mich. App. 1970). *Contra, Heath v. State*, 94 Idaho 101, 482 P.2d 76 (1971).
75. *Warden, Maryland Penitentiary v. Palumbo*, 214 Md. 407, 135 A.2d 439 (1957).
76. *Commonwealth v. Tinson*, 433 Pa. 328, 249 A.2d 549 (1969).
77. *United States ex rel Bey v. Board of Parole*, 443 F.2d (2d Cir. 1971); *Goolsby v. Gagnon*, 322 F. Supp. 460 (E.D.Wis. 1971); *Warren v. Michigan Parole Board*, 23 Mich. App. 754, 179 N.W. 2d 684 (1970).
78. *See* People *ex rel. Combs v. LaVallee*, 29 A.D.2d 128, 130–31, 286 N.Y.S.2d 600, 603, *appeal dismissed*, 22 N.Y.2d 857, 293 N.Y.S.2d 117, 239 N.E.2d 743 (1968); *Menechino v. Division of Parole*, 57 Misc.2d 865, 293 N.Y.S.2d 741 (1968); *compare* People *ex rel. Och v. LaVallee*, 60 Misc.2d 627, 303 N.Y.S.2d 772 (1968) *with* People *ex rel. Och v. LaVallee*, 60 Misc.2d 629, 303 N.Y.S.2d 774 (1969). However, another New York court, adhering to the traditional theory, ruled recently that there is no constitutional right to counsel on revocation of parole:

The discretionary nature of the Board's determination and the special expertise the Board brings to the ultimate question of whether the parole violator still constitutes a good parole risk despite his transgression render an adversary-type proceedings unwarranted and completely inappropriate. . . . Involved here is not judicial power, but State prison discipline. The Parole Board having exclusive authority over execution of the sentence (be it served within or without the prison walls), its revocation of the privilege of parole, without a full-blown judicial-type proceeding, does not constitute a denial of due process.

People *ex rel. Smith v. Deegan*, 32 A.D.2d 940, 303 N.Y.S.2d 789, 792 (App. Div. 1969).

There are, of course, differences between Washington's deferred sentencing procedure, probation revocation and parole revocation but, in our view, such differences cannot militate against the need for a lawyer where revocation of parole results in the deprivation of liberty. . . . The principle which underlies the decision in *Mempa* is sufficiently broad to encompass the revocation of parole as well as of probation. In both, the decision to deprive an individual of his liberty turns on factual determinations, and "the necessity for the aid of counsel in marshaling the facts, introducing evidence of mitigating circumstances and in general aiding and assisting the defendant to present his case . . . is apparent."[79]

A federal district court recently ruled that a parolee facing revocation must be provided with an opportunity to confront and cross-examine the government agents relied on by the parole board in making its decision.[80] The court based its ruling on the Supreme Court decision that required due-process protections to be afforded to welfare recipients before benefits are terminated.[81]

In 1969 a comprehensive legislative scheme governing parole revocation, which, interestingly, was recommended by the Board of Prison Terms and Paroles, was adopted in the state of Washington.[82] The statutes provide for prompt written notice to the parolee of the factual allegations of the violation of parole conditions; hearings held reasonably near the place where the alleged violation occurred; representation of the parolee by retained or, in the case of indigents, appointed counsel; subpoena power for the attendance of witnesses or the production of evidence; the recording of hearings; and the protection of parolees who are "requested to testify" from the use of their testimony in any criminal prosecution. The legislation does not give parolees the right to inspect the records in the board's possession; nor does it create a right of appeal from an adverse determination. However, it does provide an example of a parole board's seizing the initiative to reform its own procedures.

When a releasee's parole is revoked, he generally is returned to prison, where he must remain until he is reparoled or released on completion of the maximum term for which he was sentenced. Gus Moeller, former assistant director of the federal Bureau of Prisons and one of the

79. People *ex rel. Menechino v. Warden, Greenhaven State Prison,* 27 N.Y.2d 367, 318 N.Y.S.2d 449 (1971), quoting *Mempa v. Rhay,* 389 U.S. 128, 135 (1967).
80. United States *ex rel. Carioscia v. Meisner,* No. 71 C 906 (N.D. Ill. Sept. 10, 1971).
81. *Goldberg v. Kelley,* 397 U.S. 254 (1970).
82. Revised Code of Washington §§9.95.120–9.95.126 (1970 Supp.).

country's more experienced correction officials, advised that sometimes offenders must go back to prison several times before they are successfully released. The returns should not be considered examples of the system's failure, he remarked to us, but rather, necessary steps in the process of adjusting back into the community.

Many parole violators are returned to prison not because of the commission of a new felony but because of the commission of a misdemeanor or the technical violation of one of the conditions of parole. Return of all parole violators to prison, regardless of the nature of the violation, is much more expensive than using jails or other local facilities for short-term stays.

In California the Department of Corrections has experimented with sending parole violators to jail or to short-term return units of prison for an average stay of three to four months. (The average stay in prison after a parole violation in that state is usually from fifteen to eighteen months.) No significant difference was found between the performance of the two groups after re-release. California has continued to use the short-term return units as a much less expensive alternative than returning parole violators to prison.[83]

Halfway houses or community correctional centers also might be used for short-term stays by parole violators or parolees having difficulty adjusting to complete freedom. Such a practice is followed for Youth Services parolees in the District of Columbia, where a Community Treatment Center functions as both a conventional halfway house and a "halfway-back" facility. In most cases a parolee who is readmitted to the center retains his job while he is there.

The possibility of discharging some parolees before the expiration of their full sentences (sometimes many years after they have been placed on parole) prompted the California legislature to pass a law in 1965 permitting parole agents to recommend discharge of parolees who have been on parole for at least two years and who have demonstrated their "rehabilitation."[84] Studies of the decisions made to implement the law reveal that there has been little consistency either in parole agents' conclusions regarding continuation or discharge from parole or in the information used by them to reach their conclusions. During the first year and a half of the law's operation only 26 percent of the cases reviewed for possible early discharge actually were discharged from parole; yet only 2 percent

---

83. Bull, "Long Jail Terms and Parole Outcome" (Research Report No. 28, California Department of Correction, October 1967); Burkhardt, *Parole in California* 8 (1968).
84. Cal. Pen. Code §2943.

of the entire group was returned to prison by the courts within one year for subsequent criminal behavior, including 3 percent of the group continued on parole and 1.3 of those discharged.

Parole is a sensible—in fact essential—concept in a society as committed to imprisonment as ours. There is an obvious need for a period of decompression and reintroduction to society after an extended time of isolation and removal from the temptations and responsibilities of the community. But beyond this use of parole as a transition are greater possibilities for the shifting of emphasis in correction from institutions to community programs.

As an example, the California Youth Authority has begun a massive program, aided by a $2 million federal grant, to improve its parole supervision and services. The goal of the program is to reduce parole revocations and consequent returns to institutions enough to make the program self-supporting within two years. According to Allen Breed, director of the Youth Authority, the program will provide parolees with a variety of services, depending on their needs, and will provide parole agents with training and consultation aimed at developing community alternatives to institutions and changing the decision-making process to favor the use of community alternatives over the revocation of parole and reinstitutionalization. The hoped-for result: reduction of crimes committed by parolees, the closing of at least 400 institutional beds and the use of the money saved to support continuation of the new parole program. At present, such a reallocation of resources from institution to parole, together with a greater emphasis on probation and other community alternatives, seems to have the greatest potential for reorienting correction from its reliance on imprisonment as the primary means of dealing with offenders.

On the other hand, while parole provides a sensible way to release those who are imprisoned as early as possible and to assist them in returning to society, when we consider the way the system operates in practice, we must raise the question of whether in fact it serves its purpose. The same system that enables prisoners to be released before expiration of their maximum sentences also enables parole boards to reimprison them for violation of technical conditions that few could obey. What in theory is a benign and reformative system too often in practice replaces assistance with surveillance and mercy with the arbitrary exercise of unbridled discretion. Instead of helping former prisoners to readjust to society, far too often the system simply creates one more hurdle for them to overcome.

VI

Clemency—Rehabilitating the Record

Clemency is a generic term covering several forms of legal processes, including pardon, commutation, reprieve and amnesty. Defined in Webster's dictionary as "a disposition to be . . . merci[ful], humane . . . mild and compassionate and to moderate possible severity of judgment and punishment," in a more artful sense clemency is a determination late in the criminal justice process by an executive authority to mitigate some consequences of a sentence.

There are four types of clemency. The chief and by far the most commonly used form is the *pardon,* which either exempts a convicted offender from all punishment or removes the civil disabilities associated with his criminal conviction. A *commutation* lessens the severity of the penalty that has been prescribed. A *reprieve* merely postpones execution of a sentence that has been imposed. An *amnesty* overlooks the crimes of a group of offenders.

Clemency can be seen as an over-all balancing mechanism that compensates for flaws in the criminal justice system; or it can be considered simply as a special, more finite tool to achieve specific aims in limited, special cases. Two divergent views about the essential nature of the pardon power were exemplified in two decisions of the Supreme Court. According to an early opinion by Chief Justice John Marshall, a pardon was considered an official but private act, an offer of grace which, like a contract, had to be accepted by the offender in order to be complete.[1] In 1926, how-

1. *United States v. Wilson,* 32 U.S. (7 Pet.) 150 (1833). The legalistic doctrine that a pardon is not valid until delivered persists. *See e.g.,* Petition of De Angelis, 139 F. Supp. 779 (E.D.N.Y. 1956), holding that a pardon is an act of grace not tantamount to a finding of not guilty or the setting aside of a verdict.

ever, the Supreme Court was presented with a case in which a prisoner had refused the President's offer to commute his sentence from death penalty to life imprisonment. Writing for the majority of the Court, Justice Oliver Wendell Holmes, Jr., said:

> A pardon in our days is not a private act of grace from an individual happening to possess power. It is a part of the Constitutional scheme. When granted it is the determination of the ultimate authority that the public welfare will be better served by inflicting less than what the judgment fixed. Just as the original punishment would be imposed without regard to the prisoner's consent and in the teeth of his will, whether he liked it or not, the public welfare, not his consent, determines what shall be done.[2]

Clemency generally serves a unique function in the administration of the criminal law. In some instances it may provide the last official chance to do justice in an individual case; it is a device to relieve undue severity or judgmental error and to temper justice with mercy by considering facts that might mitigate guilt.

In an ideal society with a perfect system of criminal justice, there would be no need for any form of clemency. But in reality the complexity of circumstances surrounding society's reaction to any individual criminal act perforce may leave questions concerning the appropriateness of the justice provided to an accused wrongdoer. There is a need in the imperfect official system for some provision for clemency which "represents the sense of human weakness, the recognition of human fallibility, the cry of human compassion. It is a confession of imperfect wisdom."[3]

The need to include clemency in any complete system of criminal justice derives from a recognition of the political and historical nature of the criminal justice system, as well as the fallibility of man. Values and motives change, and the system sometimes must have a way to recognize these changes in individual cases. Sir Francis Bacon felt that the essence of the king's clemency power was to individualize the law; the classical criminologist Cesare Beccaria felt it was a technique to cure severe punishments more so than to correct individual judgments; the Attorney General's exhaustive 1939 *Survey of Release Procedures* suggested that it is a procedure for updating and modernizing the justice system. All were right.

2. *Biddle v. Perovich*, 274 U.S. 480, 486 (1926).
3. Smithers, *Executive Clemency in Pennsylvania* 61 (1909).

The right to appeal from a criminal conviction is relatively recent. Before these developments in appellate procedure, almost the only recourse of an innocent man convicted of a crime was to apply for an executive pardon. Even today, cases arise in which, due to the technical limitations on the traditional, legalistic post-conviction remedies, no way exists other than the pardon power to rectify a wrongful conviction.

Broad discretionary executive powers of clemency have been considered necessary, as one writer has stated, "to temper retribution with mercy, to correct error, to do justice where the rigorous inflexibility of a judicial system has not adjusted to compelling social needs."[4] It provides some remedy for the exceptional case. And it may spotlight institutional or procedural shortcomings and suggest reforms. While it may be used to correct errors, resolve doubts or temper sentences, most frequently the clemency process is used to restore rights lost as a collateral effect of conviction.

More than recognizing errors or adapting to changing times and values is involved in the extraordinary clemency process. A moral element exists as well; and it goes to the heart of the philosophic goals of any criminal justice system. It is most apparent in cases of civil disobedience. Throughout our history there have been notable examples where good men of decent intent violated laws for reasons of conscience. Is suffering punishment for one's acts a necessary part of the moral component which characterizes civil disobedience? If gesture alone is the symbolic purpose, punishment need not follow, or, if it does, it is appropriate for it to be reviewed and ameliorated in the future. If, however, the act is stripped of its meaning without punishment or the martyrdom is diminished when the act escapes retribution, clemency might serve as a tactic to dissipate moral actions. Social protest has increased in this country in recent years from the days of the labor movement early in this century to the civil-rights movement in mid-century to the war resistance surrounding our military involvements in Indochina. Many individuals have become convicts less out of conventional outlawry or misconduct than from defiant acts of symbolic protest. How they are treated in the future will determine, to some extent, the sense of our system in years to come.

4. Foote, "Pardon Policy in a Modern State," 39 *The Prison Journal* 3 (April 1959).

Pardon

A pardon is an act of grace and forgiveness which either totally or partially relieves the person pardoned from some of the ramifications of the punishment the law originally inflicted upon him. After a person has been convicted of a crime and exhausted his judicial appeals, theoretically he may apply for a pardon at any time, whether he is in prison, on probation or parole or has been discharged completely. (In a minority of states and in the federal system, a pardon may be granted before trial.) The pardoning authority has broad discretion to exercise its power to fit the circumstances of each individual case. Before parole was established as a regular method of early release from prison, pardons were more necessary than they are today. At present, the greatest majority of pardons are granted to people who are no longer incarcerated but who wish to regain certain civil rights, such as the right to vote, testify, serve on a jury, hold public office or practice a profession, which have been lost or suspended as a result of their conviction.

There is some confusion and some difference of opinion about whether a pardon only retroactively eliminates the official ripples of recrimination following conviction of an offense, or whether it totally abnegates the offense. The wiser and more authoritative view is that a pardon does not imply innocence or cancel guilt but simply eliminates prospectively some of the pending collateral sanctions of the original conviction. In the clear words of Reed Cozart, former U.S. Pardon official: "A pardon does not erase the conviction and does not signify the innocence of the petitioner . . . it does not erase the record . . . it only forgives the offense and . . . assists the recipient to regain some rights."[5]

Acceptance of a pardon is generally considered to carry an imputation of guilt. Consequently, the Supreme Court once ruled that a witness might claim the Fifth Amendment's immunity from coerced self-incriminating testimony, despite the offer of a Presidential pardon for any crime in which he might implicate himself.[6]

On the other hand, pardons are sometimes the only means of establishing a person's innocence in cases where the technical prerequisites for

5. Cozart, "Clemency Under the Federal System," 23 *Federal Probation* 6 (September 1959); Cozart, "The Benefits of Execution Clemency," 32 *Federal Probation* 34 (June 1968).
6. *Burdick v. United States*, 236 U.S. 79, 94 (1915).

setting aside a conviction by judicial means are not present. The federal statute that gives the court of claims jurisdiction over damage suits against the United States Government for unjust conviction permits the plaintiff to use as proof of his innocence either a "certificate of innocence" issued by a federal district court or a pardon that recites that it was granted after the applicant had exhausted all recourse to the courts and that the time for any court to exercise jurisdiction has expired.[7]

A conviction does not take away all a convict's rights automatically. It is not an additional part of the sentence that, for example, one may not vote; that further deprivation comes from the operation of local and state laws. Thus, a pardon does not give back these rights but makes it possible for them to be returned to the ex-convict if local and state law so provide. Therefore, a pardon does not remove an existing adjudication of guilt except in certain exceptional cases when such a specific declaration is the basis of the pardon, nor does a pardon itself always return lost rights. It forgives the offense, though not eradicating it, and it makes way for a return of rights while not automatically and unilaterally returning them.

ORIGIN OF PARDON

Most ancient cultures had no place for pardon. Crime was considered to be an evil of society which had to be exorcised; thus a pardon would intrude on the community's means for social defense. To more primitive cultures which deemed crimes offenses to the deity, only God could pardon the wrongdoer, never man.

The idea of pardon by the public authority presupposes that criminal responsibility is owed to some collective political entity rather than solely to the victim or his relations as was the case in ancient times. The strongest early impediment to clemency was the custom of blood revenge. It was considered the religious duty of a victim's next of kin to avenge his death. It was thought that the dead man's ghost would not rest until his murderer was killed.

The increasing sovereign powers of the Jewish kings gradually eroded the blood revenge. According to a Biblical story, the two sons of an old woman had a quarrel, and one killed the other. Their relatives announced that the remaining son must die to avenge the murder. The woman petitioned King David that "if he would hinder this slaughter of

7. 28 U.S.C. §§1495, 2513.

her son by those that wished for it, he would do her a great favor, because the kindred would not be restrained from their purpose by anything else than by the fear of Him."[8] David made a religious oath to protect the woman's son from the avengers and thus, in effect, "pardoned" the murderer from his private punishment. Similarly, in cases of accidental homicide, a person who slew another "unwittingly" could flee to the six "cities of refuge . . . appointed for all the children of Israel," where he would be safe.[9]

Under Biblical law, however, some crimes could not be pardoned. Many tribal regulations were considered to be ordained by God's will. Breaking them offended God, and no one but God could pardon the offender.

Ancient Greek criminal law emphasized private restitution to the victim of crime in money or property of comparable value. Only penalties given for public wrongs could be pardoned. Sovereignty lay in the people of Athens, and the people had the state power to grant pardons through the "Adeia." At least 6,000 citizens, meeting in a public assembly, had to support the individual seeking the motion for pardon in a secret ballot. The offender was allowed to appear before the assembly, present his case, offer testimony from friends and plead for clemency. Due to the difficulty of assembling 6,000 people in favor of Adeia, few such pardons are reported in Greek history: the recall of Alcibiades in the year 408 B.C., the pardon of Demosthenes in 323 B.C. and the recalls of Thucydides and of Aristides after three years of banishment are examples.

Under Roman law, the power to grant pardons was vested in both the judiciary and the Senate. The Roman courts had the power to remit a penalty at any time. Later, in the time of the Emperors, the Senate was given the power to pardon or to absolve a person from criminal prosecution. In fact, however, pardon always depended on the will of the Emperor, and the Senate merely executed his decisions. A "partial pardon" afforded minor solace: it allowed a condemned man to choose the mode of his death and to execute a valid will.

Along with vesting these branches of the Roman republic with some sort of pardoning power, the gods were not forgotten. A doomed criminal who accidentally encountered a vestal virgin on his way to the place of execution was automatically pardoned, but the meeting had to be an accidental one.

8. Josephus, *Antiq.* VII, Ch. VIII:4.
9. Joshua 20:2–6; Josephus IV, 7, 4.

The Germans developed more forms of pardon than any other people. Prior to the ninth century, the country was divided into tribal units. The entire tribe assembled, tried, sentenced and occasionally pardoned a wrongdoer. After the unification of Germany, the clemency power was transferred to the king. Each king required an oath of allegiance which bound each subject to the king's rules. A subject who committed a crime had violated the king's right to be respected and obeyed, in effect committing a personal crime against the king himself. Consequently, the king, morally wronged, had the power to pardon. Often trial by ordeal was employed: "Many forms of the old German death penalty were sacrifices to the angered gods. By ordeal, the gods were asked whether they wanted victim or not. If the gods refused the gift, the criminal was automatically pardoned. Other very ancient punishments, such as exposure in a leaky ship or in a ship without a rudder, were similar inquiries to the deity whether it would accept the victim or not."[10]

These conventional procedures of monarchial power were not widely practiced; when they were, they were less related to functions of the criminal justice system than to notions of religion and superstition. In many executions one of the doomed men was pardoned with the condition that he had to execute his companions. Some executions were halted by evidence of divine intervention. For example, if the rope broke in a hanging, a pardon was granted immediately. In the city of Basle, every woman sentenced to drown was set free if she reached a certain place downstream alive. This may be traced to the practice of trial by ordeal. Some pardons seemed to have been used to mark notable events, such as the birth of an heir to the throne or the beginning of a reign. Not so easily explainable was the random practice in mass executions of pardoning every tenth man at the will of the executioner.

In England, the pardoning power was first recorded in the Laws of King Ine, King of Wessex (688–725 A.D.): "let him forfeit his shire, unless the king is willing to be merciful to him." These first laws of pardon were not based on a general discretionary power to pardon all subjects. The practice of private vengeance by powerful nobles limited the king's pardoning power to crimes committed by members of the king's household or crimes committed against the personal security or authority of the king.

In the eleventh century when William conquered England, he sought to enhance the stability of his newly acquired lands through the increased

10. 3 *Attorney General's Survey of Release Procedures*, "Pardon" 13–14 (1939).

responsibility of land ownership. All lands emanated from the king. "Every man, noble and simple alike, should hold his land as a pledge of good behavior."[11] Every man had to have a lord to answer in court for his misdoings. And feudal justice gave each feudal lord the power to condemn, punish and grant pardons within the boundaries of his estate. Each lord's estate was his jurisdiction, and therefore, at each local level, there was a parochial pardoning power. Of course the king was preeminent as the lord of the entire kingdom and had the final pardoning power.

The English kings granted pardons freely. Whenever a war broke out, the king needed the support of his lords. An offender need only convince some lord to apply to the king for his pardon. An entry would then appear upon the rolls testifying to the innocence of the accused.

Royal pardons could be purchased. The *London Chronicles* of the reign of Richard II (1377–99) mentioned individuals who "hadde made grete ffynes and Raunceons, and hadde purchased hem of the kyng his patent lettres off pardon." In one recorded case a king pardoned three church officials charged with murder on condition that they pay 500 pounds currency to the family of the victim.[12]

Contention between the Crown and Parliament for the pardoning power existed in England from 1066 to 1535. Gradually, in connection with the growing nationalization of England, the Crown's pardon prerogative became increasingly solidified. In 1535, after many unsuccessful attempts at limiting the king's power, Parliament passed an act giving the king alone the power to pardon felonies. In the next century, however, when Parliament became the supreme governing authority in England, among its victories was the recognition of its power to pardon by legislative enactment.

Another historical aspect of the pardoning power in England was the struggle in the twelfth century between the Church and the state over clerics charged with crime. Benefit of clergy excused those in position to claim it from the jurisdiction of lay courts. Generally, benefit of clergy excused a wrongdoer from capital punishment and substituted minor penalties, such as branding or imprisonment for less than one year for serious offenses. Although originally benefit of clergy was extended only to clerics, eventually it was made applicable to all who could read. Al-

11. Edward Jenks, *A Short History of English Law* 27 (1922).
12. Thornbury, I *Old and New London, Its History, Its People and Its Places* 242 (1889).

though more serious crimes gradually were made exempt from benefit of clergy, the practice was not abolished formally until 1827.

When the first settlers landed in America, having escaped an oppressive power in England, they had no intention of recreating broad, absolute powers in their government. The settlers established popular legislative bodies with the power to make laws and to pardon. Gradually, as the king's control over the colonies tightened, the pardoning power gravitated to the royal governors, who represented the king.

After the Revolution, Americans were suspicious of all executive power. Early state constitutions placed various restrictions, such as approval by the executive council, on the governors' right to pardon. Others gave the pardoning power to the state legislatures.

By the time the federal Constitution was written, the tenor of political thought had shifted and the usefulness of some concentration of executive power was recognized. This shift included delegation of the pardoning power to chief executives. Writing in *The Federalist,* Alexander Hamilton approved of an unencumbered executive pardoning power: "Humanity and good policy conspire to dictate that the benign prerogative of pardoning should be as little as possible fettered or embarrassed."

Article II, Section 2 of the United States Constitution gives the President the exclusive federal power "to grant Reprieves and Pardons for Offenses against the United States except in Cases of Impeachment." Many states followed the lead of the federal government and increased the governors' powers and abolished those of the executive councils. Virtually all the states admitted to the Union after the adoption of the Constitution gave their governors the sole discretion to pardon.

In this country the pardoning power now is vested primarily in the state governors. In many states a pardon attorney or board, frequently the parole board, makes recommendations to the governor in individual cases. In three states the governors are members of the pardon boards, with no greater voting power than any other member. The legislatures, unless specifically prohibited by state constitutions, may pass procedural rules to regulate pardoning applications and hearings, but they may neither pardon nor veto executive pardons. The courts have no power to grant pardons, nor to review pardons granted by the executive.[13] Generally, a decision to grant a pardon comes after all available judicial remedies have been exhausted.

---

13. *Ex parte* United States, 242 U.S. 27 (1916). The prosecutor's power to drop or reduce a charge, and consequently to lessen the ultimate sentence, traditionally has not been considered a species of clemency.

In general, modern practice the pardoning power has remained primarily an executive power. Yet, one court has written, the power to pardon is in the United States "neither inherently nor necessarily an executive power, but is a power of government inherent in the people, who may by constitutional provision place its exercise in any official, board or department of government they choose."[14]

In a small minority of the states, the governor alone has the power to grant pardons, with no advisers or boards to aid or restrain him. A minority of states, along with the federal government, vest the power in the chief executive but provide for a pardon attorney to aid in processing and preparation of cases. Another small group of states vest the power in the governor, with the advice and consent of an executive council.

The largest number of states now provide for an advisory board to make recommendations to the governor. In some states, creation of the boards followed a period of corruption in the granting of pardons. In others, the boards were established to reduce the governors' growing workloads. This plan is favored because it eliminates absolute power, which is conducive to abuse, by shifting the responsibility to the board. While involving the chief executive in the decisions, it shares his responsibility with the community.

The degree to which the chief executive is bound by the board's recommendations varies. In some states the executive is completely free to adopt or reject the board's recommendation. In others, the governor's power of pardon is contingent upon a favorable recommendation by the board. In about one-fifth of the states, the board, of which the governor is a member, is the ultimate pardoning authority.

Board composition varies but may include any combination of the following officers and citizens: governor, lieutenant governor, attorney general, secretary of state, state penal director, prison trustees, state supreme-court justices, presiding judge, special investigators and private citizens appointed by the governor. Over two-thirds of the states have boards, yet each is organized differently.

As a general rule, the courts have no power to grant any form of clemency.[15] In what was a gratuitous comment in an otherwise extraordinary case involving the execution of the Rosenbergs, former Justice Felix Frankfurter commented about the interrelationship between judicial powers and those of executive clemency, thus providing one of the rare mentions of the subject in legal literature:

14. *Jamison v. Flanner,* 116 Kan. 624, 634, 228 P. 82, 87 (1924).
15. *Ex parte* United States, 242 U.S. 27 (1916).

It is not for this Court even remotely to enter into the domain of clemency reserved by the Constitution exclusively to the President. But the Court must properly take into account the possible consequences of a stay or of a denial of a stay of execution of death sentences upon making an appeal for clemency. Were it established that counsel are correct in their assumption that the sentences of death are to be carried out at 11 P.M. tonight, I believe that it would be right and proper for this Court formally to grant a stay with a proper time limit to give appropriate opportunity for the process of executive clemency to operate.[16]

However, some courts, particularly those that sentence misdemeanants, have retained the power to reduce their sentences after some time has been served.

The actions of the clemency authority are purely discretionary and hence are not subject to judicial review. The Oregon Supreme Court stated the rule and its rationale:

. . . it is not within judicial competency to control, interfere with, or even to advise the [clemency authority] when exercising his power to grant reprieves, commutations, and pardons. . . .

Where the constitution . . . confers unlimited power on the Governor to grant reprieves, commutations and pardons, his discretion cannot be controlled by judicial decision. The courts have no authority to inquire into the reasons or motives which actuate the Governor in exercising the power, nor can they decline to give effect to a pardon for an abuse of discretion.[17]

That these executive decisions are not subject to judicial review seems only logical in view of the underlying theory that clemency is itself a review of judicial excessiveness. An effective check against injustice thus is achieved only by vesting an exclusive clemency power in a branch of government other than the branches which write or interpret the laws. To subject executive clemency decisions to judicial review would contradict or negate its very purpose and effectiveness.

On the other hand, while ordinarily there is no review of the merits of individual clemency decisions, the constitutional argument might be

16. *Rosenberg v. United States,* 346 U.S. 322 (1953).
17. *Eacret v. Holmes,* 215 Ore. 121, 333 P.2d 741, 743–44 (1958).

made that an executive who used the clemency power in a generally discriminatory fashion was denying applicants the equal protection of the laws. Several studies indicate, for example, that of all the people who are given death sentences, a larger percentage of whites than blacks have their sentences commuted to life imprisonment.[18]

The role of the legislature in the pardoning process varies among states. One theory, once supported by a number of court decisions, was that the executive possesses an exclusive power which cannot be modified or impaired by legislative enactments. Laws authorizing courts to suspend sentences or place defendants on probation occasionally were attacked as being an invalid delegation of the pardoning power to the judiciary:

> [A court that suspends sentence] may in this way indirectly grant a reprieve, commute a penalty, or remit any part of a sentence, and thus practically exercise powers which the constitution confers exclusively upon the Governor.[19]

Similarly, the enactment of parole laws temporarily was shackled at the turn of the century by decisions which held that paroles were similar in nature to conditional pardons and therefore were improper attempts to grant legislative pardons.[20]

More generally accepted is the theory that the pardoning power, while "exclusive" with respect to infringements by the other branches of government, is not an "absolute" executive power. Legislatures have imposed various procedural requirements regarding pardons, such as their publication either as reports to the legislature or in notices in newspapers or public records. Legislatures also have established pardon boards and set procedures that must be followed before them by applicants.[21] In addition, some legislatures have limited the executive pardoning power to specific offenses. In a majority of the states, both treason and impeachment are non-pardonable, at least by the executive alone.

18. Wolfgang, Kelly and Nolde, "Comparison of the Executed and the Commuted Among Admissions to Death Row," 53 *Journal of Criminal Law, Criminology and Police Science* 301, 311 (1962). ("[T]here is reason to suspect—and statistically significant evidence to support the suspicion—that Negroes have not received equal consideration for commutation of the death penalty."); Johnson, "Executions and Commutations in North Carolina" (1957), in Bedau, *The Death Penalty in America* 452, 462 (1964); *see* Wolfgang and Cohen, *Crime and Race—Conceptions and Misconceptions* 85–86 (1970).
19. *Neal v. State*, 104 Ga. 509, 511, 30 S.E. 858, 859 (1898); *see* 3 *Attorney General's Survey of Release Procedures*, "Pardon" 105, 124–25.
20. *People v. Cummings*, 88 Mich. 249, 50 N.W.310 (1891); *State v. Board of Corrections*, 16 Utah 478, 42 P. 1090 (1898).
21. *Zink v. Lear*, 28 N.J. Super. 515, 101 A.2d 72 (1953); *People ex rel. Smith v. Jenkins*, 325 Ill. 372, 156 N.E. 290 (1927).

Under the federal Constitution and in a great number of states, only impeachment is not pardonable. In a few states, there are no restrictions on pardonable offenses. In a majority of the states where treason is excepted from the executive pardoning power the executive is allowed to delay execution of the sentence until the legislature next meets, at which time the legislature may pardon the wrongdoer.

In most states, pardons may be granted only after conviction. In the remaining states and in the federal system, while pardon theoretically could be granted before or after conviction, in fact it is limited to a post-conviction process. In addition, pardons frequently are granted after a sentence has expired in order to enable the released convict to regain rights that he lost upon conviction.

Notwithstanding such legislative regulations, the pardoning power is broad in nature, and where it is allowed it is not subject to review by any other government agency. Parole statutes, on the other hand, frequently contain detailed regulations concerning eligibility, the procedures for granting and revoking parole and the length and conditions of parole supervision. Consequently, it has been argued that legislatures should refrain from restricting the applicability of parole statutes lest they thereby abdicate the releasing function to the executive clemency power which is beyond legislative control.

Governors have varied widely in their willingness to grant pardons. For example, the governor of Texas from 1925–26, Mrs. Miriam E. Ferguson, granted approximately 3,500 pardons in a two-year period. Her predecessor had granted only seventeen pardons in four years.

The clemency system is vulnerable to political pressure. By granting a pardon, a politician may make himself many friends at election time. In addition, political debts often call for favors, and a requested pardon may be the way some supporters attempt collection. If for no other reason, a system whereby the pardoning official does not alone have all the decision-making power avoids some of this pressure. Still, applications for pardons commonly include letters from the applicant's political allies, a practice which in some places is as counter-productive as it is useful in others.

PARDONING PROCEDURES

The manner in which applications for clemency are to be presented is usually prescribed by local administrative rules, statutes or constitutional provisions. The regulations are based on the need to provide for the orderly presentation of applications with all necessary information and to notify the public and all concerned parties so that objections to granting of the pardon may be heard.

Nearly half the states require notices of applications to be published in a newspaper in the county where the crime occurred. In some states, an applicant must notify the prosecuting attorney and the judge who presided over his trial. Other states require notification of the chief of police in the town where the crime was committed, the prison warden or the chairman of the board of county commissioners.

The written application usually is required to include reasons why a pardon is sought. In addition, aside from the applicant's name, among the items typically required in applications are any aliases, the dates of his sentence, the offense, trial judge, prosecuting attorney, place where the trial was held, age, birthplace, occupation and previous residences. Several states also require recommendations from the presiding judge, prosecuting attorney, the prison warden or even private citizens to be included in the application. Court records also are required in five states.

In many states, the procedure for filing the completed pardon application is so complex that applicants would do well to have lawyers to assure their rights. And in addition to complicated procedural rules, much of the required information may not be readily accessible to those applicants who are still in prison. Nonetheless no court has required the assignment of counsel to represent indigents petitioning for clemency.[22]

In nearly every state there is some investigation of an applicant's background, which may be conducted by the staff of the pardon board (often consolidated with the parole board) or by the governor's legal counsel. All investigative reports include some minimal biographical data, such as age, marital status, criminal record and any available pre-sentence, institutional and parole reports. In only a few states does the investigation proceed beyond the collection of reports to interviewing the applicant, members of his family, his defense counsel or others who know him. Psychological and psychiatric reports are included if they were compiled during the applicant's prison term. Occasionally, special psychiatric examinations are conducted at the request of the pardoning authority.

In those states in which the governor makes the decision to pardon

22. *See, e.g., United States ex rel. Callman v. Denno,* 313 F.2d 457 (2d Cir. 1963), which held that the 14th Amendment does not require a state to provide counsel during the post-appellate period.

without the aid of any advisory board (as the chief executive does in the federal system) there usually is no formal hearing. Where there is an advisory board to aid the governor, or a pardon board of which the governor is a member (approximately two-thirds of the states have this), there is a formal hearing. The states which conduct hearings are about equally divided among public, semi-public (admission only to the press and people connected with the case) and closed hearings. Pardon hearings are held in the state capitol or at the prison. Although the procedure in most states includes an interview with the applicant, in some states he is not even allowed to appear. Attorneys are allowed to appear on the applicant's behalf in most states, but they are not provided for indigents.

In surprisingly few states is there any provision for a representative of the state to appear at the hearing. Presumably the prosecutor may appear if he wishes or if his attendance is requested, but participation by both the district attorney and the judge who tried the case generally is confined to the submission of written recommendations.

Clemency hearings are not appeals and are non-judicial. The pardoning authorities are bound neither by legal precedents nor by rules of evidence and can base their decisions on whatever considerations seem persuasive. For example, a former governor of Ohio is reported to have granted clemency on the basis of the applicant's testimony under the influence of sodium amytal (truth serum).

With only one exception,[23] courts have held that a clemency hearing is not required and that if a hearing is granted, it need not comply with the procedural requirements of due process of law.[24] The Constitution does not guarantee a clemency review. Yet, where states have made provision for offenders to apply for clemency, the need is obvious for those who apply to have a fair treatment, however short of a full quasi-judicial hearing on the merits of their case that may be.

EFFECTS OF A PARDON

When an applicant receives a pardon, the board may grant a partial pardon, which absolves the person pardoned from only a portion of the legal consequences surrounding the crime. These are rare. A pardon once granted may be revoked until it has been delivered to the applicant or

23. In *McGee v. Arizona State Board of Pardons and Paroles*, 92 Ariz. 317, 376 P.2d 779 (1962), the Arizona Supreme Court held that a defendant sentenced to death had the right to a full clemency hearing.
24. *Green v. Teets*, 244 F.2d 401 (9th Cir. 1957).

someone acting on his behalf. Conditional pardons, which may be revoked if the conditions are violated,[25] were the forerunners of parole. Their use now is rare, their need having been sharply reduced since parole became the standard method of conditional release from prison. A conditional pardon contained the same restrictions on the releasee's liberty as parole, although with pardons the conditions might be tailored to individual cases without regard to any applicable statutory conditions required to be placed on parolees.

Some conditions attached to pardons and held valid by courts are reimbursing the state for trial expenses, not claiming property sold under federal confiscation laws and accepting confinement in a hospital for the insane. The Supreme Court of Utah recently held valid a pardon granted on condition that a felon leave the state permanently. The pardon was revoked when he was found living in Salt Lake City.[26]

Submission to supervision by parole officers is not commonly annexed to a conditional pardon. Thus a prisoner required by statute to serve a minimum portion of his sentence before he is eligible for parole may not only be released by a conditional pardon before the minimum term expires but may be released without the supervision that characterizes parole. It is possible for the executive to commute the minimum sentence to make a prisoner eligible for parole. His release then will be under the usual parole supervision. This use of pardons to circumvent overly rigid restrictions on the granting of parole illustrates one modern way of using clemency to escape the rigidity of other features of the criminal law.

A conditional pardon always may be revoked by the authority that granted it. In some states, neither notice to the releasee nor a hearing is required for revocation.[27] In addition, some courts have claimed the power to determine whether a condition of a pardon has been breached.[28]

Increasingly the most common type of pardon has been the pardon after completion of sentence. The chief purpose of such a pardon is to allow restoration of all rights lost upon conviction. In most states conviction of a crime carries with it the automatic and wholesale loss of civil rights, regard-

25. *Fehl v. Martin*, 155 Ore. 455, 64 P.2d 631 (1937).
26. *Mansell v. Turner*, 384 P.2d 394 (1963); *see* Brent T. Lynch, "Exile Within the United States," 11 *Crime and Delinquency* 22 (1965).
27. *E.g., In re Saucier*, 122 Vt. 208, 167 A.2d 368 (1961); *Ex parte Pitt*, 151 Tex. Dr. R. 219, 206 S.W.2d 596 (1947); *contra, Guy v. Utecht*, 216 Minn. 255, 12 N.W.2d 753 (1944).
28. *Pippin v. Johnson*, 192 Ga. 450, 15 S.E.2d 712 (1941); *contra, Reilly v. Dale*, 133 Vt. 1, 28 A.2d 637 (1942).

less of their relation to the offense. In different places this has included such things as the rights to vote, contract, hold office and most importantly to hold certain jobs. In other places, requirements are made of ex-convicts, such as registering with police officials. All these continuing encumbrances may be removed by pardons.

State law is affected most by clemency. Except for a few federal exceptions, the restoration of rights lost as a result of criminal convictions is determined by state laws which vary and control their own parochial situations.

A felony conviction results in the permanent loss of the right to vote in thirty-nine states, the right to hold public office in twenty-seven states and the right to serve on a jury in twelve states. Conviction of a felony is a ground for divorce in thirty-six states. In some places felons are deprived of the capacity to testify or to enter contracts and receive or transfer property.

At least nine states bar former offenders from certain occupations. The United States Supreme Court recently affirmed a New York statute's exclusion from the position of secretary-treasurer of a longshoremen's local union of a man who thirty-five years earlier had pleaded guilty to the charge of attempted grand larceny and received a suspended sentence.

Some states and many local jurisdictions require ex-convicts to register and keep officials informed of their movements. In some places the requirements are onerous and potentially embarrassing. (In one city, for example, anyone convicted of any of certain enumerated crimes must register with the chief of police within two hours of his arrival, undergo a complete booking procedure and carry an identification card.)[29]

In seven states, the forfeited rights are restored automatically when a sentence expires. A former offender may apply for restoration of his rights to the sentencing court in two states, to the parole board in one state, to the legislature in another state and to a special commission in still another. In the great majority of cases, however, restoration may be achieved only by means of a pardon.

Many incidental rights or access to them also are blocked by a criminal record—such things, for example, as the denial of insurance coverage, credit ratings, business loans, even a driver's license. An ex-convict has been quoted by a news columnist as saying: "As things stand now, every person convicted of a felony is given what amounts to a life sentence, part

29. *Mason v. State*, 267 Ala. 507, 103 So.2d 341, *cert. denied*, 358 U.S. 934 (1958).

of it to be served behind bars, the rest amounting to permanent restrictions on civil rights."

The legal effects of a pardon are confused. Although one ground for seeking a pardon has been deemed to be the establishment of innocence, many courts have held that a pardon implies not innocence but guilt.[30] There is disagreement on the question whether a pardoned conviction may be counted for purposes of a habitual-offender statute. Although most rights lost on conviction are automatically restored by a full pardon, others, such as the right to own a gun[31] or to return to a public office forfeited by the conviction,[32] are not. In the crucial area of licensing for a trade or profession, the licensing board has been deemed to have discretion to continue any disqualification even after a pardon. And, although a pardon removes the disqualification from holding a public position,[33] according to a recent Massachusetts decision a pardoned offender, even a disabled veteran with top preference on a Civil Service list, need not be appointed to a position if the appointing authority believes that the crime for which he was pardoned had an adverse influence on his moral character. This unforgiving, punitive attitude has been criticized:

> . . . Our system of criminal law is largely flawed in one of its most basic aspects: it fails to provide accessible or effective means of fully restoring the social status of the reformed offender. We sentence, we coerce, we incarcerate, we counsel, we grant probation and parole, and we treat—not infrequently with success—but we never forgive.[34]

To avoid the lingering effects of criminal convictions which may bar ex-offenders from routine transactions such as obtaining credit or purchasing automobile liability insurance, as well as imposing serious impediments to rehabilitation such as preventing employment, authorities have advocated expungement through destruction or sealing of records of offenders after their release from probation or incarceration and the passage of a period of time. Unlike pardons, which are exceptional and

30. *Burdick v. United States*, 236 U.S. 79, 90 (1915); *Manlove v. State*, 153 Ind. 80, 53 N.E. 385 (1899); *Roberts v. State*, 160 N.Y. 217, 54 N.E. 678 (1899); *see* 3 *Survey*—"Pardon" 267–70.
31. *Mason v. State*, 267 Ala. 507, 103 So.2d 341, *cert. denied*, 358 U.S. 934 (1958).
32. *Hultan v. Thornton*, 205 Ga. 753, 55 S.E.2d 115 (1949).
33. *Commission of the Metropolitan District Commission v. Director of Civil Service*, 348 Mass. 184, 203 N.E.2d 95 (1964).
34. Gough, "The Expungement of Adjudication Records of Juvenile and Adult Offenders: A Problem of Status" 1966 *Washington University Law Quarterly* 147, 148.

specific acts of grace granted by the chief executive, expungements could be provided by legislatures as general administrative processes of regular and widspread application.

California, Michigan, Minnesota, New Jersey and Texas have statutory provisions for expunging the records of adult offenders. The benefits of most of the statutes are restricted to first offenders. Alaska, Arizona, California, Indiana, Kansas, Minnesota, Missouri and Utah have provisions expungement limited to juvenile adjudications. Under the Federal Youth Correction Act,[35] if a court unconditionally discharges an offender before his sentence expires, his conviction automatically is set aside.

Two states have attempted to provide mechanisms through which an offender can earn back his lost civil rights—and perhaps also his sense of self-respect—without the risks and vicissitudes inherent in applying for pardon. In New York and California, a convicted offender who has served his sentence and violated no other laws may apply for a certificate of good conduct or rehabilitation.

The procedure in California[36] requires that an applicant be a resident of the state for three years. He begins the process by filing with the county clerk and the local chief of police or sheriff a notice of his intent to petition for a certificate of rehabilitation. He must submit to the supervision of the police chief or sheriff for the period of rehabilitation, usually about three years. During that time he is expected to "live an honest and upright life . . . conduct himself with sobriety and industry . . . exhibit a good moral character . . . and conform to and obey the laws of the land." At the end of this period the applicant files in court a request for a certificate of rehabilitation. He has a right to counsel, and filing fees are waived. His conduct is investigated by the district attorney, and the supervising peace officer makes a report. The court may then issue the certificate and recommend a full pardon to the governor.

There has been a drastic reduction in requests for clemency in New York since the certificate of good conduct became available in 1945. In 1966, a simplified procedure whereby first offenders may apply to the parole board for certificates of relief became available. In less than three years, more than 1,000 certificates of relief were issued.

Although certificates of rehabilitation restore all civil rights, the return of professional licenses remains discretionary with the state licensing boards. Court decisions in California have upheld the denial of reinstate-

35. 18 U.S.C. §5021 (1964).
36. *See* Calif. Penal Code §§4852.01–4852.2.

ment to two attorneys who had earned certificates of rehabilitation.[37] A dissent criticized that result, arguing that the certificate "is not like the ordinary pardon where the motive or basis may be merely sympathy or forgiveness." When such a certificate is earned its legal effects should be clear, and licensing authorities should not have the discretion to ignore it.

There is a paucity of literature on the subject of clemency. State agencies have incomplete and irregular records. But we have determined generally through personal correspondence with state officials that there are fewer pardons than commutations, rare conditional pardons, few reprieves, no amnesties, some scattered expungement and remission practices; and all are controlled under varying state procedures. Rates of clemency have remained rather even through the years, with some reduction in the number of pardons and some increase in commutations in recent years. Executive autonomy is maintained over the clemency decision-making process. Although initial work is done by separate state agencies which make recommendations to the governors (state boards of pardon and parole, pardon officials, special counsel and assistants to the governors), these recommendations are followed 95 percent of the time or more by the governors.

The general clemency mechanism was designed primarily to remedy wrongful convictions and unduly harsh sentences; the pardon process is in many cases also the only way to eradicate the troublesome collateral effects of a criminal conviction. For the latter function it may be questioned whether procedures could be devised which are less erratic and cumbersome for applicants and less time-consuming to state governors and the President.

The right to clemency, at least the right to reinstatement of lost civil rights, ought to be capable of being earned after a sentence is served and a convict has performed his actual and his social restitution. If for whatever reason this cannot be done, certainly the convict should have returned those civil rights that are not related to the crime for which he was convicted. For example, a druggist convicted of illegal dispensing of drugs might with reason have his druggist's license withheld, but there is no reason to withhold his right to vote. The idea of making a pardon a right to be earned instead of a grace to be bestowed makes sense. It would be less political, more efficient and more humane.

37. *Roth v. State Bar*, 40 Cal.2d 307, 253 P.2d 969 (1953); *Feinstein v. State Bar*, 39 Cal.2d 541, 248 P.2d 3, 12 (1952).

THE FEDERAL SYSTEM

Along with our survey of state practices, we interviewed numerous federal officials from the Pardon Attorney's Office, the Justice Department and the White House who have been responsible for making federal pardon and commutation decisions to learn how the process actually worked during three different national administrations with varied personnel during the decade from 1960 through 1970. Most of them agreed that this is a subject of great mystique and little lore but that it involves a sensitive and potentially valuable correctional power.

Approximately 500 to 600 applications are made each year to the office of the Pardon Attorney. To be eligible, applicants must not be on probation or parole; they must wait three years after release (or after conviction if there was no imprisonment) before applying for a pardon except where they were convicted of crimes involving public trust, narcotics, income-tax laws, perjury, when the waiting period is five years. Applicants receive a standard letter to determine their eligibility before being sent the proper forms—the Petition for Commutation of Sentence and the Petition for Pardon After Completion of Sentence.

Petitioners are required to include in their applications certain vital statistics, the history of the applicant, a number of endorsements and character affidavits. When the standard application is received at this level, each case is docketed and a memorandum is sent to the FBI requesting an investigation. This investigation is supposed to be done discreetly to avoid embarrassing applicants. This process usually takes a month or two. In about 25 percent of the cases, applicants at this stage are represented by attorneys.

Recommendations are solicited from the U.S. attorney who prosecuted the individual's case and the sentencing judge (who usually does not comment). Comments usually arrive within two months. The Bureau of Prisons is requested to check its records; it in turn elicits an up-to-date report from the institution where the applicant resides or has resided. Correction officials, we are told, are more liberal about clemency than prosecutors and judges. The Bureau of Prisons sends its report to the Pardon Attorney, usually without a recommendation of its own. In 95 percent of the cases it simply passes on the institution's recommendation. Occasionally, staff at the bureau feels the local institution's report is wrong or inconsistent (such as a case where co-defendants in different institutions were treated differently), but it acts essentially as a middle man and generally does not attempt to superimpose its evaluations.

On rare occasions the bureau itself will institute a proceeding, such as suggesting commutation for an inmate with a terminal illness. Sometimes the Pardon Attorney or even the Attorney General will suggest the initiation of applications. This was done during Robert Kennedy's Attorney Generalship when the submission of applications for commutation of excessive narcotics sentences was suggested by the Justice Department to individual wardens.

The Pardon Attorney and his three lawyer assistants who review all the cases give "a great deal of weight" to the recommendations of the officials who have had varying direct contacts with the individual applicants. The chief concern is with the applicant's rehabilitation after release, not the crime he originally committed or his early history. The total circumstances of each case are reviewed. In the cases of about half the applicants received, the Pardon Attorney says, relief is granted.

In relation to the number of prisoners released from prisons each year, the number of individuals receiving some form of clemency is small. For example, 15,491 prisoners were released from federal institutions in fiscal year 1967. That same year 222 federal pardons and twenty-three sentence commutations were granted.[38] In one state (Kentucky), some form of clemency was given two prisoners in fiscal 1967; 746 prisoners were paroled.

While there is no direct communication between the Pardon Attorney and the President (there is between him and Presidential staff men), he tends to follow the pace of the individual President whose policies eventually sift down to the inmates in the institutions as well. While he has no control at all over the volume of the influx of cases, the Pardon Attorney does find that the prison population reacts to the varying practices of the particular President in office.

In most cases, the Pardon Attorney's recommendations are followed. He is reversed in about 5 percent of the cases in which he recommends clemency to the higher authorities; he is rarely reversed in a decision to deny the relief sought. A man whose application is denied may reapply for a pardon in two years (although the Attorney General can reopen a case at any time). In the cases of commutations, there is no waiting period for reapplications, but one year is preferred to allow an opportunity for changed circumstances to be demonstrated. The average time for a

38. Federal Bureau of Prisons, Statistical Report, fiscal years 1967 and 1968.

case to maturate from initiation to final decision is about six months; but vicissitudes unrelated to the clemency process itself can prolong this, sometimes quite a while.

The Pardon Attorney's complete file on each applicant, with his own recommendations, goes to the Attorney General and then to the President. At each interval, there is a reconsideration of both recommended denials and grants. When the Attorney General and President have acted, the case is returned to the Pardon Attorney, who notifies the applicant of the action taken in his case. Reasons for the action taken are not, as a matter of policy, provided to the applicant, nor are sources of the information relied on in making the decision. Sometimes advice is given, such as to clear up pending court actions or creditors' claims, traffic tickets and fines (which are automatically remitted by pardon) if this conduct influenced the decision adversely.

From the Pardon Attorney's office groups of cases with complete files and recommendations of the Pardon Attorney are sent to the Attorney General. It has been customary for this phase of the Attorney General's responsibility to be delegated to his special assistant, who is briefed by and maintains contact with the Pardon Attorney, and, in turn, educates the Attorney General and evolves with him a general policy for Justice Department action in this area. Occasionally, in the unusual case with a special background, the opinions of other Justice Department officials (such as the Assistant Attorney General in charge of the Criminal Division) are elicited by the Attorney General's special assistant to determine whether special factors might be present in the background of the case which warrant weight in the applicant's clemency consideration.

General rules and intramural common law have evolved to guide the decision-making process at the Justice Department. For example, nonresident aliens are not considered for pardons since there is little reason to bother and no opportunity for the standard investigation. Commutation is rarely granted in situations where the federal parole authorities could act. In narcotics cases involving excessive sentences, though, where parole is not possible, commutation could be considered since here the clemency process would not conflict or compete with the parole process. In cases involving terminal illness, commutation generally is granted routinely, although President Eisenhower did not exercise the commutation power at all, feeling that it was not a proper area for his intrusion.

Commutations are issued only for men in federal custody (not for men in state institutions with federal detainers outstanding against them). Cases where relief is needed for employment purposes or to satisfy other real requirements of state law are preferred for pardons over cases where the sole purpose is to satisfy the conscience of the applicant or to give him a psychological boost. No petitions for pardons are entertained from applicants who have been pardoned of a previous federal offense. This "no second helping" precedent was initiated by the Attorney General in November 1949. No posthumous pardons are granted.[39]

No formal hearing is permitted before the Attorney General, although an informal interview is permitted with the Pardon Attorney or the special assistant to the Attorney General. A list of everyone who communicated with Justice officials about any applicant accompanies each file.

All officials, at all stages of the federal clemency process, professed pointedly that they recoiled from political pressures. Each political inquiry is, they say, referred perfunctorily to the standard procedural channel in the process. The Pardon Attorney is kept the "focal point" of the process. Each high public official charged with clemency powers is supersensitive to claims of improper political influence. In fact, attempts at political influence generally do more harm than good. Once a case is flagged as including non-routine elements or potential public interest, it is likely to take longer to wend its way through the labyrinth of the clemency process. In one case described to us a notorious convict was about to be pardoned when a Senator called the Pardon Attorney in his behalf. The case was called back and held for one year to avoid the appearance that the inevitable was a result of political pressure. As one clemency official told us: "There should be no politics in clemency, period!" Still, on occasions, the Pardon Attorney has been instructed what action is going to be taken by his superiors and must himself take the appropriate steps to make the decision effective.

From the Justice Department, groups of files and recommendations go to the President. Actually, the President has little to do with these cases. His special counsel receives all the files, reads the investigations accompanying each case, succinctly summarizes them and makes his recommendations with brief synopses of the cases to the President. No further hearings are held at this stage. The White House staff's preference is to do this work quietly (sometimes anonymously) without fanfare, to eliminate politics and to avoid unnecessarily hurting the individuals involved.

39. In August 1956 the Attorney General decided that the President had no legal power to issue a pardon posthumously since there is a legal requirement that the pardon be delivered and accepted.

The President receives the Attorney General's recommendations with a master warrant for his signature, granting the clemency requested for that group of cases. After the President's action, the Pardon Attorney notifies the applicant of the action taken. If the Attorney General recommends favorable action, it is ineffective until the President signs the warrant; where the Attorney General recommends negative action, the application is deemed denied if the President takes no action within thirty days.

During the Truman Administration, the Pardon Attorney was discouraged from sending negative recommendations to the President. "Why send me cases to turn down?" President Harry S Truman asked Attorney General Tom Clark. So the practice of sending negative recommendations ceased for several years until the Kennedy Administration. Then the practice reverted, since the legal authority to deny pardon applications without Presidential consideration was questioned. Now the President acts on all recommendations, positive or negative.

Most cases are routine, clear-cut, and the action recommended by the Pardon Attorney is adopted and affirmed. Usually, the only discussion with the President involves sensitive cases with potential political repercussions; the rest are treated perfunctorily. The standards applied in making these judgments perforce are personal and subjective, but most officials say that the individual's demonstrated rehabilitation and useful reintegration into the community are the keys to clemency. The overall infrequency of pardons, however, does not bespeak this philosophy.

The President essentially relies on the earlier screens at the Justice Department level to filter the cases to him, and he usually follows the recommendations he receives. He has little time to give this function much attention—and, in fact, has little to gain and much to risk in any action he takes. With changes of Administrations, newcomers to jobs in the clemency process are briefed about the established patterns by their predecessors and by the relevant professionals who remain in office. Then they usually discuss general policy approaches with their superiors, the Attorney General or the President.

While all the officials interviewed generally agreed upon the fundamental role of clemency and followed essentially the same procedures, rates of Presidential actions varied radically during different Administrations on the basis of irrelevant and fortuitous events that did not reflect either the general law-enforcement moods or specified pardon policies of those Administrations. For example, during the early part of the

Johnson Presidency pardons and commutations reached an all-time high. Then one relatively unimportant case caused a frivolous but loud and persistent local newspaper campaign attacking the President for leniency. A Senator seized on this and criticized the President in a speech before Congress for a new attitude of leniency "in opening the prison doors through accelerated approval of pardons and sentence commutations." As a result, clemency stopped completely for the remainder of the Johnson years. Aides said it was because the President had decided not to bind the incoming Administration, but the circumstances make it appear that the sensitivity of the office and the political dangers of executive clemency actions more likely were the reasons.

If publicity and politics are a problem, and if clemency is a merciful right to be earned and not merely a reward to be dangled and withdrawn for parochial, political and personal reasons having nothing to do with criminal justice policy, perhaps the system should be altered to operate more by its own impersonal force. Discretion then would be minimized. Criteria could be devised and administered by officials for the President. In the case of pardons, which involve the exercise of a constitutional power, any such change probably would have to be authorized by a constitutional amendment. But some delegation might speed and improve the process.

There is no need to bother the President of the United States with, as one official said to us, "licensing bartenders in Kansas City." He does little except sign the formal papers anyway, and delegation would relieve him of unwanted political pressures in relatively unimportant matters. Executives are criticized for mistakes in this area and are careful; they rarely receive credit for being expansive, enlightened and compassionate toward convicts. The clemency process should be made more a rehabilitative reward to be achieved after a successful correctional experience. Commutations could be handled by the courts or lower federal officials. If the restoration of all rights lost by conviction of a crime was provided for by statute, as is the case in certain circumstances, pardon would not be necessary. It could be questioned why all rights lost should not automatically be restored after sentence is served.

Some feel that clemency is a very personal prerogative for the President alone to exercise and that it is a measure which should be used very sparingly, as it dilutes the criminal justice process by putting personal notions about justice over objective facts. On the other hand, the ordinary case for clemency should not demand so precious an action as personal Presidential involvement, except in extraordinary situations.

In many states, by contrast, pardons are not necessary. Some states' statutes provide that no rights are lost upon conviction, thus no action for restoration is necessary. In other states, statutes provide that rights are restored automatically after sentence is served, again eliminating the need for requesting executive restoration of lost rights. But even in states where a pardon is needed for the restoration of rights, it could be said that it is not the pardon power itself that restores the rights but the statutes controlling those particular rights.

Several state governors have the right to restore released convicts' rights, again making official gubernatorial or Presidential pardon unnecessary. And in some instances interpretations of state laws make any executive pardon irrelevant. In one state, for example, a former convict was not allowed to serve on a local jury even though he had been pardoned because state law disqualified individuals who had been "convicted" of a felony. Thus, it was deemed that in this instance the pardon had to defer to the local statute.

All this analysis should be qualified by the consideration that some former convicts assert all their rights and are not challenged, so do not really need official clemency; others do not need it because they do not care about these rights and go through life without voting or exercising their accouterments of citizenship.

Those who administer the federal pardon office say they view their function to be to facilitate clemency, not to defeat it or manipulate the process for any other ends. Others involved in the process have been more inhibited. Some of the conservatism about granting clemency is due to a widely held misunderstanding about its actual essence and effect. Ordinarily, its function is not to determine innocence retroactively, or to excuse, vindicate or exonerate past convictions. The function of pardon is to terminate some few federal- (loss of retirement annuity benefits and certain veterans' rights) but mostly state-imposed disabilities, such as the deprivation of veterans' eligibility for bonding or for a license to conduct certain kinds of work.

While to some extent the granting of executive clemency is an act of mercy which many men seek for its own cleansing sake and is a morale builder, it really serves a more pragmatic function, essentially to allow full restoration of rights lost as a result of conviction. Many individuals do not want clemency because it exhumes their past to present unknowing family, friends or employers; others (mostly white-collar criminals) do want it to prove their rehabilitation to these same people. It is a useful rehabilitative technique and an element of compassion in the otherwise generally retributive criminal justice system.

Commutation

A commutation is a reduction of a sentence—"a substitution of a lesser for a greater punishment";[40] it has even been described as "a pardon upon condition that the convict voluntarily submits to a lighter punishment."[41] It is granted, according to one text, "for any reason that the commuting authority deems adequate: the health of the prisoner; the needs or unusual circumstances of his family; the judgment of the commuting authority that the original sentence was excessive, having regard for the nature of the offense and the state of public opinion in the community at the time of trial and sentencing. Commutation on occasion has been granted also as a reward for heroic or self-sacrificing conduct on the part of offenders while in custody, as in cases where prisoners have volun teered for dangerous medical experiments, risking life and health in the interest of the social good."[42] Mostly, it is used to allow prisoners with terminal illnesses to die out of prison, to make prisoners eligible for parole and to avoid capital punishment.

Necessary to the idea of commutation is a criminal law that recognizes different degrees of punishment. Thus when capital punishment was the mandatory penalty fixed for most crimes instead of imprisonment for a term of years, commutation could not be used. Before 1850, no state constitution included the power to commute sentences. However, it has been considered unnecessary to make explicit provision for commutation, since presumably the power is simply a lesser form of pardon. The power to commute sentences has been held to be implicit in the general grant of the pardoning power in the states whose constitutions do not mention commutation and in the federal system.[43]

The power to commute is vested in the same person or body which

40. State ex rel. Murphy v. Wolfer, 127 Minn. 102, 148 N.W. 896 (1814).
41. In re Opinion of the Justices, 190 Mass. 616, 78 N.E. 311 (1906).
42. M. Cherif Bassiouni, Criminal Law and Its Processes 25.
43. See, e.g., Lupo v. Zerbst, 92 F.2d 362 (5th Cir.), cert. denied, 303 U.S. 646 (1937); United States v. Wright, 56 F. Supp. 489 (D. Ill. 1944); Imprisonment of Indian See-See-Sah-Ma, 5 Op. Atty. Gen. 370 (1851).

possesses the pardoning power. Thus in federal cases only the President can commute a death penalty. And, much like pardon, the power to commute has been limited by statutes in many states. For example, in Colorado, the governor may commute death sentences to life imprisonment or a term not less than ten years. In Kansas, "The Governor may . . . commute a sentence . . . if in a capital case, to imprisonment for life, or for a term not less than 10 years at hard labor. . . ." In Texas and South Carolina, the governor may commute a death sentence only to life imprisonment.

The most frequent use of the power to commute has been to make eligible for parole prisoners who for some reason are excluded from or who are not yet eligible for parole. For example, many statutes except prisoners serving life sentences from parole eligibility. By commuting a life sentence then, a prisoner may be made eligible for parole. Many states also require that a minimum sentence be served before a prisoner may be eligible for parole. Here again, commutation can be granted to make such a prisoner eligible for parole. Although the granting of pardons has remained fairly constant in recent years, the rate of commutation of sentences has risen. Often state parole boards will recommend that their governor commute a sentence.

Another common use for commutation is to reduce death sentences, most often to life imprisonment. This is one of the more difficult decisions of the clemency authority—politically as well as intellectually. Approximately half of the American jurisdictions automatically review all capital cases for a clemency determination. The remaining jurisdictions act only upon a defendant's request, as is the case with pardons.

In capital cases provision of legal counsel for clemency application has not presented a serious problem. State officials and judges often urge appointed counsel to stay with the defendant through commutation proceedings. Volunteer attorneys, frequently associated with organizations which are opposed to capital punishment, commonly take cases at this stage.

Different states emphasize different aspects of the commutation investigation. One survey concluded that "the inclusion and exclusion of certain types of data seem . . . to reflect the amenability of the particular state toward the clemency decision."[44] In California, for example, the

44. Marvin E. Wolfgang, "Murder, the Pardon Board and Recommendations by Judges and District Attorneys," 50 *Journal of Criminal Law, Criminology and Police Science* 338 (1959).

major part of the report is devoted to the mental state of the defendant, including psychiatric condition and physical brain damage, which has been the most frequently cited reason for granting commutations in capital cases. Arizona refuses to consider any background of social deprivation.

While not exhaustive, investigative reports in capital cases are less perfunctory than for other clemency applications. Comments of prison officials, the presiding judge and prosecutors are included, as well as the results of psychiatric and psychological tests conducted during incarceration. California goes so far as to employ electroencephalograph examinations in cases of suspected brain damage.

Since the clemency decision is supposed to follow the exhaustion of all other available judicial remedies, commutation hearings are scheduled as close to the scheduled date of execution as possible. This has created the impression that the commutation hearing is the final appeal, a court of last resort. By scheduling the hearing close to execution, the clemency authority is reasonably free to make a decision without interruption from continued litigation or interference with the ordinary judicial process. However, this practice can raise tensions unnecessarily. In Connecticut, the commutation hearing is scheduled on the morning of the day of execution and the doomed prisoner is required to attend.

A majority of the states do not allow the prisoner to attend the commutation hearing, although many require that he be personally interviewed at prison. The requirement that the prisoner not attend the hearing is predicated on the supercilious and specious theory that his participation would not add to the proceeding but instead would create a highly emotional atmosphere. However, the majority of the states do provide for some sort of public hearings. While all states publicly announce the commutation decision, only a minority of the states publicly provide the reasons for their decisions.

While it is impossible to know which considerations are most influential when commutation of a death sentence is at stake, several obvious factors probably influence the decision. Mitigating circumstances surrounding the crime often are reconsidered by clemency authorities. Such factors as intoxication, provocation and duress, while not legally sufficient to reduce a crime in degree, may be the basis of a commutation. The viciousness of the crime and the degree to which society has been outraged no doubt are important factors in this decision. The fairness of the prisoner's trial also is considered by the clemency authority, although appeals more often reverse convictions deriving from obviously unfair trials. In considering the issue of fairness, the clemency authority will examine the attendant publicity, the general atmosphere at the trial and any tensions existing during the trial.

Doubts as to the guilt of the prisoner seeking commutation also may be considered. In fact, this is the only standard that one state's board has accepted. According to a study by the *New York University Law Review*, "Executive clemency as conceived by the Arizona Board is nothing more than an escape valve designed to avoid the possibility that an innocent man will be sentenced to death."

A question as to the defendant's guilt may be occasioned by the development of new evidence, or the uncovering of evidence previously suppressed, overlooked or presented unclearly. Or a close question in a case may be viewed as grounds for commutation. During his term of office in the 1920s, Governor Alfred E. Smith of New York followed the practice of commuting all death sentences where the court of appeals was divided in affirming the conviction.

Most states still have no procedure for appellate review of criminal sentences. The use of commutations in these cases provides another example of the role of the clemency power in compensating for gaps in the law. In cases in which many people are charged with the commission of the same crime the question of relative guilt may be a factor in granting a commutation. The individual's role in the crime becomes essential to any later consideration of his sentence. If a defendant had played a minor role, yet was given the most severe sentence, or the same sentence as the most vicious participant in the crime, a reasonable basis for commutation exists.

The same crime in various geographical areas within a jurisdiction may result in different sentences. This ground for commutation has been applied rarely and almost exclusively to situations in rural areas involving the death penalty for sex crimes.

When there has been a prolonged delay, as a result of appeals, stays of execution or reprieves, between sentencing and scheduled execution, the clemency authority may commute the death penalty on the ground that the doomed prisoner died the proverbial "thousand deaths." And if during the period between sentencing and execution (a time usually covering a period of years) it can be shown that in some extraordinary way the prisoner has rehabilitated himself, a commutation may be granted. The best example of this was the celebrated commutation of Paul Crump by the governor of Illinois. There, the only evidence presented to the governor at the commutation hearing by Crump's attorney was that the unusual defendant had completely rehabilitated himself during his nine years awaiting execution.

The clemency authority generally seeks the advice of the prosecuting attorney and the presiding judge when considering commutation. However, one empirical examination of the recommendations made in 368 cases disclosed that in two-thirds of the cases evaluated the judge and the prosecuting attorney disagreed on whether to grant commutation. Nonetheless, the positive recommendation of at least one of these parties is essential, according to that survey. And a unanimous recommendation does not lead inevitably to a favorable ruling, although it is unlikely without this recommendation. In only 7 percent of the total murder cases surveyed was commutation granted when both the prosecution and the presiding judge submitted negative evaluations to the reviewing clemency authority.[45]

Some lawyers attempt to stimulate favorable publicity in order to augment their client's chance for a commutation. For obvious reasons, clemency officials resent publicity; and they have insisted that it does not influence their decisions. However, the different fate of the applications for commutation in two Illinois capital cases, which were decided in the same month in 1962 by the same governor, indicate that favorable publicity may well influence a decision to commute.

The case of Paul Crump, who had been convicted of killing a watchman during an armed robbery of a packing plant, was given extensive coverage by the press. Sympathetic feature stories were published in national magazines—*Ebony*, for example, referring to the newly rehabilitated prisoner as "minister to the sick, protector of the weak, and keeper of the conscience of men who have no conscience." Former Governor Kerner commuted Crump's death sentence to life imprisonment.

James Dukes was convicted of murdering a police officer in the course of a gun battle. His application for clemency was considered shortly after Crump's. According to his lawyer, the subject of commuting death sentences had received so much recent attention in the news media because of Crump that it ceased to be newsworthy. Dukes received very little attention from the press. Governor Kerner decided not to commute his sentence.

Along with the general public interest in cases, the view of the clem-

45. *Ibid.*

ency authority on capital punishment certainly is an important factor in the commutation decision. The executive may feel that the death penalty is too severe, or that it is inappropriate in a particular case, or he may have strong personal convictions that are drawn into his considerations. An example of the latter situation was Lee Cruce, governor of Oklahoma from 1911 to 1915, who considered capital punishment legalized murder. He commuted twenty-two death sentences to life imprisonment. More recently, former governors Edmund Brown of California and Endicott Peabody of Massachusetts both were on record as being opposed to capital punishment. While Governor Peabody followed the pattern of Governor Cruce, commuting all death penalties, Governor Brown commuted selectively, feeling that it also was his duty to uphold the laws of California. With both the morality and the constitutionality of capital punishment subjected increasingly to widespread questioning, several governors recently have stayed all death sentences. One, Governor Milton Shapp of Pennsylvania, has announced that no prisoner will die while he is governor.

Whether a governor should allow his personal views on the propriety of a legislatively prescribed sentence to determine his commutation decisions is a debatable question. The Oklahoma Supreme Court objected strongly to Governor Cruce's course of action:

> No Governor has the right to say, directly or substantially; . . . "I think that capital punishment is wrong. I know that it is taught in the Bible, and is provided for in the laws of Oklahoma, but I occupy a higher plane than this. . . . Therefore, notwithstanding my official oath, I will place my judgment above the law, both human and divine, and will make my will supreme in the state, and will not permit capital punishment to be inflicted in Oklahoma, no matter what the law is, or how atrocious the offense committed may have been." : . .[46]

The views of a pardoning authority regarding the propriety of a particular kind of punishment inevitably play a large part in his decisions. Indeed, the very purpose of clemency is to allow a personalized kind of justice where unusual circumstances warrant it and to avoid the application of laws widely felt to be generally outmoded or inapt in specific situations. In any event, capital punishment is on the wane, having been abolished in many states already. Short of such statutory or judicial abolition, clemency frequently can serve the function of making rigid laws

46. *Henry v. State,* 10 Okla. Cr. 369, 389, 136 P. 982, 990 (1913).

or emotional situations comport with more detached public ideas of what is just and balanced.

The use of commutation to make prisoners eligible for parole illustrates still another area in which the clemency device is used to ameliorate other laws which are inflexible or unjust. Commutations will be necessary until paroling authorities are given complete authority to determine eligibility for parole. Should legislatures continue to make minimum prison terms mandatory for certain crimes, commutations may become more frequent than they are today.

The whole subject of appropriate policies to guide the clemency process has been given sparse attention. We agree with one of the rare reviews of the subject which concluded that much of the present reliance upon the forms of clemency could be reduced:

> Adequate court procedures for the post-conviction correction of error and reformed parole and sentencing practices could greatly reduce present necessity of reliance upon the pardon power to correct abuse. Reform of the law relating to the effects of criminal convictions and abolition of the death penalty would still further narrow the scope of executive clemency into workable channels. The trend of the past 75 years has been for the courts and administrative agencies to take over more and more of the functions of correction and adjustment which formerly could be handled only by a pardon. Continuation of this trend will leave the executive power to pardon free to deal with the unusual case which defies ordinary solution and to correct arbitrary administrative misuse of power.[47]

Until that more perfect time, however, the clemency power of commutation will continue to be a useful technique for assuring criminal justice.

Reprieve

A reprieve is merely a respite, a postponement of the execution of a sentence, usually granted in order to provide the executive authority with an opportunity for final action on an application for a pardon or commutation. A reprieve does not lessen the severity of the sentence; it merely allows a period of grace after the sentence has begun.

47. Foote, "Pardon Policy in a Modern State," 39 *The Prison Journal* 7 (April 1959).

Historically, reprieves applied only to capital cases; but now in some states a reprieve may be granted regarding any criminal sentence. In Texas, for example, the Board of Pardons and Paroles may temporarily release on furlough a convicted offender from jail or prison either before he has started to serve his sentence or during his term. Reprieves are generally granted for medical reasons or for the critical illness or death of a member of a prisoner's immediate family. The power to reprieve necessarily includes the power to fix a later date for execution of a sentence. The executive power to reprieve has been limited in many states. For example, in Texas, the governor may grant only one reprieve of not more than thirty days in any one case without the consent of the Board of Pardons and Paroles.

The procedure for reprieve is usually the same as for pardons, except that the formalities frequently are relaxed. For example, if the next meeting of the pardon board is after the scheduled execution of sentence, the applicant may go directly to the governor for reprieve.

Since reprieves are used primarily in capital cases to delay execution while pardon or commutation is sought, the procedure is no longer very important in states which do not allow capital punishment. However, a reprieve occasionally may be granted to allow consideration of an application for pardon before the applicant is actually imprisoned. Reprieves are sometimes granted when by state law an execution date for sentences cannot be set more than a fixed number of days after conviction and entry of judgment. A reprieve may be necessary then in order for the prisoner to have the time to prepare an appeal.

Since a reprieve does no more than postpone the execution of sentence, it is a special, limited form of clemency. It sometimes is a necessary first step to the substantive granting of commutation or pardon.

Amnesty

Amnesty is a rather esoteric and extraordinary procedure, less an integral part of the criminal justice system than a special political power tangential to it. Nonetheless, however special the technique may be, it does raise a profound moral question about the absolute need for punishment in a criminal justice system and the appropriate role of political grace in that system.

Amnesty is a general pardon, extended by the chief executive to groups of persons without regard to the special circumstances of the individual cases of specific members of the group. Usually amnesty is granted in forgiveness of political offenses, such as treason or rebellion. It differs from pardon in three respects: it entirely overlooks the offense, it pertains to groups, and it may refer to unnamed individuals, while a pardon usually does not excuse the particular offense and pertains to specific individuals. While this technique is a part of the laws of England and the United States, amnesties have not been used with the same frequency in this country as they have in Europe. It is particularly useful in other countries where private and judicial techniques for redressing injustices are less available. In fact, there is an international organization, Amnesty International, which oversees cases worldwide where amnesty seems appropriate.

Historically, the act of amnesty has had a much broader purpose than the usual grant of any other form of clemency. The other forms of clemency are acts of mercy and compassion toward individuals and, while derivately they may be said to serve the public welfare, essentially they are limited inquiries into the mitigating circumstances of certain offenses and the character and personality of the individual applicants. Other, totally different, criteria are applied regarding grants of amnesty.

Political offenses are deemed to uniquely threaten the sovereign, and while the tendency (as with all criminal acts) may have been to prosecute, in some cases it turns out to have been undesirable to have pursued that course. In a national crisis, such as a war, rebellion or civil disorder, the most important national virtue may be unity. When a class or community has committed a political offense, unity is not always achieved through prosecution. Sometimes, as was the case with the civil disorders in April 1968 in Washington, D.C., police restraint works better than retaliation. It may serve the nation better to overlook some threatening acts than to prosecute them. The granting of amnesty, similarly, may be deemed to benefit the nation as a whole more so than the individuals relieved.

Amnesties have been known to the law for nearly 2,500 years. The first recorded amnesty took place in Greece at the end of the Peloponnesian War. A junta had seized Athens after the war and banished the city's officials. For two years, 404–403 B.C., this group, called "The Thirty Tyrants," ruled the city. At first reform-minded but soon repressive, these occupiers soon became unpopular.

One of the ousted leaders, Thrasybulus, recruited an army of exiles in the city of Thebes and eventually, after battle, ousted the junta and restored democratic rule to Athens. In what was called "one of those epochal moments in the maturation of civilization" the returning regime decided not to punish the Athenian officeholders or citizens who had co-operated with the junta and not to adjudge the severe punishments usually reserved for traitors and collaborators. "Instead he invited them to participate in rebuilding a democratic Athens . . . the impact of the amnesty edict was to bind Athens together in a unity it had seldom achieved before."[48] Solidarity of the people was the purpose of the amnesty grant; in emergencies such as wartime this can be a very important element of the legal system.

In Greece, to obtain "Adeia," 6,000 persons had to vote in a secret ballot for an individual seeking pardon. It was very difficult for one person to get 6,000 persons to vote (only a few such pardons were granted), but in the case of a whole class or group, obtaining such a form of clemency was not difficult. Some of these ancient Greek amnesties excluded certain individuals. The amnesty of Solon, for example, "did not cover criminals who had committed murder or were fugitive because of acts of 'tyranny.'"

In the early nineteenth century, Napoleon used amnesty as a means of gaining the public support necessary to mobilize armies. On March 13, 1815, after escaping from the isle of Elba, Napoleon granted a general amnesty, excepting only thirteen people. Napeoleon was neither the only nor the first political leader to grant amnesties to mobilize his forces. One historian notes that (in England) "[a]s soon as war was declared, it was the custom to issue a proclamation in which a general pardon of all homicides and felonies was granted to everyone who would serve for a year at his own cost."[49]

The United States Constitution says nothing about amnesties. The Supreme Court has ruled that there is no legal distinction between amnesties and pardons.[50]

During the American Civil War, amnesties were employed on a broad basis for reasons other than the mobilization of armies. Among Northerners, there was little doubt that all who participated in the "rebellion" were guilty of treason, a crime that carried the death penalty.

The Confiscation Act of July 17, 1862, consequently made some major adjustments in the law relating to treason. The death penalty was

48. Cox, "Amnesty for America's Exiles," 28 *Christianity and Crisis—A Christian Journal of Opinion* (1968).
49. Pike, I *History of Crime in England* 294 (1873).
50. *Knote v. United States,* 95 U.S. (5 Ott) 149, 152–53 (1877).

to be only the most extreme of a range of graduated punishments; some offenses were defined out of the category of treason; and, finally, the President's pardoning power was stated by Congress to be applicable on a mass scale, enabling him to proclaim general amnesties:

> . . . the President is hereby authorized, at anytime hereafter, by proclamation, to extend to persons who may have participated in the existing rebellion in any State or part thereof, pardon and amnesty, with such exceptions and at such time and on such conditions as he may deem expedient for public welfare.[51]

Although he granted individual pardons before that time, President Abraham Lincoln waited to use his amnesty power until December 8, 1863, when the military successes of the Union had increased to the point where it seemed possible to persuade some Southerners to desert the Confederacy and surrender to the Union. Lincoln appears to have used the amnesty power as a wartime measure to weaken the will of the Confederacy and regain the loyalties of its members. Lincoln offered amnesty to all supporters of the Confederacy, except for those "who are, or shall have been, civil or diplomatic officers or agents of the so-called Confederate Government . . ." who would take an oath of allegiance to the United States:

> . . . Whereas, it is now desired by some persons heretofore engaged in said rebellion to resume their allegiance to the United States, and to reinaugurate loyal state governments within and for their respective states: Therefore—
>
> I, Abraham Lincoln, President of the United States, do proclaim, declare, and make known to all persons who have, directly or by implication, participated in the existing rebellion, except as hereinafter excepted, that a full pardon is hereby granted to them and each of them, with restoration of all rights of property, except as to slaves . . . and upon the condition that every such person shall take and subscribe an oath . . . [to uphold the Constitution, all valid Acts of Congress and Presidential proclamations concerning slavery].[52]

For President Andrew Johnson, the amnesty and pardoning powers were a method—perhaps the only possible method—of reuniting the coun-

---

51. 37th Cong., 2d Sess., Chap. 195, Sec. 13, July 17, 1862, 12 *United States Statutes at Large*, 592.
52. Proclamation by the President of the United States of America, Dec. 8, 1863, 13 *United States Statutes at Large*, 737–38.

try once the war was over. However, Johnson felt that "treason is a crime and must be made odious"; thus, he increased the classes of people excepted from his Amnesty Proclamation of May 29, 1865, to include anyone connected with the Confederate Government. Although he said he did not expect to deny pardons to many of the individuals in the excepted classes, he intended they should sue for pardon and realize the enormity of their crime. Indeed, Johnson was later to be criticized bitterly for the wholesale granting of individual pardons. (By September 1867, when Johnson issued his second amnesty proclamation, approximately 13,500 individual pardons had been granted, and 150,000 people remained under some kind of disability.)[53]

In subsequent proclamations, Johnson gradually granted amnesty to the excepted classes. Finally, in a Christmas Proclamation delivered in 1868, Johnson granted a "universal amnesty":

> Whereas . . . the authority of the Federal Government having been re-established in all the States and Territories within the jurisdiction of the United States, it is believed . . . that a universal amnesty and pardon for participation in said rebellion extended to all who have borne any part therein will tend to secure permanent peace, order, and prosperity throughout the land, and to renew and fully restore confidence and fraternal feeling among the whole people, and their respect for and attachment to the National Government, designed by its patriotic founders for the general good:
>
> Now, therefore, be it known that I, ANDREW JOHNSON, President of the United States, by virtue of the power and authority in me vested by the Constitution, and in the name of the sovereign people of the United States, do hereby proclaim and declare unconditionally, and without reservation, to all and to every person who directly or indirectly participated in the late insurrection or rebellion, a full pardon and amnesty for the offence of treason against the United States, or of adhering to their enemies during the late civil war, with restoration of all rights, privileges, and immunities under the Constitution and the laws which have been made in pursuance thereof.[54]

After this proclamation, Congress clashed with the President over his Reconstruction policies. The Fourteenth Amendment and the Recon-

53. See McKitrick, Andrew Johnson and Reconstruction 143–50 (1960).
54. Proclamation by the President of the United States, Dec. 25, 1868, 15 United States Statutes at Large, 711–12.

struction Acts provided that former Confederates could not vote or hold public office, regardless of whether they had received executive clemency. Since these laws specified that only Congress could restore rights removed by legislative action, Congress later issued its own amnesties. By special bills passed between 1868 and 1872, Congress amnestied several thousand former Confederates. The General Amnesty Act of May 22, 1872, restored political privileges to all but a few hundred.

If the goal of an amnesty is to unify, it seems to be most effective after the war, rebellion or disorder is over. After World War I, Germany granted many amnesties (on August 4, 1920; July 21, 1922; August 17, 1925; July 14, 1928; October 24, 1930; and finally on August 7, 1934). Very similar to the American Civil War experience, the German amnesties at first contained many exceptions. Each new amnesty included more of the previously excepted persons, until finally a general, unconditional amnesty was proclaimed on August 7, 1934, after Hitler had taken power.

There were four important amnesty proclamations in recent American history. All were granted at Christmastime—in 1945, 1947 and two proclamations in 1952. The first proclamation was a general pardon, and stated, in part:

> NOW, THEREFORE, I, HARRY S TRUMAN, President of the United States of America, do hereby grant a full pardon to all persons convicted of violation of any law of the United States or of the Territory of Alaska, except the laws for the government of the Army and the Navy, who on or after the twenty-ninth day of July, 1941, and prior to the date hereof, entered, enrolled in, or were inducted into the armed forces of the United States and who after serving in active status for not less than one year have been or shall hereafter be honorably discharged or separated therefrom. . . .[55]

The second amnesty followed a review by a special Amnesty Commission. It granted a full pardon "to those persons convicted of violating the Selective Training and Service Act of 1940."[56] Over 1,500 individuals (1,523) were covered by this amnesty grant. It may well prove to be a relevant precedent today.

The third recent amnesty granted by the United States followed the

55. Proclamation by the President of the United States, Dec. 24, 1945, 60 *United States Statutes at Large*, Part 2, p. 1335.
56. Proclamation by the President of the United States, Dec. 23, 1947, 62 *United States Statutes at Large*, Part 2, pp. 1441–42.

Korean war and benefitted those soldiers who prior to their induction had been convicted of non-military crimes and thereby had lost various civil rights. The amnesty excused the convictions and restored their rights.[57]

The fourth recent amnesty grant benefitted all persons who deserted from the armed forces of the United States between August 14, 1945, and June 25, 1950. The amnesty removed the harsh penalties imposed for deserting "in time of war," since there was no actual combat, but a formal state of war existed.

Thus the purpose of the amnesties granted by the United States has been to unify the country after a war so that the frictions which the war generated could be smoothed and perhaps also the judgments that later in peacetime might have appeared unwise could be corrected. (It is interesting to speculate whether a similar amnesty will follow the Vietnam war regarding the unusually high number of violators of the Selective Service Act.

Late in 1971, Senator Robert Taft, Jr., introduced legislation which would provide for what he called "conditional amnesty." This proposed law would eliminate future prosecution of draft dodgers if within one year of the passage of the bill they agreed to return to the country and serve three years either in the military or in some federal agency such as the Public Health Service. Those draft dodgers already convicted and serving sentences also would be eligible. Estimates reported at the time indicated the bill could apply to 70,000 expatriates and about 500 men in prisons.

It was time, Senator Taft said, for the nation to be magnanimous by offering this chance for rehabilitation of conscience-stricken young men. The arguments against amnesty are that it is unfair to those who served and that it would wreck the draft system. President Richard M. Nixon in a television interview on January 2, 1972, said he would not grant amnesty to draft dodgers so long as the war continued and there were prisoners of war; only after that, he said, would he consider amnesty. In addition to questions of policy, a separation-of-powers question of constitutional proportion might be raised by such legislation as that proposed by Senator Taft if the President was opposed to granting amnesty to those already convicted. However, the Supreme Court did once approve the power of Congress to grant amnesty, in 1896.[58]

57. Proclamation by the President of the United States, Dec. 24, 1952, 67 *United States Statutes at Large,* pp. C23–24.
58. *Brown v. Walker,* 161 U.S. 591; *see also Springer v. Philippine Islands,* 277 U.S. 211 (1928).

Since amnesty seems to imply guilt of a crime, some American violators do not want it, as they do not consider themselves guilty. As James Reston, Jr., has said in arguing for universal amnesty and against the Taft bill, ". . . amnesty means clearing the books of charges made or anticipated for war resistance, placing the burden on the bookkeeper, not on the accused." If these men are not criminals, the argument goes, they should not have to bear any stigma of criminality.)

A recent and widely publicized amnesty was granted in Israel in 1967 during the six-day war. Its purpose was the traditional one, to unify the nation at a time of crisis, as well as a pragmatic one, to swell the ranks of its small army.

Although amnesties have been used to promote national unity and, perhaps, to correct the overly zealous prosecution of violators of the so-called "political" laws that typically come into play during wartime, they have not been used as a technique of correctional reform. One authority has suggested that every state occasionally conduct an amnesty program as an appropriate means of reviewing prison populations and clearing them of prisoners who could be released safely prior to the time other correctional processes would get around to them.[59] Such a use of amnesties would conform to a primary function of clemency in general: to relieve the criminal justice system from the unpropitious effects of an overly rigid, unresponsive set of laws.

In 1958, the governor of Louisiana established a committee, popularly known as the "Forgotten Man's Committee," to study the state's prison system. Subcommittees made individual studies of each prisoner's case. As a result, the committee took 222 names to the state pardon board, which pardoned 107 inmates.

A study made in Florida after the involuntary amnesties which followed the Supreme Court's *Gideon* decision indicated that persons released through such methods may be no more likely to repeat their crimes than people released later by the ordinary methods. Retroactive release of prisoners due to changes in the law is not unusual. Special procedures such as this—even the common statutes of limitations for crimes—are forms of clemency in that they undo punitive features of the criminal justice system for reasons unrelated to the correctional aspects of individual cases. Some prison officials are critical of these procedures because they feel that they are unfair to other unaffected prisoners and thus undermine the system. Nonetheless, to the extent that the moral aspects of

59. Rubin, *The Law of Criminal Correction* 693–94 (1963).

the law prevail over positivistic, legal ones, the criminal justice system is infused with a humanistic, political element whose purpose, we feel, cannot be planned into the system but whose value to it cannot be underestimated.

In each of the areas where clemency is used today, it is possible to see how the function could be served more consistently and, perhaps, more efficiently by some other method. For example, direct post-conviction remedies unhampered by technical restrictions would solve the problem of people who are innocent but have exhausted all judicial remedies. Continuing review of sentences by courts or parole boards—without the limitations imposed by statutory minimum sentences—would remove the necessity for pardons or commutations based on mitigating circumstances or second thoughts about the appropriateness of sentences. The abolition of capital punishment would make the frequent commutations in this area unnecessary. More rational policies about depriving offenders of their civil rights, together with procedures designed expeditiously to restore the rights that are lost, would better serve the needs of a large class of people.

Even if all these changes were made, however, a need for executive clemency would remain. No judicial system can ever be perfect, and while it is impossible to foresee all the specific areas in which some safety valve will be necessary, the possibility for resort to some ameliorating device is salutory.

There always must be some way available to do justice in a case where, for whatever reason, a way is not provided for by usual procedures. To the extent that the criminal justice system needs to take account of changing political judgments by changing the results of the standard criminal processes in a particular case, the forms of clemency may provide that power. Finally, clemency may provide a worthwhile psychological effect on an offender by reducing the feelings and the stigma which come from conviction. A sovereign act of forgiveness is a state act of ultimate mercy.

VII

Redressing Prisoners' Grievances

Prisoners have rebelled against the prison system since its inception. But in recent years prison riots have become a regular phenomenon throughout the United States. In penitentiaries in New York, California, Ohio and Virginia, in jails in New York and New Jersey, in a military stockade in California—to name a few illustrative instances—rampaging prisoners have refused to work, taken hostages and destroyed prison property. One noted prison authority reported that between 1950 and 1958 alone he knew of "105 riots or serious disturbances in American prisons."[1]

These violent disturbances represent more than the venting of hostility by people in confinement; they often are a justified but frustrated cry for help. People in jails and prisons destroy property, injure others, hold hostages, even maim themselves in symbolic protest. Lacking a public press or pulpit from which to speak, or sympathetic ears to hear them, few prisoners have effective, legitimate means to communicate their grievances. Inevitably, the prisoners themselves are hurt most as a result of their rioting—they are shot, gassed, punished and segregated; but sometimes their complaints are considered and even heeded. As one convict related to the authors: "It may seem stupid, but this is the only time someone ever listened to us." Prison riots, like ghetto riots, signify a kind of civil-rights revolution by people who too long have been without ordinary institutions, adequate representatives, or any other means to redress strongly felt grievances. Riots are a warning phenomenon: that prisoners will no longer march silently in lock step, accepting everything done to them in the name of "correction."

1. Clemmer, *The Criminal Community* (1958).

Common to all prison riots are demands for decent conditions and civil treatment. Inevitably, the protesting inmates announce a list of specific grievances which form the basis of their complaints. Fundamental to them all is a desire to be treated with some measure of personal dignity. As one particularly enlightened prison administrator has advised:

> [M]y belief is that [the prisoners'] real problem is their frustrated desire to be treated in a more human way and with more fairness in all the subtle contacts between inmates and staff. . . .
>
> We have given prisoners a little more of academic education, vocational training and relaxed rules which permit them to talk in the dining room and to walk casually down the hall. . . . These changes suggest to the prisoner that maybe he should be treated like a human being, so this whets his appetite for a more complete accomplishment of a goal of human dignity. However, having whetted his appetite, we have denied him fulfillment in actuality because the prison is still a place where custodial personnel view prisoners as unworthy beings and in countless little ways reinforce this view with meaningless rules and endless punishments.[2]

Imprisonment perforce entails many inherent deprivations, but not necessarily those that give rise to riots. Most prisoners agree that the most difficult and damaging aspect of imprisonment is the demeaning and dehumanizing stripping away of personal identity that begins upon entering the institution's receiving room. An ex-convict recently released from a federal prison plaintively described this painful process:

> During their stay they were preached at: "Don't serve time; let time serve you"—even as their genitals were examined for contraband in the receiving rooms. . . . [T]he inmates are treated as a subspecies of humanity—lower than the meanest hack (guard) and less significant than the animals on prison farms.
>
> This policy of dehumanization, not lack of finances or facilities, is the single largest barrier to prisoner rehabilitation. . . .
>
> In the name of . . . discipline, the most idiotic and demeaning sort of conformity is required of all inmates, deliberately robbing them of every shred of individuality and denying them any sort of meaningful choice or control of their lives.

2. Letter from Paul W. Keve, former Commissioner of Correction, state of Minnesota, to the President's Commission on the Causes and Preventions of Violence, October 9, 1968.

A few examples suffice:

Mustaches, beards, hair longer than three inches, and long sideburns are prohibited. No decorations other than two photographs of "approved" relatives or friends are permitted in inmates' quarters. (No photographs that include the inmate himself are allowed, as though the image of the prisoner in happier times and non-prison clothes would reinforce his ego.) . . .

Individual initiative is discouraged and in many cases punished. Disobedience of the most whimsical commands of any hack is punishable by a series of sanctions including lengthening of incarceration by loss of time off for good behavior. . . .

In prison, every convict knows that conformity is nothing more than a tool designed by his keepers to make his custodial task easier.[3]

Not all of the problem addressed here is attributable to the rigors of the institutional experience. A significant part of the dilemma is assigned all prisoners by the law itself; it is the system's sentence for all convicted criminals in addition to the time imposed by the judge.

A more formal part of the correctional initiation process is the convict's loss of his civil rights. A criminal conviction subjects virtually all of a person's activities to regulation by correctional officials, particularly if he is sent to an institution rather than placed on probation. In addition, a prison sentence (or, in some states, any conviction of a felony) may affect the convict's legal status for the rest of his life.[4]

A felony conviction results in the permanent loss of the right to vote in thirty-nine states, the right to hold public office in twenty-seven states and the right to serve on a jury in twelve states; it is a ground for divorce in thirty-six states; in some states felons are deprived of the capacity to testify or to enter contracts and receive or transfer property.[5] The fre-

3. Ostro, "Why U.S. Prisons Are Failing," *National Catholic Reporter*, Aug. 27, 1969, at 1–2.
4. In California, for example, "[a] sentence of imprisonment in a state prison for any term suspends all the civil rights of the person so sentenced, and forfeits all public offices and all private trusts, authority, or power during such imprisonment." California Penal Code §2600 (Deering 1969 Supp.). The only rights excepted from the California statute are the rights to inherit property, correspond with attorneys and public officeholders, own manuscripts written while in prison and receive publications not disapproved by prison authorities.
5. American Correctional Association, *Manual of Correctional Standards* 271–72 (3d ed. 1966). *See* President's Commission on Law Enforcement and Administration of Justice, Task Force Report: *Corrections* 88–91 (1967). *Cf. Barsky v. Board of Regents*, 347 U.S. 442 (1954) (power of a state medical board to suspend the license to practice medicine of a doctor who had been convicted of failing to produce documents subpoenaed by a Congressional committee upheld).

quently quoted judicial declaration that "[a] prisoner retains all the rights of an ordinary citizen except those expressly, or by necessary implication, taken from him by law"[6] has little meaning in practice. Much of the legislation related to the collateral consequences of a conviction is extremely ambiguous. A convict frequently is unaware of what rights he has lost or how long they have been suspended until he attempts to exercise them.

Some deprivations of liberty are the necessary result of confinement in an institution. For example, sharp curtailment of freedom of movement and conformity to some basic regulations are inevitable for all prisoners. Many restrictions, however, need not result from custody; they flow from the dated myth that jailers hold all the strings and prisoners are their total subjects. This view, stated most explicitly by a Virginia court in 1871, in denying application of the Virginia Bill of Rights to felons, has been as tenacious as the fortress-like prison walls which were built to effectuate it, or as one judge visualized it, "as the ball and chain which he [the convict] drags after him."

> A convicted felon [is one] whom the law in its humanity punishes by confinement in the penitentiary instead of with death. . . . For the time being, during his term of service in the penitentiary, he is in a state of penal servitude to the State. He has, as a consequence of his crime, not only forfeited his liberty, but all his personal rights except those which the law in its humanity accords to him. He is for the time being the slave of the State.[7]

This attitude, traditionally reflected in prison administrations, remains the cause of the majority of inmate complaints. Even the questions prisoners raise with attorneys frequently are not related solely to obtaining release from confinement. Prisoners have a great reservoir of unresolved grievances concerning prison administration, practices and routines.

Historically, there have been few effective routes through which inmates could complain about their treatment or have any effect on the decisions that are made about virtually every facet of their lives. One former convict stated what has become a standard complaint:

6. *Coffin v. Reichard,* 143 F.2d 443, 445 (6th Cir. 1944), *cert. denied,* 325 U.S. 887 (1945).
7. *Ruffin v. Commonwealth,* 62 Va. (21 Gratt.) 790, 794–96 (1871).

All inmate requests and efforts outside the standard daily prison routine are purposely made extremely difficult: adding names to the list of approved correspondents or visitors; applications for job or quarters changes; special letters to persons not on mailing lists, etc. It is often weeks or months before a simple request is answered; sometimes they are not answered at all.[8]

Correctional administrators traditionally have justified their broad authority free from judicial control on the basis of statutory delegations of power or the practical needs of running large custodial institutions. This disbursement of powers means, according to a recent critique, that

> once an offender has been convicted and sentenced, the entire responsibility for determining his circumstances during the term of his sentence is entrusted to the professional judgment of correctional personnel. The offender may make *requests*, not *demands*; he may be accorded *privileges*, but he has no *rights* other than those specifically preserved to him by statute.[9]

Statutes regulating the maintenance and care of prisoners and the power of their keepers to control them are rare. The legislative standards that do exist are for the most part vague and unenforced. For example, laws in some states direct that prison food and clothing must be "wholesome," "coarse," "cheap," "plain" or "sufficient to sustain health."[10] Facilities may be required to be "clean and healthful."[11] Laws relating to institutional programs or classification of prisoners are even more rare. The statutes that deal with the employment of inmates are concerned primarily with prohibiting certain methods of production or competition with private business. Thus, prison officials have virtually unlimited discretion to deal with people in custody. Their only constraints are created by inadequate budgets, obsolete physical facilities and insufficient, untrained personnel.

In the absence of effective statutory regulation of administrative discretion, prisoners have attempted to take their grievances to court. Although most of the legal complaints filed by prisoners attack their crimi-

8. Ostro, "Why U.S. Prisons Are Failing," *National Catholic Reporter*, Aug. 27, 1969, at 2.
9. Kimball and Newman, "Judicial Intervention in Correctional Decisions: Threat and Response," 14 *Crime and Delinquency* 1, 4 (1968).
10. *E.g.*, Ala. Code tit. 44, §176 (1958); Ind. Ann. Stat. §13–238 (1956); Mass. Ann. Laws ch. 126, §33 (1965); Mich. Stat. Ann. §28.1395 (1954); N. Mex. Stat. Ann. §42–2–5 (1953).
11. *E.g.*, Ala. Code tit. 45, §174; Ill. Ann. Stat. ch. 108, §32 (Smith-Hurd 1952).

nal convictions and continued custody, a growing number challenge the treatment they have received since entering prison. It is perhaps not surprising that the courts, accused of being overly solicitous of the rights of people accused of crime, traditionally have refused to elucidate or enforce the rights of these same people once they have been convicted. Once a criminal sanction has been imposed, many judges (and lawyers as well) have abdicated to correctional administrators and, occasionally, behavioral scientists their responsibility for imaginatively applying the criminal law. According to a typical judicial statement, the "supervision of inmates of . . . institutions rests with the proper administrative authorities and . . . courts have no power to supervise the management and disciplinary rules of such institutions."[12]

The "Hands-Off" Doctrine

Correctional administrators' claims to autonomy have been supported by a policy of judicial abstention termed the "hands-off doctrine."[13] Some courts have gone so far as to deny that they have any jurisdiction to review the management of penal institutions.[14] In declining jurisdiction to protect prisoners' rights, courts most often rely upon language used by the Supreme Court in *Price v. Johnston*[15] that "[l]awful incarceration brings about the necessary withdrawal or limitation of many privileges and rights, a retraction justified by the considerations underlying our penal system." That case involved an attempt by a federal prisoner, although represented by a court-appointed attorney, per-

12. *Sutton v. Settle,* 302 F.2d 286, 288 (8th Cir. 1962).
13. The phrase originated in Fritch, *Civil Rights of Federal Prison Inmates* 31 (1961). Its implications and effect in denying prisoners legal redress are explored in Note, "Beyond the Ken of the Courts," 72 *Yale Law Journal* 506 (1963). Cases expressing various formulations of the "hands-off" doctrine are catalogued therein at 508 n.12.
14. *E.g., Garcia v. Steele,* 193 F.2d 276, 278 (8th Cir. 1951). "The Courts have no supervisory jurisdiction over the conduct of the various institutions. . . ." *Dayton v. Hunter,* 176 F.2d 108 (10th Cir. 1949), *cert. denied,* 338 U.S. 888 (1950). *See* Note, "Constitutional Rights of Prisoners: The Developing Law," 110 *University of Pennsylvania Law Review* 985 (1962):

> [A] study of the cases involving alleged mistreatment indicates that the courts have been so influenced by the dogma of the independence of prison authorities that judicial intervention has been limited to the extreme situation. Some courts have even stated the dogma in language which suggests that the courts have no jurisdiction over these matters.

Id. at 986–87 (footnote omitted).
15. 334 U.S. 266, 285 (1948).

sonally to argue his appeal from a trial court's order denying his fourth petition for *habeas corpus*. In question was a restriction on the freedom of movement of prisoners—an integral part of institutional custody.[16] Consequently, the language of the opinion is not precedent when a prisoner's constitutional rights are at issue. However, the widespread resort to and reliance on the court's language by other courts as justification for judicial abstention has gone far beyond the narrow situation involved in the *Price* case.

This judicial reluctance to interfere in internal prison affairs appears to be based on three distinct rationales: the theory of separation of powers;[17] the lack of judicial expertise in penology; and the fear that intervention by the courts will subvert prison discipline.[18]

Generally, courts, which have always decided constitutional questions, have not permitted the separation-of-powers doctrine to preclude judicial review of legislatively delegated authority. Even statutes providing that action by an administrator is "final" have not been interpreted by the courts to exclude review outside of administrative channels. If accepted, the claim of administrative expertise would eliminate all judicial willingness to hear complaints that administrative procedures fail to respect constitutional and statutory rights. In fact, courts presently are showing increased willingness to scrutinize the standards and procedures used by administrators in comparable areas which heretofore were practically immune from review. In one recent survey, several clues for the evolution of correctional law were traced to developments in the fields of public welfare, juvenile justice, commitment of the mentally ill and student rights.[19]

As for the third rationale—the possible effect of judicial review on

16. The court limited the sphere of its decision, observing that "[o]ral argument on appeal is not an essential ingredient of due process and it may be circumscribed as to prisoners where reasonable necessity so dictates." *Id.* at 286. The statute, 28 U.S.C. §1651 (1964), *formerly* 28 U.S.C. §377 (1940), gave the courts of appeals discretion whether to issue an order commanding that a prisoner be brought to court to argue his appeal. The opinion emphasized that no oral argument of an appeal is required by the Constitution.

17. "The prison system is under the administration of the Attorney General . . . and not of the district courts." *Powell v. Hunter,* 172 F.2d 330, 331 (10th Cir. 1949).

18. In *Golub v. Krimsky,* 185 F. Supp. 783, 784 (S.D.N.Y. 1960), a prisoner was denied the right to sue the warden of a federal prison for damages allegedly resulting from the defendant's failure to furnish proper medical care on the ground that "to allow such actions would be prejudicial to the proper maintenance of discipline."

19. Cohen, *The Legal Challenge to Corrections: Implications for Manpower and Training* 2–10 (1969). Hereinafter cited as Cohen. The Supreme Court recently held that the due-process clause of the Fourteenth Amendment prohibits a state from terminating public-assistance payments without giving the recipient the opportunity for an evidentiary hearing. *Goldberg v. Kelley,* 397 U.S. 254 (1970).

prison discipline—some judges have acknowledged that the need for discipline may provide too ready an excuse for denying prisoners' rights. One New York court of appeals judge, dissenting from a holding that refused to remove all limitations on prisoners' freedom to communicate with government officials, stated that:

> No valid reason, other than the shibboleth of prison discipline, has been advanced for the denial of this right in the case before us. I believe that courts should look behind inappropriate slogans so often offered up as excuses for ignoring or abridging the constitutional rights of our citizens.[20]

The "hands-off" doctrine has been used by both state and federal courts. When federal courts have been presented with the claims of state prisoners, avoidance of potential federal-state conflict has provided a further rationale for declining jurisdiction. A typical reason given by federal courts for rejecting petitions from state prisoners is that "[i]t is not the function of federal courts to interfere with the conduct of state officials in carrying out such duties under state law."[21] Even claims based on the violation of rights guaranteed by the federal Constitution have been rejected by the federal courts:

> A prisoner may not approve of prison rules and regulations, but under all ordinary circumstances that is no basis for coming into a federal court seeking relief even though he may claim that the restrictions placed upon his activities are in violation of his constitutional rights.[22]

The Abrogation of "Hands-Off"

The "hands-off" doctrine frequently has closed the courts to prisoners seeking redress of legitimate grievances. However, the doctrine has not been applied so consistently that all suits by prisoners have been barred. Even at the height of judicial abstention, there were a few judges who were so shocked by prisoners' claims that they attempted to fashion

20. *Brabson v. Wilkins,* 19 N.Y.2d 433, 438, 227 N.E.2d 383, 386, 280 N.Y.S.2d 561, 566 (1967) (dissenting opinion).
21. United States *ex rel. Lawrence v. Ragen,* 323 F.2d 410, 412 (7th Cir. 1963).
22. United States *ex rel. Morris v. Radio Station WENR,* 209 F.2d 105, 107 (7th Cir. 1953).

some remedy.[23] The first group of cases in which the judiciary agreed to accept jurisdiction on a regular basis in this class of litigation involved the protection of access to the courts themselves. Although the complaints involving impediments on the right of access to court were generally related to prisoners' efforts to challenge their original convictions in traditional ways,[24] recognition of the barriers which could be created by the actions of prison administrators led the courts for the first time to speak of an emerging new phenomenon—prisoners' rights. In addition, the right of access to court, although only partially protected, assured inmates of some forum in which to present complaints, some of which eventually would be recognized as legitimate.

Despite these cases, the "hands-off" doctrine generally survived intact until the decade of the 1960s. Two groups of Supreme Court cases, neither of which related directly to the rights of convicted criminals, contributed to a lessening of the traditional judicial reluctance to intervene in cases involving prisoners' grievances. The Court began to scrutinize various aspects of police and prosecutorial conduct that allegedly prejudiced the rights of defendants and to fashion ways to enforce these rights when law-enforcement officials ignored them.[25] It became increasingly anomalous to ignore completely claims of convicted criminals, leaving them at the mercy of correctional personnel.

At the same time, but in a different context, the Court was resurrecting a nineteenth-century statute which had been passed to enable blacks to enforce their newly granted constitutional rights against state officials. In 1961, in a suit by citizens against local policemen,[26] the Court delineated the requirements for bringing suit under the federal Civil

23. Civil damage suits against individual jailers for injuries unnecessarily inflicted on prisoners by the officials themselves or negligently allowed to be inflicted by other prisoners have long been an accepted, if inadequate, remedy. *See* section on Civil Suits Against Officials *infra*. A federal court of appeals broadened the reach of *habeas corpus* to enable a prisoner to question the terms as well as the legality of his confinement. *Coffin v. Reichard*, 143 F.2d 443 (6th Cir. 1944), *cert. denied*, 325 U.S. 887 (1945).

However, the facts of the few cases in which prisoners were given relief do not seem to have been any more compelling than many of the claims that were denied. As recently as 1962, for example, a court dismissed petitions which claimed that a prisoner's head was split open by guards, *In re* Riddle, 57 Cal. 2d 848, 850, 372 P.2d 304, 305, 22 *California Reporter* 472, 473 (1962), and that another's right eye was knocked out of its socket, *In re* Jones, 57 Cal. 2d 860, 861, 372 P.2d 310, 311, 22 *California Reporter* 478, 479 (1962).

24. *See, e.g., Ex parte* Hull, 312 U.S. 546 (1941); *Bailleaux v. Holmes*, 177 F. Supp. 361 (D. Ore. 1959), *rev'd sub nom. Hatfield v. Bailleaux*, 290 F.2d 632 (9th Cir.), *cert. denied*, 368 U.S. 862 (1961).

25. *E.g., Miranda v. Arizona*, 384 U.S. 436 (1966); *Escobedo v. Illinois*, 378 U.S. 478 (1964); *Mapp v. Ohio*, 367 U.S. 643 (1961).

26. *Monroe v. Pape*, 365 U.S. 167 (1961).

Rights Act.[27] The opinion, written by Justice Douglas, gave the act such an expansive reading that it became clear that federal courts had a duty to hear claims of interference with federally protected rights by state officials, regardless of whether the petitioners had first exhausted their state remedies.[28]

In 1964 the Court explicitly confirmed the fact that state prisoners are entitled to the protections of the Civil Rights Act.[29] Even before that decision, lower federal courts had begun to alter the way in which they handled prisoners' complaints. Although courts frequently continue to defer to the supposed needs of prison discipline,[30] the renewed use of the Civil Rights Act has permitted the federal courts to examine the claims of state prisoners to determine whether constitutional rights have been violated.[31] In state courts, however, prisoners' remedies are still quite limited.[32]

The Warren Court considered very few cases in the area of correction.[33] Two cases decided near the end of its tenure, however, indicate

27. 42 U.S.C. §1983 (1964). Federal court jurisdiction of cases based on the Civil Rights Act is based on 28 U.S.C. §1343 (1964).
28. This position was reaffirmed in *McNeese v. Board of Education,* 373 U.S. 668 (1963), a school-segregation case.
29. *Cooper v. Pate,* 378 U.S. 546 (1964).
30. *See, e.g., Roberts v. Pepersack,* 256 F. Supp. 415 (D. Md. 1966), *cert. denied,* 389 U.S. 877 (1967); United States *ex rel. Henson v. Myers,* 244 F. Supp. 826 (E.D. Pa. 1965).
31. *Compare* United States *ex rel. Hancock v. Pate,* 223 F. Supp. 202 (N.D. Ill. 1963), with *Swanson v. McGuire,* 188 F. Supp. 112 (N.D. Ill. 1960). In *Hancock,* the district court refused to follow an earlier decision of its own court of appeals, *Siegel v. Ragen,* 180 F.2d 785 (7th Cir.), *cert. denied,* 339 U.S. 990 (1950), which had enunciated a "hands-off" rationale. The district court reasoned that the Supreme Court's decision in *Monroe v. Pape,* 364 U.S. 167 (1961), had vitiated the earlier precedent. 223 F. Supp. at 204. *See also Wright v. McMann,* 387 F.2d 519, 522–23 (2d Cir. 1967).
32. *See Marcellin v. Scott,* 59 Misc, 2d 38, 298 N.Y.S.2d 43 (Sup. Ct. 1969), in which a New York court declined to hear a prisoner's claims of cruel and unusual punishment, forbidden by both the New York and the federal constitutions. Citing *Wright v. McMann,* 387 F.2d 519 (2d Cir. 1967), the court declined to proceed absent a legislative mandate for it to follow. 59 Misc. 2d at 38, 298 N.Y.S.2d at 44. The case was reversed on appeal when the New York legislature amended its correctional law. *Marcellin v. Scott,* 33 App. Div. 588, 304 N.Y.S.2d 299 (Sup. Ct., App. Div. 1969). *But see, Lewis v. State,* 176 So. 2d 718 (La. App. 1965) (parents of boy who died because of flogging by employees of state industrial school may recover damages from state); *Mahaffey v. State,* 392 P.2d 279 (Idaho 1964) (conditions of solitary confinement may constitute cruel and unusual punishment); People *ex rel. Brown v. Johnston,* 9 N.Y.2d 482, 174 N.E.2d 725, 215 N.Y.S.2d 44 (1961) (*habeas corpus* may be used to challenge place of confinement).
33. *McDonald v. Board of Elections,* 394 U.S. 802 (1969); *Johnson v. Avery* 393 U.S. 483 (1969); *Wilson v. Kelley,* 393 U.S. 266 (1969) (*per curiam*); *Houghton v. Shafer,* 392 U.S. 639 (1968) (*per curiam*); *Lee v. Washington,* 390 U.S. 333 (1968) (*per curiam*); *Mempa v. Rhay,* 389 U.S. 128 (1967); *United States v. Demko,* 385 U.S. 149 (1966); *Cooper v. Pate,* 378 U.S. 546 (1964) (*per curiam*); *United States v. Muniz,* 374 U.S. 150 (1963). *See* Rubin, book review, 16 *Crime and Delinquency* 112 (1970).

that the correctional system is not immune from judicial scrutiny. *Mempa v. Rhay*,[34] a case concerned with the revocation of probation, applied the due-process requirement of the Fourteenth Amendment to the operations of the correction system. In *Johnson v. Avery*,[35] the Court attempted to ensure prisoners' access to court by forbidding officials from denying inmates the aid of "jail-house lawyers" (other prisoners) so long as no other counsel was available. As a result, the Court provided added impetus to judicial review of prison regulations and administrative actions that affect constitutional rights.[36]

Chief Justice Burger has indicated a special interest in the function of correction as an integral part of the criminal-justice system. In a 1969 speech to the American Bar Association convention the new Chief Justice, who already had the image of a law-and-order advocate, said:

> For many years we neglected the entire spectrum of criminal justice. Slowly but with increasing pace we have corrected procedural inequities. . . . In time we must take stock of what we have done and see whether all of it is wise and useful and constructive.
>
> Meanwhile we must soon turn increased attention and resources to the disposition of the guilty once the fact-finding process is over. Without effective correctional systems an increasing proportion of our population will become chronic criminals with no other way of life except the revolving door of crime, prison and more crime.[37]

34. 389 U.S. 128 (1967).
35. 393 U.S. 483 (1969).
36. *See, e.g.*, United States *ex rel. Schuster v. Herold*, 410 F.2d 1071, 1078 (2d Cir. 1969), *cert. denied*, 390 U.S. 487 (1969):

"There is no doubt," as the Supreme Court has recently remarked, "that discipline and administration of state detention facilities are state functions. They are subject to federal authority only where paramount federal constitutional or statutory rights supervene. It is clear, however, that in instances where state regulations applicable to inmates of prison facilities conflict with such rights, the regulations may be invalidated." *Johnson v. Avery*. . . . It is not too difficult, in this regard, to discern that a transfer [from a prison to a state hospital for the criminally insane] of the character confronting us involves rights of the nature described by the Supreme Court.

37. Although it is too early to predict the position of the Burger Court, early decisions indicate that it will not reverse the trend established by its predecessor. *See Younger v. Gilmore*, 404 U.S. 15 (1971) (*per curiam*); *Haines v. Kerner*, 92 S.Ct. 594 (1972) (*per curiam*); *but see Cruz v. Beto*, 40 U.S. *Law Week* 3452 (Mar. 20, 1972) (Rehnquist, J., dissenting).

Prisoners' Rights

Although prisoners are said to retain all rights not specifically taken from them by operation of law,[38] the opposite is true. Except for a few changes in procedure established administratively, usually under the threat of unfavorable judicial rulings, virtually the only way prisoners have been able to acquire any legal rights at all has been through litigation.

The rights that prisoners have attempted to establish fall into four categories. The first category, still insufficiently protected by the courts, involves inmates' rights to physical security and the minimal conditions necessary to sustain life. The second category, which has received varying degrees of recognition, includes rights usually termed "civil rights" when applied to persons who are not in prison: freedom of religion, freedom of expression, freedom from racial discrimination, the right of privacy, the right to vote and the right to defend oneself against criminal charges. The third category, long considered important by the courts, protects prisoners' access to court to challenge the legality of their criminal convictions. Finally, just beginning to be recognized, is a prisoner's right to demand that he be given the benefit of reasonable standards and procedural protections when decisions are made that have a significant effect on him.

RIGHT TO DECENT TREATMENT: CRUEL AND UNUSUAL PUNISHMENT

Without an enforceable fundamental right to protection of his health and safety, a prisoner's other rights are meaningless. Some states have statutes that require prisons to conform to general standards of health and sanitation,[39] and courts that have been willing to take jurisdiction of legal actions concerning prisons generally have recognized the basic right to physical security.

Despite this apparently sweeping recognition of a governmental duty to treat captives humanely, recent testimony before Congressional committees and reports by responsible governmental and private groups have

38. *Coffin v. Reichard,* 143 F.2d 443, 445 (6th Cir. 1944), *cert. denied,* 325 U.S. 887 (1945).
39. *E.g., New York Correctional Law* §46 (McKinney 1968) (Commissioner of Correction has duty to protect and preserve the health of the inmates); 18 U.S.C. §4042 (1964) (Bureau of Prisons shall furnish suitable quarters and provide for the safekeeping, care, and subsistence of all persons charged with or convicted of a federal offense).

documented the existence of conditions of such filth and nightmarish brutality that no civilized person could contend that they are necessary for the rehabilitation, deterrence or even the punishment of criminals. For far too many prisoners, the right to minimum standards of decent food, clothing, shelter and medical care, the right to be protected from physical assault while incarcerated and the right not to be disciplined by torture exist only in theory and rarely can be enforced.

Protection of Physical Health and Integrity. Most claims involving the failure of prison officials to provide the minimal conditions necessary to health, to furnish reasonable medical care and to protect prisoners from assault by other inmates have been actions for damages against prison officials or the state and federal governments themselves brought by convicts after their release from prison. For example, jailers have been held liable for failure to take reasonable steps to protect inmates from beatings or sexual attacks by other prisoners.[40] But recoveries are rare.

Even in the elemental areas of food and medical care, judges hesitate to impinge on the discretion of prison officials. A Utah court dismissed a prisoner's petition for a writ of *habeas corpus* complaining that he was not being given sufficient food for his sustenance and comfort. After hearing testimony by the prison doctor that there had been no cases of malnutrition for at least five years, the court ruled that hunger pains are subjective and dismissed the petition.[41] Another court rejected prisoners' complaints about the food they were served when confined to an isolation unit. According to the judge, "while 'grue' is not appetizing and is not served attractively,[42] it is a wholesome and sufficient diet for men in close confinement day after day. The Court observed all of the petitioners, and none of them appeared to be suffering from malnutrition."[43] Recently,

40. *Ratliff v. Stanley,* 224 Ky. 819, 7 S.W.2d 230 (1928); *Hixon v. Cupp,* 5 Okla. 545, 49 P. 927 (1897); *Riggs v. German,* 81 Wash. 128, 142 P. 479 (1914); *see also United States v. Muniz,* 374 U.S. 150 (1963); *Whitree v. State,* 56 Misc. 2d 693, 290 N.Y.S.2d 486 (Ct. Cl. 1968); *but see Adams v. Pate,* 445 F.2d 105 (7th Cir. 1971) (prisoner's complaint that he was beaten repeatedly by inmate nurses on orders of prison guards and that the warden, although informed of the beatings, did nothing to stop them, fails to state a claim against the warden); *cf. Carter v. Carlson,* 447 F.2d 358 (D.C. Cir. 1971) *cert. granted sub nom. District of Columbia v. Carter,* 40 U.S. *Law Week* 3314 (U.S. Jan. 2, 1972).
41. *Hughes v. Turner,* 14 Utah 2d 128, 378 P.2d 888 (1963).
42. "Grue" consists of meat, potatoes, eggs, oleo, syrup and seasoning, baked together in a pan and served in four-inch squares.
43. *Holt v. Sarver,* 300 F. Supp. 825, 832 (E.D. Ark. 1969). Several months later, however, the same court ruled that the method of serving these meals to prisoners in isolation must be changed so that the food "gets to them in more sanitary and palatable condition." *Holt v. Sarver,* 309 F. Supp. 362, 385 (E.D. Ark. 1970).

however, a federal court of appeals ruled that a complaint alleging that a warden had withheld all food for fifty-one hours during an apparent riot, without further information, stated a claim for deprivation of constitutional rights, and a district court invalidated the use of the traditional diet of bread and water for punishment.[44]

Recent court decisions involving the provision of needed medical care have given prisoners an enforceable right to have their illnesses diagnosed and treated by a physician.[45] Rulings by New York courts have established the general principle that "[p]rison physicians owe no less duty to prisoners who must accept their care, than do private physicians to their patients who are free to choose."[46] Prison officials have, however, retained wide discretion concerning the nature and extent of medical treatment offered and the prisoner's right to seek medical assistance elsewhere.[47] Although judges have had some difficulty in defining the limits of a state's duty to care for the prisoners in its custody, there is no doubt that there exists a responsibility to provide minimal food, shelter and medical care. Some courts have ruled that refusal by the state prison authorities to provide an inmate with needed medical care is actionable under the federal Civil Rights Act.[48] In *Talley v. Stephens*,[49] a federal district court ordered Arkansas prison officials to provide inmates with

---

44. *Dearman v. Woodson*, 429 F.2d 1288 (10th Cir. 1970); *Landman v. Royster*, 337 F. Supp. 621 (E.D. Va. 1971).

45. *Cf. In re* Owens, 9 *Criminal Law Reporter* 2415 (Cir. Ct., Cook County, Ill., July 9, 1971) (tranquilizing drugs may not be administered to juveniles confined in the Illinois Industrial School for Boys without examination by physician and report to court-appointed guardian).

46. *Piscano v. State*, 8 App. Div. 2d 335, 340, 188 N.Y.S.2d 35, 40 (1959); *Whitree v. State*, 56 Misc. 2d 693, 290 N.Y.S.2d 486 (Ct. Cl. 1968).

47. A federal court has upheld a refusal by Wisconsin prison authorities to permit an inmate's use of the mails to solicit medical assistance from the Veterans Administration regarding a foot ailment that prison doctors had been unable to cure. *Goodchild v. Schmidt*, 279 F. Supp. 149 (E.D. Wis. 1968). *See also Willis v. White*, 310 F. Supp. 205 (E.D. La. 1970) (rejection of syphilitic prisoner's request for out-of-prison treatment).

48. *See McCollum v. Mayfield*, 130 F. Supp. 112, 114–15 (N.D. Cal. 1955). *But see Gittlemacker v. Prasse*, 428 F.2d 1 (3d Cir. 1970); *Owens v. Alldridge*, 311 F. Supp. 667 (W.D. Okla. 1970); *Willis v. White*, 310 F. Supp. 205 (E.D. La. 1970). *Isenberg v. Prasse*, 433 F.2d 449 (3d Cir. 1970); United States *ex rel. Hyde v. McGinnis*, 429 F.2d 864 (2d Cir. 1970). Pennsylvania *ex rel. Gatewood v. Hendrick*, 368 F.2d 179 (3d Cir. 1966), *cert. denied*, 386 U.S. 925 (1967). In general, actions may be brought under the Civil Rights Act to redress violations of constitutional rights perpetrated by persons acting under color of law. *See* 42 U.S.C. §1983 (1964).

In *Ramsey v. Ciccone*, 310 F. Supp. 600, 604–605 (W.D. Mo. 1970), the court ruled that a federal prisoner's remedy for any possible negligent medical treatment was not in *habeas corpus* but in an action for damages under state law. The court distinguished between negligent medical treatment, a simple tort, and the intentional, reckless, callous or grossly negligent denial of needed medical care. Only the latter constitute a violation of the Eighth Amendment.

49. 247 F. Supp. 683 (E.D. Ark. 1965).

reasonable medical attention and enjoined them from requiring prisoners in poor physical condition to perform physical labor beyond their capacity.

Courts have provided less protection when inmates were brutalized by prison officials or other inmates.[50] In one unusual case, however, a federal court refused to extradite an escaped prisoner to Georgia.[51] Based on testimony by the prisoner and other escapees, as well as articles from national magazines, the court concluded "that it was the custom of the Georgia authorities to treat chain-gang prisoners with persistent and deliberate brutality [and] that Negro prisoners were treated with a greater degree of brutality than white prisoners." When the Georgia authorities failed to offer any contradictory testimony, the court refused to order extradition.

Every prisoner has a right to be free from violence, including sexual threats or assaults. These intra-inmate brutalities, however, often exist free from interference by prison officials. After listening to extensive testimony, a federal judge noted with horror that on Arkansas prison farms:

> An inmate who is physically attractive to other men may be, and frequently is, raped in the barracks by other inmates. No one comes to his assistance; the floor walkers do not interfere; the trusties look on with indifference or satisfaction; the two free world people on duty appear to be helpless. Sexual assaults, fights, and stabbings in the barracks put some inmates in such fear that it is not unusual for them to come to the front of the barracks and cling to the bars all night.[52]

Unfortunately, legal remedies in this area are particularly difficult to find and, in all probability, will neither compensate the victim nor protect him from further attack; indeed, any action he takes against other stronger or more sophisticated prisoners is likely to bring retaliation.[53] By analogy to decisions that subject prison authorities to damages for

50. *But see Allison v. Wilson*, 434 F.2d 646 (9th Cir. 1970) (allegations of physical abuse by warden and two guards state cause of action under federal Civil Rights Act).
51. *Johnson v. Dye*, 175 F.2d 250 (3d Cir.), *rev'd per curiam on other grounds*, 338 U.S. 864 (1949).
52. *Holt v. Sarver*, 309 F. Supp. 362, 377 (E.D. Ark. 1970), *aff'd* 442 F.2d 304 (8th Cir. 1971).
53. Prisoners attending a nine-day workshop in Annapolis, Maryland, disputed a social worker's claim that he could protect an inmate who reported threats of sexual attacks to the authorities from retaliation by other inmates.

> It's a jungle. Why, I could get to that man three times a day because I bring food to the cells. I could dash a pot of coffee in his face . . . anything. He'd be worse off than before. He'd be branded a rat for squealing by the whole institution. *Time*, June 27, 1969, at 78.

negligently failing to protect prisoners from injuries by other prisoners,[54] both the officials and the Government should be liable for failing to protect against the well-known and predictable dangers of homosexual attacks.[55] Recently some attorneys, presumably aware of the inefficacy of the specter of future damage suits to give their clients immediate protection, have petitioned for the release of prisoners whom officials have been unable to keep safe from attack. Although courts naturally have viewed the release of threatened prisoners as a last resort to ensure their safety, there is a sprinkling of reported instances in which judges have ordered untried prisoners released from jail[56]—or transferred to another jail[57] for their own safety. In an unprecedented decision, a West Virginia judge set aside the sentence of a prisoner serving a ten-year term in the West Virginia Penitentiary because of his conclusion that further imprisonment there, in the face of unhealthy conditions, the absence of rehabilitative programs, together with the prisoner's very real fear for his own life, would constitute cruel and unusual punishment. The court was influenced by the fact that two recent murders had taken place in the prison, one of a prisoner who had filed a similar petition for release, and by testimony from both the prosecutor and a deputy warden that they could not protect a prisoner's life if other inmates wished to take it. The decision was reversed by the West Virginia Supreme Court of Appeals.[58]

In *Holt v. Sarver*,[59] a federal district judge agreed to go beyond these individual remedial measures and permitted a suit on behalf of all the inmates of the Cummins Farm Unit of the Arkansas State Penitentiary. A chief complaint by the prisoners was that most of them were housed

54. *But see Simmons v. Maslysnky*, 45 F.R.D. 127 (E.D. Pa. 1968); *Upchurch v. State*, 51 Hawaii 150, 454 P.2d 112 (1969).
55. In *Roberts v. Williams*, 302 F. Supp. 972 (N.D. Miss. 1969), *aff'd* 9 *Criminal Law Reporter* 2052 (5th Cir., Apr. 1, 1971), a claim·by a prisoner against the prison official who permitted a trustee inmate to handle a shotgun which discharged and injured the plaintiff, was ruled actionable under the federal Civil Rights Act. According to the court, callous indifference on the part of officials toward the safety of prisoners may constitute cruel and unusual punishment even where there is no specific intent to inflict harm.
56. A young defendant who was detained in the Philadelphia Jail prior to his trial was ordered released by Court of Common Pleas Judge Alexander F. Barbieri, in an unpublished order dated Sept. 26, 1968, when the judge found that prison authorities had been unable to protect him from ten homosexual attacks. The district attorney agreed that keeping the defendant in prison under these circumstances would constitute cruel and unusual punishment. New York *Times*, Sept. 28, 1968 at 65, col. 8.
57. Commonwealth of Pennsylvania *ex rel. Bryant v. Hendrick*, 7 *Criminal Law Reporter*, 2463 (Court of Common Pleas for Philadelphia County, Aug. 11, 1970), *aff'd* 444 Pa. 83, 280 A.2d 110 (1971). The court noted that the petitioners' lives were in danger at Holmesburg.
58. State of West Virginia *ex rel. Pingley v. Coiner*, HC No. 70–181 (Cir. Court of Randolph County, May 6, 1971) *rev'd*—W.Va.—186 S.E.2d 220 (1972).
59. 300 F. Supp. 825 (E.D. Ark. 1969).

in open barracks, patrolled only by inmate "floorwalkers," who were in-effective in preventing nighttime assault.[60] The court recognized a con-stitutional right of prisoners to a reasonable degree of protection by the state while they are incarcerated:

> It is plain . . . that the State must refrain from imposing cruel and unusual punishments on its convicts. And the Court is con-vinced that the State owes to those whom it has deprived of their liberty an even more fundamental constitutional duty to use ordinary care to protect their lives and safety while in prison. . . .

The court noted the inadequate resources that the state had allocated to its prison farms; yet it ordered the Commissioner of Corrections generally to allocate the department's limited resources in such a way that there would be a substantial start toward alleviating the unsafe conditions.

Although the petitioners in *Holt* did not challenge the use of in-mates to perform the functions of prison guards, this question was raised in a subsequent suit,[61] where the court agreed that a system that relies on trusties for security and houses inmates in open barracks, leaving them open to "frequent assaults, murder, rape and homosexual conduct," is unconstitutional.

Clearly, some way must be found to protect the safety of confined prisoners and prevent the violence done to them in prisons. One possible way to decrease the danger of sexual attack might be for courts to order prison officials to institute some program of conjugal visiting. Provision for voluntary heterosexual contacts would do much to reduce the inci-dence of prison assaults, so many of which are sexually motivated.

Many courts have deferred taking even modest, progressive steps, usually on separation-of-powers grounds. Simple changes, such as the provision of an individual room or cell for every prisoner, or the hiring of sufficient guards to ensure security, have been denied because they would cost more money than legislators have appropriated for correc-tion.[62] Remedial steps have not been ordered because they might "dis-

---

60. During an 18-month period there had been seventeen stabbings, four of them fatal. *Id.* at 830–31.
61. *Holt v. Sarver,* 309 F. Supp. 362 (E.D. Ark. 1970), *aff'd* 442 F.2d 304 (8th Cir. 1971).
62. *Cf. Upchurch v. State,* 51 Hawaii 150, 152, 454 P.2d 112, 114 (1969). While recognizing that the state legislature might be at fault for failing to appropriate the funds needed for a modern prison, the court refused to find the state liable on that theory.

rupt the Penitentiary or leave [prison authorities] helpless to deal with dangerous and unruly convicts."[63] Yet it is unlikely that many prisons will have available even the minimum precautions necessary for the safety of the inmates without judicial intervention. Legislatures traditionally have shown little readiness to provide the authority or the funds for basic institutional changes. This continued inaction will require courts to assume the responsibility of ordering changes of conditions, up to and including the condemnation of unsafe prison buildings where that is necessary to achieve the rights of the prisoners. The district court in *Holt*, although at first reluctant to order changes that would cost more money than officials then had available, recognized that nothing would change unless it took the responsibility for requiring broad reform. The court of appeals agreed and ordered the district court to continue to monitor the progress of correctional officials in curing constitutional violations.[64] In a suit by inmates of the Orleans Parish Prison, a federal district court ordered New Orleans city officials to correct unsafe conditions despite its finding that the sheriff responsible for the jail was "doing the best he can with the facilities and means available to him."[65]

Discipline. For inmates living in ordinary prison conditions, life can be unhealthy and unsafe; for those who are being punished for infractions of prison rules, it can be unbearable. Behavioral psychologists, may be convinced that the most effective way to change behavior is to reward the traits that are desired; American prisons, however, traditionally have offered few rewards for good behavior. Consequently, infractions can be punished only by making a prisoner's life even less pleasant than usual. In 1969 a federal judge faced with a decision concerning the disciplinary facilities at a state prison farm noted the dearth of disciplinary alternatives under the present system:

> Convicts still work long hours in the fields and in institutional facilities; they are paid nothing, either actually or constructively, for their labor; they have few privileges and few incentives to be cooperative, rules-observing members of the prison community. . . .

63. *Holt v. Sarver,* 300 F. Supp. 825, 833 (E.D. Ark. 1969).
64. *Holt v. Sarver,* 442 F.2d 304 (8th Cir. 1971).
65. *Hamilton v. Schiro,* C.A. No. 69–2443 (E.D. La., June 25, 1970). *See also* State of West Virginia *ex rel. Pingley v. Coiner,* HC No. 70–181 (Cir. Ct. Randolph County, May 6, 1971) *rev'd*—W.Va.—186 S.E. 2d 220 (1972): "Should the legislative and executive branches of government fail to provide funds and correct penology deficiencies in West Virginia, then by a separate and distinct action it may be imperative that the inherent powers of the judiciary be tested."

Confinement in isolation is now the only stringent disciplinary measure available at Cummins since the Court of Appeals has enjoined the use of the strap. If confinement of that type is to serve any useful purpose, it must be rigorous, uncomfortable, and unpleasant.[66]

Prison disciplinary measures are meted out by prison administrators for the violation of what may be an unwritten regulation with neither criminal charges nor a hearing procedure to protect the convict's rights. It is difficult to reconcile these added punishments with the theory that

[T]he crowning glory of the criminal jurisprudence of the English-speaking peoples is and ever has been that the life, liberty, and property of the humblest citizen could only be invaded by the law, and in strict conformity to that law. . . . Nor does a conviction of crime alter the rule. The sentence pronounced must be only that which the law annexes to the offense.[67]

Nevertheless, statutes in several states specifically authorize punishments by prison officials, including solitary confinement, corporal punishment[68] (despite the fact that legislation in all states but one has abolished corporal punishment as a sentence for crime),[69] the use of chains and shackles, forfeiture of earnings, reduction in diet and the loss of statutory "good time." Where statutes limit the use of corporal punishment or the amount of time that an inmate can be kept in solitary confinement, they are easily circumvented.[70] Until the late 1960s, courts consistently refused to review the punishments imposed on prisoners by their keepers. Surprisingly enough, in the process of abrogating their "hands-off" attitude, judges condemned the tortures involved in prison discipline considerably

66. *Holt v. Sarver*, 300 F. Supp. 825, 829–33 (E.D. Ark. 1969). *See also Jackson v. Bishop*, 404 F.2d 571, 575 (8th Cir. 1968) (because there were so few privileges to withhold and facilities for segregation and solitary confinement were limited, whipping was the primary disciplinary measure used in the Arkansas penal system before it was enjoined).
67. *Howard v. State*, 28 Ariz. 433, 435, 237 P. 203, 203–204 (1925); *see In re* Bonner, 151 U.S. 242 (1894).
68. As of 1968, administrative regulations authorized prison personnel to whip inmates only in Mississippi and Arkansas. *See Jackson v. Bishop*, 404 F.2d 571, 575 (8th Cir. 1968).
69. *See State v. Cannon*, 55 Del. 587, 190 A.2d 514 (1963) *rev'd on other grounds*, 55 Del. 597, 196 A.2d 399 (1963).
70. The warden of a Massachusetts jail told the authors that the state's limitation of solitary confinement to ten consecutive days, Mass. Ann. Laws ch. 127, §§39–41 (1965), is complied with by allowing a prisoner to leave his cell and walk around the cell block once before being put back for another ten-day period.

later than they acted to redress the deprivation of access to court or of freedom of religion.

The prohibition of "cruel and unusual punishment" found in the Eighth Amendment is directly applicable to cases of prison brutality. It has, however, received little use or practical development in this country, despite the fact that many of the disciplinary practices that are common in American prisons are scarcely more enlightened than the punishments the amendment was designed to condemn.[71]

The few cases in which the Supreme Court has used the Eighth Amendment to eliminate some form of criminal punishment have all been somewhat bizarre: in 1910 the Supreme Court condemned the chaining of prisoners and the "hard and painful" labor for making false entries in a public record;[72] in 1958 the Court invalidated a federal statute that penalized a deserter from military service in time of war with the loss of his citizenship;[73] and finally, in 1962, the Court held that a drug addict, who is sick, cannot be deemed a criminal on that ground alone without running afoul of the Eighth Amendment.[74]

Other penalties, however, including sterilization,[75] capital punishment for rape,[76] the civil disabilities that accompany a conviction,[77] and the ingenious methods devised to employ the death penalty,[78] seem to be at least as barbarous but have escaped the Court's condemnation.

In two cases the Supreme Court has been asked to apply the Eighth Amendment to the treatment of prisoners rather than to the statutory

71. The Eighth Amendment proscribes punishments that are "manifestly cruel and unusual, as burning at the stake, crucifixion, breaking on the wheel, or the like," or those that "involve torture or a lingering death." *In re* Kemmler, 136 U.S. 436, 446–47 (1890).

72. *Weems v. United States,* 217 U.S. 349 (1910).

73. *Trop v. Dulles,* 356 U.S. 86 (1958). Noting the rarity of the imposition of statelessness as punishment for crime, the four concurring Justices suggested that "any technique outside the bounds of these traditional penalties [fines, imprisonment and execution] is constitutionally suspect." *Id.* at 110.

74. *Robinson v. California,* 370 U.S. 660 (1962). This case marked the first time the Court ruled that the prohibitions of the Eighth Amendment apply to the states. *Cf. Powell v. Texas,* 392 U.S. 514 (1968).

75. *Buck v. Bell,* 274 U.S. 200 (1927), *distinguished, Skinner v. Oklahoma ex rel.* Williamson, 316 U.S. 535 (1942) (petitioner had based his argument primarily on the Eighth Amendment; statute voided on equal-protection grounds).

76. *Rudolph v. Alabama,* 275 Ala. 115, 152 So.2d 662, *cert. denied* 375 U.S. 889 (1963); *but see Ralph v. Warden, Maryland State Penitentiary,* 438 F.2d 786 (4th Cir. 1970) (capital punishment for rape violated Eighth Amendment where victim's life was not endangered).

77. *Barsky v. Board of Regents,* 347 U.S. 442 (1954).

78. *E.g.,* Louisiana *ex rel. Francis v. Resweber,* 329 U.S. 459 (1947) (first attempt to execute defendant failed but second did not); *McElvaine v. Brush,* 142 U.S. 155 (1891) (electrocution); *Ex parte* Medley, 134 U.S. 160 (1889) (hanging); *Wilkerson v. Utah,* 99 U.S. 130 (1878) (shot in public).

sentence for a crime. In both, escaped prisoners contested that serious prison brutality already experienced in Georgia and Alabama prisons, and the expectation of more upon return, would render extradition a cruel and unusual punishment. Refusing to reach the merits, the Court ordered the return of both escapees for their failure to exhaust state remedies.[79] In a dissenting opinion, Justice Douglas protested the effect of the Court's insistence on technicalities:

> [I]f the allegations of the petition are true, this Negro must suffer torture and mutilation, or risk death itself to get relief in Alabama. . . . I rebel at the thought that any human being, Negro or white, should be forced to run a gamut of blood and terror in order to get his constitutional rights. . . . The enlightened view is indeed the other way.[80]

In discussing the amendment, however, the Court has interpreted the ban on cruel and unusual punishment in language destined to be more significant to prisoners than the limited, frequently unfavorable decisions. It has said that "[t]he Eighth Amendment expresses the revulsion of civilized man against barbarous acts—the 'cry of horror' against man's inhumanity to his fellow man."[81] The amendment's basic concept "is nothing less than the dignity of man. . . . [It] must draw its meaning from the evolving standards of decency that mark the progress of a maturing society."[82] Despite the fact that much of this rhetoric is taken from concurring or dissenting opinions, some lower federal courts have concluded that "the totality of the language used" evidences "the basic attitude of the entire Court to the Eighth Amendment."[83]

For years, lower federal courts, presented with complaints of the most brutal conditions of solitary confinement,[84] ruled that the Eighth

79. *Sweeney v. Woodall*, 344 U.S. 86 (1952); *Dye v. Johnson*, 338 U.S. 804 (1949) (*per curiam*). *See also Stewart v. State*, 475 P.2d 600 (Ore. 1971).
80. 344 U.S. at 92–93 (dissenting opinion).
81. *Robinson v. California*, 370 U.S. 660, 676 (1962) (Douglas, J. concurring).
82. *Trop v. Dulles*, 356 U.S. 86, 100–101 (1958) (separate opinion). *See also Weems v. United States*, 217 U.S. 349, 372–73 (1910).
83. *Jackson v. Bishop*, 404 F.2d 571, 579 (8th Cir. 1968). *See also Jordan v. Fitzharris*, 257 F. Supp. 674, 679 (N.D. Cal. 1966).
84. *Ford v. Board of Managers*, 407 F.2d 937 (3d Cir. 1969) (confinement in filthy cell without running water and with bread and water only, except one full meal every third day); *Roberts v. Pepersack*, 256 F. Supp. 415 (D. Md. 1966), *cert. denied*, 389 U.S. 877 (1967) (confinement without clothing in forty-degree temperatures); *Ruark v. Schooley*, 211 F. Supp. 921 (D. Colo. 1962) (deprivation of food, water and toilet paper for fifty-two hours); *Blythe v. Ellis*, 194 F. Supp. 139 (S.D. Tex. 1961) (confinement subsequent to major surgery in cell subject to frequent flooding necessitated further surgery).

Amendment does not prohibit such forms of punishment.[85] However, in 1966, in *Jordan v. Fitzharris*,[86] a federal district judge held a full hearing at the Soledad Correctional Training Facility in California to determine the truth of a prisoner's charges regarding the twelve days he had spent in solitary confinement in a "strip" cell as punishment for a disciplinary infraction.[87] Testimony by Jordan and other prisoners substantiated the allegations that the strip cells at Soledad lacked adequate heat, light and ventilation. In addition, Jordan's cell was filthy, there was no way for him to clean it, and while in it he was denied a bed, bedding, clothing, adequate medical care or any means of keeping himself clean. The court, although recognizing that judges ordinarily should not interfere with the administration of prisons, was convinced that intervention was required in this case

> [t]o restore the primal rules of a civilized community in accord with the mandate of the Constitution of the United States. . . .
> In the opinion of the court, the type of confinement depicted in the foregoing summary of the inmates' testimony results in a slow-burning fire of resentment on the part of the inmates until it finally explodes in open revolt, coupled with their violent and bizarre conduct. Requiring man or beast to live, eat and sleep under the degrading conditions pointed out in the testimony creates a condition that inevitably does violence to elemental concepts of decency.

85. *E.g., Ford v. Board of Managers*, 407 F.2d 937 (3d Cir. 1969); United States *ex rel. Knight v. Ragen*, 337 F.2d 425 (7th Cir. 1964), *cert. denied*, 380 U.S. 985 (1965); *Williams v. Wilkins*, 315 F.2d 396 (2d Cir.), *cert. denied*, 375 U.S. 852 (1963); *Roberts v. Pepersack*, 256 F. Supp. 415 (D. Md. 1966), *cert. denied*, 389 U.S. 877 (1967); *Roberts v. Barbosa*, 227 F. Supp. 20 (S.D. Cal. 1964); *Ruark v. Schooley*, 211 F. Supp. 921 (D. Colo. 1962); *Blythe v. Ellis*, 194 F. Supp. 139 (S.D. Tex. 1961). *But see Fulwood v. Clemmer*, 206 F. Supp. 370, 377 (D.D.C. 1962) (two years' solitary confinement not "reasonably related" to disturbance of prison peace); *accord, Wright v. McMann*, 321 F. Supp. 127, 145 (N.D.N.Y. 1970) (seventeen months' segregation unconstitutionally disproportionate to offense of refusing to sign safety sheet).
    State courts continue to refuse to apply prohibitions of cruel and unusual punishment to prisoners. *See, e.g., Marcellin v. Scott*, 59 Misc. 2d 38, 298 N.Y.S.2d 43 (Sup. Ct. 1969), *rev'd*, 33 App. Div. 2d 588, 304 N.Y.S.2d 299 (1969). *But see Mahaffey v. State*, 392 P.2d 279, 281 (Idaho 1964).
86. 257 F. Supp. 674 (N.D. Cal. 1966).
87. Part of the trial was conducted at the prison and, according to the presiding judge it

> represented an intensely human drama of some precedential value. It may be noted that this is the first occasion that the United States District Court in this circuit has undertaken to inquire into the procedures and practices of a State penal institution in a proceeding of this kind.

Id. at 679. It may well have been the first time anywhere. The judge was so appalled by the physical layout of the "strip cell" that he appended pictures to his opinion.

The court issued a permanent injunction against the imposition of cruel and unusual punishment as part of solitary confinement. Under its order, "use [of a strip cell] must be accompanied by supplying the basic requirements which are essential to life, and . . . as may be necessary to maintain a degree of cleanliness compatible with elemental decency in accord with the standards of a civilized community." It then advised the defendants that adoption of the disciplinary practices recommended by the American Correctional Association[88] would satisfy constitutional requirements.

A year later, in *Wright v. McMann*,[89] the United States Court of Appeals for the Second Circuit reversed a district court's dismissal without a hearing of a prisoner's request for an injunction and damages.[90] The court of appeals held without dissent that if Wright could prove he had been subjected to the "debasing conditions" alleged, he would establish a violation of his Eighth Amendment rights. Citing the Supreme Court's opinion in *Weems v. United States*,[91] the court ruled that

> civilized standards of humane decency simply do not permit a man for a substantial period of time to be denuded and exposed to the bitter cold of winter in northern New York State and to be deprived of the basic elements of hygiene such as soap and toilet paper. . . . [Such] subhuman conditions . . . could only serve to destroy completely the spirit and undermine the sanity of the prisoner. The Eighth Amendment forbids treatment so foul, so inhuman and so violative of basic concepts of decency.[92]

Again, the standards of outside, "enlightened" correctional administrators were considered persuasive. In judging the constitutionality of New York's practices, the federal court considered it "of some interest" that

---

88. American Correctional Association, *Manual of Correctional Standards* 414–15 (3d ed. 1966). The standards limit punitive segregation on a restrictive diet to a maximum of fifteen days and suggest that the cells be evenly heated, adequately lighted and ventilated and contain toilets, washbowls and bathing facilities.
89. 387 F.2d 519 (2d Cir. 1967), *rev'g* 257 F. Supp. 739 (N.D.N.Y. 1966).
90. Wright alleged he had been kept in a strip cell for consecutive periods of thirty-three and twenty-one days, under conditions similar to those in *Jordan v. Fitzharris*. The district court had ruled that the complaint did not sufficiently show a denial of Wright's constitutional rights and that his remedy, if any, was in the state courts. *Wright v. McMann*, 257 F. Supp. 739, 745 (N.D.N.Y. 1966).
91. 217 U.S. 349, 378 (1910).
92. *See also Sostre v. Rockefeller*, 312 F. Supp. 863 (S.D.N.Y. 1970), *aff'd in part, modified in part, rev'd in part sub nom. Sostre v. McGinnis*, 442 F.2d 178 (2d Cir. 1971) (*en banc*); *Hancock v. Avery*, 301 F. Supp. 786 (M.D. Tenn. 1969).

directives of the United States Bureau of Prisons[93] would not permit the treatment that Wright said he had received. On remand, the district court found that Wright indeed had been subjected to the treatment he claimed, awarded him $1,500 in damages and ordered state authorities to draw up new rules for confinement in "observation" cells.[94]

The Supreme Court has never considered a challenge to methods of prison discipline based on the Eighth Amendment. However, the Court's unanimous action in an appeal questioning the validity of a confession by a prisoner who had spent fourteen days in the punishment cell of a Florida prison may indicate the action it would take in a case similar to *Jordan* or *Wright*.

The prisoner had been convicted of participating in a prison riot. After the riot, he was confined in a punishment cell with two other inmates. For fourteen days the only outsider he saw was the prison's investigating officer. The Court ruled that the confinement of the prisoner voided his confession:

> For two weeks this man's home was a barren cage fitted only with a hole in one corner into which he and his cell mates could defecate. For two weeks he subsisted on a daily fare of 12 ounces of thin soup and eight ounces of water. For two full weeks he saw not one friendly face from outside the prison, but was completely under the control and domination of his jailers. These stark facts belie any contention that the confession extracted from him within minutes after he was brought from the cell was not tainted by the 14 days he spent in such an oppressive hole . . . . The record in this case documents a shocking display of barbarism which should not escape the remedial action of this Court. . . .[95]

Evidence of the squalid, brutal, dehumanizing conditions of many American prisons is sufficient to warrant an invigorated judicial review

93. U.S. Bureau of Prisons, Policy Statement 7400.5, app. A, at 2 (Nov. 28, 1966), which provides in part:
> The quarters used for segregation shall be well ventilated, adequately lighted, appropriately heated and maintained in a sanitary condition at all times. . . . All inmates shall be admitted to segregation (after thorough search for contraband) dressed in normal institution clothing and shall be furnished a mattress and bedding. In no circumstances shall an inmate be segregated without clothing except when prescribed by the Chief Medical Officer for medical or psychiatric reasons. . . . [S]egregated inmates shall be fed three times a day on the standard ration and menu of the day for the institution. . . . Segregated inmates shall have the same opportunities to maintain the level of personal hygiene available to all other inmates. . . .
94. *Wright v. McMann*, 321 F. Supp. 127 (N.D.N.Y. 1970).
95. *Brooks v. Florida*, 389 U.S. 413, 414–15 (1967) (*per curiam*).

of prisoners' cases claiming cruel and unusual treatment. There is no good reason why courts should hesitate to require humane living standards in American prisons; the cruel and unusual punishment clause of the Eighth Amendment is the obvious constitutional basis for judicial intervention.

Corporal punishment. Disciplining prisoners by the use of any type of corporal punishment is prohibited by statute or administrative regulation in the federal[96] and in practically every state[97] penal system. Notwithstanding statements of official policy, however, instances of corporal punishment are common in prisons throughout the country. Where statutes specifically prohibit its infliction, it should be possible for prisoners who are beaten by guards or subjected to other sadistic forms of punishment to bring legal action under the statutes. However, statutes providing criminal sanctions[98] may preclude civil suits by the injured prisoners.[99] Prosecutors are likely to be reluctant to prosecute fellow officials and, even if prosecuted, it would do the injured prisoner little good. A civil action for damages or for an injunction, predicated on the standards dictated by the Eighth Amendment,[100] may provide the only remedy for the injured prisoner.

In 1968, only Arkansas and Mississippi had regulations officially sanctioning the flogging of prisoners.[101] Although the latter have not been challenged, a federal district court, relying on the historical interpretations of cruel and unusual punishment, refused to rule that flogging with a large leather strap in an Arkansas prison was proscribed by the Eighth Amendment. The court would only impose certain limitations on the practice; for example, an inmate must be fully clothed while he is being flogged.[102]

96. 18 U.S.C. §3564 (1964).
97. *E.g.,* N.Y. Laws of 1970, ch. 479 ("No inmate . . . shall be subjected to degrading treatment, and no officer or other employee . . . shall inflict any blows whatever upon any inmate, unless in self-defense, or to suppress a revolt or insurrection"); Cal. Penal Code Ann. §§2652–53 (Deering 1961); N.D. Cent. Code §12–47–26 (1960); *Lewis v. State,* 176 So.2d 718 (La. App.), *appeal denied,* 248 La. 364, 178 So.2d 655 (1965).
98. *E.g.,* Cal. Penal Code Ann. §§2652–53 (Deering 1961).
99. *Cf. Ridgway v. Superior Court,* 74 Ariz. 117, 122, 245 P.2d 268, 272 (1952).
100. Under the federal Civil Rights Act, 42 U.S.C. §1983 (1964), it is possible for a court to award damages to a prisoner whose constitutional rights have been violated.
101. *See Jackson v. Bishop,* 404 F.2d 571, 575 (8th Cir. 1968). A Delaware statute authorizes corporal punishment as an alternative sentence to imprisonment. *See* Del. Code Ann. ch. 39, §§631, 811, 3905–08 (1953); *see also Cannon v. State,* 55 Del. 597, 196 A.2d 399 (1963); *Balser v. State,* 195 A.2d 757 (Del. 1963) (inclusion of twenty lashes as part of a sentence for robbery does not constitute cruel and unusual punishment).
102. *Talley v. Stephens,* 247 F. Supp. 683 (E.D. Ark. 1965).

Prison authorities, no doubt heartened by this decision, disregarded even these minimal safeguards. Two years later, the district court attempted to impose "appropriate safeguards" on the use of corporal punishments. This time a more abashed court of appeals reversed and in *Jackson v. Bishop*[103] held that "the use of the strap . . . irrespective of any precautionary conditions which may be imposed, offends contemporary concepts of decency and human dignity and precepts of civilization which we profess to possess. . . ."[104]

After the September 1971 uprising and taking of hostages at New York's Attica prison, prisoners sought a federal-court injunction against further physical reprisals by guards. Prisoners and one National Guardsman testified that

> . . . beginning immediately after the State's recapture of Attica on the morning of September 13 and continuing at least until September 16, guards, state troopers and correctional personnel had engaged in cruel and inhuman abuse of numerous inmates. Injured prisoners, some on stretchers, were struck, prodded or beaten with sticks, belts, bats or other weapons. Others were forced to strip and run naked through gauntlets of guards armed with clubs which they used to strike the bodies of the inmates as they passed. Some were dragged on the ground, some marked with an "X" on their backs, some spat upon or burned with matches, and others poked in the genitals or arms with sticks. According to the testimony of the inmates, bloody or wounded inmates were apparently not spared in this orgy of brutality.

Despite its acceptance of the testimony for the purposes of its decision, the district court denied the injunction because of the assurances of prison authorities that the reprisals would not continue.

103. 404 F.2d 571 (8th Cir. 1968) *rev'ing Jackson v. Bishop*, 268 F. Supp. 804, 815–16 (E.D. Ark. 1967).
104. *Id.* at 579. The court was particularly concerned about the problems involved in granting broad discretion over discipline to lower-echelon personnel, where it was easily subject to abuse in the hands of the sadistic and unscrupulous. A similar concern was central to Judge Sobeloff's opinion in *Landman v. Peyton*, 370 F.2d 135, 139–41 (4th Cir.), *cert. denied*, 385 U.S. 881 (1966). *See also Mason v. Peyton*, Civ. No. 53–69–R (E.D. Va., consent decree, Aug. 13, 1968) (injunction against the indiscriminate use of tear gas and chemical MACE on prisoners in Virginia); *In re* Birdsong, 39 F. 599, 600–601 (S.D. Ga. 1889).

These problems seem to be less involved with the nature of the punishments that may be imposed, a question to be determined under the Eighth Amendment, than with the procedures that must be followed in meting out any discipline. The latter question seems to be amenable to solution under the traditional requirements of due process of law.

The court of appeals reversed, holding that "even if some corporal punishment may be permitted under the Constitution, the mistreatment of the inmates in this case amounted to cruel and unusual punishment in violation of their Eighth Amendment rights." In the circumstances, the appellate court was not satisfied with the officials' assurances, in the absence of further proof:

> If the abusive conduct of the prison guards had represented a single or short-lived incident, unlikely to recur, or if other corrective measures had been taken to guarantee against repetition, injunctive relief might be denied, despite the heinous character of the conduct. . . .
>
> Here, however, the conduct of some of the prison guards, state police and correctional personnel, as testified to, was not only brutal but it extended over a period of at least several days, with one serious incident occurring much later.[105]

The Problem of Standards. In *Jordan, Wright* and *Jackson,* the courts had no difficulty in declaring the challenged disciplinary practices to be both cruel and unusual in violation of the Eighth Amendment. While it is temptingly easy to so restrict the scope of the Eighth Amendment to punishment that is both cruel *and* unusual, such an interpretation unduly restricts the potential for enforcing standards of decency and humanity in prisons.[106]

It has been recommended that federal courts adopt administrative regulations to establish minimal standards of constitutionality in this area.[107] Recently, however, a federal district judge refused to do so and denied that the failure to meet such standards was at issue in constitutional challenges of prison practices:

105. *Gonzalez v. Rockefeller,* 10 *Criminal Law Reporter* 2227 (2d Cir., Dec. 1, 1971).
106. In *Trop v. Dulles,* 356 U.S. 86, 99 (1958), the Supreme Court refused to consider the death penalty "as an index of the constitutional limit on punishment," since it "has been employed throughout our history, and, in a day when it is still widely accepted, it cannot be said to violate the constitutional concept of cruelty." *Cf. Rudolph v. Alabama,* 375 U.S. 889 (1963) (dissent from denial of *certiorari*).
107. Hirschkop and Millemann, "The Unconstitutionality of Prison Life," 837 *Virginia Law Review* 795 (1969).

> The continued abuse of discretion by local school boards forced the courts to adopt the HEW guidelines. By similar logic, the present misuse of unfettered discretion by state penal authorities justifies the adoption of the federal prison regulations. Such action would effect an instantaneous improvement in Virginia prison conditions.

Cf. Rubin, "Needed—New Legislation in the Correctional Field" (unpublished paper presented to the Annual Conference of the Oregon Correction Association, Oct. 15, 1969), which suggests that the standard be established by statute rather than administrative regulation.

A practice that may be bad from the standpoint of penology may not necessarily be forbidden by the Constitution. And a prison system that would be excellent from the point of view of a modern prison administrator may not be required by the provisions of the Constitution with which the Court is concerned.[108]

However, the court had previously warned state prison officials that

Where an unconstitutional situation is found to exist in a given prison, the prison authorities cannot escape responsibility for it by merely pointing to the existence of the same situation in other prisons, or by establishing that conditions in their prisons are "better" or "no worse than" conditions prevailing elsewhere.[109]

For example, solitary confinement is an accepted method of discipline, and courts have consistently refused to rule that it constitutes cruel and unusual punishment *per se*,[110] or that its duration must be to a specified period.[111] Yet, as prison officials themselves have admitted, the psychological effects of solitary confinement, which deprives a prisoner of exercise, companionship and mental stimulation, can be extremely severe.[112] Cruelty need not involve the infliction of bodily pain,[113] for even

108. *Holt v. Sarver*, 309 F. Supp. 362, 369 (E.D. Ark. 1970), *aff'd* 442 F.2d 304 (8th Cir. 1971).
109. *Holt v. Sarver*, 300 F. Supp. 825, 828 (E.D. Ark. 1969) (dictum).
110. "Solitary confinement in and of itself does not violate Eighth Amendment prohibitions, and the temporary inconveniences and discomforts incident thereto cannot be regarded as a basis for judicial relief." *Ford v. Board of Managers*, 407 F.2d 937, 940 (3d Cir. 1969); *accord, Burns v. Swenson*, 430 F.2d 771, 777–78 (8th Cir. 1970). *Courtney v. Bishop*, 49 F.2d 1185 (8th Cir.) *cert. denied*, 396 U.S. 915 (1969); *Abernathy v. Cunningham*, 393 F.2d 775, 777 (4th Cir. 1968); *Graham v. Willingham*, 384 F.2d 367 (10th Cir. 1967); *Holt v. Sarver*, 300 F. Supp. 825, 827 (E.D. Ark. 1969); *see Stroud v. Johnston*, 139 F.2d 171 (9th Cir. 1943) (confinement of the "Bird Man of Alcatraz" in an isolation cell for life accepted as within the range of administrative discretion); *cf. Ray v. Neil*, Civ. No. 5590 (M.D. Tenn., order entered, Dec. 29, 1969) (warden ordered to permit James Earl Ray some time out of his isolation cell for recreation, work and exercise).
111. *Sostre v. McGinnis*, 442 F.2d 178 (2d Cir. 1971); *Beishir v. Swenson*, 331 F. Supp. 1227 (W.D. Mo. 1971).
112. A strip cell is a necessary part of prison discipline owing to the fact that a prisoner when being punished for breach of prison discipline is placed in solitary confinement or segregation, [where] he often becomes violent and destroys property, tears the cell up and sets fires and otherwise conducts himself as to be dangerous to himself and others.
Wright v. McMann, 387 F.2d 519, 526 n.15 (2d Cir. 1967) (statement of prison warden); *see also Wright v. McMann*, 321 F. Supp. 127, 138–39 (N.D.N.Y. 1970) (on remand).
In the most recent edition of its *Manual for Correctional Standards* 413 (1966), the American Correctional Association stated:
Perhaps we have been too dependent on isolation or solitary confinement as the principal method of handling the violators of institutional rules. Isolation may bring short-term conformity for some, but brings increased disturbances and deeper grained hostility to more.
113. *Weems v. United States*, 217 U.S. 349, 372–73 (1910).

"enforced idleness can be cruel punishment, particularly when it is only to protect [the prisoner] from bodily harm [by his fellow prisoners]."[114]

In *Sostre v. Rockefeller*,[115] a New York prisoner spent thirteen months in solitary confinement. He was not permitted to use the prison library, read newspapers, see movies or attend classes. According to the federal district court that enjoined continuation of this form of punishment, "the crux of the matter is human isolation—the loss of 'group privileges.'" The district court, going beyond existing definitions of cruel and unusual punishment, which heretofore had required extreme physical conditions accompanying solitary confinement, found that

> punitive segregation . . . is physically harsh, destructive of morale, dehumanizing in the sense that it is needlessly degrading, and dangerous to the maintenance of sanity when continued for more than a short period of time which should certainly not exceed fifteen days. . . .
>
> Subjecting a prisoner to the demonstrated risk of the loss of his sanity as punishment for any offense in prison is plainly cruel and unusual punishment as judged by present standards of decency.

The court of appeals reversed.[116] Despite its recognition that prolonged segregation might be "counterproductive as a correctional measure and personally abhorrent," the court found that the conditions in this case, which included rudimentary implements of personal hygiene, a reasonable diet and the opportunity for daily outdoor exercise and communication with other prisoners, were "several notches above those truly barbarous and inhumane conditions" previously found cruel and unusual. The court noted the absence of any testimony that the confinement threatened the prisoner's physical or mental health and pointed out that a physician visited him daily. The appeals court refused to place an upper limit on the duration of the punishment, pointing out that the continued confinement in this case could have been ended by the prisoner's agreement to abide by institutional rules.

At the opposite extreme from isolation is the punishment inherent

114. *Washington Post*, Dec. 30, 1969, §A, at 7, col. 1, *discussing Ray v. Neil*, Civ. No. 5590 (M.D. Tenn., order entered, Dec. 29, 1969). *See also Davis v. Lindsay*, 321 F. Supp. 1134 (S.D.N.Y. 1970) (segregation of detainee because of her notoriety violates her right to equal protection despite availability of same facilities given rest of the jail population).
115. 312 F. Supp. 863 (S.D.N.Y. 1970).
116. *Sostre v. McGinnis*, 442 F.2d 178 (2d Cir. 1971) (*en banc*).

in the inhuman overcrowding that plagues so many prisons and local jails. As a report to the National Commission on Violence recognized, hostility often cannot be contained when a prisoner is thrust into an overcrowded cell where "he must fight for space on the floor to sleep, let alone be accorded the simple comfort of a bed."[117]

The court in *Holt v. Sarver* went beyond standards set by correctional administrators and the policies underlying the prohibition against cruel and unusual punishment in ruling that overcrowded conditions ran afoul of the Constitution:

> Without undertaking to state with specificity the exact point at which one of the isolation cells becomes "overcrowded" rather than simply "crowded" . . . the Court finds that the cells have been chronically overcrowded. . . .
>
> [T]here are limits to the rigor and discomfort of close confinement which a State may not constitutionally exceed. . . . [T]he prolonged confinement of numbers of men in the same cell under the conditions that have been described is mentally and emotionally traumatic as well as physically uncomfortable. It is hazardous to health. It is degrading and debasing; it offends modern sensibilities, and, in the Court's estimation, amounts to cruel and unusual punishment.[118]

In several recent cases, indignant courts have ordered an end to overcrowded and unsanitary conditions in jails and detention centers. A federal district court ruled that the population of a New Mexico jail must not exceed sixty prisoners.[119] It therefore ordered the immediate release of the inmates who had served the longest terms in order to reduce the number of confined prisoners to sixty. Other federal courts have ordered relief, based on the Eighth Amendment, from overcrowding, lack of light, sanitation, ventilation, exercise or adequate supervision, in jails in New Orleans,[120] Little Rock[121] and two California counties.[122] According to the opinion of one of the district judges:

117. Report of the Task Force on Law and Law Enforcement to the National Commission on the Causes and Prevention of Violence, *Law and Order Reconsidered* 579 (1969).
118. 300 F. Supp. 825, 833 (E.D. Ark. 1969).
119. *Curley v. Gonzales,* Civ. No. 8372 (D.N.M., Feb. 13, 1970).
120. *Hamilton v. Schiro,* C.A. No. 69–2443 (E.D. La., June 25, 1970).
121. *Hamilton v. Love,* 328 F. Supp. 1182 (E.D. Ark. 1971).
122. *Brenneman v. Madigan,* No. 70–1911 (N.D. Cal., Mar. 11, 1971); *Dean v. Young,* No. 123849 (N.D. Cal., Mar. 17, 1971). *See also Wayne County Jail Inmates v. Wayne County Board of Commissioners,* Cir. Action No. 173217 (Cir. Ct., Wayne County, Mich., May 18, 1971).

I have come to the inescapable conclusion that Greystone should be razed to the ground. Confinement in cells at Greystone, under the almost unbelievable conditions which prevail there, offends elemental concepts of decency and is of such shocking and debasing character as to constitute cruel and unusual punishment for man or beast.[123]

A three-judge state court ordered two pre-trial detainees transferred out of the Holmesburg Prison in Philadelphia, where conditions were termed "an affront to the dignity of man" and outside "the limits of civilized standards" and gave authorities thirty days in which to correct the most flagrant abuses, after which the court presumably would act on similar petitions.[124]

Recent scientific studies have shown that marked, demonstrable physiological and psychological damage is done to animals isolated for prolonged periods or overcrowded beyond permissible territorial imperatives. Studies in "sensory deprivation," where men were placed in dark, soundproofed, but comfortable rooms, have demonstrated that confinement resulted in definite biochemical and neurological changes of an indefinite duration. Although no similar experiments have been undertaken with prisoners as subjects, it is likely that forced and uncomfortable solitary confinement or overcrowding may have unknown and possibly drastic effects.

In *Lollis v. New York State Department of Social Services*,[125] a court faced with a challenge to the solitary confinement of a fourteen-year-old girl in an unfurnished "strip room" at a New York training school relied heavily on the opinions of several experts in adolescent psychology concerning the harmful effects of such confinement. One witness warned of the danger in prolonged exposure to sensory deprivation—"a state of

123. *Brenneman v. Madigan* at 4. *See also Anderson v. Nosser*, 438 F.2d 183 (5th Cir. 1971) (conditions of pre-trial detention of racial protest demonstrators at the Parchman State Prison in Mississippi).
124. Commonwealth of Pennsylvania *ex rel. Bryant v. Hendrick*, No. 1567 (Court of Common Pleas for Philadelphia County, Aug. 11, 1970), *aff'd* 440 Pa. 83, 280 A.2d 110 (1971). When untried detainees are involved, any conditions beyond those necessary to ensure presence at trial are subject to challenge as punishment without due process of law, forbidden by the Fifth and Fourteenth Amendments, as well as under the more stringent Eighth Amendment standard. *See Jones v. Wittenberg*, 323 F. Supp. 93 (N.D. Ohio 1971): "[Detainees] are not to be subject to any hardship except those absolutely requisite for the purpose of confinement only, and they retain all the rights of an ordinary citizen except the right to go and come as they please." *See also Tyler v. Ciccone*, 299 F. Supp. 684 (W.D. Mo. 1969); *Anderson v. Nosser, Hamilton v. Love, Brenneman v. Madigan*, Commonwealth of Pennsylvania *ex rel. Bryant v. Hendrick, supra*.
125. 322 F. Supp. 473 (S.D.N.Y. 1970).

affairs which will cause a normal adult to begin experiencing psychotic-like symptoms, and will push a troubled person in the direction of serious emotional illness. . . . [I]solation is a condition of extraordinarily severe psychic stress; the resultant impact on the mental health of the individual exposed to such stress will always be serious, and can occasionally be disastrous." The court ruled that the confinement violated the Eighth Amendment's ban on cruel and unusual punishment.

Such considerations raise new questions concerning the proper application of the cruel and unusual punishment prohibitions to the egregious prison conditions and the prototype prison forms. In light of these findings, new standards of decency for acceptable punitive measures must be established. Traditionally, all prisoners have been subjected to rigid controls in order to control the few truly violent inmates. These overly repressive measures were required for the sake of security.[126] A federal court of appeals, however, recently ruled that a mental patient must be treated according to the "least restrictive alternative."[127] A similar provision should be applied to prisons.[128] In *Wright v. McMann*,[129] the court indicated that the Eighth Amendment forbids prison officials from subjecting all prisoners to coercive methods needed to control a few. In a footnote, the court answered defendant's contention that strip cells "are only used to avoid the dangerous consequences of placing a prisoner in a segregated area immediately upon his being sentenced to . . . punishment":

> But apparently no determination was made that this *particular* prisoner was or would have become violent. Indeed, the Warden's answer admits that "The treatment of Wright was strictly routine treatment for a violation of prison discipline. . . ."[130]

126. *Jordan v. Fitzharris*, 257 F. Supp. 674, 680–81 (N.D. Cal. 1966).
127. *Covington v. Harris*, 419 F.2d 617, 623–25 (D.C. Cir. 1969).
128. See *Palmigiano v. Travisono*, 317 F. Supp. 776 (D.R.I. 1970) (prison officials may only use legitimate means to prevent introduction of contraband, choosing the least restrictive alternative).
129. 387 F.2d 519 (2d Cir. 1967).
130. *Id.* at 526 n.15; *cf. Hancock v. Avery*, 301 F. Supp. 786, 789 (M.D. Tenn. 1969). *Compare* complaint filed in federal court by the New York "Panther 21," *Shakur v. McGrath*, 69 Civ. 4493 (S.D.N.Y. 1969). The complainants were held on high bail for trial on charges of conspiracy in various jails throughout New York City.
   Two separate questions appear to be involved in the complaint. The first concerns the procedure (or lack thereof) through which particular inmates were singled out to be handled more vigorously than others. The second involves the rational relationship between the risks these inmates were thought to pose and the treatment they received. The court did not consider whether the methods that had been used to control the prisoners were constitutional. *Shakur v. McGrath*, 69 Civ. 4493, at 6, 10–12 (S.D.N.Y., mem., Dec. 31, 1969).

If prisoners are to realize the potential scope of Eighth Amendment protections, other common prison practices should be challenged as cruel and unusual punishment. Chief among these are the denial of heterosexual relations, the requirement that the prisoners work for little or no pay and the warehousing of prisoners with no attempt at rehabilitation.

Sexual Deprivation. One of the classic problems in American prisons is caused by the deprivations resulting from long periods of confinement of men (or women) without normal means for release of their natural sexual urges. This onerous, unnatural condition causes great anxieties and perversions among prisoners. Long, enforced sexual abstinence, especially among young people, is a cruel and unnecessary form of punishment which must irritate and undoubtedly frustrates any chance of rehabilitation. In addition, the refusal to allow married prisoners sexual relations with their wives must increase their alienation and the disruptive effect of imprisonment on family life. To date, no court has ruled that a prisoner has a right to sexual relations while he is in prison, and somewhat surprisingly, apparently no prisoner has attempted to obtain such a ruling.[131]

Approximately thirty countries[132] allow furloughs or conjugal visits, usually limited to married men. Six countries[133] even permit certain inmates to live with their families in special penal colonies. In certain Latin American countries even single prisoners are allowed sexual release outside prison. The California Correctional Institute at Tehachapi recently began a practice of allowing inmates near the end of their sentence to spend a weekend with their wives in apartments on the prison grounds. Louisiana permits furloughs, but with one exception, no American prison allows normal sexual relations inside the prison.

It is interesting that despite the reputation of Southern prisons for being the most brutal and least progressive, a program of conjugal visitation is flourishing at the Mississippi State Penitentiary. The practice began, oddly enough, as part of the segregation policy of the prison. Black

131. In one case a wife tried unsuccessfully to obtain a court order allowing her conjugal visits with her incarcerated husband. *Payne v. District of Columbia*, 253 F.2d 867 (D.C. Cir. 1958) (*per curiam*).
132. Argentina, Belgium, Czechoslovakia, Denmark, West Germany, Great Britain, Greece, Ireland and the Sudan (furloughs only), Burma, Chile, Costa Rica, Ecuador, El Salvador, Guatemala, Honduras, Japan, Mexico, Peru, the Philippine Islands, the Soviet Union (conjugal visits only), Bolivia, Brazil, Canada, Colombia, India, Pakistan, Poland, Puerto Rico, Sweden, Venezuela (conjugal visits and home furloughs). Hopper, *Sex in Prisons, The Mississippi Experiment with Conjugal Visiting* 6 (1969).
133. Burma, India, Mexico, Pakistan, the Philippines and the Soviet Union. *Id.* at 9.

prisoners, assumed somehow to be driven by especially strong sexual impulses, were allowed to have private visits for the purposes of engaging in intimate sexual release. The practice spread and eventually was adopted throughout the system.

According to a recent study, the conjugal visiting program in Mississippi is successful because the staff and inmates have a balanced attitude about the subject, jealousies and exploitation do not exist, privacy is respected and the practice is maintained without unnecessary rules and regulations through a sense of mutual cooperation.

Most American correction officials seem to oppose conjugal visits on the ground that it would heighten tensions, cause administrative problems, violate prevailing community mores, trigger public criticism, appear too improvident and lenient and (by some stretch of the imagination) make adjustment to prison life more difficult for inmates. Other correction authorities appear to favor introducing the practice not only for obvious reasons of humanitarianism but also as the best way to check one of the most critical problems in prisons—rampant and often violent homosexuality.

The taboo of sex and the conventional shortsighted pseudo-moralism of prison administrations in America make it unlikely that conjugal visitations will be allowed generally without a judicial declaration that it may not be denied.

Prison Labor. In many states and counties and in the federal system, prison labor is used to reimburse the Government for some or all of the expense of operating the prisons. Although several Southern states formerly leased their prisoners to private employers, public criticism, coupled with the needs of state and local governments to build roads, manufacture license plates and provide supplies for government agencies, led to the replacement of the convict lease system with chain gangs laboring on public works outside the prisons and the operation of farms and "state-use" industries inside the prisons.[134]

In many cases, unpaid maintenance work is the only job available. Where there is other work to do, job assignments generally are unrelated to possibilities for employment after release; according to a former inmate, "getting the garbage removed is far more important than the remover's future."

134. For example, the Federal Penitentiary in Atlanta produces mail bags. The state of Maryland has a minimum-security prison where inmates do all the laundry for the state's hospitals and prisons. Practically all state prisons manufacture license plates.

When they are assigned a job, prisoners may not refuse to work.[135] And despite the fact that prison working conditions, particularly those associated with farm labor in the South, frequently are extremely brutal, a federal court refused to interfere with a prisoner's assignment to work in the field unless he could demonstrate some serious physical injury.[136]

The profits of the various systems of prison industries depend on paying the prison laborers extremely low wages or none at all.[137] Yet the prisoners are required to purchase their own personal items, such as supplies for shaving, writing or smoking and are not even furnished with shoes, warm clothing or bad-weather gear, although they are required to work in bad weather. Arkansas prisoners are so exploited that in 1966 the state actually made a profit of close to $300,000 after deducting all expenses. Ohio prisoners recently received their first pay raise in seventeen years. Inmates with outside dependents now can earn up to nine and one half cents an hour, single inmates up to five cents an hour.

Courts have consistently ruled, however, that prisoners have no right to wages for work performed while in prison.[138] Recently a federal court of appeals rejected an indigent prisoner's challenge, on equal-protection grounds, to a Vermont statute that allows a prisoner five days of his sentence for each month worked if he chooses to forego his wages of ten cents an hour.[139] Furthermore, prisoners are not entitled to compensation for injuries; workmen's compensation plans are presumed to apply only to those employed voluntarily by the state, while "a prisoner's status is that

---

135. See Watson v. Industrial Commission, 100 Ariz. 327, 414 P.2d 144, 148 (1966): "A prisoner is compelled by statute to perform manual labor as punishment for his criminal offense and has no alternative except to be disciplined for his failure to work."
136. Bryant v. Harrelson, 187 F. Supp. 738 (S.D. Tex. 1960); cf. Talley v. Stephens, 247 F. Supp. 683, 687 (E.D. Ark. 1965) (injunction against requiring prisoners in poor physical condition to do work they are physically unable to perform).
137. In Arkansas,

> [c]onvicts still work long hours in the fields and in institutional facilities; they are paid nothing, either actually or constructively, for their labor. . . . The only legitimate way in which a convict at Cummins can earn money is to sell blood to the prison blood bank.

Holt v. Sarver, 300 F. Supp. 825, 829 (E.D. Ark. 1969).
138. E.g., McLaughlin v. Royster No. 13,881 at 1–2 (4th Cir., mem., Sept. 8, 1969).

> [t]here is no constitutional requirement that prisoners be paid at all for work required to be performed during the terms of imprisonment. Small payments are made to prisoners by the Commonwealth of Virginia, and we perceive no constitutional violation in requiring prisoners to purchase with that income items of personal convenience and comfort.

See also State Board of Charities and Corrections v. Hays, 190 Ky. 147, 227 S.W.282 (1920).
139. Baldwin v. Smith, 446 F.2d 1043 (2d Cir. 1971).

of involuntary servitude which is a consequence of his conviction and incarceration.[140]

Prisoners from Georgia[141] and Arkansas[142] penitentiaries recently claimed that forced labor, performed for the economic benefit of the state, violates the Thirteenth Amendment's ban on slavery and involuntary servitude. However, since the Thirteenth Amendment specifically exempts work done as "punishment for crime" it appears to offer little hope to prison inmates.[143] In *Holt v. Sarver*, forced prison labor was labeled "involuntary servitude."[144] Yet from the language of the Thirteenth Amendment and the fact that convict labor was commonly used when the amendment was written, the court concluded the amendment's proscription was inapplicable to convicted criminals.

When prison labor is used for the profit of the state, however, the servitude imposed seems less as "punishment for crime" than as a means of enriching the state. Perhaps at that point this otherwise unconstitutional system of peonage can no longer be rationalized or sustained on correctional theories.

A more fruitful line of argument is that requiring prisoners to work without due compensation constitutes cruel and unusual punishment prohibited by the Eighth Amendment. Enlightened prison administrators feel that prisoners should be paid at least the minimum wage and be required to pay for their room, board and any extra food and personal items they care to purchase in prison, and to contribute to the support of their dependents. Under this system, the families of prison inmates could be taken off public welfare. More important, the self-supporting

140. *Watson v. Industrial Commission*, 100 Ariz. 327, 414 P.2d 144, 148 (1966); *accord, Lawson v. Travelers' Insurance Company*, 37 Ga. App. 85, 139 S.E. 96 (1927); *Miller v. City of Boise*, 70 Idaho 136, 212 P.2d 654 (1949); *Moats v. State*, 215 Md. 49, 136 A.2d 757 (1957); *Greene's Case*, 280 Mass. 506, 182 N.E. 857 (1932); *Brown v. Jamesburg State Home for Boys*, 60 N.J. Super. 123, 158 A.2d 445 (County Ct. 1960); *Murray County v. Hood*, 163 Okla. 167, 21 P.2d 754 (1933).

141. *Wilson v. Kelley*, 294 F. Supp. 1005 (N.D. Ga. 1968), *aff'd per curiam*, 393 U.S. 266 (1969).

142. *Holt v. Sarver*, 309 F. Supp. 362, 364 (E.D. Ark. 1970); *aff'd* 442 F.2d 304 (8th Cir. 1971).

143. *See Butler v. Perry*, 240 U.S. 328 (1916); *United States v. Reynolds*, 235 U.S. 133 (1914); *Draper v. Rhay*, 315 F.2d 193 (9th Cir.), *cert. denied*, 375 U.S. 915 (1963); *Lindsey v. Leavy*, 149 F.2d 899 (9th Cir. 1945); *Blass v. Weigel*, 85 F. Supp. 775, 781 (D.D.C. 1949). *But see Pollock v. Williams*, 322 U.S. 4, 17 (1944), where the Supreme Court condemned peonage and declared that the Thirteenth Amendment was designed "not merely to end slavery but to maintain a system of completely free and voluntary labor. . . ." *See also* Shapiro, "Involuntary Servitude: The Need for a More Flexible Approach," 10 *Rutgers Law Review* 65 (1964).

144. 309 F. Supp. 362, 372 (E.D. Ark. 1970):

> The Arkansas system of working convicts is not "slavery" in the constitutional sense of the term. The State does not claim to own the bodies of its prisoners. The situation does involve "servitude," and there is no doubt whatever that the "servitude" is "involuntary."

inmates would have more self-respect and a sense of responsibility. In addition, the need to pay a realistic wage for labor might encourage prison industries to use more modern equipment, thereby increasing the applicability of the techniques learned to industrial processes outside the prisons.

A related area that appears amenable to the same kind of challenge is the prevalent practice of refusing to allow prisoners to carry on legitimate business, such as publishing manuscripts[145] or patenting inventions.[146] Although the confiscation of some personal property from inmates is necessary for prison security,[147] deprivations of property that cannot be justified as essential security measures could be considered as cruel and unusual punishment prohibited by the Eighth Amendment, if not by state laws, or forbidden as a deprivation of property without due process of law prohibited by the Fifth and Fourteenth Amendments.

Warehousing: Right to Rehabilitation. Two recent cases have raised this novel and potentially explosive legal question: Can a state place a convicted criminal in prison without making any effort to rehabilitate him? Arkansas prisoners sought, with some success, an injunction prohibiting prison officials from incarcerating them "without providing meaningful rehabilitative opportunities" and requiring the authorities "to formulate and implement a plan of rehabilitation including adequate vocational, educational, medical and other programs for all inmates of the institutions operated by defendants."[148] In Georgia, prisoners unsuccessfully sought a judicial declaration that sentencing convicts to county work camps, where no effort was made to rehabilitate them, constituted cruel and unusual punishment.[149]

The notion of a right to rehabilitation seems to have arisen as a con-

---

145. *United States v. Maas*, 371 F.2d 348 (D.C. Cir. 1966); *Stroud v. Swope*, 187 F.2d 850 (9th Cir.), *cert. denied*, 342 U.S. 829 (1951); *Davis v. Superior Court*, 175 Cal. App. 2d 8, 345 P.2d 513 (Dist. Ct. App. 1959); *see Numer v. Miller*, 165 F.2d 986 (9th Cir. 1948).
146. United States *ex rel. Wagner v. Ragen*, 213 F.2d 294 (7th Cir.), *cert. denied*, 348 U.S. 846 (1954).
147. *See Lanza v. New York*, 370 U.S. 139, 144 n.14 (1962):

> Saws have been secreted in bananas, in the soles of shoes, under the peaks of caps, and drugs may be secreted in cap visors, under postage stamps on letters, in cigars and various other ways. . . . Cells should be systematically searched for materials which would serve as a weapon or medium of self-destruction or escape. Razor blades are small and easily concealed.

148. *Holt v. Sarver*, 309 F. Supp. 362, 364 (E.D. Ark. 1969), *aff'd* 442 F.2d 304 (8th Cir. 1971).
149. *Wilson v. Kelley*, 294 F. Supp. 1005, 1012 (N.D. Ga. 1968), *aff'd per curiam*, 393 U.S. 266 (1969): "[A] work camp per se does not constitute such 'inhuman, barbarous or torturous punishment' as to violate the Eighth Amendment."

comitant of the developing "right to treatment"[150] in the area of civil commitment. The treatment received by patients after confinement was first questioned in 1966 when the Court of Appeals for the District of Columbia ruled that a statute providing for the mandatory commitment of defendants acquitted of criminal charges by reason of insanity[151] gives them a right to treatment while institutionalized.[152] Although no court has ordered a patient released from a mental hospital because of inadequate treatment, the Massachusetts Supreme Court has ordered a state mental hospital to institute a more adequate treatment program where a patient was receiving nothing more than custodial care.[153]

A New York defendant, committed as unfit to stand trial and retained eleven years more than the maximum criminal sentence, was awarded $300,000 damages from the state as compensation for the twelve years and four months he had spent in a state hospital.[154] According to the court, an adequate psychiatric examination and treatment would have resulted in a much earlier release.[155] New York courts also have ruled that convicted criminals sentenced to indefinite terms for sexual or narcotics-related offenses instead of the definite sentence provided for the offense[156] are given the alternative sentence for the purpose of rehabilitation; consequently they have a right to receive some rehabilitative treatment.[157] Another New York case recognized that "[a]dequate psychological and psychiatric services are indispensable to the whole concept of 'one day to life' sentence and without them the 'one day' is meaningless

150. The phrase "right to treatment" first was used by Birnbaum, "The Right to Treatment," 46 *American Bar Association Journal* 499 (1960). *See also* editorial, "A New Right," 46 *American Bar Association Journal* 516 (1960).
151. D.C. Code Ann. §24–301(d) (1967).
152. *Rouse v. Cameron,* 373 F.2d 451, 453, 455 (D.C. Cir. 1966). The court intimated that even if there had been no applicable statute, it might have found a constitutional right to treatment.
153. *Nason v. Superintendent of Bridgewater State Hospital,* 353 Mass. 604, 233 N.E.2d 908 (1968). The patient had sought a transfer to a different institution where treatment would be available.
154. *Whitree v. New York,* 56 Misc. 2d 693 290 N.Y.S.2d 486 (Ct. Cl. 1968).
155. *Cf. Maatallah v. Warden, Nevada State Prison,* 470 P.2d 122 (Nev. 1970).
156. *See* New York Mental Hygiene Law §208 (McKinney Supp. 1968).
157. *People ex rel. Ceschini v. Warden,* 30 App. Div. 2d 649, 291 N.Y.S.2d 200 (1968) (*per curiam*) (remanded to determine whether petitioner, who claimed he was segregated from other prisoners as a homosexual and denied participation in educational or vocational training, was receiving any treatment). In *People ex rel. Blunt v. Narcotic Addiction Control Commission,* 295 N.Y.S.2d 276 (Sup. Ct.), *aff'd mem.,* 296 N.Y.S.2d 533 (App. Div. 1968), the court agreed with a prisoner who complained that he was being held in the custody of the Narcotic Addiction Control Commission beyond the maximum penal sentence and that in the absence of rehabilitative treatment his continued confinement would be "purely custodial and legally . . . untenable." Recognizing the experimental nature of treatment for addiction and the inadequate personnel and facilities used by the commission, the court decided not to "thwart the legislative purpose in enacting . . . the Mental Hygiene Law by prematurely interfering in its mechanics." *Id.* at 281–82.

and the 'life' may well be the end result."[158] A federal court, upholding the constitutionality of Maryland's Defective Delinquent Act,[159] has reached a similar conclusion.[160]

There are substantial problems in applying the "right to treatment" rationale to prison inmates. First, unlike foreign criminal codes, which frequently specify rehabilitation as a central purpose of imprisonment,[161] American criminal statutes give little guidance as to the over-all policy reasons for incarcerating criminals.[162] According to the American Correctional Association, whose statement of the purposes of the prison system is widely accepted (on paper), the purpose of rehabilitation is basic to our entire correctional system.[163] However, the only judge to have considered the question refused to adopt the primacy of rehabilitation:

> In years past many people have felt, and many still feel, that a criminal is sent to the penitentiary to be punished for his crimes

158. People *ex rel. Kaganovitch v. Wilkins*, 23 App. Div. 2d 178, 183, 259 N.Y.S.2d 462, 466 (1965).
159. Md. Ann. Code art. 31B (1957).
160. *See Sas v. Maryland*, 334 F.2d 506, 509 (4th Cir. 1964) (statute held constitutional on its face, but remanded to determine "whether the proposed objectives of the Act are sufficiently implemented to its actual administration to support its categorization as a civil procedure and justify the elimination of conventional criminal procedural safeguards"), *on remand*, 295 F. Supp. 389, 420 (D. Md. 1969) (statute held constitutional in its "interpretation, application, administration and results").
161. *E.g.*, Swedish Penal Code ch. 1, §7: "In the choice of sanctions, the court, with an eye to what is required to maintain general law obedience, shall keep particularly in mind that the sanction shall serve to foster the sentenced offender's adaptation to society." The Penal Code of Sweden (Sellin translation 1965); U.S.S.R. Criminal Code art. 20:

> *Purpose of punishment.*—Punishment not only constitutes a chastisement for a committed crime, but also has the purpose of correcting and reeducating convicted persons . . . [and] also has the purpose of preventing the commission of new crimes both by convicted persons and others.
> Punishment does not have the purpose of causing physical suffering or the lowering of human dignity.

Soviet Criminal Law and Procedure 151 (Berman and Spindler translation 1966).
162. *But see* Mont. Const art. III, §24, which provides that "laws for the punishment of crime shall be founded on the principles of reformation and prevention. . . ." *See also* N.C. Const art. XI, §2; Nev. Acts 3075, ch. 817, §6 (1969); Mo. Ann. Stat. §216.090(1) (1962); La. Rev. Stat. Ann. §15–854 (1967); Ga. Code Ann. §77–319 (Supp. 1968).
163. American Correctional Association, *Manual of Correction Standards* xix (3d ed. 1966):

> Correctional institutions and agencies can best achieve their goal of rehabilitation by focusing their attention and resources on the complete study and evaluation of the individual offender and by following a program of individualized treatment. Principle XXII: To assure the eventual restoration of the offender as an economically self-sustaining member of the community, the correctional program must make available to each inmate every opportunity to raise his educational level, improve his vocational competence and skills, and add to his information meaningful knowledge about the world and the society in which he must live. Principle XXIII: To hold employable offenders in correctional institutions without the opportunity to engage in productive work is to violate one of the essential objectives of rehabilitation.

and to protect the public from his further depredations. Under that view, while there is no objection to rehabilitation, it is not given any priority. . . .

Given an otherwise unexceptional penal institution, the Court is not willing to hold that confinement in it is unconstitutional simply because the institution does not operate a school, or provide vocational training, or other rehabilitative facilities and services which many institutions now offer.[164]

If rehabilitation is not accepted as an obvious purpose of imprisonment, it would be persuasive to demonstrate that correctional treatment decreases recidivism and, hence, contributes to the protection of the public.[165] However likely this may seem, there is unfortunately little empirical proof that such is the case.[166] Nor is there a consensus on what

164. *Holt v. Sarver*, 309 Supp. 362, 379 (E.D. Ark. 1970), *aff'd* 442 F.2d 304 (8th Cir. 1971). On appeal, one judge's concurring opinion would have had the district court retain jurisdiction until "immediate and continuing emphasis is given to an affirmative program of rehabilitation." Courts occasionally have implied from the existence of special correctional programs that rehabilitation is a central goal of criminal sentences. *See Williams v. New York*, 337 U.S. 241 (1949); *People v. Cotter*, 267 N.Y.S.2d 679 (App. Div. 1966); *Abbott v. City of Los Angeles*, 53 Cal. 2d 674, 687, 349 P.2d 974, 982–83 (1960).
In the case of juveniles, determining the type of detention should present no such problem. Most states have statutes requiring that "when the child is removed from his own family, the court shall secure for him custody, care and discipline as nearly as possible equivalent to that which should have been given to him by his parents." D.C. Code Ann. §16–2316(3) (Supp. V 1966); *see, e.g.,* Cal. Welf. and Inst'ns Code §502(c) (1966). Relying on section 2316(3), the United States Court of Appeals for the District of Columbia has twice held that a child who needs psychiatric assistance and is not provided with it should be released from custody. *In re* Eelmore, 382 F.2d 125 (D.C. Cir. 1967); *Creek v. Stone*, 379 F.2d 106 (D.C. Cir. 1967).
165. *See* American Correctional Association, *Manual of Correctional Standards* 10 (3d ed. 1966):

> Penologists in the United States today are generally agreed that the prison serves most effectively for the protection of society against crime when its major emphasis is on rehabilitation. They accept this as a fact that no longer needs to be debated.

166. In a recent experiment in New York City with 400 potentially deviant girls, half were referred to the Youth Consultation Service, a private social agency, where they were given individual counseling and group therapy by trained case workers. The other half were given no special services. At the end of the period there were some differences in the attitudes of the control and the experimental cases. In the areas of school performance and behavior, the incidence of out-of-wedlock pregnancy and trouble with the police, however, there were virtually no statistically significant differences between the two groups. Meyer, Borgatta and Jones, *Girls at Vocational High* (1965). It should be noted, however, that the professional efforts were directed only toward self-understanding and attitudes, while the practical problems of getting through school, finding a job and developing social grace were hardly touched. In addition, the goals of treatment were not clear, and researchers consequently found it difficult to specify the criteria of success. Finally, only immediate changes in behavior were tested.
Some professionals in the field of correction admit that they must accept the efficacy of treatment as an article of faith. Interview with Marguerite Q. Warren, Director of Research, Community Treatment Project, California Youth Authority, Sacramento, California, Dec. 2, 1968. *But see* Warren, "The Case for Differential Treatment of Delinquents," 381 *Annals* 47 (1969). *Cf. Holt v. Sarver*, 309 F. Supp. 362, 379 (E.D. Ark. 1970), *aff'd* 442 F.2d 304 (8th Cir. 1971).

constitutes correctional "treatment." Is it a series of "group therapy" sessions run without professional participation or supervision?[167] Is it vocational training on outdated machinery?[168] A totally therapeutic community? Or can any effort to impel prisoners to engage in some useful activity, even if only to perform janitorial services, be termed "treatment"?[169]

The right-to-treatment cases have been based, at least in part, on judicial suspicion of the deviation of civil commitments and alternative sentences from the conventional safeguards of criminal procedure. If this is a crucial consideration, it may preclude the extension of the principle to ordinary criminal sentences. However, in a recent federal decision that prohibited the transfer of a state prisoner to a mental hospital without affording him the procedural safeguards of a civil commitment hearing,[170] the Second Circuit Court of Appeals cited cases dealing with the right to treatment and intimated that they might apply to a prisoner who is transferred to a mental institution while serving a criminal sentence.

On the other hand, in *Wilson v. Kelley*,[171] a three-judge federal court rejected an argument by Georgia prisoners that they had a right to treatment, despite the fact that a state statute mandated a "program of rehabilitation."[172] The court made this telling and rather honest appraisal: "Other than the constitutional rights which follow a man into confinement, no duty is absolutely owed a prisoner other than to exercise ordinary care for his protection and to keep him safe and free from harm." The court rejected the argument that since some Georgia prisons had access to rehabilitative programs, the others should as well:

> Humane efforts to rehabilitate should not be discouraged by holding that every prisoner must be treated exactly alike in this respect. . . . To order the maximum for each and every person confined, as sought by plaintiffs here, would be financially pro-

167. Brief for Relator-Appellant at 3–5, People *ex rel. Blunt v. Narcotic Addiction Control Commission*, 58 Misc. 2d 57, 296 N.Y.S.2d 533 (App. Div. 1968). *Cf.* Minton and Rice, "Using Racism at San Quentin," *Ramparts*, January 1970, at 17, 22: "[g]roup counseling courses . . . under the direction of prison officials turn into sessions in which one inmate 'finks' on another or on himself."
168. *See Holt v. Sarver*, 309 F. Supp. 362, 370, 380 (E.D. Ark. 1970), *aff'd* 442 F.2d 304 (8th Cir. 1971).
169. *Cf. Ray v. Neil*, Civ. No. 5590 (M.D. Tenn. order entered Dec. 29, 1969). It should be noted that courts have not yet come to grips with the criteria for *adequate* treatment for the mentally ill. *See* Halpern, "A Practicing Lawyer Views the Right to Treatment," 57 *Georgia Law Journal* 782, 790–94 (1969).
170. United States *ex rel. Schuster v. Herold*, 410 F.2d 1071 (2d Cir. 1969).
171. 294 F. Supp. 1005 (N.D. Ga. 1968), *aff'd per curiam*, 393 U.S. 266 (1969).
172. Ga. Code Ann. §§77-310 (Supp. 1961).

hibitive for this state and could result in a reduction of rehabilitative efforts rather than an implementation.

One commentator predicts that, since judicial orders requiring legislative appropriations could not be enforced, judges may prefer to deny
that any right to treatment exists rather than admit stalemate. On the
other hand, while their powers to create programs on their own initiative
are limited, judges do have the ability to force the issue by refusing to
sentence convicts to an institution that fails to offer any hope of rehabilitation or by ordering their transfer to another institution. In addition, a
right to rehabilitation can serve as a rationale for forbidding arbitrary
interference by prison officials with self-improvement projects. According
to one prisoner whose allegations are supported by claims made in
court,[173]

> self-righteous prison tyrants decide whether a desired corre-
> spondence study is "practical" or "realistic" training or not. . . .
> For example, this writer has sought for over two years Bureau
> of Prisons approval to pursue a Correspondence Course in law
> study. But these self-righteous charlatans have denied this plea
> for knowledge and self-improvement by declaring it as being
> "impractical and unrealistic study for prisoners since they would
> not be able to practice law once released."

Potentially even more useful is the theory that, while a state may not
be required to attempt to rehabilitate a prisoner in its custody, it may be
forbidden to imprison him under conditions that make it more difficult
for an inmate to rehabilitate himself: "The absence of an affirmative program of training and rehabilitation may have constitutional significance
where in the absence of such a program conditions and practices exist
which actually militate against reform and rehabilitation."[174]

The most serious problem in adopting the treatment rationale is
posed by the actual uses to which it has been put. Sol Rubin, experienced
commentator, recently remarked that

> [T]reatment may *not* be humanitarian . . . treatment may be
> an invasion of civil rights . . . treatment may be harmful. . . .

173. *See, e.g., Carey v. Settle,* 351 F.2d 483 (8th Cir. 1965) (books necessary for
prisoner's correspondence course confiscated from his cell because of five-book limit);
cases cited in note 145 *supra.*
174. *Holt v. Sarver* 309 F. Supp. 362, 379 (E.D. Ark. 1970), *aff'd* 442 F.2d 304 (8th
Cir. 1971).

[B]efore one decides on treating a person, even a convicted criminal, one must consider whether leaving him alone may not be better, better for him and better for society. . . .

I agree [that a right to treatment] is an important right, and it must become a protection for individuals. But it must *not* become a cover for depriving people of their liberty. . . .

[W]e freely commit people and call it treatment.[175]

His contention is not that prison inmates should receive no rehabilitative treatment but that decisions to incarcerate offenders, or even to place them on probation, should be made only for the purposes of public safety, not for the purposes of treatment: "I do not accept rationalizing imprisonment by the uses of treatment." A similar fear was expressed by Professor Francis Allen more than ten years ago:

Measures which subject individuals to the substantial and involuntary deprivation of their liberty are essentially punitive in character, and this reality is not altered by the facts that the motivations that prompt incarceration are to provide therapy or otherwise contribute to the person's well-being or reform. As such, these measures must be closely scrutinized to insure that power is being applied consistently with those values of the community that justify interferences with liberty for only the most clear and compelling reasons.[176]

There is some evidence that these fears might be realized in the prison setting. In California, the philosophy of treatment, emphasizing education, vocational training and various forms of therapy, was central in the mid-twentieth-century expansion of the penal system from three prisons to ten. Prisoners were led to believe that participation in prison programs would equip them to cope with the outside world. Yet a recent survey of California parolees disclosed that over half felt that the pro-

175. "The Illusion of Treatment in Sentences and Civil Commitments" at 2, address by Sol Rubin at the University of South Carolina, March 29, 1968, printed with changes at 16 *Crime and Delinquency* 79 (1970). *See also* President's Commission on Law Enforcement and Administration of Justice, Task Force Report: *Correction* 58–59 (1967):

There is a decided danger that the existence of special facilities will imply a comparable existence of special expertise encouraging society to shuffle off on correctional institutions problems that should be dealt with elsewhere. There are many indications that this has been the result, for example, of schools for defective delinquents and programs for sexual psychopaths.

176. Allen, "Criminal Justice, Values and the Rehabilitative Ideal," 50 *Journal of Criminal Law, Criminology and Police Science* 226, 230 (1959).

grams were ineffective and rates of recidivism had not been reduced.[177] The inmates viewed the entire treatment program as "a grand hypocrisy in which custodial concerns, administrative exigencies and punishment were all disguised as treatment." In addition, many staff members and administrators were likewise disillusioned.

It could be argued that prisoners should be accorded a constitutional right to treatment. At a minimum, this should include for each prisoner the development of a rehabilitative plan designed to develop his talents and meet his particular needs. Plans might encompass schooling, professional or vocational training, medical or psychiatric attention and provision for earning money to support dependents. The treatment rhetoric should not, however, be used to deny prisoners their liberty unnecessarily or paradoxically to deprive them of their constitutional rights.

Cumulative Effect of Unconstitutional Conditions. In 1970 a federal district judge in Arkansas, rather than limiting his decision to a consideration of specific abuses practiced on particular prisoners, ruled that conditions in the Arkansas system, including a delegation of authority over prisoners to armed trusty inmates, the physical danger to prisoners from trusties and other inmates in the open barracks and the complete absence of efforts to rehabilitate the inmates confined there, made it cruel and unusual punishment to sentence anyone to an Arkansas prison:

> After long and careful consideration the Court has come to the conclusion that the Fourteenth Amendment prohibits confinement under the conditions that have been described and that the Arkansas Penitentiary System as it exists today, particularly at Cummins, is unconstitutional. . . .
>
> It is one thing for the State to send a man to the Penitentiary as a punishment for crime. It is another thing for the State to delegate the governance of him to other convicts, and to do nothing meaningful for his safety, well being, and possible rehabilitation. It is one thing for the State not to pay a convict for his labor; it is something else to subject him to a situation in which he has to sell his blood to obtain money to pay for his own safety, or for adequate food, or for access to needed medical attention.[178]

177. Irwin, "Correctional Treatment and the Inmate Sense of Injustice" 4 (unpublished paper prepared for the Center for Law and Society, Berkeley, California, 1968).
178. *Holt v. Sarver,* 309 F. Supp. 362, 381 (E.D. Ark. 1970), *aff'd* 442 F.2d 304 (8th Cir. 1971).

Although the Arkansas system is somewhat unique because of its history of running prisons for profit and reliance on inmates to perform tasks and exercise authority generally given to "free-world" personnel, this decision should have far-reaching effect. It establishes the precedent that, while specific and sometimes trivial prison conditions may not in themselves be outlawed on constitutional grounds, together they may be sufficient to convince a court that an entire system of corrections is constitutionally deficient.

CIVIL RIGHTS IN PRISON

Many of the claims that prisoners bring to court concern rights that elsewhere have been held to be protected by the Constitution from governmental interference. These claims concern prisoners' right to practice a religion, to be free from racial discrimination, to communicate freely, to vote, to enjoy privacy and to have the same rights as others when they are accused of crimes. Although special difficulties derive from the inherent constraints of large institutions with special problems of discipline, the courts that have heard these cases (particularly those that granted the prisoners' requests) have relied heavily on precedents outside the prison area. Consequently, many decisions, particularly the numerous cases dealing with religion and with racial segregation, essentially represent extensions of general civil liberties law into the field of correction.

Religion. Apart from the cases affirming prisoners' right of access to court, it was in the area of religious freedom that the courts were first impelled to abandon their "hands-off" attitude toward the restrictions imposed by imprisonment. Not only is freedom of religion enshrined as "one of the fundamental 'preferred' freedoms guaranteed by the Constitution,"[179] but religion in prison is thought to serve "the rehabilitative function by providing an area within which the inmate may reclaim his dignity and reassert his individuality."[180] Yet some courts recognize that "quite ironically, while government provides prisoners with chapels, ministers, free sacred texts and symbols, there subsists a danger that prison personnel

179. *Pierce v. LaVallee,* 293 F.2d 233, 235 (2d Cir. 1961).
180. *Barnett v. Rodgers,* 410 F.2d 995, 1002 (D.C. Cir. 1969). *See also Brown v. Peyton,* 437 F.2d 1228, 1230 (4th Cir. 1971): "One of the principal purposes of incarceration is rehabilitation and rehabilitation is a moral and intellectual process. Criminals and prison communities may be benefitted by the free exercise of religion."

will demand from inmates the same obeisance in the religious sphere that more rightfully they may require in other aspects of prison life."

In fact, judges often refuse to allow prison officials the same latitude that is granted when rights they consider less crucial are at stake.[181] As in the non-prison religious cases,[182] courts distinguish between a prisoner's absolute right to religious beliefs[183] and his qualified right to engage in religious practices.[184] Much of the litigation involving religion in prison has revolved about the question of what restrictions on religious practices are reasonable in the prison setting. Recent judicial expressions have ranged from a willingness to defer to the "considered professional opinion" of prison authorities[185] to an insistence on a showing of "reasons imperatively justifying the particular retraction of rights."[186]

In the past decade, many religious-freedom claims have concerned Black Muslims, whose religious beliefs, including political doctrines of black racial supremacy, were not originally deemed protected by the First Amendment.[187] In addition, Muslim demands for special diets and visits and correspondence with their ministers, many of whom are ex-convicts, have created difficult administrative problems for prison personnel.

181. "Whatever may be the view with regard to ordinary problems of prison discipline . . . we think that a charge of religious persecution falls in quite a different category." *Pierce v. LaVallee,* 293 F.2d 233, 235 (2d Cir. 1961); *see Howard v. Smyth,* 365 F.2d 428 (4th Cir. 1966) (inmate may not be punished for refusal to divulge names of Black Muslims in prison population); *Roberts v. Pegelow,* 313 F.2d 548 (4th Cir. 1963); *Sewell v. Pegelow,* 291 F.2d 196 (4th Cir. 1961) (district court must hear complaint that all Muslim prisoners were being kept in isolation and deprived of normal privileges because of the hostility of prison officials toward the Muslim faith); *Fulwood v. Clemmer,* 206 F. Supp. 370 (D.D.C. 1962) (where prisoner had broken prison rules by proclaiming religiously derived racist doctrines in the inflammatory setting of the prison baseball field, punishment by more than two years' solitary confinement, the denial of normal privileges and facilities and the practice of his religion, and transfer to another prison to suppress the Muslim religion held too severe for the offense).
182. *E.g., Cantwell v. Connecticut,* 310 U.S. 296, 303–304 (1940).
183. *E.g., Pierce v. LaVallee,* 293 F.2d 233, 235 (2d Cir. 1961); *Sewell v. Pegelow,* 291 F.2d 196 (4th Cir. 1961).
184. "Within the prison society as well as without, the practice of religious beliefs is subject to reasonable regulations, necessary for the protection and welfare of the community involved." *Long v. Parker,* 390 F.2d 816, 820 (3d Cir. 1968).
185. *Abernathy v. Cunningham,* 393 F.2d 775, 779 (4th Cir. 1968) (prison officials may prohibit the receipt of Black Muslim publications).
186. *Barnett v. Rodgers,* 410 F.2d 995, 1001 (D.C. Cir. 1969) (jail officials must make an effort to accommodate dietary restrictions of Black Muslim prisoners).
187. *In re* Ferguson, 55 Cal. 2d 663, 361 P.2d 417, 12 *California Reporter* 753, *cert. denied,* 368 U.S. 864 (1961); *cf. In re* Jones, 57 Cal. 2d 860, 372 P.2d 310, 22 *California Reporter* 478 (1962). *But see Fulwood v. Clemmer,* 206 F. Supp. 370 (D.D.C. 1962); Delaware *ex rel. Tate v. Cubbage,* 210 A.2d 555 (Del. 1965); *Brown v. McGinnis,* 10 N.Y.2d 531, 180 N.E.2d 791, 225 N.Y.S.2d 497 (1962).
Some officials, however, continue their refusal to recognize the Muslim religion. The supervisor of the Nassau County Jail recently testified in a New York court that Islam is not accepted as a religion at the jail. New York *Times,* Dec. 12, 1969, at 57, col. 7.

Application of the equal-protection principle to different religions[188] has been significant for small or less conventional groups.[189] Many states actually provide chaplains,[190] chapel facilities[191] and even religious medals[192] to be worn by prisoners of various faiths. Some courts have ruled that state statutes or administrative regulations prohibiting racial or religious discrimination or granting inmates the right to hold religious services in prison chapels must be applied to all religious groups.[193] Others have reached similar conclusions on the constitutional grounds of freedom of religion and equal protection of the laws.[194]

Some courts have recognized that it may not always be practical for prison officials to treat members of all religious groups with strict equality. Exceptions are allowed, however, only when officials can demonstrate their reasonableness. For example, a state need not provide a full-time chaplain for every denomination.[195] However, prison authorities may not deny a group the right to hold its own religious services because it is "not recognized."[196]

In some areas Muslim prisoners have gone beyond demands for equal protection to seek special treatment in order to practice their religion. The most difficult area in which to accommodate Muslim practices

188. *See, e.g.,* Delaware *ex rel. Tate v. Cubbage,* 210 A.2d 555 (Del. 1965).
189. *But see Jones v. Willingham,* 248 F. Supp. 791, 794 (D. Kan. 1965), where the court ruled that a warden's actions in refusing to allow Muslims the same privileges given members of other religious faiths was not arbitrary, capricious or unlawful. In fact, the warden "not only was fully justified in imposing on the plaintiff and others professing Muslim beliefs the restrictions of which the plaintiff now complains, but it was his duty to so act."
More recently, three ministers associated with the Church of the Crossroads and eight sailors imprisoned in the Pearl Harbor Naval Prison filed suit in federal court to challenge the refusal of Navy officials to allow the ministers in the prison. The refusal was based on the "unusual" or "unconventional" nature of the services conducted at the church. *Bridges v. Davis,* Civ. No. 3078-80 (D. Hawaii, filed Feb. 26, 1970).
190. *See Walker v. Blackwell,* 411 F.2d 23, 28 & n.6 (5th Cir. 1969).
191. *See McBride v. McCorkle,* 44 N.J. Super. 468, 130 A.2d 881 (App. Div. 1957).
192. *See Fulwood v. Clemmer,* 206 F. Supp. 370 (D.D.C. 1962).
193. *Sewell v. Pegelow,* 291 F.2d 196 (4th Cir. 1961), *appeal dismissed per stipulation,* 304 F.2d 670 (4th Cir. 1962); *Fulwood v. Clemmer,* 206 F. Supp. 370 (D.D.C. 1962); *Shaw v. McGinnis,* 14 N.Y.2d 864; 200 N.E.2d 636 (1964); *Brown v. McGinnis,* 10 N.Y.2d 531, 180 N.E.2d 791, 225 N.Y.S.2d 497 (1962).
194. *E.g., Cooper v. Pate,* 378 U.S. 546 (1964) (*per curiam*) (purchase of religious publications); *Long v. Parker,* 390 F.2d 816 (3d Cir. 1968) (provision for religious medals; use of prison chapel; special dietary arrangements and receipt of religious publications, which may be excluded if officials demonstrate a "clear and present danger" to prison security or discipline); *Northern v. Nelson,* 315 F. Supp. 687 (N.D. Cal. 1970) (provision of The Holy Qur'an and other religious materials to Muslims); Delaware *ex rel. Tate v. Cubbage,* 210 A.2d 555 (Del. 1965) (facilities for religious services, permission to wear religious symbols). *But see Gittlemacker v. Prasse,* 428 F.2d 1 (3d Cir., 1970) (prison is under no duty to supply an inmate with a clergyman of his own sect).
195. *Gittlemacker v. Prasse,* 428 F.2d 1 (3d Cir. 1970); *see Rockey v. Krieger,* 306 N.Y.S.2d 359 (Sup. Ct. 1969); *Konigsberg v. Ciccone,* 285 F. Supp. 585, 593-96 (W.D. Mo. 1968); *cf. Sharp v. Sigler,* 408 F.2d 966 (8th Cir. 1969).
196. *Theriault v. Carlson,* 10 *Criminal Law Reporter* 2479 (N.D. Ga., Feb. 25, 1972).

is that of diet: The Muslim religion forbids all consumption of pork and requires special foods and mealtimes during the month of December (Ramadan). One federal court of appeals dismissed allegations that Muslim prisoners were subjected to a diet that offended their religious practices.[197] Yet when Muslim inmates of the District of Columbia jail complained that two-thirds of their meals contained pork, including several main dishes of pork and frequent servings of vegetables seasoned with pork, the Court of Appeals for the District of Columbia[198] reacted differently:

> There is no finding as to whether any particular "considerations underlying our penal system" warrant the tax on conscience that the jail's food service policies require appellants to endure. Nor is there a finding as to whether that program could not be administered in such a way as to lighten or eliminate its burden on free religious exercise. . . .
>
> Certainly if this concession is feasible from the standpoint of prison management, it represents the bare minimum that jail authorities, with or without specific request, are constitutionally required to do, not only for Muslims but indeed for any group of inmates with religious restrictions on diet.[199]

This case is particularly significant as it is the first to require prison officials to make some special provisions for unconventional religious practices. On the other hand, courts have not required authorities to make special arrangements for Ramadan on the basis "that considerations of security and administrative expense outweigh whatever constitutional deprivation petitioners may claim."[200] And the growing number of challenges to regulations requiring prisoners to cut their hair and shave their beards have not been aided by appeals to religious principle.[201]

Similarly, cases dealing with subscriptions to religious publications, correspondence with religious leaders and reception of religious radio broadcasts have been decided on the basis of reasonable restrictions on freedom of religion, rather than as limitations on freedom of speech. One

197. *Walker v. Blackwell*, 411 F.2d 23, 25–26 (5th Cir. 1969). The point seems to have been confused with the Muslims' special requests concerning Ramadan discussed below.
198. *Barnett v. Rodgers*, 410 F.2d 995 (D.C. Cir. 1969).
199. *Id.* at 1001–03. *Cf. SaMarion v. McGinnis*, 35 App. Div. 2d 684, 314 N.Y.S.2d 715 (1970).
200. *Walker v. Blackwell*, 411 F.2d 23, 26 (5th Cir. 1969).
201. *Brooks v. Wainwright*, 428 F.2d 652 (5th Cir. 1970); *Glenn v. Wilkinson*, 309 F. Supp. 411 (W.D. Mo. 1970); *cf.* People *ex rel. Rockey v. Krueger*, 306 N.Y.S.2d 359 (1969) (regulation applied unequally to Black Muslims and Orthodox Jews); *Seale v. Manson*, 326 F. Supp. 1375 (D. Conn. 1971) (regulation unconstitutional as applied to prisoner in pre-trial detention who had not been convicted of any crime).

recent decision by a federal court of appeals upheld a ban on publications written by Black Muslims based on officials' predictions of the probable effect of the materials on relations among the prisoners,[202] despite contrary policy in other prisons. By contrast, the Court of Appeals for the Third Circuit has held that where prisoners of other faiths are permitted to receive religious literature, Muslim prisoners may not be denied the same right unless the authorities can prove to the satisfaction of the court that the literature creates a "clear and present danger" to prison discipline.[203] The Fifth Circuit has added that, "should the newspaper ever develop a substantially inflammatory effect on prison inmates," officials could act to avoid "imminent prison violence."[204]

A Federal Bureau of Prisons regulation prohibiting correspondence by an inmate with the head of his church has been questioned by one official and undermined by two recent cases. One directed that Black Muslim prisoners be permitted to correspond with Elijah Muhammad "for the limited purpose of seeking spiritual advice";[205] the other ordered officials to allow a prisoner who claimed that he was the reincarnation of Jesus Christ to communicate his revelation to the Pope.[206]

Although other problems concerning religion have not yet been challenged in court, certain regulations seem unrelated to valid, official interests. For example, before 1966, inmates in federal prisons were prohibited from changing their religious affiliation while in custody. Another rule limited attendance at services of other religions. Even now, according to the Legal Counsel to the Bureau of Prisons, it is

> recognized that the prison setting is anything but a natural environment, and that the change of religion under these circumstances very well could not be intelligently or deliberately made. It is suggested that the chaplain encourage an individual to defer his identifying with a new religious denomination, so long as he is confined.[207]

Constitutional objections lie not only in official interference with religion but in its encouragement. Atheists and agnostics have com-

202. *Abernathy v. Cunningham*, 393 F.2d 775 (4th Cir. 1968); *but see Brown v. Peyton*, 437 F.2d 1228 (4th Cir. 1971).
203. *Long v. Parker*, 390 F.2d 816, 822 (3d Cir. 1968); *cf. Knuckles v. Prasse*, 435 F.2d 1255 (3d Cir. 1970) (Black Muslim literature could constitute clear and present danger to institution).
204. *Walker v. Blackwell*, 411 F.2d 23, 29 (5th Cir. 1969).
205. *Ibid.*
206. *Peek v. Ciccone*, 288 F. Supp. 329, 333–34 (W.D. Mo. 1968).
207. Barkin, "Impact of Changing Law Upon Prison Policy," 48 *Prison Journal* 19 (1968); *see* Bureau of Prisons, Policy Memorandum 7300.4 (Apr. 6, 1966).

plained about policies of releasing prisoners to attend religious services while banning alternative activities by non-religious groups. In addition, parole boards often favor religious involvement by prisoners and give weight to letters of recommendation from chaplains as indications of rehabilitation. Even more questionable is the delegation to chaplains of authority over prisoners. A District of Columbia prisoner recently stated that his request to get married had been denied on the basis of the opinion of the Protestant chaplain (who was "not of our faith") opposing the marriage.

Free Expression. In 1963, a law-journal survey concluded that prison inmates have no legal right to freedom of speech and assembly:

> Forms of expression traditionally protected by the First Amendment are subject to severe and even total curtailment in prison. Severe infringements on freedom of speech and association in prison have been upheld by the courts or ignored by them under the rubric of the hands-off doctrine. . . . The broad principles of censorship and restricted mailing lists have been approved by the courts as a non-reviewable exercise of the discretion entrusted to prison authorities.[208]

Today, despite progress in other areas, the law regarding free expression in prison remains virtually unchanged. Judicial rulings that have resulted in increased freedom to speak, write or assemble have been based on some other protection, such as access to court or equal protection of racial or religious groups,[209] leaving prison officials unchecked by the speech and assembly provisions of the First Amendment. For example, prison authorities are free to censor communications[210] and screen out "reasonably objectionable,"[211] "inflammatory"[212] or "subversive"[213] articles or pub-

208. Note, "Beyond the Ken of the Courts," at 537–38.
209. *See e.g. Edwards v. Duncan*, 355 F.2d 993 (4th Cir. 1966); *Lee v. Tahash*, 352 F.2d 970 (8th Cir. 1965). For a discussion of the freedoms related to racial or religious groups, see section on Religion *supra*, at notes 178–207. *See also Rockey v. Krueger*, 306 N.Y.S.2d 359 (Sup. Ct. 1969) (rights to wear a beard if religion so requires); *Long v. Parker*, 390 F.2d 816 (3d Cir. 1968) (right to receive religious or racially oriented publications); *cf. In re* Harrell, 2 Cal. 3d 675, 420 P.2d 640, 87 *California Reporter* 504 (1970) (pursuant to Cal. Penal Code §2600 prisoners may receive all printed matter except those in prohibited categories).
210. *Brabson v. Wilkins*, 19 N.Y.2d 433, 227 N.E.2d 383, 280 N.Y.S.2d 561 (1967); *Wilson v. Kelley*, 294 F. Supp. 1005 (N.D. Ga. 1968), *aff'd per curiam*, 393 U.S. 226 (1969); *see also* section on Remedies *infra*.
211. *Jackson v. Godwin*, 400 F.2d 529, 540 (5th Cir. 1968).
212. *Walker v. Blackwell*, 411 F.2d 23, 29 (5th Cir. 1969).
213. *Rivers v. Royster*, 360 F.2d 593 (4th Cir. 1966).

lications.[214] A recent federal decision did permit inmates who belonged to the Black Panther party to read *Panther,* the party's weekly magazine, but left the authorities free to restrict the dissemination of the publication to other inmates and to decide "when and how" the Panthers could read it.[215] Moving yet one step further, another court enjoined officials from screening out all but "hard core pornography," basing its ruling on the freedom of publishers to circulate printed materials to prisoners.[216]

A federal district court recently broke new ground by ruling that, although "certain literature may pose such a clear and present danger to the security of a prison or to the rehabilitation of prisoners that it should be censored," protection of prisoners' limited First Amendment rights required several procedural safeguards when reading materials are withheld. Specifically, the court ordered that literature cannot be screened by prison officials without: notice to a prisoner that literature addressed to him has been censored or withheld; an opportunity to present arguments, either oral or written, in favor of a finding that the literature is acceptable; and a decision by a body that can be expected to act fairly.[217]

California prisoners have a statutory right to receive all reading material accepted by the United States Post Office except for literature that is obscene, tends to incite violent crime or concerns gambling or a lottery.[218] Interpreting the statute, the California Supreme Court invalidated a regulation banning materials found not to be "conducive to rehabilitation":

> It may well be that even persons who have committed antisocial acts warranting their imprisonment may derive greater rehabilitative benefits from a relatively free access to the thoughts of all mankind as reflected in the published word than they would derive from a strictly controlled intellectual diet.[219]

214. In *Sostre v. McGinnis,* 442 F.2d 178 (2d Cir. 1971) (*en banc*), the court ruled that a prisoner cannot be punished for possession of "inflammatory" or "racist" literature. However, the court approved the less restrictive course of confiscating literature that might "subvert prison discipline," leaving open the question of the constitutional standards necessary to justify the confiscation. The district court's order requiring officials to submit regulations governing the receipt, distribution, discussion and writing of political literature was reversed.
215. *Shakur v. McGrath,* 69 Civ. 4493, at 8–9 (S.D.N.Y., mem. Dec. 31, 1969).
216. *Palmigiano v. Travisono,* 317 F. Supp. 776 (D.R.I. 1970).
217. *Sostre v. Otis,* 330 F. Supp. 941 (S.D.N.Y. 1971). The court found that the recent establishment of a broadly based review panel of prison officials from different disciplines satisfied the third criterion.
218. Cal. Penal Code, §2600 (West 1968).
219. *In re* Harrell, 2 Cal. 3d 675, 703–704, 470 P.2d 640, 645, 87 *California Reporter* 504, 509 (1970).

Outside these narrowly circumscribed areas of protection, judicial fear of the incendiary potential of free speech has left officials with a free rein to silence convicts in their custody. For example, one federal court supported the use of severe disciplinary sanctions to curtail a prisoner's urgings for a sit-down demonstration to protest "mistreatment, inequities, and criminal neglect by state correctional officials and civil personnel":

> Roberts has no judicially enforceable right to advocate open defiance of authority within the prison walls. . . . Supreme Court statements to the effect that there is no absolute right to freedom of speech means that attempts to speak in a milieu where such speech may incite an insurrection against the authorities must be tempered. . . . In a prison environment, where the climate tends to be more volatile than on the streets, strong restraints and heavy penalties are in order.[220]

Another federal court refused to invalidate the segregation and transfer of a Virginia prisoner for "agitating" by posting on the prison bulletin board and circulating copies of a letter he had sent to the governor suggesting prison reform and urging prisoners to make their grievances known.[221]

Admittedly, the "clear and present danger" that speech may create[222] can be greater in prison than elsewhere.[223] But it is highly questionable whether there is sufficient justification for the judicial declaration that "a propagandist has no judicially enforceable right to propagandize within the prison walls, whether his propaganda be directed to other inmates or to outsiders."[224] Until courts begin to address the First Amendment question of free expression in prison, such declarations will remain accurate statements of the law, blocking important outlets for prisoners' feelings of frustration as well as their constructive and creative ideas.

220. *Roberts v. Pepersack*, 256 F. Supp. 415, 429–30 (D. Md. 1966), *cert. denied* 389 U.S. 877 (1967).
221. *Landman v. Peyton*, 370 F.2d 135 (4th Cir. 1966).
222. *Cf. Gitlow v. New York*, 268 U.S. 652, 672–73 (1925) (dissenting opinion); *Schenck v. United States*, 249 U.S. 47, 52 (1918).
223. *Cf. In re* Van Geldern, 14 Cal. App. 3d 838, 92 Cal. Rptr. 592 (1971).
224. *McCloskey v. Maryland*, 337 F.2d 72 (4th Cir. 1964) (anti-Semitic propaganda). *But see Sostre v. Rockefeller*, 312 F. Supp. 863, 876 (S.D.N.Y. 1970), *aff'd in part and rev'd in part sub nom. Sostre v. McGinnis*, 442 F.2d 178 (2d Cir. 1971) (*en banc*) holding that officials may not punish an inmate for writing militant letters, possessing political literature or refusing to answer questions about a political organization, where his activities caused no reasonable apprehension of a disturbance or security risk. "It is not a function of our prison system to make prisoners conform in their political thought and belief to ideas acceptable to their jailers." *See also Carothers v. Follette*, 314 F. Supp. 1014 (S.D.N.Y. 1970).

Racial Discrimination and Segregation. Racial tensions and aggressions have been termed second only to sexual frustration in the informal system of exploitation in prison.[225] Discrimination against minorities in the treatment of prisoners and the hiring and promotion of guards and other employees continues to exist in virtually all prisons but is most obvious in the South, where black prisoners perform most of the menial tasks and black employees are virtually nonexistent.[226] On the other hand, the special living conditions and disciplinary problems of penal institutions make life particularly difficult for whatever group is in the minority (in a few prisons this is the whites), and partly for this reason prisons were the last public institutions to be desegregated by court order.

Despite some early "hands-off" cases,[227] courts have had little difficulty invalidating policies that clearly discriminate against racial minorities. Prison regulations that deny black prisoners the right to receive "non-subversive" newspapers and magazines that are oriented toward blacks, while allowing white prisoners to receive publications of general circulation, have been deemed a denial of equal protection.[228] Devious methods may not be employed to discriminate against a racial minority; for example, a policy of allowing prisoners to receive only "home town" newspapers where newspapers of general circulation are written primarily for the white majority was invalidated as establishing an unreasonable racial classification.[229]

The first federal court to be presented with a claim involving racial

225. Report of the Task Force on Law and Law Enforcement to the National Commission on the Causes and Prevention of Violence, *Law and Order Reconsidered* 581 (1969); *see* Minton and Rice, "Using Racism at San Quentin," *Ramparts,* January 1970, at 17.
226. *See, e.g., Wilson v. Kelley,* 294 F. Supp. 1005 (N.D. Ga. 1968), *aff'd per curiam,* 393 U.S. 266 (1969).
227. *E.g., United States ex rel. Morris v. Radio Station WENR,* 209 F.2d 105 (7th Cir. 1953) (black prisoners allegedly denied opportunity to participate in radio programs sponsored by prison authorities).
228. *Jackson v. Godwin,* 400 F.2d 529 (5th Cir. 1968); *Rivers v. Royster,* 360 F.2d 593 (4th Cir. 1966). *See also Owens v. Brierley,* 452 F.2d 640 (3rd Cir. 1971).
229. *Id.* The courts relied on a line of racial classification cases from outside the prison area, *e.g., McLaughlin v. Florida,* 379 U.S. 184 (1964) (invalidating a statute prohibiting racially mixed cohabitation).
  As yet, no court has granted prisoners standing to challenge discriminatory practices in hiring prison employees. *See Wilson v. Kelley,* 294 F. Supp. 1005, 1010–11 (N.D. Ga. 1968), *aff'd per curiam,* 393 U.S. 226 (1969). In a recent case involving segregated state mental hospitals, however, patients were given such standing:

> We agree that the plaintiffs do not have standing to challenge the practices as potential employees, but we must conclude that they do have standing because of the secondary effects on the plaintiffs as patients of the discrimination against staff personnel. The plaintiffs stand in the same relationship to the hospital staff as students in the public schools stand to their teachers. . . .

Marable v. Alabama Mental Health Board, 297 F. Supp. 291, 297 (M.D. Ala. 1969).

segregation of prisoners (including a walled-off compartment for blacks in the dining hall) rejected it summarily on the theory that "by no parity of reasoning can the rationale of *Brown v. Board of Education* . . . be extended to State penal institutions."[230] Since then, however, several courts have upheld such challenges under the equal-protection clause of the Fourteenth Amendment, without requiring specific proof of discrimination or unequal facilities. The first case involved institutions for juveniles, since there the analogy to public education was the most obvious.[231] More recently, state prisons and local jails in Alabama, Georgia, Arkansas and Virginia have been ordered to desegregate,[232] and the existence of segregated prisons is no longer considered to present a substantial constitutional question.[233]

Of course, racial tensions do continue to present serious problems in prisons. Prison officials have been unable, however, to demonstrate that court-ordered integration enhances the problems of prison violence. A federal district judge cited this lack of evidence as the reason for rejecting a request by five white and five black Georgia prisoners to enjoin the application of the mandatory desegregation order and replace it with freedom of choice.[234] The prisoners predicted that violence would result from involuntary integration.

The judicial decisions desegregating the prisons do not preclude officials from considering disciplinary problems.[235] But the federal judicial

230. *Nichols v. McGee*, 169 F. Supp. 721, 724 (N.D. Calif.), *appeal dismissed*, 361 U.S. 6 (1959).
231. *See State Board of Public Works v. Myers*, 224 Md. 246, 167 A.2d 765, 769 (1961): "But if we assume, without deciding, that the distinction between penal institutions and public schools is tenable, it does not follow that educational programs offered in the training schools may be on a segregated basis." *See also Board of Managers v. George*, 377 F.2d 228, 232 (8th Cir. 1967) (whether juvenile institutions are termed "educational" or "penal," wholesale and arbitrary discrimination by state statutes is far removed from disciplinary administrative matters by prison officials); *Singleton v. Board of Commissioners*, 356 F.2d 771 (5th Cir. 1966) (juvenile institutions termed "educational" by statute); *Crum v. State Training School for Girls*, 413 F.2d 1348 (5th Cir. 1969); *Montgomery v. Oakley Training School*, 426 F.2d 269 (5th Cir. 1970) (unitary integrated system ordered). *But see Edwards v. Sard*, 250 F. Supp. 977 (D.D.C. 1966).
232. *Holt v. Sarver*, 309 F. Supp. 362, 382 (E.D. Ark. 1970) *aff'd* 442 F.2d 304 (8th Cir. 1971); *Mason v. Peyton*, Civ. No. 5611–R (E.D. Va., order entered, Oct. 16, 1969); *Wilson v. Kelley*, 294 F. Supp. 1005 (N.D. Ga. 1968), *aff'd per curiam*, 393 U.S. 266 (1969); *Washington v. Lee*, 263 F. Supp. 237 (M.D. Ala. 1966), *aff'd per curiam*, 390 U.S. 333 (1968). *See also Bolden v. Pegelow*, 329 F.2d 95 (4th Cir. 1964) (injunction against segregated barber shops in District of Columbia prison).
233. *Board of Managers v. George*, 377 F.2d 228 (8th Cir. 1967) (three-judge court not required); *Major v. Sowers*, 298 F. Supp. 1039 (E.D. La. 1969) (three-judge court not required for order to desegregate juvenile institutions in Louisiana).
234. *Rentfrow v. Carter*, 296 F. Supp. 301, 303 (N.D. Ga. 1968).
235. *See Washington v. Lee*, 390 U.S. 333, 334 (1968) (*per curiam*) (concurring opinion), in which three justices made it clear that prison authorities "acting in good faith and in particularized circumstances," may "take into account racial tensions in maintaining security, discipline, and good order in prisons and jails."

policy generally has been that "the danger to security, discipline, and good order must presently exist and be apparent to justify any segregation. This prohibits any standard policy or program of segregated custody at state, county, or local level."[236] An exception has occurred in a District of Columbia case, where a district judge ruled that in a prison with a ratio of approximately ten black inmates for every white, the policy of having six integrated and sixteen all-black dormitories could not be considered discriminatory.[237] Arkansas officials were excused temporarily where "to order immediate desegregation of the barracks would create disciplinary problems that Respondents are not able to solve at the moment and would tend to make the already bad situation at the Penitentiary substantially worse than it is."[238]

More subtle, and less readily dealt with than official policies of segregation, is the fact that racial tensions often permeate every informal aspect of prison life. Race is the most obvious division among prisoners and the most available avenue for venting the frustrations caused by imprisonment. According to former inmates of New York State prisons, separation of the races is almost total. There are black and white baseball fields, black and white areas in the recreation yard, black and white jobs, black and white sections of the dining room. Although there is no official policy of segregation (administrators explain that the inmates prefer the separation), guards foster the antagonisms by granting privileges and meting out punishments according to race and by isolating or transferring prisoners who attempt to unify the different groups.

Former employees at San Quentin have written that from the summer of 1968 until early 1969 inmate groups banded together to report to outsiders on conditions at the prison and to petition the state legislature for improvements. The prisoners published a newspaper, spent a weekend locked in their cells to dramatize the unity of their protest and presented their grievances to a legislative committee that visited the prison. According to the report, the response of prison officials was to destroy the prisoners' unity in order to stifle their protest:

236. *Wilson v. Kelley*, 294 F. Supp. 1005, 1009 n.5 (N.D. Ga. 1968), *aff'd per curiam*, 393 U.S. 266 (1969).
237. *Edwards v. Sard*, 250 F. Supp. 977 (D.D.C. 1966); *cf. Dixon v. Duncan*, 218 F. Supp. 157 (E.D. Va. 1963) (District of Columbia prison officials may not force white prisoners to live in integrated dormitories while giving black prisoners a choice between integrated and all-black dormitories).
238. *Holt v. Sarver*, 309 F. Supp. 362, 381–82 (E.D. Ark. 1970), *aff'd*, 442 F.2d 304 (8th Cir. 1971). "It must be remembered that we are not dealing here with school children. We are not dealing with free world housing; we are not dealing with theatres, restaurants, or hotels. We are dealing with criminals, many of whom are violent, and we are dealing with a situation in which the civilian personnel at the Penitentiary are not in control of the institution."

Activities at the prison were kept to a minimum, and once again guards were passing manufactured threats among the antagonistic racial groups whose hatreds had just barely been brought under control. Worst of all, inmates watched helplessly as guards smuggled guns, knives and raw materials for weapons into the hands of those most likely to use them on other inmates. The system by which the prison ran was imperiled and the power structure struck back at the inmates' organization by once again dividing to conquer.[239]

Racial skirmishes were renewed, and the old suspicions replaced the temporary solidarity. "[T]he only box score convicts care about now is by color: three blacks murdered and one badly wounded; one white murdered and eight in the hospital."

The problems of racial differences in prison are not restricted to the South. The legal right to integrated prisons will not solve this problem. Racial antagonism may be endemic in a society marked by racial tensions and insistent on imprisoning its offenders.

Privacy. The few courts that have considered the question have ruled that prisoners, who are "public figures in whose misadventures the community has a consuming interest,"[240] have no protection from exploitation by the news media.[241] Thus, for example, a prisoner whose parole hearing was filmed for use in a television documentary without his knowledge or consent was given no right to sue either the broadcasting station or the parole board.[242]

Within the prison, inmates have no right to claim constitutional immunity from searches of their persons or their personal property. "It is obvious that a jail shares none of the attributes of privacy of a home, an automobile, an office, or a hotel room. In prison, official surveillance has traditionally been the order of the day."[243]

But denial of privacy has gone beyond these physical aspects that

239. Minton and Rice, "Using Racism at San Quentin," *Ramparts,* January 1970, at 18, 24.
240. *Travers v. Paton,* 261 F. Supp. 110, 117 (D. Conn. 1966).
241. Id.; *Raynor v. American Broadcasting Co.,* 222 F. Supp. 795 (E.D. Pa. 1963); *Miller v. National Broadcasting Co.,* 157 F. Supp. 240 (D. Del. 1957); *Bernstein v. National Broadcasting Co.,* 129 F. Supp. 817 (D.D.C. 1955), *aff'd,* 232 F.2d 369 (1956).
242. *Travers v. Paton,* 261 F. Supp. 110 (D. Conn. 1966). *Cf. Commonwealth v. Wiseman,* 356 Mass. 260, 249 N.E.2d 610 (1969) (showing of *Titicut Follies* enjoined at behest of state authorities).
243. *Lanza v. New York,* 370 U.S. 139, 143 (1962). *But see Palmigiano v. Travisono,* 317 F. Supp. 776 (D.R.I. 1970):

Though this court has focused mainly on the issue before it as it relates to the First Amendment, it is of the opinion that the conduct of the . . . of-

ostensibly are connected to prison security. Not only are all consensual sexual relations forbidden, whether they be heterosexual or homosexual, but prisoners are forbidden to contract marriages (without cohabitation) unless they have official permission.[244] No court has yet ruled that this complete control over every aspect of a prisoner's existence is impermissible, no matter how it relates to his criminal career or his security in custody and regardless of the propriety of the criteria imposed.

Voting. Despite the obviously punitive nature of the common practice of permanently disenfranchising prisoners, there have been few constitutional challenges to these statutes by ex-convicts.[245] Some prisoners who were not disqualified from voting by law have complained of refusals by election officials to allow them to cast ballots while they were in prison. So far, these challenges have been unsuccessful.

In 1967, a Pennsylvania prisoner asked a federal court to require state election officials to set up voting equipment in state prisons,[246] arguing that since neither state laws generally nor his sentence in particular included the explicit forfeiture of his right to vote, the refusal to permit him to do so constituted an additional penalty not authorized by law.[247] The court's response was that the provision of a state statute[248] pertaining to absentee electors did not include persons confined in a prison or mental institution and that the provision violated none of the inmates' constitutional rights:

> It is only where fundamental, humane and necessary rights are breached that the constitutional protections become involved.
> These do not include the right to vote, nor can they include any rights which interfere with the Warden's duty and function

---

ficials of indiscriminately opening and reading all prisoner mail including that of unconvicted awaiting trial inmates, whether the same be from the inmates or members of the free society, is a violation of the Fourth Amendment.

244. *See Complaint, Parman v. Montilla,* Civ. No. 469–70 (D.D.C., filed Feb. 17, 1970). Where "the classification counselor . . . the prison chaplain and the warden all agreed that this young man should not marry this girl," such permission was denied despite the fact that the girl was pregnant with his child and both families approved of the marriage. Washington *Evening Star,* Nov. 15, 1969, at A–22, col. 1.

245. *See Green v. Board of Elections of New York* 380 F.2d 445 (2d Cir. 1967), *cert. denied,* 389 U.S. 1048 (1968) (refusal to convene three-judge district court upheld); *Beacham v. Braterman,* 300 F. Supp. 182 (S.D. Fla. 1969), *aff'd without opinion,* 396 U.S. 12 (1969) (three-judge court convened but disqualification upheld); *Stephens v. Yeomans* Civ. No. 1005–70 (D. N.J., Oct. 30, 1970) (three-judge court ordered to consider felon's right to vote).

246. *Ray v. Commonwealth,* 263 F. Supp. 630 (W.D. Pa. 1967).

247. *Cf. Coffin v. Reichard,* 143 F.2d 443, 445 (6th Cir. 1944), *cert. denied,* 325 U.S. 887 (1945) (a prisoner retains all the rights of an ordinary citizen except those expressly, or by necessary implication, taken from him by law).

248. Pa. Stat. tit. 25, §2602(y) (1941).

of seeing to the enforcement of the incarceration and the fulfillment of sentence after conviction.

The court's conclusion that the right to vote is not fundamental is inconsistent with an earlier Supreme Court case[249] overturning an electoral
regulation that effectively deprived servicemen of the right to vote.
"States may not casually deprive a class of individuals of the vote because
of some remote administrative benefit to the State." On the other hand,
the Court interpreted an Illinois election law as not affording unconvicted prisoners awaiting trial the right to absentee ballots and declined
to rule that the law denied prisoners the equal protection of the laws.[250]
While the decision appears to diminish the importance of the right to
vote, according to the Court's opinion, "there [was] nothing to show that
a judicially incapacitated pretrial detainee [was] absolutely prohibited
from [voting];" thus it was not unreasonable for the Legislature to refuse
them absentee ballots while granting ballots to persons who could show
an "absolute inability to appear at the polls."

Charges of Criminal Conduct in Prison. When a prisoner is suspected
of committing a crime while in prison, he is supposed to be "entitled to the
rights of any suspect who is walking the streets."[251] The only exceptions appear to relate to Fourth Amendment search and seizure protections.[252] A
difficult problem of double jeopardy[253] occurs, however, when a prisoner's
conduct is made the basis of a criminal charge in addition to intramural
disciplinary action by prison authorities. For example, an inmate convicted of participating in a prison riot was sentenced to a term of nine
years and eight months, to run consecutively with the term he was then
serving. In addition, prison officials ordered him confined to a punishment
cell for 35 days.[254] In another case, a prisoner who stood trial for killing

---

249. *Carrington v. Rash*, 380 U.S. 89 (1965).
250. *McDonald v. Board of Election Commissioners*, 394 U.S. 802 (1969). Ill. Rev.
Stat., ch. 46, §§19–1 and 19–3 (1967).
251. Barkin, "Prison Policy," at 19; *see, e.g., Mathis v. United States*, 391 U.S. 1
(1968) (warning of rights); *Brooks v. Florida*, 389 U.S. 413 (1967) (voluntariness
of confession); *Blyden v. Hogan*, 320 F. Supp. 513 (S.D.N.Y. 1970) (warning of
rights before inmates signed consent-to-interview forms following riots); Bureau of
Prisons, Policy Statement 2001.1 (Feb. 19, 1968) (warning of rights, counsel, self-
incrimination).
252. *See Lanza v. New York*, 370 U.S. 139 (1962); *cf. People v. Dorado*, 62 Cal. 2d
338, 356–67, 398 P.2d 361, 371–72, 42 *California Reporter* 169, 179–80, *cert. denied*,
381 U.S. 937 (1965).
253. *See Benton v. Maryland*, 395 U.S. 784 (1969).
254. *Brooks v. Florida*, 389 U.S. 413 (1967) (*per curiam*). The lower-court decision
was reversed on other grounds, the contention of double jeopardy apparently not
having been raised.

a guard and was acquitted of murder on a plea of self-defense was "pad-locked" by the prison superintendent in a solitary cell.[255] More than a year after the acquittal, a federal district court, in deference to the dis-cretionary authority of the superintendent over disciplinary matters, denied the prisoner's request for release into the general prison popula-tion.

In *Clutchette v. Procunier,* the double-jeopardy argument was not made. However, the court examined a further problem created by sub-jecting the same conduct to criminal prosecution and administrative discipline. Although a criminal suspect has the right to remain silent in the face of police questioning, since *Miranda v. Arizona,* a prisoner choos-ing to do so may have to sacrifice the right to explain his conduct to the prison disciplinary committee before being punished. According to the court:

> The prisoner, warned that anything he says may be used against him in a criminal prosecution, is put to the choice between re-maining silent and sacrificing his right to defend himself before the committee, or speaking to the committee and risking in-criminating himself in a future prosecution. The trap is unavoid-able.[256]

Because of the difficulty involved in making this choice, the court ruled that any prisoner charged with a prison-rule violation that may be pun-ishable by state authorities must be provided with counsel.

After the uprising at the Attica prison in September 1971, there were extensive interrogations of inmates by state authorities. Although the state provided inmates with forms on which they could request or waive counsel, prisoners claimed that refusal to cooperate with the investiga-tion, regardless of the possibilities of self-incrimination, could lead to administrative reprisals. Consequently, they requested an injunction against any interrogations except in the presence of counsel.

A federal court of appeals upheld the denial of injunctive relief, citing the dearth of evidence of improper questioning of prisoners and the existence of the adequate legal remedy of excluding any illegally ob-tained evidence from future trials. According to the court, "Plaintiffs' incarceration as the result of prior convictions for unrelated offenses, while it does not strip them of Sixth Amendment rights . . . does not

255. *Jones v. Peyton,* 294 F. Supp. 173 (E.D. Va. 1968).
256. *Clutchette v. Procunier,* 328 F. Supp. 767 (N.D. Cal. 1971); *Miranda v. Arizona,* U.S. 486 (1965).

confer upon them greater rights to counsel than those of citizens outside of the prison walls." A dissenting opinion, emphasizing the subtle pressures that could be applied to deter prisoners from requesting counsel and the resulting dilemma of choosing between possible prosecution and administrative reprisal, concluded that a prisoner's need for counsel may exceed that of a suspect in the usual criminal investigation.[257]

Detainers. A prosecutor who has unresolved charges against a prisoner in the custody of another jurisdiction may lodge a detainer against him. The result of the detainer is that on the expiration of his present sentence or on his being granted parole,[258] the prisoner must be turned over to the authority lodging the detainer. The detainer increases a prisoner's uncertainty concerning his future, while increasing the time that lapses before trial,[259] thus making it more difficult to secure witnesses and defend against the charges. In 1967 the Supreme Court ruled that the Sixth Amendment's guarantee of a speedy trial applies to the states.[260] Since that time, federal courts have given post-conviction relief to prisoners claiming that state convictions obtained after long delays while the defendants served prison terms in other states prejudiced their rights to a fair trial.[261]

Similar post-conviction relief was not, at first, granted to federal prisoners attempting to have state detainers dismissed. According to the federal courts, state courts lacked jurisdiction to try federal prisoners

257. *Gonzalez v. Rockefeller*, 10 *Criminal Law Reporter* 2227 (2d Cir., Dec. 1, 1971).
258. No matter how weak the case, the existence of the detainer generally prevents a prisoner from being assigned desirable work allowing minimum security. *See Pitts v. North Carolina*, 395 F.2d 182, 187 (4th Cir. 1968) (accusations in a detainer need not be proved; no judicial officer is involved in issuing a detainer); Note, "Effective Guaranty of a Speedy Trial for Convicts in Other Jurisdictions," 77 *Yale Law Journal* 767 (1968). Many detainers are apparently filed for punitive reasons; they are withdrawn shortly before the convict's release, having served their purpose by curtailing prison privileges and preventing parole. According to one estimate, as many as one half the detainers are never pursued by the requesting authority. Note, "Detainers and the Correctional Process," 1966 *Washington University Law Quarterly* 417. A recent federal regulation prevents a detainer from *automatically* precluding consideration for parole. 28 C.F.R. §2.9 (1970).
259. *See, e.g., Gregory v. Page*, 289 F. Supp. 316 (E.D. Okl. 1968); United States *ex rel. Magucci v. Follette*, 272 F. Supp. 563 (S.D.N.Y. 1967); *Troyan v. United States*, 240 F. Supp. 383 (D. Kan. 1964).
260. *Klopfer v. North Carolina*, 386 U.S. 213 (1967). Prisoners have long had such a right when the charges were federal. *See, e.g., Fouts v. United States*, 253 F.2d 215 (6th Cir.), *cert. denied*, 358 U.S. 884 (1958); *Taylor v. United States*, 238 F.2d 259 (D.C. Cir. 1956). *See also Pellegrini v. Wolfe*, 225 Ark. 459, 283 S.W.2d 162 (1955); *People v. Bryarly*, 23 Ill. 2d 313, 178 N.E.2d 326 (1961); *People v. Winfrey*, 20 N.Y.2d 138, 288 N.E.2d 808, 281 N.Y.S.2d 823 (1967); in which state courts ruled that it was necessary for prosecutors to make reasonable efforts to extradite for speedy trial prisoners held in another state.
261. *E.g., Pitts v. North Carolina*, 395 F.2d 182 (4th Cir. 1968).

until after their release from federal custody.[262] In 1969, however, the Supreme Court ruled in *Smith v. Hooey*[263] that a federal prisoner has a right to a speedy trial on all pending state charges but left open the question of when and how that right could be enforced.[264] The consensus of lower federal court opinions was that the courts' lack of jurisdiction over state prosecutors who lodged the detainers,[265] coupled with the doctrine requiring exhaustion of state remedies,[266] precluded prisoners from attacking the state indictments on which the detainers were based while they were still serving prison terms for previous convictions.[267] The Supreme Court took up the question again the following year in *Dickey v. Florida*,[268] overturning a state conviction that had been obtained after a lapse of nearly eight years, during which the defendant had been in federal prison and had made repeated demands for a speedy trial.

Although *Dickey* dealt with the right of a federal prisoner to demand a speedy trial by state authorities,[269] it left unsettled the effect of unresolved detainers on an inmate's treatment by prison authorities. One federal district court,[270] however, established a procedure for federal prisoners to remove the burdensome restrictions imposed by prison au-

262. *Petty v. Georgia*, 395 F.2d 770 (5th Cir. 1968); *Henderson v. Circuit Court*, 392 F.2d 551 (5th Cir. 1968); *McCary v. Kansas*, 281 F.2d 185, 187 (10th Cir. 1960).
263. 393 U.S. 374 (1969).
264. *See Lawrence v. Blackwell*, 298 F. Supp. 708, 715 (N.D. Ga. 1969): "While Smith v. Hooey clearly establishes a right to speedy trial for federal prisoners with pending State charges, it gives precious little practical guidance to the lower courts about the effectuation of that right."
265. If the federal court in the state where the prisoner is incarcerated has jurisdiction—*see Sanders v. United States*, 297 F. Supp. 375 (N.D. Ga. 1969)—it usually will be impossible to get jurisdiction over the state prosecuting authorities. *See Carnage v. Sanborn*, 304 F. Supp. 857 (N.D. Ga. 1969); *Lawrence v. Blackwell*, 298 F. Supp. 708 (N.D. Ga. 1969). *See also Dixon v. Tennessee*, 404 F.2d 27 (6th Cir. 1968). In *Carnage v. Sanborn, supra*, the court rested its decision on its inability to issue a writ in the nature of mandamus against a state (as opposed to a federal) official. *See* 28 U.S.C. §1361 (1964).
266. United States *ex rel. Houghton v. Scranton*, 272 F. Supp. 960 (E.D. Pa. 1966), *rev'd sub nom. Houghton v. Shafer*, 392 U.S. 639 (1968) (*per curiam*); *Monroe v. Pape*, 365 U.S. 167 (1961) (federal district court has concurrent jurisdiction under federal Civil Rights Act); Amsterdam, "Criminal Prosecution Affecting Federally Guaranteed Civil Rights: Federal Removal and Habeas Corpus Jurisdiction to Abort State Court Trial, 113 *University of Pennsylvania Law Review* 793, 884–96 (1965); Note, "Habeas Corpus—Effect of Supreme Court Change in Law on Exhaustion of State Remedies Requisite to Federal Habeas Corpus," 113 *University of Pennsylvania Law Review* 1303 (1965). *See generally*, section on Remedies *infra*.
267. *See White v. Tennessee*, 304 F. Supp. 661 (N.D. Ga. 1969); *Smith v. Londerholm*, 304 F. Supp. 73 (D. Kan. 1969); *Lawrence v. Blackwell*, 298 F. Supp. 708 (N.D. Ga. 1969); *Sanders v. United States*, 297 F. Supp. 375 (N.D. Ga. 1969).
268. 398 U.S. 30 (1970).
269. The Court's opinion left many possible questions unsettled, including the necessity of a demand for a speedy trial and the allocation of the burden of proving prejudice to the defendant. *See* Brennan, J., concurring, 398 U.S. at 39.
270. *Lawrence v. Blackwell*, 298 F. Supp. 708 (N.D. Ga. 1969).

thorities because of the unresolved detainers. Once informed of the existence of a state detainer, the prisoner must make demand for a speedy trial to the appropriate state authorities, wait a "reasonable time" for the state to act—generally 180 days—then petition the federal court for the removal of restrictions:

> The state [authorities] are under a constitutional obligation to make a diligent, good-faith effort to try the plaintiffs within a reasonable time. . . . It will be for the state trial judges to decide what the plaintiffs must show to merit dismissal of their indictments. . . .
> However . . . if the states involved have not made a "diligent, good-faith effort" to bring the prisoners to trial within a reasonable time after this order, the . . . federal penitentiary authorities must remove the restrictions flowing from these detainers. . . . When diligence is lacking, the prison authorities must then permit these prisoners to enjoy the privileges to which they would otherwise be entitled, absent the detainers.[271]

In other words, although the courts may not be willing or able to remove the detainers themselves, they can order prison officials to minimize their punitive effect.[272] Following the *Dickey* decision, Congress enacted the Interstate Agreement on Detainers.[273] The act provides that anyone imprisoned by a state or the federal government with unresolved charges against him in another jurisdiction may file written notice of the place of his imprisonment and a request for final disposition of all outstanding charges in that state. Once such a request has been received, the prisoner must be brought to trial within 180 days unless the appropriate court grants a continuance for good cause. Any request by a prisoner under the act operates as a waiver of his extradition.

ACCESS TO COURT

Although prison officials consistently have been accorded wide powers to limit and censor inmates' communications with the outside world,[274] the

271. *See also Weiss v. Blackwell*, 310 F. Supp. 360 (N.D. Ga. 1969).
272. *See Carnage v. Sanborn*, 304 F. Supp. 857 (N.D. Ga. 1969).
273. Public Law 91–538, 91st Cong., 2d Sess. Dec. 9, 1970.
274. *E.g.*, State Board of Corrections of Georgia, Rule 36, *cited in* Brief for Plaintiff at 47, *Wilson v. Kelley*, 294 F. Supp. 1005 (N.D. Ga. 1968), *aff'd per curiam*, 393 U.S. 266 (1969); Missouri State Penitentiary, Inmate Informational Pamphlet: *Rules and Procedures* 14 (Sept. 1967); Leopold, "What Is Wrong with the Prison System?" 45 *Nebraska Law Review* 33, 50 (1966); Note, "Prison Restrictions—Prisoner Rights," 59 *Journal of Criminal Law, Criminology and Police Science*, 386, 387–88 (1968);

deprivation of reasonable access to the courts to air legal grievances is not a necessary concomitant of imprisonment,[275] and administrative restrictions on correspondence may not operate to deny prisoners this right.[276]

The Supreme Court affirmed the right of access to court in 1941,[277] when it held invalid a state regulation that all *habeas corpus* petitions must be approved by the parole board's "legal investigator" as "properly drawn" before they would be transmitted to a court. The Court ruled that although the aim of regulation might be laudable, it had the effect of abridging prisoners' rights to apply to federal courts for *habeas corpus*, and the question "whether a petition for writ of *habeas corpus* addressed to a federal court is properly drawn and what allegations it must contain are questions for the court alone to determine."[278]

Other cases have held that both the due-process and the equal-protection clauses of the Fourteenth Amendment (and, presumably, the due-process clause of the Fifth Amendment) prohibit the application of even reasonable prison regulations to keep a prisoner from filing a timely appeal from his conviction.[279] These cases involved prisoners' efforts to attack the criminal convictions that led to their incarceration. In addition, courts have recognized that in situations where inmates can secure their rights only through judicial decrees, protection of their access to the courts is basic to the enforcement of all other rights.[280] Thus, courts have reaffirmed the access principle in cases where prisoners claimed mistreat-

---

accord, Palmigiano v. Travisono, 317 F. Supp. 776 (D.R.I. 1970); *Burns v. Swenson,* 430 F.2d 771 (8th Cir. 1970). For further discussion, see section on Remedies *infra.*
275. *Edwards v. Duncan,* 355 F.2d 993 (4th Cir. 1966) (dictum); *see* cases cited at notes 279–80 *infra.*
276. *Lee v. Tahash,* 352 F.2d 970 (8th Cir. 1965).
277. *Ex parte* Hull, 312 U.S. 546 (1941).
278. *See also White v. Ragen,* 324 U.S. 760, 762 n.1 (1945) (right of access by state prisoners to state courts).
A federal district court recently suggested that prison officials should refrain from screening petitions for obscene, abusive or "otherwise objectionable allegations," and should limit their perusal to a determination that the addressee is a court official and the subject related to judicial relief. *Talley v. Stephens,* 247 F. Supp. 683, 690 n.4 (E.D. Ark. 1965).
279. *E.g. Dowd v. United States ex rel.* Cook, 340 U.S. 206 (1951); *Cochran v. Kansas,* 316 U.S. 255 (1942); *Hymes v. Dickson,* 232 F. Supp. 796 (N.D. Cal. 1964); *People v. Howard,* 166 Cal. App. 2d 638, 334 P.2d 105 (Dist. Ct. App. 1958); *Warfield v. Raymond,* 195 Md. 711, 71 A.2d 870 (1950).
Although the due-process clause may not require a state to provide criminal appeals, *see Douglas v. California,* 372 U.S. 353 (1963); *Griffin v. Illinois,* 351 U.S. 12 (1956), where appeals are available, the arbitrary denial by prison authorities of a prisoner's right to appeal constitutes a denial of the equal protection of the laws. *Dowd v. United States ex rel.* Cook, 340 U.S. 206 (1951); *Cochran v. Kansas,* 316 U.S. 255 (1942).
280. *Coleman v. Peyton,* 362 F.2d 905, 907 (4th Cir.), *cert. denied,* 385 U.S. 905 (1966) (dictum); *Stiltner v. Rhay,* 322 F.2d 314, 316 (9th Cir. 1963), *cert. denied,* 376 U.S. 920 (1964).

ment in prison, as well as in those where their release was sought.[281]

There has been far less concern about the effect of prison officials refusing to permit inmates to file civil suits that are not related to their personal liberty. According to one federal court of appeals,[282]

[o]therwise, penitentiary wardens and the courts might be swamped with an endless number of unnecessary and even spurious law suits filed by inmates in remote jurisdictions in the hope of obtaining leave to appear at the hearing of any such case, with the consequent disruption of prison routine and concomitant hazard of escape from custody.[283]

Thus, litigation not related to actual personal liberty can be instituted only after the prisoner is released. The effect of the restriction creates a number of problems for the prisoner. Injunctive relief to protect the interests of the prisoner-plaintiff, while incarcerated, is thereby denied.[284] Furthermore, by forcing the prisoner to wait years to bring a suit for damages, problems will arise similar to those created by the detainer system—witnesses may no longer be available and evidence may have grown stale. Where courts refrain from invalidating these restrictive prison rules, the prisoner-plaintiff is denied judicial review of his complaint on its merits. For example, one federal court[285] refused to issue

281. *E.g., Talley v. Stephens,* 247 F. Supp. 683 (E.D. Ark. 1965); *Fulwood v. Clemmer,* 206 F. Supp. 370 (D.D.C. 1962); *In re* Riddle, 57 Cal. 2d 848, 372 P.2d 304, 22 *California Reporter* 472 (1962); *In re* Ferguson, 55 Cal. 2d 663, 361 P.2d 417, 12 *California Reporter* 753, *cert. denied,* 368 U.S. 864 (1961); *Kahn v. LaVallee,* 12 App. Div. 2d 832, 209 N.Y.S.2d 591 (Sup. Ct. 1961) (dictum).
282. *Tabor v. Hardwick,* 224 F.2d 526 (5th Cir. 1955).
283. *See Seybold v. Milwaukee County Sheriff,* 276 F. Supp. 484 (E.D. Wis. 1967), in which the court refused to permit a prisoner to argue a motion for injunction against copyright infringement:

We can conceive of no greater interference with prison officials or prison discipline than requiring that prisoner-plaintiffs who wish to appear in civil actions unrelated to their imprisonment be transported from prison to this court by prison guards, housed in this area and released from their normal duties at the institutions during proceedings in their cases.

See also Diaz v. Chatterton, 229 F. Supp. 19 (S.D. Calif. 1964) (federal funds not available to transport prisoners from state prison to appear at trial or pretrial hearings in ordinary civil action); *Kirby v. Thomas,* 336 F.2d 462, 464 (6th Cir. 1964).
284. *E.g., Seybold v. Milwaukee County Sheriff,* 276 F. Supp. 484 (E.D. Wis. 1967).
285. *Kirby v. Thomas,* 336 F.2d 462 (6th Cir. 1964). Prison regulations forbade prisoners to mail any legal papers except "those which constitute a part of *habeas corpus* or *coram nobis* proceedings in which the inmate seeks to test the validity of the judgment of conviction under which he is confined and if successful in his contentions to obtain a new trial or his freedom." *Id.* at 462–63 n.1. The court did not explore either the availability of attorneys to handle civil claims for indigent prisoners or the possible violation of the equal-protection clause if only those inmates who could afford to hire private attorneys were permitted to pursue their claims. *Id.* at 464.

a writ of *mandamus* ordering a prison warden to allow an inmate to mail pleadings he had prepared to a federal district court. A prisoner-plaintiff may consequently be precluded from filing even civil-damage actions against prison officials, as permitted under the federal Civil Rights Act,[286] where prison rules deny his access to the court.

Other prison regulations permeate prison life so as to block access to the courts notwithstanding judicial efforts to the contrary.[287] For example, censorship of the mail alerts prison officials to complaints even before they reach the courts.[288] Although prisoners may not be disciplined for bringing suit against prison officials,[289] reprisals do occur.[290]

Under the present system, neither a reason nor a hearing need be given before a prisoner is punished.[291] Indeed, it may be impossible to show that disciplinary measures resulted from an attempted exercise of constitutional rights. When prisoners are able to inform the courts that such punishments stemmed from legitimate efforts to air grievances in court, judges have no problem in condemning the reprisals and enjoining their repetition.[292]

286. See *Jackson v. Bishop*, 404 F.2d 571 (8th Cir. 1968); *Wright v. McMann*, 387 F.2d 519 (2d Cir. 1967); *Smartt v. Avery*, 370 F.2d 788 (6th Cir. 1967); *Howard v. Smyth*, 365 F.2d 428 (4th Cir.), cert. denied, 385 U.C. 988 (1966); *Jordan v. Fitzharris*, 257 F. Supp. 674 (N.D. Cal. 1966); United States ex rel. *Hancock v. Pate*, 372 P.2d 304, 22 *California Reporter* 472 (1962):
287. E.g., *Spires v. Bottorff*, 317 F.2d 273 (7th Cir. 1963) cert. denied, 379 U.S. 938 (1964), where the court held that a prisoner might have a cause of action under the Civil Rights Act against a state judge who claimed he was "agitated with" the prisoner's demands for copies of the charges that had led to his conviction, and induced the warden to prevent him from corresponding with him or the clerk of his court; *Fulwood v. Clemmer*, 206 F. Supp. 370 (D.D.C. 1962); In re Riddle, 57 Cal. 2d 848, 372 P.2d 304, 22 *California Reporter* 472 (1962):

> [I]f, when a prisoner, as he must, submits his proposed petition to the prison officials for their perusal, and the petition charges the officials with misconduct, the prison officials can summarily decide that his charges are false and punish him for making them, there is a form of coercion that will very effectively prevent access to the courts.

288. See, e.g., *Carothers v. Follette*, 314 F. Supp. 1014, 1020 (S.D.N.Y. 1970) (copies made of any letters to a judge in which a prisoner complains of his treatment).
289. United States ex rel. *Cleggett v. Pate*, 229 F. Supp. 818, 821–22 (N.D. Ill. 1964).
290. In *Sostre v. Rockefeller*, 312 F. Supp. 863, 869 (S.D.N.Y. 1970), aff'd in part, modified in part, and rev'd in part sub nom. *Sostre v. McGinnis*, 442 F.2d 178 (2d Cir. 1971) (en banc) a prisoner was confined to his cell during July 4th celebrations for having dust on his cell bars. The court found that the charge and punishment were imposed in retaliation for the prisoner's success in obtaining a court order releasing him from punitive segregation the day before. See also *Meola v. Fitzpatrick*, 9 *Criminal Law Reporter* 2404 (D. Mass., Feb. 8, 1971). *Carothers v. Follette*, 314 F. Supp. 1014 (S.D.N.Y. 1970).
291. Punishment may be imposed at the discretion of prison authorities for infractions of prison rules as defined by the prison authority. See generally *Howard v. Smyth*, 365 F.2d 428 (4th Cir. 1966).
292. E.g., *Meola v. Fitzpatrick*, 322 F. Supp. 878 (D. Mass. 1971). In *Smartt v. Avery*, 370 F.2d 788 (6th Cir. 1967), a federal court invalidated a parole-board regulation

The court in *Talley v. Stephens*[293] recognized that the problem of reprisal is particularly acute where a convict complains to a court about physical mistreatment inside the institution and that "a theoretical right of access to the courts is hardly actual and adequate if its exercise is likely to produce reprisals, physical or otherwise, from Penitentiary personnel." A related but as yet unresolved issue is whether inmates may be denied access to court while they are being punished for some other, unrelated infraction.[294]

Other issues in defining what is "reasonable" access to court concern the practical problems of initiating a legal action from a prison cell. Some administrative regulations, such as the limitation on an inmate's paper supply (a few pieces per week), seem petty and unreasonable. Others may represent an effort to accommodate individual rights and the necessary practical restrictions which inevitably must be imposed by the institutional setting. In the latter group are problems related to obtaining and conferring with counsel or other legal help and, for those who must represent themselves, obtaining access to legal materials.

Counsel. Several years ago, the California Supreme Court[295] recognized the crucial relationship between the ability to afford and secure an attorney and a prisoner's ability to exercise his legal right of access to court. The court ruled that prison authorities could not use their power to censor prisoners' mail to screen out letters to attorneys even when the mail criticizes the prison regime. Yet prisoners continue to complain that their letters documenting prison abuses to attorneys subject them to reprisals by the authorities.

Although the New York Court of Appeals has enjoined prison offi-

---

that postponed for one year the parole eligibility of any inmate who filed a *habeas corpus* petition in court. The court ruled that the parole board could not penalize prisoners for exercising their constitutional and statutory right of access to court by withholding a privilege (consideration for early release) that would otherwise have been granted.
293. 247 F. Supp. 683 (E.D. Ark. 1965).
294. In Virginia, prisoners confined to "meditation" cells as punishment may not correspond with courts or attorneys unless they have litigation actually pending. One prisoner testified that he was prevented from communicating with a court or his attorney for forty-three days. According to the Director of the Department of Welfare, writing to court is one of the "privileges" an inmate loses when he goes into "meditation." Record at 24, *Mason v. Peyton*, Civ. No. 53–69–R (E.D. Va., consent decree, Aug. 13, 1968).
295. *In re* Ferguson, 55 Cal. 2d 663, 361 P.2d 417, 12 *California Reporter* 753, *cert. denied*, 368 U.S. 864 (1961). *Cf. McCloskey v. Maryland*, 337 F.2d 72 (4th Cir. 1964) (prisoner has no constitutional right to seek legal assistance in spreading anti-Semitic propaganda).

cials from withholding communications addressed to a prisoner's attorney if they concern the legality of his detention or the treatment he is receiving in prison, the letters may be censored by authorities and any material unrelated to these subjects may be deleted.[296] A federal court of appeals,[297] limiting a more liberal district court decision,[298] agreed.[299] The federal practice of opening mail to attorneys only for the purpose of inspecting for contraband or planned illegal activities[300] has been judicially approved. However, several federal courts have been insisting lately there is no purpose for which mail to or from attorneys may be read by officials. In one case, although an agreement permitting the opening of mail from attorneys in order to inspect for contraband was approved by the court, officials were required to do so only in the presence of the inmate addressee. According to the court, "if the opening occurs in the absence of the inmate, his attorney will still be reluctant to communicate fully with his client because of the fear that his correspondence will be read by others. The 'chilling effect' on the inmates' right to the effective assistance of counsel is apparent."[301]

Inmates have the right to consult privately with their attorneys in the institution at reasonable times.[302] Although visual surveillance of a

---

296. *Brabson v. Wilkins*, 19 N.Y.2d 433, 227 N.E. 2d 204, 280 N.Y.S.2d 561 (1967); *Lee v. Tahash*, 352 F.2d 970, 974 (8th Cir. 1965). Cf. *McDonough v. Director of Patuxent*, 429 F.2d 1189 (4th Cir. 1970) (obtaining of psychiatric, financial and legal assistance for court hearing to redetermine finding of defective delinquency).
In *Rhinehart v. Rhay*, 314 F. Supp. 81, 82–83 (W.D. Wash. 1970), prison authorities were permitted to withhold letters to an inmate's attorney because they referred to "boundless" acts of "oral sodomy" among the prison population and thus violated prison regulations against letters containing vulgar or obscene matter or complaining about prison policies.
297. *Sostre v. McGinnis*, 442 F.2d 178 (2d Cir. 1971) (en banc).
298. *Sostre v. Rockefeller*, 312 F. Supp. 863 (S.D.N.Y. 1970).
299. See also *Wright v. McMann*, 321 F. Supp. 127, 142 (N.D.N.Y. 1970); *Freeley v. McGrath*, 314 F. Supp. 679 (S.D.N.Y. 1970).
300. *Cox v. Crouse*, 376 F.2d 824 (10th Cir.), cert. denied, 389 U.S. 865 (1967); *Konigsberg v. Ciccone*, 285 F. Supp. 585, 597 (W.D. Mo. 1968); *Haas v. United States*, 344 F.2d 56, 67 (8th Cir. 1965).
Palmigiano v. Travisono, 317 F. Supp. 776 (D.R.I., 1970) (prison officials enjoined from inspecting correspondence between inmates and judges, clerks, attorneys, public officials, legislators and correction officials); *Freeley v. McGrath*, 314 F. Supp. 679 (S.D.N.Y. 1970) (censorship of mail to all New York attorneys enjoined); *People v. Wainwright*, 325 F. Supp. 402 (M.D. Fla. 1971) (censorship of mail to local attorneys enjoined).
301. *Smith v. Robbins*, 328 F. Supp. 162 (S.D. Me. 1971).
One commentator has questioned whether restrictions on what prisoners may tell their attorneys by mail but not by personal interview gives an unfair advantage to the prisoner with sufficient funds to pay his lawyer to visit him. Muraskin, "Censorship of Mail: The Prisoner's Right to Communicate by Mail with the Outside World," 48 *Prison Journal* 33, 37 (1968).
302. *Rhem v. McGrath*, 326 F. Supp. 681 (S.D.N.Y. 1971). *In re* Allison, 425 P.2d 193, 57 *California Reporter* 593 (Sup. Ct.), cert. denied, 389 U.S. 876 (1967).

prisoner's interview with his attorney is permitted,[303] electronic eaves-dropping is not; obviously a criminal defendant cannot be properly represented by counsel unless he can be assured of confidentiality.[304]

Although indigent defendants are entitled to appointed counsel at their trial and appeal, the appointment of lawyers to represent prisoners seeking post-conviction relief in federal court from their conviction or sentence or from some aspect of confinement is left to the discretion of the court.[305] To convince a court that his case warrants appointed counsel, an inmate must prepare and submit his own petition. Although some states provide counsel for indigent prisoners attacking their convictions,[306] most do not. For inmates attacking prison conditions through civil suits, the appointment of counsel is rare;[307] for those confronted by private legal problems such as divorce or Social Security claims, it is virtually nonexistent. Despite the fact that many prisoners are totally or functionally illiterate and incarceration prevents their seeking evidence and witnesses, prisoners generally must represent themselves.

Prisoner self-representation results in much wasted time by the inmates, an overburdening of the courts by a flood of irrelevant, untimely and inaccurate petitions and a feeling of frustration and hostility on the part of prisoners, who often "become convinced that their claims are being denied, not because they are without merit but because they are uneducated laymen who do not know the tricks of litigation."[308]

Under these conditions, frivolous claims may be heard while many

303. *Konigsberg v. Ciccone*, 285 F. Supp. 585, 596–97 (W.D. Mo. 1968).
304. The defendant need not show that the information actually was transmitted to the prosecutor. *State v. Cory*, 62 Wash.2d 371, 382 P.2d 1019 (1963). *Cf. Lanza v. New York*, 370 U.S. 139 (1962). See Annot., 5 A.L.R.3d 1360, 1375–79 (1966).
305. *E.g.*, United States *ex rel. Manning v. Brierley*, 392 F.2d 197 (3d Cir.), *cert. denied*, 393 U.S. 882 (1968); *Barker v. Ohio*, 330 F.2d 594 (6th Cir. 1964). See *Aubut v. State of Maine*, 431 F.2d 688 (1st Cir. 1970) (court will not appoint counsel for a prisoner who is unable to show in his petition a reasonable probability of error).
306. *See* Ill. Rev. Stat., ch. 38, §122–24 (1961); Ore. Rev. Stat. §138.590 (1964); *Honore v. Washington State Board of Prison Terms and Parole*, 466 P.2d 485 (Wash., 1970) (equal protection requires appointment of counsel for indigent petitioner's hearing or appeal where petition in good faith raises significant issues which are neither frivolous nor repetitive and require professional legal assistance to be presented and considered fairly). *People v. Shipman*, 62 Cal. 2d 226, 397 P.2d 993, 42 *California Reporter* 1 (1965) (counsel appointed after petitioner makes out *prima facie* case).
307. *See* United States *ex rel. Gardner v. Madden*, 352 F.2d 792, 794 (9th Cir. 1965); *Smart v. Heinze*, 347 F.2d 114, 116 (9th Cir.), *cert. denied*, 382 U.S. 896 (1965). *Weller v. Dickson*, 314 F.2d 598, 601, 604 (9th Cir. 1963), *cert. denied*, 383 U.S. 953 (1966); *Roberts v. Pepersack*, 256 F. Supp. 415, 435–37 (D. Md. 1966), *cert. denied*, 389 U.S. 877 (1967); *Temple v. Pergament*, 235 F. Supp. 242, 243 (D.N.J. 1964); *Jefferson v. Heinze*, 201 F. Supp. 606, 607 (N.D. Cal. 1962).
308. Cherry, "A Look at Prisoner Self-Representation," 48 *Prison Journal* 30 (1968).

meritorious claims never receive proper consideration.[309] Courts are unrealistic in relying on such hollow moralisms as: prisoners need not know the law to file a petition; they need only supply "a short, simple and intelligible statement" of the facts that entitle them to relief;[310] and inmates have no right to aid in finding legal loopholes in presumptively valid judgments.[311] Experienced, practicing attorneys recognize the difficulty of engineering the complicated and often elusive routes of the law, distinguishing between law and fact and separating the essential facts from the irrelevant.[312] Efforts to circumvent the need for real counsel by instructing convicts in the law or providing forms for *habeas corpus* petitions[313] have done little to solve the problem. These inadequate substitute procedures, avoidable only by the more affluent convict, may well violate the equal-protection clause of the Fourteenth Amendment.

Due to the large number of illiterate and poorly educated prisoners without adequate counsel, many inmates ask other, more sophisticated prisoners to do their legal work. These "jailhouse lawyers" may cause problems of prison discipline and generally provide their "clients" with inferior representation and false hopes of success while they flood the courts with spurious claims. Consequently, prison regulations uniformly forbade prisoners to assist or receive assistance from other inmates in the preparation of legal documents.

In *Johnson v. Avery*,[314] when a Tennessee prisoner was transferred to a maximum-security cell as punishment for writing writs for other

309. For example, in *Ford v. Board of Managers*, 407 F.2d 937, 940 (3d Cir. 1969), the court denied relief for the reason that the conditions of solitary confinement of which prisoners complained were not as barbaric as those held unconstitutional in *Wright v. McMann*, 387 F.2d 519 (2d Cir. 1967), and *Jordan v. Fitzharris*, 257 F. Supp. 674 (N.D. Cal. 1966). In the latter cases, however, the courts were impelled to order relief by briefs and even photographs, submitted by appointed counsel. In *Ford*, the court had not appointed an attorney to detail the challenged conditions.
310. *Johnson v. Avery*, 252 F. Supp. 783, 787 (M.D. Tenn. 1966) (dictum), *rev'd*, 382 F.2d 353 (1967), *rev'd and remanded*, 393 U.S. 483 (1969).
311. *Cf. Lee v. Tahash*, 352 F.2d 970, 973–74 (8th Cir. 1965); *Hatfield v. Bailleaux*, 290 F.2d 632, 640–41 (9th Cir.), *cert. denied*, 368 U.S. 862 (1961); *Roberts v. Pepersack*, 256 F. Supp. 415, 433–34 (D. Md. 1966).
312. "[I]t is necessary to understand what one's rights are before it is possible to set out in a petition the facts which support them. . . ." *Johnson v. Avery*, 393 U.S. 483, 501 (1969) (dissent). See Krause, "A Lawyer Looks at Writ-Writing," 56 *California Law Review* 371, 374 (1968).
313. *See* Sokol, *A Handbook of Federal Habeas Corpus* 53–54, 192–200 (1965). The forms attempt to elicit short statements of the essential facts. However, they still include questions that call for legal knowledge, such as, "In what way were you deprived of due process of law?" Krause, "Writ-Writing," *supra* note 312, at 374 n.13. The form in use in Wisconsin directs the prisoner to "state concisely the grounds on which you base your allegation that you are being held in custody unlawfully." Note, "Legal Services for Prison Inmates," 1967 *Wisconsin Law Review* 514, 522.
314. 252 F. Supp. 783 (M.D. Tenn. 1966).

prisoners, a federal district court ordered his release. The court ruled that this prison regulation had the effect of barring illiterate prisoners from access to a federal writ of *habeas corpus,* and consequently was void. "For all practical purposes, if such prisoners cannot have the assistance of a 'jailhouse lawyer' their possibly valid constitutional claims will never be heard in any court." The court of appeals viewed the conduct in question as the unauthorized practice of law, and reversed.[315] The Supreme Court, in a rare entry into the field of correctional law, reversed the court of appeals and reinstated the district court's order.[316] Although the Court recognized the intramural administrative problems inherent in representation of some prisoners by others, it considered the federal right of access to court to be paramount. The Court held that as long as Tennessee provided no "reasonable alternative" to the assistance of other inmates, it could not outlaw the jailhouse lawyer.

The *Johnson* decision was followed by successful challenges to regulations barring jailhouse lawyers in several states.[317] In two instances, however, courts have ruled that the provision of legal services by law students, supervised by attorneys, satisfied the "reasonable alternative" requirement.[318]

In a concurring opinion to *Johnson v. Avery,*[319] Justice Douglas noted that there are presently insufficient legal-aid offices and public defenders to serve men in prison.[320] In a growing number of projects law students have provided legal assistance to inmates at various federal and state institutions. The response of prison officials to these programs has been encouraging. According to the legal counsel of the federal Bureau of Prisons:

---

315. 382 F.2d 353, 356–57 (6th Cir. 1967).
316. 393 U.S. 483 (1969).
317. *Beard v. Alabama Board of Corrections,* 413 F.2d 445 5th Cir., 1969); *Carothers v. Follette,* 314 F. Supp. 1014 (S.D.N.Y. 1970).
    In *Sostre v. McGinnis,* 442 F.2d 178 (2d Cir. 1971) (*en banc*) the court ruled that, although it could not prohibit legal assistance by prisoners, it could require a prisoner to apply to the warden for permission to help others. The California Supreme Court invalidated prison regulations providing that an inmate's briefs, petitions and other legal papers must remain in his possession. The court refused, however, to set aside regulations preventing jailhouse lawyers from corresponding with "clients" in other prisons, interviewing inmates in isolation or gaining access to their clients' disciplinary records. *In re Harrell,* 2 Cal. 3d 675, 420 P.2d 640, 87 *California Reporter* 504 (1970).
318. *Novak v. Beto,* 320 F. Supp. 1206 (S.D. Tex., 1970) (single attorney for 1,300 inmates, with promise of further effort to use law students); *Ramsey v. Ciccone,* 310 F. Supp. 600 (W.D. Mo. 1970); *Ayers v. Ciccone,* 303 F. Supp. 637 (W.D. Mo. 1969), *aff'd,* 431 F.2d 724 (8th Cir. 1970); *cf. Williams v. United States Department of Justice,* 433 F.2d 958 (5th Cir. 1970) (eighteen-month delay in rendering of legal aid by law students unreasonable).
319. 393 U.S. at 491.
320. *See also United States v. Simpson,* 436 F.2d 162, 166–67 (D.C. Cir. 1970).

The experience at Leavenworth [with law students from the University of Kansas] has shown that there have been very few attacks upon the administration; that prospective frivolous litigation has been screened out and that where the law school felt the prisoner has a good cause of action relief was granted in a great percentage of cases. A large part of the activity was disposing of long outstanding detainers lodged against the inmates. In addition, the program handled civil matters such as domestic relations problems and compensation claims. Even where there has been no tangible success, the fact that the inmate had someone on the outside to listen to him and analyze his problems had a most beneficial effect.[321]

In the past few years, public and private agencies have begun to furnish grants to law schools for the development of legal-aid programs for prisons and jails. Nonetheless, as Justice Douglas noted, these programs, "resting on a shifting law school population . . . often cannot meet the daily prison demands."[322] He suggested that laymen, both inside and outside of prison, be permitted to act as "next of friend" to prisoners in the preparation of legal documents.

Practical Requirements of Prisoner Self-Representation. At present, self-representation remains the only realistic way for most prisoners to get into court. And as long as prisoners are preparing legal documents, they will require an opportunity to prepare petitions and will need access to relevant legal materials. Yet despite this need for legal materials, prison libraries are grossly inadequate,[323] both in the number and type of law books owned and in the physical capacity to accommodate the large numbers of inmates who wish to use them.

Courts traditionally held that inmates have no right to engage in legal research and hence have refused to require prison officials to furnish prisoners with legal materials or to allow them to own their own law

321. Barkin, "Prison Policy," *supra* note 207, at 8–9.
322. *Johnson v. Avery,* 393 U.S. 483, 496 (concurring opinion).
323.   Like newly landed immigrants who do not speak the language, they must use law libraries to become conversant with law. Antiquated law books and insufficient time allocated for legal research ill prepare prisoners to handle their own cases. The ancient law books obstruct rather than assist them in their research. Without other legal reference sources, prisoners with no money must dig out decisions to use as citations. Unknown to them, many of the citations they collect have been overruled or modified by later decisions.
Larsen, "A Prisoner Looks at Writ-Writing," 56 *California Law Review* 353 (1968).

books.[324] Restrictions have been upheld on the amount of time a prisoner may spend in the prison library,[325] the number and type of books a prisoner may purchase himself,[326] the source from which books may be purchased (only directly from publishers),[327] and the use and storage of books in prisoners' cells.[328] The withholding of all legal materials from prisoners in disciplinary cells has been approved.[329]

In a few cases, however, judges have determined that these restrictions should be eliminated because they had the effect of hampering a prisoner's access to court.[330] Since these decisions are based on specific

324. *E.g., Lee v. Tahash*, 352 F.2d 970, 973–74 (8th Cir. 1965); *Siegel v. Ragen*, 180 F.2d 785 (7th Cir. 1950), *cert. denied*, 339 U.S. 990: "Obviously the right to practice law or to maintain a law department within the confines of a state penitentiary is not a right secured by the Constitution of the United States." *Id.* at 788; *Robinson v. Birzgalis*, 311 F. Supp. 908 (W.D. Mich. 1970). *Roberts v. Pepersack*, 256 F. Supp. 415, 434 (D. Md. 1966); *Johnson v. Avery*, 252 F. Supp. 783, 787 (M.D. Tenn. 1966); *aff'd*, 393 U.S. 483 (1969); *United States ex rel. Henson v. Myers*, 244 F. Supp. 826 (E.D. Pa. 1965); *Barber v. Page*, 239 F. Supp. 265 (E.D. Okla. 1965), *aff'd*, 390 U.S. 719 (1968); *Chessman v. Superior Court*, 44 Cal. 2d 1, 279 P.2d 24 (1955). *But see* American Correctional Association, *Manual of Correctional Standards* 268 (3d ed. 1968): "No impediments shall be imposed upon the rights of any prisoner to free access to books of law." U.S. Bureau of Prisons, Policy Statement 2001.1 (Jan. 21, 1966):

> It is the intent of the Bureau to afford inmates reasonable access to legal material, legal counsel and a reasonable opportunity to prepare their legal documents. . . . If the inmate has the financial means to purchase a lawbook, he shall be allowed to do so unless there is a compelling reason to the contrary.

The statement requires a minimal law library to be maintained in each institution. *See generally,* Cohen, "Reading Law in Prison," 48 *Prison Journal* 21 (1968).
325. *Hatfield v. Bailleaux*, 290 F.2d 632, 640–41 (9th Cir.), *cert. denied*, 368 U.S. 862 (1961).
326. *Walker v. Pate*, 356 F.2d 502 (7th Cir. 1966); *Hatfield v. Bailleaux*, 290 F.2d 632, 640 (9th Cir. 1961); *Grove v. Smyth*, 169 F. Supp. 852 (E.D. Va. 1958); *In re Harrell*, 2 Cal. 3d 675, 420 P.2d 640, 87 Cal. Rptr. 504, 518–19 (1970); *People v. Matthews*, 46 Misc. 2d 1024, 261 N.Y.S.2d 654 (1965).
327. *Lockhart v. Prasse*, 250 F. Supp. 529 (E.D. Pa. 1965); United States *ex rel. Wakely v. Pennsylvania*, 247 F. Supp. 7 (E.D. Pa. 1965).
328. *Carey v. Settle*, 351 F.2d 483 (8th Cir. 1965); United States *ex rel. Lee v. Illinois*, 343 F.2d 120 (7th Cir. 1965); *Hatfield v. Bailleaux*, 290 F.2d 623 (9th Cir. 1961); *Piccoli v. State Board of Trustees*, 87 F. Supp. 672 (D.N.H. 1949).
329. *Hatfield v. Bailleaux*, 290 F.2d 632, 637–38 (9th Cir. 1961) (no one kept in isolation for more than two weeks); *cf. Wright v. McMann*, 387 F2d 519 (2d Cir. 1967):

> [T]he withholding of all legal materials from Wright for the first few days of confinement in the "strip cell" may be reasonable . . . but withholding for 36 days materials such as the trial record that might be essential for the prosecution of a pending appeal seems dubious.

Id. at 527 n.17.
330. United States *ex rel. Mayberry v. Prasse*, 225 F. Supp. 752 (E.D. Pa. (1963) (use of Pennsylvania Rules of Procedure purchased at prison bookstore during pending litigation); *Bailleaux v. Holmes*, 177 F. Supp. 361 (D. Ore. 1959), *rev'd sub nom., Hatfield v. Bailleaux*, 290 F.2d 632 (9th Cir.) *cert. denied*, 368 U.S. 862 (1961) (use of legal materials in cells, purchase of law books, confiscation of legal documents found outside library); *In re* Schoengarth, 57 *California Reporter* 600, 425 P.2d 200 (Sup. Ct. 1967) (use of materials in cells); *People v. Superior Court*, 273 P.2d 936 (Cal. Dist. Ct. App. 1954), *rev'd sub nom. In re* Chessman, 44 Cal. 2d 1, 279 P.2d 24 (1955) (access to law library). For a discussion of *Bailleaux v. Holmes, see* Cohen 70–72.

factual determinations, they could be overruled by a contrary finding that a prisoner in fact had "reasonable" access.[331] Even those decisions not reversed on appeal could be limited to their "peculiar" facts.[332]

The Supreme Court's opinion in *Johnson v. Avery*,[333] which evidenced concern for the practical implications of indigency and lack of education and sophistication on the right of access to courts, indirectly affected the rationales concerning legal materials and the opportunity to prepare. In light of this landmark opinion, it became increasingly difficult to justify statements such as these, from two previous federal decisions:

> Prison regulations are not required to provide prisoners with the time, the correspondence privileges, the materials or other facilities they desire for the special purpose of trying to find some way of making attack upon the presumptively valid judgments against them.[334]
>
> Prisons are not intended, nor should they be permitted, to serve the purpose of providing inmates with information about methods of securing release therefrom.[335]

Following the *Johnson* decision, a three-judge federal court invalidated a California regulation limiting the law books in state prison libraries to a prescribed list. Despite the state's asserted need for economy and standardization, the court found that the effect of the regulation

---

331. See, e.g., *Argentine v. McGinnis*, 311 F. Supp. 135 (S.D.N.Y. 1969). In *Bailleux v. Holmes*, 177 F. Supp. 361 (D. Ore. 1959), rev'd sub nom., 290 F.2d 632 (9th Cir. 1901), the district court ruled that:

> Plaintiffs need more time than they are presently afforded to prepare their legal matters adequately. With no legal training, many are forced to represent themselves under conditions which an experienced attorney would find intolerable.

Id. at 363. The court of appeals, however, ruled that since four of the petitioners had instituted legal actions since becoming prisoners, they in fact had access to court:

> If the purpose [of restrictive regulations] was not to hamper inmates . . . gaining . . . access to the courts with regard to their respective criminal matters, and if the regulations and practices do not interfere with such reasonable access, . . . [t]he fact . . . that access could have been further facilitated without impairing effective prison administration is likewise immaterial.

290 F.2d at 640. See Note, "Beyond the Ken of the Courts," at 556.
332. See *Roberts v. Pepersack*, 256 F. Supp. 415, 435 (D. Md. 1966); United States ex rel. *Wakeley v. Pennsylvania*, 247 F. Supp. 7 (E.D. Pa. 1965), which refused to follow United States ex rel. *Mayberry v. Prasse*, 225 F. Supp. 752 (E.D. Pa. 1963).
333. 393 U.S. 483 (1969).
334. *Lee v. Tahash*, 352 F.2d 970, 973 (8th Cir. 1965).
335. *Roberts v. Pepersack*, 356 F. Supp. 415, 433 (D. Md. 1966); cf. American Bar Association Project on Minimum Standards for Criminal Justice, Standards Relating to Post-Conviction Remedies §3.1 (approved draft, 1968).

was to deny prisoners access to court and perhaps to deny equal protection to the indigent. (Affluent prisoners were permitted to consult with private counsel and purchase personal law books.) The court recognized that "the wording of the statute and the wishes of the scholars notwithstanding, . . . more than simple 'facts' are needed in order to file an adequate petition for relief by way of *habeas corpus* . . . 'Access to the courts' . . . encompasses all the means a defendant or petitioner might require to get a fair hearing from the judiciary on all charges brought against him or grievances alleged by him."[336] On November 8, 1971, the Supreme Court unanimously affirmed.

Despite recent evidence of judicial concern for access to court, the most frequently cited reason for denying relief in these cases—one not likely to disappear while the present mentality of correctional law prevails—is that the prisoner whose claim is at issue obviously has gained access to court even if his route has been slow and difficult: "[T]he fact that he was able to bring this action makes it highly improbable that he was prevented from filing his petition. . . . It is true, that in the past, certain prisoners were prevented from filing such petitions, but that situation has been remedied."[337]

In one California case,[338] the state supreme court reversed a lower-court order giving a notorious prisoner the right to send letters to court, engage in legal research and consult with his counsel, because at the time of his hearing it did not appear that he was being deprived presently of these rights. A dissenting opinion noted:

> Judicial protection of the rights of a prisoner would indeed be a mockery if the courts would always accept the pious protestations of the prison authorities that the rights would be accorded and then blithely disregard them the next day, leaving the prisoner to commence again his weary journey through the court process toward a chimerical goal.

The situation of the prisoners who get to court but are denied relief is not as pathetic as that of prisoners who are never heard from at all.

336. *Gilmore v. Lynch,* 319 F. Supp. 105, 110 (N.D. Calif. 1970), *aff'd sub nom. Younger v. Gilmore,* 404 U.S. 15 (1971) (*per curiam*).
337. *Siegel v. Ragen,* 88 F. Supp. 996, 1000 (N.D. Ill. 1949), *aff'd,* 180 F.2d 785 (7th Cir.), *cert. denied,* 339 U.S. 990 (1950). *See also Hatfield v. Bailleaux,* 290 F.2d 632 (9th Cir.), *cert. denied,* 368 U.S. 862 (1961); *Roberts v. Pepersack,* 256 F. Supp. 415, 434 (D. Md. 1966); Note, "Constitutional Rights of Prisoners," *supra* note 14, at 990–91.
338. *In re* Chessman, 44 Cal. 2d 1, 279 P.2d 24 (1955).

Some prisoners, completely barred from the courts, never get an opportunity to raise their complaints in any forum. It is ironic if not suspicious that so many of the known complaints against prison conditions come from California, a state with a relatively progressive penal system, and so few from other states whose systems are notorious. It is less likely that these other prisoners are satisfied than that they are being denied adequate means to make their grievances public.

Remedies

The most obvious judicial power over the administration of correctional facilities, that of sentencing individual defendants, rarely has been used as a vehicle for reform.[339] In a District of Columbia case decided under the Federal Youth Correction Act,[340] however, a federal district judge held an "ancillary factfinding hearing in aid of sentencing" to question the recommendation of correctional authorities that a defendant, although amenable to youthful-offender treatment, be sentenced as an adult, since "meaningful treatment cannot be provided due to overcrowding and inadequate facilities." Stating that "the Court is entitled to have facilities provided sufficient to make the Act effective and the Court must insist that its sentencing orders are implemented . . ." the court ordered the director of the federal Bureau of Prisons and the Mayor-Commissioner of the District of Columbia to take immediate steps to make additional facilities available for Youth Act cases. The court based its exercise of supervisory power on its "inherent authority to direct action which is found essential to the continued effective functioning of the Federal Courts. . . . Unless adequate facilities are made available, the Court's role in sentencing becomes merely advisory and it loses the 'judicial power' to enforce its orders of commitment under the Act."[341]

It is unlikely that inmates can interject the issue of denial of their rights in prison into an appeal challenging their original convictions.[342]

339. *Cf.* State of West Virginia *ex rel. Pingley v. Coiner,* HC No. 70–181 (Cir. Ct. of Randolph County, May 6, 1971), *rev'd,* 186 S.E.2d 220 (W.Va. 1972).
340. 18 U.S.C. §§5005 *et seq.*
341. *United States v. Alsbrook,* 336 F. Supp. 973 (D.D.C. 1971).
342. In *State v. Williams,* 157 Conn. 114, 249 A.2d 245 (1968), the defendant was precluded from using his mistreatment in jail before trial as a basis for attacking the judgment of conviction. No case has been found in which a prisoner attempted to attack a conviction on the basis of mistreatment in prison after the conviction.

Some means must therefore be found to raise the issue in a separate proceeding. In moving away from judicial abstention, courts have fashioned several devices, each with its own requirements,[343] which prisoners may use to remedy certain deprivations: civil suits for damages against prison officials or against the state or federal government; damage suits or injunctions against state officials under the federal Civil Rights Act; *mandamus* against correction officials; *habeas corpus*; criminal prosecutions against officials who act illegally; contempt for failure to obey court orders to keep prisoners safe; and class actions.

Civil Suits Against Officials

The traditional and most widely accepted technique for recovering for injury due to the negligence of prison officials has been a tort suit for damages.[344] Most of these cases have involved a failure to provide minimal food, clothing, shelter, medical care or protection from physical assault. To this genre of cases, courts generally have applied the usual standard of civil liability for negligence—requiring that prison officials exercise due care to ensure the safety of prisoners in their custody.

> A sheriff owes to a prisoner placed in his custody a duty to keep the prisoner safe and free from harm, to render him medical aid when necessary, and to treat him humanely and to refrain from oppressing him.[345]

343. Courts have said that if an unrepresented prisoner seeks an inappropriate type of relief, they will interpret his complaint as asking for whatever relief is warranted by the facts of his case. *Richey v. Wilkins*, 335 F.2d 1 (2d Cir. 1964); *Kregger v. Posner*, 248 F. Supp. 804, 806 (E.D. Mich. 1966); *Roberts v. Pepersack*, 256 F. Supp. 415, 420–21 (D. Md. 1966); *Beckett v. Kearney*, 247 F. Supp. 219 (N.D. Ga. 1965); United States *ex rel. Henson v. Myers*, 244 F. Supp. 826 (E.D. Pa. 1965). *But see Bennett v. California*, 406 F.2d 36, 39 (9th Cir. 1969).

344. *See, e.g., Hill v. Gentry*, 280 F.2d 88 (8th Cir. 1958), cert. denied, 364 U.S. 875 (1960); *Asher v. Cabell*, 50 F. 818, 827 (5th Cir. 1892); Indiana *ex rel. Tyler v. Gobin*, 94 F. 48 (D. Ind. 1899); *Magenheimer v. State ex rel.* Dalton, 120 Ind. App. 128, 90 N.E.2d 813 (1950); *Smith v. Miller*, 241 Iowa 625, 40 N.W.2d 597 (1950); *Topeka v. Boutwell*, 53 Kansas 20, 35 P. 819 (1894); *Ratliff v. Stanley*, 244 Ky. 819, 821–22, 7 S.W.2d 230, 231–32 (1928); *O'Dell v. Goodsell*, 149 Neb. 261, 30 N.W.2d 906 (1948); *Hixon v. Cupp*, 5 Okla. 545, 49 P. 927 (1897); Annot. 14 A.L.R.2d 353 (1950).

345. *Thomas v. Williams*, 105 Ga. App. 321, 326, 124 S.E.2d 409, 413 (1962); *Kendrick v. Adamson*, 51 Ga. App. 402, 403, 180 S.E. 647, 648 (1935). *See also Ex parte* Jenkins, 25 Ind. App. 532, 58 N.E. 560 (1906); *Farmer v. State ex rel.* Russell, 224 Miss. 96, 79 So. 2d 528 (1955); State *ex rel. Morris v. National Surety Co.*, 162 Tenn. 547, 39 S.W.2d 581 (1931); *Kusah v. McCorkle*, 100 Wash. 318, 170 P. 1023 (1918). In an Oklahoma case a jury found a sheriff negligent for failing to isolate an inmate's smallpox-ridden cellmate, as a consequence of which the sick prisoner's roommate contracted the disease and died. The court allowed the inmate's wife to recover from the sheriff in a wrongful-death action. *Hunt v. Rowton*, 143 Okla. 181, 288 P. 342 (1930).

Where statutes impose a duty of care upon prison officials, that duty may be interpreted by the courts as giving prisoners a civil cause of action against officials for non-compliance. For example, a New York court found the failure of a warden and a prison physician to provide an injured prisoner with medical care to constitute "the neglect of a duty imposed by law."[346] Similarly a West Virginia court held that the administratrix of a deceased prisoner, who alleged that the prisoner's death was attributable to the failure of his jailer to furnish medical care, had stated a *prima facie* case under a statute providing that "when any prisoner is sick the jailer shall see that he has adequate medical attention and nursing."[347] A Kentucky court interpreted a statute requiring jailers to "treat prisoners with humanity, and furnish them with proper food and lodging during their confinement," to impose liability where a jailer knew of the predatory activities of an inmate "kangaroo court" and failed to protect a prisoner from them.[348] In three states, however, courts have refused to find prison officials liable for failing to exercise due care in discharging their duties. In Maryland and Massachusetts the "hands-off" attitude of the courts precluded prisoners' tort suits against negligent officials without a showing of malice or an intent to cause the prisoner bodily harm.[349]

> It is inconsistent with the purpose for which prisons are established, and with the discipline which must be maintained over prisoners, that the officers should be responsible to the prisoners, in private actions, for mere negligence in the performance of their duties.[350]

In Illinois the court of appeals ingeniously construed a statute requiring each jailer to "furnish necessary . . . medical aid for all prisoners under his charge"[351] as creating a quasi-judicial rather than a ministerial duty.[352] Consequently, the court imposed no liability for a jailer's "mere negligent omission" to provide adequate medical care.[353] In addition, the

346. *McCrossen v. State*, 277 App. Div. 1160, 101 N.Y.2d 591, 592 (Sup. Ct.), *appeal denied*, 302 N.Y. 950, 98 N.E.2d 117 (1950). The court noted a statutory duty to "protect and preserve the health of inmates." New York Correctional Law, §46 (McKinney 1968).
347. *Smith v. Slack*, 125 W. Va. 812, 26 S.E.2d 387 (1943).
348. *Ratliff v. Stanley*, 224 Ky. 819, 7 S.W.2d 230 (1928).
349. *O'Hare v. Jones*, 161 Mass. 391, 37 N.E. 371 (1894); *Carder v. Steiner*, 225 Md. 271, 170 A.2d 220 (1961). *See also* State *ex rel. Clark v. Ferling*, 220 Md. 109, 151 A.2d 137 (1959); *Williams v. Adams*, 85 Mass. (3 Allen) 171 (1861).
350. *O'Hare v. Jones*, 161 Mass. 391, 392–93, 37 N.E. 371, 372 (1894).
351. Ill. Rev. Stat. ch. 75, §19 (1961).
352. *Bush v. Babb*, 23 Ill. App. 2d 285, 162 N.E.2d 594 (1959).
353. 23 Ill. App. 2d at 288, 162 N.E.2d at 597.

court noted that any duty imposed was owed to the public and not to individual prisoners; thus a violation could result only in a statutory penalty, not in civil liability.

Even though the majority of states allow damage actions against negligent prison employees, tort suits often are unsatisfactory remedies for prison abuses. One commentator has noted the extreme difficulties in proving an inmate's cause to the satisfaction of a jury:

> One cannot read a juror's mind; but certainly the fact that the plaintiff is a convicted criminal will adversely affect the weight given to his testimony. Getting one's witnesses to testify is also a problem, for where the alleged tortious acts were witnessed by fellow inmates, they may be unwilling to come forward for fear of incurring disfavor with the prison staff.[354]

More fatal than the difficulties of proof are some states' restrictions preventing prisoners from bringing civil suits as long as they remain in prison. Although a prisoner may be sued and a judgment enforced against him,[355] courts in states where the legislatures have suspended convicts' civil rights during imprisonment have interpreted these statutes as precluding the right to file any complaints except those challenging an original conviction.[356] The inability to file civil suits applies to private claims that accrued before the inmate was imprisoned, as well as to claims for damages arising during the prison term. In response to this obstruction, over half the states have statutes making imprisonment a disability which tolls the statute of limitations.[357] In California, for example, the statute of limitations on a prisoner's claim is extended until six months after his civil rights have been reinstated.[358]

Thus most civil suits by prisoners in state courts are brought after the period of confinement which may be years after the alleged tort oc-

354. Sneidman, "Prisoners and Medical Treatment," 4 *Criminal Law Bulletin* 459 (1968).
355. Twelve states have statutory provisions for serving prisoners with civil complaints: Alabama, Arizona, Maine, Massachusetts, Michigan, Mississippi, Nevada and Tennessee; California, Idaho, Montana and Utah provide for service in county prisons. Rubin, *The Law of Criminal Correction* 615 n.25 (1963).
356. See *Wright v. McMann*, 387 F.2d 519, 523 (2d Cir. 1967). See also *McCollum v. Mayfield*, 130 F. Supp. 112, 116 (N.D. Cal. 1955) (construing statute in the absence of any decisions by the California Supreme Court); Rubin, *The Law of Criminal Correction* 615 (1963); Note, "California Public Entity Immunity from Tort Claims by Prisoners," 19 *Hastings Law Review* 573, 573–74 (1968).
357. Rubin, *The Law of Criminal Correction* 615 n.26 (1963).
358. Cal. Gov't Code §945.6(b) (West 1966). In order to be entitled to the additional time to sue, however, a convict must have taken certain prescribed steps within the usual period of the statute of limitations. §§900–935.6.

curred.[359] In addition to the burdens of proof already mentioned, the plaintiff must further overcome the inevitable practical problems of stale evidence, imperfect memories and unavailable witnesses. This later problem may be particularly acute where it is necessary to use inmate witnesses who have since been released. Consequently, the mere tolling of the statute of limitations does not prevent all prejudice to the convicts rights[360] and civil actions remain ineffective remedies for prisoner-plaintiffs.

CIVIL SUITS AGAINST FEDERAL, STATE AND LOCAL GOVERNMENTS

Another problem faced by a prisoner with a cause of action against a prison employee is the financial inability of most lower-level custodial employees to pay significant money judgments rendered against them. Ordinarily a plaintiff would benefit from the rule of *respondeat superior,* which requires an employer to assume liability for injuries inflicted by his employees in the scope of their employment. Where a government—in this case a federal or local correction institution—is the employer, however, use of this doctrine falls victim to the more venerable, however questionable, doctrine of sovereign immunity which dictates that a sovereign generally may not be sued without its consent.

In the past few years the federal government,[361] the District of Columbia[362] and over one-third of the states[363] have abrogated to some extent this rule of immunity by means of statutory amendment or judi-

359. Prisoners with life sentences may be entirely precluded from suing. *See McCollum v. Mayfield,* 130 F. Supp. 112, 116 (N.D. Cal. 1955).
360. *But see Tabor v. Hardwick,* 224 F.2d 526, 529 (5th Cir. 1955).
361. Federal Tort Claims Act, 28 U.S.C. §1346(b) (1964).
362. *See Spencer v. General Hospital,* 425 F.2d 479 (D.C. Cir. 1969) (*rehearing en banc*); *Carter v. Carlson,* 447 F.2d 358 (D.C. Cir. 1971), *cert. granted sub nom. District of Columbia v. Carter,* 40 *U.S. Law Week* 3314 (U.S., Jan. 2, 1972) (District may be sued for injuries intentionally inflicted by its agents in the discharge of non-discretionary activities); *Baker v. Washington,* 448 F.2d 1200 (D.C. Cir. 1971) (defense of sovereign immunity rejected in claim for damages for a beating of a prisoner by guards).
363. *See, e.g., Stone v. Arizona Highway Commission,* 93 Ariz. 384, 381 P.2d 107 (1963); *Muskopf v. Corning Hospital District,* 55 Cal. 2d 211, 359 P.2d 457, 11 Cal. Rptr. 89 (1961); *Hargrove v. Cocoa Beach,* 96 So. 2d 130 (Fla. 1957); *Molitor v. Kaneland Community Unit District No. 302,* 18 Ill. 2d 11, 163 N.E.2d 89 (1959); *Haney v. City of Lexington,* 386 S.W.2d 783 (Ky. 1964); *Williams v. City of Detroit,* 364 Mich. 231, 111 N.W.2d 1 (1961); *Spanel v. Mounds View School District No. 621,* 264 Minn. 279, 118 N.W.2d 795 (1962); *Rice v. Clark County,* 79 Nev. 253, 382 P.2d 605 (1963); *McAndrew v. Mularchuk,* 33 N.J. 172, 162 A.2d 820 (1960); *Kelso v. City of Tacoma,* 63 Wash. 2d 913, 390 P.2d 2 (1964) (abrogation partly based on statute); *Holytz v. City of Milwaukee,* 17 Wis. 2d 26, 115 N.W.2d 618 (1962).

cial decision.[364] Even where new statutes grant a specific right to sue for money damages, however, prisoners have encountered problems in enjoying the statute's apparent protection. For example, despite the fact that the Federal Tort Claims Act does not specifically exclude prisoners from the act's waiver of immunity, federal courts consistently found that the benefits of the act did not extend to prisoners.[365] The rationale derived from the previously mentioned "hands-off" policy: suits by prisoners against the United States would have a detrimental effect on prison discipline and would involve the judiciary in the unwanted task of administering the federal penal system. Congress could not have intended such an "extreme" result.[366]

The Supreme Court first faced the question of whether the Federal Tort Claims Act applies to prisoners in 1963 in *United States v. Muniz*.[367] Noting that prisoners were not specifically excluded from the protections of the act, the Court refused to create judicial exceptions and held that prisoners may recover damages from the United States Government for personal injuries sustained in federal prison due to the negligence of prison employees. The court of appeals for the District of Columbia recently went beyond *Muniz* and ruled that a federal prisoner, injured while being held by local authorities in a local jail, may sue the United States for damages under the Federal Tort Claims Act.[368]

364. *See* Van Alstyne, "Governmental Tort Liability: A Decade of Change," 1966 *University of Illinois Law Forum* 919; Morris, "The Disappearing Doctrine of Governmental Immunity from Tort Liability," 26 *Georgia Bar Journal* 435 (1964).
365. Citations to prior cases are collected in Judge Kaufman's dissent to *Winston v. United States*, 305 F.2d 253, 258 (2d Cir. 1962), *aff'd*, 374 U.S. 150 (1963).
366. *Sigmon v. United States*, 110 F. Supp. 906 (W.D. Va. 1953). *But see United States v. Muniz*, 374 U.S. 150 (1963) (Government's "hands-off" argument rejected). In California, the sovereign-immunity doctrine as applied to local governments was overturned by judicial decision in 1961. *Muskopf v. Corning Hospital District*, 55 Cal. 2d 211, 359 P.2d 457, 11 *California Reporter* 89 (1961); *Lipman v. Brisbane Elementary School District*, 55 Cal. 2d 224, 359 P.2d 465, 11 *California Reporter* 97 (1961). When the state legislature responded by passing the California Tort Claims Act, Cal. Gov't Code §§810–996.6 (West 1966), and explicitly granted public entities immunity from liability for injuries to prisoners, *id.* §844.6, the state courts found so many ways to avoid that interpretation that the law surrounding prisoners' claims was thrown into confusion. *See Garcia v. State*, 247 Cal. App.2d 7, 56 *California Reporter* 80 (1967) (widow and child may recover for wrongful death of prisoner killed by collapse of negligently maintained weight-suspension rack); *Sanders v. County of Yuba*, 247 Cal. App.2d 748, 55 *California Reporter* 852 (1967) (prisoner may recover under another section of the statute for negligent failure of prison authorities to provide medical care); Note, "California Public Entity Immunity from Tort Claims by Prisoners," 19 *Hastings Law Review* 573 (1968).
367. 374 U.S. 150 (1963).
368. *Close v. United States*, 397 F.2d 686, 687 (D.C. Cir. 1968).

> Since the Congress has clearly committed the custody and safekeeping of federal prisoners upon conviction to the Attorney General, then it must be true that in this instance the . . . jailer was serving as the Attorney General's jailer; and it must also be true . . . that . . . the Attorney General had some degree of power, commensurate with his continuing responsibility, to supervise the jailer in his handling of this particular prisoner.

Yet the Federal Tort Claims Act may not be used in all cases of negligently caused injuries to federal prisoners. Three years after *Muniz,* the Supreme Court ruled that a 1934 statute enacted twelve years before the Tort Claims Act, authorizing payment of compensation to inmates for prison work-related injuries by the Federal Prison Industries, Inc.,[369] precluded suit under the Tort Claims Act where the injuries were covered by the compensation statute.[370] The Court determined that statutes passed for the purpose of providing compensation administratively for injured workmen almost always have been construed as substitutes for, not supplements to, common-law tort actions. The dissenting opinion by Justices White and Douglas pointed out, however, that the statutory remedy for injured prisoners was neither as certain nor as comprehensive as the compensation laws that generally are construed as exclusive remedies. This statutory scheme permitted but did not require compensation, and the amount of the award was entirely within the discretion of the Attorney General, provided it did not exceed the amount that would have been payable under the Federal Employees' Compensation Act. In addition, an injured prisoner received no compensation until released from prison and none then if he has recovered. If he died in prison, his survivors received nothing. Finally, even when compensation was awarded, it did not become a vested right, and payments could be suspended immediately if the claimant was convicted of another crime. According to the court of appeals, whose decision was reversed by the Supreme Court, "[w]hat emerges on examination . . . is a severely restrictive system of compensation permeated at all levels by the very prison control and dominion which was at the origin of the inmate's injury."[371]

The erosion of the federal law of sovereign immunity in prisoners' cases is salutary and has resulted in the compensation of injured prisoners in some cases. It must be remembered, however, that federal prisoners comprise less than 10 percent of the prison population and generally are confined under better conditions than their state counterparts. The development of remedies that benefit only the inmates of federal institutions leaves the major part of the problem untouched.

Even where federal or state prisoners have been allowed to bring a tort claim against a government entity, they must contend with yet an-

---

369. 18 U.S.C. §4126 (1964). The coverage of the act was expanded in 1961 to include not only injuries suffered in "any industry" but also in "any work activity in connection with the maintenance or operation of the institution where confined." *Id.*
370. *United States v. Demko,* 385 U.S. 149 (1966).
371. 350 F.2d 698, 701 (3d Cir.), *rev'd,* 385 U.S. 149 (1966).

other obstacle. Intentional torts, such as assault or battery, may not be included in the statutory abrogation of immunity.[372] And, even more damaging to claims by prisoners, the statutes almost always except actions by officials that are based on a statute or an administrative regulation or that involve an official's exercise of discretion.[373] In cases where the defense of sovereign immunity is raised, officials can be expected to claim that the act in question was discretionary and that to hold them responsible would unfairly hamper and second-guess them in their important work.

The distinction between governmental acts that are discretionary and those that are "ministerial" has not been drawn with precision. It is clear that a parole board's decision on whether to release an inmate before the expiration of his maximum sentence is discretionary.[374] Beyond this, however, there is little agreement. As one court recognized: "It would be difficult to conceive of any official act, no matter how directly ministerial, that did not admit of some discretion in the manner of its performance, even if it involved only the driving of a nail."[375]

It has been argued that the considerations of risk allocation and moral responsibility favoring the abrogation of sovereign immunity in prisoners' suits support a narrow construction of the exception for discretionary acts. Accordingly, in *United States v. Muniz*,[376] the Supreme Court refused to dismiss two prisoners' complaints, one alleging that a prison doctor had failed to diagnose a tumor and the other claiming that a prison guard had locked the plaintiff in a dormitory with twelve other inmates who the guard knew were trying to attack him.

In a recent opinion involving a medical malpractice suit against a public hospital, two federal judges distinguished between the discretionary formulation of policy and its ministerial execution:

372. *E.g.,* Federal Tort Claims Act, 28 U.S.C. §2680(h) (1964) (exemptions to liability): "Any claim arising out of assault, battery, false imprisonment, false arrest, malicious prosecution, abuse of process, libel, slander, misrepresentation, deceit, or interference with contract right." *Ibid.*
373. *E.g., id.* §2680(a):

Any claim based upon an act or omission of an employee of the Government, exercising due care, in the execution of a statute or regulation, whether or not such statute or regulation be valid, or based upon the exercise or performance or the failure to exercise or perform a discretionary function or duty on the part of a federal agency or an employee of the Government, whether or not the discretion involved be abused.

374. *Bennet v. California,* 406 F.2d 36 (9th Cir. 1969); *Silver v. Dickson,* 403 F.2d 642 (9th Cir. 1968).
375. *Ham v. Los Angeles County,* 46 Cal. App. 148, 162, 189 P. 462, 468 (1920).
376. 374 U.S. 150 (1963).

Where the injury proximately resulted from a deliberate choice in the formulation of official policy, characterized by a high "degree of discretion and judgment involved in the particular governmental act," immunity would remain. To inquire into such decisions in a tort suit might "jeopardiz[e] the quality and efficiency of government itself," and endanger the creative exercise of political discretion and judgment through "the inhibiting influence of potential legal liability asserted with the advantage of hindsight." On the other hand, where the injury was inflicted by negligent official acts or omissions other than in the formulation of public policy—"ministerial acts"—liability could be asserted.[377]

The judges went on to say that where the discretion involved in a case is medical, rather than governmental, the private law of malpractice could be relied on to determine the question of liability. The degree of discretion given officials in the performance of their duties would then be merely one consideration in determining the issue of "reasonable care."

Some of this analysis is inapplicable to prisons which have no private counterparts. It would be difficult, however, to assert that the decisions of a prison guard are intricately bound up with "the formulation of public policy" and therefore demanding of immunity.[378] This ministerial-discretionary dichotomy has finally been brought into focus in a District of Columbia case.[379] Complainant, an epileptic, alleged that she was denied her medicine while in a punishment cell. The District of Columbia denied responsibility, claiming that the complaint referred to discretionary acts protected by the sovereign immunity doctrine. The plaintiff urged that providing her prescribed pill each evening, a medically required routine, was a simple ministerial act. The case was dismissed by the district court but remanded for trial by the court of appeals.[380] After a jury trial the plaintiff was awarded substantial damages.

The exceptions for official actions authorized by statute or adminis-

377. *Spencer v. General Hospital*, 425 F.2d 479, 488 (D.C. Cir. 1969) (Wright and Bazelon, J.J., concurring), *citing Elgin v. District of Columbia*, 337 F.2d 152, 154–55 (D.C. Cir. 1964).
378. Where private counterparts can be found, however, courts in states that have moved away from sovereign immunity have applied the standards of private negligence law. *E.g., Pisacano v. New York*, 8 App. Div. 2d 335, 340, 188 N.Y.S.2d 35, 40 (1959); "Prison physicians owe no less duty to prisoners who must accept their care, than do private physicians to their patients who are free to choose."
379. *Anthony v. District of Columbia*, No. 32,010 (D.C. Cir., Dec. 2, 1969) (remanded for reconsideration in light of *Spencer v. General Hospital*, 425 F.2d 479 (D.C. Cir. 1969)).
380. *Ibid.*

trative regulation were discussed in a recent Hawaii case involving the
beating of a prisoner by other inmates.[381] The prison rules prescribed
that an inmate whose safety was threatened be put in "Corridor C." After
threats were made against a prisoner, prison guards put him in Corridor C. Despite this precaution, the other inmates reached the prisoner
and injured him. Although Hawaii had waived sovereign immunity from
liability for the torts of state employees,[382] the statute made an exception
for

> any claim based upon an act or omission of any employee of the
> State, exercising due care, in the execution of a statute or regula-
> tion, whether such statute or regulation be valid, or based upon
> the exercise or performance or the failure to exercise or perform
> a discretionary function or duty on the part of a state officer or
> employee, whether or not the discretion involved be abused.

The court held that the adoption of internal prison rules was a discretionary function. In order to recover, the prisoner-plaintiff would have
to prove that the guards had failed to follow the pertinent regulations,
or that they had failed to use ordinary care in doing so.[383] The court rejected the contention that the Supreme Court's decision in *Muniz*, involving similar statutory language,[384] required a finding of liability in the
present case. The court agreed with the plaintiff's claim that the Hawaii
State Prison is antiquated and inadequate for the safety and security of
the inmates confined there and ascribed the basic fault to the legislature
for failing to appropriate funds for a modern prison. Nonetheless, the
court was not prepared to undertake the political problems of judicially
translating its factual findings into legal ones; it refused to hold the state
liable for having failed to provide a safe place in which to confine its
prisoners.

The Use of Civil Damage Suits

Two recent cases, both from states that have waived the sovereign-
immunity defense, indicate some potential in using civil damage suits to

381. *Upchurch v. State*, 51 Hawaii 150, 454 P.2d 112 (1969).
382. Hawaii Rev. Laws §245A-2 (Supp. 1965) renders the state liable "in the same
manner and to the same extent as a private individual under like circumstances."
383. 51 Hawaii at 152, 454 P.2d at 115.
384. *Muniz* involved the applicability of the Federal Tort Claims Act, 28 U.S.C.
§2680 (1964), to prisoners.

provide compensation to former prisoners or their families and to deter state employees from at least the most flagrant abuse of prisoners' rights. In Louisiana, the state was held liable for over $13,000 in damages to the parents of a boy who had died following a punishment by flogging administered by employees of a State Industrial School for Colored Youths.[385] Liability was based on a state statute which prescribed that "masters and employers are answerable for the damage occasioned by their servants and overseers, in the exercise of the functions in which they are employed."[386] The state claimed that since the Director of Institutions had not authorized prison employees to prescribe or administer corporal punishment, the employees were not acting within the scope of their employment. Although conceding that the announced policy of the Board of Institutions prohibited corporal punishment, the court concluded that the policy was rarely enforced and the severity of the flogging administered in this case was no greater than punishments normally inflicted on inmates for similar infractions. Consequently, the beating could be interpreted to have occurred within the scope of employment "inasmuch as the said employees were performing their assigned task of maintaining discipline in a manner inferentially if not expressly permitted and authorized, any alleged rules to the contrary notwithstanding."

Whitree v. New York[387] was less explicit. Committed as unfit to stand trial, a former inmate of a state mental institution had been kept in the "hospital" for eleven years more than the maximum term for which he could have been sentenced to prison had he been found guilty of the crime charged. Although Whitree did not question the validity of his original commitment, the court found that the length of his stay resulted from the failure of the state's doctors to examine him carefully and to treat any disorders that may have existed. The important dimension of the case for present considerations is that the court, in allowing recovery against the sovereign, applied the same law of medical malpractice it would have used in a case against a private hospital.

FEDERAL CIVIL RIGHTS ACT

The federal Civil Rights Act of 1871 provides a basis for redressing prisoners' grievances when state officers are involved:

385. *Lewis v. State,* 176 So. 2d 718 (La. App. 1965).
386. La. Civ. Code Ann. art. 2320 (West 1952).
387. 56 Misc.2d 693, 290 N.Y.S.2d 486 (Ct. Cl. 1968).

> Every person who, under color of any statute, ordinance, regula-
> tion, custom, or usage, of any State or Territory, subjects, or
> causes to be subjected, any citizen of the United States or other
> person within the jurisdiction thereof to the deprivation of any
> rights, privileges, or immunities secured by the Constitution or
> laws, shall be liable to the party injured in an action at law, suit
> in equity, or other proper proceeding for redress.[388]

For many years the general "hands-off" doctrine, aggravated by the federal courts' reluctance to inject themselves into state administrative problems,[389] prevented the Civil Rights Act from becoming an effective remedy for prisoners. A federal district court, as recently as 1960, determined
that the act must be construed

> so as to respect the proper balance between the States and the
> federal government in law enforcement. . . . The fact that a
> prisoner is assaulted, injured, or even murdered by state offi-
> cials does not necessarily mean that he is deprived of any right
> protected or secured by the Constitution or laws of the United
> states.[390]

Even courts that recognized the applicability of the act to claim by state
prisoners required an exhaustion of state remedies before suit could be
brought in federal court.[391]

In 1961, however, the Supreme Court revitalized the Civil Rights Act
in *Monroe v. Pape*.[392] Although that case did not involve the rights of
prison inmates, its far-reaching principles were later held to apply to prisoners,[393] thus creating a most significant judicial remedy for prison abuses.

388. 42 U.S.C. §1983 (1964). This post-Civil War legislation was originally enacted
to protect the newly freed American Negro. It has only recently been applied to protect the rights of citizens generally.
389. *See, e.g., Siegel v. Ragen,* 180 F.2d 785, 788 (7th Cir. 1950): "The Government of the United States is not concerned with, nor has it the power to control or
regulate the internal discipline of the penal institutions of its constituent states."
390. *Swanson v. McGuire,* 188 F. Supp. 112, 115–116 (N.D. Ill. 1960). *See also
Oregon ex rel. Sherwood v. Gladden,* 240 F.2d 910 (9th Cir. 1957); United States
ex rel. Atterbury v. Ragen, 237 F.2d 953 (7th Cir. 1956), *cert. denied,* 353 U.S. 964
(1957); *Wagner v. Ragen,* 213 F.2d 294 (7th Cir. 1954), *cert. denied,* 348 U.S. 846
(1954); United States *ex rel. Morris v. Radio Station WENR,* 209 F.2d 105 (7th
Cir. 1953); *Kelly v. Dowd,* 140 F.2d 81 (7th Cir.), *cert. denied,* 321 U.S. 783
(1944); *Nichols v. McGee,* 169 F. Supp. 721 (N.D. Cal.), *appeal dismissed,* 361
U.S. 6 (1959); *Curtis v. Jacques,* 130 F. Supp. 920 (W.D. Mich. 1954); *Piccoli v.
State Board of Trustees,* 87 F. Supp. 672 (D. N.H. 1949).
391. *E.g., Kelly v. Dowd,* 140 F.2d 81 (7th Cir.), *cert. denied,* 321 U.S. 783 (1944).
392. 365 U.S. 167 (1961).
393. *Cooper v. Pate,* 378 U.S. 546 (1964).

In *Monroe*, the Court reversed a lower court's dismissal of a suit under the Civil Rights Act against Chicago police officers for breaking into a family's home, searching it and detaining the father, with neither a search nor an arrest warrant. After reviewing the legislative history of the act, Justice Douglas, writing for the majority, concluded that the purpose of the Civil Rights Act was to provide a federal remedy for violations of constitutional rights by officials whom a state had clothed with authority.[394] Any claimed violation of petitioners' rights to due process or equal protection of the law, whether by recurrent or isolated abuse, would be sufficient to establish federal jurisdiction to consider the claim. The complaint of infringement need not have been authorized by state law and, in fact, may have been prohibited expressly by state statute or constitutional provision. Since the statute provides civil rather than criminal remedies, liability does not depend on the officers' having acted willfully; the statute should be construed "against the background of tort liability that makes a man responsible for the natural consequences of his actions."

Since one purpose of the act had been "to provide a federal remedy where the state remedy, though adequate in theory, was not available in practice," federal courts should have concurrent jurisdiction in cases brought under the act, without a requirement that state remedies be exhausted. Hence, in *Monroe*, the fact that the Illinois constitution barred unreasonable searches and seizures was no barrier to a federal suit under the Fourteenth Amendment.

In many federal courts, the *Monroe* decision largely undid the "hands-off" attitude toward state prisoners suing under the Civil Rights Act.[395] To a large degree these decisions have made federal court action the most direct route for resolution of state prisoners' grievances. In order to state a claim under the Civil Rights Act, however, a prisoner must allege that the state deprived him of a federal statutory right[396] or a con-

---

394. 365 U.S. at 180.
395. *E.g.*, *Jackson v. Bishop*, 404 F.2d 571 (8th Cir. 1968); *Wright v. McMann*, 387 F.2d 519 (2d Cir. 1967); *Smartt v. Avery*, 370 F.2d 788 (6th Cir. 1967); *Howard v. Smyth*, 365 F.2d 428 (4th Cir.), *cert. denied*, 385 U.S. 988 (1966); *Jordan v. Fitzharris*, 257 F. Supp. 674 (N.D. Cal. 1966); United States *ex rel. Hancock v. Pate*, 223 F. Supp. 202 (N.D. Ill. 1963).
396. An example of a Civil Rights Act suit based on a federal statute occurred in *Smartt v. Avery*, 370 F.2d 788 (6th Cir. 1967), where a federal court enjoined the Tennessee Pardon, Parole and Probation Board from enforcing regulations which postponed for one year the eligibility for parole of any inmate who filed a petition for *habeas corpus*. In addition to its objections on constitutional grounds, U.S. Const. art. I, §9 (suspension of the writ of *habeas corpus* prohibited), the court voided the regulation as infringing the federal statutory right of a state prisoner to petition a federal court for a writ of *habeas corpus*, 370 F.2d at 790.

stitutional right guaranteed by the Fourteenth Amendment.[397] Courts generally have interpreted the scope of Fourteenth Amendment rights to be enforced by the act quite liberally.[398] For example, in an early case decided under the act, a district court ruled that the refusal by county jail officials to furnish medical care to a severely injured inmate could amount to a deprivation of life itself in violation of the Fourteenth Amendment.[399] Where, however, a court ruled that the common-law tort of invasion of privacy was not a constitutional right, there was no basis for the prisoner's suit under the Civil Rights Act.[400] After stating that "all torts are not violations of rights 'secured by the Constitution and laws,'" the court distinguished an earlier decision that had allowed a suit for invasion of privacy under the Civil Rights Act[401] on the basis that the photographic intrusions in that case were so shocking "as to outrage the community's sense of decency."[402] In any case, prisoners, by virtue of their crimes and subsequent trials are rendered public figures having no right to privacy.

The requirement that actions challenged in a suit brought under the Civil Rights Act must have been "under color of state law" has been interpreted to mean the "misuse of power, possessed by virtue of state law and made possible only because the wrongdoer is clothed with the authority of state law."[403] Thus an early case against a prison physician was

397. See generally, Benton v. Maryland, 394 U.S. 784 (1969); Palko v. Connecticut, 302 U.S. 319 (1937).
398. See Roberts v. Pepersack, 256 F. Supp. 415, 421 (D. Md. 1966), cert. denied, 389 U.S. 877 (1967).
399. A refusal to furnish medical care when it is clearly necessary, such as is alleged here, could well result in the deprivation of life itself. . . . This amounts to the infliction of permanent injuries, which is, to some extent, a deprivation of life, of liberty and of property. Since these rights are protected by the Fourteenth Amendment to the Federal Constitution, the complaint sufficiently alleges the deprivation of a right, privilege or immunity secured by the Constitution and laws of the United States.

McCollum v. Mayfield, 130 F. Supp. 112, 115 (N.D. Cal. 1955). Accord, United States ex rel. Knight v. Ragen, 337 F.2d 425, 426 (7th Cir. 1964) (dictum), cert. denied, 380 U.S. 985 (1965); Elsberry v. Haynes, 256 F. Supp. 738, 739 (W.D. Okla. 1966); Gordon v. Garrson, 77 F. Supp. 477, 479 (E.D. Ill. 1948); contra, Isenberg v. Prasse, 433 F.2d 449 (3d Cir., 1970); Gittlemacker v. Prasse, 428 F.2d 1 (3d Cir. 1970); United States ex rel. Hyde v. McGinnis, 429 F.2d 864 (2d Cir. 1970); Owens v. Alldridge, 311 F. Supp. 667 (W.D. Okla. 1970); Willis v. White, 310 F. Supp. 205 (E.D. La. 1970); see Ramsey v. Ciccone, 310 F. Supp. 600, 604–605 (W.D. Mo. 1970).
400. Travers v. Paton, 261 F. Supp. 110 (D. Conn. 1966). The prisoner had claimed that his right to privacy had been violated by a television station's secret filming, without his consent, of his parole hearing. The court limited the Supreme Court's decision in Griswold v. Connecticut, 381 U.S. 479 (1965), to cases involving the marital relationship, 261 F. Supp. at 112–13.
401. York v. Story, 324 F.2d 450 (9th Cir. 1963), cert. denied, 376 U.S. 939 (1964).
402. 261 F. Supp. at 115.
403. United States v. Classic, 313 U.S. 299, 326 (1941).

dismissed because the complaint did not state that the doctor had a duty as a state agent to treat an inmate of the prison.[404] The requirement of action "under color of state law" was broadened, however, in a notorious federal prosecution of a Mississippi sheriff, deputy sheriff and patrolman and several private individuals for conspiring to deprive three young civil-rights workers of their civil rights (they were murdered) under color of state law.[405] The district court dismissed the indictments against the private individuals. The Supreme Court reversed, holding that

> Private persons, jointly engaged with state officials in the prohibited action, are acting "under color" of law for purposes of the statute. To act "under color" of law does not require that the accused be an officer of the State. It is enough that he is a willful participant in joint activity with the State or its agents. . . . Those who took advantage of participation by state officers in accomplishment of the foul purpose alleged must suffer the consequences of that participation.

Consequently, anyone clothed with authority by a state correctional system—a prisoner who is made a trusty and given power over other prisoners, for example—or even private persons acting in concert with state correctional officers, could be held liable under the act.

Damages. The Civil Rights Act is phrased in terms of both legal and equitable remedies.[406] Although some cautious courts have determined that prison officials, acting within the scope of their authority, enjoy a sweeping immunity under the Civil Rights Act,"[407] this conservatism has not been reflected in most opinions. Courts generally have recognized that "to hold that all state officials in suits brought under section 1983 enjoy an immunity similar to that they might enjoy in suits brought under state law 'would practically constitute a judicial repeal of the Civil Rights Act.' "[408] Yet federal courts have been reluctant to award compensatory

404. *Gordon v. Garrson,* 77 F. Supp. 477, 480 (E.D. Ill. 1948).
405. *United States v. Price,* 383 U.S. 787 (1966).
406. Any person who deprives a citizen of his constitutional rights "shall be liable to the party injured in an action at law, suit in equity, or other proper proceedings for redress." 42 U.S.C. §1983 (1964).
407. *Delaney v. Shobe,* 235 F. Supp. 662, 666 (D. Ore. 1964) (suit against warden detaining prisoner pursuant to an invalid judgment); *cf. Selico v. Jackson,* 201 F. Supp. 475, 478 (S.D. Cal. 1962) (suit against police officers for acting outside the scope of their authority by assaulting prisoners whom they had arrested illegally).
408. *Jobson v. Henne,* 355 F.2d 129, 133 (2d Cir. 1966), *citing Hoffman v. Haldren,* 268 F.2d 280, 300 (9th Cir. 1959); *Roberts v. Pepersack,* 256 F. Supp. 415, 425 26

damages to prisoners in cases brought under the act.[409] No doubt, judges are loath to hold officials personally liable for their exercise of poor judgment.

In *Sostre v. Rockefeller*,[410] however, the court ordered both the warden and the state commissioner of corrections to compensate an inmate for physical, mental and even intangible injuries resulting from unwarranted punishment.[411] In addition, in an order apparently unprecedented in a prisoner's case, the court awarded punitive damages against both officials:

> The bad faith and malice toward Sostre (based in large part upon political disagreement with him) that motivated Follette [Warden of Green Haven Prison] to put plaintiff in punitive segregation and in effect, to "throw the key away," and McGinnis' [New York Commissioner of Correction] failure to act after being notified of Sostre's confinement . . . are quite reprehensible; an award of exemplary damages is in order.

The court of appeals in *Sostre v. McGinnis* reversed the award of punitive damages, noting that the warden's improper conduct in segregating Sostre "so far as appears reflected no pattern of such behavior by himself or by other officials." The court approved the award of compensatory damages; however, the warden against whom they were levied had died

---

(D. Md. 1966), *cert. denied* 389 U.S. 877 (1967). *See also Sostre v. Rockefeller*, 312 F. Supp. 863, 877–880 (S.D.N.Y. 1970), *aff'd* in part and *rev'd* in part *sub nom. Sostre v. McGinnis*, 8 *Criminal Law Reporter* 2437 (2d Cir., Feb. 24, 1971). *But see Westberry v. Fisher*, 309 F. Supp. 12 (D. Me. 1970) (district court, although conceding that the Civil Rights Act allows equitable suits against state officials, ruled that such a doctrine should not be extended to a damage action against the State Welfare Commissioner, because actions at law would affect state treasuries); *Gilmore v. Gordon*, 433 F.2d 860 (2d Cir. 1970); *Robinson v. Largent*, 311 F. Supp. 1032 (E.D. Pa. 1970) (parole board members and parole agent held immune from Civil Rights Act suit).

409. *See, e.g., Jordan v. Fitzharris*, 257 F. Supp. 674 (N.D. Calif. 1966) (injunction issued against continuation of certain aspects of punitive segregation held to violate the Eighth Amendment; costs of action reimbursed to appointed counsel; damages against officials refused without comment). *But see Monroe v. Pape*, 221 F. Supp. 635 (N.D. Ill. 1968) (on remand) ($13,000 in damages were assessed against the policemen for unconstitutional search and seizure).

410. 312 F. Supp. 863 (S.D.N.Y. 1970) *aff'd in part, modified in part, rev'd in part sub nom. Sostre v. McGinnis*, 442 F.2d 178 (2d Cir. 1971) (*en banc*).

411. The prisoner had been kept in solitary confinement for 372 days as punishment for his legitimate legal activities and black-militant views. The court ordered compensation for the following injuries at a rate of twenty-five dollars for each day spent in punitive segregation: (1) severe physical deprivations—*i.e.*, loss of energy-giving food and loss of exercise; (2) needless degradation; (3) loss of work opportunities of a rehabilitative nature; (4) loss of money which might have been earned by working; (5) loss of schooling and training opportunities; (6) loss of self-improvement through reading books of one's own choice; and (7) great mental anguish. *Id.* at 885.

since the suit began and there was "no party before [the court] against whom appropriately to award damages."

When a district court finally heard the claims of the prisoner in *Wright v. McMann*,[412] it found that he had been kept nude, with neither mattress, bedding nor heat, for a total of thirty-two winter days. The court ruled that this treatment violated the Eighth Amendment; yet due to the absence of "the usual propositions of doctor bills, loss of wages, physical injury and possible future physical impairment," the prisoner was awarded only $1,500 plus his costs. Punitive damages were denied.

Even if the more expansive interpretation of the court in *Sostre* were to prevail, "[t]he right to bring lawsuit against an impecunious policeman can scarcely be considered a complete and effective remedy."[413] Unfortunately the doctrine of sovereign immunity survives as a bar to the liability of many states and municipalities under the Civil Rights Act. Although the Supreme Court ruled in *Monroe* that the complainants had a cause of action against the individual policemen, it refused to hold that there was a cause of action against the City of Chicago, the policemen's employer, which was absolved from liability under state law. The Court concluded that according to the act's legislative history, Congress did not undertake to bring municipal corporations within the ambit of the statute.[414] Thus the official is presumed to be acting as an agent of the state for purposes of the "under color of state law" requirement, but is "stripped of his official or representative character and is subject in his person to the consequences of his individual conduct" when he acts illegally or unconstitutionally.[415] In denying governmental responsibility, the sovereign-immunity doctrine prevents the Civil Rights Act from serving as an adequate means to compensate prisoners for the effects of illegal actions by prison personnel. The federal court of appeals for the District of Columbia recently ruled that the District may not raise the defense of municipal sovereign immunity to defeat its liability under the act.[416]

412. 321 F. Supp. 127, 143–44 (N.D.N.Y. 1970).
413. *Negrich v. Hohn*, 246 F. Supp. 173, 182 (W.D. Pa. 1965); *see Roberts v. Pepersack*, 256 F. Supp. 415, 421 n.4 (D. Md. 1966), *cert. denied*, 389 U.S. 877 (1967).
414. *Monroe v. Pape*, 365 U.S. 167, 187–92 (1961). See *Eddings v. Commonwealth of Pennsylvania*, 311 F. Supp. 944 (E.D. Pa. 1970) (neither the state nor the city is a "person" within the meaning of §1983). *Cf. Hesselgesser v. Reilly*, 440 F.2d 901 (9th Cir. 1971) (vicarious liability of sheriff for actions of his deputy depends on state law).
415. *Ex parte* Young, 209 U.S. 123, 159–60 (1908). See Wright, *Federal Courts* 157–61 (1963). *Cf. Larson v. Domestic and Foreign Commerce Corp.*, 337 U.S. 682 (1949) (claim that official was exceeding statutory powers or acting unconstitutionally).
416. *Carter v. Carlson*, 447 F.2d 358 (D.C. Cir. 1971), *cert. granted sub nom. District of Columbia v. Carter*, 40 U.S. Law Week 3314 (U.S., Jan. 2, 1972); *Baker v. Washington*, 448 F.2d 1200 (D.C. Cir. 1971).

Injunctions. The means for compensating prisoners or punishing prison officials for misconduct to inmates are tenuous and, at best, provide only partial relief. Even where damage suits against government entities are available, courts can only hear individual cases on a piecemeal, after-the-fact basis. When a prisoner is beaten or starved, transferred to a mental institution, forbidden to practice his religion or held incommunicado, it is of little comfort that some day he may be able to collect damages from the responsible officials or the state, or that a jailer who is guilty of gross malfeasance conceivably may be held criminally liable. The convict needs a means to adjudicate his rights quickly and prospectively in order to force prison administrators to respect these rights. Although non-judicial resolutions may exist, presently the most effective way for prisoners to accomplish this objective is to bring action for injunctive relief.

There is an obvious need for injunctions in prison settings where abuses generally are long-standing and may be expected to continue unless prevented. Although injunctions are the traditional remedy where legal remedies are inadequate, their use on behalf of convicts has been surprisingly rare. In fact, no case has been found in which a state court issued an injunction on behalf of the rights of prisoners. Even though courts in every state have some sort of equity jurisdiction, even where separate equity courts no longer exist, it is not clear whether most state courts would even consider a prisoner's petition for injunctive relief in the absence of a statute directing them to do so. Very few state legislatures have passed such statutes.[417]

Although federal district courts have general jurisdiction to issue equitable decrees,[418] the federal courts that have responded to prisoners' complaints generally rely on *habeas corpus* and, very rarely, *mandamus* writs, both of which are specifically provided for by federal statutes. Injunctions were not used in cases involving civil rights until the Supreme Court resurrected the Civil Rights Act in *Monroe*. Since that time, the states' failure to develop judicial procedures for controlling the widespread disregard of prisoners' rights has made equitable relief from some of the most flagrant abuses primarily the province of the federal courts

---

417. *See Wright v. McMann,* 387 F.2d 519, 523–24, 528 (2d Cir. 1967), in which the court discussed the failure of the New York legislature to give state prison inmates the right to apply for injunctive relief against improper treatment. Following this discussion the applicable New York statute was amended to provide: "Nothing . . . shall . . . deny a convict . . . injunctive relief . . . where such treatment violates his constitutional rights." N.Y. Civ. Rights Law §79-C (McKinney Supp. 1970).
418. U.S. Const. art. III, §2; *see Payne v. Hook,* 74 U.S. (7 Wall.) 425, 430 (1868); *United States v. Howland,* 17 U.S. (4 Wheat.) 108, 115 (1819).

operating under the Civil Rights Act.[419]

Even before *Monroe,* however, a district court had ruled that a state prisoner could file a federal claim under the Civil Rights Act despite state statutory provisions suspending his capacity to bring a civil action for the duration of his imprisonment.[420] Although the Federal Rules of Civil Procedure make a person's capacity to sue dependent on the law of his domicile or the state in which the federal district court is located, the court concluded that a literal application of the rules "would bring about an artificial and erroneous result. . . . The logical corollary of defendant's argument is that if plaintiff were imprisoned for life, his remedy for the alleged invasion of his federally protected constitutional right would be completely lost through the operation of a local statute.[421]

419. *Cf. Wright v. McMann,* 387 F.2d 519, 528 (2d Cir. 1967) (concurring opinion):

> It is clear that there is no administrative or judicial body with an unmistakable mandate to entertain an application by Wright for an order that would prevent recurrence of the treatment of which he complains. . . . Thus, while all would agree that it is far better that the states should formulate, supervise and enforce their own rules for the treatment of recalcitrant prisoners, we are faced with asking a district court to write some of the rules.

There is some question of whether a three-judge court is required, pursuant to 28 U.S.C. §2281, to issue an injunction when officials act in accordance with statewide prison regulations. The Supreme Court did not allude to the issue in *Houghton v. Shafer,* 392 U.S. 639 (1968), although the regulations in question were "said to be strictly enforced throughout the entire correctional system in Pennsylvania." However, the Ninth Circuit required a three-judge court in *Gilmore v. Lynch,* 400 F.2d 228 (9th Cir.), *cert. denied,* 393 U.S. 1092 (1968). In *Seale v. Manson,* 326 F. Supp. 1375 (D. Conn. 1971), the court concluded that a three-judge court was unnecessary where no state statute was challenged and the regulations at issue were not issued to effectuate a specific statute.

420. *McCollum v. Mayfield,* 130 F. Supp. 112 (N.D. Cal. 1955).

421. 130 F. Supp. at 116. *Contra, Weller v. Dickson,* 314 F.2d 598, 601 (9th Cir.), *cert. denied* 373 U.S. 930 (1963). In *Weller* the district court denied the right to file a federal complaint *in forma pauperis,* a discretionary act under 28 U.S.C. §1915 (1964), on the basis that since state law tolled the running of the statute of limitations on a convict's claims during his imprisonment, "the action, surviving the term of imprisonment, can be brought in a more favorable atmosphere, namely, after the potential plaintiff has become a member of free society." *Ibid.* at 601.

Denial of leave to file *in forma pauperis* could effectively preclude a large number of indigent prisoners from filing suit. In a concurring opinion, Judge Duniway proposed that district judges use this discretionary power to discourage prisoners from exercising their statutory right to sue prison officials:

> [T]he district judge should have a broader discretion in civil actions brought by prisoners against their jailers than in other civil actions. We know from sad experience with habeas corpus and [section] 2255 cases that imprisoned felons are seldom, if ever, deterred by the penalties of perjury. They do not hesitate to allege whatever they think is required in order to get themselves even the temporary relief of a proceeding in court.

Id. at 601–602. *See also Higgins v. Steele,* 195 F.2d 366, 369 (8th Cir. 1952).

These decisions would seem to undercut access to the courts solely on the basis of the poverty of the claimant. Such a result would appear to be inconsistent with recent decisions to expand access to the judiciary for immediate relief. *But see Brown v. Brown,* 368 F.2d 992, 993 (9th Cir.), *cert. denied,* 385 U.S. 868 (1966); *Stiltner v.*

Exhaustion of Remedies. In *Monroe v. Pape*,[422] the Supreme Court explicitly held that an exhaustion of state remedies was not a prerequisite to bring a suit under the Civil Rights Act. Similarly, lower courts have reiterated the principle that state prisoners claiming a denial of their constitutional rights need not exhaust state administrative or judicial remedies before seeking relief in the federal courts.[423] Yet these opinions show confusion over whether the Civil Rights Act excuses exhaustion of state and administrative remedies in every case, or only where application for relief through state channels clearly would be futile.[424] The Supreme Court has added to this confusion by reiterating that exhaustion is unnecessary[425] while taking care to examine available state remedies and demonstrate their inadequacy for dealing with the claims raised.[426]

In *Houghton v. Shafer*,[427] prison officials confiscated materials necessary for an inmate to conduct a *pro se* appeal from his burglary

---

Rhay, 322 F.2d 314 (9th Cir. 1963), *cert. denied sub nom. Stiltner v. Washington*, 376 U.S. 920 (1964):

> It may appear . . . that although a cause of action is formally alleged the proceeding is nonetheless frivolous. . . . [T]he preferable procedure for the District Court to follow is to grant leave to proceed in forma pauperis if the requirements of 28 U.S.C.A. §1915(a) are satisfied on the face of the papers submitted, and dismiss the proceeding under 28 U.S.C.A. §1915(d) if the court thereafter discovers that the allegation of poverty is untrue or the action is frivolous or malicious.

Id. at 316–17. *See also Smith v. Bennett*, 365 U.S. 708, 709 (1961) (to interpose any financial consideration between an indigent prisoner and his exercise of a state right to sue for his liberty is to deny that prisoner the equal protection of the laws); *Cruz v. Hauck*, 92 Sup. Ct. 313 (1971) (*per curiam*).

422. 365 U.S. 167 (1961).
423. *E.g., Edwards v. Schmidt*, 321 F. Supp. 68 (W.D. Wisc. 1971); *Talley v. Stephens*, 247 F. Supp. 683, 686 (E.D. Ark. 1965).
424. *See Eisen v. Eastman*, 421 F.2d 560, 569 (2d Cir. 1969); *Sostre v. Rockefeller*, 312 F. Supp. 863, 881–83 (S.D.N.Y. 1970) *aff'd in part, modified in part, rev'd in part sub nom. Sostre v. McGinnis*, 442 F.2d 178 (2d Cir. 1971) (*en banc*); Comment, "Section 1983 Jurisdiction: A Reply," 83 *Harvard Law Review* 1352, 1358 (1970); Note, "Limiting the Section 1983 Action in the Wake of Monroe v. Pape," 82 *Harvard Law Review* 1486, 1498–1501 (1969).
425. *McNeese v. Board of Education*, 373 U.S. 668 (1963); *Houghton v. Shafer*, 392 U.S. 639 (1968) (*per curiam*).
426. *E.g., McNeese v. Board of Education*, 373 U.S. 668, 674–76 (1963):

> It is immaterial whether respondents' conduct is legal or illegal as a matter of state law. . . . Such claims are entitled to be adjudicated in the federal courts. . . .
>
> Moreover, it is by no means clear that Illinois law provides petitioners with an administrative remedy sufficiently adequate to preclude prior resort to a federal court for protection of their federal rights. . . .
>
> When federal rights are subject to such tenuous protection, prior resort to a state proceeding is not necessary.

But see Damico v. California, 389 U.S. 416 (1967), holding that adequate administrative remedies need not be exhausted.
427. 392 U.S. 639 (1968) (*per curiam*).

conviction. The officials justified the confiscation on the basis that the materials had been found in another cell in violation of prison rules prohibiting the unauthorized lending of books to other inmates. The owner of the materials petitioned in federal district court for their return, but his complaint was dismissed for failure to allege exhaustion of state administrative remedies.[428] According to the inmates' handbook, prisoners could take their problems to the "Classification and Treatment Clinic," the superintendent of the institution, the Deputy Commissioner of Correction, the Commissioner of Correction and, as a final appeal, the state attorney general. The inmate in this case approached only the deputy superintendent, who reportedly told him to "leave well enough alone."[429]

The Supreme Court, in reversing the district court's dismissal, noted that

> the rules of the prison were validly and correctly applied to petitioner; these rules are further said to be strictly enforced throughout the entire correctional system in Pennsylvania. In light of this it seems likely that to require petitioner to appeal to the Deputy Commissioner of Correction, the Commissioner, or to the Attorney General *would be to demand a futile act. In any event, resort to these remedies is unnecessary in light of our decisions. . . .*[430]

Thus, although theoretically the exhaustion of state remedies is clearly not necessary in federal suits under the Civil Rights Act, the question remains whether the rule would be different in a case where resort to state procedures might not be futile.[431]

This question may soon reach the courts in relation to a statute recently passed by the Maryland legislature in response to a far-reaching federal court decision changing the disciplinary procedures in Maryland

428. United States *ex rel. Houghton v. Scranton*, 272 F. Supp. 960 (E.D. Pa. 1966).
429. 392 U.S. at 640.
430. *Id.* (italics added).
431. See *Holland v. Beto*, 309 F. Supp. 784 (S.D. Tex. 1970) (§1983 suit unavailable to prisoner claiming interference with his use of the mails who has not exhausted state remedies, which in this case are available and adequate).
   In *Carothers v. Follette*, 314 F. Supp. 1014, 1018–19 (S.D.N.Y. 1970), the court noted that, although exhaustion of state judicial remedies is no longer necessary, there may still be some question of whether exhaustion of state administrative remedies is required. The court declined to settle the question, since it considered the possibility of writing a letter to a prison warden protesting disciplinary action "clearly inadequate and hardly worthy of classification as an administrative procedure. . . ." Cf. *Hall v. Garson,* 430 F.2d 430 (5th Cir. 1970): "It may be that exhaustion of administrative remedies is still required at least to the extent that it is necessary to have an authoritative institutional decision or pronouncement."

prisons.[432] The statute[433] creates an Inmate Grievance Commission to receive complaints from state prisoners, hold hearings (with certain procedural protections for the complainants) where complaints are found to have merit, order changes. If changes are ordered, the order is forwarded to the Secretary of Public Safety and Correctional Services, who may affirm, reverse or modify it. The complainant may seek review of an adverse decision in a state court. The statute provides that "no court shall be required to entertain an inmate's grievance or complaint within the jurisdiction of the Inmate Grievance Commission unless and until the complaint has exhausted the remedies as provided in this section."

Related to the exhaustion doctrine but distinguishable from it is the further pitfall of abstention. In *Wright v. Mann*,[434] a leading case regarding injunctions against cruel and unusual punishment under the Civil Rights Act,[435] the appellate court determined that although the New York Court of Claims had jurisdiction to award damages for injuries inflicted by state prison employees, no state court had jurisdiction to issue preventive injunctive relief. The court recognized that

> money damages are small consolation for a man serving a potentially long sentence and complaining of debasing prison conditions which he endured and fears he might have to endure again. . . . And so we have grave doubt as to the existence of a state remedy adequate in either theory or practice.[436]

A concurring opinion reluctantly agreed with the conclusion that the district court must hear Wright's complaint.[437] It indicated, however, that if a state's courts had jurisdiction to give state prisoners injunctive relief from brutal treatment, federal courts should abstain for a reasonable period[438] from consideration of the complaints until the state courts had the opportunity to act:

432. *Bundy v. Cannon,* 328 F. Supp. 165 (D. Md. 1971).
433. Ann. Code of Md., Art. 41, §204 F. (1971).
434. 387 F.2d 519 (2d Cir. 1967).
435. *See* section on Right to Decent Treatment: Cruel and Unusual Punishment *supra.*
436. 387 F.2d at 523–24. *See Wilwording v. Swenson,* 404 U.S. 249 (1971) (*per curiam*); *rev'g* 439 F.2d 1331 (8th Cir. 1971).
437. The failure of New York to provide a forum whereby the state

> will listen to complaints of those whom it imprisons leaves us no choice but to open the doors of the federal courts to such prisoners who make claims of cruel and oppressive treatment which, if true, would establish violation of constitutional rights.

Id. at 527.
438. Abstention, a voluntary abnegation of federal judges' power to enjoin state action, recently has been limited by the Supreme Court to "narrowly limited 'special circumstances.'" *Zwickler v. Koota,* 389 U.S. 241, 248 (1967). The majority in *Wright,*

I do not agree that recent decisions of the Supreme Court mandate or were intended to mandate action by federal courts in all cases involving the treatment of prisoners in state institutions, without a suitable period of abstention where state courts are empowered to hear the case and where there is reason to believe that the state would grant relief if the complaint were well-founded. . . . As it is not certain that New York will entertain a request to enjoin improper correctional treatment and it only affords money damages after the fact, the federal courts have a duty to listen and to act if it be shown that constitutional rights are being disregarded.[439]

In response to *Wright,* the New York legislature passed a statute[440] empowering state courts to grant injunctive relief to state prisoners. Subsequently a federal district court accepted jurisdiction of a prisoner's request for an injunction without requiring resort to a state court under the statute.[441] The court reasoned that intervening decisions of the Supreme Court[442] had established that state equitable remedies, no less than legal remedies, need not be exhausted before federal relief is sought. Furthermore, the court declined to abstain from exercising its concurrent jurisdiction, reasoning that the state had no complex administrative system that would be disrupted by federal intervention and that federal constitutional standards, rather than unresolved questions of state law, necessarily would govern any decision in state or federal court.[443]

In a suit for an injunction, the problem of exhaustion is further compounded by the traditional principle that an injunction will not issue unless there is no adequate remedy at law.[444] Thus the majority opinion

---

citing *McNeese v. Board of Education,* 373 U.S. 668, 673–74 (1963), concluded that "cases involving vital questions of civil rights are the least likely candidates for abstention." 387 F.2d at 525. *See also Jones v. Wittenberg,* 323 F. Supp. 93, 98 (judgment), 330 F. Supp. 707 (order) (N.D. Ohio 1971): "[I]t would be a tremendous triumph of hope over reality to think that what has been developed in more than a century by conflicting political interests and by public indifference and hostility will be changed by those who are completely embroiled in the resultant mess."
439. 387 F.2d at 528. *Cf. Rodriguez v. McGinnis,* 10 *Criminal Law Reporter* 2365 (2d Cir., Jan. 25, 1972) (Friendly, C.J., concurring) ("abstention would mean abdication in any case where the state afforded a fair hearing, whether the proper constitutional standards were applied or not").
440. McKinney's Consol. Laws, c.6, §79-c.
441. *Carothers v. Follette,* 314 F. Supp. 1014 (S.D.N.Y. 1970).
442. *Houghton v. Shafer,* 392 U.S. 639 (1968); *King v. Smith,* 392 U.S. 309 (1968); *Damico v. California,* 389 U.S. 416 (1967).
443. *See also Clutchette v. Procunier,* 328 F. Supp. 767 (N.D. Cal. 1971).
444. The preference for legal remedies, based on a reluctance to curtail the right to jury trials, the rigors of procedures for enforcing injunctions and the restrictiveness of

in *Wright* observed that although federal courts have concurrent jurisdiction in cases under the act, "the Supreme Court did not intend *Monroe*
and *McNeese* to abrogate the historic principle that federal courts will
not entertain a suit in equity when 'plain, adequate and complete' remedy
may be held at law."[445] Subsequent to the *Wright* decision, a district
court refused to allow an inmate of the Milwaukee County Jail to file a suit
for an injunction under the Civil Rights Act *in forma pauperis*.[446] Although the court recognized that a case brought under the Civil Rights
Act is not subject to the exhaustion requirement, it refused to consider a
claim for an injunction without a showing that there was no adequate
remedy at law.[447] While phrased in terms of the prerequisites to equitable
remedies, however, the requirement appears very much like that of ex-
haustion-of-state remedies.

Declaratory Judgments. In addition to coercive relief, federal courts considering prisoners' claims under the Civil Rights Act may issue declaratory
judgments which define the rights and obligations of the parties to a case.
Once, such a judgment is obtained, prison officials determine what appropriate action is required.[448] The court may retain jurisdiction, however,
should coercive relief prove necessary in the future.[449] Declaratory judgments are useful where judicial action may be warranted but the court is
reluctant to enter an area of supposed administrative expertise or where

---

preventive relief, has survived the merger of law and equity. Comment, "Federal Injunctions Against State Actions," 35 *George Washington Law Review* 744, 753 (1967).
However, in cases where compensatory damages are difficult to determine, legal remedies are considered inadequate. *E.g., Dehydro, Inc. v. Tretolite Co.*, 53 F.2d 273
(N.D. Okla. 1931); *see Orloff v. Los Angeles Turf Club, Inc.*, 30 Cal. 2d 110, 180
P.2d 321 (1947). Some courts have presumed that legal remedies are inadequate
where constitutional rights are at stake. *Reynolds v. Sims*, 377 U.S. 533, 585 (1964)
(dictum); *Clemons v. Board of Education*, 228 F.2d 853, 857 (6th Cir.), *cert. denied*, 350 U.S. 1006 (1956). *But cf. Gong v. Bryant*, 230 F. Supp. 917 (S.D. Fla.
1964); *Sincock v. Duffy*, 215 F. Supp. 169 (D. Del. 1963), *aff'd sub nom. Roman v.
Sincock*, 377 U.S. 694 (1964).
445. 387 F.2d at 523, *citing Potwora v. Dillon*, 386 F.2d 74 (2d Cir. 1967).
446. *Miller v. Purtell*, 289 F. Supp. 733 (E.D. Wis. 1968).
447. Plaintiff has not shown that he has made any attempt . . . to
    invoke the aid of state authorities or courts which should have the oppor-
    tunity, in the first instance, to correct improper conditions of custody. This
    failure warrants denial of resort to the equitable remedy here requested.
Id. at 734.
448. Declaratory Judgment Act, 28 U.S.C. §2201 (1964): "In a case of actual controversy within its jurisdiction . . . any court of the United States, upon the filing of an
appropriate pleading, may declare the rights and other legal relations of any interested party seeking such declaration, whether or not further relief is or could be
sought."
449. "Further necessary or proper relief based on a declaratory judgment or decree
may be granted, after reasonable notice and hearing, against any adverse party whose
rights have been determined by such judgment." *Id.* §2202.

its decision would necessitate an appropriation of additional funds by a state legislature.[450]

Recently, inmates complaining of physical assaults by other inmates in prison barracks and unhealthy conditions in isolation cells[451] were afforded both injunctive and declaratory relief:

> The Court has recognized heretofore the financial hardships under which the Penitentiary system is laboring, and the Court knows that Respondent cannot make bricks without straw.
>
> However, the Court is convinced that given the will Respondent with means now available to him . . . can make a substantial start toward alleviating the conditions that the Court has found to be unconstitutional. He will be ordered to do so.
>
> The Court will not undertake at this time to prescribe any specific immediate steps to be taken by Respondent. The Court would like to know first what Respondent thinks that he can do, and what he is willing to undertake to do.

This decision led to some improvements in conditions at the prison. Continuing inmate complaints, however, and indications that conditions were beginning to revert to their former state, prompted a consideration of the constitutionality of the entire Arkansas penal system.[452] The second opinion declared that the system was being operated unconstitutionally and ordered officials to take steps to remedy the situation. Again the officials were allowed time to prepare a plan of action to conform the system to constitutional standards; this time, however, the court was more explicit about its minimum standards. Furthermore, it added the warning that "unless conditions at the Penitentiary farms are brought up to a level of constitutional tolerability, the farms can no longer be used for the confinement of convicts." The federal court refused to delegate responsibility for prison conditions to any other governmental organ.

Limitations of the Civil Rights Act for Federal Prisoners. While suits under the Civil Rights Act have proved helpful to state prisoners, federal prisoners have not been able to obtain similar equitable remedies under the act. Federal district court jurisdiction is restricted to the specific cate-

450. Cf. *Upchurch v. State,* 51 Hawaii 150, 153, 454 P.2d 112, 114 (1969).
451. *Holt v. Sarver,* 300 F. Supp. 825 (E.D. Ark. 1969).
452. *Holt v. Sarver,* 309 F. Supp. 362 (E.D. Ark. 1970), aff'd 442 F.2d 304 (8th Cir. 1971). The decision included three complaints that had been consolidated for trial in 1969 and five more added for the second trial.

gories of cases authorized by Congressional legislation.[453] Since the Civil Rights Act is limited by its own terms to intrusions carried out under color of *state* law, it cannot be used to obtain judicial relief against *federal* officials. The only other federal statute authorizing injunctive relief similar to that provided under the Civil Rights Act is one granting federal courts jurisdiction over cases involving the federal constitution or a federal statute.[454] However, unlike cases involving deprivations of civil rights under color of state law,[455] the general federal-question jurisdiction is limited to cases where there is a minimum of $10,000 in controversy.[456]

Although no cases deal with the question, a federal court presumably would have to abdicate jurisdiction over a prisoner's request for injunctive relief unless the petitioner could show that the right he sought to protect had the requisite monetary value.[457] As the Supreme Court has recognized, however, claims involving personal liberty rather than property are "inherently incapable of pecuniary valuation." No federal statute has waived the jurisdictional amount requirement for claims alleging violations of inmates' constitutional rights by federal prison officials. Thus, while federal prisoners have sued the United States for damages[458] and have sought relief through writs of *habeas corpus*[459] and, occasionally, *mandamus*,[460] they have not sought injunctive relief.[461]

---

453. *See Briggs v. United Shoe Machine Co.*, 239 U.S. 48, 50 (1915) (federal equitable powers may be exercised only where court has been given jurisdiction over subject matter of suit); *see generally* Comment, "Federal Injunctions Against State Actions," 35 *George Washington Law Review* 744, 751–53 (1967).
454. 28 U.S.C. §1331 (1964).
455. 28 U.S.C. §1343 (1964). *Hague v. CIO*, 307 U.S. 496, 529 (1939) (separate opinion of Stone, J.); *accord, Douglas v. City of Jeannette*, 319 U.S. 157, 161 (1943); *see* Wright, *Federal Courts* 90–91 (1963), Comment, "Federal Injunctions Against State Actions," 35 *George Washington Law Review* 744, 752 (1967).
456. 28 U.S.C. §1331(a) (1964); *see Ex parte* Young, 209 U.S. 123, 145 (1908).
457. *See Hague v. CIO*, 307 U.S. 496, 507–508 (1939) (separate opinion of Roberts, J.).
458. *E.g., United States v. Muniz*, 374 U.S. 150 (1963); *Close v. United States*, 397 F.2d 686 (D.C. Cir. 1968).
459. *E.g., Barnett v. Rodgers*, 410 F.2d 995 (D.C. Cir. 1969); *Peek v. Ciccone*, 288 F. Supp. 329 (W.D. Mo. 1968).
460. *E.g., Walker v. Blackwell*, 411 F.2d 23 (5th Cir. 1969); *Fulwood v. Clemmer*, 295 F.2d 171 (D.C. Cir. 1961).
    28 U.S.C. §1361 (1964) gives federal courts jurisdiction, without regard to amount in controversy, of actions in the nature of *mandamus* against federal officers or agencies. In the first appeal of *Walker v. Blackwell*, 360 F.2d 66 (5th Cir. 1966), the district court's dismissal of a suit by Black Muslim prisoners against the warden of a federal penitentiary was reversed. Although the court of appeals agreed that the suit could not be brought against federal officials under the Civil Rights Act, it ruled that the complaint stated a cause of action against the warden under 28 U.S.C. §1361. *Id.* at 67.
461. The use of the federal Civil Rights Act also ensures the availability of liberal discovery rules under the federal Rules of Civil Procedure. The availability of discovery in a suit for *habeas corpus* or *mandamus* is in doubt.

A broader and more useful rule would permit any case involving the interpretation of personal rights based on federal law to be heard in federal court. Such a rule would provide for federal prisoners the remedies currently available to state prisoners in federal courts.[462]

MANDAMUS

Prison officials may be forced to take affirmative action respecting prisoners' rights where prisoners are successful in obtaining a writ of *mandamus*. Although *mandamus* could provide an efficient means for courts to oversee administrative action, legislatures and courts have imbedded within the remedy so many intricacies that it is seldom used in prisoners' cases.[463] *Mandamus* is the appropriate procedure for controlling the ministerial (non-discretionary) acts of executive officials, for requiring officials to exercise their discretion and for preventing the abuse of administrative discretion. *Mandamus* may not be used, however, to control the manner in which discretion is exercised. The difficulty lies in applying this theory to specific instances. As with sovereign immunity, lines must be drawn distinguishing ministerial from discretionary acts. In addition, correction of abuse of administrative discretion must be differentiated from substitution of judicial for administrative judgment.

The law of *mandamus* is unclear in most states and varies greatly among different jurisdictions. In one state, for example, issuance of the writ requires proof that the official involved has shown " 'not merely error of judgment, but perversity of will, passion, prejudice, partiality, or moral delinquency.' "[464] Other courts have been more liberal. In New York, a writ "in the nature of *mandamus*" was granted to compel the Commissioner of Correction to permit a Black Muslim prisoner the free exercise

---

462. *Cf. Bolling v. Sharpe*, 347 U.S. 497, 500 (1954), which held that although the terms of the equal-protection clause apply literally only to the states, "it would be unthinkable that the same Constitution would impose a lesser duty on the federal government."

463. *See* 3 Davis, *Administrative Law Treatise* §23.09 (1955). The "hands-off" attitude is reflected in decisions denying writs of *mandamus*. *See, e.g., Sturm v. McGrath*, 177 F.2d 473 (7th Cir. 1949), where the court held that it lacked the power "to superintend through mandamus . . . the administrative conduct of a penitentiary or its discipline." *Ibid.* at 474.

Occasionally, however, courts have issued a writ of *mandamus* against prison officials without discussing their reasons or the requirements that must be met in future cases. *See Brabson v. Wilkins*, 19 N.Y.2d 433, 440, 227 N.E.2d 383, 386, 280 N.Y.S.2d 561, 566 (1967) (Keating, J., dissenting in part); *State ex rel. Tate v. Cubbage*, 210 A.2d 555 (Del. Super. Ct. 1965).

464. *State ex rel. Shafer v. Ohio Turnpike Commission*, 159 Ohio St. 581, 591, 113 N.E.2d 14, 19 (1953).

of his religion.[465] The commissioner was directed to promulgate regulations dealing with all prisoners' rights to practice their religion subject to necessary security measures, as provided by a state statute.[466]

Even the use of *mandamus* to compel compliance with statutory duties[467] is of limited value. Most statutes dealing with the rights of prison inmates are extremely broad and ambiguous. In the majority of cases, denial of these rights by officials cannot be corrected simply by requiring adherence to existing legislation.[468] In one federal case,[469] *mandamus* was refused prisoners claiming denial of freedom to practice their religion where there was no statute to implement the constitutional right to free exercise of religion. The court stated that *mandamus* cannot be issued unless the duty of the administrative officer to act is clearly established and defined and the obligation to act is peremptory. In addition, administrative remedies must be exhausted before this type of judicial relief is sought.[470] The court did not inquire, however, whether any administrative remedies existed in fact.

Although the writ of *mandamus* has been abolished in the federal system, a writ "in the nature of *mandamus*" is available.[471] Prior to 1962, federal district courts outside the District of Columbia denied that they had jurisdiction to grant writs of *mandamus*, mandatory injunctions or other relief calling for affirmative action by executive officers.[472] In 1962, Congress gave all federal district courts original jurisdiction of any action in the nature of *mandamus* to compel an officer, employee or any agency of the United States to perform a duty owed to a petitioner.[473]

Despite this increased jurisdiction, troublesome limitations exist. The Supreme Court's requirements for *mandamus* continue to present pitfalls in all but the clearest of cases:

465. *Brown v. McGinnis*, 10 N.Y.2d 531, 180 N.E.2d 791, 225 N.Y.S.2d 497 (1962). Three judges concurred in result only because the inmate had made no specific demand to the warden which the court could require him to act upon. The dissenters argued that "a mandamus order can only be issued to compel the performance of prescribed acts to which the petitioner has a clear legal right." *Id.* at 536, 180 N.E.2d at 793, 225 N.Y.S.2d at 501. See concurring opinion of Desmond, C.J., *id.* at 536, 180 N.E.2d at 793, 225 N.Y.S.2d at 501.
466. New York Correc. Law §610 (McKinney 1968).
467. *See also Shaw v. McGinnis*, 14 N.Y.2d 864, 200 N.E.2d 636, 251 N.Y.S.2d 971 (1964).
468. *See Wright v. McMann*, 387 F.2d 519, 523–24 (2d Cir. 1967).
469. *White v. Clemmer*, 295 F.2d 132 (D.C. Cir. 1961).
470. The court relied on the requirements set forth in *Hammond v. Hull*, 131 F.2d 23, 25 (D.C. Cir. 1942), *cert. denied*, 318 U.S. 777 (1943). *See also Walker v. Blackwell*, 411 F.2d 23 (5th Cir. 1969); *Walker v. Blackwell*, 360 F.2d 66 (5th Cir. 1966); *Fulwood v. Clemmer*, 295 F.2d 171 (D.C. Cir. 1961).
471. Fed. R. Civ. P. 81(b). *See* cases cited in Moore, *Federal Practice* §81.07 (1955).
472. *E.g., Green v. United States*, 283 F.2d 687 (3d Cir. 1960). *See* 3 Davis, Administrative Law Treatise §23.09 (Supp. 1965).
473. 28 U.S.C. §1361 (1964).

[M]andamus . . . [is] a remedy long restricted . . . in the main, to situations where ministerial duties of a nondiscretionary nature are involved. Where the matter is peradventure clear, where the agency is clearly derelict in failing to act, where the action or inaction turns on a mistake of law, then judicial relief is often available. . . . But where the duty to act turns on matters of doubtful or highly debatable inference from large or loose statutory terms, the very construction of the statute is a distinct and profound exercise of discretion. . . . We must then infer that the decision to act or not to act is left to the expertise of the agency. . . .[474]

In addition, a federal court will not order *mandamus* against a state official,[475] and the refusal of courts to use *mandamus* to control discretionary actions remains.[476]

HABEAS CORPUS

Habeas corpus has long been the primary method for prisoners to challenge the legal authority for their confinement.[477] Before the Civil War this classic writ, considered by state courts to have been authorized by common-law tradition, as well as by statute, was used more by state than federal courts. Although provided for generally in the Constitution and specifically mentioned in section 14 of the Judiciary Act of 1789,[478] it was not until 1867 that Congress authorized the federal courts to grant *habeas corpus* "in all cases where any person may be restrained of his or her liberty in violation of the constitution, or of any treaty or law of the United States. . . ."[479] Both state[480] and federal[481] prisoners then began using the federal courts to challenge their detention on constitutional grounds.

For the better part of a century, however, both state and federal courts would entertain *habeas corpus* petitions only where a prisoner chal-

474. *Panama Canal Co. v. Grace Line, Inc.*, 356 U.S. 309, 317–18 (1958) (citations omitted).
475. *In re* Wolenski, 324 F.2d 309 (3d Cir. 1963) (*per curiam*).
476. *E.g., Smith v. United States*, 333 F.2d 70 (10th Cir. 1964); *Armstrong v. United States* 233 F. Supp. 188 (S.D. Calif. 1964).
477. *E.g., Ex parte* Watkins, 27 U.S. (3 Pet.) 193, 203 (1830); *see* Longsdorf, "Habeas Corpus: A Protean Writ and Remedy," 8 F.R.D. 179 (1948); Glass, "Historical Aspects of Habeas Corpus," 9. *St. John's Law Review* 55 (1934).
478. *See* 28 U.S.C. §§2241–2255 (1964).
479. Act of Feb. 5, 1867, ch. 28, §1, 14 Stat. 385.
480. *See* 28 U.S.C. §2254 (1964). *Townsend v. Sain*, 372 U.S. 293 (1963), required federal district judges to hold full evidentiary hearings into the prisoners' claims where the state had not provided such a hearing.
481. *See* 28 U.S.C. §2255 (1964) (statutory substitute for *habeas corpus*).

lenged the legality of his original conviction and where a granting of the writ on that basis would lead to his release or a new trial.[482] The courts generally based this restrictive view of *habeas corpus* on the 1934 decision of the Supreme Court in *McNally v. Hill.*[483] There, the Court held that a prisoner serving two consecutive sentences could not challenge the validity of the second sentence until he had begun to serve it—even though the allegedly void sentence rendered him ineligible for parole on the first. The Court interpreted the writ's historical purpose as limiting judicial relief to the discharge of the prisoner or his admission to bail where his detention was deemed unlawful.

> There is no warrant in either the statute or the writ for its use to invoke judicial determination of questions which could not affect the lawfulness of the custody and detention, and no suggestion of such a use has been found in the commentaries on the English common law.[484]

This rigid rule was altered, however, by a more generous interpretation of the historic power of *habeas corpus*. In 1944 a federal court of appeals, in *Coffin v. Reichard,*[485] created a new remedy for prison inmates who, while admittedly confined pursuant to a valid judgment of conviction, claim that the conditions of their imprisonment violate constitutional guarantees. The Sixth Circuit Court of Appeals ordered the district court to hold a hearing on the petition of an inmate who claimed that he "suffered bodily harm and injuries and was subjected to assaults, cruelties and indignities from guards and his co-inmates." The court ruled that

> A prisoner is entitled to the writ of habeas corpus when, though lawfully in custody, he is deprived of some right to which he is lawfully entitled even in his confinement, the deprivation of

482. Habeas corpus may not be used to secure judicial decision of any question which, even if determined in the prisoner's favor, could not result in his immediate release. The only relief authorized is the discharge of the prisoner, and that only if his detention is found to be unlawful.

United States *ex rel. Binion v. United States Marshal*, 188 F. Supp. 905, 908 (D. Nev. 1960), *aff'd*, 292 F.2d 494 (9th Cir. 1961) (*habeas corpus* will not issue where there is any period of imprisonment that petitioner is legally obliged to serve). *See also Snow v. Roche*, 143 F.2d 718, 719 (9th Cir. 1944) (complaint alleging inadequate food and medical treatment dismissed for failure to question legality of confinement); *Robinson v. Director*, 3 Md. App. 222, 238 A.2d 124 (1968).

483. 293 U.S. 131 (1934), *overruled, Peyton v. Rowe*, 391 U.S. 54 (1968) (allegation that inmate confined as a "defective delinquent" not receiving adequate treatment may not be raised in *habeas corpus* or other post-conviction proceeding as it does not relate to the validity of the original judgment on the criminal offense).

484. 293 U.S. at 136–37.

485. 143 F.2d 443 (6th Cir. 1944).

which serves to make his imprisonment more burdensome than the law allows or curtails his liberty to a greater extent than the law permits.

According to the *Coffin* opinion, "the judge is not limited to a simple remand or discharge of the prisoner, but he may remand with directions that the prisoner's retained civil rights be respected. . . ."[486]

This more flexible view of *habeas corpus* expressed in the *Coffin* case was underscored and perhaps expanded two years later by Judge Learned Hand:

> We can find no more definite rule than that the writ is available, not only to determine points of jurisdiction, stricti juris, and constitutional questions; but *whenever else resort to it is necessary to prevent a complete miscarriage of justice.*[487]

The italicized phrase would seem to make the writ available in any situation where a proper legal challenge is raised. In 1963 the Supreme Court expressed its approval of the expanded use of the writ.[488] In permitting a prisoner released on parole from a state prison to challenge his original conviction on federal constitutional grounds, the Court noted that although

> the chief use of habeas corpus has been to seek the release of persons held in actual, physical custody in prison or jail. . . . [B]esides physical imprisonment, there are other restraints on a man's liberty, restraints not shared by the public generally,

486. *Ibid.* Interestingly, the *Coffin* court, which first advocated this expanded view of *habeas corpus*, also abjured the then prevalent "hands-off" attitude. Other courts' continued adherence to the policy of abstention in cases involving claims by prison inmates limited the full potential of this writ as a means of overseeing the terms of confinement:

> Since the prison system of the United States is entrusted to the Bureau of Prisons . . . courts have no power to supervise the discipline of the prisoners nor to interfere with their discipline, but only on habeas corpus to deliver from imprisonment those who are illegally detained.

Williams v. Steele, 194 F.2d 32, 34 (8th Cir. 1952). *But see Holland v. Ciccone*, 386 F.2d 825 (8th Cir.), *cert. denied*, 390 U.S. 1045 (1968).

In other cases, while conceding that *habeas corpus* would be appropriate where prisoners' constitutional rights had been violated, courts denied petitions on the ground that inmates had failed to prove "exceptional circumstances," amounting to "cruel, inhuman, or excessive punishment." *In re* Baptista's Petition, 206 F. Supp. 288 (W.D. Mo. 1962); *Hughes v. Turner*, 14 Utah 2d 128, 378 P.2d 888, *cert. denied*, 374 U.S. 846 (1963); *In re* Riddle, 57 Cal. 2d 848, 372 P.2d 304, 22 *California Reporter* 472, *cert. denied*, 371 U.S. 914 (1962).

487. United States *ex rel. Kulick v. Kennedy*, 157 F.2d 811, 813 (2d Cir. 1946) (italics added), *rev'd on other grounds*, 332 U.S. 174 (1947) (*habeas corpus* cannot be used where direct appeal is permitted).

488. *Jones v. Cunningham*, 371 U.S. 236 (1963).

which have been thought sufficient in the English-speaking world to support the issuance of habeas corpus. . . . [The writ] is not now and never has been a static, narrow, formalistic remedy; its scope has grown to achieve its grand purpose—the protection of individuals against erosion of their right to be free from wrongful restraints upon their liberty.

Furthermore, in 1968 the Court overruled *McNally* and held that prisoners may attack sentences they have not yet begun to serve.[489] The restrictions surrounding *habeas corpus* were relieved even further when, in another case that term, the Court allowed a state prisoner whose sentence had expired during the pendency of his federal *habeas corpus* proceedings to continue the challenge of his original criminal conviction.[490]

In these far-reaching decisions the Court recognized that the collateral consequences of criminal convictions were so significant that the inmate's release from prison did not serve to make his case moot. The Court delineated the possible dispositions of a *habeas corpus* petition in a way that should end the debate, at least in the federal court, on the use of the writ as a remedy for prison abuses:

> [T]he [Federal Habeas Corpus] statute does not limit the relief that may be granted to discharge of the applicant from physical custody. Its mandate is broad with respect to the relief that may be granted. It provides that "[t]he Court shall . . . dispose of the matter as law and justice require. . . ." The 1966 amendments to the habeas corpus statute [providing for "release from custody or other remedy"] seem specifically to contemplate the possibility of relief other than immediate release from physical custody.

Finally, in the recent decision in *Johnson v. Avery*,[491] the Court affirmed a federal district court's use of *habeas corpus* to release a state prisoner from solitary confinement, although not from imprisonment, for violating a prison regulation.

489. *Peyton v. Rowe*, 391 U.S. 54, 67 (1968).
490. *Carafas v. LaVallee*, 391 U.S. 234 (1968).
491. 393 U.S. 483 (1969), *aff'g* 252 F. Supp. 783 (M.D. Tenn. 1966). The district court recognized that the relief sought "is, in fact, to release the petitioner from custody—from the very real custody of solitary confinement which is, in a sense, a jail within a jail." 252 F. Supp. at 787. *Cf.* United States *ex rel. Katzoff v. McGinnis*, 441 F.2d 558 (2d Cir. 1971) (*habeas corpus* is proper for challenging administrative actions, such as the withdrawal of earned good time, which may result in a failure to allow release according to law).

Recently, most federal and some state courts have shown a willingness to use *habeas corpus* in cases where judges have been particularly shocked by the mistreatment of prisoners. An Idaho court,[492] although agreeing with prison officials that prison supervision and maintenance is an executive function, ordered a hearing on a petition for *habeas corpus* in which a prisoner alleged that he had been beaten, denied medical care, forced to live under extremely unsanitary conditions and unjustly held in solitary confinement for prolonged periods of time. A West Virginia court granted a *habeas corpus* petition and vacated the prison sentence of a defendant it had sentenced for robbery on the basis of testimony about unsafe and antirehabilitative conditions in the penitentiary. The judge reasoned that "courts should have an interest in the welfare as well as the rehabilitation of the defendants whom they commit to penal institutions. This concern should not end at the date of sentencing." However, his bold action was reversed on appeal.[493] A Pennsylvania court used *habeas corpus* to transfer two pre-trial detainees from the Holmesburg Prison to another jail because of its conclusion that conditions at Holmesburg constituted cruel and unusual punishment.[494] One federal district court, while recognizing the expanded use of *habeas corpus*, imposed the requirement that the denials of rights challenged must not relate to "past wrongs, not involving the validity of the confinement, and not of a continuing or probably continuing nature," and that the deprivations must be such that they amount to an "unlawful administration of sentence."[495]

Two decisions in the early 1960s, one by a New York state court and

492. *Mahaffey v. State*, 87 Idaho 228, 392 P.2d 279 (1964).
493. State of West Virginia *ex rel. Pingley v. Coiner*, HC No. 70–181 (Cir. Ct. of Randolph County, May 6, 1971) *rev'd*—W.Va.—186 S.E.2d 220 (1972).
494. Commonwealth of Pennsylvania *ex rel. Bryant v. Hendrick*, 7 *Criminal Law Reporter* 2463 (Court of Common Pleas for Phila. County, Aug. 11, 1970), *aff'd*, 444 Pa. 83, 280 A.2d 110 (1971). Recognizing the possibility of a large number of *habeas corpus* petitions from other untried prisoners, the court announced that it would decline to hear them for a thirty-day period in order to give officials the opportunity to eliminate the most flagrant abuses. Surprisingly, no further petitions were filed.
495. *Konigsberg v. Ciccone*, 285 F. Supp. 585, 589 (W.D. Mo. 1968), *aff'd*, 417 F.2d 161 (8th Cir. 1969), *cert. denied*, 397 U.S. 903 (1970). Employing this rationale, the court dismissed complaints by an inmate that he was struck by prison personnel, subjected to institutional censorship of letters and telephone calls to his attorney, deprived of adequate water while confined in a maximum-security cell and taken incognito to testify before a grand jury without the knowledge of his family and attorney. These actions were deemed "past events not likely to recur, and not amounting to any type of mistreatment that would justify habeas corpus relief." *Id.* at 600. Since this was a case in which the court reviewed each contention in a lengthy opinion (that at one point accused the inmate of abusing the *habeas corpus* process, *id.* at 597) and dismissed all but one claim, it seems likely that the court felt that the dismissed challenges did not reach constitutional proportions. *Cf. Ramsey v. Ciccone*, 310 F. Supp. 600, 606 (W.D. Mo. 1970).

one by a federal court of appeals, found *habeas corpus* particularly suitable for testing the appropriateness of the place in which prisoners are being confined. In People *ex rel. Brown v. Johnston*,[496] a convict challenged the validity of his transfer from the Attica State Prison to the Dannemora State Hospital, an institution for prisoners considered insane. Two lower courts denied the inmate's petition for a writ of *habeas corpus* on the ground that once a convict is validly committed to prison, *habeas corpus* proceedings are inappropriate for testing the place of his detention.[497] The New York Court of Appeals reversed and ordered the trial court to consider the petition. The court recognized that the restraints imposed by confinement in the hospital were greater than those inherent in ordinary imprisonment and expressed a willingness to subject to inquiry "any *further* restraint *in excess* of that permitted by the judgment. . . ."[498] In expansive language, the court sketched a potentially significant role for *habeas corpus* in enforcing the requirements of due process of law when prison administrators impose deprivations of inmates' liberty greater than those envisioned by the sentencing judge.[499]

Similarly, in *Shone v. Maine*,[500] a juvenile who had been adjudicated delinquent and committed to a juvenile training center was deemed "incorrigible" by the institution's administrators and transferred to a state prison for young adult offenders. Although the transfer was carried out pursuant to state law,[501] it was considered invalid by the federal court

496. 9 N.Y.2d 482, 174 N.E.2d 725, 215 N.Y.S.2d 44 (1961).
497. 11 App. Div. 2d 819, 203 N.Y.S.2d 353 (1960).
498. 9 N.Y.2d at 482, 174 N.E.2d at 726, 215 N.Y.S.2d at 46 (1961).
499. An individual, once validly convicted and placed under the jurisdiction of the Department of Correction . . . is not to be divested of all rights and unalterably abandoned and forgotten by the remainder of society. If these situations were placed *without* the ambit of the writ's protection, we would thereby encourage the unrestricted, arbitrary and unlawful treatment of prisoners, and eventually discourage prisoners from cooperating in their rehabilitation.

    Since the writ of habeas corpus has traditionally been relied upon to alleviate the oppression of unlawful imprisonment and abuses of similar character, it can be invoked to obtain a hearing to test the validity of a commitment in an institution for the criminally insane. We cannot merely by virtue of the valid judgment sanction the subsequent abrogation of lawful process.

    The State's right to detain a prisoner is entitled to no greater application than its correlative duty to protect him from unlawful and onerous treatment . . . mental or physical. "Relief other than that of absolute discharge should be forthcoming. . . ."
Id. at 482, 174 N.E.2d at 726, 215 N.Y.S.2d at 46. *See* sections on Classification of Prisoners; Degrees of Custody; Transfers, *infra*, and Punishment of Prisoners for Infractions of Prison Rules, discussing similar lack of hearing or other adequate protection of prisoners' rights.
500. 406 F.2d 844 (1st Cir.), *vacated as moot*, 396 U.S. 6 (1969).
501. Me. Rev. Stat. Ann., tit. 15, §2717 (1964).

for having failed to employ procedures required by due process of law. The court issued a writ of *habeas corpus* directing the return of the prisoner to the training center.[502]

This expansive view of *habeas corpus* is not unanimous, however, particularly among state courts.[503] Recently, a Florida prisoner, whose request for prison officials to forward a written complaint to the United States Attorney General by certified mail was refused, filed a petition for a writ of *habeas corpus* in the state court. The court ruled that even if the prisoner's constitutional rights had been violated by the officials' inaction, a writ of *habeas corpus* cannot be issued to a prisoner not entitled to immediate release from confinement.[504] The Supreme Court denied *certiorari*, and the decision was later cited with approval by a court in another state.[505]

Even where available, federal court review of prison practices through *habeas corpus* can be an extremely lengthy process. Procedurally, prisoners must still exhaust all alternate remedies before seeking the writ.[506] The statutory and case law pertaining to exhaustion of remedies has already been developed in the context of challenges to criminal convictions. The extent to which the exhaustion requirement applies to *habeas corpus* attacks on prison conditions is not clear.[507]

The requirement of exhaustion of remedies is more exacting when state prisoners are involved. Before his petition for a federal writ of *habeas corpus* can be considered, the federal statute requires

---

502. 400 F.2d at 849. *Cf. Darsey v. United States*, 318 F. Supp. 1346 (W.D. Mo. 1970).
503. *See Wilwording v. Swenson*, 439 F.2d 1331 (8th Cir. 1971) (absent exceptional circumstances complaints concerning conditions of confinement are not generally within the proper scope of *habeas corpus*); *rev'd per curiam on other grounds*, 404 U.S. 249 (1971). *Granville v. Hunt*, 411 F.2d 9 (5th Cir., 1969); *McNeal v. Taylor*, 313 F. Supp. 200 (W.D. Okla. 1970).
504. *Schack v. State*, 194 So. 2d 53 (Fla. Dist. Ct. Appeals), *cert. denied*, 386 U.S. 1027 (1967).
505. *Brown v. Justice's Court*, 83 Nev. 272, 428 P.2d 376 (1967).
506. 28 U.S.C. §2254 (1964); *Johnson v. Dye*, 338 U.S. 864 (1949) (*per curiam*).
507. A statutory provision applying to federal prisoners requires that before applying for *habeas corpus* a prisoner first must apply for relief to the court that sentenced him, "unless it . . . appears that the remedy by motion is inadequate or ineffective to test the legality of his detention." 28 U.S.C. §2255 (1964). This jurisdictional requirement is inappropriate where the original sentence is not under attack, and, in fact has not been mentioned in recent *habeas corpus* proceedings involving alleged deprivations of federal prisoners' rights. *E.g., Barnett v. Rodgers*, 410 F.2d 995 (D.C. Cir. 1969); *Peek v. Ciccone*, 288 F. Supp. 329 (W.D. Mo. 1968); *Konigsberg v. Ciccone*, 285 F. Supp. 585 (W.D. Mo. 1968), *aff'd*, 417 F.2d 161 (8th Cir. 1969), *cert. denied*, 397 U.S. 963 (1970). *But see Lowe v. Hiatt*, 77 F. Supp. 303, 305 (M.D. Pa. 1948), where the court referred to the establishment of a "prisoners' mail box" by the U.S. Bureau of Prisons as a form of administrative relief.

that the applicant has exhausted the remedies available in the courts of the State, or that there is either an absence of available State corrective process or the existence of circumstances rendering such process ineffective to protect the rights of the prisoner. An applicant shall not be deemed to have exhausted the remedies available in the courts of the State . . . if he has the right under the law of the State to raise, by any available procedure, the question presented.[508]

The federal courts that have considered the question have deemed this requirement applicable to cases where the validity of the original conviction is not at issue.[509] Although the Supreme Court's decision in *Fay v. Noia*[510] expanded the use of *habeas corpus* to question criminal convictions, it had no direct relevance to direct attacks on prison restrictions. Thus, the technicalities of exhaustion still may make the right to apply for *habeas corpus* meaningless. For example, when an inmate awaiting state trial in the Manhattan House of Detention for Men claimed that he was being denied adequate access to the legal materials necessary for him to prepare for his trial,[511] his petition for a writ of *habeas corpus* was dismissed for failure to exhaust state remedies.[512] More than three months earlier, he had made his request to the New York County Court of General Sessions, and the request was denied. He then attempted to appeal the denial and was informed by a law clerk that the New York Code of Criminal Procedure "does not authorize an appeal from the orders of the General Sessions Court denying your application to be furnished with law books. Under the circumstances, there is no further action to be taken by this Court in the matter." The federal petition was then filed. Yet a memorandum filed in federal court by an assistant New York county district attorney informed the court that the prisoner still might apply for relief from the Supreme Court of the State of New York. Consequently, the federal petition was dismissed "without prejudice to petitioner's right to bring another application . . . should his state remedies

508. 28 U.S.C. §2254(b)-(c) (1964).
509. *E.g.,* United States *ex rel. Thompson v. Fay,* 197 F. Supp. 855 (S.D.N.Y. 1961). (State prison authorities withheld letter from prisoner to U.S. Attorney General's Commission; prisoner's failure to show exhaustion of state remedies as required by 28 U.S.C. §2254 precluded consideration of petition for writ of *habeas corpus*); *but see Edwards v. Schmidt,* 321 F. Supp. 68 (W.D. Wisc. 1971).
510. 372 U.S. 391 (1963) (exhaustion requirement of §2254 refers only to a failure to exhaust the state remedies still available to the applicant at the time he files his application for *habeas corpus* in federal court).
511. *See* section on Access to Court, *supra.* The petitioner was unrepresented by counsel. *Cf. Gideon v. Wainwright,* 372 U.S. 335 (1963).
512. *Barone v. Warden,* 209 F. Supp. 309 (S.D.N.Y. 1962).

prove to be time-barred."[513] Whether this man's request ever received consideration by a federal court before the time of his criminal trial is not known. But the enormous deterrent these procedural requirements impose upon the unsophisticated inmate may render the remedy ineffective.

One short cut developed for challenging criminal convictions through *habeas corpus* might provide a relaxation of the exhaustion requirement in cases involving prisoners' grievances: where a state does not provide a procedure for consideration of an alleged violation of a federal right, it is not necessary for a prisoner to go through the motions of applying to the state courts.[514] Accordingly, the Supreme Court remanded a case which had held that no federal rights were violated where petitions for post-conviction relief were denied without a hearing.[515] The Court held that the existence of the Illinois Post-Conviction Hearing Act[516] did not automatically mean that Illinois afforded an adequate post-conviction remedy:

> On remand, petitioners should be advised whether their claims that constitutional rights were infringed at their trials may be determined under the Post-Conviction Hearing Act, or whether that Act does not provide an appropriate state remedy in these cases. If petitioners' claims may be resolved in a proceeding under the Act . . . such resolution may proceed without further action by this Court. *If Illinois does not provide an appropriate remedy for such a determination, petitioners may proceed without more in the United States District Court.*

Failure to exhaust theoretically available but ineffective state remedies has been excused where there was a showing that procedural obstacles were overwhelming, such as the imposition of state court fees that the prisoner is unable to pay, or the impending execution of a death sentence too early to permit application for appellate review. In many cases involving prisoners' grievances, the requirements for resolution by state courts are frequently so inadequate, complicated or ambiguous[517] that exhaustion of remedies such as *mandamus* or state *habeas corpus* might be excused. This seems to have been the approach taken by the district court in *John-*

513. *Id.* at 310. The court suggested that the petitioner might be more successful with a petition under the federal Civil Rights Act. *Id.*
514. *Young v. Ragen*, 337 U.S. 235 (1949); *see* Note, "Effect of the Federal Constitution in Requiring State Post-Conviction Remedies," 53 *Columbia Law Review* 1143 (1953).
515. *Jennings v. Illinois*, 342 U.S. 104 (1951).
516. *See* Ill. Rev. Stat. ch. 38, §§826–32 (1961), *as amended, id.* §122 (1964).
517. See the extended discussion of possible state remedies in *Wright v. McMann*, 387 F.2d 519, 523–24 (2d Cir. 1967).

son v. Avery,[518] excusing resort to the state courts where "under present state rulings the *habeas corpus* remedy in Tennessee would not be adequate to reach this question on its merits."

Although the requisite exhaustion of judicial remedies may prove less damaging to *habeas corpus* petitions challenging unconstitutional prison restrictions than to petitions challenging criminal convictions, the requirement that administrative remedies be exhausted could become crucial. At present, few departments of correction have established procedures for hearings or other methods of resolving prisoners' grievances. If some administrative complaint procedures should be developed in the future, courts could be expected to require prisoners to use these administrative channels before taking their grievances to court.[519]

In an effort to avoid the complications and delays inherent in the exhaustion requirement and, perhaps, to gain the advantage of liberal discovery proceedings,[520] prisoners' attorneys have begun to file an increasing proportion of suits under the federal Civil Rights Act rather than *habeas corpus*. To date, the efforts of the courts to distinguish between the two types of action have been futile and confusing. In *Rodriguez v. McGinnis*,[521] a prisoner sued officials under both the Civil Rights Act and federal *habeas corpus*, claiming that he had been improperly deprived of good time which, if credited to his sentence, entitled him to immediate release. The district court ruled that the case was predominantly a Civil Rights Act claim, with a *habeas corpus* petition included as an adjunct to ensure full relief if the prisoner should prevail. The appellate court reversed, holding that, since the complaint sought relief from custody, it was in fact an application for *habeas corpus* and required the exhaustion of state remedies. Another federal court of appeals ruled that a complaint seeking relief from solitary confinement could be brought only through *habeas corpus*,[522] other courts, faced with only slightly varying

---

518. 252 F. Supp. 783 (M.D. Tenn. 1966), *rev'd*, 382 F.2d 353 (6th Cir. 1967), *aff'd*, 394 U.S. 718 (1969).
519. Exhaustion of federal administrative remedies was required in *Paden v. United States*, 430 F.2d 882 (5th Cir., 1970); *O'Brien v. Blackwell*, 421 F.2d 884 (5th Cir. 1970); *Hess v. Blackwell*, 409 F.2d 362 (5th Cir., 1969); *Smoake v. Willingham*, 359 F.2d 386 (10th Cir. 1966). An analogous problem to the one just discussed could arise if an administrative route were open in theory but in fact never resolved inmates' complaints. *Cf. Houghton v. Shafer*, 392 U.S. 639 (1968).
520. The discovery provided for in the federal Rules of Civil Procedure is available as a matter of course in suits brought under the Civil Rights Act. In *habeas corpus* proceedings, on the other hand, limited discovery is available only upon application to the court. *See Harris v. Nelson*, 394 U.S. 286 (1969).
521. 307 F. Supp. 627 (N.D.N.Y. 1969); *rev'd*, 451 F.2d 730 (2d Cir. 1971).
522. *Jones v. Decker*, 436 F.2d 954 (5th Cir. 1970). However, the court reversed the dismissal of the portions of the complaint seeking a declaratory judgment and damages under §1983. *See also Denney v. State of Kansas*, 436 F.2d 587 (10th Cir. 1971).

factual situations, have concluded differently.[523] A federal district court, after reviewing several such decisions, as well as the legislative history of the federal *habeas corpus* statutes, concluded that the original purposes of the exhaustion requirement apply only when state judicial proceedings are challenged and, consequently, exhaustion is required only when the validity of a criminal conviction or sentence is at issue, regardless of whether a particular action is brought under *habeas corpus* or the Civil Rights Act.[524]

Most recently, the Supreme Court, over the lone dissent of Chief Justice Burger, summarily reversed the dismissal of a federal *habeas corpus* petition for failure to exhaust all conceivable state judicial remedies. The Court ruled that, even if further exhaustion were required under the statute, the complaint, which challenged conditions of maximum-security confinement in a state penitentiary, might also be read as pleading a cause of action under the Civil Rights Act, not subject to the requirement of exhaustion.[525] Following the decision in *Wilwording*, the Court of Appeals for the Second Circuit reconsidered its decision in *Rodriguez v. McGinnis* and this time voted to affirm the decision of the district court.[526] However, the existence of seven separate concurring and one dissenting opinion offers graphic evidence of the continued confusion.

CRIMINAL ACTIONS AGAINST OFFICIALS

In theory it is always possible to seek a criminal prosecution for assault and battery or even for murder against officials who grossly abuse prisoners in their custody. Some state statutes explicitly provide that "the person of a prisoner sentenced to imprisonment in the State prison is under the protection of the law, and any injury to his person, not authorized by law, is punishable in the same manner as if he were not convicted or sentenced."[527] Courts, in denying prisoners other forms of civil relief,

---

523. *Sinclair v. Henderson,* 435 F.2d 125 (5th Cir. 1970) (conditions of death row); United States *ex rel. Hill v. Johnston,* 321 F. Supp. 818 (S.D.N.Y. 1971) (*habeas corpus* petition seeking transfer from a state hospital for the criminally insane to a state mental hospital for the civilly committed dismissed for failure to exhaust state remedies; dismissal specifically stated to be without prejudice to any suit under §1983 that might be under the facts).
524. *Edwards v. Schmidt,* 321 F. Supp. 68 (W.D. Wisc. 1971).
525. *Wilwording v. Swenson,* 404 U.S. 249 (1971) (*per curiam*) *rev'g* 439 F.2d 1331 (8th Cir. 1971).
526. *Rodriguez v. McGinnis,* 10 *Criminal Law Reporter* 2365 (2d Cir., Jan. 25, 1972) (*en banc*).
527. Cal. Pen. Code §2650 (West 1970). *See, e.g.,* Ariz. Rev. Stat. Ann. §31–127 (1956); Fla. Stat. Ann. §952.14 (1944); Nev. Rev. Stat. §212.010 (1968).

often cite the possibility of criminal prosecution as the only available remedy.[528]

Unfortunately, this is perhaps the least satisfactory of all recourses for prisoners to redress grievances. Although there are reported instances of criminal sanctions against jailors under the English common law,[529] modern prosecutors understandably have been reluctant to invoke local criminal statutes against fellow officials. Only in North Carolina does there seem to have been any effort to hold prison employees accountable for their crimes against prisoners. In 1916, a North Carolina jury found a prison road-camp guard guilty of assault and battery for exceeding the instructions of his superintendent by whipping a prisoner between fifteen and twenty times.[530] According to the North Carolina Supreme Court, this punishment was "excessive and unnecessarily humiliating." Several years later, the same court reversed an assault conviction of a prison-camp superintendent for flogging a prisoner with a leather strap, on the ground that the state legislature had specifically authorized corporal punishment for disciplining "unruly" prisoners.[531] When a prisoner caught "talking on the road" was handcuffed to the bars of his cell for seventy hours, however, the court rejected the superintendent's argument that the corporal punishment was not cruel and unusual because it was authorized by the prison rules.[532]

In some cases, legislatures have enacted special penal statutes to regulate the treatment of prisoners. In California, for example, it is a misdemeanor

> to use in the prisons, any cruel, corporal or unusual punishment or to inflict any treatment or allow any lack of care whatever which would injure or impair the health of the prisoner, inmate or person confined; and punishment by the use of the strait jacket, gag, thumb-screw, shower-bath or the tricing up of prisoners, inmates or persons confined is hereby prohibited.[533]

528. *E.g., Bush v. Babb,* 23 Ill. App. 2d 285, 162 N.E.2d 594 (1959) (statutory duty to provide medical care owed to public but not to individual prisoners; only state can sue for violation); *Ridgway v. Superior Court,* 74 Ariz. 117, 245 P.2d 268, 272 (1952) (criminal statutes concerning offenses against children cited as the proper remedy for floggings and other punishments of boys in institutions for juveniles).
529. 1 Hawk. Pl. Cr. ch. 31 §§10, 119 (1777); *see* Rubin, *The Law of Criminal Correction* 386–87 (1963).
530. *State v. Mincher,* 172 N.C. 895, 90 S.E. 429 (1916). The guard had been instructed to whip the prisoner five or six times.
531. *State v. Revis,* 193 N.C. 192, 136 S.E. 346 (1927).
532. *State v. Carpenter,* 231 N.C. 229, 240, 56 S.E.2d 713, 721 (1949) (lower court decision reversed on other grounds).
533. Cal. Pen. Code §§2652, 2653 (West 1970).

In addition, any person who treats a state prisoner in his custody with "wilful inhumanity or oppression" may be fined up to $2,000 and removed from office. But these statutes have not been enforced, and for all practical purposes they are a dead letter. When sensational publicity and investigations by state and federal authorities resulted in the prosecution of several Arkansas prison employees under a state statute making it a felony to exceed punishments prescribed by the State Penitentiary Board,[534] the Arkansas Supreme Court upheld the dismissal of all charges, holding the statute void as an unconstitutional delegation of legislative power.[535]

In a few extreme cases, almost all of them involving Southern prisons, the United States Department of Justice has reacted to the failure of states to prosecute by obtaining federal indictments of local officials under the criminal provisions of the federal Civil Rights Act. That statute provides in part that

> Whoever, under the color of any law, statute, ordinance, regulation, or custom, willfully subjects any inhabitant of any State, Territory, or District to the deprivation of any rights, privileges, or immunities secured or protected by the Constitution or laws of the United States . . . shall be fined not more than $1,000 or imprisoned not more than one year, or both.[536]

In three cases decided in the 1950s,[537] federal appeals courts ruled that summary or corporal punishment of convicts could violate the statute, regardless of whether the punishments were authorized by state law.[538]

534. Ark. Stat. Ann. §46–158 (1964).
535. *State v. Bruton*, 246 Ark. 288, 437 S.W.2d 795 (1969). In the absence of an adequate yardstick for the guidance of the board, it could set minimums or extremes of punishment without restraint. The effect of this statute is to authorize an administrative body to impose criminal liability upon penitentiary employees based upon rules fixed by it. *Id.* at 289, 437 S.W.2d at 796.
536. 18 U.S.C. §242 (1964).
537. *United States v. Jackson*, 235 F.2d 925 (8th Cir. 1956); *United States v. Walker*, 216 F.2d 683 (5th Cir. 1954); *United States v. Jones*, 207 F.2d 785 (5th Cir. 1953).
538. A convicted prisoner remains under the protection of the Fourteenth Amendment except as to those rights expressly or by necessary implication taken from him by law. He still has his right to be secure in his person against unlawful beating done under color of law willfully to deprive him of the right.
United States v. Jackson, 235 F.2d 925, 929 (8th Cir. 1956).
[f]ederal laws may be violated within prison walls, and federal crimes committed therein . . . and the fact that state officers are violating state as well as federal laws does not exonerate them from penalties under the latter. . . . Color of law, as used in the statute, means pretense of law; it may include, but does not necessarily mean, under authority of law.
United States v. Jones, 207 F.2d 785, 786–87.

After the Arkansas Supreme Court had precluded state prosecution of prison employees,[539] federal indictments were returned against fifteen employees and former employees for inflicting cruel and unusual punishment on state and county prisoners.[540] Juries voted to acquit in six of the cases. In a seventh case, the jury could not agree, and the defendant, a former superintendent of the Tucker State Prison Farm, changed his plea to *nolo contendere* and was fined $1,000.[541] The judge who sentenced him imposed the maximum fine allowable under the statute but decided not to send the defendant to prison:

> I don't believe you could live 60 days in a Federal Penitentiary or a jail.
> I think that long before that time, some one or more of these persons or their friends with whom you have dealt in the past as inmates of the Arkansas Penitentiary will kill you. . . . The court doesn't want to give you a death sentence.

Recently, federal indictments were returned against deputy sheriffs in Alameda County, California, for violating the civil rights of persons arrested in connection with the "People's Park" incidents in Berkeley.[542] Two of the deputies were accused of "forcing a prisoner to place his head against a metal pole at the jail and then clubbing the opposite side of the pole." Three others were accused of "holding, beating, choking and striking" a prisoner while booking him. According to the county sheriff, the United States attorney responsible for the indictments had "taken these deputies and thrown them to the wolves," setting a "terrible example of law enforcement."[543]

CONTEMPT

The contempt power is the traditional legal weapon by which courts have enforced their orders. By definition, one is held to be in contempt upon disobedience to an existing order. Although courts may implement this power in virtually any situation involving such non-compliance, it rarely has been used to support prisoners who are seeking enforcement of court orders.

In 1889 a federal district judge in Georgia sentenced a defendant to

539. *State v. Bruton,* 246 Ark. 288, 437 S.W.2d 795 (1969).
540. *See* New York *Times,* Nov. 23, 1969, at 32, col. 1.
541. New York *Times,* Jan. 19, 1970, at 37, col. 2.
542. Washington *Post,* Feb. 4, 1970, at A-3, col. 1.
543. *Id.*

a local jail.[544] Later he read in a newspaper of the prisoner's disorderly conduct and the consequent disciplinary measures imposed by the jailer: "He was chained by the neck to the grating of the cell, and by the time he stands up until this morning, and lives a day or two on bread and water, he will probably be willing to be disciplined." Outraged by this treatment of a prisoner he had sentenced, the judge ordered an investigation and directed the jailer to show cause why he should not be held in contempt of court. Upon a failure to show cause, the jailer was fined fifty dollars plus court costs—the fine to be suspended as long as the offense was not repeated. This is the first reported case of a sentencing judge's use of the broad, inherent contempt power to discipline a jailer for violating his implicit responsibility for the safekeeping of prisoners committed to his custody by the court. Although there was no precedent for this use of the contempt power, the judge reasoned that the abuse of power was so extreme and so dangerous that some judicial remedy simply had to be established.[545]

A few years later, the Supreme Court itself used the contempt power to punish disobedience of a federal court order that a Negro be detained safely pending appeal of a rape conviction.[546] The Court ruled that the county sheriff and other defendants could be held in contempt for allowing the prisoner to be lynched. Justice Oliver Wendell Holmes, Jr., characterized the alleged offense as a conspiracy "to break into the jail for the purpose of lynching and murdering [the prisoner] with intent to show contempt for the order of this court. . . ." The conclusion that disrespect of the court was the essence of the misconduct may seem farfetched. Nevertheless, the case provides another example of a court searching for an inherent power with which to remedy the abuse of prisoners where other governmental action seems unlikely.

544. *In re* Birdsong, 39 F. 599 (S.D. 1889).
545. Now, can it be pretended that the court is powerless to compel the jailer to the performance of his duty, or to prevent or punish its non-performance in the presence of this important relation to the administration of justice imposed by law? . . .
  [N]either this court, nor, indeed, the highest court in the land, would assume, even after a full hearing, to exercise the power to chain up by the neck a prisoner for disorderly conduct, even the most atrocious, and even though committed in the actual presence of the court. Had any judge of America done with the most degraded convict what this jailer admits he did with the person of this prisoner, his impeachment would be inevitable. Well, may a jailer arrogate to himself powers which are withheld from the courts? Is it competent for the jailer in his discretion to inflict penalties and to exercise arbitrary powers which are not deemed safe or appropriate to be entrusted to the judges? The proposition is unworthy of any intelligent mind trained in the letter or the philosophy of the law.
Id. at 600–601.
546. *United States v. Shipp*, 203 U.S. 563 (1906).

Two state courts have discussed the possible use of the contempt power to ensure the safekeeping of prison inmates. In *Howard v. State*, decided in 1925,[547] the Supreme Court of Arizona affirmed a lower court's decision to hold the superintendent of an adult prison in contempt for his apparent unduly harsh treatment of a prisoner:

> When . . . the superintendent of the prison receives the commitment, which is his only authority for detaining any man within that prison, he may only do what that commitment orders him, to wit, "receive and safely keep" the defendant for the time specified therein. If, without legal justification, he does more than is necessary to so safely keep him, he is violating the law just as much as he is in releasing him before the expiration of his minimum term of sentence. . . .
>
> When a court of record in a civil action orders a party to do or not to do a certain thing, and its order is disobeyed the remedy is the invocation of that inherent power existing in all such courts to punish a violation of its order as a contempt. . . . We see no reason why this power does not exist as well in criminal cases. . . .
>
> The superintendent of the state prison is ex officio an officer of each superior court of the state for the purpose of carrying out its proper sentences, and is subject to attachment for contempt if he departs therefrom. . . .

In 1952, however, the superintendent of a boys' training school successfully petitioned the same court to quash a juvenile court's contempt proceedings against him and other employees of the school.[548] The employees had subjected two court-committed juveniles to disciplinary measures that included floggings, long hikes in bare feet, barefoot labor in briar patches and standing at attention without food in the mess hall while the other boys ate their meals. Denying the authority of the *Howard* case, the court held that the commitment order constituted nothing more than an order to the superintendent to receive and keep the child until he reaches his twenty-first birthday or is discharged sooner by law. According to the court, judges only have power to commit juveniles, thereby abrogating responsibility over sentenced prisoners to executive officials. A dissenting opinion argued that the juvenile court has exclusive and continuing juris-

547. 28 Ariz. 433, 237 P. 203 (1925), *overruled, Ridgeway v. Superior Court*, 74 Ariz. 117, 245 P.2d 268 (1952).
548. *Ridgway v. Superior Court*, 74 Ariz. 117, 245 P.2d 268 (1952).

diction in all matters affecting juvenile children—a fact recognized but considered irrelevant by the majority—and urged that this jurisdiction gave the court the power to protect the children it commits.

Several years later, the Supreme Court of Rhode Island[549] ruled that a petition to adjudge a warden or custodial officer in contempt of a court's order of commitment is an appropriate means of correcting prison abuses. The court limited this use of contempt to cases of cruel and unusual punishment, refusing to broaden its applicability to include cases involving inappropriate classification of inmates into degrees of security.

When a federal court sentences a convicted defendant, it commits him to the custody of the Attorney General. Although the prisoner's "safekeeping" is not made an explicit condition of the commitment order, a recent court-of-appeals decision pointed out that "Congress has clearly committed the custody and safekeeping of federal prisoners upon conviction to the Attorney General. . . ."[550] Such reasoning might be used to support a contempt citation against federal correction officials who act callously and violently to prisoners in their charge.

Employment of the contempt power could be expanded to provide another appropriate recourse for prisoners' claims of maltreatment. It is unlikely, however, that it would be available for frequent use because of the political nature of the remedy and the practical problems of proof, even in cases of egregious misconduct. Nonetheless, conscientious judges could change the local climate in prisoner-correctional official relationships by acknowledging a responsibility to assure the integrity of their sentences in appropriate cases.

On the other hand, even where contempt may be the only means of enforcing a judicial decree, courts have been reluctant to use this extraordinary remedy even in civil cases.[551] Prisoners have not yet attempted to have officials held in contempt for failure to carry out judicial orders. The success of such an endeavor is unlikely since the persistent rationale of prison discipline may be expected to make judges even more loathe to

---

549. *State v. Brant,* 99 R.I. 583, 209 A.2d 455 (1965). The court, however, refused to invoke its contempt power against a warden who had carried out an invalid decision of a classification board to keep a prisoner in administrative segregation for purposes of security.
550. *Close v. United States,* 397 F.2d 686, 687 (D.C. Cir. 1968).
551. In the field of labor law, where many contempt actions have been brought to enforce court orders, courts have been reluctant to use the remedy where there is any question of whether a judicial decree has in fact been violated. *See, e.g., N.L.R.B. v. American Aggregate Co.,* 335 F.2d 253 (5th Cir. 1964) (court reversed master's finding that company should be held in contempt for failing to abide by court order to bargain in good faith with union).

use their contempt power. For example, in one of a series of federal court cases dealing with the Arkansas prison system, an otherwise sympathetic district judge was "not persuaded"[552] that the court orders[553] in question had been violated.

In addition to questions surrounding judicial willingness to use contempt to enforce decrees, there is the question of who may bring an action for such enforcement. When judges determine issues on a case-by-case basis, the result may be a ruling that is of use only to the original plaintiff:

> While this court, faced with the facts in *Howard* and *Landman,* spoke quite harshly of the uses made of "C" Building, we certainly did not intend to imply that a prisoner's confinement there may not be justified and represent a valid exercise of the judgment and discretion of prison officials in the difficult area of penitentiary discipline.[554]

Where a court refuses to expand the applicability of its findings, a prisoner not party to that action cannot claim the benefits of a favorable judicial decision without litigating anew.

CLASS ACTIONS

Class actions, in which suits are brought by or against representatives of a class and a decree in favor of or against representatives of a group binds all members of the class, were developed by courts of equity as an answer to the practical problems of multiparty litigation: the unwieldy number of interested parties to the suit, the difficulty of subjecting all the members to service of process and the likelihood that the membership of so large a group may change during the course of the suit. The nature of actions like this is made to order for litigation by prisoners aimed at general conditions. Judgments in favor of the representatives to a suit would then apply to the entire class and could be enforced by any member of the class. It would be useful, too, for prison

552. *Holt v. Sarver,* 300 F. Supp. 825, 828 (E.D. Ark. 1969).
553. *Jackson v. Bishop,* 404 F.2d 571 (8th Cir. 1968).
554. *Abernathy v. Cunningham,* 393 F.2d 775, 777 (4th Cir. 1968), *cert. denied,* 385 U.S. 988 (1966), in which the court emphasized its earlier opinions, citing *Howard v. Smyth,* 365 F.2d 428 (4th Cir. 1966), and *Landman v. Peyton,* 370 F.2d 135 (4th Cir. 1966).

administrators, who could reduce multiple litigation through precedential test cases.

In *Jordan v. Fitzharris*,[555] a federal district court enjoined California prison authorities from subjecting plaintiff to violations of the Civil Rights Act by confining him in a "strip cell" which lacked the "essentials for survival." The court's opinion was worded in terms that could benefit all inmates of the Soledad prison, or perhaps of the entire California penal system:

> If the defendants intend to continue with the use of the so-called "strip" or "quiet" cell as device in the general plan of solitary confinement, then its use must be accompanied by supplying the basic requirements which are essential to life, and by providing such essential requirements as may be necessary to maintain a degree of cleanliness compatible with elemental decency in accord with the standards of a civilized community. . . .
>
> Primitive segregation cells should be so constructed that all parts are visible to the patrolling officer from the corridor. Such cells or at least some of them should be sound proofed. . . .

Yet, if the defendants continued using "strip cells" to discipline other prisoners without conforming to the standards set out by the court,[556] the other affected prisoners probably would have to initiate another lawsuit for their relief, relying on the *Jordan* decision as precedent. If, on the other hand, the *Jordan* suit initially had been a class action, any members of the class included in the decree later could attempt to enforce it by bringing an action for contempt against the prison officials.

Where prisoners are uneducated, unaware of their rights or of the means for implementing them, or unrepresented by counsel, a class suit could provide the only practical means for presenting their grievances to a court. Moreover, class suits are frequently more efficient and economical than individual actions and save time for the courts, the defending prison officials and the attorneys. For example, when Georgia prisoners succeeded in a class action in federal court to desegregate all correctional institutions in the state,[557] other prisoners who later sought to block

555. 257 F. Supp. 674 (N.D. Cal. 1966). *See* notes 86–88 *supra* and accompanying text.
556. *See* Cal. State Legislature, Black Caucus Report: *Treatment of Prisoners at California Training Facility at Soledad Central* (1970).
557. *Wilson v. Kelley*, 294 F. Supp. 1005 (N.D. Ga. 1968), *aff'd per curiam*, 393 U.S. 266 (1969).

the integration in one prison were precluded from pursuing endless litigation on the ground that they were within the class of plaintiffs represented by the earlier action.[558]

Presently, the disadvantage of a class suit by prisoners is that many judges continue to be reluctant to issue broad orders in prison cases. For example, although condemning the abuses associated with punitive segregation of prisoners, no court has been willing to forbid the use of solitary confinement as punishment in all cases. Specific decisions ordering changes in prison conditions often are said to be based on "exceptional circumstances" present only in the case under consideration. A judge presented with a class action might well be hesitant to order sweeping changes that must apply throughout a state or federal prison system.[559] Perhaps this judicial reluctance could be reduced by suing on behalf of a smaller group than the inmates of an entire prison system.[560] A typical class action might be brought by prisoners incarcerated in a single prison or part of a prison, such as death row or a maximum-security unit. Other "classes" might represent inmates of particular religion.

Although class actions are permitted by state statutes, their use has been relatively rare. In fact, there is not a single decision by a state court in which prisoners were allowed to bring a class suit against prison officials. New Jersey,[561] Florida[562] and Colorado[563] courts have denied prisoners the right to bring class suits for *habeas corpus* or other post-conviction relief from their original convictions. According to the New Jersey opinion, "a commitment to prison acts individually on each person committed, and a writ seeking his discharge on *habeas corpus* must likewsie be individual."[564] The Colorado court agreed that "the very nature of *habeas corpus* proceedings forfends class actions."[565]

The adoption of a modified Rule 23 of the Federal Rules of Civil Procedure in 1966 brought federal class actions into greater prominence

---

558. *Wren v. Smith,* 410 F.2d 390 (5th Cir. 1969). Unfairness in this regard should be minimized by the notice and intervention provisions of Fed. R. Civ. P. 23(c).
559. *Cf. Ford v. Board of Managers,* 407 F.2d 937 (3d Cir. 1969).
560. *See Rakes v. Coleman,* 318 F. Supp. 181 (E.D. Va. 1970) (alcoholics confined in state prisons); *Blyden v. Hogan,* 320 F. Supp. 513 (S.D.N.Y. 1970) (untried jail inmates who had signed consent-to-interview forms following New York riots); *Valvano v. McGrath,* 8 *Criminal Law Reporter* 2397 (S.D.N.Y., Jan. 15, 1971) (inmates seeking injunction against reprisals for riot).
561. Petition of Santiago, 104 N.J. Super. 110, 248 A.2d 701 (1968) (defendants tried as disorderly persons improperly denied juries).
562. State *ex rel. Williams v. Purdy,* 242 So.2d 498 (Fla. 1971).
563. *Riley v. City and County of Denver,* 137 Colo. 312, 324 P.2d 790 (1958) (challenge to void judgments of municipal courts).
564. 104 N.J. Super. at 114, 248 A.2d at 704.
565. 137 Colo. at 313, 324 P.2d at 791.

than they had enjoyed previously and simplified the requirements surrounding them. Under the new rule, there are four requirements for the maintenance of any class action in federal court: (1) The class must be so numerous that it is impractical to bring them all before the court; (2) There must be questions of law or fact common to the class; (3) The claims or defenses of the representative parties must be typical of the claims or defenses of the class; (4) The representative parties must be able to protect the interests of the class fairly and adequately.[566]

In addition to the four general requirements, a class action must fall into one of three categories. First, the prosecution of separate actions must create a risk of inconsistent adjudications or impede the ability of other members of the class to protect their own interests.[567] Second, the party opposing the ·class must have acted or refused to act on grounds generally applicable to the class.[568] And, third, a court may allow a class action where "the questions of law or fact common to the members of the class predominate over any questions affecting only individual members, and that a class action is superior to other available methods for the fair and efficient adjudication of the controversy."[569]

No court has considered these three categories with reference to class actions by prisoners. The federal courts in Arkansas have permitted class actions by state prisoners under the Civil Rights Act.[570] In three cases thus far, courts have decided that Arkansas prisoners had meritorious complaints and fashioned relief that would apply to all other prisoners in the state.[571] A complaint attacking disciplinary procedures and punishments at San Quentin recently was permitted to proceed as a

566. Fed. R. Civ. P. 23(a).
567. See Booth v. General Dynamics Corp., 264 F. Supp. 465 (N.D. Ill. 1967).
568. Fed. R. Civ. P. 23(b)(2); see Eisen v. Carlisle and Jacqueline, 391 F.2d 555, 564 (2d Cir. 1968); Note, "Proposed Rule 23: Class Actions Reclassified," 51 Virginia Law Review 629, 648–49 (1965).
569. Fed. R. Civ. P. 23(b)(3); see Esplin v. Hirschi, 402 F.2d 94 (10th Cir. 1968), cert. denied, 394 U.S. 928 (1969); Hohmann v. Packard Instrument Co., 399 F.2d 711 (7th Cir. 1968).
570. Jackson v. Bishop, 404 F.2d 571, 573 (8th Cir. 1968): "We are also satisfied, as were the district judges, that the cases are appropriately to be regarded as class actions within the scope and reach of Rule 23, Fed. R. Civ. P." Holt v. Sarver, 300 F. Supp. 825, 827 (E.D. Ark. 1969): "The petitions were submitted by the inmates pro se. The Court permitted them to be filed and prosecuted as class actions in forma pauperis and consolidated them for hearing."
571. In Jackson v. Bishop, the court enjoined the superintendent "and all personnel of the penitentiary system from inflicting corporal punishment, including the use of the strap, as a disciplinary measure." 404 F.2d at 581. In Holt v. Sarver, the court combined an injunction with a declaratory judgment and gave the Arkansas Commissioner of Correction thirty days to report on the steps he planned to take that would "make a substantial start toward alleviating the conditions that the Court has found to be unconstitutional." 300 F. Supp. at 833.

class action on behalf of all inmates affected by the challenged practices.[572]

Most of the growing number of challenges to conditions of local jails have been brought as class actions. Courts have permitted class actions on behalf of inmates of the Cook County Jail,[573] the New Orleans Parish Prison,[574] the county jail in Little Rock, Arkansas[575] and two county jails in California.[576] In a case involving a successful challenge to conditions in a local Ohio jail, a federal district court concluded:

> It is apparent . . . that this action can only be maintained realistically as a class action. . . . The claims of any particular individual could easily become moot at any time, and must become moot within a relatively limited period. It is also very difficult to demonstrate that any one individual has suffered a specific wrong which can be righted without regard to the totality of wrongs in the system.[577]

On the other hand, a federal district judge refused to permit an action on behalf of inmates of the Milwaukee County Jail because of his doubts that adequate notice could be given to the members of the class, many of whom were transients and held in jail for only a short time.[578] Since any judgment in the case would have little effect on these "transients," it is not clear why this obstacle was considered insurmountable.

A federal court in New Jersey refused to allow a class action on behalf of New Jersey prisoners protesting solitary-confinement conditions, even though all of the prisoners were potentially exposed to the challenged deprivations. The court reasoned that a class suit was improper where the circumstances surrounding the imposition of punishment varied according to individual cases.[579]

These cases appear to fall into the second category of class actions under Rule 23, where the group has been treated as a class by the other

---

572. *Clutchette v. Procunier*, 328 F. Supp. 941 (S.D.N.Y. 1971); *cf. Bundy v. Cannon*, 328 F. Supp. 165 (D. Md. 1971).
573. *Inmates of the Cook County Jail v. Tierney*, No. 68 C 504 (N.D. Ill. 1968).
574. *Hamilton v. Schiro*, 328 F. Supp. 1182 (E.D. Ark. 1971).
575. *Hamilton v. Love*, 9 *Criminal Law Reporter* 2293 (E.D. Ark., June 2, 1971).
576. *Brenneman v. Madigan*, No. 70–1911 (N.D. Cal., Mar. 11, 1971); *Dean v. Young*, No. 123849 (N.D. Cal., Mar. 17, 1971).
577. *Jones v. Wittenberg*, 323 F. Supp. 93 (judgment), 330 F. Supp. 707 (order) (N.D. Ohio 1971).
578. *Shank v. Peterson*, 8 *Criminal Law Reporter* 2397 (E.D. Wisc., Jan. 12, 1971).
579. *Ford v. Board of Managers*, Civ. No. 946–67 (D. N.J. decided April 30, 1968), aff'd on other grounds, 407 F.2d 937 (3d Cir. 1969) (*per curiam*).

party to the suit.[580] Although designed primarily to deal with civil rights cases involving discrimination against large groups such as racial minorities, the provision is not limited to these cases. "[A]ction or inaction is directed to a class within the meaning of this subdivision even if it has taken effect or is threatened only as to one or a few members of the class, provided it is based on grounds which have general application to the class."[581] This explanatory language of the Advisory Committee seems to refute the argument of the New Jersey court that differing circumstances of disciplinary action preclude a class action. So long as all prisoners may be subjected at some time to the questioned deprivations, a class action would seem appropriate.[582]

Several class actions for the desegregation of state and local prisons[583] have been successfully brought under the third category of Rule 23. This subsection permits judicial discretion to allow a class suit where common questions predominate.[584] The Supreme Court has affirmed this use of class actions.[585]

Class actions for *habeas corpus* present more difficult problems. No substantial reason has been offered to distinguish class actions in prisoners' *habeas corpus* suits under the Civil Rights Act. Yet, although *habeas corpus* actions are considered "civil" suits,[586] the extent to which the Federal Rules of Civil Procedure apply to such actions is unclear. Nevertheless, federal courts frequently have applied the provisions of particular rules to *habeas corpus* actions when they seemed useful.[587] And, in a recent decision, the Supreme Court ruled that, although Rule 23 does not apply to *habeas corpus* proceedings, a federal district court may fashion

---

580. Prisoners, each having been convicted of a crime, are generally treated as a class in being denied civil rights given other citizens.
581. Fed. R. Civ. P. 23 (Advisory Committee notes).
582. *But see Wright v. McMann,* 321 F. Supp. 127, 137 (N.D.N.Y. 1970) (on remand; class action inappropriate in suit for damages and injunction where damages, liability and defenses affect different individuals in different ways).
583. *Training School for Boys v. George,* 377 F.2d 228 (8th Cir. 1967); *Singleton v. Board of Commissioners,* 356 F.2d 71 (5th Cir. 1966) (Florida state reform schools); *Wilson v. Kelley,* 294 F. Supp. 1005 (N.D. Ga. 1968), *aff'd per curiam,* 393 U.S. 266 (1969) (all Georgia penal institutions); *Washington v. Lee,* 263 F. Supp. 327 (M.D. Ala. 1966), *aff'd per curiam,* 390 U.S. 333 (1968) (all Alabama penal institutions).
584. Fed. R. Civ. P. 23(2) (3).
585. *Lee v. Washington,* 390 U.S. 333 (1968) (*per curiam*).
586. *E.g., U.S. v. Williamson,* 255 F.2d 512 (5th Cir.), *cert. denied,* 358 U.S. 941 (1958); *Estep v. Texas,* 251 F.2d 579 (5th Cir. 1958).
587. *E.g., Schiebelhut v. United States,* 318 F.2d 785 (6th Cir. 1963) (rule 33); *United States ex rel. Seals v. Winman,* 304 F.2d 53, 63–64 (5th Cir. 1962), *United States ex rel. Tillery v. Cavell,* 294 F.2d 12, 18 (3d Cir. 1961), *cert. denied,* 370 U.S. 945 (1962) (rule 60(a)); *Estep v. United States,* 251 F.2d 579, 581–83 (5th Cir. 1958) (rules 45(c) & 41(a)(1)); *Bowen v. Bowles,* 258 F. Supp. 111, 113 (N.D. W. Va. 1966) (rule 6(b)(2)), *cert. denied,* 372 U.S. 915, 924 (1963) (rule 36).

suitable discovery procedures in actions for *habeas corpus*.[588]

The Supreme Court has left open the question whether Rule 23 may be applied in a *habeas corpus* action.[589] The three lower federal courts that have dealt with this question reached only tentative—and differing— conclusions. Prisoners on death row in California[590] and Florida[591] each attempted to bring class actions to challenge death sentences imposed in unrelated trials.[592] The California action was on behalf of all persons "who are presently under sentences of death by the State . . . or who have been convicted of capital crime and are hence subject to the death penalty under the laws of the State. . . ."[593] The district court decided that in order to determine conclusively the merit of every claim that each prisoner could raise, it would require individual rather than class petitions:

> We do not say that a class action for a writ of habeas corpus could never under any circumstances be maintained but determine at this time that because of the procedural problems inherent in this proceeding, use of such a class suit does not appear the most practicable vehicle to determine the issues presented.

Following a preliminary hearing, the Florida court decided that the factual record was insufficient to determine whether a class action was appropriate. The court then ordered prison officials to permit the petitioners' attorneys to interview all death-row inmates not already represented by counsel to determine the status of their legal proceedings.[594] It is too soon to ascertain whether this is an implicit acknowledgment that under correct circumstances class actions will be appropriate in these cases.

588. *Harris v. Nelson*, 394 U.S. 291 (1969). Rule 81(a)(2) can be read as merely denying the direct applicability of particular federal rules and not precluding their indirect application or the development of parallel or quite different procedures.
589.   The applicability to habeas corpus of the rules concerning joinder and class actions has engendered considerable debate. . . . The only issue before the Court in this case is the applicability to habeas corpus proceedings of those rules which deal with discovery. We intimate no view on whether the Federal Rules may be applicable with respect to other aspects of a habeas corpus proceedings.
Harris v. Nelson, 394 U.S. 291, 295 n.5.
590. *Hill v. Nelson*, 272 F. Supp. 790 (N.D. Cal. 1967).
591. *Adderly v. Wainwright*, 272 F. Supp. 530 (M.D. Fla. 1967).
592. Federal courts routinely have allowed joint petitions for *habeas corpus* by petitioners convicted at the same trial. *E.g.*, United States *ex rel. Poret v. Sigler*, 361 U.S. 375 (1960); *DeGrandis v. Fay*, 335 F.2d 173 (2d Cir. 1964); *Curtis v. Bolger*, 331 F.2d 675 (8th Cir. 1964).
593. *Hill v. Nelson*, 272 F. Supp. 790, 792 (N.D. Cal. 1967).
594. *Adderly v. Wainwright*, 272 F. Supp. 530, 532–33 (M.D. Fla. 1967).

In another federal *habeas corpus* case, three inmates of the Baltimore City Jail, along with the American Civil Liberties Union, challenged convictions based on curfew violations that occurred during the April 1968 riots as "next friends on behalf of an estimated fifty persons similarly situated."[595] Since the petition was dismissed for failure to exhaust state remedies, questions of the propriety of class actions and the standing of the plaintiffs to represent a class of convicts were not reached.

The suggestion has been made that the appropriateness of class actions in *habeas corpus* proceedings challenging the legality of prisoners' detention should be determined by balancing the importance of the issues common to the individual claims against the importance of variations in the relevant facts.[596] A similar criterion could be employed where the *habeas corpus* petition challenges the treatment of inmates, rather than the legality of their original convictions or sentences. Possibly this balancing approach, like that employed in cases heard under Rule 23, will result in a greater number of class suits in the prisoners'-rights cases than in those involving the legality of the detention, where variations in the crimes charged and in individual trials must be considered.

In the class desegregation suits one question that has been raised frequently is the appropriateness of the individual plaintiffs and defendants to raise and defend particular issues on behalf of an affected class. It appears to be settled, at least where statewide statutes and policies are involved, that prisoners may sue on behalf of all the inmates of a state penal system and that the plaintiffs need not include a representative of each institution that will be affected by the judgment.[597] Similarly, in

---

595. *Mitchell v. Schoonfield*, 285 F. Supp. 728 (D. Md. 1968).

596. Note, "Multiparty Federal Habeas Corpus," 81 *Harvard Law Review* 1487–88 (1968).

597. *See Marable v. Alabama Mental Health Board*, 297 F. Supp. 291, 297 (M.D. Ala. 1969):

> It is no more necessary for the plaintiff to be confined in every facility administered by the Mental Health Board than it was for the plaintiff-inmates in *Washington v. Lee* . . . who were held to be a proper class to challenge practices at all Alabama correctional institutions to be incarcerated at every such institution.

Cf. Ford v. Board of Managers, 407 F.2d 937 (3d Cir. 1969), in which the denial of a class suit on behalf of all New Jersey prisoners may have been motivated partly by the fact that the prisoner in whose name the suit had been brought was soon to be released and thus was not the appropriate party to protect the interests of the other prisoners. In addition, another prisoner had moved to intervene on the ground that "My interest is not adequately protected by Plaintiff Ford in that Ford had little or no knowledge of legal matters or procedure, whereas I do." *Id.* at 939. In *Wilson v. Kelley*, 294 F. Supp. 1005 (N.D. Ga. 1968), aff'd *per curiam*, 393 U.S. 266 (1969), the plaintiffs, white and black inmates of various penal institutions in Georgia, were permitted to challenge segregation practices on behalf of the 10,000 prisoners in the state. Other inmates were thereafter precluded from attacking the court's order to inte-

Washington v. Lee,[598] six inmates of various Alabama prisons and jails sued the Commissioner of Correction, members of the State Board of Correction, a sheriff and the warden of the Birmingham City Jail to force desegregation of the entire system. The sheriff and the warden objected that they did not represent all the wardens, jailers and sheriffs in the state. A three-judge district court responded that class defendants need not be identically situated and that it was immaterial that in this case only the officials in charge of the largest jails had been included:

> It would be extremely difficult, if not impossible, to find members of a class to serve as representative defendants in a case, such as this one, where there are not some material differences in the physical facilities and operations involved. But since the rule requires only that there be questions of law and fact common to these defendants and the members of the class which they represent . . . then it becomes immaterial whether certain of these class defendants are not otherwise identically situated.

Furthermore, once deemed a proper party, a change of a plaintiff's status will not defeat litigation in this class of cases. Plaintiffs in desegregation suits have been permitted to continue representing a class of prisoners even if they are released during the pendency of the action, as long as they can show "past use of the facilities, where feasible, and right to, or a reasonable possibility of future use."[599] This possibility exists, for example, where a juvenile is released from a reform school conditionally,[600] or perhaps simply where he is of juvenile-court age.[601]

But the representative status must be clear to the court. Black prisoners were not permitted to attack the employment practices of Georgia penal institutions where only thirteen of the 857 employees of the State

---

grate the prisons. However, when the same plaintiffs attempted to challenge the system of sentencing to county public-works camps, they were not permitted to do so on the ground that "there is considerable doubt as to plaintiffs' standing as representatives of a class. The court is far from convinced that all prisoners at county public works camps would prefer being inmates at the Reidsville State Penitentiary." *Id.* at 1009–12.

598. 263 F. Supp. 327 (M.D. Ala. 1966), *aff'd per curiam,* 390 U.S. 333 (1968).

599. *Singleton v. Board of Commissioners,* 356 F.2d 771, 773 (5th Cir. 1966). Once released, however, it is not necessary for the plaintiffs, adult or juvenile, "to show an intention to violate the laws of the State . . . or the City . . . in such a manner that would subject one or more of them in the future to imprisonment in these locations." 253 F. Supp. at 329–30.

600. *Singleton v. Board of Commissioners,* 356 F.2d 771, 774 (5th Cir. 1966).

601. *Id.* at 774 n.4. *But see State Board of Public Works v. Myers,* 224 Md. 246, 167 A.2d 765, 768 (1961) (dictum) (male juvenile has no standing to attack operation of reform school for girls since he is not eligible for admission).

Board of Correction were black,[602] even though blacks composed 56 percent of the state prison population:

[N]ot a single plaintiff or witness offered has ever even applied for a job in any such capacity. As prisoners they constitute a proper class for contesting their segregated status. However, as a proper class under Rule 23 for employment purposes they obviously do not.[603]

As the prisoners' brief pointed out,[604] and one of the judges recognized, the effect on black prisoners of discriminatory hiring of prison employees is analogous to the effect on black school children of racially segregated faculties. Pupils now have standing to challenge the existence of segregated faculties.[605] In an analogous case, another three-judge court allowed patients of state mental institutions to attack discriminatory hiring practices based on this secondary-effect argument.[606]

At least it is clear that the class suit can be used widely and imaginatively by inmates questioning internal operations and practices of correctional institutions which affect them directly. In at least one case,[607] a federal district judge cited the broad settlement and supervisory discretion under Rule 23 as support for an active judicial role in mediating, investigating and enforcing a settlement of the suit. The same is not true,

602. *Wilson v. Kelley,* 294 F. Supp. 1005 (N.D. Ga. 1968), *aff'd per curiam,* 393 U.S. 266 (1968). In addition, since the defendants all were separate employers, presumably with independent hiring policies, the court doubted that a judgment against them could bind prison officials of other local jurisdictions. *Cf. Sostre v. Rockefeller,* 312 F. Supp. 863 (S.D.N.Y. 1970) *aff'd in part, modified in part, rev'd in part sub nom. Sostre v. McGinnis,* 442 F.2d 178 (2d Cir. 1971) (*en banc*), *citing Washington v. Lee,* 263 F. Supp. 327 (M.D. Ala. 1966) for the proposition that "[p]laintiff, of course, has standing to challenge any racially discriminatory practices pursued by state officials in the state's prisons where he resides and is subject to reside," but concluding that the prisoner-plaintiff had failed to prove "that the paltry number of non-white guards and other personnel . . . resulted from racial discrimination against qualified applicants or a conspiracy to deny blacks and Puerto Ricans their rights." 312 F. Supp. at 876–77.
603. *Wilson v. Kelley,* 294 F. Supp. 1005, 1010 (N.D. Ga. 1968).
604. Brief for Plaintiff at 10 *Wilson v. Kelley,* 294 F. Supp. 1005 (N.D. Ga. 1968).
605. *E.g., United States v. Jefferson County Board of Education,* 372 F.2d 836, 883–86 (1966), *aff'd on rehearing en banc,* 380 F.2d 385 (5th Cir.), *cert. denied,* 389 U.S. 840 (1967); *Lee v. Macon County Board of Education,* 267 F. Supp. 458, 472, *aff'd sub nom. Wallace v. United States,* 389 U.S. 215 (1967).
606. *Marable v. Alabama Mental Health Board,* 297 F. Supp. 291, 297 (M.D. Ala. 1969):

We agree that plaintiffs do not have standing to challenge the practices as potential employees, but we must conclude that they do have standing because of the secondary effects on the plaintiffs as patients of the discrimination against staff personnel. Plaintiffs stand in the same relationship to the hospital staff as students in the public schools stand to their teachers.

607. *Morris v. Travisono,* 310 F. Supp. 857 (D. R.I. 1970).

however, where the prisoners challenge the administrative policies of correction agencies themselves.

The broadest use of the prisoners' class action to date occurred early in 1970.[608] A federal district court in Arkansas combined eight separate complaints and permitted the petitioners to sue on behalf of themselves, other prisoners and "other persons who may in the future be confined at Cummins or at Tucker [prison farms]." Although the court rejected the petitioners' individual claims, it concluded that the "overall situation" at the prisons made the operation of the entire system unconstitutional:

> It appears to the Court . . . that the concept of "cruel and unusual punishment" is not limited to instances in which a particular inmate is subjected to a punishment directed at him as an individual. In the Court's estimation confinement itself within a given institution may amount to a . . . punishment prohibited by the Constitution where the punishment is characterized by conditions and practices so bad as to be shocking to the conscience of reasonably civilized people even though a particular inmate may never personally be subject to any disciplinary action. . . . [O]verall conditions . . . may be so bad that it amounts to an unconstitutional cruel and unusual punishment to *expose* men to those conditions, regardless of how those conditions may operate fortuitously on particular individuals.

Regulating the Discretion of Prison Administrators

The practical problems of ensuring access to court and of successfully prosecuting a legal action make it essential to develop ways of holding prison authorities accountable for the fair and reasonable exercise of their broad discretion without taking every decision to court. Ironically, as criminal sentences became more flexible and different types of correctional programs with varying degrees of freedom and rehabilitative potential developed, the unchecked and almost complete discretion of correctional administrators over convicts increased. The President's Crime Commission recently noted that

608. *Holt v. Sarver*, 309 F. Supp. 362 (E.D. Ark. 1970), *aff'd* 442 F.2d 304 (8th Cir. 1971).

Today . . . an offender may be sentenced for an indeterminate length of time, with his release depending on the decision of correctional authorities. . . . And he may be subjected to special discipline or punishment on the basis of determinations from which he has no appeal.

Legislation ordinarily provides little guidance for these correctional decisions. Correctional administrators have been slow to develop policies and procedures to guide correctional officials and protect the rights of offenders. And trial and appellate courts have been reluctant to review either the merits of such decisions or the procedures by which they are made.

Yet it is inconsistent with our whole system of government to grant such uncontrolled power to any officials, particularly over the lives of persons. . . .

[E]xpert judgments in the field of corrections are no less fallible than judgments by labor boards or other administrative agencies.[609]

Within the authority of correctional administrators are decisions that are as crucial to the administration of justice as the adjudication of guilt, and hence in need of greater procedural safeguards. For example, correction and prison authorities determine the initial assignment or transfer of inmates to various institutions or halfway houses, their classification into degrees of custody, jobs and training programs, discipline for infractions of prison rules, revocation of good-time credits and granting of furloughs, work or school release. At a different level, affecting the mundane daily life of every prisoner, is the unsupervised, often unreviewed discretion of the lowest echelon of employees: the undereducated and undertrained guards. One attorney who has been active in litigation on behalf of inmates views this as the central problem in prisons:

Prisoners often have their privileges revoked, are denied the right of access to counsel, sit in solitary, or maximum security or lose "good time" on the basis of a single, unreviewed report of a guard. When the courts defer to administrative discretion, it is this guard to whom they delegate the final word on reasonable prison practices. This is the central evil in prison. It is not homosexuality, nor inadequate salaries, nor the cruelty and

609. President's Commission on Law Enforcement and Administration of Justice, *The Challenge of Crime in a Free Society* 179 (1967); Task Force Report: *Corrections* 82–83 (1967).

physical brutality of some of the guards. The central evil is the unreviewed administrative discretion granted to the poorly trained personnel who deal directly with the prisoners.[610]

This complete control over every aspect of an inmate's existence frequently deprives prisoners of their lives, their liberty and their property without due process of law.[611] Yet recent judicial opinions commonly assume that the due-process clauses of the Fifth and Fourteenth Amendments do apply to prisoners.[612] A federal court of appeals recently ruled that, although imprisonment necessarily brings about the withdrawal or limitation of many rights and privileges, acceptance of that fact "does not preclude recognition by the courts of a duty to protect the prisoner from unlawful and onerous treatment of a nature that, of itself, adds punitive measures to those legally meted out by the court."[613]

Despite these and similar pronouncements, significant problems remain in the application of due process to correctional decisions. Most courts have ignored the due-process clause entirely, confining their discussions to irrelevant labels, such as "privileges," "grace" and "vested" or

---

610. Hirschkop and Millemann, "The Unconstitutionality of Prison Life" 811–12, 55 *Virginia Law Review* 795 (1969). Affirming the dismissal of a complaint brought by a prisoner confined to the maximum-security unit of the Virginia State Penitentiary, Circuit Judge Simon Soboloff warned that

> Superintendent Peyton admitted that he does not make periodic inspections of the building and that while he "suppose[d]" that he has made surprise visits, he could not recall a single instance. . . .
> [I]nvestigations are limited to discussions with the guards involved; never, he stated, does he talk with the prisoners. . . .
> The record thus establishes that the fate of inmates confined in segregation or meditation is left largely to the unsupervised and unreviewed discretion of the guard staff assigned to "C" building. While written regulations governing their conduct have been promulgated, these are insufficient if no attempt is made to insure their observance.

Landman v. Peyton, 370 F.2d 135, 139–40 (4th Cir.) (dicta) (footnotes omitted), *cert. denied,* 385 U.S. 881 (1966).
   A consultants' report attributed a "guard riot"—a sweep of a District of Columbia prison for "trouble-makers" that left several prisoners seriously injured—to the lack of administrative supervision over the guards, as well as the guards' feelings of hostility toward their supervisors and the prisoners. Report on the Lorton Complex Incident, November 18, 1968, Submitted to The Honorable Walter E. Washington, District of Columbia, by the Mayor-Commissioner's Temporary Committee to Investigate Activities at the Lorton Correctional Complex.
611. This "arbitrary power in a prison-keeper to iron a prisoner, or indeed, to select at his pleasure a penalty which he thinks adequate as a disciplinary measure for real or fancied misconduct" was characterized over eighty years ago by a federal judge as "intolerable among a free and enlightened people" and having "no place among English-speaking nations." *In re* Birdsong, 39 F. 599, 600 (S.D. Ga. 1889).
612. *E.g., Washington v. Lee,* 263 F. Supp. 327, 331 (M.D. Ala. 1966), *aff'd per curiam,* 390 U.S. 333 (1968).
613. *Jackson v. Godwin,* 400 F.2d 529, 532 (5th Cir. 1968).

"contingent" rights.[614] Furthermore, even in the cases where courts have determined that some procedural protections are called for, except for a few significant and quite recent exceptions, they have neither defined the nature and extent of the procedures required nor supplied any reliable criteria for determining when the protections apply. The problems of imputing constitutional doctrine to the daily prison routine may be illustrated by an examination of several types of important decisions that are commonly made by prison authorities.[615]

PUNISHMENT OF PRISONERS FOR INFRACTIONS OF PRISON RULES

Prisoners generally are disciplined through imposition of special deprivations such as solitary confinement and the withdrawal of the few, simple remaining rewards of their existence by loss of privileges. The one sanction most complained about by prisoners, however, is the postponement of release dates by removal of statutory "good-time" credits (commonly awarded for time served without disciplinary infractions or for work done in prison industries).[616] Since judges normally take parole eligibility and good-time credits into account when sentencing convicted defendants, the subsequent administrative decision to postpone release in effect increases the sentence that was intended by the judge.

Although some correction departments publish inmates' handbooks listing the regulations that prisoners are expected to obey, most do not, and an inmate may have no idea of the rule he has violated until he is punished.[617] Even where written rules exist, they may be so vague as to be meaningless. For example, a pervasive regulation outlaws any manifestation of "disrespect" toward correctional officers. Thus, although courts have attempted to prevent punishment of prisoners exercising

614. *E.g., Sigler v. Lowrie,* 404 F.2d 659 (8th Cir. 1968), *cert. denied,* 395 U.S. 940 (1969); *Douglas v. Sigler,* 386 F.2d 684 (8th Cir. 1967). *Cf.* Van Alstyne, "The Demise of the Right-Privilege Distinction in Constitutional Law," 81 *Harvard Law Review* 1439 (1968).
615. The crucial, decision of whether and when to grant parole is generally made by an independent parole board. Despite a large number of challenges in recent years, courts have refused to impose any substantive or procedural requirements on the parole decision. *See, e.g., Bennett v. California,* 406 F.2d 36 (9th Cir.), *cert. denied,* 395 U.S. 940 (1969); *Padilla v. Lynch,* 398 F.2d 481 (9th Cir. 1968); *Sturm v. California Adult Authority,* 395 F.2d 446 (9th Cir. 1967), *cert. denied,* 394 U.S. 966 (1969).
616. *See, e.g.,* 18 U.S.C. §§4161 & 4165 (1964). Unlike the discipline by solitary confinement, there is no question of the constitutionality of postponing a prisoner's release date (within the limits of his sentence) for misbehavior in prison. What is questioned here is the procedures by which the decisions are made.
617. *See Howard v. Smyth,* 365 F.2d 428 (4th Cir. 1966) ("for the good of the institution").

their constitutional or statutory rights,[618] there is no adequate protection where prison officials impose punishment for violation of some unwritten (and possibly *ad hoc*) regulation.[619] Scant progress has been made in establishing in prison the usual standard of criminal law—namely, that conduct may be punished only when forbidden by a written regulation drawn with enough specificity to inform potential violators of just what conduct is forbidden.[620]

Despite the seriousness of adding to a prison sentence or of exposing someone to the hardships of solitary confinement, very few departments of correction have attempted to establish a reliable method for determining whether an infraction in fact has occurred. The federal Bureau of Prisons has regulations requiring that decisions to put a prisoner in solitary confinement be made by either an "Adjustment Committee" or a "Treatment Team" of at least three members.[621] Good-time credits may be withheld for up to one month by this committee with no special procedures. However, to justify the forfeiture of accrued credits, the in-

---

618. *E.g., Johnson v. Avery,* 394 U.S. 483 (1969); *Smartt v. Avery,* 370 F.2d 788 (6th Cir. 1967); *Howard v. Smyth,* 365 F.2d 428 (4th Cir. 1966).
619. *See Landman v. Peyton,* 370 F.2d 135, 139 (4th Cir. 1966):

> In [*Howard v. Smyth*] we held that where from the uncontradicted testimony the only reasonable inference is that prison officials have acted arbitrarily and have infringed protected First Amendment rights, relief is due. This record, however, comes to us replete with conflicting testimony, and we are not prepared to say that the findings are clearly erroneous. *Cf. Rodriguez v. McGinnis,* 451 F.2d 730 (2d Cir. 1971).

620. *But see In re* Owens, 9 *Criminal Law Reporter* 2415, 2416 (Cir. Ct. Cook County, Ill., July 9, 1971) (before taking disciplinary action that could result in solitary confinement or "confinement to room" officials responsible for the Illinois Industrial School for Boys must set forth rules, applicable punishments and procedures to be followed for imposing punishment "in clear and concise language understandable to any ward . . . reduced to writing and . . . distributed to each ward upon his admission to the institution"). *See also Jones v. Wittenberg* 323 F. Supp. 93 (judgment), 330 F. Supp. 707, 720 (order) (N.D. Ohio 1971):

> Discipline imposed shall have a direct relationship to the institutional rule violated. . . . This obviously requires that the rules of the jail, and the penalties for violation, must be established in advance, and made clearly known to all inmates.

In *Landman v. Royster,* 333 F. Supp. 621 (E.D. Va. 1971), the court, noting that "the purposes of the constitutional requirement of reasonable specificity—fair warning so that one may conform to the rules, and exactness so that arbitrary penalties or penalties for protected conduct will not be imposed—have been ill-served by the rules enforced against Virginia prisoners," condemned the punishment of prisoners for such vaguely defined offenses as "misbehavior" and "agitation." On the other hand, the court refused to disallow the offenses of "insolence," "harassment" and "insubordination."
621. Bureau of Prisons Policy Statement 7400.5A (mimeo, July 2, 1970); *cf.* American Correctional Association, *Manual of Correctional Standards* 408–411 (3d ed. 1966); Model Penal Code §304.7 (Proposed Official Draft, 1962), both of which require notice and a hearing whenever a prisoner is punished for a breach of discipline. The National Council on Crime and Delinquency's Model Act for the Protection of Prisoners §4 (1972) requires a hearing and representation by counsel or some other person of the prisoner's choice whenever punishment is imposed that may affect an inmate's sentence or eligibility for parole.

mate must be given a hearing and he is entitled to be assisted by a staff member of his choice and to appeal the decision to the director of the Bureau of Prisons.[622]

In most states, there are no hearings before inmates are put in solitary confinement; reports filed with prison officials by guards sometimes suffice to keep prisoners in solitary for many months. Officials uniformly have the power to segregate troublesome inmates in emergencies. In a recent case, a court refused to invalidate the use of this power to keep a prisoner in segregation for seven months before he was given any type of hearing.[623]

Even where "hearings" are held, they are not hearings in the legal sense of the term. In Wisconsin, for example, there are hearings before a Disciplinary Committee whenever a prisoner is punished for a "substantial" violation. However, based on his observations of the procedures at the State Reformatory, a legal intern concluded: "In essence, the committee takes the facts as stated in the [guard's] conduct report to be true, thus creating a presumption of guilt which is difficult if not impossible for the inmate to overcome."[624] Our observations of hearings in prisons in other states bear out this conclusion. When there is substantial question of a prisoner's guilt, the usual practice is to find him guilty but give him a mild sentence. This is small comfort when, as is generally the case, every infraction is recorded in a prisoner's record and affects his opportunities for parole, minimum custody, furloughs or work release.

Notwithstanding their acknowledgment of the general application of the Fifth and Fourteenth Amendments, most courts have not imposed procedural requirements on administrative decisions regarding prison discipline. Recently, a court summarily rejected a prisoner's complaint that he should have been given a hearing before or shortly after being

622. Bureau of Prisons Policy Statement 7400.6 (mimeo, Dec. 1, 1966) (written summary of the proceedings provided for appeal).
623. *Burns v. Swenson*, 430 F.2d 771 (8th Cir. 1970); cf. *Williams v. Robinson*, 432 F.2d 637 (D.C. Cir., 1970); cf. *Carter v. McGinnis*, 320 F. Supp. 1092 (M.D.N.Y. 1970); *Smoake v. Walker*, 320 F. Supp. 609 (S.D.N.Y. 1970).
624. Note, "Administrative Fairness in Corrections," 1969 *Wisconsin Law Review* 587, 595. The hearing is conducted as follows:

> [T]he associate warden [reads] the conduct report to the inmate. The inmate is then given an opportunity to admit or deny the charge and to explain. He is not permitted to bring in evidence or witnesses or support his case.
>
> Committee procedure does permit the committee to call the complaining staff member as witness if it is deemed desirable. However, this is rarely done and in fact even in the most confusing situations no such procedure was observed during the summer. . . . After the inmate has spoken in his own behalf, he is excused and the committee determines what action it will take. The inmate is then recalled and informed of the disposition of his case.

placed in solitary confinement where prison rules did not entitle an inmate to a hearing.[625] The court reasoned that prison discipline relates to the internal affairs of a penal institution, and the lack of a hearing did not deprive the complaining prisoner of any fundamental right.

The past two years have seen a growing number of challenges to the power of correctional officials to discipline prisoners without giving them due-process protections. In the case of *Sostre v. Rockefeller*,[626] a federal district court ruled that a prisoner retains his right to procedural due process while incarcerated. This protection "applies to charges for which he may receive punitive segregation or any other punishment for which earned good-time credit may be revoked or the opportunity to earn good-time credit is denied." Specifically, the court held that before a prisoner could be sentenced to punitive segregation, he was entitled to the protection of enumerated procedural safeguards. A prisoner who "was, in effect, 'sentenced' to more than a year in punitive segregation without the minimal procedural safeguards required" was entitled to collect damages from the officials responsible for his summary punishment.[627]

This portion of the decision was reversed on appeal. Over strong dissent, a majority of the full federal court of appeals ruled that "[a]ll of the elements of due process recited by the district court are not necessary to the constitutionality of every disciplinary action taken against a prisoner." The court stated that it did not consider the present case an appropriate vehicle for spelling out the due-process requirements to apply to New York prisons; it did add, however, that it "would not lightly condone the absence of such basic safeguards against arbitrariness as adequate notice, an opportunity for the prisoner to reply to charges lodged against him and a reasonable investigation into the relevant facts—at least in cases of substantial discipline."[628]

In *Morris v. Travisono*,[629] another recent federal case, the district judge mediated negotiations between lawyers representing Rhode Island prisoners and those representing prison officials. As a result, the officials agreed to the adoption of provisional regulations to govern disciplinary procedures. The regulations require that the following steps be taken before disciplinary action may be imposed: There must be a written

625. *Courtney v. Bishop*, 409 F.2d 1185 (8th Cir.), *cert. denied*, 396 U.S. 915 (1969).
626. 312 F. Supp. 863 (S.D.N.Y. 1970).
627. *See also Wright v. McMann*, 321 F. Supp. 127, 141–42 (N.D.N.Y. 1970).
628. *Sostre v. McGinnis*, 442 F.2d 178 (2d Cir. 1971) (*en banc*).
629. 310 F. Supp. 857 (D. R.I. 1970).

charge by the reporting officer or employee; preliminary investigation by a superior officer, including interviews with the reporting officer, the inmate and other inmates and employees; written notice to the inmate and sufficient opportunity to prepare a defense; a hearing before a disciplinary board at which the inmate, assisted by a classification counselor if he so desires, may present evidence to refute the charge; a written decision, based on substantial evidence, with its rationale and consequences stated explicitly; and automatic review of the record by the warden of the institution.

Some federal courts presented with broad challenges to various disciplinary practices have begun to adopt the position that the degree of procedural protection afforded depends on the severity of the punishments that can be meted out.[630] In Maryland, eighty-two prisoners, suing in two separate actions, claimed that they had been illegally transferred from minimum- or medium-security institutions to segregation in the maximum-security unit of the Maryland Penitentiary and deprived of substantial amounts of good-conduct time for allegedly participating in work stoppages or being "not amenable to the program security level" of the institution. The court ordered that the procedures used were inadequate in failing to give each inmate charged with an infraction:

> (1) adequate notice of the alleged misconduct or of the time when the hearing would be held; nor (2) an opportunity to question the person charging him with an offense or to present witnesses on his own behalf; nor (3) an impartial "Adjustment Team," since the correctional officer pressing the charge was a member of the Adjustment Team which heard his case.[631]

After the court issued an interim order, the Maryland Division of Correction adopted regulations, which were accepted by the court, distinguishing between "major" and "minor" violations—the former involving penalties of more than fifteen days' solitary confinement or loss of more than five days' good time. (Unfortunately, this distinction in practice is made on an *ad hoc* basis, apparently based as much on the identity of the offender as on his offense.) Written notice and a hearing before an impartial board are required in all cases. Each board is expected to include a hearing officer from outside the institution as soon as budgetary con-

---

630. *See also Nolan v. Scafati,* 430 F.2d 548 (1st Cir., 1970). *Compare Meola v. Fitzpatrick,* 322 F. Supp. 878 (D. Mass. 1971), *with Brown v. Brierley,* 316 F. Supp. 236 (W.D. Pa. 1970).
631. *Bundy v. Cannon,* 328 F. Supp. 165 (D. Md. 1971).

straints allow. A written decision and review by the warden are provided. In the case of major violations, the inmate must be represented by another inmate or a volunteering staff member (staff members are not used frequently, since they are not expected to respect the confidentiality of information given them by their clients; lawyers still are not allowed) and may be permitted to call witnesses at the discretion of the board; in minor cases, the inmate may be represented and may not call witnesses.[632]

In *Clutchette v. Procunier*,[633] prisoners at San Quentin brought a class action challenging all of the disciplinary procedures in use at the prison. The court ordered officials to promulgate rules that would satisfy the requirements of "rudimentary due process"—namely, notice of the charge, the right to call and cross-examine witnesses, counsel or a counsel substitute, decision by an unbiased fact-finder and equal access to any right to appeal. The court mentioned that all these safeguards might not be necessary in every case and suggested guidelines, such as the length of time in isolation (ten days) or the possibility of increasing a prisoner's sentence, to delineate those instances in which protections would be required. In cases in which a prisoner is charged with a rule violation which also could be prosecuted by state authorities as a crime, the *Clutchette* court went beyond other decisions and required that the prisoner be provided with a lawyer, not a counsel substitute, to represent him at the disciplinary hearing, due to the difficult choice "between remaining silent and sacrificing his right to defend himself before the Committee, or speaking to the Committee and risking incriminating himself in a future prosecution."

In *Landman v. Royster*[634] a federal district court in Virginia, after careful consideration of the applicability of due-process protections to the prison setting, concluded that the same procedural requirements prescribed in *Clutchette* should prevail whenever any time in solitary confinement, transfer to maximum security or loss of good time is imposed or a prisoner is padlocked in his own cell for more than ten days. When lesser penalties are imposed, all of these "minimum due process standards" (representation, written notice and appellate review) are not required; however, verbal notice, the opportunity for a hearing before an

632. Maryland Dept. of Public Safety and Correctional Services, Department of Correction, Adjustment Procedures (1971).
633. 328 F. Supp. 767 (N.D. Cal. 1971).
634. 333 F. Supp. 621 (E.D. Va. 1971); *see also McCray v. Maryland*, Misc. Pet. 4363 (Circuit Court for Montgomery County, Md., Nov. 11, 1971).

impartial decision-maker with cross-examination of the complaining officer and the presentation of testimony in defense may not be omitted.

When a prisoner's sentence is lengthened by administrative decree, no "internal discipline" rationale can apply. The Supreme Court once held that eligibility for parole is a "privilege . . . a question of state policy exclusively for the state to decide, as is also the procedure to ascertain the fact, as well as the kind or amount of evidence upon which to base its determination."[635] In the past few years, however, the concept of "privilege" has been eroded. Particularly in the areas of public employment[636] and public welfare,[637] where the potential controls by government over the private lives of individuals are particularly pervasive, it is becoming clear that citizens must have some protection in the form of enforceable rights, from arbitrary governmental action. The case for the protection of basic individual rights seems even stronger in a prison setting, where the government controls every aspect of the inmates' existence.

In 1963, a federal district court[638] distinguished between decisions relating to discipline within a prison and those that may affect the date of a prisoner's release:

> It is the added penalty of postponement of eligibility for parole, when viewed in the light of the allegations made here, that distinguishes this case from those where the "internal discipline" doctrine applies. . . . Warden Pate's decision is not limited to curtailing plaintiff's rights in prison; it goes to the more basic question of how long he is to be deprived of his liberty. True, plaintiff has no unqualified right to be free. His right to be heard with regard to parole, however, is as much a part of his sentence as is the terminal date set by the judge. The Pardon and Parole Board may deny the request for parole on the basis of information which it feels pertinent to the question of the prisoner's ability to maintain a lawful existence in society. That decision is within the province of the Board. To me, defendant and his agents over-reach their authority—limited as it is to the supervision of prisoners while in state custody—when they bar or

635. *Ughbanks v. Armstrong,* 208 U.S. 481, 488 (1908).
636. *See McAuliffe v. Mayor of New Bedford,* 155 Mass. 216, 220, 29 N.E. 517 (1892), where the then Judge Holmes made the oft-quoted statement that "the petitioner may have a constitutional right to talk politics but he has no constitutional right to be a policeman."
637. *See Goldberg v. Kelley,* 397 U.S. 254 (1970).
638. United States *ex rel. Hancock v. Pate,* 223 F. Supp. 202 (N.D. Ill. 1963).

postpone the consideration of parole in normal course, a decision which trespasses upon the power granted to another agency of the state, the Pardon and Parole Board.

In 1968, a federal court of appeals issued the potentially significant ruling that when a demotion results in the postponement of a prisoner's eligibility for parole, which represents "a chance for at least qualified liberty," the prisoner is entitled to a hearing to refute the charge that formed the basis of his demotion.[639]

Outside of these two cases dealing with the Illinois merit system, few cases have dealt with the procedural requirements necessary to postpone a prisoner's eligibility for parole. However, in a recent decision requiring a hearing before a prisoner could be transferred from a prison to an institution for insane criminals,[640] the court was influenced by the fact that one effect of the transfer was to postpone the prisoner's eligibility for parole—in that case, for over twenty years.

The courts have shown far less concern for procedural regularity when a prisoner is deprived of good-time credits, despite the direct effect of administrative action in this area on a prisoner's liberty.[641] Although one court has conceded that "the forfeiture of a prisoner's good-time for no reason at all might amount to the type of arbitrary and capricious conduct warranting relief,"[642] most of the cases dealing directly with the question generally have supported prison officials.[643] State statutes

639. United States ex rel. Campbell v. Pate, 401 F.2d 55, 57 (7th Cir. 1968), cert. denied, 395 U.S. 947 (1969). The prisoner was demoted when guards found a powder in his cell that he claimed was a soft-drink mix and they claimed was something else, presumably a drug. The guards refused to have the powder analyzed. This kind of factual conflict occurs frequently when prisoners are disciplined on the basis of charges made by guards.

Cf. Sturm v. California Adult Authority, 395 F.2d 446, 450 (9th Cir. 1967) (Browning, J., concurring in denial of petition for rehearing):

[I]t seems inconsistent at the least to say that appellant's equal protection argument must fail because his longer term was justified by the infractions of prison regulations and that his due process contention must fail because his longer term was not a "penalty" for those infractions.

640. United States ex rel. Schuster v. Herold, 410 F.2d 1071, 1076 (2d Cir.), cert. denied, 396 U.S. 847 (1969):

Schuster would have become eligible for parole in 1948, had he remained in Clinton. His present situation is far different; the district court judge observed that the present policy of the Parole Board appears to preclude the possibility of parole for any prisoner as long as he is in Dannemora Hospital.

641. But see Nolan v. Scafati, 430 F.2d 548, 550 n.2 (1st Cir. 1970).

642. Outten v. Peyton, Civ. No. 12,141 at 2 (4th Cir., order entered Dec. 3, 1968) (dictum).

643. In Sostre v. Rockefeller, 312 F. Supp. 863 (S.D.N.Y. 1970) aff'd in part, modified in part, rev'd in part sub nom. Sostre v. McGinnis, 442 F.2d 178 (2d Cir. 1971) (en banc), the district court ordered that procedural requirements be applied whenever

regulating good-time credits have withstood the challenge that they are unconstitutionally vague.[644] The courts consider the granting or denial of good time by prison administrators to be "discretionary with the executive officer" who administers the provision: "its allowance is a matter of grace rather than a right."[645] The right to good time is conditional until a prisoner is released and before then can be withdrawn freely at any time.[646]

Similar reasoning was used to uphold a state statute that allowed the cancellation of a portion of a prisoner's spending account (the wages earned from prison labor) "for the violation of a rule, want of propriety or other misconduct, as a matter of discipline. . . ."[647] According to the federal court that upheld the statute, the "spending account" was analogous to statutory good-time credits:

> The Nebraska Legislature has provided . . . that a prisoner will be paid for labor at a rate to be regulated by the director of prisons. There exists no constitutional right for such payment and it is readily apparent that such compensation is by grace of the state. . . . A state legislature may grant a favor to a convicted criminal, but it also may attach such conditions to the granting of the favor as it deems proper.[648]

---

earned good-time credit is revoked or the opportunity to earn good time denied, and required prison officials to credit a prisoner with the 124⅓ days of good-time credit he was unable to earn while wrongfully confined to punitive segregation. The court of appeals reversed the requirement of procedural protections to be applied in every case but ruled that, since the prisoner in this case had been unlawfully confined to punitive segregation because of his political beliefs and legal activities, the lost good time should be restored.

644. In *Douglas v. Sigler*, 386 F.2d 684 (8th Cir. 1967), the court ruled that Neb. Rev. Stat. §29–2633 (1964), which provides that whenever a charge of misconduct is sustained by the warden against a prisoner, the prisoner loses the good time earned to the date of the infraction, "or as much as the warden deems proper," but that the prisoner may regain all or part of the time lost, at the discretion of the warden, "as a suitable reward for subsequent good conduct," is "explicit and in clear terms affords any prisoner in the Nebraska Complex the privilege of earning a diminution of his sentence by good behavior and the observance of the rules, regulations and requirements of that institution." *Id.* at 686.

645. *Id.*; see also *Brown v. Warden*, 351 F.2d 564 (7th Cir. 1965); *Hiatt v. Compagna*, 178 F.2d 42 (5th Cir. 1949), *aff'd per curiam*, 340 U.S. 880; *Douglas v. King*, 110 F.2d 911 (8th Cir. 1940); Annot., 95 A.L.R.2d 1267 (1964). *Cf. Sawyer v. Sigler*, 8 *Criminal Law Reporter* 2317 (D.Neb., Dec. 23, 1970) (statutory good time, mandatory under state statute, may not be withheld from prisoners physically unable to work).

646. *Uryga v. Ragen*, 181 F.2d 660, 663 (7th Cir. 1950); *Lupo v. Zerbst*, 92 F.2d 362 (5th Cir. 1937); *State ex rel. Menard v. Nichols*, 167 Neb. 144, 91 N.W.2d 308 (1958).

647. Neb. Rev. Stat. §83–439 (1966).

648. *Sigler v. Lowrie*, 404 F.2d 659, 661–62 (8th Cir. 1968).

CLASSIFICATION OF PRISONERS;
DEGREES OF CUSTODY; TRANSFERS

Traditionally, courts have accorded correctional administrators complete freedom in assigning prisoners to different prison programs. Officials exercise broad discretion in deciding appropriate security measures and the relative freedom each prisoner may be allowed. "[Even though] one is given greater freedom of movement than another, or if one becomes a trusty, while many do not, such routine matters of prison administration [have not been considered proper] subjects of judicial controversy."[649]

Clearly, correctional routine requires that professionals be given flexibility to deal with different types of offenders. On the other hand, a person who feels that he is not being treated fairly will not be receptive to reformative programs. According to a President's Commission report:

> [T]he "collaborative regime" advocated . . . is one which seeks to maximize the participation of the offender in decisions which concern him, one which seeks to encourage self-respect and independence in preparing offenders for life in the community. It is inconsistent with these goals to treat offenders as if they have no rights, and are subject to the absolute authority of correctional officials.[650]

Circumscribing crucial decisions by procedural requirements protecting the prisoner's rights and ensuring his participation may impair efficiency somewhat, but should aid both rehabilitation and the protection of individual rights.

Recently, prisoners have begun to question the assumption that they are completely subject to administrative discretion. For example, under what circumstances can some prisoners be assigned to work for the profit of the state while others receive schooling and vocational training?[651] Can defendants who are being detained prior to their trial be subjected

649. *Roberts v. Pegelow*, 313 F.2d 548, 550 (4th Cir. 1963). In the federal system, the Attorney General's exclusive statutory authority and responsibility "to classify federal prisoners for the purposes of confinement, care and treatment," 18 U.S.C. §4082 (1964), have been interpreted as precluding judicial review of "his determinations, made in exercise of that authority." *Garcia v. Steele*, 193 F.2d 276, 278 (8th Cir. 1951); *Frost v. Ciccone*, 315 F. Supp. 899 (W.D. Mo. 1970); *Peek v. Ciccone*, 288 F. Supp. 329, 338 (W.D. Mo. 1968).
650. President's Commission on Law Enforcement and Administration of Justice, Task Force Report: *Correction* 83 (1967).
651. *See* Complaint, *Wilson v. Kelley*, 294 F. Supp. 1005 (N.D. Ga. 1968), *aff'd per curiam*, 393 U.S. 266 (1969).

to more onerous conditions than other convicted inmates of a jail because officials consider them special security risks?[652] Can a convicted murderer be required to spend all his time locked in a maximum-security cell in order to protect him from other prisoners?[653]

In *Morris v. Travisono*,[654] Rhode Island prisoners confined to a "Behavioral Control Unit" challenged the procedures by which prisoners were classified as unable to adjust to the general prison population or constituting a serious threat to the security of the institution. New regulations adopted through negotiations between the prisoners and administrators provided for periodic review of inmates' classifications by an institutional classification board, written notice to inmates whose classifications may be downgraded, hearings with an opportunity for inmates' defense, announcement of explicit classification decisions and rationales based on substantial evidence and demonstrating consideration of an inmate's entire record, and an opportunity for review by the Assistant Director of the Department. The judge retained jurisdiction of the case and announced that he would review the reclassifications of the complaining prisoners.

In the past few years, prisoners have had some success challenging their transfers to more restrictive institutions.[655] Indeed, the New York

652. Complaint at 11, *Shakur v. McGrath*, 69 Civ. 4493 (S.D.N.Y., filed Oct. 1969). The complainants, 13 of the "Panther 21" defendants, argued that
[s]ince plaintiffs have not been charged with infraction of any detention center rules or regulations, and since there has been no explicit or implicit reason given for their treatment, such treatment . . . constitutes cruel and unusual punishment, for, where there has been no crime, any form of punishment must be looked upon as being cruel and unusual.
Other inmates subjected to such onerous conditions allegedly had committed some serious infraction of institutional regulations after entering the jail. *Id.* at 11–12. In an interview, Commissioner of Correction George F. McGrath stated that the special treatment was justified because the defendants' high bail indicated that they were security risks and because their presence in the jail population might cause a riot. New York *Times*, Feb. 28, 1970, at 36, col. 3.
653. *See Ray v. Neil* (M.D. Tenn., order entered, Dec. 29, 1969). In handing down his temporary order that Ray be given some recreation, work and exercise, Judge William E. Miller said: "[E]nforced idleness can be cruel punishment, particularly when it is only to protect him from bodily harm." Washington *Post*, Dec. 30, 1969, at A–7, col. 1.
654. 310 F. Supp. 857 (D. R.I. 1970).
655. As yet there have been no challenges to the grant and subsequent revocation of programs involving minimum confinement, such as correctional camps, work release and halfway houses. *But see* President's Commission on Law Enforcement and Administration of Justice, *The Challenge of Crime in a Free Society* 181 (1967). *But cf. Landman v. Peyton*, 370 F.2d 135, 137–38 (4th Cir. 1966); *Peek v. Ciccone*, 288 F. Supp. 329, 338 (W.D. Mo. 1968); *Roberts v. Pepersack*, 256 F. Supp. 415, 431–32 (D. Md. 1966); *Lewis v. Gladden*, 230 F. Supp. 786, 787–88 (D. Ore. 1964); *Bell v. Warden*, 207 Md. 618, 113 A.2d 482, *cert. denied sub nom.*, *Bell v. Maryland*, 350 U.S. 852 (1955); *Clutchette v. Procunier*, 328 F. Supp. 767, 780–81 (N.D. Cal. 1971): "While prisoners may have no vested right to a certain type of confinement or certain privileges, it is unrealistic to argue that the withdrawal of those privileges they do have, or the substitution of more burdensome conditions of confinement would not,

Court of Appeals hinted in 1962 that a transfer without a hearing of one in prison to an institution for the criminally insane might be unconstitutional.[656] A few years later in *Baxstrom v. Herald*,[657] the Supreme Court rejected a statutory procedure under which a prisoner was civilly committed upon expiration of his penal sentence at the request of the director of a state hospital as a denial of equal protection of the laws. All other persons civilly committed were entitled to a jury trial on the question of sanity (and more proof of dangerousness) before being transferred.

Although *Baxstrom* involved a person no longer under criminal sentence, the case can be used as precedent when a prisoner is transferred and accorded less exacting procedural safeguards than members of the general public. However, even after *Baxstrom* was decided, a Massachusetts court refused to apply its equal-protection rationale to a law permitting post-trial commitment of "sexually dangerous persons."[658] The court concluded that it was reasonable to treat prisoners, even those sentenced for unrelated crimes, differently from everyone else, since prison officials had the opportunity to observe inmates and discover "sexually deviate behavior and tendencies."[659]

Two federal court of appeals cases decided in 1969 applied *Baxstrom* to situations where no extension of the length of sentence was involved. In United States *ex rel. Schuster v. Herold*,[660] a prisoner who had been sentenced to twenty-five years to life for second-degree murder was transferred to Dannemora State Hospital for the Criminally Insane when a prison doctor certified that he was "in his opinion insane." The court rejected the state's contention that the transfer merely represented a change in the place of detention and thus was beyond the purview of judicial review:

---

under their 'set of circumstances,' constitute a 'grievous loss.' . . . Procedural due process must obtain whenever the individual is subject to 'grievous loss' at the hands of the state. . . ."
656. People *ex rel. Brown v. Johnston*, 9 N.Y.2d 482, 174 N.E.2d 725, 215 N.Y.S.2d 44 (1961). *But see* People *ex rel. Harris v. LaVallee*, 16 App. Div.2d 990, 229 N.Y.S.2d 321 (1962). The New York legislature later enacted a law preventing transfer of a prisoner to such institutions without hearings. New York Correctional Law §383 (McKinney 1968).
657. 383 U.S. 107 (1966).
658. *Commonwealth v. Major*, 345 Mass. 666, 241 N.E.2d 822 (1968). In *Specht v. Patterson*, 386 U.S. 605 (1967), the Supreme Court held that a convicted sex offender was entitled to a further hearing on the question of illness before he could be sentenced to an indefinite term as a "habitual offender and mentally ill." *See also* People *v. Bailey*, 21 N.Y.2d 588, 237 N.E.2d 205 (1968), 289 N.Y.S.2d 943.
659. 345 Mass. at 668, 241 N.E.2d at 823.
660. 410 F.2d 1071 (2d Cir. 1969).

[A] transfer of the character confronting us involves [paramount federal, constitutional or statutory] rights. . . . Not only did the transfer effectively eliminate the possibility of Schuster's parole, but it significantly increased the restraints upon him, exposed him to extraordinary hardships, and caused him to suffer indignities, frustrations and dangers, both physical and psychological, he would not be required to endure in a typical prison setting.

Consequently, the court concluded that "before a prisoner may be transferred to Dannemora, he is entitled to substantially the same procedures including periodic review of the need for continued commitment in a mental institution and jury trial as are granted to civilians when they are involuntarily committed to a mental hospital."[661]

In *Shone v. Maine*,[662] the *Baxstrom* principle was applied to the transfer of an "incorrigible" juvenile delinquent to a men's prison. The court ruled that before a person "in the custodial care of the state" can be transferred to a "functionally distinct institution on the basis of a critically new finding of fact," he is entitled to the same protections as those who are not in custody.[663] In this case, since the original adjudication of delinquency had included no finding of "incorrigibility," the petitioner was entitled to a hearing with the assistance of an attorney.[664]

Where due-process protections apply to a transfer from the general prison population to more restrictive custody for disciplinary reasons, it should be irrelevant whether prison authorities label the restriction "punitive" (punishment for a disciplinary infraction) or "administrative" (for the order of the institution). At least one court has so ruled [665]

THE FUNCTION OF REVIEW

As prisoners succeeded in having administrative decisions invalidated by the courts, the principle that courts have the power and responsibility to review certain types of correctional decisions emerged. The threat of increasing judicial review should influence correctional administrators to be more conscious of the quasi-judicial procedures they follow in arriving at their decisions. Correctional agencies can learn from the

661. *Id.* at 1084. *See also Matthews v. Hardy*, 420 F.2d 607 (D.C. Cir. 1969), *cert. denied*, 90 S. Ct. 1231 (1970).
662. 406 F.2d 844 (1st Cir. 1969).
663. 406 F.2d at 848.
664. *Id.* at 847, 848–49 n.13. *Accord*, People *ex rel. Goldfinger v. Johnston*, 53 Misc. 2d 949, 280 N.Y.S.2d 304 (Sup. Ct. 1967) (youth entitled to hearing before transfer from correctional school to institution for "defective delinquents"). *Cf. Specht v. Patterson*, 386 U.S. 605, 608–609 (1967).
665. *Urbans v. McCorkle*, 334 F. Supp. 161 (D.N.J. 1971).

recent experiences of police and prosecutors, who, despite repeated judicial warnings, failed to institute rational procedures on their own accord and eventually found themselves obliged to adhere to procedures imposed on them by the courts.[666]

Recently, the Crime Commission agreed that in the first instance it would be preferable for administrative officials to formulate their own standards for controlling decision-making:

> It is important that correctional administrators, who are most knowledgeable about the problems involved, develop policies and procedures which will accommodate the needs of the system as well as the interests of convicted offenders. The more adequate such internal controls are, the less it will be necessary for courts to intervene to define necessary procedures or to review the merits of correctional decisions.[667]

In *Sostre v. Rockefeller*,[668] the district court not only awarded damages as compensation for punishments imposed without minimal procedural safeguards but also ordered prison officials to prepare and submit for court approval regulations governing disciplinary procedures and the receipt, writing and distribution of political literature.[669] In *Morris v. Travisono*,[670] the court went even further and mediated negotiations for new regulations. It then retained jurisdiction for an eighteen-month period to ensure enforcement of the regulations and to permit either side to propose changes in the new rules. Where similar decisions are lacking, however, it would be useful for such standards to be written into appropriate statutes.

It is time to recognize the truth of what one expert in criminal law has been urging for years—that "the correctional agency is not sui generis, but another administrative agency which requires its own administrative law if it is to make its maximum contributions harmoniously with the values of the general social order in which it functions."[671] There are possibilities for administrative review within correctional hierarchies

666. *Burns v. Swenson*, 288 F. Supp. 4, 9–10 (W.D. Mo. 1968).
667. President's Commission on Law Enforcement and Administration of Justice, Task Force Report: *Correction*, 83 (1967). *See also* "Needed—New Legislation in the Correctional Field," address by Sol Rubin to the Oregon Correction Association Annual Conference, Medford, Oregon, Oct. 15, 1969.
668. 312 F. Supp. 863 (S.D.N.Y. 1970).
669. The court of appeals reversed, terming the submission of rules an "extra-ordinary procedure." *Sostre v. McGinnis*, 8 *Criminal Law Reporter* 2437 (2d Cir., Feb. 24, 1971) (*en banc*).
670. 310 F. Supp. 857 (D. R.I. 1970).
671. Kadish, "Legal Norm and Discretion in the Police and Sentencing Processes," 75 *Harvard Law Review* 904, 930–31 (1962).

themselves; for example, review of lower-echelon personnel by a panel of correctional administrators, inmates and disinterested outsiders; or perhaps a reviewing body of detached specialists modeled after the Court of Military Appeals or Tax Court, that could develop its own specialized procedures and expertise.[672] One former correctional official has proposed that parole boards be given the function of reviewing institutional decisions on appeal from inmates.[673]

Where departments of correction have attempted to create administrative procedures, the courts have evidenced a willingness to abide by them. For instance, judges have referred prisoners to administratively established grievance procedures[674] and required that they channel their complaints through them before coming to court.[675] In a system where correctional decisions are based on explicit standards and carefully regulated procedures, the function of judicial review would no longer be to examine the correctness of any individual decision but simply to judge the adequacy of the criteria and procedures used in reaching the decision.[676]

Less obvious than the need for administrative criteria, procedures and review is the distinction between the types of decisions that require a trial-type hearing in the first instance and those that are less important

672. "This looseness in the imposition of serious disciplinary punishment is particularly questionable when weighed with the fact there are no official written channels for authoritative and formal review and appeal." *Wright v. McMann*, 321 F. Supp. 127, 142 (N.D.N.Y. 1970). The problem with an appellate authority within an administrative agency, however, is its potential inclination to vindicate the judgments of the officials whose decisions are under review.
673. Bixby, "A New Role for Parole Boards," *Federal Probation* (June 1970) at 24, 27–28.
674. *Sewell v. Pegelow*, 304 F.2d 196 (4th Cir. 1962).
675. *Burns v. Swenson*, 288 F. Supp. 4, 11 (W.D. Mo. 1968); *Cupp v. Swenson*, 288 F. Supp. 1 (W.D. Mo. 1968). In *McBride v. McCorkle*, 44 N.J. Super. 468, 130 A.2d 881 (1957), the court stated that the correction department is a state administrative agency; consequently, it is relevant to discuss the doctrine of exhaustion of administrative remedies.
    One commentator expressed the fear that the burden of exhausting administrative remedies before going to court might be too great for "the indigent semi-illiterate prisoner who prepares his own papers without benefit of counsel. . . . For him, administrative reform may turn out to be an unfulfilled promise." Muraskin, "Censorship of Mail: The Prisoner's Right to Communicate by Mail with the Outside World," 48 *Prison Journal* 33, 36 (1968). This possibility could be obviated by providing attorneys or law students to advise prisoners of their rights. *See* notes 305–22 *supra* and accompanying text.
676. *See* Kimball and Newman, "Judicial Intervention in Correctional Decisions: Threat and Response," 14 *Crime and Delinquency* 1, 7 (1968):

> Judicial review of discretionary decisions ordinarily asks not whether the decision was the best alternative but only whether the substantive rules applied are illegitimate, whether the procedures failed to comply with the statutory requirements and the rudiments of fairness, and whether the decision was so unreasonable that no sensible, well-intentioned man could accept it. This sort of review leaves room for correction to make policy, establish procedures, and decide particular cases with a minimum of interference.

and may be handled summarily and, if necessary, corrected later after review.[677] While some commentators have opposed the introduction of adversary procedures into correction, fearing that adversary techniques will impair correctional efficiency and public safety without any compensating gain in the soundness of decisions,[678] courts have followed the general rule of administrative law that a person who has a significant interest in the outcome of governmental action is entitled to an adversary hearing with representation by counsel.[679]

While this kind of distinction is necessary to the administration of a "total institution,"[680] where every aspect of a person's existence is regulated by authorities, it should be kept in mind that the "stripping process" referred to at the outset of this chapter involves many minor sanctions that are often unnecessarily damaging to personal dignity. A compulsory haircut may be as crucial to a prisoner's self-image as denial of his right to attend religious services. Perhaps we must accept the reality that the only way to preserve personal dignity in the involuntary institutional setting of a prison is to surround intramural decision-making with so many safeguards that the system becomes too cumbersome to work. On the other hand, if correctional institutions are to have any chance of releasing prisoners who are less likely to commit crimes than they were before their imprisonment, ways for resolving grievances must be found.

Non-Judicial Alternatives for Resolving Grievances

No doubt courts are hesitant to extend their review of prisoners' grievances for fear of being inundated with claims. Given even minimal

677. See President's Commission on Law Enforcement and Administration of Justice, Task Force Report: *Correction* 84 (1967):

>   What is needed is to provide offenders under correctional authority certain protections against arbitrary action, not to create for all correctional decision-making a mirror image of trial procedure. What sorts of protections are proper will depend upon the importance of the decision. . . .
>   It is too early to define absolute standards in this area but it is of utmost importance that a beginning be made in considering and experimenting with a variety of methods of safeguarding the rights of offenders.

678. Burdman, "The Conflict between Freedom and Order," 15 *Crime and Delinquency* 371 (1969).

679. 1 Davis, *Administrative Law Treatise* §7.04 (1958).

680. The phrase was originated by Goffman, "Characteristics of Total Institutions," in *Symposium on Preventive and Social Psychiatry* (1957). See generally Goffman, *Asylums* (1961).

research facilities, prisoners who have little else to keep themselves busy can generate an enormous amount of litigation. In 1964, federal and state prisoners filed 6,240 petitions in federal district courts alone. By 1971 this figure had nearly tripled—to 16,266.[081]

In the absence of legal advice most prisoners cannot assess their cases' chance of success. One way to screen out the many groundless complaints would be to provide some mechanism for furnishing prisoners with legal advice on a regular basis. According to a committee of the American Bar Association:

> The best way to stem the flow of worthless applications and, conversely, to bring forward meritorious applications, is to educate the prisoner population on the respective utility and futility of applying. The optimal form of education would involve face-to-face interviews between prisoners and attorneys who could advise them of the probable merits or lack of merit in their grievances.[682]

Legal assistance would also save the courts time by producing petitions that are better drafted and contain less irrelevant material than those written by unaided inmates.

In addition to legal counseling, prisoners need access to private citizens and non-judicial government agencies to help them deal with their problems. Prison administrations might be more likely to relieve some of the unnecessary deprivations of prison life if private citizens pointed out their irrationality and, if necessary, put pressure on the officials to eliminate them.[683] But prisons and prisoners present low-visibility social

---

681. Administrative Office of the United States Courts, Annual Reports of the Director —1964 and 1971.

682. American Bar Association Project Minimum Standards for Criminal Justice, *Standards Relating to Post-Conviction Remedies* 50 (approved draft 1968).

683. "Another factor in the apathy of the people was the fact that the . . . evils of leasing were hidden from public view. . . . Hence the masses of people were actually unaware of the evil conditions that obtained." Green, "Some Aspects of the Convict Lease System in the Southern States," in *Essay in Southern History* 112, 123 (Green ed. 1949), *quoted in* Plaintiff's Brief at 47 n.2, *Wilson v. Kelley,* 294 F. Supp. 1005 (N.D. Ga., 1968), *aff'd per curiam,* 393 U.S. 266 (1969). *Cf.* President's Commission on Law Enforcement and Administration of Justice, Task Force Report: *Correction* 85 (1967):

> The mere presence of outsiders would serve to discourage illegal, unfair or inhumane practices. The potential dangers of leaving the correctional system entirely isolated from the outside world are illustrated by the recent investigation of conditions in the Arkansas prison system, which included widespread corruption and physical abuse. . . .

On the other hand, many of the administrative changes that were suggested to prison officials by the prisoners, judges, state legislators, law-enforcement officials and private citizens present at a conference held in Annapolis, Maryland, in June 1969 were implemented quickly and voluntarily. *See generally* National College of State Trial Judges, *A Positive State Program: Crime and Correction Workshop* (1969).

problems. People forget them and really do not want to be reminded about them once offenders are caught and convicted. But this need not remain the case; it is not the case elsewhere in the world.

KRUM is an influential public association dedicated to prison reform in Sweden. It has counterparts in Denmark (KRIM), Norway (KROM) and Finland (the November Movement). The organization is composed of students, professors, businessmen, some politicians and other members of the general community, along with present and former convicts—all of whom share the central commitment that the correction system needs to be watchdogged and liberalized, that prisoners should be treated decently and that alternatives to prisons should be promoted. Some cities in Sweden provide communal subsidies to local branches of KRUM; the national organization is seeking a state subsidy. Meanwhile, volunteers visit institutions, follow relevant affairs and lobby for changes to secure greater protections of prisoners' rights. The group's charter reads like an enlightened bill of rights for prison problems.

Organizations such as these could exist in this country and could accomplish two major improvements: the creation of an effective outlet for airing legitimate grievances of inmates and the involvement of the community in the correctional process.

In the past, riots, occasional investigations and court actions have been the only avenues of exposing senseless restrictions and brutal conditions in prisons. In some cases prisoners with access to court, whether or not they succeeded in obtaining a judgment, have been able to achieve some beneficial administrative changes.[684] In one instance, an assistant attorney general, called upon to defend conditions of solitary confinement challenged by a state prisoner, admitted the conditions were

---

684. *Pope v. Daggett,* 350 F.2d 296 (10th Cir. 1965), *vacated,* 384 U.S. 33 (1966) (prison rules that denied prisoner right to send letter to his probation officer changed during litigation); *Sewell v. Pegelow,* 304 F.2d 670 (4th Cir. 1962) (appeal dismissed by stipulation when District of Columbia Commissioners adopted new regulations concerning Muslims' right to engage in religious practices); *Hatfield v. Bailleaux,* 290 F.2d 632 (9th Cir.), *cert. denied,* 368 U.S. 862 (1961) (capacity of library enlarged during suit); *Burns v. Swenson,* 288 F. Supp. 4 (W.D. Mo. 1968) (during action Missouri Department of Correction, working with court and counsel for plaintiffs, adopted revised set of rules concerning inmate conduct that resulted in release of plaintiffs from maximum-security unit); *Jordan v. Fitzharris,* 257 F. Supp. 674, 681 (N.D. Cal. 1966) (while prisoner was seeking Supreme Court review of unfavorable judgment in a state court, California Department of Correction sought to correct "some questionable practices . . . with respect to strict adherence to rules and regulations"); *McBride v. McCorkle,* 44 N.J. Super. 468, 130 A.2d 881 (1957) (in case challenging inability of prisoners in segregation wing to attend religious services, court informed at oral argument that request of the Department of Institutions and Agencies for funds to erect a small chapel in the segregation wing—a request first made in 1953—had finally been met).

"terrible" and "should not be permitted to exist."[685]

Unfortunately, prison inmates rarely obtain such access to sympathetic outsiders to voice their grievances; they are not usually permitted to publish books[686] or articles in magazines of general circulation[687] or even to give sermons to those on the outside.[688] One of the most recent judicial opinions on the subject, concerning an inmate's letters to *Playboy* magazine, stated that "if . . . the purpose of the correspondence was to effect publication of a critique of [Maryland's] defective delinquency law and its implementation at Patuxent with deleterious effect upon institutional control and discipline, treatment programs and other inmates, the administration of the institution would not be powerless in its discretion to suppress it." The court cited the possibility of adverse effects of making known the inmate's apparent defiance and critical attitude on other inmates and on future juries convened to determine defective delinquency status.[689] There is an old saying among prisoners that "the wall is there to keep people *out*."

The chief barrier to communication with the outside world is the complete control by officials of a prisoner's visitors, his correspondents, the number of letters he may write and the subject matter and language that his letters may contain.[690] For example, administrative regulations in Georgia direct wardens and all correctional personnel to prevent unauthorized outside contacts:[691]

685. *Wright v. McMann*, 387 F.2d 519, 525 (2d Cir. 1967). *See also Mahaffey v. State*, 87 Idaho 228, 392 P.2d 279, 281 (1964) (district attorney's brief admitted that, if facts alleged were true, some were "inexcusable and shocking").
686. *Stroud v. Swope*, 187 F.2d 850 (9th Cir.), *cert. denied*, 342 U.S. 820 (1951) (prisoner prohibited from corresponding with publishers in an effort to secure publication of his manuscript); *Numer v. Miller*, 165 F.2d 986 (9th Cir. 1948); (permission for inmate to take correspondence course in English withdrawn when officials discovered purpose of his taking course was to enable him to write a book exposing prison conditions).
687. Prisoners generally are allowed to write articles for institutional newspapers and magazines only. When an exception is made, it is only with extremely stringent limitations and censorship requirements. *See* U.S. Bureau of Prisons, Policy Statement 7300.14 (mimeo, Sept. 7, 1966).
688. *Berrigan v. Warden*, 8 *Criminal Law Reporter* 2396 (D. Conn., Jan. 22, 1971).
689. *McDonough v. Director of Patuxent*, 429 F.2d 1189, 1193 (4th Cir. 1970).
690. Most prisons do not permit inmates to use telephones. *Cf. Konigsberg v. Ciccone*, 285 F. Supp. 585 (W.D. Mo. 1968), *cert. denied*, 397 U.S. 963 (1970). Yet many prisoners are unable to write letters and may be embarrassed to have other inmates write for them. At the District of Columbia's Lorton Reformatory and Youth Center, three direct telephone lines to Washington were recently installed. Inmates may now talk with friends or relatives each evening by paying 20 cents. Even with the unexpectedly heavy use, officials have found it unnecessary to provide more than a cursory monitoring of calls. The availability of telephones may help to diffuse tensions by enabling prisoners readily to obtain information about family crises.
691. Georgia State Board of Correction Rule 36, *cited in* Brief for Plaintiff at 47, *Wilson v. Kelley*, 294 F. Supp. 1005 (N.D. Ga. 1968), *aff'd per curiam*, 393 U.S. 266 (1969). *See also Mahaffey v. State*, 87 Idaho 228, 392 P.2d 279, 281 (1964).

Inmates' letters are censored, and those containing information or statements known to be untrue, or not in accordance with known facts, will be disapproved and rejected. . . . Names of other inmates . . . and derogatory or abusive remarks about the personnel or critical remarks about the institution and administration [are forbidden, as are] detailed information or descriptive data regarding the institution or its operation.[692]

Violations of these proscriptions subject an inmate not only to muzzling but to disciplinary action. A Maryland prisoner reportedly was held in solitary confinement and his parole date delayed for criticizing prison conditions and personnel in a letter to a friend.[693] Virginia prisoners have been subjected to reprisals for seeking the help of civil-liberties and civil-rights organizations.[694] Even letters to relatives and clergymen are censored on the superciliously paternalistic ground that they may "worry or upset" the recipient. According to a former long-term prisoner, censorship rules in some institutions "are so rigorous that it is virtually impossible to comment on anything but the state of one's health (and there must be no complaints!) and the weather."[695]

Prison regulations generally limit the volume as well as the contents of outgoing mail. If letters are to be searched for contraband and screened for "unacceptable" contents, such limitation may be an administrative necessity. However, the regulations often go beyond the volume limitation to a restriction on the number of persons with whom an inmate may correspond.[696] This rigidity may well serve to deter prisoners from discussing their problems with outside citizens and groups, since they are not likely to be on his approved mailing list.

The courts generally have endorsed restrictions on the use of the mails as a necessary incident of incarceration:

Prisoners lawfully confined to state penitentiaries have no absolute right to the use of the mails. As with many civil rights and

692. Georgia State Board of Correction Rules 18–20, *cited in* Brief for Plaintiff at 47, *Wilson v. Kelley*, 294 F. Supp. 1005 (N.D. Ga. 1968), *aff'd per curiam*, 393 U.S. 226 (1969).
693. Washington *Post*, Sept. 22, 1969, at A15, col. 1. *But see Carothers v. Follette*, 314 F. Supp. 1014 (S.D.N.Y. 1970).
694. Hirschkop and Millemann, "The Unconstitutionality of Prison Life," 823–24, 55 *Virginia Law Review* 795 (1969).
695. Leopold, "What Is Wrong with the Prison Systems?" 45 *Nebraska Law Review* 33, 50 (1966).
696. *E.g.*, Missouri State Penitentiary, Inmate Informational Pamphlet, *Rules and Procedures* 14 (Sept. 1967): "You are permitted a maximum of ten approved correspondents and you may write three personal letters a week to them on one side only of the stationery provided."

privileges, this one yields to the internal discipline of a large prison. . . . Thus, the mere withholding of petitioner's letter by prison authorities is not a violation per se of any federal right.[697]

Similarly, a prisoner on death row for nine years was denied an injunction against the refusal by prison authorities to permit correspondence with anyone with whom access was not specifically provided to a condemned prisoner by statute.[698] Another court approved the cancellation by a federal warden of a prisoner's right to send letters to a woman he claimed as his common-law wife.[699] The prisoner's first letter had been returned by the superintendent of a state reformatory where the woman was imprisoned. The superintendent noted that the male prisoner "appears to be only the most recent in a series of paramours." Therefore, assuming there were no "constructive elements whatever in their relationship," he did "not see that any useful goal will be attained by permitting correspondence between them while they are institutionalized."[700] Judges have sustained not only the prohibition of unacceptable correspondents but also of "unacceptable sentiments and points of view."[701]

Prison officials may refuse to mail an inmate's business letter on the ground that it is too vague,[702] or forbid him entirely to engage in business correspondence.[703] With the statement that "a prisoner who persists in abusing a privilege . . . is in no position to complain of unequal treatment if that privilege is taken away from him," a court refused to interfere with the discontinuation of an inmate's correspondence course in

697. United States ex rel. Thompson v. Fay, 197 F. Supp. 855, 856 (S.D.N.Y. 1961); accord, Lee v. Tahash, 352 F.2d 970 (8th Cir. 1965).
698. Labat v. McKeithen, 361 F.2d 757 (5th Cir. 1966). The relevant statute provided for correspondence with the prisoner's lawyer, doctor, minister and close relatives.
699. Fussa v. Taylor, 168 F. Supp. 302 (M.D. Pa. 1958). See also Huffman v. Nebraska Bureau of Vital Statistics, 320 F. Supp. 154 (D. Neb. 1970); Adams v. Ellis, 197 F.2d 483 (5th Cir. 1952); Abamine v. Murphy, 108 Cal. App. 2d 294, 238 P.2d 606 (1951).
700. 168 F. Supp. at 303. But see Morales v. Schmidt, No. 71-C-29 (W.D. Wis., Apr. 6, 1972), in which a federal judge enjoined prison officials from interfering with correspondence between an inmate and his sister-in-law, claimed to be the mother of his illegitimate child. In the light of the fundamental First Amendment freedom involved, the court was "not persuaded that the government's interest in diminishing the likelihood of . . . future unlawful sexual activity by one convicted of a past crime, as contrasted with one not convicted of a past crime, is so compelling as to permit the vindication of this interest by inference with this correspondence. . . ."
701. McClosky v. Maryland, 337 F.2d 72 (4th Cir. 1964) (censorship of anti-Semitic statements termed an "essential adjunct of prison administration").
702. Krupnick v. Crouse, 366 F.2d 851 (10th Cir. 1966).
703. Stroud v. Swope, 187 F.2d 850 (9th Cir. 1951) ("Birdman of Alcatraz" forbidden to engage in correspondence to secure publication of a book); see Powell v. Hunter, 172 F.2d 330 (10th Cir. 1949).

English on the discovery by officials that his objective was to write a book exposing the brutality of prison authorities after his release.[704]

Although accepting the doctrine that "certain restrictions on expression to persons outside the prison are clearly justified," a federal district court concluded recently that such restrictions should not be applied to a prisoner's letter to his parents in which he charged that "the prison system in New York State stinks. . . . The people in charge are not qualified. . . . Half the employees did not get out of high school. . . ." The court reasoned that there was no indication that the prisoner's remarks threatened either prison security or his own rehabilitation, "unless that word is to be defined as abject acceptance of all prison conditions, however unjustifiable. . . . [W]e doubt whether preparation of a prisoner for return to civilian life is advanced by deadening his initiative and concern for events within the prison itself."[705]

In a unique opinion[706] dealing with a Rhode Island prison, another federal district court recently ruled that

[O]fficials at the Adult Correctional Institution have used such controls to suppress any criticism of the institution or institutional officials. I fail to appreciate such an attitude which smothers information to the public about prisoners and prison life—it serves no rational social purpose supportive of prison objectives. It merely serves to destroy one of the few vehicles prisoners have of informing the public about their existence—a public which should know so that it can exercise its responsibility in a meaningful way. Furthermore, it is my view that censorship for such reason is an unconstitutional infringement of the First Amendment rights of the plaintiffs, including the right to petition for redress of grievances.

Officials of the Adult Correctional Institution have also taken it upon themselves to read and screen outgoing mail to protect the public, including the courts, from insulting, vulgar letters. This is not their function—they are not the protectors of the sensibilities of the public which can protect itself.

The court enjoined prison officials from opening, reading or inspecting any outgoing mail without a search warrant and from reading (as opposed to inspecting for contraband) letters to prisoners from correspondents on their approved mailing lists.

704. *Numer v. Miller,* 165 F.2d 986, 987 (9th Cir. 1948).
705. *Carothers v. Follette,* 314 F. Supp. 1014, 1021, 1025 (S.D.N.Y. 1970).
706. *Palmigiano v. Travisono,* 117 F. Supp. 776 (D.R.I. 1970).

Despite the allowance of virtually unlimited discretion to prison officials to control mailing and visiting rights, courts have made an inroad into this area in cases involving complaints to non-judicial government officials. A prisoner's letter to a state Senator describing conditions of the Virginia State Penitentiary was intercepted by an official who did not believe "it is the prisoner's place to be describing to the State Senator his description of how we operate the penitentiary."[707] In ruling that prison authorities may not suppress complaints to executive officials, the court of appeals recognized that

> If the operation of the prisons and the treatment of the inmates is lodged solely in the Executive, generally without any possibility of judicial restraint, there ought to be open avenues of complaint by prisoners to those in general charge of their immediate jailers. Executive capacity to prevent abuses and excesses on the part of subordinate officials would be greatly impaired if the most fruitful sources of information are damned up or diverted.[708]

Likewise, a federal district court prohibited District of Columbia prison officials from punishing a prisoner for making "false accusations" against the officials in a complaint to the District Commissioners.[709] The complaint had been made in accordance with procedures approved by the commissioners, and the ensuing punishment therefore interfered with the prisoner's right to seek redress of his grievances.

A recent case before the New York Court of Appeals questioned the breadth of the rule of restricted communications.[710] The trial court had enjoined prison officials from intercepting and withholding communica-

707. Deposition of R. W. Oliver, Assistant Superintendent, Virginia State Penitentiary, Feb. 7, 1969, at 139, *Mason v. Peyton,* Civ. No. 5611-R (E.D. Va., order entered, Oct. 16, 1969), *quoted in* Hirschkop and Millemann, "Prison Life" at 806.
708. *Roberts v. Pegelow,* 313 F.2d 548, 551 (4th Cir. 1963). The U.S. Bureau of Prisons has established a "Prisoners' Mail Box" from which letters may be sent directly, without censorship, to designated officials, including the President, Vice President, Attorney General, director of the Bureau of Prisons, members of the U.S. Parole Board, the Surgeon General, U.S. Public Health Service and members of Congress. According to the general counsel of the Bureau of Prisons: "The inmate may thus discuss his problems with government officials not immediately responsible for his custody and discipline. . . . Complaints against the institutional personnel cannot be throttled by them." Barkin, "Impact of Changing Law Upon Prison Policy," 48 *Prison Journal* 3, 15 (1968).
   In a recent ten-month period over 6,000 letters were sent through the Prisoners' Mail Box. (The total population of the twenty-eight federal prisons is approximately 20,000.) Hearings on S. 1195 before the Subcomm. on Administrative Practice and Procedure of the Senate Comm. on the Judiciary, 90th Cong., 2nd Sess. 36 (1968).
709. *Fulwood v. Clemmer,* 206 F. Supp. 370 (D.D.C. 1962).
710. *Brabson v. Wilkins,* 19 N.Y.2d 433, 227 N.E.2d 204, 280 N.Y.S.2d 561 (1967).

tion to attorneys or to any court, law-enforcement agency or executive officials of the state or federal government.[711] The court limited the recipients to whom letters would be protected and the subjects that could be discussed freely to

> any court and any communications addressed to any executive official of the Federal or State Government concerning . . . unlawful treatment by prison authorities and any communications addressed to his attorney concerning the legality of his detention and treatment received while incarcerated, all however, subject to the right of the prison authorities to censor such communications and strike therefrom any material not relating to the foregoing.[712]

In a dissenting opinion,[713] one judge argued that communications to other officials should be treated no differently from those to courts, which the Supreme Court long ago had ruled could not be screened by prison personnel:[714]

> The [Court] overlooked the fact that judges and courts are not the only persons or agencies capable of granting relief to prisoners complaining about the illegality of their treatment or detention. For this reason, I see no basis for distinguishing between letters to courts, to the prisoner's attorney or to government officials. In all these cases only the recipient of the letters should be permitted to determine whether the contents warrant their intervention and not the very person whose jurisdiction and conduct are being questioned.[715]

This dissenting opinion was specifically adopted by a federal district court in New York.[716] The complaint before that court alleged that an in-

---

711. *Id.*, 45 Misc. 2d 286, 256 N.Y.S.2d 693 (Sup. Ct. 1965).
712. 19 N.Y.2d at 436, 227 N.E.2d at 206, 280 N.Y.S.2d at 563.
713. *Id.* at 438, 227 N.E.2d at 207, 280 N.Y.S.2d at 564.
714. *Ex parte* Hull, 312 U.S. 546 (1941); *see* note 277 *supra* and accompanying text.
715. 19 N.Y.2d at 439, 227 N.E.2d at 208, 280 N.Y.S.2d at 565. *Cf. Peek v. Ciccone,* 288 F. Supp. 329 (W.D. Mo. 1968), in which the court ordered officials of the U.S. Medical Center for Federal Prisoners to allow an inmate who claimed that he was the reincarnation of Jesus Christ to communicate his revelation to the Pope:

> No question of prison discipline or administration is involved. There is no evidence or reason to suppose that the Pope needs the protection of the Medical Center. Therefore, the petitioner should be allowed to communicate his religious experience and claims to the Pope. To forbid this is an invidiously discriminatory and arbitrary denial of religious freedom.

Id. at 334.
716. *Sostre v. Rockefeller,* 312 F. Supp. 863 (S.D.N.Y. 1970).

mate's letters with his attorney had been examined by prison officials who deleted those portions they deemed irrelevant. The court enjoined the officials from censoring, refusing to mail or refusing to deliver to the inmate any communication between him and any court, public official or agency, or lawyer. The court of appeals upheld the order insofar as it prohibited officials from refusing to mail or give to the prisoner, or from deleting material from, any communication between the prisoner and any court, any public official or agency or any lawyer. However, only matters related to his conviction or complaints concerning prison administration might be discussed with his attorney. In order to ensure that these protected communications were not used as a subterfuge to discuss "restricted matters," the court permitted officials to open and read all correspondence.[717]

Prisoners clearly should have access to government administrators and executives to voice their complaints. But without some pressure of publicity or judicial action the officials, who usually have other, more pressing constituencies and responsibilities,[718] are not always willing to listen. Meaningful access to court, lawyers and outside officials and organizations requires someone, whether within the Government or outside it, whose first responsibility is to receive and deal with the complaints of prisoners.

Many complaints concern relatively minor practices that, while easily resolved, can escalate into major confrontations when left unheeded. Administrative practices regarding food, schedules, mail, visits,

---

717. *Sostre v. McGinnis*, 442 F.2d 178 (2d Cir. 1971) (*en banc*); *accord, LeVier v. Woodson*, 443 F.2d 360 (10th Cir. 1971); *Shaffer v. Jennings*, 314 F. Supp. 588 (E.D. Pa. 1970); *cf. Meola v. Fitzpatrick*, 322 F. Supp. 161 (D.N.J. 1971) (censorship of correspondence with the courts violates the Fifth Amendment).

718. *See, e.g.*, Deposition of O. L. Brown, Director, Virginia Department of Welfare at 49, 52, *Landman v. Royster*, Civ. No. 170–69–R (E.D. Va., filed Apr. 30, 1969):

> [Y]ou have never gone to see any of these gentlemen and asked them what their problems were, or had them brought to you, have you?:
> A. No.
> Q. Is this for security reasons?
> A. No.
> Q. This is just your policy not to talk to prisoners?
> A. That's right.
>   . . . .
> Q. In fact, all letters, isn't it true, concerning conditions inside the penitentiary go to the Division of Corrections, up or down the line, may go to Mr. Peyton, may go to Mr. Cunningham, or—
> A. There is no one else to send them to.
> Q. Except some independent evaluation by your office. But you never do that, do you?
> A. No. I have no method for independent evaluation.

treatment by custodial employees, racial slurs, rude comments and crude handling are the types of situations that cause riots or escalate into major lawsuits. Yet they can be coped with sensitively where there is a fair and effective mechanism for handling complaints. Creation of such a mechanism for resolving these problems short of recourse to the full panoply of the legal process would be most desirable.

In Denmark confidential complaints from prisoners are often sent to ombudsmen. Where the ombudsman is not able to resolve problems with prison officials on the scene, he has access to administrative channels and may even deal directly with the Director of Prisons. The ombudsman provides a number of services for the prison community. His visits to penal institutions assist inmates in making ther complaints known. Yet spurious claims are not burdensome since the ombudsman is on the scene to investigate the matter. He is able to distinguish clearly individual problems from those affecting a class of prisoners.[719]

Since the first office of ombudsman to defend citizens from official wrongs was created in Sweden in 1809, the idea has flourished around the world. Although the former director of the federal Bureau of Prisons, Myrl E. Alexander, testified that our federal prison system did not require an ombudsman, he admitted that "Any system or device which would help us manage these highly volatile prisons and institutions and provide an outlet for, many times, these rather emotionally disturbed persons, can be no serious problem to us."

In Italy the position of surveillance judge (*giudice di sorveglianza*) was created to make decisions concerning the transfer and release of prisoners and to ensure that the prisons were being administered according to law. His responsibilities include regularly visiting the prisons in his jurisdiction and investigating whether, for example, prisoners who are supposed to be paid for their work are actually receiving money. Although the visiting judge has no power to order prison officials to change their procedures, he can report irregularities to his superior, the minister of justice. A similar institution, *judge de l'application des peines*, has been created in France.

According to one observer, transplanting the idea of the surveillance judge in the United States might cause some problem of judicial delay, since prison populations here are so much larger than in Europe. Nonetheless, "the presence of a surveillance judge on the prison grounds would undoubtedly reinforce the rights of prisoners. And the prisoners'

719. Interview with Dr. Steven Hurwitz, Copenhagen, Denmark, Oct. 31, 1968.

morale might be boosted considerably by the knowledge that a prestigious judicial official is striving to protect their rights and interests."[720]

At a recent meeting of the National Association of Attorneys General, Chief Justice Warren Burger described the Netherlands inspection procedure. There, a three-member team from the Ministry of Justice, trained in law, psychology and counseling, make regular visits to all institutions where people are confined. Their responsibility is to inquire into the bases for confinement, listen to the prisoners' grievances and report to the Minister of Justice on cases that appear to call for a remedy. According to Chief Justice Burger:

> In a sense these trained teams are like bank examiners, or health inspectors. Their method provides a regular avenue of communication designed to flush out the rare case of miscarriage of justice and the larger number of cases in which the prisoner has some valid complaint or deserves reexamination of his sentence. The mere existence of such an avenue of communication exercises a very beneficial influence which is in many respects far superior to our habeas corpus process. With us, the prisoner hopes that some distant proceeding before a remote judge will enable him to have his cries heard; with them, the prisoner meets face to face with trained counselors who give him a sympathetic hearing, ask questions, make a record of his complaints, and bring his valid grievances to the attention of higher authority.

The National Council on Crime and Delinquency recently recommended that every state correctional department establish a grievance procedure under which all grievances communicated by prisoners to the head of the department would be investigated by a person or agency outside the department and a written report of the findings would be submitted to the department and the prisoner.[721]

The Maryland legislature recently created an Inmate Grievance Commission, consisting of five members, at least two of them attorneys. Any state prisoner may complain to the commission, which, unless it finds his complaint "on its face wholly lacking in merit," will give him a hearing. At the hearing the prisoner may call and question witnesses and, if

720. Seewald, "The Italian Surveillance Judge," 45 *Nebraska Law Review* 96, 97–98 (1966).
721. A Model Act for the Protection of Rights of Prisoners §5 (1972).

he can afford it, be represented by an attorney. The commission's order must include its findings of facts, its conclusions and its disposition of the complaint. If the decision is in favor of the complainant, in whole or in part, it is reviewed by the Secretary of Public Safety and Correctional Services. The statute attempts to limit judicial review to "a review of the record of the proceedings before the Commission and the Secretary's order, if any, pursuant to such proceedings."[722]

Professor Gellhorn, an American authority on the ombudsman concept, noted that

> Nowhere is the need for external examination of grievances greater than in America's prisons, jails, and other places of detention. . . . [I]nmates, many of them ill adjusted socially and resistant to discipline, live perforce in an authoritarian setting; they are poorly equipped by nature or training to participate in rational planning for themselves or their companions. Those whom a court has condemned to loss of freedom cannot expect, then, to find behind prison walls a fully fashioned democracy, keenly sensitive to individual wishes. Nonetheless, the man under detention continues to be a man. He is not free, but neither is he without rights. The question to be considered is how the prisoner's residual rights can best be protected without destroying a penal institution's discipline. . . .
>
> If a state ombudsman existed, he would be a preeminently suitable person to inquire into conflicts between convicts and their keepers. Foreign ombudsmen have successfully reconciled disciplinary demands and inmates' interests. Their work in this respect has been a social service of high order. An American counterpart is badly needed.[723]

A bill passed by the California Legislature but vetoed by the Governor[724] would have created a correctional ombudsman responsible to the legislature to receive complaints from prisoners and attempt to resolve those found to have merit by recommending changes to the administrators involved or suggesting new legislation. A recent proclamation by the Governor of Minnesota established the first state correctional ombudsman, responsible to the Governor, with the authority to investigate complaints from prison and jail inmates, their families, probationers, parolees and

722. Ann. Code of Md., Art. 41, §204 F(1971).
723. Gellhorn, *When Americans Complain* 145–51 (1966).
724. Assembly Bill No. 1181, introduced Mar. 25, 1971.

correctional staff. The ombudsman's office will be funded on a pilot basis by a federal grant. The federal Bureau of Prisons has an Office of Review, staffed by lawyers, to investigate institutional complaints. In Oregon, the superintendent of the penitentiary has appointed an employee, formerly a prison guard, to act as prison ombudsman. Although the use of a prison employee as ombudsman is hindered by his dependence on the administration he is supposed to criticize, both inmates and staff members at the institution report that the ombudsman has done much to relieve tensions by calling individual injustices or oversights to the attention of the superintendent. What began as a three-month experiment has been made permanent.

The greatest potential for the use of non-judicial remedies to effect broader, systemic change appears to lie in the work of private groups outside of the bureaucracy. The Pennsylvania Prison Society received the approval of authorities for putting an ombudsman employed by it into the Philadelphia prison system. However, after the ombudsman, an ex-offender originally approved by prison officials, served for thirty days, the officials asked that he be removed and replaced with someone else.

The Center for Correctional Justice, a private, non-profit organization in the District of Columbia, has a grant from the United States Office of Economic Opportunity to develop nonjudicial remedies for prisoners' grievances. During the first few months of its operation, the center has provided offenders in the District of Columbia with access to legal counseling and representation in both civil and criminal matters through contracts with community legal-services agencies. Where offenders' complaints involve their treatment within the correctional agency, the center assumes the role of an ombudsman, attempting to resolve grievances through negotiation with administrators. If this should fail, an effort will be made to resolve grievances through techniques of collective bargaining. Litigation will be used as a last resort where it appears essential to eliminating egregious practices or expanding the frontiers of correctional law.

Originally developed voluntarily by labor and management groups as an alternative to strikes and other methods of economic disruption, the flexibility of collective-bargaining techniques as a method of absolving disputes short of court action has been demonstrated in the fields of public employment, student-university relations and community conflicts. The purpose of collective bargaining is to resolve specific grievances in a more expeditious, less expensive manner than going to court. According to one experienced arbitrator:

Collective bargaining is particularly designed for the reconciliation of group differences that are not susceptible to solution
through the dictates of law. Although a law can set guidelines,
it cannot resolve the claims of competing groups that fall within
the framework of these legal standards. In such circumstances,
the conflicting demands can be resolved only by an accommodation that is mutually acceptable.[725]

These principles could be readily applied to correctional institutions. They
are particularly appropriate in those instances where prisoners have begun to organize into unions, generally led by ex-prisoners, to bargain for
higher rates of pay and better working conditions, as well as for more general improvements. Although no prisoners' union has yet received recognition as the official bargaining agent for its members, a California union has
announced that it will file suit in federal court to achieve such recognition.

The outlines of correctional law must first be established by legislation
and court interpretations of statutes and constitutional provisions. Within
these confines, however, there remains a large area to be negotiated between prisoners and officials;[726] and that includes many of the petty an-
noyances that make prison life so unbearable and prison atmosphere so
volatile.

Although it may be questioned whether there are sufficient incentives for prison authorities, who are under no legal obligation to do so, to
agree to arbitration, the same could be said of the merchants, landlords,
educators and bureaucrats who have accepted arbitration. In fact, there
are several significant incentives. One is the avoidance of frequent litigation, which is a nuisance to both the prison officials called upon to testify
and the public attorney obligated to defend prison practices. Another is
the potential that collective bargaining might generate a feeling of fairness in prisoners that could reduce institutional tensions. In educational
institutions and in ghetto populations administrators and businessmen

725. Keel, *Monthly Labor Review,* Jan., 1969, at 3.
726. As one judge urged in deciding a difficult prison case in 1966:

There should be conferences or hearings at which prisoners can air their
grievances over disciplinary measures taken against them. . . . Courts are
not called upon and have no desire to lay down detailed codes for the conduct of penal institutions, state or federal. And it is not our purpose to do
so. . . . Experience teaches that nothing so provokes trouble for the management of a penal institution as a hopeless feeling among inmates that they
are without opportunity to voice grievances or to obtain redress for abusive
or oppressive treatment.

Landman v. Peyton, 370 F.2d 135, 140–41 (4th Cir. 1966).

have discovered that riots or boycotts are often the alternative to fair treatment.

The procedures for arbitration that have been developed in the context of labor relations make the technique particularly adaptable to prison problems. To begin with, the umpires need not be professional arbitrators; even in the labor field more than eight out of ten are not. Thus third-party neutrals who have particular expertise in correction may be chosen by both prisoners and the officials. Furthermore, the parties could stipulate in advance the rules to be followed and the issues to be settled. Some can be designated for binding adjudication (arbitration) and others only for negotiation (mediation). The arbitrators would have no jurisdiction beyond the issues stipulated and would be required to act within the limits set by the prevailing statute, case law or administrative standards agreed upon by the parties. Although administrators may be reluctant to arbitrate substantial problems, experience with the procedure could convince them of its efficacy and lead to the creation of a new administrative institution to which prisoners and officials alike would turn whenever problems arose within the interstices of the law.

A new challenge to lawyers and administrators alike is the recent advent of prisoners' unions and the effort to provide them with recognition by officials, as well as the legal status to operate and impose sanctions. Two unions in California and one in New York (the latter with the backing of a recognized outside union) have sought to bargain collectively with officials concerning standard union demands for higher wages and better working conditions. In addition, one of the California unions has addressed itself to general problems of inadequate medical care, indeterminate sentencing laws, and parole practice.

To date, none of the officials involved has agreed to recognize a prisoners' union. In fact, legal battles are under way simply to establish the unions' right to send their newsletters into the prisons. The fight for recognition undoubtedly will reach the courts, where lawyers for the fledgling unions can be expected to raise both the First Amendment issues of freedom of association and right to assemble and petition for redress of grievances, and the more specific right of unions to achieve recognition under federal labor laws. The way in which these issues are resolved will do much to determine the shape of the prisoners'-rights movement for the next several years.

Aside from helping prisoners, some administrative problems in the criminal-justice system would be relieved if there were a direct and expeditious means to filter and handle prisoners' complaints. An effective administrative procedure would sift through spurious claims and still provide a direct and expeditious route for resolving valid charges. For example, complaint to an ombudsman might be required as a condition precedent to airing grievances in court. In the long run, such a procedure would save considerable time and expense; and it would defuse many incendiary but minor problems. As Professor Gellhorn has noted, the availability of a suitable technique to air prisoners' grievances can be valuable as a way "to invigorate supervisors" more than to "punish miscreants."[727] Chief Justice Burger recently stated:

> We need not and should not abandon or even modify habeas corpus. What we need is to supplement it with flexible, sensible working mechanisms adapted to the modern condition of overcrowded and understaffed prisons . . . a simple and workable procedure by which every person in confinement who has, or who thinks he has, a grievance or complaint can be heard promptly, fairly and fully.[728]

While introducing a measure of due process into penal institutions can go far to ameliorate present conditions, no legal procedures will ever be sufficient to make large, maximum-security prisons workable, rehabilitative institutions. All that can be done is to make them somewhat less horrible than they are today.

Conclusion

After two centuries of simply sending convicted criminals to prison, some judges finally have begun to accept responsibility for what happens to convicts after they are sentenced. Recently the courts have abandoned their "hands-off" attitude toward prisons and begun to assume an activist and sometimes almost a crusading role. Judicial decisions concerning the rights of prisoners may be viewed as a little-noticed by-product of a larger judicial revolution in civil rights and criminal procedure. The Warren Court actually decided very few of the cases brought by prison-

727. Gellhorn, *When Americans Complain* 90 (1966).
728. Address by Chief Justice Warren E. Burger to the National Association of Attorneys General, Washington, D.C., Feb. 6, 1970.

ers against correctional officials. Yet its emphasis on the rights of poor and frequently powerless individuals may well have set the stage for several imaginative and impatient lower-court judges to intervene on behalf of prisoners, traditionally thought to possess no rights. The Burger Court, led by a Chief Justice who has expressed particular interest in correction, can be expected to extend the movement.

The federal courts have been more receptive than their state counterparts to claims involving prisoners' grievances. Yet it has been predominantly state-prison practices that have impelled federal courts to act. A few district judges consistently have decided the cases brought by prisoners. These judges have developed an expertise and an almost paternalistic feeling of responsibility for the prisoners under their jurisdiction, and a disproportionate number of the innovative decisions in this area can be credited to their sense of outrage. Several of the judges whose courts are located near large prisons have listened to prisoner's complaints in their courtrooms and, in a few cases, have held hearings inside the prisons. What they have seen and heard often has shocked them. The first decision condemning conditions of solitary confinement was made by a federal district judge who went into a California prison (far from the worst) and became convinced that the "responsible prison authorities" had "abandoned elemental concepts of decency by permitting conditions to prevail of a shocking and debased nature. . . ."[729] Whatever may have been the theoretical problems in judicial intervention, the realities of the prison system screamed for some legal justifications for providing systemic reform.

Assuming an ombudsman-like role, these federal judges have exercised more control of the prisoners' cases than would be expected in an ordinary lawsuit—sometimes consolidating cases, appointing attorneys and even framing the issues to be considered. In *Holt v. Sarver*, it was Chief Judge J. Smith Henley who first posed the question whether the Arkansas Penitentiary System, which was operated by inmate labor and relied on trusty guards, was unconstitutional. In *Johnson v. Avery*,[730] federal judge William E. Miller took a complaint by a prisoner being held in solitary confinement for serving as a "jailhouse lawyer" and broadened the issue to consider the pressing need for lawyers to represent all indigent prisoners. The widely publicized Supreme Court opinion of Justice Abe Fortas

729. *Jordan v. Fitzharris*, 257 F. Supp. 674, 680 (N.D. Cal. 1966). Feeling that no words could describe what he had seen, Chief Judge George B. Harris appended pictures of solitary "strip cells" to his opinion.
730. 309 F. Supp. 362 (E.D. Ark. 1970), *aff'd*, 442 F.2d 304 (8th Cir. 1971).

did little more than reinstate Judge Miller's landmark decision which had been reversed by the court of appeals.[731] Similarly, in *Morris v. Travisono*,[732] Judge Pettine succeeded in persuading Rhode Island prison officials to negotiate new procedures for classifying and disciplining prisoners (a broader issue than that first posed by the complaint), in return for which the complaining prisoners agreed to clean up food and excrement that was causing a health hazard in their cells. The judge held frequent conferences with lawyers for both sides and conducted an independent review of their proposed settlement.[733] When a settlement had been reached, the court retained jurisdiction for eighteen months to ensure that the regulations that had been agreed on were followed and to modify them if it should appear desirable. Finally, the judge suggested that the prisoners' attorneys might want to consider further litigation on behalf of dissatisfied inmates to challenge the conditions of life associated with punitive segregation. Such active judicial participation marks a dramatic departure from the courts' long-standing attitude of "hands-off."

The central role of the trial judge in cases brought by an unrepresented and frequently uninformed prison inmate, however, does not always aid the complaining prisoner; in fact, it can have the opposite effect. An unsympathetic judge often can quash a prisoner's case simply by declining to appoint an attorney to present his claims. In a recent federal case involving conditions of solitary confinement at the New Jersey State Prison,[734] the court concluded that the treatment of prisoners there was not as barbaric as it was in the two cases[735] where other federal courts had granted relief. Crucial to this conclusion, it seems, was the failure of the district court to have the conditions in New Jersey detailed by a lawyer appointed by the court. Cases like this underscore the need to develop alternate techniques for resolving prison grievances; courts can and should do only a part of the necessary watchdogging.

The influence of federal district judges also has created some paradoxical regional variations in the decisions concerning prisoners' rights. Courts in New York, California, Arkansas, Virginia, and Tennessee have been the most active proponents of decent treatment for captives. The first

731. 252 F. Supp. 783 (M.D. Tenn. 1966), *rev'd*, 382 F.2d 353 (6th Cir. 1967), *rev'd*, 393 U.S. 483 (1969).
732. 310 F. Supp. 857 (D.R.I. 1970).
733. The judge consulted with well-known penologists and solicited the opinions of the entire prison population—through sealed, uncensored letters. *Id.* at 859, 863.
734. *Ford v. Board of Managers*, 407 F.2d 937, 940 (3d Cir. 1969) (*per curiam*) (district court opinion unreported).
735. *Wright v. McMann*, 387 F.2d 519 (2d Cir. 1967); *Jordan v. Fitzharris*, 257 F. Supp. 674 (N.D. Cal. 1966).

two states, for whatever reason, do seem to have more than their share of active writ-writers. But that does not tell the whole story. It is not clear whether the handful of judges responsible for innovative decisions are motivated by a special, perhaps aristocratic, feeling of responsibility for the poor and powerless or simply are sensitive men who have been unusually exposed to the brutalities and irrationalities of the correction system. It is ironic that a few Southern judges from states renowned for having the worst systems have issued landmark decisions which have provided a broad precedential basis for judicial reform.

Other judges have expressed the fear that judicial efforts to oversee the treatment of prisoners will open "Pandora's Box," leading to "judicial supervision of penal institutions in such minute detail as to encompass even the selection and makeup of daily menus and the direction of the service of coffee three times a day. . . ."[736] In fact, even the judges who are the most willing to order changes in prison practices seem frustrated by their inability to fashion remedies without tearing down the entire prison structure and committing resources to transform it into a more effective, less dehumanizing institution. Judicial decisions, confined as they are to individual after-the-fact complaints, are essentially negative— orders to officials to cease certain offensive practices or to make restitution in money damages as rough compensation for harm already done. Judges cannot institute rehabilitative programs, rebuild prisons or order legislatures to commit more resources to correction.[737] Even the most sympathetic judges have not rid themselves completely of the idea that prisons exist to punish lawbreakers. One said, for example: "the food is not appetizing; it is not intended to be, and the Constitution does not require that prisoners in isolation be served tasty or attractive dishes."[738]

Courts can perform only a small part of the role of overseeing the correctional system. A law professor, considering the part to be played by litigation in prison reform, recently wrote:

> . . . Certainly the well wrought opinions of thoughtful
> judges in some recent prisoners' rights cases have through media

736. *Barnett v. Rodgers*, 410 F.2d 995, 1004 (D.C. Cir. 1969) (Tamm, J., concurring in the result).
737. In one instance where the Attorney General's office claimed that the case was "nothing more than an effort to coerce the . . . Legislature into appropriating more money for the System, and that the court was without jurisdiction to entertain such an action," the court summarily denied the claim, heard the case and ordered extensive changes. *Holt v. Sarver*, 309 F. Supp. 362, 364 (E.D. Ark. 1970), *aff'd*, 442 F.2d 304 (8th Cir. 1971).
738. *Holt v. Sarver*, 300 F. Supp. 825, 828 (E.D. Ark. 1969).

dissemination heightened the public concern over prison conditions. Just as civil rights litigation served in the early sixties to dramatize and personalize discrimination (litigation, by focusing on a single plaintiff's plight, can be more stunning than any impersonal, composite analysis), prison cases may have this value even when the direct reform achieved by a plaintiff's verdict is negligible.[739]

While it always will be necessary to keep judicial avenues open as a last resort when grievances cannot be resolved through other means, it is essential for other governmental agencies, as well as the private sector, to assume a more active role. Standard-setting legislation is sorely needed. The involvement of private citizens in correction would go far to open up the system to public view and ensure that correctional programs make sense. Finally the development of non-judicial methods for settling disputes is necessary to provide a more efficient, inexpensive and responsive system than will ever be possible where the protection of individual rights is entrusted to courts alone.

Perhaps there always will be a sense of futility in these efforts to protect society by caging dangerous criminals while at the same time meaningfully protecting the constitutional rights of those incarcerated. Although the worst abuses can be curbed, it is within the nature of total institutions like prisons to repress the individuality of the people confined there. This inevitable problem stresses the importance of subjecting only the most dangerous, hopeless criminals to the complete control of prisons. If the current emphasis on law and order leads to more and larger prisons, the errors and failures of our correction system will only be compounded and continued. This survey of prisoner's grievances provides another example of the growing recognition that the present prison system is antirehabilitative, inhumane and capable only of aggravating the crime problem.

739. Fry, *Prisons and Lawyers* (unpublished, 1971).

VIII

Community Correction

In this chapter, we include those attempts that are being made to build bridges back to the community from the world of correction. First we discuss correctional programs being run in the free community by correctional agencies; then we discuss community programs that are being run by private agencies both in correctional institutions and in the community. Both techniques, we feel, are essential and should be encouraged and expanded.

Correction in the Community

In the past decade, correctional agencies have made some effort to develop programs which, while retaining stricter custody of offenders than traditional probation or parole, attempt to provide a bridge back to the free community. Generally, these programs are introduced after offenders have undergone some period of imprisonment. The two major programs are work release and residence in a halfway house.

Work Release

Work release, also known as "work furlough" or "day parole," is a program that enables selected prisoners to be released from confinement during certain hours, usually for the purpose of private employment, and

527

to return to confinement during their non-working hours. Some variations of work-release programs enable women to return home during working hours in order to keep house and attend to the needs of their families or permit part-time release to participate in academic or vocational training programs or voluntary service in the community.[1]

Some form of work release has existed on an informal basis in the United States since the early days of the prison system. In several states it was a common practice to place women prisoners in the custody of private families to serve as indentured domestics. The practice of binding out women prisoners to domestic service was authorized by legislation in Massachusetts in 1880 and continues to be followed in a few states for female juveniles as well as adults.

In the early 1900s, a New Hampshire sheriff released some of his prisoners to work in the community by day and to serve nights and weekends in the jail. His actions were not authorized by law, but he received considerable favorable publicity as a result. Even today, sheriffs have used work release informally in states without formal legislation.

In 1873 a widely circulated report by the Wisconsin State Board of Charities and Reform decried the idleness that caused jail inmates to deteriorate:

> Here are scores and hundreds of men, some of them young and in vigorous health, who are compelled to spend from a few days to a year, and sometimes two years, in absolute idleness, while the taxpayers of the various counties are supporting them.
> What a waste of labor! What an injury to the men themselves to keep them in a state of enforced idleness! What an unwise expenditure of public funds to support healthy, able-bodied men in such idleness![2]

In 1913 the Wisconsin legislature enacted the Huber Law, which authorized judges and magistrates to impose conditional sentences on certain misdemeanants to enable them to retain their jobs while serving sentences in local jails. The purpose of the law, according to its sponsor, was to permit jail inmates to support their dependents. The Huber Law, since expanded to cover jail inmates sentenced for non-payment of a fine or contempt of court, as well as misdemeanants, was employed sporadi-

1. Florida Code §945.09(1)(b).
2. Wisconsin Department of Public Welfare, Division of Correction and Bureau of Research and Statistics, "Private Employment for County Jail Inmates" 1 (Research Bulletin C-2, 1957).

cally in a few Wisconsin counties after its enactment. The labor shortage during the Second World War caused the program to be used more widely. By 1956, fifty-two out of seventy-one counties had a work-release program, and out of the 7,682 adults sentenced to Wisconsin jails in that year, over one-third (2,654) were sentenced under the Huber Law. The great majority of the work-release prisoners were in metropolitan areas. However, for practical reasons related to the job market, sentencing under the Huber Law could not automatically assure employment; almost one-third of the prisoners sentenced under the Huber Law were unemployed.

For more than forty years, no state followed Wisconsin's lead. Then a North Carolina statute,[3] enacted in 1957 and amended in 1959, became the first law devising a work-release program for felons and to be implemented throughout a state. For many years, a North Carolina judge had been putting convicted offenders on probation on condition that they find jobs and turn their pay over to the clerk of the court, who disbursed their earnings and kept their savings for them.

The introduction of work release into North Carolina was based primarily on economic necessity. Since 1933, North Carolina prisons have been under the jurisdiction of the State Highway Commission, which used prisoners to construct and maintain state roads. With greater mechanization, the use of unskilled prison labor became less economical, and the prisons were separated from the Highway Commission in 1957. Thus, at a time when correctional authorities were trying to institute rehabilitative programs, pressure was brought to end diversion of highway funds to support correctional agencies. The state constitution required all penal institutions to be as nearly self-supporting as possible. Internal prison enterprises were expanded somewhat, but resistance from the private sector restricted what labor could be done in prisons.

Governor Luther Hodges appointed a committee to study the Wisconsin program and its provisions for reimbursement to the counties for the room and board of work-release prisoners. The committee drafted a bill providing that any state prison inmate could be granted work-release privileges on recommendation of the sentencing court. The legislature enacted a substitute measure restricting eligibility for work release to misdemeanants with less than six months previously spent in prison.

During the first two years of the law's operation, sentencing courts recommended only sixteen inmates for work release, and half of those

3. General Statutes of North Carolina §148–33.1.

recommended were unable to find suitable employment. The law was amended in 1959 to permit a judge imposing a sentence to state prison for five years or less to recommend that the prisoner be given the option of serving his sentence under the work-release plan. Subsequently, the law was liberalized further to permit the parole board to authorize work release for any prisoner without the necessity of a recommendation by the sentencing court, provided that where a prisoner had not served one-fourth of his sentence, the board would consider any recommendation of the sentencing judge.

North Carolina's work-release program included over 6,000 prisoners in its first five years of operation. According to George W. Randall, former Director of Prisons in North Carolina, the program reduced crime, providing direct economic benefits to the state as well:

> By reducing the recidivism, work release has played an important role in curtailing our prison population. Four years ago, it had reached an all-time high of more than 12,000. Today, in spite of a fast-growing State population, our prison population has been reduced to 10,600, 3,700 below a prediction made by University of North Carolina social scientists in 1956. . . .
>
> Our work-release program has many appeals. First in public appeal is the program's relief to the taxpayer. In the North Carolina Prison System today, more than 1,000 work-release inmates support themselves. Without work-release privileges, these offenders would be a tax burden on the State. The 6,080 participants approved for the program between its inception and May 1, 1965, have earned a total of $4,482,796. From this amount the prison department has deducted $1,502,000 for their keep and $370,000 for transportation.[4]

By 1965, twenty-four states had passed laws providing for some form of work release. Many of the statutes had rigid limitations, extending work release only to some counties or to prisoners with short sentences or in some cases to those sentenced for non-support of dependents. Only North Carolina and Maryland extended the provisions of their work-release statutes to felons as well as misdemeanants. Work release also was employed in several foreign countries: in Denmark for alcoholics and young adult prisoners, in Sweden as pre-release preparation for long-

4. Testimony before the Senate Ad Hoc Subcommittee of the Committee on the Judiciary, 89th Congress, 1st Session, July 29, 1965, at 16–17.

term prisoners, in Norway for prisoners who had served a substantial portion of their sentences and in France for both short-term prisoners and prisoners having served all but one year of a long sentence.

The Federal Prisoner Rehabilitation Act, enacted by Congress in 1965, enabled any federal prisoner selected at the discretion of the Attorney General to "work at paid employment or participate in a training program in the community on a voluntary basis while continuing as a prisoner of the institution or facility to which he is committed."[5] The proponents of the federal statute emphasized the positive effect of new community programs on the reduction of crime rather than any economic benefits that could be expected to accrue. According to Nicholas Katzenbach, then Attorney General:

> This measure is designed to help facilitate rehabilitation. It is designed to help make first offenders last offenders. It is also designed, therefore, to help reduce the continuing rise in the rate of crime. It is written to help us break what President Johnson described as the intolerable "endless, self-defeating cycle of imprisonment, release, and re-imprisonment which fails to alter undesirable attitudes and behavior."[6]

In order to allay the fears of union representatives, the Justice Department submitted an amendment to the bill, which, as enacted, provided that before a prisoner was put on work release, representatives of local unions would be consulted, that prisoners' employment could not result in the displacement of other workers or be in a field in which there was a labor surplus and that the rates of pay and other conditions of employment of work-release employees would be similar to those paid or provided to free workers in the same community.

After the federal legislation was enacted, several states passed similar legislation based on the federal model. By the end of 1968, thirty-four states and the District of Columbia had legislation authorizing some work-release program. In all but seven of the states, the program applied to prison inmates throughout the state.

Two primary advantages frequently are ascribed to work-release programs: the economic benefits to society and the psychological effects on the offender. According to one account:

5. P.L. 89–176, 89th Congress, 1st Session, 1965, amending 18 U.S.C. Section 4082.
6. Statement before the Senate Ad Hoc Subcommittee of the Committee on the Judiciary, 89th Congress, 1st Session, July 29, 1965, at 7.

Traditional incarceration punishes both the offender and society. The offender loses his freedom and his job, and he may also be fined; society is required to pay the cost of his keep, treatment, and supervision, and it may also have to support his family through public assistance of some kind in addition to incurring losses to the economy in manpower, buying power, and taxes.

The psychological losses are equally damaging. . . . Withdrawing the opportunity and responsibility for performing the major adult role tasks in our society is not a constructive act, yet it is the most frequent official response to crime in the U.S. today.[7]

Work release also provides one solution to the long-standing problem of prison labor. Opposition from private industry and labor unions has restricted prison industries to the production of products for government use. In addition, the low cost of prison labor has permitted administrators to tolerate inefficient methods of production, with little relation to the methods used by private industry. Prison industries offer prisoners neither the economic incentives nor the job training of the free labor market. At a minimum, work-release programs can give an offender the opportunity to return to his normal economic role; at best, they can provide valuable training, while combining work with other resources, such as schooling and medical services, available in the community.

USES OF WORK RELEASE

Various parts of the correction system make different uses of work release. The program can be employed as a sentencing measure, similar to a condition of probation, whereby a judge sentences a minor offender to work release for his entire term. In some jurisdictions, work release is even being used as a pre-conviction condition of bail. On the other hand, several jurisdictions use work release as a pre-release measure to ease a prisoner back into the community prior to his discharge from imprisonment.

Depending on which phase of a sentence work release will cover, assignment to the program may be made by different agencies. Where work release is used as a pre-release measure, the decision generally is made by prison or parole authorities, occasionally with veto power in the sen-

7. Zalba, "Work-Release—a Two-Pronged Effort," 13 *Crime and Delinquency* 521 (1967).

tencing court.[8] Where work release is used for the entire term of a minor offender, the commitment to work release generally is made by the sentencing court. In the latter case, the correctional officials administering the program generally have the power to suspend a participant from work release temporarily for violating regulations; however, removal from the program must be by the sentencing court. This feature is occasionally a source of friction between judges and correctional officials, since the latter officials object to administering a program over which they lack full control.

ELIGIBILITY FOR WORK RELEASE

After initial hesitancy, most of the states with work-release laws recently extended their programs to cover felons, frequently after several years' successful experience in using work release only for misdemeanants. The authorizing legislation generally makes no exceptions based on the offense committed. A few statutes limit the duration of work release to the last few months of a prisoner's term.

Although statutory limitations are now relatively rare, many offenders are excluded from work release by administrative practice. Only one of the programs included in a recent survey of work-release programs permitted convicted homosexuals to participate in work release, and work release appeared to be used predominately for younger offenders. There are good reasons for concentrating rehabilitative efforts on young offenders, who presumably are more amenable to correctional programs. On the other hand, older prisoners generally are more stable and frequently can complete community programs without incident. Since work-release programs involve no outlay of scarce correctional resources, there is no good reason for limiting them to younger prisoners.

Federal regulations exclude from consideration for work release "offenders identified with large-scale, organized criminal activity, [and] others whose presence in the community is likely to evoke adverse public reaction toward the inmate or the government." In addition, "offenders convicted of serious crimes against the person, or whose records include such offenses, and offenders whose offenses involved violations of financial trust, shall not be placed on Work Release without prior Bureau approval." Administrators in North Carolina automatically exclude prisoners

8. *See, e.g.*, General Statutes of North Carolina, §148–33.1(b).

who have escaped, have a detainer pending or are serving life sentences. An inmate's chances for selection are "diminished" if he is serving his second or third sentence, if he has been convicted of public drunkenness or if he has violated prison rules.

In addition to limitations based on the type of offense, some administrators have determined that work release should be used only for prisoners with special needs. According to the federal Bureau of Prisons:

> Work Release is not intended as a program or status to be made available automatically to all who may be technically "eligible." There must be indicated need for the opportunities and responsibilities which Work Release provides. This is a Classification Committee judgment to be related to the pre-release, family need or other individual circumstances for which Work Release is particularly appropriate. . . .[9]

> Just as all prisoners are not suitable candidates for Community Work . . . so Community Work, as a correctional treatment tool, has little or nothing to offer certain offenders. As a practical matter a gangster or other professional criminal is ordinarily not sentenced to imprisonment with any significant intent that he will be "corrected" or "rehabilitated." Rarely does the typical "white collar" offender need any of the rehabilitation services which a correctional system may offer, and his commitment, more often than not, is a reflection of public policy. In the light of present knowledge, there is grave doubt about how much can be done to change the ways of the chronic repeater who seems to "do life on the installment plan" with successive commitments to prisons and jails.

> The predominant focus of correctional effort now and over the years ahead is on the younger offender who comes, typically, from a deprived economic, social and family background. He is most likely to be markedly deficient in educational attainment, without work skills and with little understanding or regard for the middle-class values upon which our society is based.

> This is the context in which the potentials of Community Work are seen. Community Work will be an effective correctional tool only to the extent that it is used wisely for specific purposes and as a means toward the attainment of goals of treatment, training and control of selected offenders.[10]

9. Bureau of Prisons, Policy Statement 7500.20(A) 4 (1967).
10. "Correctional Research Associates, Community Work—An Alternative to Imprisonment" 4 (1967).

Other restrictions, which apply primarily to felons, require that a prisoner serve a certain portion of his sentence before being eligible for work release. According to a recent survey:

Two administrative patterns are found in measuring eligibility according to the proportion of sentence already served. Measuring from the beginning of the sentence, Illinois requires that half of the minimum sentence be served, and Rhode Island, one-sixth of the sentence. Reflecting the concept of work release as a bridge between penal confinement and life in the free community, some other states measure eligibility from time of probable release to the community. Michigan and Nebraska require that there be less than a year to serve; and the District of Columbia, Hawaii, Utah, and Florida, less than six months. Hawaii and Florida provide exceptions for cases of unusual merit. In Indiana, the inmate must be within six to ten months of eligibility for a parole hearing.[11]

The federal Bureau of Prisons ordinarily limits work-release placements for pre-release purposes to a period of from three to six months preceding an inmate's probable release date. When prisoners participate in educational or training courses in the community, however, they normally are permitted to remain in them for the duration of the course—an academic year, for example.

To deliberate policy restrictions such as these are added practical considerations. Most prisons and some jails are located far from population centers, and public transportation to job sites frequently is unavailable. The absence of suitable local places of confinement was given as the primary reason why one-fourth of the inmates actually approved for work release in one state were not placed in the program. In addition, since many prisoners are housed far from the areas to which they will return after release, some prison officials consider it of little value to have them working at jobs that they cannot keep.

Such restrictions, in addition to an occasional statutory limitation on proportion of the total prison population that may participate in a work-release program at any one time, have sharply curtailed the number of work-release prisoners. In fiscal year 1969, the federal Bureau of Prisons, in its fourth year of operating a work-release program, had only

11. Johnson, "Report on an Innovation—State Work-Release Programs," 16 *Crime and Delinquency* 417, 421–22 (1967).

2 percent of its total prisoner population on work release. A recent survey showed that only North Carolina, Maryland and the District of Columbia had implemented work-release programs to a significant extent in state prisons. Even in North Carolina, by far the most active program, the approximately 1,000 inmates on work release constitute only 10 percent of the total prison population. Despite a great local demand for unskilled and semi-skilled labor at the minimum wage rate and employers' indications that they desired more work-release employees, the typical work-release employee in North Carolina was chosen conservatively and had the following characteristics: He was about thirty-four years old and had had some high-school or trade-school training; he had a history of successful employment before entering prison, having been employed approximately 92 percent of the time he was not in prison; he had never received unemployment compensation and preferred to work rather than receive it; he was a low-skilled worker and had received an annual income of approximately $3,169 before going to prison; he had a deep feeling of responsibility toward his dependents.[12]

ADMINISTRATION OF WORK-RELEASE PROGRAMS

The fact that work release was used for several years almost solely for misdemeanants in local jails established a pattern of county administration. State work-release laws frequently are implemented only in some counties. Although a few states have a work-release adviser in the state department of correction, county officials determine whether to institute work-release programs in county jails and have complete responsibility for administering the programs. In addition, some state prisoners participating in work-release programs are housed in local jails and supervised by local officials under contract with the state in order to give them an opportunity to find employment in their home communities.[13]

The key position generally occupied by county sheriffs in work-release programs prompted a survey of their attitudes toward employment of prisoners in the community. In 1963, a questionnaire was sent to 492 sheriffs in forty-two states, and 218 (37 percent) responded. Thirty-six percent reported having had experience with work-release prisoners. Interestingly, while only half the sheriffs from states with work-release

12. Cooper, "Employers and Employees in the Work-Release Program in North Carolina," 16 *Crime and Delinquency* 427, 432–33 (1970).
13. *See, e.g.,* California Penal Code, §§1208(a) and 2910; West's Minnesota Statutes Annotated §241.26(2).

legislation actually had experience with work release, the survey showed that 23 percent of the sheriffs from non-work-release states reported having informal experience with some type of program. In the states that had work-release laws, only 18 percent of those reporting currently had any work-release prisoners. Fifty-one percent of those with work-release experience reported they had had ten or fewer work-release prisoners in their total experience. Only 16 percent reported having more than fifty such prisoners.

Sheriffs displayed considerable misinformation about work-release laws, and, curiously, this ignorance was more pronounced among those sheriffs from states which had work-release laws. The majority of sheriffs responded favorably to the idea of work release, particularly those who had had experience with the program. However, 84 percent of the sheriffs responded that they had neither the personnel nor the physical facilities to handle work-release prisoners. The study was able to identify no significant personal or social variables associated with the sheriffs' attitudes toward work release.

Only 39 percent of the respondents felt that prisoners should have a job at the time of sentencing in order to qualify for work release. Eighty-three percent agreed that some persons, such as persons who had committed "all felonies," "serious felonies" or "crimes of violence," should be excluded from this type of program. Forty-four percent would exclude those sentenced to less than an unspecified certain minimum term.

Seventy-two percent of those experienced with work-release prisoners reported administrative problems such as transporting prisoners from and to work, departures from work at different times, men returning to jail drunk and walkaways.

The sheriffs cited the following advantages of the work-release program: It enables the prisoner to support his family; he is not a county burden; he is able to keep his job; he is able to support himself; the jail experience is not so demoralizing. The chief disadvantage, according to 68 percent of the sheriffs, was that work release defeats the punitive purpose of sentencing. Other disadvantages listed were the special handling required, loss of control over the prisoner, security problems, excessive administrative costs and resentment of work-release prisoners by prisoners not in the program.

In another survey performed by the Wisconsin Division of Correction in 1967, sixty-nine Wisconsin judges with criminal-court jurisdiction were asked their opinions regarding the advantages and disadvantages of the state's Huber Law. The advantage to the communities mentioned most frequently was the economic one: the ability given inmates to support their dependents and pay their existing debts and to the communities to defray the costs of imprisonment. The judges praised the law for allowing inmates to continue their regular employment, relieving the idleness of county jails and aiding in rehabilitation. Seventeen of the sixty-nine judges saw no disadvantages in the law. Others cited drawbacks: Offenders are given no real penalty if they are required to spend only non-working hours in jail; offenders receive too much freedom and insufficient supervision; administering the law overburdens jailers and jail facilities; use of the law is not feasible in areas in which there is little or no industry; transporting inmates to and from their place of employment presents difficulties.[14]

EMPLOYMENT

One of the crucial facets of any work-release program is, of course, finding jobs for the participating inmates. In a recent survey of twenty-six California counties employing work release, all but one reported that their programs exclude some types of jobs, primarily those related to alcoholic beverages, commission work or jobs without a fixed location. The federal program, on the other hand, has no specified restrictions on the kinds of work-release jobs for which prisoners may be considered.

Where misdemeanants are assigned to work release immediately after sentencing, generally they keep the same jobs they held before conviction. Approximately 86 percent of the misdemeanants in one Minnesota work-release program held the same jobs in jail that they had held previously. Administrators of local work-release programs in California have stressed the importance of minimizing the time between sentencing and the start of work release when an employee plans to return to his old job:

> The importance of speedy and flexible classification for those who are employed at the time of sentencing stems from the probability of job loss if the subject is away too long. Often the applicant is only marginally employable, and a special effort to maintain existing employment is more than justified. In some

14. Grupp, "Work Release—The Sheriff's Viewpoint," 13 *Crime and Delinquency* 513 (1967); Wisconsin Division of Correction and Bureau of Research and Statistics, "Private Employment for County Jail Inmates" 8–14 (1967).

jurisdictions probation departments are investigating the possibility of work furlough prior to commitment, and judges are sentencing eligible offenders to surrender on their days off, thereby minimizing both the loss of time and the risk of termination of employment.[15]

According to George W. Randall it is possible for some offenders recommended for work release by the sentencing judge to begin work (and their sentence) the following day.

For inmates without a job or for those who are not put on work release immediately after sentencing, finding acceptable employment frequently presents major problems. A survey of work release in Wisconsin jails revealed that lack of available employment, together with the extra workload placed on jail personnel, were the most important reasons for limited application of the Huber Law. A review of North Carolina's experience found that as the program was expanded, the proportion of available skilled jobs declined consistently. Although skilled workers comprised more than 40 percent of work-release prisoners between 1957 and 1960, in 1963, when more than ten times the number of prisoners were in the program, they comprised slightly more than 15 percent. The major source of failure in the program was loss of jobs. Most jobs lost were in seasonal occupations, where workers were laid off regularly. Employers rarely fired employees for unsatisfactory job performance.[16]

The situation is different, for obvious reasons, for long-term prisoners. State work-release administrators surveyed recently reported little reliance on returning long-term prisoners to their pre-conviction employment. The low skill level of most work-release employees makes it essential to develop community vocational-training programs as part of work-release programs. Institutional training does not suffice. Data collected during the first year of the federal work-release program revealed that only 29 percent of the prisoners studied were placed in jobs closely related to their institutional job training; 16 percent held jobs that were "moderately" related; and 55 percent had assignments unrelated to their institutional training.[17] Federal prisons were much more successful in obtaining jobs for inmates that provided on-the-job training than they

15. Hoover, *Work Furlough Practices in California* 9 (1968).
16. Johnson, "Work-Release—A Study of Correctional Reform," 13 *Crime and Delinquency* 521, 528–29 (1967).
17. Bureau of Prisons, *New Bridges to the Community: A Collection of Studies on the First Year's Experience with the Work-Release Program* 33–35 (1967).

were in finding jobs related to previous prison training. Fifty-nine percent of the inmates studied were placed in jobs that provided "much" training, and only 19 percent received little or no training.

A unique experiment undertaken jointly by the District of Columbia Department of Correction and the District's public-housing agency is employing work-release prisoners to renovate vacant or vandalized public-housing units. The prisoners, many of them skilled laborers, live in the housing projects they are renovating, receive full union wages for their work and in some cases receive job training from the contractors supervising the project. One official reported: "We are rehabilitating people and houses at the same time."

Once a job has been obtained, the majority of work-release prisoners appear to perform to their employers' satisfaction. Seventy-six percent of the sixty-five employers responding to a survey of work release in North Carolina indicated that the performance of their work-release employees was of approximately the same quality as that of the average non-prison employee doing similar work at the same wage rate. Twenty percent indicated that the work releasees' performance was superior to that of the other employees; only 4 percent said that it was inferior. Of the work-release employees then employed by the firms surveyed, employers expected almost half to continue employment with the same firm after release from prison; approximately 16 percent had done so in the past. On the other hand, of the one hundred work-release employees surveyed, more than three quarters said that they intended to remain with their present employers after their release from prison, that they would accept a job similar to their work-release job if they were free from prison supervision and that the most important reason for accepting work-release employment was to support their families. (Twenty percent wanted work experience, and only 4 percent said that their most important reason was a desire to escape the prison atmosphere.)

An early survey of the federal work-release program revealed that, in 78 percent of the 1,043 cases studied, employers expressed a willingness to hire work-release employees permanently on their release from the institution; employers actually rehired 288 released inmates; seventy-one employees were hired by another employer in an occupation related to their work-release occupation.[18]

The federal Civil Service Commission has devised a system under which federal work-release prisoners may be employed by Government

18. *Ibid.*, 26, 28 (1967).

agencies. However, there are a number of restrictions. Agencies may employ prisoners only in those positions with a shortage of regular recruits. No person may serve under the special appointing authority, which obviates the need to follow normal Civil Service requirements, longer than one year after he is released from custody. At that time, convicted offenders must apply for competitive appointment under regular examining procedures.

EARNINGS OF WORK-RELEASE PRISONERS

A typical work-release statute prescribes the procedure for distributing prisoners' earnings:

> From [a prisoner's] earnings the administrator shall pay the prisoner's board and personal expenses, both inside and outside the jail, and shall deduct so much of the cost of administration of this section as is allocable to such prisoner and in an amount determined by the administrator, shall pay the support of the prisoner's dependents, if any. If sufficient funds are available after making the foregoing payments, the administrator may, with the consent of the prisoner, pay, in whole or in part, the pre-existing debts of the prisoner. Any balance shall be retained until the prisoner's discharge and thereupon shall be paid to him.[19]

Operating under this statute, the more than 5,000 prisoners and county jail inmates participating in work release in California in fiscal year 1968 earned more than $2 million in after-tax income (an average of $400 per prisoner), of which more than $600,000 was paid to support dependents, over $200,000 was paid for inmates' personal expenses, more than $500,000 went to them at the time of their release, and over $650,000 was collected by correction authorities for maintenance charges. Maintenance charges ranged from zero in one county to a maximum of $12 per working day for certain work-release prisoners in another county. The average charge was $3.50 per day. Four counties varied the charge in relation to a prisoner's income. In one California county alone, between July 1, 1968, and June 30, 1969, participants in the County Work Furlough Program earned a total of $370,364 and paid maintenance charges of $84,983.[20]

19. California Penal Code, §1208(E).
20. San Mateo County Work Furlough Program (mimeographed, 1969).

A survey of the Minnesota Department of Correction Work-Release Program determined that the 178 felony offenders who spent an average of four months in the program in 1969 earned a median net income of $666.32 each, from which they contributed a total of $4,528 for support of dependents, $96,259 for their own support (including room and board, payment on past indebtedness and weekly expenses) and $39,891 in taxes.[21] A study of the District of Columbia's work-release program concluded that it costs twice as much to keep an offender in an institution as to put him on work release.[22]

One innovative use of earnings from work release could be to make restitution to the victims of prisoners' crimes. This has not been done to date, although we view it as a promising technique for expanding the uses of work release.

ADMINISTRATIVE PROBLEMS

In addition to finding jobs for work-release prisoners, administrators are responsible for accounting for work-release prisoners' funds. Most programs do not permit inmates to carry money with them when they are inside the institution. Over half of the California programs surveyed require that employers transmit the pay of work-release prisoners directly to the administrator of the program instead of to the employee. Some employers have objected to this practice because of the administrative chores involved. In addition, critics point out that not allowing an employee to pick up his own pay detracts from his dignity and sense of responsibility. In other programs, prisoners are paid by their employers but are required to turn over their earnings to prison administrators.

Other administrative problems include the difficulty of transporting inmates to and from jobs and the effect on prison routines of employees working different shifts. A few officials have complained that the failure to provide separate housing for work-release prisoners allows them to bring contraband into the institution and that other prisoners pressure them to do errands during their time at work. Others have noted that there are likely to be harmful effects of the presence of work-release prisoners on general prison discipline.

There is a difference of opinion among correctional officials as to whether separate housing is essential to a work-release program. Some feel that an effective program must provide separate housing facilities;

21. Bartholomew, Ryan and Mandel, *Analysis of Work Release for Felons in Minnesota* 21–22 (1970).
22. Cost Analysis of the District of Columbia Work-Release Program (1969).

others think that work-release prisoners can be housed with other mini-mum-custody inmates. A few statutes require separate housing.[23] This requirement, together with the failure of legislatures to appropriate funds for special work-release facilities, has precluded the existence of work-release programs in many jails.

Institutions for state prisoners may be located many miles away from employment, with little or no access to public transportation, unless special housing is provided. Furthermore, the location of remote central-ized prison facilities often precludes the possibility of an inmate finding employment that he can maintain after his release from prison. Different states have experimented with various solutions to the housing problem. In North Carolina, work-release prisoners live in old highway-maintenance camps. In addition, several special work-release facilities have been con-structed at state prisons. Other states house some state work-release pris-oners in local jails, halfway houses, farms or prison honor dormitories.

Administrators of some of the most active programs have determined that work release should not hinge on the availability of separate housing facilities. A 1961 amendment to the North Carolina statute deleted the requirement that work-release prisoners be housed "apart from other prisoners serving regular sentences," in order to permit the State Prison Department to determine the extent to which separate housing was nec-essary.[24] The Bureau of Prisons has directed federal institutions that

> Work Release inmates may live in specially designated quarters; however, the exclusive use of outside quarters for housing Work Releasees is not possible nor necessarily desirable at this time Under no circumstances should the lack of outside quarters cur-tail the number of participants.[25]

The administrator of Florida's work-release program reports that, since the legislature failed to appropriate funds for the establishment of sepa-rate centers or institutions for work-release prisoners, Florida's program was inaugurated from existing institutions.

PERFORMANCE OF WORK-RELEASE PRISONERS

There are records of some of the work-release programs' "successes" and "failures." These categories vary according to the definitions given them by different program administrators. Generally, however, a "suc-

23. See, e.g., Annotated Laws of Massachusetts, C. 127, Section 86D.
24. See General Statutes of North Carolina, §148–33.1(c).
25. Bureau of Prisons, Policy Statement 750.20A6 (1967).

cess" is defined as a prisoner who remains on work release until the end of his prison term and a "failure" as a prisoner who is removed from the program, for whatever reason, prior to the expiration of his institutional sentence. Viewed in this way, the federal program, from its initiation in October 1965 to July 1969, had a success rate of 66 percent. The other one-third of the participants were terminated for the following reasons: "disciplinary problems" (9 percent); escape (5.9 percent); job abolished (2.4 percent); inmate request (2.2 percent); "intra-institutional infractions" (1.8 percent); "lack of skill" (1.6 percent); and "other" (11 percent).[26] Half the federal escapes occurred either during the first month on the program or after an inmate had been on the job for at least six months—the latter attributed to problems arising from the "Cinderella-like" status of a long-term work-release prisoner.

Of more than 5,000 prisoners, mostly misdemeanants, placed on work furlough in California during fiscal 1968, almost 90 percent completed the program successfully. The principal reason for failure was the use of alcohol by work-furlough prisoners (which may amount to taking only one drink). Most of the remaining failures were attributed to unauthorized absence from the job, side trips, such as visits home or elsewhere, and returning late from work.

Two hundred twenty-three inmates of the Bucks County Prison in Pennsylvania were placed on work release in a recent three-and-one-half-year period. Of this group, seven men violated prison regulations and twelve failed to return to the Rehabilitation Center at the proper time. Men in the latter group returned later voluntarily or called the center and asked to be picked up. "Thus," according to Warden John D. Case, "although about 9 percent of work releasees can be said to have actually been 'over the hill' since the program has been operating, only 3 percent were 'walk-aways' serious enough to be considered escapees."

A study of Minnesota's work-release program for felons reported that, of 140 prisoners for whom work release was terminated during 1969, 56 percent were defined as successes and 44 percent were defined as failures. No one was returned for a new criminal offense. About half the failures violated prison rules, and the other half absconded. Researchers viewed the findings optimistically:

> Initial reaction to the findings of this analysis of Work Release activity may be skepticism as the failure rate was about the

26. The substantial percentage of terminations reported in the "other category may include escapes, disciplinary problems and intra-institutional infractions." Bureau of Prisons, Operations Memorandum 7500.53 Attachment 1 (1969).

same as if a coin were flipped. However, a second look at the data indicates that the failures were of a relatively harmless nature. Not one work releasee was returned to a correctional institution for commission of a new offense, but rather for violation of rules such as drinking, not returning to the facility after work, missing work, etc. This type of behavior may well be expected from one who has been locked up for eighteen months.[27]

Between 1957 and 1963 in North Carolina, the number of prisoners selected for work release increased sharply due to liberalized legislation and administrative policy. The failure rate, defined as violation of rules or escapes, rose from 18.3 percent between 1957 and 1960 to 25.6 percent in 1963. However, it was down to 18 percent by 1970. The category of rule violations declined to 12 percent, perhaps because prison employees came to respond more liberally to infractions. According to one report, violations were "more a product of accommodation to the half-free status of work-release inmates than a threat to the internal security of the prison or the security of the free community. The half-free status permitted the prisoner to receive visitors at the place of work, presented opportunity for difficulties with employers or fellow employees, opened the way to traffic violations and drunkenness, and so on."[28]

The reasons advanced most frequently by both prison administrators and work-release prisoners for escapes from work-release programs concern drinking, desire to be with women and marital conflicts. In most jurisdictions, the rules by which prisoners on work release agree to abide are extremely stringent. For example, an inmate in Bucks County, Pennsylvania, must agree to travel to and from work by the quickest route, with no stops, not to visit family or friends, not to drink any intoxicating beverages, not to make any telephone calls while away from the prison. Some administrators have emphasized the importance of liberalizing in-prison visiting provisions for work-release prisoners in order to reduce the probability of illicit visits during the period of release for work.

EVALUATION

While there has been considerable debate about the ongoing efficacy of work-release programs, there have been very few attempts to evaluate

27. Bartholomew, Ryan and Mandel, *Analysis of Work Release for Felons in Minnesota* 23–24 (1970).
28. Johnson, "Work-Release—A Study of Correctional Reform," 13 *Crime and Delinquency* 521, 529 (1967).

them in terms of the performance of participants after their release from prison. No study has compared the performance of work-release participants with that of a randomly selected control group that did not participate in the program. A one-year follow-up study of ninety-nine federal prisoners who completed the work-release program successfully and left prison during the program's first six months revealed that

> . . . Eighty-four percent of these offenders have succeeded to the extent that they have maintained themselves in the community for at least one year without further serious convictions. Men with no prior commitments succeeded at the rate of 88%, while men with one or more prior commitments succeeded at the rate of 81%. . . .
>
> . . . maximum benefit was apparently derived by those men falling into the poorer risk categories. Men who were good risks succeeded at or near the rates expected. Those offenders who were poorer risks succeeded at much higher than their expected rates.

A study of the model work-release program in Bucks County, Pennsylvania, attempted to determine whether sentencing prisoners to work release involves any increased risk to the community. The study compared recidivism rates of a "pre-work-release" group of inmates of the Bucks County Prison in 1961 with that of a group of work-release participants in 1965. Recognizing the obvious limitations of a comparison between the performance of jail inmates in different years, the study concluded that at the very least there was no increase in recidivism rates for work-release prisoners as compared with a sample group of prisoners who served out their terms in the county jail, and there was some data indicating that the group that did not participate in the work-release program experienced a slightly higher rate of recidivism than the work-release inmates.[29]

The results of a follow-up study of the 281 offenders (156 felons and 125 misdemeanants) who participated in the District of Columbia's work-release program between its inception in April 1966 and the end of July 1967 were less favorable to work release. Of the 156 felony offenders, almost one-third absconded or were removed from the program prematurely. A post-release follow-up of all the felony participants showed,

29. Newman and Bielen, *Work Release: An Alternative in Correctional Handling* (1967).

one year after their release, approximately 25 percent had been detained in the District of Columbia jail; the remaining 75 percent were considered "successes." Of the 125 misdemeanants, more than one quarter absconded or were removed from the program prematurely. One year following release, almost one quarter of the total misdemeanant group had been detained in the District of Columbia jail.

The 75 percent success rate for the felony offenders on work release was somewhat lower than the 85 percent success rate for the 432 felony offenders released from the District of Columbia's reformatory in 1965. However, the study pointed out that the work-release participants may have been a high-risk group, since they were drawn primarily from groups that ordinarily are released at the expiration of their sentences rather than on parole. The study also raised the possibility that work release may be effective differentially, helping some groups of participants but unsuited to others.[30]

In discussions preceding the enactment of the federal work-release legislation, officials of the Bureau of Prisons predicted that they would be able to determine in advance which prisoners could benefit from participation in a work-release program by using established techniques of diagnosis and prediction. This forecast now seems overly optimistic; it is yet to be determined with any reliability which prisoners benefit from work release and what characteristics are associated with successful performance.

Even without demonstrable research results, it seems clear that work-release programs are sensible economically and give prisoners whatever psychological value there is in supporting themselves and their families. Work release enables an offender to support himself and his family, to be a productive, tax-paying member of society, to reimburse the state or county for his keep and to leave the institution with considerable savings on his release. In addition, work release may make it easier for prisoners to find jobs on their release and give them an opportunity to associate with co-workers in an informal setting. Finally, by involving private employers, work-release programs create new resources for correction and new pressure groups for sensible correctional programs.

At the very least, a commitment to work release or, in some cases, a sentence to serve weekends in jail is a way to provide criminal sanctions

30. Adams and Dellinger, *In-Program and Post-Release Performance of Work-Release Inmates: A Preliminary Assessment of the Work-Release Program* (Research Report No. 13, 1969).

that are less damaging, disruptive, embarrassing and expensive than the usual prison term. A sentence to work release recognizes explicitly that in many cases the safety of the community does not require custody of prisoners and that incarceration is for purposes of punishment or deterrence only. Neither public denunciation nor total loss of freedom need be added. Work-release programs, as characterized by one authority,

> . . . break hard and fast forms of punishment and modify them into patterns which conserve the offender. For some classes of correctional clients, these plans seem to be all that is necessary: they serve their nights or weekends in jail and sin no more. . . . Pending the interesting research which could be done, the value of the Huber Plan, and its derivatives, is in the demonstration that exile need not be total.[31]

In more serious cases, where a "taste of jail" without the pretense of treatment does not seem sufficient, the greatest potential of work release lies in using private employment in conjunction with other community resources, academic, vocational and recreational, and with residence in publicly or privately operated halfway houses.

FURLOUGHS

We noted earlier the incredible tensions that can build up in prisons, where men are locked up for years with no access to women or, indeed, to any outside society. One technique for lessening these tensions is to allow as many prisoners as can be released safely to spend short but frequent periods out of prison on furlough. Furloughs, though commonly used in European countries, have been used less frequently here.

The opportunity for a prisoner to spend time with his family provides one of the most compelling reasons for a liberal use of furloughs. We suggested earlier that instituting the practice of conjugal visiting would do much to minimize personal tensions as well as the occurrence of perversion and homosexual attacks in prisons. For prisoners who safely can be granted furloughs, this practice offers an additional alternative that is less cumbersome than conjugal visiting, requires no special facilities and should invite less public criticism.

In addition to their use to reduce institutional tensions and keep

31. Conrad, *Crime and Its Correction* 274 (1967). *See also* Grupp, "Work Release and the Misdemeanant," 29 *Federal Probation*, June 1965.

families intact, furloughs give prison administrators needed flexibility to deal with the situations where parole is delayed for administrative reasons or for lack of a job or place to live. Furthermore, some halfway houses allow a few residents to be on "out count," living at home but reporting in regularly, thus aiding a gradual transition from imprisonment to freedom.

Some statutes authorizing work-release programs include provisions giving administrators discretion to grant furloughs to selected prisoners. Although some of the statutes permit furloughing of any prisoners at the discretion of prison administrators, others limit furloughs to prisoners on work release. Statutory provisions range from Florida's narrowly limited permission to "visit, for a period not to exceed twenty-four hours exclusive of travel time, a specifically designated place or places for the purpose of visiting a dying relative, attending the funeral of a relative, arranging for employment or for a suitable residence for use when released, or for another compelling reason consistent with the public interest . . ." to federal legislation allowing administrators to authorize a prisoner to "visit a specifically designated place or places for a period not to exceed thirty days. . . . An extension of limits may be granted only to permit a visit to a dying relative, attendance at the funeral of a relative, the obtaining of medical services not otherwise available, the contacting of prospective employers, or for any other compelling reason consistent with the public interest."[32]

Before the federal law was passed, the Bureau of Prisons, in line with the common practice in many state correctional systems, permitted trusted prisoners to travel to their home communities in emergencies under the escort of a prison guard. The prisoners or their families paid all transportation expenses, salaries and expenses of the accompanying employees. The purpose of the new law was to permit travel without an escort. According to former Attorney General Nicholas Katzenbach:

> . . . if a prisoner or his family cannot afford the cost of a guard, or no employee is available to volunteer his time, the prisoner cannot see a dying relative or attend the funeral, or accept a job interview. His resentment is understandable, and the setback to his rehabilitation is avoidable.
>
> Our request is simply to permit qualified and trusted prisoners to undertake such travel alone. The trust reposed in such

32. 18 U.S.C. §4082(1).

prisoners would, assuredly, encourage and assist in rehabilitation.

Needless to say, the authority would be used most judiciously and applied only to prisoners who do not present a threat to the community. It involves no costs to the Government.[33]

Correction officials in the District of Columbia have gone beyond the federal practice and authorized "evaluative furloughs" for inmates with good behavior records. Under the program minimum-security prisoners may spend one day each month with their families. Despite the high success rate of the program (only six prisoners out of 363 have failed to return on time) and its easing effect on prison tensions, it is under attack.

Even in some of the jurisdictions without special legislation, furloughs may be granted as part of work-release programs. For example, the sheriff responsible for the Milwaukee County, Wisconsin, jail reports that:

> Occasionally Huber prisoners request special release privileges because of some emergency. The court or Sheriff does not have this authority specifically spelled out in the Statutes. However, the court may exercise its discretion to authorize such special releases and may also parole a Huber prisoner for a portion or all of his sentence for cause. With permission of the sentencing court the Huber prisoner may be paroled to spend the Thanksgiving and Christmas holidays with his family. This procedure has been followed for a number of years with notable success.[34]

The use of furloughs as part of a work-release program provides a way to reduce the number of failures attributable to unauthorized absences. The administrators of five county work-release programs in California recently suggested that work-furlough administrators be given statutory authority to grant short leaves for home visits, doctors' appointments, funerals and "other valid purposes." According to the administrator of one successful program:

---

33. Testimony before the Senate Ad Hoc Subcommittee of the Committee on the Judiciary, 89th Congress, 1st Session, July 29, 1965, at 9.
34. Purtell, "Milwaukee County Jail—Huber Law Fact Sheet" at 2, in American Correctional Association, Ad Hoc Committee on Work Release, *Work Release in the United States* (1968).

Such a change seems reasonable. Work furloughees are already permitted to leave the institution essentially without supervision for one purpose, and it logically follows that such trust should be extended to other comparable areas. Home visits would be not only an extra privilege to supplement other methods of control, but should also sharply reduce the number of failures caused by unauthorized side trips and visits during work or travel time.[35]

Some correctional administrators conceive of work release, together with furloughs, as affording an opportunity for participation in other community activities in addition to employment. For example, a memorandum prepared by the federal Bureau of Prisons allows

. . . participation in community religious, educational, social, civic and recreational activities . . . when there is reason to believe that such participation will contribute significantly to the offender's learning and exercise of personal responsibility. Similarly, within the statutory 30 day limit, furloughs may be authorized as program resources, but not as rewards. When used, these are to be scheduled progressively as a "tapering-off" technique.[36]

North Carolina prisoners who have been on work release for thirty to sixty days generally are allowed home visits if they can demonstrate satisfactory job performance, prison conduct and home circumstances. For inmates who qualify, home visits are usually allowed for two nights once each month.

However, a recent survey of state work-release practices regarding felons reports that many states flatly prohibit attendance by work-release employees at social events, even those sponsored by their employers. Ironically, even more states prohibit visits by work-release prisoners to their families. According to the survey:

Official reluctance to extend the boundaries of work-release privileges specifically to include visits to the family is indicated by the high number of states (fourteen) prohibiting this practice. Oregon reports that six-hour leaves can be arranged for sports events, family visits, and so on "usually accompanied by a

35. Hoover, *Work Furlough Practices in California* 10–11 (1968).
36. Bureau of Prisons, Policy Statement 7500.20A 6–7 (1967).

sponsor." South Carolina apparently permits home leaves for inmates in pre-release status. Alaska, Colorado, Connecticut, the District of Columbia, and Minnesota report that home visits can be authorized. Hawaii provides thirty-hour weekend furloughs with immediate families. North Carolina grants home leaves to "eligible" inmates for one weekend every thirty days.

The survey concludes that:

Although there is universal acclaim for the work-release goal of strengthening or maintaining the prisoner's affiliation with his family, it is a different matter when the issue involves official sanctioning of the prisoner's release for an unsupervised visit with his family.

Why this distinction? The release of inmates into the community runs counter to the idea that the convicted criminal poses a threat to life or property and that his release into the community erodes the punitive purpose of prison confinement. These issues are less likely to be raised when the period of relative freedom is tied directly to employment, because the economic advantages to the prison and the presumed supervision of the inmate by the employer offer justification for work release. Furthermore, this type of release does not emphasize gratification of the personal interests of the inmate.[37]

HALFWAY HOUSES

For almost two hundred years, religious and humanitarian groups have made sporadic attempts to offer temporary shelter and food to people without homes, families or means of support. In Europe and in England, people with mental disturbances have been housed in homes in the community since the end of the nineteenth century. And as early as 1788, the Philanthropic Society of London organized several small cottages for children who had been arrested for begging or stealing.

The first formal authorization of community residences for offenders occurred in 1914, when British judges were authorized to impose residence in a probation hostel as one of the conditions of probation for young offenders. Approximately thirty-five hostels now operate in Britain under private, frequently religious, auspices. Operation of the hostels

37. Johnson, "Report on an Innovation—State Work-Release Programs," 16 *Crime and Delinquency* 417, 425 (1970).

has been subsidized partially by government funds since 1928.

On the other hand, until quite recently private efforts to establish residences for offenders in the United States were carried out in the face of public indifference and even hostility. The first suggestion of a special residence for offenders occurred in the report of a commission appointed by the Massachusetts legislature in 1817 to study the prison system and recommend changes. The legislature failed to adopt the proposal. Although it was suggested again in 1830, it was disapproved on the basis of an objection filed by the Inspectors of the State Prison, who feared that prisoners living in any sort of halfway house would contaminate one another.

Crofton's "Irish System," which provided for a graduated series of steps to move offenders from maximum-security confinement to parole supervision in the community, was adopted in parts of Britain beginning in the 1860s.

In the United States, where the official system was less responsive to the need for transitional steps between custody and freedom, a few halfway houses did open under private auspices. The Isaac T. Hopper Home in New York, established by a group of Quakers in 1845, is still in operation. In 1864, a group of Bostonians opened the "Temporary Asylum for Disadvantaged Female Prisoners" to house women discharged from jails and houses of correction. It operated for almost twenty years. A "House of Industry" opened in Philadelphia in 1889.

At about this time a committee of the American Prison Association expressed its opposition to the proliferation of halfway houses, which, oddly, it charged would perpetrate "prison stigma" and create a permanent class of undesirable citizens. Despite such official hostility, Maud and Ballington Booth, with support from the Volunteers of America, a missionary religious society, opened Hope Hall in New York in 1896 to provide temporary shelter for prisoners released from Sing Sing Prison— it was to be a place that would be a real home and not an institution. The police were persuaded to stop their harassment of the residents through the intervention of Theodore Roosevelt, then Police Commissioner of New York.

In succeeding years, the Booths opened other Hope Halls in several cities, including Chicago, San Francisco, New Orleans. However, with the advent of parole as a method of release from prison, correctional authorities argued that there was no longer any need for Hope Halls and, ironically, that residence in halfway houses would cause prisoners to violate parole regulations against associating with ex-convicts. After the Depression, which forced the Volunteers of America to cut back its funding, all the Hope Halls gradually were closed.

Although the Salvation Army and the Volunteers of America continued to admit former prisoners to their dormitories and social-service centers on the same basis as other homeless men, it was not until after World War II that correctional officials in the United States became interested in halfway houses as a means of aiding the transition of prisoners from prison back to the community. Parole, which, it had been thought, would provide a system of graduated supervision and services, had been adopted in every state; yet many released prisoners were committing further crimes, a large proportion in the first few months following release. Others were being returned to prison for violating the many and frequently technical terms of their parole. In 1946, a report to a National Conference on Juvenile Delinquency suggested:

A post-training school hostel would solve many of the difficulties arising from emotional disturbances when release is delayed, and ease the transition from the institution to the community. For various reasons it seems advisable that the hostels should be controlled by the training school itself and should be regarded as part of the institution setup. . . ."[38]

During this period, several state prisons in the Midwest, and the federal Bureau of Prisons instituted pre-release programs in an attempt to ease this crucial and often difficult transition. Prisoners nearing the end of their prison terms were housed in separate dormitories or in pre-release camps located outside the prisons, where they received extra privileges and participated in group discussions of potential common-problem areas, such as employment, family relations and drinking. However, it soon became clear that these prisoners could not cope effectively with problems of reintegration into the community while they continued to be isolated from the community. When they finally were released, their problems remained. According to a report by the Bureau of Prisons:

For many inmates, the lectures, discussions and small increase in privileges were no important gain. These offenders, away without family, lacking meaningful friendships, poorly trained

38. National Conference on Prevention and Control of Juvenile Delinquency, "Report on Institutional Treatment of Delinquent Juveniles" 47 (1946).

and with little self-confidence, found it difficult to obtain the employment and residence that were often prerequisites for release on parole. Those completing a sentence saw only the barest chance of survival where their total assets were a small cash gratuity and a "dress-out" prison suit.[39]

In the 1950s, in an effort to deal with the problems of offenders in a community setting, private groups again opened residences for released prisoners. The first examples of what was to become a new halfway-house movement owed their existence to the efforts of a few dedicated individuals.

In London, Merfyn Turner, a schoolteacher who had been imprisoned as a conscientious objector during the Second World War, volunteered to visit friendless prisoners. He was assigned to Pentonville Prison, where he found a large number of "homeless, friendless, destitute . . . inadequate offenders," who he was convinced need not have been sentenced to prison in the first place but who, having been incarcerated, perhaps could be prevented from returning by adequate after-care. Turner decided that in order to "settle to the acceptable mode of living which they said they wanted," released prisoners needed a "home and family tailor-made for them where they would be accepted for what they were and supported, supervised and directed into a satisfactory and satisfying way of life. . . ."

In 1954, having convinced the London Parochial Foundation to finance it, Turner bought a large Victorian house in north London, to which he invited selected prisoners whom he thought he could help. Despite the assurance of skeptics that "you could not run a house of criminals . . . and live with them without inviting calamity and catastrophe, which the Old Testament prophets could not have bettered," Turner and his wife lived with their charges, ate with them, counseled them and befriended them. As Turner later wrote:

> The homeless men . . . who come to Norman House . . . need to learn to live with their fellow men. In the past, the process of learning has not proceeded far because they had no anchorage, nobody to help protect them from their own immature reactions to simple situations which well-integrated members of society take in their stride. Norman House offers that anchor.

39. U.S. Bureau of Prisons, "The Residential Center: Correction in the Community" iii (1968).

> Living in a state of belonging, accepted as members of the
> family, and not . . . as society's rejects and objects of charity,
> they see for the first time in their lives, the true nature of
> "going straight."[40]

Men remained at Norman House for an average of four months.
Turner found that the residents' criminal activities ceased while they
lived at Norman House, perhaps out of deference to the attentions of
Turner and his wife. When they left the house, however, approximately
half of the residents relapsed into unemployment, homelessness and,
sometimes, crime. Concluding that for some of these people short-term
residence in a halfway house was not enough, the Turners opened a
boarding house, where some residents could remain indefinitely. In this
house the turnover of residents was small, the average length of stay
being three years.

In the past ten years Norman Houses and other halfway houses modeled after them have proliferated throughout England and Northern
Ireland. Today they receive financial support from the government, and
the services they provide for unattached former prisoners are considered
an integral part of the National After-Care Service.

In this country, at about the same time, Father Charles Dismas
Clark, a Jesuit priest whose efforts on behalf of Missouri prisoners already had earned him the nickname "The Hoodlum Priest," became
convinced that the only real rehabilitation of criminals could be accomplished outside prisons by private citizens, without interference from
the state. But under the present system, a prisoner is released from a
long term in prison with no help from the free community and few non-
criminal opportunities.

Father Clark approached Morris Shenker, a criminal lawyer in St.
Louis, and persuaded him to raise enough money to buy a house. This
unusual partnership established Dismas House (Dismas was the name
given to the good thief who died next to Jesus) in 1959 to offer shelter
and assistance to recently released prisoners until they could find jobs and
homes of their own. Dismas House welcomed the ex-prisoners whom no
one else wanted. Soon Dismas House, along with St. Leonard's House, a
similar place opened in Chicago by James Jones, an Episcopalian minister, and 308 West Residence in Wilmington, Delaware, operated by a

40. Turner, "The Lessons of Norman House," 381 *The Annals of the American Academy of Political and Social Science* 39, 41 (1969); Turner, *Safe Lodging* (1961).

prisoners' aid society in a house owned by the state, had gained public and official support that astounded even their founders.

The publicity given these private efforts, together with the growing professional interest in pre-release programs, was instrumental in generating Congressional support for a recommendation by then Attorney General Robert F. Kennedy in 1961 that federal funds be appropriated for the establishment of the first publicly operated halfway house under federal auspices.

Several months later, the Bureau of Prisons opened its first pre-release guidance centers in New York and Chicago to receive young federal prisoners who had been committed under the Federal Juvenile Delinquency Act or the Federal Youth Correction Act, were scheduled to be released within ninety days and planned to make their homes within a fifty-mile radius of one of the centers. The apparent success of the centers led to an expansion of the program. Under the Prisoner Rehabilitation Act of 1965, the Bureau of Prisons was authorized to establish community-based residences for adult pre-release prisoners as well as for youthful offenders and to transfer federal prisoners to approved residential community treatment centers maintained by non-federal agencies.

Although a few states and several counties have followed the lead of the federal government in establishing halfway houses for newly released prisoners, halfway houses for adults for the most part have remained privately operated. The operators of these facilities, most of which have sprung up independently under local sponsorship, met in 1963 and formed the International Halfway House Association. In 1968 the association, with more than thirty members, was accepted as an affiliate of the American Correctional Association.

The sporadic and independent growth of halfway houses, together with the innovative and experimental nature of some of their programs, make it difficult to define their essential features. We have included in this category any facility, located within or near a population center, to which a convicted offender is assigned and that provides a greater degree of supervision and services than does the standard probation and parole process, while avoiding the security, regimentation and massive size of a prison. Within this broad definition, however, distinctions become blurred.

Commitments to halfway houses may be made by courts or departments of correction or, usually in the case of private halfway houses, offenders may apply for admission. Although most halfway houses are residential, some offenders may participate in programs without living in, and a few programs provide daytime activities only. Halfway-house staff members may find jobs for residents or expect them to use existing employment services in the community. Special vocational training or recreational activities may be provided, or all activities may take place outside the house.

Some programs offer only food and shelter; others require conformity to a fairly rigid set of regulations and offer counseling that can range from an occasional group discussion to a highly structured therapeutic community with compulsory attendance at group meetings for as many as six hours a day. Some houses have experienced virulent opposition from their neighbors; some exist in the community with little opposition and little contact with their surroundings; a few have become true community facilities with a variety of activities involving outsiders.

The growth of the halfway-house program, which, according to a recent account, "has eclipsed its historical antecedents . . . [confounding] its sponsors no less than its opponents,"[41] can be attributed to a general dissatisfaction with the lack of any alternative between warehousing an offender in a maximum-security prison and releasing him to supervision in the community so minimal that it amounts to a suspended sentence. In addition to the opportunities for intensive supervision and access to community resources that community facilities offer, they have received public support recently as a far less expensive correctional alternative than institutionalization.

Although intensive programs in the community for offenders are considerably more expensive than traditional probation or parole supervision, generally they cost far less than institutional confinement. Halfway houses can be leased or constructed far more cheaply than custodial institutions. And even with generous professional staffing, community programs cost less to operate than maximum-security prisons. Money is not diverted to custodial uses, and many educational, training and recreational resources that already exist in the community may be inexpensively used instead of having to be duplicated in the institutions. The short duration of most community programs greatly reduces the cost per offender. Group-care homes operating in the homes of foster parents cost still less—and non-residential programs least of all. The federal government's Law Enforcement Assistance Administration has come to recog-

41. Keller and Alper, *Halfway Houses: Community-Centered Correction and Treatment* 9 (1970).

nize that, in view of the enormous commitment of resources that would be required to improve correctional institutions, community programs offer the only practical alternative:

> It may be true that institutions do not have to be as depressing and as destructive as they are. But the hard facts are that it will take many years—perhaps generations—and a good deal of money to make them significantly better. . . . Nearly all of these facilities are inadequate, merely from a physical point of view, for purposes of rehabilitation. With costs of construction now running nearly $25,000 per patient or inmate, it appears that even at today's prices, more than $12 billion would be required for more and better personnel and for new and improved institutional programs.
>
> In economic terms alone then, we have no alternative but to turn to the community and its resources if we are to do anything meaningful in the rehabilitation of offenders.[42]

Recognition of the potential of community correctional programs, pronounced the most promising development in correction today by the President's Crime Commission, should not eclipse an awareness of their still very minor place in the present system. Though halfway houses have been said to represent the most important breakthrough in this century for increasing the rate of prisoner rehabilitation, only a small proportion of offenders presently participate in any halfway-house program. For example, there are six halfway houses in San Francisco, which, in aggregate, can house 100 men. There are 1,400 parolees in San Francisco.

The latest edition of the International Halfway House Association directory lists 247 facilities in the United States and fifty-one in Canada (over half of which opened since 1965); however, most of these serve no more than twenty people at a time, and the majority still seem to be religious missions that offer free bed and lodging to a few transient alcoholics. Others may serve drug addicts or mental patients in addition to offenders under correctional supervision. A reasonable estimate is that each of the halfway houses in the United States houses twenty offenders under correctional supervision at one time; thus the total number of halfway-house residents constitutes approximately one-third of

42. Skoler, "Future Trends in Juvenile and Adult Community-Based Correction" (paper presented by Director, Office of Law-Enforcement Programs, LEAA, to the Centennial Congress of the American Correctional Association, October 14, 1970).

one percent of the total of 1.3 million offenders that are under correctional supervision at any one time.

HALFWAY-HOUSE PROGRAMS

The first halfway houses were established to deal with the problems inherent in moving from a custodial institution to freedom in the community. Whether for pre-release offenders still technically in the status of prisoners or offenders released from prison on parole or at the expiration of their sentences, this transitional "halfway-out" function is still the primary use of halfway houses.

In addition to their role in dealing with the problems created by incarceration, halfway houses have begun to be used as an innovative way of avoiding those problems. Beginning with Highfields in 1950, a few small community facilities have provided highly structured, short-term programs for youthful offenders in the community in lieu of institutionalization ("halfway in"). In addition, there are some less structured programs for adults that attempt to replace prison with community programs. Finally, in a few places, selected offenders who are having difficulties on probation or parole can be sent to halfway houses for a short period as an alternative to a revocation of their probation or parole and recommitment to an institution ("halfway back").

PRE-RELEASE PROGRAMS:
FEDERAL COMMUNITY TREATMENT CENTERS

Halfway houses can be used as an intermediate release step for two groups of offenders: those who have not yet been paroled or those who are paroled on condition that they live in a halfway house. In the former category, prisoners are transferred to a halfway house by the correction department without participation by the parole board; in the latter, prisoners without families whose parole boards require them to have a place to live and some prospect of employment before they will release them on parole apply for admission. In some cases the directors of private halfway houses go into the prisons to interview applicants. In return for providing men with an address so that they can be paroled, some halfway houses require applicants to commit themselves to participating in their regular counseling program.

Where residents retain the status of prisoners, halfway-house rules regarding curfews and sign-outs generally are more strict. Any unexcused absence may be regarded as an escape, and residents may be returned to prison without a formal order by a court or a parole board. Although the director of a halfway house may expel parolees from the program for interference with other residents or for flaunting the rules, a parolee may not be returned to prison unless he commits a crime or violates the terms of his parole.

The best known of the governmentally operated halfway houses, with programs typical of pre-release facilities, are the community treatment centers operated by the federal Bureau of Prisons. Originating in 1961 when they were called "pre-release guidance centers" for youthful offenders and expanded in 1965 to include adults,[43] the program now extends to eight facilities in New York City, Chicago, Detroit, Atlanta, Kansas City, Los Angeles, Oakland and Houston. All these facilities together can house approximately 400 offenders at a time, or 1,200 inmates in a year out of a total federal prisoner population of close to 21,000. In addition, the Bureau of Prisons contracted with thirty state, county and private community treatment centers and local jails in fiscal 1969 to house 160 federal prisoners on work release or in need of halfway-house facilities. Since the 1965 legislation, the centers have accepted some adults. However, they continue to give preference to young offenders and better than average risks.

The most frequent crime committed by community treatment center residents involves property offenses, primarily interstate auto theft. Although the Bureau of Prisons has attempted to expand the function of the centers and, according to a spokesman, "the pre-release guidance centers ceased to exist in 1965," our own observations, backed by testimony from Bureau of Prisons officials, is that federal community treatment centers continue to be used primarily for pre-release prisoners and to perform the same function as the original pre-release guidance centers.

Figures supplied by the bureau indicate that in fiscal 1969 more than 95 percent of all center residents were transferred from federal institutions. Almost 3 percent were committed directly by the courts for diagnostic observation or under "split sentences"; the rest were returned escapees, parole violators or state offenders accepted under contract.

Since the centers are operated by the Bureau of Prisons, jurisdictional problems arise when an attempt is made to commit to them an unsentenced offender or one who is on probation or parole, all of whom

43. Federal Prisoner Rehabilitation Act, P.L. 89–176, 18 U.S.C. §4082.

are in the custody of the courts or other independent agencies. To meet these jurisdictional problems, the Justice Department introduced and Congress enacted legislation to make residential community treatment centers available to persons on probation, on parole or released because of good-time credits. The legislation provides that, in cases where the Attorney General certifies that adequate treatment facilities, personnel and programs are available, the sentencing court or the United States Board of Parole may require a person to reside in or participate in the program of a residential community treatment center as a condition of his probation, parole or release. However, the limited capacity of these centers, which presently can accommodate a total of only thirty-six additional offenders within existing facilities, and their operation by the Bureau of Prisons, which has responsibility for institutions but not for probation or parole, make it likely that a significant number of new facilities will have to be opened before any significant expansion can be expected. The Bureau of Prisons may request that the committing court or parole board terminate an offender's participation if it appears that he can derive no further benefit from the program or if his residence or participation adversely affects the rehabilitation of others in the program.

Under the present program, the majority of federal center residents are transferred to the centers three to four months prior to their expected parole date. They travel to the center by public transportation without escort. Newly arrived residents are interviewed by a counselor and an employment specialist. They are informed of the few basic rules, including the curfew, mandatory counseling sessions and prohibitions against driving, drinking or using drugs. After his first two days at the center, the new resident is expected to seek work or to enroll in a vocational-training program or school. He is provided with pocket money until he finds employment, although once he finds a job he is expected to pay for his meals and to turn his check over to center staff members so that they can put a portion in the bank for him.

As a resident spends more time at the center, his privileges are increased. Gradually his evening curfew advances from 9:00 until 11:00 P.M. At the end of the first week he generally will be permitted to spend a day with his family; the next week he may spend two days at home. After approximately four weeks a resident may obtain an overnight pass. A small number of men nearing the end of their stay may be permitted to live outside the center on "out-count" as long as they check in periodically and return to the center for group discussions.

COMMUNITY CORRECTION / 563

Some restrictions, however, apply to all residents in federal centers, regardless of the length of their stay. All residents must sign out when leaving the center and sign in on returning, stating their intended destination and time of return. Anyone still serving the prison portion of his term who leaves the center without permission may be considered an escapee. A resident can be sent back to prison by the center staff if he fails to adjust. However, other less drastic sanctions, such as the loss of weekend and evening passes, are available for disciplining recalcitrant residents. Staff members anticipate that men recently released from prison will have some difficulty adjusting to freedom and generally prefer to see problems surface at this stage rather than later when the men will be free from all supervision.

According to statistics supplied by the Bureau of Prisons, in-program failures, defined as the proportion of residents who escape or are returned to prison, comprised 15.3 percent of those in centers in fiscal year 1967 (10.9 percent escaped and 4.4 percent returned to custody), 19.3 percent in fiscal year 1968 (12.8 percent escaped and 6.5 percent returned to custody) and 19.9 percent in fiscal year 1969 (12.6 percent escaped and 7.3 percent returned to custody). The bureau considers this increase in the percentage of failures a small one and attributes it to a trend toward receiving a greater proportion of offenders due for release at the expiration of their sentences or mandatory release who presumably are worse risks than prisoners who are released early through parole.[44]

Directors and counselors at federal centers frequently are rotated from the Bureau of Prisons regular staff. Thus, institutional case workers are given an opportunity to observe some of the problems that prisoners will encounter on their release. In addition, since the full-time staff generally do not live in the centers, part-time students are employed to provide supervision during the late-night hours and weekends. Federal probation officers, who will supervise the offenders when they are released on parole, are expected to participate in the counseling activities of the centers. However, since these officers are not responsible to the Bureau of Prisons but to the courts, there has been some difficulty in coordinating their activities with those of the center staff.

None of the residences attempts to achieve the atmosphere of a

44. Bureau of Prisons, Composite Report of Community-Based Programs, Fiscal Year 1969 Data, Table IV (Operations Memorandum 7500.51, August 27, 1969). In fiscal year 1967, 15.2 percent of the centers' population were released at the end of their sentences by expiration or mandatory release. In fiscal year 1969 this percentage had more than doubled, to 36.4 percent.

therapeutic community. Periods of residence are short (the average was seventy-two days in fiscal year 1969), and the terms of various residents are staggered. Prisoners are encouraged to spend time in the community rather than attend frequent group meetings. However, mandatory group discussions are held in some centers to discuss common problems or to hear talks by outside speakers concerning employment, family counseling or management of money. Individual counseling is available to any resident with a problem. Both individual and group-counseling sessions focus on day-to-day problems such as applying for a job, opening a bank account or re-establishing family ties rather than on deep-seated emotional problems, which staff members hope have been dealt with in the institution and which they do not feel could be solved at any rate within the restrictions of the center's program.

We visited the federal facilities in Los Angeles, Chicago, New York City and Atlanta and discussed their operations with the administrators and a number of the residents. The New York center, in operation since January 23, 1968, is housed in a dilapidated hotel in the middle of New York City and holds forty people. Aside from sixteen others at a local youth center and some narcotics centers, this is the whole halfway-house activity for New York. The federal government is now considering setting up additional houses in Brooklyn or Queens and in New Jersey.

The annual budget is $82,000. The staff is composed of a director, unit manager, administrative assistant, four part-time (twenty hours a week) counselors, one correctional counselor, three night-time supervisors. Interviewers see eight people a day and manage in-depth counseling a few times a week for each person. There are group-discussion activities three nights a week. Staff members want as residents those who need the center, who are without ties, have an unstable employment history or a broken home; they think they can benefit them the most by helping their adjustment. The focus of the director's interest is "the day-to-day problems of post-release adjustment, like money management, employment and the like."

The center in Chicago is similar. Run in a YMCA in a deadbeat part of town since 1961, it presently services about thirty men, mostly young but recently as old as thirty-five. Some men (90 to 95 percent of the population) come on their way out of institutions in a fifty-mile radius; some (5 percent) come on direct commitment from the courts for study and observation for ninety days. The average stay is forty-five to sixty days. The classification committees at the prison institutions decide who comes, although the center can veto a man. Most men (there were also two women when we were there) are young, car thieves, check bouncers, a few addicts but rarely men sentenced for violent crimes.

While originally the men who were sent to the institutions did not need it (case workers sent men as a reward for their adjustment to prison), now problem people are sent who need the assistance of the social services offered. "This is not for the professional criminal or the guy with a family and job waiting," we were advised. However, the administrators admitted that their supervision is superficial ("You can't correct a man in forty-five days"), that some men feel it adds pressures to their transition back to the community and that they are overcrowded, impoverished and limited in what they can do ("the staff must react in set ways") by official regulations. In Atlanta and Los Angeles and, we take it, in the other centers we did not see, the setup is very much the same.

In addition to transferring prisoners to its own community treatment centers, the Bureau of Prisons contracts with state and private facilities to receive its pre-release prisoners in areas where there are no federal centers. Fifty-seven federal prisoners were released from such facilities in fiscal year 1968 and 106 in fiscal year 1969. Since only eight states and the District of Columbia currently operate halfway houses for adult pre-release prisoners or parolees, most of the federal contracts are with privately operated centers.

The over-all reality is that as yet an extremely small percentage of all adults released from prison spend any time in a halfway house. There are even fewer pre-release halfway houses (as opposed to community institutions) for juveniles released from training school than for adults released from prison, and virtually all the juvenile facilities are operated by states or counties. Private groups have been reticent to accept juveniles, who present greater disciplinary problems than adults and who frequently cannot work to pay bed-and-board fees.

There can be little question that generally the services and the increased supervision that halfway houses can offer to people released from prison make sense as a way of coping with the problems involved in the transition from imprisonment to freedom. In fact, some correctional administrators feel that any offender who is dangerous enough to be imprisoned should be released by means of some intermediate community residential center. At any rate, it seems likely that the use of pre-release halfway houses will increase substantially.

HALFWAY HOUSES IN LIEU OF IMPRISONMENT

Beyond this obvious function of halfway houses as a pre-release measure, an even greater potential use of community centers lies in their implementation as a means for avoiding incarceration completely. To date, most of these facilities have been exclusively for juveniles. In this category, at present, are group homes and therapeutic communities for juveniles, work-release centers for adults and non-residential programs.

Administrators of halfway houses for juveniles have found that the turnover of residents is much slower than in halfway houses for adults. Youths without stable homes (generally the only ones sent to halfway houses in the first place) are unable to progress through the program in the usual two to three months and then find a place to live independently. Consequently, terms of residence in halfway houses for juveniles range up to two years.

The long periods of residence necessary for juveniles in need of home substitutes have led to the development of group foster homes. An extension of the idea of foster care to provide long-term placement for delinquent children released from training school or placed in the homes as a condition of their probation, group homes for correctional purposes began to be used in Wisconsin in 1955. The Wisconsin Welfare Department's Division of Correction presently licenses and subsidizes both what it refers to as "boarding homes" to care for one to four delinquent children and "group homes" for five to eight children. In 1966 Wisconsin had thirty-one group homes caring for a total of 133 children.

In 1960 the Youth Division of the Michigan Department of Correction used a foundation grant to develop foster homes as temporary placements for some youthful parolees. A parole agent was designated to recruit foster parents and pay them an allowance for each child placed in their homes. A variety of group homes was developed, including some established boarding houses that were paid to house parolees. Although the formal program ended when the foundation support expired, some group homes continued to be used for Michigan parolees.

Minnesota began to use group homes extensively in response to a survey by a citizens' group in 1964 that discovered that, in the two preceding years, 250 children had been detained in training schools beyond their dates of scheduled release because their own homes were thought inadequate to receive them and foster placement was unavailable.

In addition to Wisconsin, Michigan and Minnesota, juvenile authorities in California, Ohio, Iowa and Colorado make some use of group homes. Foster parents generally are recruited from middle-aged couples who have raised families of their own. Foster fathers generally continue to work outside the home. Group parents are paid boarding fees for each child and, in some states, are guaranteed a monthly subsidy for each available bed, regardless of whether it is occupied. Additional payments may be made for clothing, medical care and pocket money. In some states the foster parents receive consulting services from state agencies as well as relief parents to enable them to take vacations. The purpose of group homes is to give children without stable homes of their own a secure, disciplined and affectionate domicile. The presence of several children in the same home has been found reassuring to children who fear intense relationships with adults.

Although group homes are sometimes arranged so that children from the same parole or probation caseload are housed together, they are not meant to provide any formal treatment. Their atmosphere is less intense and their residents less involved in correctional programs than in some of the small, specialized public institutions for juveniles. Foster parents usually have no formal training in dealing with delinquents, although most have had prior experience raising children.

Since foster parents own or rent their own homes, group homes involve no capital outlay by the state. No staff members need to be hired to supervise the children, and even with generous subsidies for room and board, group foster care costs a state less than half the price of institutional care. The only commonly noted drawback to group homes is their transient nature. The demanding nature of the foster parents' role means that most couples do not remain foster parents for many years. Death or illness of a parent may require immediate removal of the children, and the parents can insist that a ward be removed when disagreements arise. Yet the drawbacks are not significantly different from those of ordinary family living, and for many children group homes have been found to be a stable alternative to institutionalization.

The New York Division for Youth has devised an adaptation of group homes. The state agency purchased a townhouse in Manhattan and a cluster of townhouses in the Bronx. It employs house parents to live in the apartments and provide a temporary home for juveniles committed there, who go to school or work in the community. A program director supervises the various operations, and relief personnel live in the homes for two days each week in order to give the house parents some time off. The division has found this arrangement more lasting than the usual group home situation, since more services are provided to foster parents and the state's ownership of the buildings and employment of the house parents gives the agency greater control over the program.

SPECIAL COMMUNITY CENTERS
FOR JUVENILES AND ADULTS

In the chapter on institutions, we described a few small community institutions for juveniles to which young offenders can be sentenced directly by the courts in lieu of institutional incarceration or detention at the traditional training school. Such alternatives for adults that would replace imprisonment by short, intensive programs in the community are virtually unknown. However, "halfway in" alternatives for adults to begin at the time of sentencing and include residence in the community may come about as an extension of work release.

The District of Columbia Work Release Act[45] permits a judge to sentence directly to work release, under terms prescribed by the courts, any defendant convicted of a misdemeanor, imprisoned for non-payment of a fine, committed to jail after revocation of probation or considered to present "such special circumstances as merit the granting of the privilege." Offenders sentenced to the work-release program are housed in community work-release centers operated or contracted by the Department of Correction. If they commit further crimes or violate the regulations of the centers, the department may suspend the work-release status for up to five days or the sentencing court may revoke work release and resentence the defendant.

In 1964, aided by a federal grant, the San Diego County, California, Department of Honor Camps opened Crofton House, a residence outside San Diego for selected jail inmates, primarily misdemeanants, and some felons serving jail terms as a condition of their probation, as an additional alternative to the five rural camps already operated by the county. All residents, carefully selected as good risks for the initial experiment with community residence, were on work release. They spent an average of four to five months at Crofton House. From their earnings they paid the county for their room and board. A professional staff conducted intensive group-counseling sessions three to five evenings a week, using

45. P.L. 89–803, 89th Congress (1966), 2nd Sess.; 24 D.C. Code §§461–470.

the guided group interaction methods. After the first three years, during which the project was subsidized by federal funds, administrators of the county camp system decided that the group process would be facilitated if the men had the same jobs. Consequently, men living at Crofton House were required to work on some public project as a group, returning to the house in the evening. Eligibility requirements were broadened to include narcotics offenders. At the same time, a new, in-town facility in a leased motel was planned for other residents, who would continue on work release.

A similar facility, stressing a therapeutic community orientation within a community residence and work, academic education or vocation training in the community, opened recently in the District of Columbia for offenders sentenced under the Federal Youth Correction Act. This program, entitled the Youth Crime Control Project, is particularly unusual, in accepting, with few exceptions, youths sentenced for felonies who ordinarily would serve their terms in a maximum-security institution. Eligible youths are sentenced at random to the community facility or the institution to facilitate evaluation of the program.

Narcotic treatment centers, both the abstinence-oriented programs modeled after Synanon and Daytop Lodge, which attempt to change an addict's entire life style, and the methadone maintenance programs currently being undertaken in several cities, offer an alternative to sentencing an addict convicted of a crime to prison or to a distant hospital, where he will be withdrawn from drugs physically but receive little long-term help. Some correction departments have begun to transfer prisoners who are addicts to halfway houses operated by independent narcotic treatment agencies.

In the probation chapter we speculated on the possibility of developing intensive, non-residential, community programs that would increase the resources available to probation officers and permit a much greater proportion of offenders to be placed on probation. As yet, no state has such a program for adults, although some California counties have taken steps in this direction with funds received from probation subsidies. However, a few promising innovations have been made in this area for juveniles.

A private, charitable organization, the Citizenship Training Group, was started in Boston in 1936 by Judge John Forbes Perkins, who thought that many juveniles needed more intensive counseling and supervision than ordinary probation but at the same time did not need to be sent to institutions. Perhaps the oldest program, the Citizenship Training Group has been housed in the same building (a YMCA) and, in conjunction with the local juvenile court, has run basically the same programs for more than thirty years. In 1965 a second unit was added in Roxbury, and in 1967 a separate girls' unit was started.

As a condition of probation, children are required to attend a program for two hours after school every weekday for a minimum of twelve weeks. They are given bus tickets to the center and expected to report straight from school. At the center they are given a complete battery of physical, reading and psychological tests, then enrolled in a structured program that includes gym classes, arts and crafts, remedial reading, group discussions and educational films.

Two probation officers, employed by the Juvenile Court, have their offices in each center. They visit the children's schools and collect background information about them and their entire families from all social agencies in the community that have worked with the families previously. (In many cases when a child comes into the program, they already have worked with some of his siblings.) Each officer generally has a caseload of about thirty children, half of whom he sees on a daily basis and half once a week.

After the first twelve weeks a conference is held among the CTG people who have worked with a child, his schoolteachers and representatives from outside agencies. Usually they decide to move him into the second phase of the program, in which he reports to his probation officer weekly and continues with some special help, such as remedial tutoring. In the third stage, which generally begins after another twelve weeks, a child may be placed in an after-school job or athletic program.

The regular CTG program operates only when school is in session. However, it operates a day-camp program in July which includes field trips, boating with volunteers from a community boat club and swimming. The purpose of the program is to keep children busy who cannot find jobs or a place in any other summer program.

Funding the program is a constant problem. More than $60,000 must be raised each year. However, for each child, the program costs less than one-tenth of an institutional program.

The chief advantage of the CTG, according to William Ahern, its executive director, is that it is the first place in many of the children's lives in which they get some personal attention and discipline. One child who went through the program recently had to be driven by staff members to a speech therapist at Boston University every day because he could neither read the subway signs nor ask directions without stuttering hopelessly. "I don't know," he told us, "if we taught John to be a good citizen, but we taught him how to talk and even to read a little."

Some of the youths return for frequent visits when they are no longer required to do so. Yet the people associated with the program recognize that it cannot change a child's entire life; its intervention is temporary, its claims modest.

Variations on the idea of after-school activity centers for juvenile probationers have been tried in different places. These programs, sponsored by local probation departments or civic groups, frequently involve weekend or summer camping experiences.

Some of the New York and New Jersey programs modeled after Highfields are non-residential but involve youths in employment and counseling programs for the entire day and early evening. By far the best known, the most carefully structured and the most diverse non-residential centers for juveniles are those developed by the Community Treatment Project in California. This program, originally established in 1961 for delinquent youths committed to the Youth Authority from two counties, has since been extended to other parts of the state. Youths considered eligible for the program are those who are committed to the Youth Authority for the first time (although they may have failed repeatedly on probation and in other county programs), who are between fourteen and eighteen years old and who have not committed a particularly serious or bizarre crime.[46] To test the program's impact, eligible delinquents are assigned at random to a juvenile correctional institution or to the project.

The Community Treatment Project divides its participants into nine "interpersonal maturity levels" and assigns them to counselors and programs that have been found to work well with their personality type. Approximately one-fourth of the participants are placed in foster homes or group homes. All are assigned to parole agents with small caseloads,

46. About 70 percent of the boys and 90 percent of the girls committed to the Youth Authority from Sacramento and Stockton and 50 percent of the boys and 75 percent of the girls committed from San Francisco have been found eligible for the program. Palmer, Community Treatment Project, Seventh Progress Report, Part 2: *Recent Research Findings and Long-Range Developments at the Community Treatment Project* 51 (CTP Research Report No. 9, Part 2, Oct. 1968). Interestingly, the delinquents judged ineligible for the community treatment program have been found to have a much lower parole violation rate than those judged eligible for the program but not admitted. This finding is consistent with other studies that have shown assaultive offenders to represent a better recidivism risk than non-assaultive offenders. Warren, "The Case for Differential Treatment of Delinquents," 381 *The Annals of the American Academy of Political and Social Science* 47, 58 (1969).

generally twelve to fifteen wards for each agent, and are supervised intensively in the community.

The project offices are housed in community centers that resemble neighborhood settlement houses. Depending on the program devised for each youth, he may come to the center only for individual or family counseling or he may be required to attend daily group sessions at the center. The center offers individual tutoring and recreation as well as counseling. Frequent parties and outings are planned jointly by the wards and staff.

A carefully devised research plan enabled the youths supervised in the community to be compared with similar youths who completed the usual institutional program. Only 28 percent of the experimental group of 270 youths had failed on parole after fifteen months in the community and 38 percent after two years. In contrast, the control group of 357 youths had a failure rate of 52 percent and 61 percent after two years.[47] When the performance of youths of the various maturity levels was compared, 48 percent of the eligible population clearly appeared to have done better in the experimental than the traditional program; 2 percent did well in both programs; for 44 percent neither program had a clear advantage. Only one category, representing 6 percent of the youth studied, appeared to be handled more effectively in the regular institutional program.

However, the directors of the Community Treatment Project emphasize that the superior results for the community group cannot be explained simply in terms of the advantages in avoiding institutionalization. Although there have been no efforts to test the random assignment of comparable cases to institutional programs and to regular parole programs, the youths paroled directly from the reception center to the community without participating in the Community Treatment Project or an institutional program had a slightly higher failure rate on parole than the control cases who went through the institutional program. Both groups

47. California Youth Authority, *The Community Treatment Project After Five Years* 5–7. The fifteen-month period studied began for the experimental group as soon as they left the reception center and for the control group when they were released from training school.

Observers have noted that these figures may be slightly misleading due to the differential use of temporary detention for the two groups. California Youth Authority agents are permitted to put wards in temporary detention for periods ranging from a few days to a month without revoking their parole. Since community treatment participants were placed in temporary detention more often than control subjects—*see id*. at 6—it is possible that temporary detention may have been used for conduct that ordinarily would have warranted revocation of parole. Keller and Alper, *Halfway Houses: Community Centered Correction and Treatment* 153 (1970).

On the other hand, since the community treatment project participants were supervised much more closely than youths in standard parole caseloads, violations may have been discovered more frequently for the experimental group than for the controls.

had a significantly higher rate of failure than the Community Treatment Project participants. According to the project's research staff, "These findings emphasize the fact that the experimental program is not only *community-located* but has been characterized, specifically, by a differential treatment approach which was not present within the control program." This idea, simple enough in theory, of classifying offenders and treating different groups in different ways is a recent and seminal development in correction.

Although no state has followed California's lead in developing extensive non-residential community programs in lieu of institutions, and, in fact, the California Youth Authority itself has not extended its community treatment project throughout the state, two California counties have modeled non-residential programs for girls on the community treatment project. In addition, the Youth Authority has opened several "community parole centers" to offer parolees facilities for intensive counseling, instruction and recreation similar to those found in the Community Treatment Project.

Several problems are common to all halfway houses, no matter what their programs. Among them are the relative advantages of public versus private sponsorships, interaction with the surrounding communities and evaluation of the effect of different programs.

Sponsorship and Funding

The early halfway houses all were privately operated and depended on donations from private citizens or religious organizations for their financing. Some of the early pioneers in developing halfway-house facilities feared that governmental operation would stifle the humanistic helping-hand attitude that had characterized the movement, replacing it with an unfeeling, perhaps even a punitive system.

Although several of the public halfway houses we have seen had bureaucratic regulations and little contact with the community, some private houses are subject to the same criticism. Private halfway houses have little contact with either the prisons from which their residents come or the parole officers with official responsibility for the residents' supervision, although some have tailored their programs to the requirements of state parole boards. The most exciting programs (Dismas House was one) have been based on the personal dedication of a private citizen or group of citizens who cooperate in fund-raising, community relations, and in the operation of the halfway-house program. However, the drawback of relying on the missionary zeal of private citizens is that it may be short-lived.

Dismas House in St. Louis is perhaps the best known example of a halfway-house program that owes its existence to the pioneering efforts of one man. However, the man is dead, and when we visited Dismas House recently we found that much of the sense of mission had died with him. Father Clark had filled almost all his staff positions with ex-convicts. At present, after problems with stolen donations and unanswered letters from unpopular prisoners, the ex-convicts have been removed from all key positions. The only ex-convict employed by Dismas House now is the house man. The remaining staff members seem to work primarily from nine to five, although the house residents generally are at work during those hours. Due to inadequate supervision in the evenings, there are no visiting hours at the house after five. Curfews are in effect for all men, no matter how long they have lived in the house. Decisions seem to be made by staff members with no participation by the residents.

The financing, as well as the innovative programming of a private halfway house, may be temporal. Many of the private facilities have been started by large donations from private individuals or a grant from a foundation or the federal government. After the first few years, the grant may expire or the donations subside.

In some cases, however, publicly operated facilities may fare no better. For example, three widely praised community correctional centers operated by the Kentucky Department of Correction under a demonstration grant from the Office of Economic Opportunity were closed when the grant funds ran out. Several county-operated institutions for juveniles have met a similar fate.

Several of the private halfway houses we have visited are in debt. Because most states have made no funds available to pay private halfway houses for accepting state parolees, several of the houses are finding it necessary economically to accept an increasing proportion of federal pre-release prisoners. Private halfway-house directors often find that they must devote a large part of their time to seeking financing and that state governments are not receptive to their pleas for governmental subsidies or even for inclusion in applications for federal bloc grants. For these reasons, one observer has predicted that governmental (mostly state) operation of halfway houses will become more prevalent and will gradually replace private operations:

There probably will always be certain well-known and successful facilities that will remain purely private, but already it is evident that many privately sponsored halfway houses falter soon after getting started because they lack the financial backing or administrative resources necessary to keep them going.[48]

It seems reasonable to expect community programs to follow the same pattern of development that has characterized the probation and parole systems, with private citizens and religious groups devising methods of aiding offenders followed by government cooperation and, eventually, takeover. As evidence of the trend toward government operation of community programs, it is noteworthy that, of the $22 million allocated in 1970 by the Justice Department's Law Enforcement Assistance Administration to support community correctional programs, the lion's share went to state departments of correction. The structure of LEAA funding, with allocation of grants by planning boards composed of state officials, is largely responsible for this kind of allocation.

However, there is another possibility, of privately operated halfway houses subsidized by government funds. Such an arrangement, though common in European countries, is relatively unfamiliar in the United States. Yet one of the first halfway houses to be established here since the Second World War, 308 West Residence, Wilmington, Delaware, was started by a private prisoners'-aid agency in a house owned by the state. Such cooperation between public and private agencies eventually could set a new pattern of correctional innovation.

The federal Bureau of Prisons increasingly is placing its pre-release prisoners in private halfway houses under contract. A few state correction departments, notably in the District of Columbia and California, have attempted to broaden the alternatives available for community placement by contracting with private halfway houses.

The broadest effort to diversify community services has been undertaken in the District of Columbia, where the Department of Correction is in the process of developing an innovative partnership arrangement with privately operated halfway houses. The department, which intends to have 50 percent of the District of Columbia's prison population (approximately 4,000) in community-based programs by 1973, has devised a method of increasing halfway-house capacity quickly by leasing space rather than building new facilities and by contracting with private groups

48. Keve, *Imaginative Programming in Probation and Parole* 227 (1967).

to operate entire residences for offenders under the department's jurisdiction. Several such contracts already have been negotiated: with the Bureau of Rehabilitation to operate an existing halfway house, with the Psychiatric Institute Foundation to operate a house concentrating on group therapy, with the Narcotics Treatment Agency (an independent city agency) to operate houses for addicts and with Efforts from Ex-Convicts, a group of ex-offenders with a successful history of finding jobs for released prisoners, to operate a program staffed entirely by ex-offenders, who, although they lack formal training, have been able to relate better to halfway-house residents than traditional professional counselors. The department intends to negotiate similar contracts with other groups so that half its total halfway-house capacity eventually will be privately operated. The groups will be freed of the traditional financial worries by a guarantee of certain minimum support from the department for the length of the contract.

Privately run halfway houses are favored in the District of Columbia because they can avoid building in a Civil Service bureaucracy with a vested interest in particular correctional methods. Contracting with private groups gives the department greater flexibility to experiment with different programs and, by avoiding the built-in permanence of government programs, to discontinue those that do not appear to work. By assigning its offenders at random to the different privately operated halfway houses and to halfway houses directly operated by the department, it should be able to evaluate the success of the different programs by comparing the recidivism rates of offenders released from each house after six months. The department will change its contracting policies depending on the various indications of success.

In addition to the value of competition among different groups operating halfway houses and of the ability to evaluate different programs, the department hopes that the involvement of various groups from different parts of the community in operating correctional programs will help to change community attitudes and to increase community participation in correctional programs.

COMMUNITY RELATIONS

In a recent national public-opinion survey concerning correction, over three-quarters of those polled supported the idea of halfway houses. When asked whether they would favor the establishment of a halfway house in their neighborhood, half the respondents said yes, although two-thirds indicated that they thought their neighbors would be opposed. In many cases where a halfway house has attempted to move into any but the most deteriorated neighborhoods there has been strong opposition from neighbors on the basis that the presence of a halfway house would cause crime rates in the area to climb and property values would suffer.

In order to avoid such problems, the Bureau of Prisons has located federal centers in marginal neighborhoods with mixed land uses, generally zoned for apartments or commercial purposes. Some of the first centers were located in YMCAs, either on one floor or in scattered rooms. These centers have the benefit of additional, complementary facilities, such as a public cafeteria and recreation areas. The use of rooms scattered throughout a facility makes it possible to accept a few women releasees along with the men. On the other hand, some of the centers have found that their location in larger buildings causes friction with other residents and makes it more difficult to establish rapport among center residents.

In a few cases neighbors have gone so far as to take legal action to prevent the location of a new halfway house in their area. Private citizens have attempted to discourage halfway houses and even have gone to court in efforts to have their presence enjoined. In one case, local businessmen claimed successfully that a proposed community work-release residence was not a rooming house but a jail and, consequently, in violation of a municipal zoning regulation. The city of Minneapolis refused to grant the necessary permits to the Volunteers of America to enable the organization to remodel a building it owned so that it could be used as a halfway house. Other cities, responding to vigorous campaigns by neighborhood residents, have refused to grant necessary zoning certificates.

Efforts have been made by the staffs of two halfway houses to determine whether the presence of halfway houses in a neighborhood increases crime or lowers property values. In both cases, surveys made several months after the house was opened discovered that property values were unchanged and that crimes in the neighborhood were committed at about the same rate as before the halfway house arrived. Directors of four other facilities report that their observations, together with informal conversations with area residents, have revealed no adverse effect on property values or crime rates due to their presence.

Although many halfway houses, both public and private, have succeeded in overcoming active opposition through the use of community advisory boards and launching active campaigns for public support, often with the cooperation of the communications media and community leaders, most of the halfway houses we have visited have made little attempt to become part of the neighborhoods that surround them. (On the other hand, one young, imaginative executive director of a halfway house sees its primary function as that of teaching ex-convicts to use their leisure time in the community. "Vocation and education are only half the story—we hope to teach these men how to play in socially acceptable ways and to change the loser image they have of themselves.") Virtually all halfway houses make use of employment and recreational resources in the community, but very few have developed any kind of informal interaction between the residents and their neighbors.

Perhaps it is unrealistic to expect that halfway houses located in hotels or YMCAs will become community centers. However, we have seen halfway houses located in large houses in residential areas that have seemed as isolated from their communities as if they were surrounded by high walls and guard towers. In one, for example, the house is located in a black ghetto. All the staff members are white and look down on their surroundings. The house is kept locked, and no one from the community is allowed inside. Rather than a community facility, this house appeared to be little more than a prison located in a city, from which men are furloughed to go to their employment.

A few halfway houses have attempted, with varying success, to encourage community members to participate in their activities. For example, Crofton House in San Diego, California, has made significant efforts to encourage residents to become active members of their community:

> We have thought of Crofton House as intimately related to the community in order that the men might develop favorable perceptions of themselves as ordinary conforming citizens and neighbors. In various ways staff and men worked toward this goal. There were Easter Egg Hunts on the big lawn for the neighborhood children, Halloween and Christmas parties, open house for the entire community to visit, and even a wedding at the house. Perhaps as a result of these efforts, the neighbors who at first found Crofton House quite threatening have come to accept it with calmness if not enthusiasm. Nevertheless, there has not developed the kind of over-the-back-fence neighborliness for which we had hoped.[49]

49. Kirby, "Crofton House: An Experiment with a County Halfway House" 33 *Federal Probation* 53, 55 (March 1969).

The District of Columbia's Youth Crime Control Project was planned with the idea that an important function of a community correctional program is to make community members accept responsibility for the program's success. Consequently, private citizens from the immediate neighborhood of the house, as well as District of Columbia judges, lawyers, doctors and clergymen, will be involved regularly in the planning and the operation of the facility. In addition, the project has taken the further step of making itself welcome in a neighborhood by providing services to the community. An entire floor of the facility is available for meetings of community groups and recreational activities to which the neighborhood is invited. Perhaps the biggest innovation in this facility is the presence of community services for non-offenders as well as for people under correctional supervision. Several local government agencies, including adult education, vocational rehabilitation, narcotics treatment and public health, will establish branch offices in the facility to serve all the eligible clients in the neighborhood.

Some of the narcotics rehabilitation houses run by former addicts have recognized that true acceptance by the community comes only when a facility makes itself a valuable part of its neighborhood. Consequently, facilities such as Odyssey and Phoenix Houses in New York have launched neighborhood clean-up campaigns in an effort to raise property values in the surrounding communities, as well as drug education programs and store-front operations to give emergency aid and counseling to addicts. As a result of neighborhood improvement programs, the Phoenix program has been able to enlist the aid of neighborhood merchants in contributing food and furniture when a new house opens.

Although observers have questioned whether these programs (in particular Synanon, the oldest and best known), which are carried out in ingrown, protective communities and do not attempt to return a large number of addicts to the community as quickly as possible, fit the usual definition of community programs, Synanon's rehabilitative program may be a community correctional program in the best sense of the term. By training former addicts as specialists who dedicate their careers to rehabilitating other addicts, these programs provide continuing service and recognize their responsibility to transform the community, as well as the particular offenders referred to them.

The 1967 President's Commission on Law Enforcement and Administration of Justice pointed out that a community correctional program must make an effort to change the community as well as the offender:

The task of correction . . . includes building or rebuilding solid ties between offender and community, integrating or reintegrating the offender in community life—restoring family ties, obtaining employment and education, securing in the larger sense a place for the offender in the routine functioning of society. This requires not only efforts directed toward changing the individual offender, which has been almost the exclusive focus of rehabilitation, but also mobilization and change of the community and its institutions.[50]

Unfortunately, in many cases halfway-house personnel have discovered that the community resources they hoped to enlist in the rehabilitation of their residents simply do not exist. As the President's Crime Commission recognized, "There is little sense in getting an offender readmitted to a slum school so poor that he will not profit from it; funds for the purchase of clinical services are useless if there are no clinics to go to."

EVALUATION

One of the reasons for the spread of halfway houses is the belief that the problems encountered by released prisoners in moving back to the free community have a direct bearing on recidivism rates, which statistics show are highest during the first few months after release. Assistance in dealing with the problems of newly released prisoners presumably should reduce the rate of recidivism of halfway-house residents. While reduction of recidivism may not be the only measure of success, it is by any standard a critical one. However, few halfway-house programs have made any attempt to measure their effectiveness by this standard.

Even where research has been conducted, the results can be questioned. With the exception of the California Youth Authority's Community Treatment Program, no program has assigned offenders to experimental and control groups on a truly random basis. Although the researchers sometimes intend to use randomly selected experimental and control groups, the plan is abandoned due to insufficient referrals, the reluctance of judges to base their sentencing on random selection, or the hesitancy of staff members to alienate correctional personnel by rejecting their referrals because of research requirements.

Researchers have attempted to compensate for the lack of random

50. The President's Commission on Law Enforcement and Administration of Justice, Task Force Report: *Correction* 7 (1967).

assignment testing by tracing the experiences of control groups with characteristics similar to those of the experimental groups. This method involves a subjective judgment on the part of researchers as to which characteristics are associated with success or failure. Particularly where so little research has been done on the success of community programs, it is almost impossible to make such a determination in advance. The use of base-expectancy scores as an alternative is limited to the few states where the scores are available and subject to limitations of timeliness (old scores may no longer be valid) and relevance to the particular population being studied (scores based on the experience of New York prisoners may not predict the experience of Illinois prisoners, for example).

While these problems plague all correctional research, others arise only in studies of halfway-house programs. For example, when the period of time spent in a halfway house is included in a follow-up study of recidivism, the question arises whether the detection of technical violations is increased by the closer surveillance of the residents. In addition, there is disagreement whether the return of a resident to prison constitutes a failure. Since the flexibility to try released prisoners in halfway houses before releasing them finally is an essential part of the rationale of the halfway-house program, administrators contend that returning a resident to prison should not necessarily be considered a failure of the program. While this theory appears valid, the total exclusion of escapees from the failure category is also questionable. Finally, the number of offenders processed through most community programs to date has been so small that any valid statistical conclusions are difficult to draw.

Most of the early research on pre-release halfway houses was conducted by the federal Bureau of Prisons. One study compared the recidivism rates of 109 offenders released from pre-release centers with general recidivism rates for federal prisoners. After one year of parole supervision the recidivism rate was about 30 percent.[51] The rate for prisoners

51. Brooks and Karacki, "Federal Prerelease Guidance Centers: Preliminary Study of the Effectiveness of Three Centers During First Full Year of Operation" (1964).

The study also determined that prisoners who completed their terms in pre-release guidance centers successfully served slightly shorter terms in confinement than those released directly to the community. However, prisoners who failed in the pre-release centers and were returned to prison served an average of an additional year in custody.

Recidivism was defined as commission of a new offense leading to a new commitment to a state or federal institution or suspension of parole.

The thirty-six pre-release center residents who were returned to prison before the completion of their stay—fourteen for failure to adjust, nine for escape and thirteen for a new offense—were not included in the study. If these men were included, the total failure rate would have been 47.6 percent.

released through a center did not differ significantly from the over-all federal rate (between 30 and 40 percent). However, when the failure rate of center releasees, all of whom were youthful offenders, was compared to that of other federal prisoners of the same age (between 40 and 50 percent), the centers appeared to be having some success.

A second study of pre-release center releasees traced the experience of 285 prisoners released from four centers during 1964 after a minimum of two years' supervision on parole. In this case, a base-expectancy study, predicting recidivism of members of the group based on their prior commitments, offense and number of co-defendants, was used. Based on these characteristics, the over-all failure rate for the entire group was estimated in advance at 52 percent. When the actual performance of the group (excluding the fifty-four men returned to prison for in-program failure at the centers) was calculated, 42 percent of the 230 men paroled from the centers actually were judged failures.

A surprising result of this study was that pre-release centers appeared to help young car thieves with previous records but might actually have harmed offenders with no previous commitments or those sentenced for offenses other than car thefts. Thus the usual predictors of success on parole, which would have considered car thieves with previous records the worst parole risks, failed to predict the effect of the centers. This failure to find factors associated with recidivism—extremely unusual for this type of study—suggests the possibility that the centers had a differential impact upon residents by which prisoners with normally poor chances of success upon release were helped considerably at the centers while prisoners with normally good chances of success upon release may actually have been harmed by their pre-release experience.[52]

This conclusion is strengthened by a one-year follow-up of 140 residents released from the Shaw Residence, a privately operated halfway house in the District of Columbia, between 1964 and 1967. Since the researchers were unable to compare the performance of Shaw residents with that of a randomly selected control group, the study compared residents released from Shaw Residence with a group of the same age, race, education, criminal history and prison conduct records. However, as the researchers recognized, the comparison sample was not strictly a control group, since its members neither applied for halfway-house residence nor were referred by correctional personnel as needing residence as a condition of their parole.

52. Hall, Milazzo and Posner, "A Descriptive and Comparative Study of Recidivism in Prerelease Guidance Center Releasees" (1966).

Comparison of the experience of the Shaw group and the control group twelve months after their release from prison (including the period the Shaw group spent in the halfway house) revealed a failure rate for the Shaw group, including technical parole violations as well as new offenses, of 38 percent and a failure rate for the control group of 34 percent. Researchers offered several possible explanations for the apparently unfavorable effect of the halfway-house experience. First, they pointed out that the technical violation rate, as opposed to new offenses, was higher for the Shaw group (almost 12 percent) than for the comparison group (almost 4 percent). This difference could be explained by the close supervision given the Shaw residents, which may have permitted more residents to be caught for technical violations. Second, although the two groups were identical in the measurable characteristics generally associated with recidivism (such as age, education and past criminal record), the researchers felt that "the one who is referred to Shaw Residence is apt to be the one about whom the parole officer is less confident as to release adjustment and who in his judgment, therefore, needs more intensive casework services."

The Shaw study disclosed the same finding made previously by the Bureau of Prisons—namely, that the outcome of the halfway-house group could not have been predicted according to the characteristics of the residents. In addition, the Shaw study found no correlation at all between the actual outcomes and the ratings of the residents' chances for success that were made by case workers who interviewed residents at the time of their application for admission.[53] These findings, buttressed by the findings of researchers for the California Community Treatment Project regarding differential treatment, indicate that residence in a halfway house may be of substantial benefit to some offenders while of no use or even harmful to others.

A one-year follow-up of sixty-six releasees from Brooke House, a private halfway house in Boston, Massachusetts, revealed that the halfway-house experience appeared to have reduced significantly the recidivism rates of the men with the least hopeful base-expectancy scores, while having little, perhaps negative, effect on the men with the lowest base-expectancy scores. Although private halfway-house directors who select their residents from a pool of applicants have used certain subjective criteria for selection, to date there has been little empirical data to discriminate among the types of offenders who will or will not benefit from halfway-house programs. This study concluded tentatively that it

53. Bureau of Rehabilitation, "Report on Shaw Residence" (1968)

might be possible to increase the over-all effectiveness of the program by selecting residents who appeared to have the poorest chances of success.[54]

Another series of studies attempted to compare the performance of youths released directly from the District of Columbia Youth Center, an institution for offenders between eighteen and twenty-six sentenced under the Federal Youth Corrections Act,[55] with that of youths paroled from the Youth Center after several weeks' residence in a halfway house. Youths are released through the halfway house when the institutional staff determines that they need the extra support and supervision of the transitional experience. One study, comparing the characteristics of youths released directly from the Youth Center with those released through the community treatment centers, discovered that those characteristics generally associated with higher risks of recidivism, including age at first arrest and number of disciplinary reports incurred in the institution, were found more frequently in the halfway-house population than in the youths released directly.

When the parole performance of all the youths released on parole between 1965 and 1969 was compared, the youths who had been released directly from the Youth Center were discovered to have performed slightly better in their first year on parole than the community treatment center releasees. Twenty-two percent of the direct releasees failed in their first year on parole as compared with 26 percent of the youths released through the community treatment center. The results of the report were considered inconclusive since the community treatment center releasees, who were agreed to be higher risks, performed only slightly worse than the direct releasees. Research has not yet determined whether those released through the halfway house performed better on parole than they would have if they had been released directly.

The fundamental question has never been answered: Is the halfway-house situation ideally a reward and relief for the good prisoner who has served his time well or an aid for the releasee who is likely to be a problem when released? If the former is the case, the halfway-house solution is solving a relatively minor correctional need, although it would be perverse to deprive the best prisoners of the benefits of this brief relief from utter institutionalization. Some few long-term prisoners, however, have so adapted to the helpless state of imprisonment that this bridge

54. Runyan, "Selection Procedures at Brooke House" (1970).
55. 18 U.S.C. §5010; see Chap. III, Sentencing.

may be necessary to ease their transition back into free society. If the latter is the case, the technique becomes a critical tool for reformation, although the risks of the program will be greater. Former Deputy Director Gus Moeller of the federal Bureau of Prisons feels that minor failures in a community treatment center experience are not necessarily indicative of a bad program but rather should be viewed as a help to a tentatively stumbling man in need of aid. Several attempts to succeed at such a center may be appropriate.

In summary, research studies on the effects of halfway houses as a pre-release experience, although giving some indication that the experience may help some prisoners, particularly the poorer risks, remain inconclusive. The one study of the use of a halfway house for adults as a substitute for institutionalization is likewise inconclusive. Selected jail inmates were divided into control and experimental groups and assigned at random to the San Diego County Honor Camp or to Crofton House. Follow-up studies made at three and nine months following release on the basis of public records of law-enforcement agencies and field investigations by halfway-house staff revealed that there was no significant difference between the post-release behavior of the experimental subjects who had been at the halfway house and of the control group who had been at the honor camp.

Researchers attempted to explain this lack of difference in the experimental and control groups in terms of the similarity of the two programs (for example, there was similar group counseling in the camp and at Crofton House, and camp staff served as weekend and vacation relief for the halfway house). They found that men who had been eligible for assignment to Crofton House but had served out their terms in the jail and then were released were found to be failing in greater proportions than either the Crofton House men or the camp controls.[56]

On the other hand, research performed on community programs for juveniles that take the place of institutionalization, including studies of the programs based on the Highfields model and the rigorously conducted research attached to California's Community Treatment Project, have shown superior results for the community programs. In addition to reduced recidivism of the community-program participants, the California project seemed to improve the self-esteem and attitudes toward others of youths assigned to it.

56. Kirby, "Crofton House: An Experiment with a County Halfway House," 33 *Federal Probation* 53 (March 1969).

There have been no attempts to test the effectiveness of group homes by assigning youths to group-care homes on their release from training school on a random basis. However, in one study of releasees from Wisconsin training schools, a group of boys released to group homes was compared with other groups released to conventional foster homes or boarding homes for one to three children, or to their own homes. The conventional indicators used to predict success on parole, such as family stability, socioeconomic group and length of time spent in an institution, all tended to show a higher expected rate of failure for the boys placed in the group homes. Using these indicators, as well as their own subjective predictions, the institutional staff and the Wisconsin Juvenile Review Board predicted a 52 percent failure rate for the group-home boys as compared to a 36 percent failure rate for boys about to return to their own homes. The results of a six-month follow-up found little difference in the boarding-home and group-home samples but discovered that boys placed in group homes had a failure rate of 30 percent, as compared to a failure rate of 48 percent for the boys returned to their own parents. This was the reverse of the predictions made in advance about the two groups.[57]

A variation of the usual halfway-house program, in which youthful reformatory releasees between the ages of eighteen and twenty-five were housed in a Knights of Columbus hotel in Gary, Indiana, for six weeks after release, given the opportunity to obtain well-paying jobs at a steel company or the vocational training and counseling necessary to acquire other employment, and provided with direction and counseling by a staff under the supervision of the University of Notre Dame, was expected to provide a promising opportunity for resettling the youths in a new city with good employment prospects. However, research results were disappointing. Of seventy-seven who completed the program at the center, sixteen, or 21 percent, were recommitted to prison, almost invariably for the commission of a new felony. Those participants who worked at the steel company had the same rate of recidivism as those whom the company rejected. The recidivism rate of participants in the program can be compared to the over-all rate of 16 percent for Indiana reformatory parolees, or to the 30 percent rate for Indiana reformatory parolees between the ages of eighteen and twenty-five.

57. Wisconsin Department of Public Welfare, Division of Correction, "Analysis of Wisconsin's Foster and Group Home Program for Delinquent Juvenile Males on Aftercare" (1965).

Researchers raised the question whether the recidivism rate for halfway-house releasees was sufficiently lower than the over-all rate to justify the money and talent that had been expended on the center. They concluded that it was; "reducing recidivism among youthful releasees by a sixth or, in the event that our projected recidivism rate is on the conservative side, even a tenth, is no mean accomplishment."[58] Furthermore, the researchers pointed out that their study had the usual shortcomings: offenders were not assigned to the center at random; those who chose to come tended to include a disproportionate share of poor parole risks; and the close supervision exercised by the center staff may have enabled them to detect misconduct more readily than ordinarily would have been the case. Finally, the evaluators suggested that youthful offenders recently released from a reformatory may require more than a six-week program to establish themselves in a new community.

Even where research results are inconclusive, that fact (particularly in light of the elementary state of research as a science) does not argue against expansion of community programs. A researcher reporting on the inconclusive evaluation of Crofton House concluded with the significant observation that it is probably naïve to expect any presently known short-term experience to influence markedly a style of life learned over twenty or thirty years. Even if superior results cannot be demonstrated in all cases, community programs cost significantly less than their institutional counterparts. In addition, it appears that their more civilized and humane atmosphere and programs must be less destructive of the personalities of the people sent there than the institutional experience, however difficult it may be to measure the difference.

MODEL COMMUNITY CORRECTIONAL CENTER

An extension of the halfway-house idea could serve as community correction in the broadest sense, by providing a range of services tailored to the needs of different kinds of offenders with various problems. The President's Crime Commission suggested:

. . . construction of a wholly new kind of correctional institution for general use . . . architecturally and methodologically the antithesis of the traditional fortress-like prison, physically

58. Vasoli and Fahey, "Halfway Houses for Reformatory Releasees," 16 *Crime and Delinquency* 202, 301 (1970).

and psychologically isolated from the larger society and serving primarily as a place of banishment. It would be small and fairly informal in structure, located in or near the population center from which its inmates came; it would permit flexible use of community resources, both in the institution and for inmates released to work or study or spend short periods of time at home. Its closest existing models are some of the residential centers developed in the special juvenile treatment programs . . . and the halfway houses that have been developed in a number of communities for released prisoners.

This type of institution would perform many functions. It would receive newly committed inmates and carry out extensive screening and classification with them. For those who are not returned quickly to community treatment, the new institutions would provide short-term, intensive treatment for placing them in the community under appropriate supervision. Still other offenders, after careful diagnosis, would be sent to the higher custody facilities required for a long-term confinement of more difficult and dangerous inmates. But they might be eventually returned to the small facility as a port of re-entry into the community.[59]

Rather than a new super-institution, we envision a constellation of small facilities leased in different parts of the metropolitan areas from which their clients come, some run by public agencies and some operated privately but subsidized from public funds. These facilities, both residential and non-residential, would have varying degrees of security and programming, according to the needs of their clients. Some of the functions that might be performed by such community correctional centers include pre-trial diagnosis and limited custody for some offenders who cannot be released on recognizance; diagnostic studies for courts to aid in sentencing and for correctional agencies to aid in classification; residence for the small proportion of probationers who need it, intensive supervision and counseling services for others; residential or non-residential centers for offenders on work release or sentenced to make restitution to their victims; and structured programs for those offenders considered in need of greater supervision and structure between prison and freedom.

We have seen some of the separate elements of this program in different parts of the country: the District of Columbia's program of leasing

59. The President's Commission on Law Enforcement and Administration of Justice, Task Force Report: *Correction* 11 (1967).

small facilities for offenders on work release; the California Community Treatment Project's variety of non-residential program for youths coupled with an extensive use of group homes; the New York Division for Youth's range of residential and non-residential programs in both rural and metropolitan areas. The Florida Division for Youth Services has prepared a theoretical scheme showing the ideal characteristics of residential correctional programs for juveniles, which would provide a continuum of security and treatment, depending on the needs of the particular youth committed to the division. But no jurisdiction has even begun to tap the potential of correctional facilities in the community that are designed to provide a variety of services to the offenders and to enlist the other agencies of the community to change both the offenders and the community itself.

The Community in Correction

In alliance with the correctional establishment, in support of it and sometimes completely on its own, the private sector has become involved with the problems of the correctional world. Especially in the areas of social services, training and work and education, private organizations have been very helpful in ameliorating some of the problems of inmates and ex-convicts. Here, perhaps more than in any other area, there is a tremendous potential for reform. Resolving social problems in the private sector is in the best American tradition of private enterprise. And it must be, after all, in the free community that the offender ultimately will succeed or fail. Without collaboration with this community the correctional world is operating in an unreal vacuum, doomed to failure.

Voluntary Agencies

Ever since there have been prisons, conditions in them have been bad and prisoners have been neglected. But there always has been some lone and intrepid individual whose outrage at prison conditions led to inspiring individual acts of mercy and, sometimes, movements for reform. In England, in the eighteenth century, John Howard, whose name now marks prison-reform organizations in the United States and abroad, was a one-man traveling prison ombudsman who devoted years to improving prison conditions; Elizabeth Fry, a Quaker who became known as "the angel of Newgate," was a pioneer at improving conditions at women's institutions. Personal efforts like these continue; they are inspirational, but perforce their impact must be limited. However, recently various private voluntary organizations and professional groups such as bar associations and organized institutions such as religious associations have begun to work in the field of correction and have evolved as another resource for reform outside the correctional establishment. Their role is vital, if still inadequate.

Voluntary efforts to "humanize" prisons and provide social services to prisoners and their families have existed in the United States since the eighteenth century. The earliest efforts were in the form of prison visits by middle-class "do-gooders" usually sponsored by religious groups. The Pennsylvania Prison Society, the oldest voluntary agency specializing in aiding prisoners, was established in 1787 under Quaker leadership. The Salvation Army, the Volunteers of America and other socially concerned and usually religiously motivated people saw the needs of prisoners as part of their Christian mission in the late 1800s and devoted time and money to developing programs that would make prisons more tolerable—providing libraries, improving food and eliminating brutal practices on the part of guards, as well as helping released prisoners to find employment and housing upon re-entry into the world outside the institution.

These early volunteer efforts were characterized by emotional involvement with the prisoner and his family and a personal humanistic approach, exemplified by Christmas baskets and personal sponsorship before parole became available. Volunteers would find jobs for offenders upon release and provide temporary financial support. Occasionally volunteers opened their homes to offenders and "hired" them as house servants or gardeners.

The Volunteers of America, through their founder, Maud Ballington Booth, portrayed this personal touch. Mrs. Booth made thousands of visits to prisons all over the country during her long life, preaching and bringing small gifts. Concerned about the medical and psychological condition of prisoners upon discharge in the late 1800s, the Volunteers established "Hope Halls," halfway-house-type residences where a prisoner could find board and room, medical care and help in finding a job.

The Volunteers also sponsored the Volunteer Prison League, the first self-help prisoner group in an American prison. When founded at Sing Sing in 1896, the league was open to any prisoner who would try to live up to five Calvinistic rules, including praying every morning and night, reading the Day book faithfully, refraining from the use of bad language, faithfully observing prison rules and becoming examples of good conduct, earnestly cheering and encouraging others in well-doing and right living. By 1923 the Volunteer Prison League group had been established in forty-six state and federal prisons with over 100,000 members. Essentially the league provided a form of group therapy for its members. Each member had a copy of the five rules hanging in his cell and wore a small button on his jacket with the league's motto, "Look Up and Hope," printed on it. Evangelistic religious programs were conducted by Mrs. Booth and her associates.

In addition the Volunteers of America did individual counseling with prisoners and their families and provided financial assistance. Efforts were made to help released prisoners in finding employment. While the efforts of the Volunteers of America were similar to those of other groups like the Quakers, Salvation Army and local prisoners'-aid societies, the size of the problem was so large that these volunteers were able to help only a small portion.

As prison administrators became aware of the need for social services, social workers, psychologists and psychiatrists were employed to provide counseling and therapy. The clash between the evangelistic, religiously inspired but untrained and unprofessional volunteer and the professional counselor, trained in the behavioral sciences, was inevitable. The dedicated volunteers moved into the background as the professional social workers took over, both as counselors inside prison walls and as probation and parole officers on the outside.

In some parts of the world, particularly in the Scandinavian countries and the British Isles, there has been a greater accommodation between professionals and volunteers, and volunteers continue to play an important role in the correctional field. Under the supervision of trained personnel the volunteer provides probation and other after-care services to a large number of prisoners. In Sweden, for example, there are 10,000 volunteers (in a total population of eight million) who supervise two-thirds of all probation and after-care cases.

Similarly, in the Netherlands there are almost 9,000 volunteers providing after-care and other services designed to ease the change from prison life to life outside the walls. One volunteer program arranges for an inmate nearing the completion of his confinement to be the weekend guest of a family of his socioeconomic class living in the area. This kind of personal hospitality is thought to be more likely to have a psychological impact on the offender where it is offered by a motivated volunteer rather than by a paid professional.

Although the first attempts to provide social services to prison inmates, probationers and parolees in the United States were organized by volunteers, the role of the voluntary worker in this country has become very limited. Counseling, supervision, employment and welfare services now are provided primarily by governmental agencies. As a supplement to these tax-supported programs, however, some voluntary groups do continue to provide services, albeit to a lesser extent than in other countries.

Many of the volunteer groups have become structured in the form of social agencies, using paid professionals to administer their programs. A group of these voluntary agencies has established the Correctional Service Federation, U.S.A., a national organization which provides information and services to its member agencies through conferences and publications intended to guide the activities of the voluntary correctional agency. In addition, the federation encourages the member agencies to conduct public-information programs about correctional processes and problems as well as supporting and initiating desirable correctional legislation. The Correctional Service Federation has a membership of twenty-three voluntary agencies. Besides serving its members, the federation's staff aids local or statewide citizen groups interested in establishing voluntary correctional service agencies.

According to the American Correctional Association, "The voluntary agency, representing unofficial and generous community interest rather than official authority, helps to facilitate the prisoner's return to free society, the rehabilitation of the offender, and the protection of society through prevention of crime." The potential strength of a voluntary correctional service agency, according to the association's manual, is in its independence of the limitations of regulations and statutory restrictions which govern public agencies. This freedom, combined with flexibility due to small size, should enable these voluntary agencies to act quickly and boldly, without concern for public or political disapproval.[60]

TYPES OF VOLUNTARY AGENCIES

Voluntary agencies fall into several categories. The largest number of agencies are oriented toward social work, emphasizing professional

60. American Correctional Association, *Manual of Correctional Standards*, Ch. 17 (3d ed. 1966).

social work concepts of treating the offender's personal problems of adjustment while providing needed material assistance. Another group of agencies might be classified as private welfare agencies, which provide material services such as food, housing and clothing to the offender and his family at times of crisis. A third category includes self-help groups designed along the lines of Synanon and Alcoholics Anonymous. The latter agencies provide a variety of services and are staffed primarily by ex-offenders.

SOCIAL-WORK AGENCIES

The majority of agencies providing services to prisoners today are traditional social-work agencies. Usually these agencies receive most of their funds from the local United Fund and are staffed by professional social workers and other "professionals" with graduate training in psychology and sociology. This is not surprising in light of the fact that most private or voluntary social agencies providing counseling services today to non-prisoners in this country are social-work agencies. Because their staff has been professionally trained to understand the dynamics of behavior, these agencies believe that they can be particularly effective in facilitating the prisoner's return to free society.

Originally these agencies provided direct assistance to prisoners, ex-prisoners and their families, supplying food and clothing, finding jobs and housing and giving emergency financial assistance. The agencies were staffed in the beginning by "untrained" volunteers. As the agencies have become more "professional" they have tended to de-emphasize material assistance by referring prisoners to various public agencies such as the Welfare Department, State Employment Service, Vocational Rehabilitation, Public Housing and private welfare agencies. The social-work agencies tend to see their present role as one of treatment of the prisoner's underlying psychological problems through individual and group counseling with the prisoner and his family. The theory is that while the offer of money, clothes or a job may solve the prisoner's immediate need, ultimately he must solve his personality problems if he is to become successfully reintegrated into free society.

In addition to casework therapy, most of the agencies engage in public-education programs. News letters, public appearances by staff members at meetings of church and service groups, as well as bringing citizens into group meetings with prisoners are some of the forms of education used. The publication and distribution of annual reports are aimed at making the community aware of the agency's goals and activities and of current needs in the field of correction.

Most of the agencies also engage in lobbying. Because of their intimate acquaintance with the prisons and offenders and their professional orientation in the area of rehabilitation, the voluntary correctional agencies believe that they can be influential in effecting change in correctional methods and prison administration.

The agencies occasionally design programs which they hope will be taken over by the state and local governments, or at least receive financial assistance from governmental sources. For example, the Alston Wilkes Society of South Carolina, a statewide agency founded in 1962 with chapters in seventeen counties, undertook an "Older Adult Offender Project" in 1967 to deal with the needs of offenders over the age of forty-five. The objectives were to find employment and housing for these older offenders as well as conducting a survey to determine their needs in prison. As a result of their survey, the Alston Wilkes Society recommended that a special institution be established for inmates who were physically handicapped or of advanced age (over sixty-five), since institutionalization under normal prison conditions did not provide the special activities and recreation needed by this group. As a direct result of the voluntary agency's project, the South Carolina Department of Correction made plans to build a special institution for aged and handicapped inmates.

This agency also has taken over a program that could not be continued by the State Department of Correction. In 1968 it assumed the operation of a halfway house that had been set up by the State Department of Correction but was discontinued when its federal grant ended. Contributions from its 4,500 members, as well as grants from private foundations, enabled the Alston Wilkes Society to operate the halfway house in Columbia and to plan the opening of additional halfway houses in South Carolina.

The American Friends Service Committee, a Quaker organization, has been concerned with people who are imprisoned since Quakers often were locked up for their religious beliefs. More recently, many members have served sentences in prison for involvement in civil-rights movements or conscientious objection to war. As an expression of their concern, Quakers have set up several halfway houses for ex-offenders. The Elizabeth Fry Center, the first halfway house for women on the West Coast, was established by the Service Committee in Los Angeles. In the San Francisco area, the Friends operate the Austin MacCormick House Center, a residence for men newly released from prison, as well as an apartment satellite program. In Iowa, the American Friends Service Committee was so successful with the halfway-house project it operated in Des Moines that the state's Bureau of Correction took over the project and submitted a program to the legislature calling for the operation of eight similar institutions throughout the state.

The Washington, D.C., Bureau of Rehabilitation is another voluntary correctional service agency which provides a residential treatment program for the national-capital area. Established in 1930, the bureau prepared case histories on convicted offenders for the United States Board of Parole and supervised District of Columbia parolees. As public agencies took over these functions, the bureau developed a program of specialized services for offenders and their families, including counseling and financial assistance. The bureau has provided counseling services to mandatory releasees who were not eligible for official parole services. Another program developed by the agency is a big-brother type of personal sponsorship for juveniles in institutions. In addition, the bureau operates four residential treatment facilities, including two halfway houses for pre-releasees and two residences established through contracts with the District of Columbia Health Department to accommodate male and female drug addicts.

The Northern California Service League, the first agency in the United States to be concerned exclusively with local jails and their inmates, was established in 1948 by four sectarian agencies in the San Francisco area which saw the need for a single specialized agency to concentrate on the rehabilitation of petty offenders. As part of their program of "demonstration and research into proposed ways to help ex-inmates become constructive citizens," the league designed a project which demonstrated that intensive rehabilitation counseling by professional case workers can be more successful than incarceration in the county jail; it can be less expensive as well.

Voluntary agencies have been instrumental in changing correctional institutions in various states by supporting legislation providing for bail reform, social-service departments in the prisons, separate institutions for children, work release, family weekend visiting of inmates, state-sponsored halfway houses and other reforms. For example, the St. Louis Bureau for Men was established in 1925 to serve the needs of men without families. The agency discovered that approximately 75 percent of these men had a history of law violation and prison. Therefore, the bureau began to provide services to the ex-offender and encouraged the institutions to solve problems identified by the bureau. As a result of a bureau project that provided a case worker in the St. Louis Medium Security Institution, the institution developed its own social-service department in 1967.

The Connecticut Prison Association, established in 1875, has been active in working for legislation to aid in the rehabilitation of prisoners. The association led the move for the indeterminate sentence in Connecticut; it also drew up the probation law that was passed by the Connecticut legislature in 1903 and staffed the first probation offices in the state. (It was not until 1955 that the state of Connecticut took over the responsibility of providing probation officers.) The Connecticut Prison Association also was instrumental in establishing the state farm and prison for women and in providing juveniles with specialized probation officers. In fact, the association claims to have been one of the major influences in the establishment of the Connecticut Department of Correction, having drafted a major portion of the authorizing legislation.

During its 187-year history, the Pennsylvania Prison Society has been attempting to bring about reform in Pennsylvania's criminal law and in the prison administrative system. The society initiated the drive to remove children from jails to special detention facilities and to institutionalize the insane in mental hospitals instead of prisons. Separate prison facilities were established for women with the help of society efforts, and the provision of separate detention facilities for untried adults has been aided by the society's support. In addition, the society claims to provide direct services, such as counseling, financial assistance and aid in finding jobs, to over 1,000 offenders per year.

Although these voluntary agencies might be able to perform a significant service to prisoners, the agencies usually are so small (often two or three full-time case workers) that they do not reach the large majority of offenders. In general, the effectiveness of a voluntary correctional service agency's role in a community seems to be determined by its size in relation to the community served, the existence and quality of public agency services in the community and the extent of support of its goals by the community and the widespread knowledge of the agency's services.

There is substantial variety among the clientele of different agencies. Some agencies, such as the Jewish Committee for Personal Service in Los Angeles, are sectarian and provide services only to Jewish men and women awaiting trial or serving time in county, state and federal penal institutions. (In the case of the Jewish agency this amounts to only 1.27 percent of the prison population in California.) Other agencies, such as the Northern California Service League, provide services only to prisoners in county jails, a group that tends to receive less in the way of casework and material services than prisoners in state and federal institutions. Some agencies, such as Special Social Services, Inc., of New York City, serve only the children and families of prisoners, while other agencies work only with released prisoners. One agency, the Quaker Committee on Social Rehabilitation of New York City, gives special services to narcotics addicts. On the other hand, the Women's Prison Association of New York provides casework and direct services only to non-addicted women.

Generally, the agencies provide direct services only to offenders and families who are referred to the agency or who voluntarily seek the agency's help. Traditionally, social workers have maintained that a person must recognize that he needs professional help with his problems before he can benefit from that help. Thus a prisoner who comes to the agency because he has been coerced into doing so is less likely to solve his problems than one who seeks casework services voluntarily.

One agency, the Connecticut Prison Association (a hybrid, since it receives 70 percent of its support from the state and 30 percent from voluntary contributions), is required by statute to see *all* discharged men from correctional centers in the state of Connecticut. This agency functions primarily as a referral service rather than giving casework services to its clients.

PRIVATE WELFARE AGENCIES

This category resembles the early efforts of volunteers in the correctional field. Personal dedication and a non-professional approach characterize these groups, who are particularly helpful in providing emergency assistance as well as spiritual guidance.

These agencies tend to be less "professionally" oriented than the social-work agencies. Usually they are staffed by volunteers or counselors who are not professionally trained in social work. While many of these agencies receive some support from the United Fund, they tend to receive the majority of their financial resources from church organizations and membership contributions. Included in the category are agencies such as the Salvation Army, Volunteers of America, Yokefellow Prison Ministry, St. Vincent de Paul and the Quakers.

These groups generally provide material services to offenders and their families, including food, emergency housing, rent, clothing, summer camp and employment. Since many of these groups are affiliated with religious organizations, they provide Bible classes and religious services in the prisons as well as special Christmas celebrations. The Jewish Committee for Personal Service, while primarily a social-work agency, also has a chaplain service to provide Jewish inmates with religious services and special celebrations on religious holidays.

Private welfare agencies seem to be attempting a transformation into social-work agencies as they move toward "professionalization" by counseling prisoners and hiring social workers to supervise the counseling provided by volunteers and untrained employees.

Since it is easier for offenders to ask for help in obtaining material things such as food, housing or a job than for counseling, and the material needs have a greater urgency, the welfare agencies serve a larger percentage of those who have been involved in the correctional process than the social-work agencies. Distrust of the white, middle-class social worker, combined with the general unwillingness to accept the theory that one's problems stem from personality defects instead of society's shortcomings, tend to keep offenders from using social-work agencies as readily as private welfare agencies.

Ex-Convict Agencies

Probably the most exciting and innovative groups involved in serving offenders are those composed of ex-offenders. What they lack in professional training and formal education often is overshadowed by their dedication, enthusiasm and credibility with clients resulting from their "having been there." In fact, some of the official correctional agencies are beginning to hire ex-convicts as counselors, although they are supervised by social workers and are part of the agency structure. For example, the Correctional Council of Delaware in Wilmington has hired an ex-convict as a counselor. The Wisconsin Correctional Service plans to organize an Ex-Inmates Advisory Group within the agency structure. Other agencies are entering contracts with ex-offender groups. For example, the District of Columbia Department of Correction pays two local ex-convict groups to run a halfway house and supervise parolees.

There is no organization or formal listing of ex-offender agencies; they attract clients by word of mouth and frequent visits to the institutions. Professional social workers traditionally do their counseling outside of institutions and are uncomfortable with the restrictions of movement and rigid schedules in prisons. In addition, voluntary agency workers are not part of the prison system and are given few privileges within it. The ex-cons, on the other hand, know the institutional procedure and hierarchy very well and, where officials permit, can operate more comfortably and effectively within it.

The convict self-help groups claim to be more effective in reducing recidivism than the correctional professionals. These claims are difficult to substantiate, since statistically acceptable records of recidivism rarely are kept by the prisons or the ex-con groups. There is little doubt, however, that the current treatment methods and procedures used by professionals leave much to be desired.

A sociologist conducting an attitudinal study of inmates in Massachusetts concluded that inmates distrust staff and will not open up to them; staff and inmates find it difficult to communicate due to their different backgrounds and levels of understanding; inmates see staff as people to be conned for the inmates' advantage; having lived a life of which they are not proud, the inmates resent having to go to an authority figure—the type of person they always hated and distrusted—for help; inmates fear being ostracized by their peers if they seek professional help.[61]

The ex-convict self-help groups have reached similar conclusions based on their own experiences. Bill Sands, a former inmate of San Quentin, stated his observations as follows:

> Most convicts can never identify with any guard or official, any judge or parole officer or policeman, any social worker or psychologist. The concern or integrity the man who wants to help might show doesn't get through to the convict. There is an invisible barrier, like a glass wall, that descends between honest

61. William C. Kuehn, "The Concept of Self-Help Groups Among Criminals," 7, 1 *Criminologica* (May 1969).

citizens and convicts, and it makes the average con stone-deaf when anyone from the non-criminal world tries to reach him.[62]

Bill Sands believed that an ex-con might be able to reach convicts on their own terms, talking to them in their own language. A professional could not create this rapport. So Sands founded The Seventh Step, a group of ex-cons who conduct pre-release classes in prisons in order to remotivate potential parolees and help them find jobs, housing, clothing and food on their release. Currently there are thirty chapters of Seventh Step Foundation nationwide. Since its establishment in 1963, the group has actively solicited the aid of businessmen and other private citizens who can provide employment and personal sponsorship for inmates on release. However, the ex-cons refuse to align their group with psychiatrists, psychologists or social workers. Sands says:

> Convicts may listen politely to educated free men, but they do not answer back. They are not polite at Seventh Step meetings and they do answer back because they are deeply involved. The movement is their own.

Similar ex-con groups have been established in the last few years, but, unlike the Seventh Step Foundation, most are limited to local areas. For example, the Self Development Group is active at the Massachusetts Correctional Institution at Concord and the Deer Island House of Correction in Boston. Oddly enough, the group began as an experiment conducted by Dr. Timothy Leary, who believed that hallucinogenic drugs might be helpful in rehabilitating criminals by providing them with dramatic insight and profound religious experiences. A group of thirty-five inmates were administered the drug psilocybin once a week during

---

62. Sands, *The Seventh Step* 27 (1967). The group is called The Seventh Step because they adopted seven rules, or steps, as guidelines:

Facing the truth about ourselves and the world around us, we decided we needed to change.
Realizing that there is a power from which we can gain strength, we have decided to use that power.
Evaluating ourselves by taking an honest self-appraisal, we examined both our strengths and our weaknesses.
Endeavoring to help ourselves overcome our weaknesses, we enlisted the aid of that power to help us concentrate on our strengths.
Deciding that our *freedom* is worth more than our resentments, we are using that power to help free us from those resentments.
Observing that daily progress is necessary, we set an attainable goal toward which we can work each day.
Maintaining our own freedom, we pledge ourselves to help others as we have been helped.

the year-long experiment. While some prison officials dismissed the experiment as little more than a pot party, a core of inmates interested in helping themselves remained after the experiment was completed. They began to conduct group meetings in the prison. No longer dependent on drugs or Dr. Leary, the group emphasized the rehabilitative goal of getting men out of prison and keeping them out.

Like the Seventh Step Foundation, membership in the Self Development Group is voluntary and open to any prisoner who has the desire to help himself stay out of prison and is willing to help others do the same. This philosophy, combined with SDG's seven points which provide the theme of discussion groups, and a desire to avoid the aid of psychiatrists, social workers and other professionals, have led several observers to compare ex-con groups with other self-help organizations such as the prominent Synanon and Alcoholics Anonymous. While all self-help groups have many structural similarities, there are some dissimilarities as well. Bill Sands pointed out one of the major differences:

> The Seventh Step program does not demand that members take an active part in reforming others once their own freedom is secure. Unlike Alcoholics Anonymous, we do not impose upon anyone any obligation for another man's success. A great many of our men want to work in the program and we love them for it. A great many move out of Seventh Step as soon as they know they're finished with crime themselves, and we love them too. I think any of our former members would give help willingly if he were asked to in any particular case. But if a man wants to be let alone, we let him alone.

Some ex-con groups provide the major part of their service to the men who are outside prison. For example, Efforts From Ex-Convicts, a group based in Washington, D.C., was established in 1966 with the primary goal of finding jobs for men who had just been released. Organized by a group of black ex-cons who had "decent jobs in community action type programs," EFEC members were impressed with the fact that existing agencies designed to help ex-cons were doing virtually nothing. Rudy Yates, one of EFEC's directors, describes the program as a kind of "nepotism": "Since some of us are in the system, we're going to bring our brothers into the system."

In addition to finding jobs for ex-convicts, EFEC members have been active in assisting community efforts to eliminate crime, particularly in acting as a buffer in troubled areas of Washington. Like the Seventh Step Foundation and SDG, EFEC members are working with juveniles who are moving in the wrong direction. Some staff members have had young offenders paroled directly to them. In addition the group runs a halfway house under contract with the District of Columbia Department of Correction. Recently EFEC organized a for-profit corporation, EFEC-tivity, Inc., to develop its own job markets in the building-maintenance business. As its successes mounted, the EFEC organization has spread nationally and is now working with affiliate chapters in other states.

Another self-help group based in the District of Columbia, Bona-Bond, works with the local juvenile court in obtaining releases for juveniles. This is only part of BonaBond's work, however. Established in 1966, the group's original purpose was to provide the fidelity bonds that many employers require before they will hire an ex-con. BonaBond has been very successful in this area. There has not been a single claim filed against a bond it arranged. BonaBond also has developed a program to provide third-party release for inmates pending trial. Under this program, men are released in the custody of BonaBond. Less than 3 percent have failed to show up for trial. Hiawatha Burris, the group's original director, attributes these successes to a hard-nosed approach and expertise:

> If the men don't show up for trial, BonaBond goes out to get them or shows them to the Marshal.
>
> We're successful because our staff is composed of ex-cons, ex-junkies, ex-hustlers, liars, thieves, some murderers, and 8th grade dropouts, and that's what's in the streets.
>
> We know what it is in the streets—what it is in the jail. We know how to relate to the people because we learned it in the street.

All of the self-help groups described thus far are non-sectarian and interracial. However, one group that has a very strong appeal in the prisons is both segregated and religiously oriented. The Black Muslims must be included as a self-help group, although their primary goal has not been rehabilitation of prisoners. Nevertheless, their organization has become very powerful inside correctional institutions. In his autobiography, Malcolm X, a former prisoner, described his religious conversion and the effectiveness of the Muslims in turning him away from a life of crime:

You let this caged-up black man start thinking, the same way I did when I first heard Elijah Muhammad's teachings: let him start thinking how, with better breaks when he was young and ambitious he might have been a lawyer, a doctor, a scientist, anything. You let this caged-up black man start realizing, as I did, how from the first landing of the slave ship, the millions of black men in America have been like sheep in a den of wolves. That's why black prisoners become Muslims so fast when Elijah Muhammad's teachings filter into their cages by way of other Muslim convicts. "The white man is the devil" is a perfect echo of that black convict's lifelong experience.[63]

Other local self-help groups run by ex-convicts include The Inn in Hartford, Connecticut; Self Improvement Group, MacNeil Island, Washington; and Adults Anonymous, La Crosse, Wisconsin. A group of ex-convict organizations presently is considering organizing all of the local groups and publishing a directory, similar to the efforts of the Correctional Federation, U.S.A. The publishing of a directory would be of real value, for some ex-cons are "lost" after they leave the community where their group was operating.

Convict self-help groups have been faced with several problems. Initially there was a great deal of professional and official hostility toward the formation of ex-convict groups. The ex-cons attribute this hostility to professional jealousy. As Sands said,

> Most of the penologists who still oppose us do so because they see the Seventh Step movement as a threat to their way of life. They are right.

Hiawatha Burris, former director of BonaBond, has said, "Don't be jealous when we do it better than the professional. Give us the chance to run our programs. We'll do it anyway."

While this kind of hostility usually has been overcome to the point that the groups have been allowed to conduct meetings inside prisons without official supervision, there have been exceptions. For example, the Fortune Society, an ex-convict group in New York, was established with the primary purpose of making the public aware of the problems in the prison system and the needs of inmates and ex-offenders. Members of the group teach a college course on criminology; in addition, the society publishes a monthly news letter and sends speakers to public affairs. De-

63. *The Autobiography of Malcolm X* (1964).

spite the fact that the news letter is received by hundreds of inmates in all fifty states and over twenty-one nations, the New York state prison system refused to allow its inmates to receive the Fortune Society news letter and barred members of the Fortune Society from visiting the institutions and talking to the inmates until a court order enjoined the state from continuing the ban.[64]

In addition to this official hostility, there also have been legal obstacles. Several states require that as a condition of parole, parolees are not permitted to associate with other criminals. If this rule were strictly enforced, the ex-con groups could work with a man while he was in prison but not after he had been released into the community. These restrictions have been relaxed to a great extent, and these organizations do meet with former prisoners on the outside. Nevertheless, some parole officers continue to warn their charges not to go into the offices of ex-convict groups and "consort" with other ex-criminals.

Despite these problems, self-help groups are a shining light in an otherwise murky area. Ex-convicts can do more at lower costs because they usually do not expect the salaries commanded by social workers, psychiatrists and psychologists; many volunteer their services. Like their counterparts in AA and Synanon, they appear to be more successful in rehabilitating themselves than in responding to professional efforts. In addition, there is reason to believe that the self-help groups are reaching the most difficult, hard-core criminals who have thus far been untouched by professionals.

The use of convicts and ex-convicts in their own rehabilitation and in the correctional process generally is a promising and as yet untapped resource. For one thing, it neutralizes potential criminals. For another, it draws from a class of hitherto outsiders that unique expertise which none other has, thus giving them a positive distinction and usefulness. Third, it provides workers who can relate to the problems and communicate with the clients in a way which no one else can.

COMMUNITY ORGANIZATIONS

A number of private social organizations that have emphasized services in other areas recently have begun to show an awareness of cor-

64. *Fortune News*, January 1971. The Fortune Society brought an action to enjoin the New York State Department of Correction from banning the distribution of their newsletter, and on December 4, 1970, the U.S. District Court (Southern District of New York) granted the injunction, thereby ending the ban that had been in effect for one and a half years. *Fortune Society v. McGinnis*, 319 F. Supp. 901 (S.D.N.Y. 1970).

rectional needs and to provide miscellaneous services to offenders and their families. For example, some local Rotary and Kiwanis clubs have run projects providing books and magazines to inmates and helping to find employment for releasees. The AFL-CIO has expressed interest in setting up vocational training projects in the prisons as well as in helping the trainees obtain jobs on release. The Family Service Association of America provides counseling on problems related to marriage and child-rearing to some ex-offenders and their families. Community centers and settlement houses provide counseling and a variety of recreational facilities for the community, including ex-offenders and their families. In addition, specialized self-help groups such as Alcoholics Anonymous hold meetings in prisons for those inmates with particular problems.

The Jaycees currently are developing chapters within prisons. Recently, the Jaycee chapter at the Maryland Penitentiary was named the outstanding chapter in the state, as well as the outstanding prison chapter nationally. The chapter provides services to the non-prison community, such as addressing envelopes for local charities; occasionally inmates are allowed to attend meetings (under guard) with local civic groups. In 1970 there were 115 Jaycee prison chapters in the United States, with more than 1,500 members.

Allowing inmates the opportunity to provide voluntary services to the community is a unique way of providing them with important contacts in the community as well as a feeling of personal accomplishment. This kind of experience should be a significant factor in the rehabilitation process.

VOLUNTEERS

Many voluntary correctional service agencies use non-professional, private citizens to provide some services to offenders. Volunteers connected with religiously oriented agencies provide inmates with parties at Christmas, toys for their children and religious services. Volunteers also supply inmates with stamps, greeting cards and toiletries when the inmate cannot afford to purchase these items himself. Businessmen volunteers, through service clubs such as Kiwanis and Rotary, occasionally provide employment counseling, but these efforts depend on the whim of the local chapter.

One group of volunteers, Job Therapy, Inc., is attempting to provide a "personal touch" and a bridge to the community by assigning inmates to businessmen sponsors. Founded by a minister in 1965, the group has matched over 500 business and professional men with 600 inmates of the Washington State Reformatory in Monroe, Washington. The sponsors (some with their wives and children) visit the inmates twice a month for about a year. The citizen sponsors escort their "friend" from the institution on the day of release and stay with him the first day out, assisting with any re-entry problems into the community that may occur. In addition, the group has provided job-placement service for inmates; they claim that 300 Seattle companies now are actively cooperating with Job Therapy, Inc.

Other volunteers are involved primarily in visiting inmates and providing various activities within the institution, such as Great Books discussion groups and classes in creative writing, sewing, typing and photography. One group, the Mensa Friends, have organized programs that are restricted to inmates having IQs of 147 or better. At Patuxent Institute in Maryland, the Mensa Friends have introduced a project in which inmates record books for the blind.

A pilot program, funded by the Administration on Aging of the U.S. Department of Health, Education and Welfare, matched one needy group with another to satisfy needs of both. The Foster Grandparent Program is working in two institutions of the California Youth Authority. Although foster grandparents are active nationally in institutions for dependent and neglected children, this program, in operation since 1967, is the first to be carried out in correctional institutions.

Low-income elderly people living near the two institutions involved are selected by the Foster Grandparent Program, given an orientation program to acquaint them with the particular needs of Youth Authority wards. Each grandparent is assigned two boys who have no families or whose families do not visit or write to them regularly. They make frequent visits to the institutions to meet with their assigned "grandchildren," developing hobbies with them and assisting them with their studies. In addition, the Foster Grandparent Program sponsors organized recreational programs in the institutions and takes boys out on field trips. Payments by the project to grandparents in several cases have permitted them to get off welfare rolls. The Foster Grandparent Program has been praised by Youth Authority officials as well as by the boys who benefit directly.   According to John Riggs, Assistant Superintendent of the O. H. Close School for Boys in Stockton, California:

I personally like having the grandparents on campus. Having elderly people as well as young students from local colleges creates much more of a community atmosphere. . . . [S]ome youngsters needing a "nurturing parent" form a close bond with some of the grandparents. Beyond their services is the "new lease on life" that some grandparents openly admit they get. For the first time in years, many of them feel that they as human beings are doing something worthwhile.

Another administrator points out that providing non-threatening adults with whom the youths may talk, the foster grandparents help to soften some of the angry feelings many of the boys have toward adults. This observation is supported by a letter from one of the boys who participated in the program:

I think that [foster grandparents] mean a lot to all the men here . . . because they are what they are, and they don't try to act like they are the boss, they just act like friends. And they are people that you can really sit down and talk to and discuss about the things that are really putting you down, or about what you can do to make life worthwhile.

For the most part, however, volunteers in correctional institutions are scarce; often they are looked on with suspicion by prison personnel, and many consider work with prisoners less satisfying than volunteer work in hospitals and other "cleaner" places. Middle-class volunteers generally have less empathy for prison inmates than for patients at mental hospitals or retarded children.

There is one area, however, where volunteers are receiving a hearty welcome. Courts dealing with juveniles and young adult misdemeanants have discovered that volunteers can greatly enhance, and occasionally institute, probation services. In the early 1960s a municipal-court judge in Royal Oak, Michigan, who was concerned about the lack of rehabilitative services available to young misdemeanants invited a handful of citizens to serve as volunteer probation officers. By 1965 over 500 citizens had volunteered. The group included professionals who could provide psychiatric evaluation as well as teachers, lawyers, housewives and retired citizens. While the volunteers originally provided all of the counseling, they now work under the supervision of paid professional probation officers on a one-to-one basis with probationers. The Royal Oak

Group received nationwide publicity, and by 1968 almost sixty courts had instituted similar volunteer programs. In 1969 Judge Keith Leenhouts resigned from the bench to become the director of Project Misdemeanant Foundation, Inc., a privately funded group working toward educating communities throughout the country about the value of citizen participation in the court system. The foundation provides consultants, workshops, films and speakers to assist courts in developing their own volunteer program.

Similar volunteer programs have been established in other juvenile courts. The Boulder County District Court, Juvenile Court in Boulder, Colorado, has over 175 volunteers participating by assisting probation officers, tutoring, supervising group discussions as well as providing clerical help. In addition, the Boulder County Court provides a clearinghouse for information on new developments in volunteer court programs throughout the country by its monthly publication of *Volunteer Courts Newsletter*.

It has been estimated that there are over 350 courts using volunteers in the United States. While practically all of the court volunteers are providing services to juveniles and young adult misdemeanants, there have been some programs involving adult felons. The Federal Probation and Parole Office in Denver, Colorado, uses a few volunteers who assist the professionals. Similarly, forty volunteers serve as case aides and work with adult felons in Colorado Springs, Colorado. The American Bar Association's Commission on Correctional Facilities and Services has used young lawyers as voluntary probation and parole officers. Each lawyer handles only one or two cases.

The benefits of an active volunteer program in the courts are manifold, according to enthusiastic supporters. Because of their varied backgrounds, volunteers bring fresh ideas to the court. Volunteers return to the community as lobbyists, exerting pressure on local civic and church groups to support the upgrading of correctional programs. The volunteer has the time to give continuous one-to-one attention to his client, unlike the probation officer, who may be able to provide a mere fifteen minutes each month to his charges because of his heavy caseload. Also, volunteers increase the range of court probation services with the diversity of their talent and experience. Programs such as remedial reading, arts and crafts, tutoring and employment counseling could not be provided by a regular court probation staff in most smaller communities. There is some evidence that court programs based on volunteer participation are more effective in reducing recidivism and improving offenders' adjustment to society than courts without such programs.[65]

Dissenting voices can be heard, however. In a recent study, probation officers had some criticisms of volunteers. The probation officers claim, among other things, that volunteers are undependable, overidentify with probationers and attempt to reap too much personal gain from their relationships with the probationers. Probation officers also expressed their concern that volunteers try to take the place of the professional.

Some volunteers direct their efforts toward promoting legislation and other means of reforming existing correctional programs rather than working directly with offenders on a personal basis. The National Council on Crime and Delinquency has organized state citizen action councils in seventeen states. Assisted by the professional resources of NCCD, the over 650 private citizens have participated in activities ranging from sponsoring a study in California to determine why some juvenile offenders are detained rather than released to campaigning for the establishment of an alcoholic pre-care and after-care program and a detoxification center in New Mexico. Each state citizen action council has NCCD staff assigned to it to supervise and direct the activities of the volunteers.

To some extent there seems to have been a revival of volunteer efforts in recent years that is reminiscent of the personal involvement by volunteers at the turn of the century. The difference is that the volunteers of today tend to work with the professionals, aiding them and being supervised by them. It could be argued that a new group of volunteers is emerging—particularly in the courts. This group could be classified as unpaid paraprofessionals. While the motivation of "doing good" still prevails, the volunteers' techniques have changed from religious preaching to professionally supervised counseling.

For correction really to move into the community, the role of private, voluntary agencies must be increased. Indeed, it has been the divorce of the correctional process from the society within which all convicts ultimately must "make it" or fail that has been a fundamental flaw of the system. The system can never do the job of correction alone.

One iconoclastic criminologist, Richard Korn, has pointed out that the most significant correctional advances have been inspired by concerned lay individuals from outside the special government agencies which monop-

---

65. National Institute of Mental Health, Preliminary Research Study Report—Royal Oak Municipal Court (1968). According to this report, courts with a volunteer program were found to be more effective in reducing recidivism than courts without such a program.

olistically compose the world of correction. He ascribes this institutional lethargy or self-defensiveness to a failure among these administrators to learn from and positively exploit the consumers of the system—the prisoners themselves—and the absence of public participation in this area of administration. Not only is there an inherent institutional reluctance to change, springing from the self-interest of prison administrators, but also a tendency whereby reformers are consumed and neutralized by absorption within the system itself. The correction world is, Korn argues, like the ancient kingdom of China, always absorbing its conquerors.

As least one thing is sure: Private community help helps.

Education and Work

It should come as no surprise that prisoners generally lack education and vocational skills. Whether this is due to the greater propensity of the uneducated and unemployed to commit crimes or to their greater likelihood of being caught, the fact remains that the prison population contains a disproportionate number of people in need of education and training.

According to the 1967 Crime Commission Report, over 80 percent of the adult felons in U.S. prisons in 1960 had not completed high school. (By way of comparison, half the general population lacked a high-school education.) More than two-thirds of the prisoners were unskilled laborers, while only slightly more than one-third of the country's labor force as a whole fell into this category. A study of federal prisoners, generally considered the elite of the criminal population, determined that during the last two years before they were imprisoned, only a quarter had been employed for 75 percent or more of the time. Over one-fourth of the prisoners had worked less than 25 percent of the time, and 6 percent had had no legitimate employment at all.[66] In the District of Columbia almost half of all adult offenders were unemployed at the time they were arrested. The prisoners' lack of education and training occurs despite the fact that no significant difference has been found between the average intelligence of prisoners and that of the rest of the community.

It seems reasonable to assume, along with James V. Bennett, former director of the federal Bureau of Prisons, that "an important motivation

66. Glaser, *The Effectiveness of a Prison and Parole System* 230 (1964).

toward crime is lack of education, using that term in its broadest sense. . . ."[67] According to Bennett, "The most important contribution that prisons can make to the fight against crime is not to punish but to educate." Various studies have shown a relationship between property crimes and unemployment. Steady employment also has been shown to be associated with the successful completion of parole by released prisoners. Nonetheless, despite these compelling conclusions that can be drawn from this data, a direct cause-and-effect relation between training or employment and reduction of crime has yet to be shown empirically.

Of course, groups in society other than prisoners face the problems resulting from inadequate education and vocational training. But if inadequate training causes some people to commit crimes, concentrating resources on their education and training may be one of the most direct and cost-effective ways to prevent them from committing further crimes. This is particularly true in the case of youthful offenders, who comprise an increasing percentage of the criminal population and have the highest rates of recidivism.

According to one commentator, "The identification of a person as an offender [should] trigger a massive social response to try to prevent him from committing another anti-social act."[68] The recent report of the President's Task Force on Prisoner Rehabilitation emphasized the importance of in-prison training to enable released offenders to secure legitimate employment:

> A constructive member of the community, by definition, is a working member. A common characteristic of offenders is a poor work record; indeed it is fair to conjecture that a considerable number of them took to crime in the first place for lack of the ability or the opportunity—or both—to earn a legal living. Therefore, satisfying work experiences for institutional offenders, including vocational training when needed, and the assurance of decent jobs for released offenders, should be at the heart of the correctional process.[69]

In a recent speech to the American Bar Association's Commission on Correctional Facilities and Services, former Secretary of Labor George

67. Bennett, *I Chose Prison* 14 (1970).
68. Trebach, "No. 1 Domestic Priority: New Careers for Criminals," 4 *City* (Oct.–Nov. 1970), at 15, 17.
69. The President's Task Force on Prisoner Rehabilitation, *The Criminal Offender— What Should Be Done?* 9–10 (1970).

Shultz pledged that several federal agencies would devote substantial attention and resources to training offenders under correctional supervision:

> . . . the significant relationship between crime and unemployment represents a key intervention point in the life-style of many offenders. Further, there is substantial reason to believe that a comprehensive approach to the employment and training problems of the offender can produce significant results. In this effort we will rely heavily on the capacities of the private sector, particularly the organized bar, labor unions, and our many volunteer organizations, to work effectively, together with state and local governments.

The increasing emphasis on educating and training offenders to become productive members of the community represents a different approach to correction from punitive, deterrent or treatment approaches examined earlier. Education and training programs, particularly when they are undertaken by private businesses and citizens' groups and by governmental agencies outside of traditional correction channels, concentrate less on the personal and psychological problems of offenders than on such realistic, existential factors as creating opportunities for legitimate activities in the community and preparing offenders to take advantage of them. As Allen Breed, director of California's Youth Authority, recently remarked, such programs tend to change the community as well as individual offenders:

> The correctional objective becomes less a matter of patching up the holes in the offender's superego and more a matter of connecting him with the opportunity systems of the community; of integrating him with the socializing and conformity institutions of organized society. Rehabilitation becomes, in part at least, a problem of creating a stake for him in the prevailing social system.

EDUCATION

Prisons were not designed to be educational institutions. Prison architecture, concentrating on the custodial function and an obsessive need for security, does not lend itself readily to being used for academic programs. As one correctional administrator told us, "the whole tone of the institution communicates its purpose, and that purpose is not educational."

Efforts to train inmates sometimes come into conflict with the feeling of prison personnel that prisons exist to punish and deter criminals and that the presence of outsiders seeking to offer innovative programs and interfering with institutional schedules is unnecessarily disruptive of prison routine. For example, when a college program was instituted at the San Quentin Prison, some of the staff members commented about the injustice of having to pay for their own and their children's education, while unworthy prisoners received an education free. Others remarked that educated prisoners probably would be more dangerous than uneducated ones.

Institutional training programs often are hindered by the administration's wasteful competition for inmate time, particularly in those prisons that have devised a variety of "make-work" tasks to keep inmates from being completely idle. Most institutions offer few incentives for prisoners to take advantage of the few training programs that exist, placing greater emphasis on institutional maintenance, unskilled industrial labor and more recently on psychological counseling sessions that have been adopted by many correctional professionals as the primary way of rehabilitating prisoners.

Outside of a few juvenile and youth institutions where all inmates are assigned to educational and vocational classes and share necessary maintenance chores, prisons are organized so that inmates work at maintenance or industrial jobs as their primary and usually their only task. Available training courses must be undertaken in free time or at night, and, although consideration for parole should be improved by participation, the institutional incentives lie in the opposite direction. For example, New York prisoners can earn up to one dollar a day by working in the prison industries; those who choose to go to school instead earn only twenty-five cents. As the superintendent of a New York prison confessed, "Unfortunately, most of them are materialistic. They like the money they can earn in a job." A recently released prisoner reports that even in federal institutions

> [J]ob assignments, potentially a useful rehabilitative tool, usually have nothing whatsoever to do with a man's potential occupation when he leaves prison: getting the garbage removed is far more important than the remover's future. . . .

. . . wages have little relationship to the quality of work performed and even less to any sort of rehabilitative goals. For example, a janitor at the Terre Haute, Ind., U.S. penitentiary receiving $10 a month meritorious pay was reassigned to a plumbing vocational training program, where his $10 monthly stipend was immediately forfeited. Since the $10-a-month was all the money he had in the world—for cigarettes, shaving cream, candy and other commissary items—he quit the vocational training program and returned to his $10 a month floor sweeping.[70]

Minor efforts to provide academic education for prisoners were made as long ago as the 1830s and 1840s. A New York State law provided for the appointment of instructors in prisons in 1847. However, educational programs in prison were token and sporadic; in fact, the reformatory movement of the late nineteenth century was begun in an effort to achieve positive changes in offenders through education and vocational training.

Although juvenile institutions commonly require attendance in school and hire full-time teachers, education never has been a principal focus of adult prisons. It is unusual for inmates to be assigned to an academic school on even a part-time basis. Those teachers who do work in prisons frequently are the castoffs of the public-school system, who are willing to work for low pay and in isolated locations. For high-school or college courses, teaching is done frequently by other inmates or through correspondence schools that send materials by mail. However, in a few states, the state educational systems are beginning to provide teaching staff and accreditation for prison classes and grant diplomas to prisoners that, sensitively, do not identify the place of instruction.

BASIC EDUCATION

Before many offenders can be trained for employment they must have additional academic education. Existing vocational training programs tend to select the relatively more qualified prisoners, leaving others with no possibility of job training. According to a chaplain at Chicago's Cook County Jail:

For years we have known that the average man we talk to in Cook County . . . Jail has about a fourth-grade education level.

70. Ostro, "Why U.S. Prisons Are Failing," *The National Catholic Reporter*, Aug. 27, 1969, at 1, 2.

The question was always there—how can anyone expect these men to adjust to society and hold a job? Some can't even fill out a job application and others fear jobs because they believe they're destined to failure before they start.[71]

"Basic education" is generally considered to mean education through the high-school level. Federal funds available in the last decade to supplement the education of economically deprived children and adults can be used to support education in correctional institutions. Institutions for neglected or delinquent children are eligible for federal aid under the Elementary and Secondary Education Act of 1965.[72] It is more difficult to obtain federal grants to support adult education in prisons; only 1/2,000 ($1.5 million of the $2 billion) of the Elementary and Secondary Education Act budget has been allocated for this purpose. However, the University of Hawaii recently received a special grant from the Office of Education under the Adult Education Act of 1966[73] to formulate goals for the field of adult basic education in correctional institutions.

In recent years significant innovations have been made in educational programs in juvenile institutions. Experiments with the use of individualized instruction and behavioral motivational techniques to help students to learn occasionally have put juvenile institutions ahead of the public schools in their educational programs. On the other hand, our visits to adult prisons where rewards are offered for successful completion of courses of study have indicated that these institutions have a long way to go toward adapting academic programs in such a way as to make them relevant to offenders' life experiences and styles.

One promising development has been in the use of programmed learning devices, which permit pupils to proceed at their own pace, obviate the need for performing before classmates and build a continual series of small academic successes into learning experiences. Teaching machines have been found particularly appropriate for the ages and skill levels that are found in prisons. Such machines for use in all federal prisons currently are being manufactured at the Lompoc Federal Correctional Institution in California.

Programmed instruction, together with individual tutoring by teachers and outside volunteers, recently have been used to provide basic

71. Erwin, "Cook County Jail's Short-Term Education Program," *American Journal of Correction* (March–April 1970), at 14.
72. 20 U.S.C. §241(c)(2).
73. 20 U.S.C. §1208.

education at different types of prisons. PACE (Programmed Activities for Correctional Education) was begun at the Draper, Alabama, Youth Center as part of a manpower training program to provide youths with vocational skills. The occupational training included basic and remedial education because many trainees were found to be such poor readers that they could not understand written instructions. Several of the participants resisted remedial education until they became convinced that it was necessary for success in the vocational program.

At Draper, programmed instructional materials were devised to provide the education necessary for participation in vocational training. Inmates who progressed well were enlisted to help other youths learn and all the students participated in developing a special educational program for their young offenders. Several students from nearby Auburn University volunteered to work with the inmates in the institution, and a few inmates who completed the high-school curriculum were released to attend classes at the university.

Officials at the Cook County (Chicago) Jail visited Draper and were so impressed with its educational program that they adapted it for a short-term program for jail inmates (who are there for relatively short periods). Representatives of private manufacturers of teaching aids and the Psychology Department of Illinois Institute of Technology joined with the jail officials to incorporate PACE as a private, non-profit organization in 1967. With privately donated equipment and college student volunteers, PACE began to operate an educational program for jail inmates, most of whom could neither read nor write. At the end of seven weeks, sixteen inmates had raised their language and arithmetic abilities an average of one and one half grade levels. Counseling and job placement were added to the elementary instruction, and the program expanded to include three full-time instructors as well as part-time tutors and volunteers. Up to this stage the entire program had been operated and financed locally. However, its over-all success rate, together with individual success stories (some inmates asked to stay in jail in order to complete courses; an alcoholic who had never worked acquired a steady job; several inmates learned to read for the first time), prompted the U.S. Department of Labor's Manpower Administration to finance expansion of the program to include vocational training as well as basic education. Recently Reverend John Erwin, the jail's chaplain, convinced local business firms to donate enough funds and equipment to provide a new building for the program.

Another basic education program for jail inmates was organized by volunteers in Westchester County, New York. Working through a county committee of the National Council on Crime and Delinquency, a small group of middle-class women organized a literacy project in the Westchester County Penitentiary that attracted enough attention to convince the state Department of Education to assume responsibility for its operation and extend the program to six other New York county jails. The program, which also uses self-teaching devices but places great emphasis on personal encouragement of the students by teachers and volunteers, began when volunteers working in the jail discovered that "in many cases the prisoner's illiteracy was a principal reason why he was in trouble. He was so tuned out of the society around him, it was almost automatic that he'd break the law."[74]

The Teacher Corps, sponsored by the United States Office of Education, began a different kind of educational program at the New York City Reformatory on Rikers Island in 1968. The primary objective of the program was to help jail inmates obtain a high-school diploma. Although this objective proved impossible in some cases, due to the inadequate educational background of the inmates, thirty-one inmates out of an enrollment of about 100 actually passed a high-school equivalency test during the year that the program was in operation. Considering the low level of proficiency at which many of the inmates started the course, an evaluation of the project by New York's Vera Institute of Justice considered this a success. In addition, more than ten of the inmates were placed in college programs on their release, and several others continued their education in street academies.

Fifteen Teacher Corps interns (including several women) received special training for their jobs at the New York University School of Education. However, they found it necessary to develop their own curriculum as they went along. Classes studied the Black Power movement, films and the operation of automobiles.

In many cases the interns maintained contacts with their students after they were released from prison. The teachers got along well with prison personnel; the Vera evaluators noticed a great deal of cooperation between the interns and the prison administrators in carrying out the educational program. But perhaps the most significant accomplishment of the program was its improvement of the self-image of many of the stu-

74. Rogers, "Why Do These Women Go to Jail? *Parade* magazine, November 2, 1969, at 124.

dents, who came to see themselves as potentially productive people. According to the evaluation:

> The vast majority of inmates at the Reformatory are blacks and Puerto Ricans from economically deprived areas of New York who have been subject to the concentration of destructive forces at work in the urban slum. Generally they are youngsters who have never been interested in education because it has not been relevant to their life-style. . . .
>
> The Teacher Corps program was exciting because it succeeded in reversing the attitude of cynicism and hopelessness pervading these prisoners and in giving inmates some positive sense of expectation about what they could accomplish with their lives. . . .
>
> . . . the inmates' enthusiasm for the program was a result of several factors. The interns and inmates were of the same generation and thus shared many values common to young people which cut across social and economic values. The curriculum included topics that were relevant to the problems of Negroes and Puerto Ricans in an urban environment. Also because the ratio of teachers to students was low, about 1 to 6, interns were able to devote a significant amount of time to private tutoring, which allowed inmates to move at their own pace.[75]

In conjunction with the Teacher Corps program, twenty-five volunteers from the United States Office of Economic Opportunity's VISTA (Volunteers In Service To America) program worked with the same inmate-students six to eight weeks before their release in an effort to provide a link to community services. When the inmates were released, the VISTA volunteers remained in contact with those of them who wished.

The VISTA project showed fewer tangible successes than the Teacher Corps classes, partially because of faulty organization unrelated to the merits of the program and partly because of the lack of community resources the volunteers were able to enlist to serve released prisoners. For example, in most cases the jobs in which the VISTA volunteers could place returning inmates were unskilled and low-paying, with little possibility of advancement. Many of the releasees were narcotics addicts, and VISTA discovered that rehabilitation services for them generally had long

75. Vera Institute of Justice, Final Report, Teacher Corps—VISTA—New York City Department of Correction 7–8 (1969).

waiting lists that precluded quick treatment. However, VISTA was successful enough to convince the Vera evaluators to recommend continuation of a better-organized program of this type.

> In many instances VISTA's developed excellent relationships with their charges and gained their confidence. Ex-inmates in the community were willing to come to their VISTA's and frankly discuss personal, family and drug problems. . . . [T]hey were perhaps most effective in working with those ex-inmates interested in furthering their education. They helped at least 10 ex-inmates to gain admission to college, programs such as SEEK, and various street academy prep schools.[76]

Other programs involving Teacher Corps interns in correction currently are under way in Georgia, Connecticut, Oregon and California. However, Office of Education personnel have found it difficult to interest schools of education in training teachers for correctional work. It appears that most teachers would prefer to work with juveniles in the community before their problems become serious enough to land them in prison.

The Vera Report recommended that academic courses to train teachers be tailored to the special problems of teaching in a prison. A recent report to the Office of Education concerning the Teacher Corps urged that the interns do more to provide improved education for young offenders in correctional institutions. The report noted that "despite a correctional population that now exceeds 300,000 an education curriculum designed specifically for the need of inmates is unknown in most institutions." It appears to us that along with the development of special curricula for correctional inmates it is urgent to devise ways to bring more teachers and volunteers from the community into correctional institutions. Where this has been done, particularly in juvenile institutions, interesting and flexible programs often followed.

In some cases, the problem of motivating people to learn may be solved more easily in prisons than on the outside. Considering the lack of diversions, it should not be difficult to devise ways to make prisoners want to go to school. In Texas the state's fourteen prisons are organized into a formal public-school district, and teachers must be certified public schoolteachers. More than 6,000 prisoners (about half the total inmate population) regularly attend classes from the first grade through junior college.

76. *Ibid.* 28 (1969).

In addition to offering one of the most comprehensive educational programs for prisoners, Texas officials have taken steps to encourage inmates
to enroll in school.

All entering inmates are given a standardized test. Those who score
below the fifth grade are required to attend school for at least six hours
each week. (Approximately 18 percent have been found unable to read
or write. Less than 2 percent have graduated from high school.) Other
prisoners who qualify through a point-incentive plan based on conduct
are permitted to go to school instead of work. If they lose points, they are
returned to a work detail until they earn enough points to re-enter school.
Education frequently appears an attractive alternative to working in hot
fields picking cotton or corn or in prison industries manufacturing brooms
and soap.

Several studies of recidivism of released prisoners show some slight
advantage for those who attend educational classes in prison.[77] Glaser's
study indicated that the longer an inmate remained in educational classes,
the better his chance for successful completion of parole. Although little
research has been conducted in this area, the few findings support the
impression that encouraging prison inmates to obtain basic education will
help them to refrain from crime on their release.

COLLEGE PROGRAMS

For the prisoners who have completed high school (approximately
12½ percent, according to a recent survey) college courses by correspondence have been available generally since the 1930s. More recently,
some prisoners have been able to attend classes conducted in prisons by
the extension divisions of nearby colleges or universities. A few systems
have begun to permit selected inmates to leave the prison to attend college by day.

A survey conducted in late 1967, to which forty-nine state correctional systems responded, disclosed that thirty-one states cooperated with
colleges and universities in providing correspondence courses to inmates;
twenty states had some live college instruction; three states offered col-

---

77. See Glaser, "The Effectiveness of a Prison and Parole System" 274–275 (1964);
Zink, "A Study of the Effect of Prison Education on Societal Adjustment" (1962);
Saden, "Correctional Research at Jackson Prison," 15 *Journal of Correctional Education* 22 (1962); Fenton, "Adult Education in the California Prison System," *Journal
of Correctional Education* (July–Oct. 1950), at 68; Schnur, "The Educational Treatment of Prisoners and Recidivism," 54 *American Journal of Sociology* 142 (1948).

lege credits through instruction by television; and four states used "college furloughs" through which students were bussed to classes by day and returned to prisons at night. The number of prisoners participating in each state ranged from one to 615 in state extension programs, from one to 129 in correspondence courses, up to seventy-eight in TV study programs and from one to seven in college furlough programs.[78]

A more recent survey conducted in 1970 revealed that approximately 121 community and junior colleges in the United States offer courses for a total of almost 7,000 prison inmates. In ninety-three of the 100 colleges that responded to the survey, instruction is live, with sixty-eight conducting classes in the prisons, seventeen conducting classes at both the prison and the college and fifteen conducting classes solely at the college. Participating prisoners are able to earn degrees (generally a two-year associate in arts or science) in only slightly more than one-third of the programs. The colleges reported awarding a total of 492 degrees since their programs began. Most of the programs are supported through college budgets, with correction departments supporting others. Most of the programs surveyed are quite new; the two oldest have been in existence for nine years, and 85 percent are less than five years old.

According to the survey, the most comprehensive arrangement between a correction department and local colleges exists in North Carolina, where about one-third of the total number of colleges offering courses to prison inmates are located. The participating colleges include community colleges, technical institutes and industrial education centers, which sponsor instruction in sixty-seven of North Carolina's seventy-two prison units for a total of nearly 1,600 inmates.

One of the first prison college programs to lead to a two-year college degree was begun at the San Quentin Prison in California in 1966, through the joint efforts of the Department of Correction and the University of California. Although the project, originally funded by the Ford Foundation, began as an effort to "research and develop a new and important departure in correctional rehabilitation through the creation of an accredited four-year college program within a correctional system," it actually developed into a two-year program, offering Associate of Arts degrees in behavioral science, general, technical and vocational education, liberal arts, English and social science.

In the first five college terms of the program, 185 inmates enrolled in

78. Adams, *College-Level Instruction in U.S. Prisons: An Exploratory Survey* (1968).

the project. Participating inmates were of "average" or "high average" intelligence. The typical student had achieved a tenth- or eleventh-grade level when he entered prison but had completed his high-school education in prison by the time he entered the college project. According to one of the students in the first college class:

> There were about 26 men in that first class. Most were very intelligent and had a deep interest in a college education. It wasn't long before the class members had formed a definite group concept and were beginning to act and talk like college students. The prison yard began to feel like a campus. . . . Fearful of not living up to college standards of excellence, many of us became over-achievers.
>
> Speakers, experts in their fields, were brought in from various campuses and academically oriented organizations. . . . The learning process was being stimulated from every conceivable angle, and its effects could be seen in the quantity and quality of term papers being written by the inmates involved in the program. Two that I know of have been accepted for publication; others I have read I am sure are publishable.[79]

An evaluation of the San Quentin project after two years concluded that it should be continued and expanded:

> . . . the San Quentin Prison College Project has demonstrated that a meaningful program of higher education can be carried on in the harsh and often turbulent setting of a major prison. Analysis of the characteristics of the student body over five semesters of instruction suggests that significant numbers of inmates (possibly up to 25 percent of the institutional population) might eventually be involved in a comprehensive educational program, given sufficient attention to the educational interests of inmates and suitable pre-college preparation and orientation.
>
> The Project demonstrated that when prison inmates without prior experience in college-level instruction are brought into lower division courses, they perform as well as, or better than students who enroll in the same courses in the outside community. It also demonstrated that not only effective learning but also significant research and writing can occur within a prison college program.

79. Walter, "What the San Quentin Prison College Means to Me," Appendix to Adams, "The San Quentin Prison College Project: Final Report, Phase I" 44–45 (1968).

There were relatively clear indications that the college program provided a stimulus to the expansion and acceleration of other educational activities at San Quentin, particularly those at the high school level.[80]

More recently, the United States Office of Economic Opportunity undertook Project NewGate, an experimental educational program in state prisons in Oregon, Minnesota, Pennsylvania, New Mexico and a federal youth center in Kentucky. NewGate combines college-level instruction in prison with special counseling for participants and aid in continuing their education when they are released. Based on a project developed at the Oregon State Penitentiary in cooperation with the Oregon State System of Higher Education, the project includes in-prison liberal-arts courses, special classes on necessary study skills and group-counseling sessions both for the in-prison inmate-students and for newly released participants. NewGate students take frequent field trips and attend lectures by members of the academic community. When they are released from prison, the project often arranges for their housing, clothing and miscellaneous living expenses until they are employed or return to school. When students continue their college education (most do), they are helped to obtain financial aid and part-time jobs.

NewGate is still a very small program. The Oregon project, the oldest, has thirty-three men and fifteen women students attending classes inside prison and thirty-seven men and twenty-five women attending college classes in the community. (The inclusion of women in prison college programs is extremely unusual.) In the other four state's programs, a total of twenty-eight students have been released to the community. All are still out, and all but two (who have jobs) are in school. Because NewGate students live in separate minimum-security quarters in prison and most of their activities are undertaken as a group, the program is considered elitist by some prisoners.

Despite the growing number of prison college programs, the actual number of inmates participating remains quite small. For example, out of more than 20,000 federal prison inmates, an educational specialist for the Bureau of Prisons reports that fewer than 200 are participating in any sort of higher-education program, including correspondence courses. Yet Andress Taylor, director of the prison college program at the Federal City College in Washington, D.C., feels that the influence of the program ex-

80. Adams, "The San Quentin Prison College Project: Final Report, Phase I" 72 (1968).

tends far beyond the number of inmates who actually participate. According to him, a prison college project has the potential of restoring to the black community some of its brightest, most talented people. "[A]ll over the country, the prisons contain our aggressive, black leadership. The idea of the Lorton project is to rescue these men and restore them to the black community."

The Lorton–Federal City College project began in the District of Columbia in 1969 with funds provided by a local foundation and the District of Columbia Department of Vocational Rehabilitation. Freshman courses in sociology, mathematics and English were offered in two prisons, one for youths and one for adults, for regular credit at Federal City College. The number of enrollees began with fifteen prisoners from each facility, each taking three courses, but rose rapidly when the project began to permit inmates to enroll in single courses. During the second year, approximately 130 prisoners attended courses given by Federal City College instructors inside the prison. Another fifteen students, all sophomores, were bussed daily from Lorton to attend classes at the college. Forty men who began their studies in prison were paroled to continue their work as regular Federal City College students. Several student parolees have been hired by the United States Department of Health, Education and Welfare, which has paid the tuition for some to continue their studies at night.

According to one experienced official, intellectually able prisoners often find college courses "such a welcome diversion from the stultifying environment of prison life that they outperform students on the outside." A review of the Federal City College project's first two terms confirms this observation. Specifically, an evaluation by the Department of Correction found that prisoners' grades were mostly A's and B's; instructors observed that prison college students performed better than the students they taught at Federal City College; of fifty-six parolees from the prison college, 80 percent had enrolled as regular Federal City College students; and only three of the parolees (slightly more than 5 percent) had violated parole and been returned to the prison.[81]

The trend toward offering beginning college courses in prison and preparing as many prisoners as possible to take advantage of them is extremely promising. But there always will be serious limitations on the number and variety of courses that can be offered inside prisons. Conse-

81. The D.C. Prison College Project: An Interim Report (District of Columbia Department of Correction Research Report No. 28, July 1970).

quently, it is important for programs to include college furloughs and help parolees to enroll as regular students. Despite the limited number of students involved to date, prison college programs offer optimistic signs of what some prisoners can achieve if given the opportunity.

The success of existing programs for both basic and higher education raises the possibility of sentencing some offenders to compulsory education, preferably in the community in conjunction with halfway-house programs. This pattern already has been established with regard to work release, and, in fact, the Federal City College program plans to establish a special halfway house for its students.

WORK

For more than a century after the inauguration of the factory system at Auburn in 1823, imprisonment at "hard labor" was a reality in the United States. Prisoners worked primarily for the profit of private employers, under two principal arrangements. Under the lease system, used mostly in the South, states contracted with private employers, who took over entire prisons, paying for the prisoners' food and custody in return for their labor. For example, in 1825 the Kentucky legislature leased the state prison to a "keeper" (private employer) for $1,000 per year. By 1932 the keeper had made a net profit of more than $80,000, which was divided equally with the state. Under the contract system, on the other hand, the state retained responsibility for prisoners' custody and upkeep but sold their labor for a fixed price to private contractors, who provided the machines and materials and supervised their work. Prison-made products were sold on the open market in competition with goods made by free labor.

During the late nineteenth century, representatives of industry, labor and private organizations began to criticize the contract and lease systems as an exploitation of the prisoners and unfair competition with private industry. In 1883 Congress enacted a statute limiting the number of prisoners who could work in any one industry, and in 1905 President Theodore Roosevelt issued an order prohibiting federal agencies from contracting for the use of state prison labor. By 1929 seventeen states had passed laws making the contract system illegal, and sixteen other states required that prison-made goods be specially labeled, thus giving them an unappealing stigma.

In 1929 Congress enacted the Hawes-Cooper Act, which permitted states that prohibited the sale of goods made in local prisons to bar the importation of prison-made goods from other states without such restrictions despite the usual rule that forbids local interference with interstate commerce. Although subsequent commentaries generally attribute the motive for this legislation to the need for alleviating the labor surplus generated by the Depression, in fact the legislation was introduced in 1928 and signed into law before the stock-market crash. The legislative history of the Hawes-Cooper Act indicates that other motives seem more likely. The chief sponsors of the act were manufacturing interests protecting their markets, supported by labor unions worried about unfair competition and the General Federation of Women's Clubs, which was concerned with the abuses of contract labor. The only organized opposition to the measure came from prison wardens, who feared that the legislation would lead to unemployment and idleness among state prisoners. The opposition succeeded only in having the effective date of the law extended until 1934. In 1935, the Ashurst-Summers Act added a penalty for violating the law by making it a federal offense to transport prison-made goods into any state where they had been outlawed.[82]

In quick succession, most of the states passed legislation restricting or prohibiting the use of prison labor to manufacture goods in competition with private industry. As a result, state prison industries, which in 1932 had employed more than 77,000 prisoners and produced goods valued at more than $71 million, in 1936 and 1937 employed only 25,000 prisoners, who produced only $20 million worth of goods annually. According to James Bennett, then director of the federal Bureau of Prisons:

> . . . the depression had struck a terrible blow to our hopes and aspirations. While some thirty per cent of our countrymen were out of work, more than eighty per cent of our prisoners had been deprived of any form of constructive, industrial occupation. Some of the more ingenious wardens were devising new ways of keeping their men busy. One warden put a man to work maintaining an electric motor that needed a drop of oil a day. Another assigned a prisoner to keeping salt shakers in straight lines down the rows of tables in the mess hall.[83]

In an effort to find some useful work for prisoners after prison-made goods were barred from sale on the open market, state and federal gov-

82. 18 U.S.C. §§1761–1762.
83. Bennett, *I Chose Prison* 87–88 (1970).

ernments turned to the "state-use" system, which permitted prisons to produce products for sale only to government agencies.

Massachusetts had established a modified state-use system in 1887, through an administrative ruling that prison goods should be sold to state and county institutions so far as possible; in 1898 these institutions were required to purchase from the prisons wherever feasible. Beginning in the 1930s, other state legislatures passed laws permitting, and in some cases requiring, government agencies to purchase from local prisons. State-operated prison industries began to produce office furnishings and supplies, institutional clothing, automobile license plates and road signs for use by the prisons themselves and by other agencies.

By taking advantage of their unique status of dependence by paying prisoners no more than a few cents a day, state governments were able to obtain products inexpensively at the same time that they solved the prison labor problem. However, the reluctance of state legislatures to invest in capital equipment because prisons had a surplus of cheap labor ensured that prisoners would work at outmoded machinery in inefficient ways and that the skills they acquired in prison would be little related to demands made of employees by private industries outside prison. The whole practice was at best a marking-time for the prisoners; more often it was a waste of time and no help in their rehabilitation.

To cite a few illustrative examples, the San Quentin Prison in California operates a cotton mill that, according to former prison employees, is the only one in the state—and thus hardly good preparation for future jobs. The irrelevance of prison labor to the world of work is not restricted to California. Recently a New York judge, on questioning a fugitive about his failure to rehabilitate himself during his imprisonment in New York's Green Haven Prison, asked whether he had been taught a trade. The defendant replied: "I was learning textile weaving, but there isn't a textile mill in the state of New York, Your Honor."[84] At a conference on crime and correction we attended in Maryland, a prisoner (a talented guitarist) interrupted a speaker who was pontificating about rehabilitation by demanding:

> What does rehabilitation mean? I came in a laborer and I will go out a laborer. They taught me to make tags, but where else can I go to make tags? I got news for you, baby. In six months you'll have me back makin' those tags!

84. Jiudice, "State Prison and the 'Free' Community," 41 New York State Bar Journal 672, 673 (1969).

Even the limited potential of the state-use market has not been realized. The President's Crime Commission found that:

> Hardly any State colleges and universities make an appreciable portion of their purchases from State prisons and there are also few sales by prisons to local school systems. In most States there also has been little utilization of the municipality markets. . . .
> Several factors have limited access of prisons to State-use markets. Political . . . pressures are effective despite a model law enacted in many States which makes it an offense punishable by fine or incarceration for a State purchasing official to procure goods from the private market without first assuring that it [sic] cannot be provided by prison industries. . . . In many cases the prison-made goods are inferior in design and workmanship to those available from private firms; their delivery has been unreliable; and, despite the availability of cheap prison labor, the State still may charge more than the price of the products on the open market. The limited market and lack of a trained labor force result in small, inefficient industrial operations . . . the use of industries for vocational training . . . is hampered by the fact that equipment is often outdated and methods heavily colored by the excess of manpower for any given task and the overriding concern with security and surveillance.[85]

The alternative to unrealistic work for little or no pay is make-work or no work at all. One who visits prisons commonly sees prisoners lying on their beds, mulling about courtyards, lifting bar bells and passing the time with other forms of indolence. Prisoners who are not assigned to prison industries are put to work keeping the institution clean. Thus most employment in prison is simple housekeeping: The maintenance of the institution overcomes the purposes of its existence. When we visited the federal penitentiary in Atlanta we discovered that half the prisoners worked in a textile mill making mail bags; the other half devoted their working hours to maintaining the institution. According to a letter we received from one inmate, "The institution is now in the ludicrous position of offering valuable training to arm convicts for jobs in a highly competitive society: plunging johns, mopping floors, mowing grass. The truth is, most time is wasted."

Some prison officials have told us that having prisoners work in fac-

85. The President's Commission on Law Enforcement and Administration of Justice, Task Force Report: *Correction* 55 (1967).

tories manufacturing products that are made nowhere else or putting city prisoners on farms to do agricultural labor is useful in forming work habits that will carry over into employment on the outside. However, an official of the Bureau of Prisons has questioned "whether the habits formed in a tightly structured and tightly supervised security situation have any carry-over value to *civilian* work habits." The same official points out that even the training opportunities present in institutional maintenance, kitchen or landscaping work are wasted.

> It is not uncommon for an inmate to spend years in institutional "construction" and "maintenance" work without really learning to be a construction worker with sufficient skills to acquire employment upon release.[86]

Industries in federal prisons followed a slightly different course from those in the states. When the Bureau of Prisons was organized and authorized to operate prison industries, in 1930, a statutory clause required all federal agencies to purchase the products they needed from federal prisons at current market prices whenever they were available and met their requirements. During the Depression, however, an amendment to an appropriations bill for the Bureau of Prisons denied funds for the production of office furniture and brushes for sale to government agencies. In order to counteract the effect of the amendment, the Bureau of Prisons proposed that a new government corporation, to be managed by representatives of business and labor as well as by the Bureau of Prisons, be created to operate prison industries. Since the corporation would have its own funds, it would not need Congregressional approval each time it wished to manufacture a product. Through the intervention of President and Mrs. Franklin D. Roosevelt, trade-union leaders were persuaded not to oppose the new corporation. Federal Prison Industries, Inc., was organized in 1937 and still continues to operate factories in federal prisons.

Since the federal government purchases a greater number and variety of products than any state, Federal Prison Industries has been more extensive than its state counterparts. According to James Bennett, who also was the first Commissioner of Prison Industries, Federal Prison Industries provide inmates with valuable skills as well as producing dividends for the government:

86. McCollum, "Education and Training of Youthful Offenders," in *Princeton University Manpower Symposium, The Transition from School to Work* 108, 113–14 (1968).

. . . in 1964, the year of my retirement, sales reached nearly forty million dollars, with four million dollars paid into the U.S. Treasury in dividends and additional profits earmarked for more vocational training. Prisoners could earn as much as seventy-five dollars per month free and clear. They were learning useful trades that would help them after their release, were gaining in self-confidence, and were absorbing their prison experience. Outside the prisons, according to our records, the men who had learned good work habits in the industry and accumulated sizable savings were far less likely to become recidivists than those who did not cooperate in the program.

On the other hand, an inmate of the Atlanta Penitentiary has written to us:

Rehabilitation is impossible when the penitentiary is geared to the manufacturing of goods. . . . For example, at the prison factory at Atlanta, 1200 to 1500 men are employed in the manufacture of mail bags and other products used by the federal government. The total population of the prison is approximately 2200 men. This means that there is no Work-Release Program at Atlanta and no opportunities for parole or honest correction; since most of the population is needed in the prison sweat shop. . . . If a convict . . . manages to rehabilitate himself while sewing up mail bags, he would probably not succeed due to the failure of the prison to prepare him for release. . . . [T]he only science the Bureau of Prisons has mastered is the art of making mail bags, homosexuals and future enemies of society.

Two recent studies determined that only about one-fourth of those released from federal prisons obtained jobs that were related in any way to the actual employment or even the work training they had received while in prison. At that, most of the related jobs were in the unskilled category. According to one of the surveys:

[I]n about one-tenth of inmate postrelease jobs there are benefits from new learning acquired in prison work, in about three or four percent of these jobs there are benefits from the preservation of old skills through practice in prison, and in about five or six per cent of the postrelease jobs the prison provided useful physical or psychological conditioning.[87]

87. Glaser, *The Effectiveness of a Prison and Parole System* 252 (1964); *see* federal Bureau of Prisons "Pre-Release Guidance Center" Study 7 (1965).

The report of the 1970 President's Task Force on Prisoner Rehabilitation recommended that the annual dividend from prison industries to the United States Treasury, which amounted to $5 million in 1969, be earmarked for prisoner rehabilitation, with special emphasis on job and job-training programs.

A variety of proposals has been made to make the work experience of prisoners more relevant to the outside work world. As former Secretary of Labor George P. Shultz recognized in a speech to business leaders in 1969:

> This means more than simply following the pattern of "train-- ing" offered by the prison industries in some present United States Training and Employment Service projects such as stamping license plates, making shoes and mail bags, and then referring the prisoner to the nearest Employment Service office.

One of the simplest innovations would be to pay all prisoners wages at the prevailing civilian rate. The failure to pay prisoners fair wages for their work frequently forces their dependents to turn to public assistance and leaves inmates without financial resources when they are released. The resulting welfare state that exists in all prisons relieves the inmates from the responsibilty of supporting themselves and their families and removes the incentive to work. As a result an unofficial barter system in prisons, in which cigarettes or favors provide the medium of exchange, replaces the role of wages on the outside. According to one account:

> Inmates generally feel that the fact that they are paid less than comparable civilian workers entitles them to produce less.
> The total result of the prevalence of these attitudes has been to reduce "imprisonment at hard labor" to a euphemism existing chiefly in the rhetoric of sentencing judges and in the minds of the uninformed public. The inmate social system not only has succeeded in neutralizing the laboriousness of prison labor in fact, but also has more or less succeeded in convincing prison authorities of the futility of expecting any improvement in output.[88]

The payment of regular wages would enable prisoners to pay taxes, to reimburse the state for their room and board and to support their depend-

88. McCorkle and Korn, "Resocialization Within Walls," 293 *Annals of the American Academy of Political and Social Science* 91–92 (1954).

ents. In addition, permitting prisoners to unionize and bargain collectively for rates of pay and working conditions would make conditions of prison work more like those in private industry. An end to the exploitation of prison labor probably would lead to the introduction of more modern, labor-saving equipment in prison industries and might even help to end the rationale of unfair competition that bars prison-made goods from the open market.

A good example of the workability of private enterprise within a correctional system is seen in the Swedish experience. In Sweden, long noted for progressive steps in its correctional programs, the accent during the past decades has been on labor. And steps have been successfully adopted to introduce prison labor into the civilian market. We visited, for example, an open prison institution, Tilberge, which operated a lumber mill producing prefabricated wood houses. Workers receive civilian wages, half of which must be saved; the men pay for their food and lodging and their taxes.

Some interesting innovations recently have been proposed in this country to increase the involvement of private industries and labor unions in operating training programs. Several California institutions for youthful offenders have organized Trade Advisory Committees, composed of local business and labor leaders, who advise shop instructors on the content and methods of vocational-training programs and current trends in the various trades, as well as help refer trained inmates to jobs when they are released on parole.

A more far-reaching change was proposed recently to the California legislature. A study[89] of the value and success of work programs in California prisons pointed out that even this state system, known as one of the country's most progressive, is a failure by economic, rehabilitative and training standards. The study found what has been the case typically throughout American correctional institutions under state correctional industries programs:

1. "Employment" in reality was little more than "idleness"; most inmates were not gainfully employed; those who were employed were paid between $.02 and $.35 per hour.
2. Few valuable work habits or skills are learned; jobs were menial or blue-collar at best.

89. California Assembly Office of Research, Report on the Economic Status and Rehabilitative Value of California Correctional Industries (1969).

3. Job performance was poor and could not compare with private enterprise.
4. Recidivism rates were not improved—they were higher (55 percent) among employed prisoners than unemployed prisoners (51 percent).
5. Later employment success was not improved.
6. Men worked with old equipment at archaic jobs; they were neither well trained nor productive.
7. Even the best-motivated prisoners could do no work that would increase their job opportunities on release.
8. At that, costs to the state were high.
9. Private businesses resented the competition of government production with cheap prison labor.

With the aid of business, labor and government experts, a plan was proposed to phase out the state correctional industries program and to evolve privately operated programs instead. With government initially providing tax incentives and job-training subsidies, the correction department providing manpower, custodial and security assistance and plant facilities, private business would provide machines, training and the expectation of future employment opportunities. Legislation was proposed to revamp the state's correction system radically—but most sensibly. Under the aegis of a Correctional Opportunities Employment Board, men in prisons would apply for jobs, work for civilian wages and benefits, support their dependents and pay the state for their room and board and taxes (costs to the state now average $8.94 per day per inmate). Prison industries would be operated as branches of private business. Products would be sold on the open market, the only differences between the prison factories and other branches of the employer's business being the location of the source of labor.

The California legislature so far has failed to enact these interesting recommendations into law. In the District of Columbia, however, correctional officers are attempting to persuade several profit-making industries to set up branch factories in the city's prisons, along the lines suggested by the California plan. The factories would be staffed almost entirely by prison inmates, who would be paid the same wages as workers on the outside. The prison would provide sufficient academic and technical training for the inmates before they were hired. The Correction Department, which is working on the plan in conjunction with the local Urban Coalition, sees the branch-factory idea as a way of enabling prisoners to learn marketable skills, support their families and establish a link with a firm that might hire them as regular workers on their release. Discussions have been held with surrounding states with a view toward establishing a region-wide program to market the products of prison factories.

The present President's Task Force on Prisoner Rehabilitation recommended that a national agency, consisting of representatives of industry, labor, voluntary agencies and the public, be established to stimulate the adoption of local programs for the training and employment of offenders, initiating programs and turning them over to private industry and correctional authorities.

FEDERAL TRAINING PROGRAMS

In addition to the reforms that would make prison industries more relevant to outside work, a few programs are attempting to change the emphasis of prison work from the production of goods to providing vocational training that will enable inmates to obtain employment on their release. Federal government agencies not previously involved in correction have begun to apply to offenders some of the training methods that have been used successfully to train other members of the labor force who are physically, socially or economically handicapped. As yet there has emerged no coordinated policy among the federal agencies involved (primarily the Departments of Labor, Justice and Health, Education and Welfare and the Office of Economic Opportunity), but a series of programs originally designed for other groups have been applied experimentally to offenders.

Since the enactment of the Manpower Development and Training Act of 1962, the U.S. Department of Labor has been heavily involved in training disadvantaged members of the labor force. Beginning in 1964, the Department's Manpower Administration funded four experimental manpower-training programs in Alabama, New York, South Carolina and the District of Columbia, designed to determine whether its job-training programs could be carried out in prisons.

The first project, which included both vocational training and basic education, was instituted at the Draper Institution, near Montgomery, Alabama, a reformatory for youthful offenders. Before the program began, most of the approximately 600 inmates, who ranged in age from sixteen to twenty-five years and had an average of six years of formal education, worked on the institution's 2,000-acre farm raising cotton, wheat, sugar cane and vegetables. The four-year demonstration project enrolled a total of 392 inmates in courses taught by craftsmen to prepare them for entry-level jobs such as auto mechanics, service-station attendants, barbers, bricklayers, appliance repairmen, welders and sign painters.

The project placed released inmates in jobs with 230 employers, helped them obtain employment bonds and furnished money for tools and other expenses until they received their first pay check. In addition, counselors working in the program found that they had to deal with the men's personal problems, which often were aggravated by their imprisonment. For example, prisoners were helped to communicate with their families and with agencies that could help them (such as obtaining Social Security cards and driver's licenses). A community sponsorship program sought to involve private individuals and service groups such as Junior Chambers of Commerce in aiding the inmates when they were released.

Of the 392 men enrolled in the Draper program, 331 completed the training program. Fifty-seven waived early parole to complete their training. Of the 290 graduates who were followed up after their release, 276 were placed in jobs, all but thirty-eight at the trade they learned in prison. Among 200 released trainees followed up for a year or more, the rate of repeat offenders dropped to 30 percent; Labor Department officials cite the usual rate of recidivism for Draper releasees as 70 percent.

When the demonstration grant that had funded Draper expired, the institution obtained funding from the Manpower Administration's operating funds for its vocational program and from the United States Office of Education for the basic educational programs that accompany the training. A new facility was built five miles from the prison to house up to 135 men participating in training and educational programs, with no bars, no guns and only two guards. The new facility is expected to train 232 men each year and to bring the costs of training down from $1,100 or $1,200 to below $1,000 for each man trained.

At Rikers Island in New York City, a vocational-training and basic educational program was combined with research to determine whether the additional services would reduce the rate of crimes committed by prisoners after their release. Youths between sixteen and twenty-one years old were divided into two groups. An experimental group of 137 trainees received an eight-week training course on IBM equipment, as well as remedial education and counseling. A control group of 127 men received none of these services. One year after release, the experiences of the two groups were compared. Almost twice as many trainees as control-group members still worked for the same employer, and twice as many of the trainees had been promoted. Forty-eight percent of the trainees had been returned to jail, as compared with 66 percent of the control group. Comparing only those inmates who were considered drug users, 55 percent of those in the training group returned to jail within the year compared to 80 percent in the control group.[90]

After the research project was completed, Rikers Island received a second grant from the Manpower Development Training Administration to give basic training to 240 youths and 120 adults in trades for which there was a current demand in the New York metropolitan area. Prisoners who wished to continue their training after release were paid a training allowance based on the number of their dependents. However, when the second grant expired, the project lapsed from lack of funding.

In 1965, as a result of the success of these early experimental programs, Congress amended the Manpower Development and Training Act to provide that

> [t]he Secretary of Labor shall . . . develop and carry out experimental and demonstration programs of training and education for persons in correctional institutions who are in need thereof to obtain employment upon release. [P]rograms . . . may include vocational education; special job development and placement activities; pre-vocational, basic, and secondary education, and counseling . . . ; supportive and follow up services and other such assistance as is deemed necessary.[91]

Despite the fact that Congress appropriated no special funds to implement the legislation, pilot projects to provide basic-skill training for a total of 4,700 state prisoners have been undertaken so far in forty-seven institutions in twenty-eight states at a total cost of $5.7 million. Training has been provided in thirty-five occupations, with inmates paid an incentive allowance of up to $20 a week to participate. According to former Secretary of Labor George P. Shultz:

> Preliminary findings . . . confirm the feasibility of training under institutional constraints, a high degree of interest by in-

90. Aller, "Lessons Learned from Vocational Training Programs Given in a Prison Setting," in University of Wisconsin Center for Studies in Vocational and Technical Education, *Education and Training in Correctional Institutions* 3, 6 (1968).
91. Manpower Development and Training Act of 1962, §251, 42 U.S.C. §§2571 *et seq.*

mates, and increasing acceptance and cooperation by correctional staff and parole authorities. Supportive services, job-finding assistance, and linkages to the private and voluntary sectors require considerable strengthening, however, if we are to fully benefit from our investment in training.[92]

The Labor Department currently plans to expand its manpower-training program for prisoners and to coordinate its separate pilot projects into a more comprehensive program that will be financed as part of the state's regular manpower-training budgets.

Another division of the Labor Department, the Bureau of Apprenticeship and Training (BAT), has established a different type of training program in fifteen state and four federal prisons. The BAT programs take longer to complete than MDTA training (anywhere from three years and 6,000 hours to five years and 10,000 hours) and prepare prisoners for skilled jobs, such as mechanics, electricians, silk-screen printers and upholsterers. Each program is registered with the Department of Labor and must meet the minimum quality standards of training recommended by the Secretary of Labor.

At each participating institution the BAT program is administered by a Multi-Trades Joint Apprenticeship and Training Committee, consisting of local labor and management representatives from each of the trade areas for which inmates are being trained. In order for a program to be established in an institution, the local labor and management groups represented on the committee must indicate their willingness to place released apprentices in existing local programs to complete their apprenticeships and to employ apprentices who have completed their training as journeymen when opportunities are available. If the trainee desires to move to another part of the country, the committee recommends him to a Joint Apprenticeship and Training Committee in that locality.

Administrators have attempted to select the youngest inmates with the greatest potential for training for the BAT program. To date, those accepted for apprenticeship have been between the ages of seventeen and twenty-six, with enough education and aptitude to satisfy the Apprenticeship and Training Committees that they can complete apprenticeship successfully. Due to the extended nature of the training programs, the BAT program has been instituted only in prisons for felons. Wherever possible,

92. Remarks by former Secretary of Labor George P. Shultz before the Commission on Correctional Facilities and Services of the American Bar Association, Washington, D.C., June 10, 1970.

the completion date of apprenticeship programs is timed to coincide with the prisoners' scheduled date of release.

VOCATIONAL REHABILITATION

Vocational Rehabilitation, a federal program established in 1920 to assist wounded veterans of World War I obtain employment, originally was concerned only with the physically handicapped. Assistance was provided in the form of medical treatment, prosthetic appliances, hospitalization and convalescent care, maintenance (transportation, lunch money, etc.), tools, licenses, counseling and job placement. The federal program currently funds vocational programs and provides basic administrative guidelines. Programs are administered by state vocational rehabilitation agencies.[93]

Traditionally designed to assist the handicapped person to enter or re-enter gainful employment, vocational rehabilitation services tend to be distributed in the following pattern. After being referred, the applicant is medically evaluated to determine if he has a physical or mental disability which can be considered a vocational handicap. Weighing the client's handicap against his vocational potential or aptitude, the counselor develops a rehabilitation plan which may involve a few or all of the regular services. Usually these services are purchased by Vocational Rehabilitation from specialized agencies or individuals and may include surgery or other medical treatment, prosthetic appliances, hospitalization and convalescent care, vocational training and training materials, financial assistance for room, board and transportation and tools, equipment and licenses. Once the plan is activated, the client must adhere to it. If he does not go along with the plan he will be dropped. However, if the client follows each step of the rehabilitation plan and finds employment, the agency considers him "rehabilitated" and ends its services to him.

In 1965 the federal legislation was amended to expand vocational services to include the socially as well as the physically handicapped. Prior to the amendment a few state Vocational Rehabilitation agencies had provided services to prisoners who had physical disabilities. With the expanded definition of disability, prison officials thought that the

93. Initially administered by the Federal Board of Education, the Vocational Rehabilitation program eventually became the responsibility of a division of the Department of Health, Education and Welfare. "Fifty Years of Vocational Rehabilitation in the U.S.A. 1920–1970." U.S. Department of Health, Education and Welfare, Social and Rehabilitation Service, Rehabilitation Services Administration (1970).

kinds of social and emotional problems manifested by criminality were a handicap to acceptable employment and therefore offenders could qualify for vocational-rehabilitation aid services.

As a result of this approach, the Vocational Rehabilitation Administration, the U.S. Bureau of Prisons, the U.S. Probation Service and the U.S. Board of Parole joined forces and designed the Federal Offenders' Rehabilitation Program in April 1965. The purpose of the four-year program was to test the effectiveness of providing intensive vocational rehabilitation services to federal offenders at various stages in the correctional process. To implement the research program, eight satellite projects were organized in Denver, Atlanta, Chicago, Springfield (Illinois), Pittsburgh, Tampa, San Antonio and Seattle.

All federal prisoners, releasees and probationers who lived near one of the project offices were considered eligible for the Federal Offenders' Rehabilitation Program (FOR) if they were between the ages of sixteen and fifty-five and had release dates prior to February 29, 1968. The 2,654 eligible offenders were assigned randomly to experimental and control groups.

Services to offenders varied, depending on the project area. For example, the Georgia Vocational Rehabilitation agency chose to give services to older, less educated offenders, primarily treating them quickly with the purchase of medical services. The Washington agency, on the other hand, served a younger population with more educational achievement and tended to provide the clients with long-term training programs. Other variations existed in terms of the size of the state agency and the employment rate of the city chosen for the FOR program. For example, Tampa had a very high rate of employment, whereas jobs were not very plentiful in San Antonio.

Vocational-rehabilitation services were provided for inmates as well as those released on probation or parole. Institutional programs varied to some extent, depending on the population. At the maximum–medium-security prisons in Atlanta and at McNeil Island, for example, vocational-training programs were conducted in machine shop, welding, masonry, electronics and barbering. In addition, academic courses ranging from basic literacy through college were available. More extensive programs were available, however, at the youth institution at Englewood, including woodworking, auto mechanics and radio and television repair and carpentry.

Training purchased in the community by vocational rehabilitation agencies included welding, auto mechanics and truck driving as well as academic courses leading to white-collar jobs. Some financial assistance was given to offenders enrolled in training programs to cover room, board, transportation and clothing.

In their final report, the FOR program found that while offenders needed services in the vocational and medical areas, their primary needs were for counseling in the area of psychosocial adjustment. The vocational rehabilitation counselors discovered that offenders needed more of their time and involvement than the physically disabled client. The study found that offenders do not resemble the traditional, physically handicapped vocational-rehabilitation clients who are patient and cooperative during the time-consuming evaluation and training process. According to the research director of FOR:

> Given what we know about the nature of the offender client, not many will be able to tolerate the long waiting periods before tangible services are available, and others will find the delayed gratification of [vocational rehabilitation] hard to accept. . . .
>
> [Vocational rehabilitation] has found and will continue to find that, in contrast to its previous clients, the [correctional rehabilitation] client is a rebel. His deviant behavior leads him to push hard for what he wants, to unmask phonies and to be generally irritating. His previously frustrating and degrading experiences with helping agencies have reinforced this pattern. He won't be a silent consumer. . . .[94]

The results of the FOR program revealed no significant differences in either employment or recidivism between the offenders who received intensive vocational rehabilitation services and the control group. Attributing this lack of positive impact partly to unrefined research techniques, the study recommended that vocational rehabilitation continue to be considered as a significant program in rehabilitating offenders, noting that some program changes might enhance effectiveness. Among the changes recommended were providing immediate and tangible services to keep the offender involved until long-range services are available. Since it may be that the offender's lack of motivation and cooperation are in fact his vocational disability, the study suggests that the offender be treated for this behavioral disability rather than rejected because of it.

94. "A Future for Correctional Rehabilitation?" Federal Offenders' Rehabilitation Report 279 (1969) (final report).

Other research and demonstration projects involving vocational-rehabilitation services in state correctional institutions have had slightly more positive results. In Oklahoma, it was concluded that public offenders could be successfully rehabilitated. The staff of the vocational-rehabilitation agency and the state penitentiary designed a demonstration project to provide rehabilitation services to handicapped inmates. The project was to develop methods of evaluating the rehabilitation potential of inmates, integrating the available vocational training into a total vocational rehabilitation program and providing job placement and follow-up. The study noted, however, that results might improve if offenders for the program were selected more carefully. As an example, it was shown that younger offenders had a better chance of being accepted into the project but older inmates had a better chance of being rehabilitated. Similarly, individuals with higher IQs tended to be accepted by the project; yet these individuals were less likely to be rehabilitated successfully. It was suggested that long-term programs were designed for the more intelligent offender and it was difficult for him to continue with the training after release when family pressures for support were dominant. In addition, it was found that, due to heavy caseloads, counselors were unable to provide the long-term counseling and supportive services needed by many of the offenders.

Since the statutory definition of "handicapped person" now may include public offenders, many state agencies have applied to HEW for funds to provide vocational rehabilitation services to offenders. So far, however, there has been little reason to believe that the traditional vocational rehabilitation approach can be successful with large numbers of offenders. Recent studies have shown that the program can rehabilitate some offenders. In order for vocational rehabilitation to have a greater impact, however, those administering the program will have to be creative and flexible rather than relying on the "tried and true methods" of the past with their time-consuming evaluation periods and long-term training programs. Physically handicapped persons and convicted offenders may have nothing in common other than the mutual problem of finding a job. The mere fact that vocational rehabilitation funds are now available for offenders, however, may aid in the development of more successful programs.

Vocational rehabilitation for offenders is a recent innovation. As the agencies begin to deal with offenders on a more regular basis, specialized techniques and new approaches may be created which will solve some of the problems encountered with the traditional vocational rehabilitation program.

EMPLOYMENT

Despite these recent efforts to train prisoners for jobs, finding employment after they are released continues to be the biggest problem facing ex-prisoners. Compounding the problems of inadequate education and training they had before they were convicted, the ex-offenders are branded by their criminal records—the scarlet letter of the twentieth century.

Glaser's study of federal prisoners revealed that during the first month after release only one out of every four was employed at least 80 percent of the time, and three out of ten were unable to find jobs at all. Three months after release, only four out of ten had worked at least 80 percent of the time, and nearly two out of ten still could not find work of any kind. A more recent survey found that in 1964 a national sample of former federal prisoners had an unemployment rate of 17 percent as compared to a 5 percent unemployment rate in the labor force at large and that a smaller proportion of the ex-offenders than of other workers was employed on a full-time basis.[95]

A recent nationwide poll revealed that over 50 percent of private employers said they would hesitate to hire an ex-offender as a salesman or a supervisor; fewer than one-third would hire him as a clerk handling money. A 1966 survey revealed that almost 40 percent of the private firms questioned indicated a reluctance to hire offenders for *any* position. Another 28 percent would hire them for specific jobs only. Even those employers willing to employ former inmates in entry-level jobs sometimes were unwilling to advance them to positions of responsibility.[96] In addition to restrictions imposed by employers, some unions flatly exclude all ex-convicts.

It is possible that the courts may begin to review the automatic use of criminal records as a bar to employment. A federal district court recently ruled that employers may not refuse to hire job applicants solely because of their arrest records. The court noted that in this case there

95. Pownall, "Employment Problems of Released Prisoners: Dimensions and Sociological Implications," in *University of Wisconsin Conference on Education and Training in Correctional Institutions* 63, 69 (1968).
96. Joint Commission on Correctional Manpower and Training, *The Public Looks at Crime and Correction* 14–15 (1968); Aller, "Lessons Learned from Vocational-Training Programs Given in a Prison Setting," in *University of Wisconsin Conference on Education and Training in Correctional Institutions* 3, 10 (1968).

was no evidence that people who have been arrested, even a number of times, but have no convictions perform less efficiently or less honestly than other employees. Since Negroes are arrested substantially more frequently than whites, the court reasoned that any policy disqualifying prospective employees on the basis of arrest records alone, even though applied without regard to race, "discriminates in fact" against Negro applicants and thus violates federal fair-employment provisions. The court stressed that its opinion should not be read to forbid a company to comply with any national-security clearance regulation and specifically declined to consider the extent to which information concerning criminal convictions as opposed to arrests might be considered by prospective employers.[97] However, its rationale might be extended to all cases where ex-offenders are refused employment without regard to the relationship between their crime and their fitness for a particular job.

Federal, state and local governments have an even worse record than private employers in their employment of offenders. Over half the states have a specific policy against employing anyone with a criminal record. Where state and local governments are not barred by statute from hiring ex-offenders, they frequently have no articulated policy on the subject at all and leave the decision to the people who do the hiring, who tend to be conservative in exercising their discretion.

In a recent study of 300 of the largest counties in the United States by the Georgetown University Law Center's Institute of Criminal Law it was found that local government jobs are almost universally closed to ex-convicts. The ex-convict is eliminated at the point of application since the application form requires him to give information regarding his arrest record in 85 percent of the counties surveyed and 75 percent of the cities. During interviews conducted with local officials it was found that most communities had not considered making a special effort to hire ex-convicts. Apathy on the part of local officials and lack of awareness of offenders' special problems appeared to be the reason for closing the employment door to an ex-offender.

One particularly disappointing finding was that only 14 percent of the state and local correctional agencies have ever hired an ex-offender.

The United States Employment Service has also been singularly unsuccessful in finding employment for ex-offenders. In most states ex-offenders receive no special assistance from the state employment agencies. In a few states a special employment counselor works with ex-

---

97. *Gregory v. Litton Systems, Inc.,* S.D. Cal., July 10, 1970, 74 *Labor Relations Reporter* 49 (1970).

offenders, but these individual efforts have not been actively supported by the state agencies. Low-level jobs such as sweeping and dishwashing are available to the ex-offender. If he works at one of these jobs for four to six months to show that he is stable, he may be considered for a higher-level position. By that time, some talented ex-offenders have been discouraged and frustrated.

One unique program in San Francisco involves a homosexual state-employment counselor who has been extraordinarily successful in finding good jobs for ex-offenders who are homosexuals. He travels into the community rather than sitting in an office waiting for employers and prospective employees to come to him. For the most part, however, state employment agencies have been useless in finding jobs for ex-convicts.

The federal government, which had a long-standing policy against hiring any ex-offenders, modified its policy in 1968 to permit agencies to hire "carefully and selectively, rehabilitated offenders for jobs where they are needed and for which they are qualified by education, training, and competitive examining procedures."[98] Before an offender may be considered for employment under the new Civil Service regulations he must demonstrate that he is "fit for the particular position which he seeks" by evidencing "complete rehabilitation through his conduct and activities." Despite the difficulty of meeting these conditions, the Civil Service Commission has no special programs to employ parolees; in fact, the commission has pointed out that "[r]ehabilitated offender applicants are required to meet the full qualifications of education, experience, medical standards, and suitability . . . for the position for which they apply." This policy, as interpreted by the President's Task Force on Prisoner Rehabilitation, means that the federal government

> will now hire ex-offenders on an individual basis, if the agency that wants their services presents a strong brief, and after an elaborate and time-consuming screening by the Civil Service Commission. In other words, it is a great deal more trouble to hire an ex-offender than somebody else. . . . The government is scarcely persuasive when it urges industry to adopt employment policies toward ex-offenders that it itself is unwilling to adopt.[99]

98. United States Civil Service Commission, "Employment of the Rehabilitated Offender in the Federal Service," C.S.C. Form 941, Feb. 1968.
99. The President's Task Force on Prisoner Rehabilitation, *The Criminal Offender—What Should Be Done?* 10 (1970).

The Department of Health, Education and Welfare recently instituted a pilot program in the Office of Education in Washington, D.C., to employ eighteen released prisoners under a work-study plan. The employees work eight-hour days and attend college in the evenings. The Government pays for their tuition and books in addition to their regular salaries. People who do well at their jobs are promoted quickly and given increasing amounts of responsibility. Although former Assistant Secretary of HEW James Farmer recommended that the program be adopted in all of HEW's Washington and Baltimore offices, expansion of the plan has been stalled so far by other officials' fear of a backlash from long-time, low-paid employees who have not been offered the same opportunities.

The licensing and bonding requirements applicable to many jobs present still further obstacles to the employment of ex-offenders. Licensing regulations, which apply to occupations ranging from law and medicine to collecting garbage and cutting hair, frequently contain broad enough standards of competency and honesty which result in flat proscriptions against all offenders. Often there is no rational connection between the restrictions placed on a former offender's occupation and the crime he committed. For example, although one of the most popular vocational training courses in the New York City Reformatory is the barber school, New York State often delays or denies applications for apprentice barber's licenses when the applicant has a prison record. Motor-vehicle departments frequently deny or delay driver's licenses to former prisoners.

Ex-offenders also have difficulty in meeting employers' requirements of bonding against theft, a common practice in many retail and service businesses. In addition, prospective employers sometimes insist on bonds from people with criminal records that they would not require from other employees. Many bonding companies flatly refuse to underwrite bonds for ex-prisoners. A few voluntary agencies have attempted to fill this gap by writing bonds themselves; some, such as BonaBond in the District of Columbia, were organized just for this purpose. In programs funded by the Department of Labor's Manpower Administration, participants can be bonded by a private company under contract with the Department of Labor. As of October 1969, 1,738 former prisoners were bonded under this program and only twenty-seven had defaulted. The bonding company reduced its premiums due to the low rate of default.

The unfavorable attitudes of hirers toward former offenders are compounded by the attitudes of employment agencies. According to the Department of Labor, 75 percent of private employment agencies refuse to refer any applicant with an arrest record. State employment services have formal ties with correctional authorities in only half the states, and fewer than 10 percent of the offenders referred to state employment services are placed in jobs.

A recent survey of former federal prisoners disclosed that only 10 percent had obtained their first post-release jobs through state employment services and 5 percent through the prison employment counselors or federal probation offices. Over 80 percent of the jobs were obtained through the help of family and friends. The study observed:

> With post-release jobs being obtained primarily in this fashion, it is understandable why there is high correlation between previous work experience and post-release employment. This might also explain why inmates who have received training and attained skills often do not obtain employment which utilizes such skills. Professional job placement assistance is needed.[100]

The Department of Labor is about to fund special services for offenders in state employment offices in Massachusetts, Arizona, Oklahoma, Pennsylvania and Georgia. The need for such services has been made much more obvious recently because of the proliferation of halfway houses, which attempt to marshal community services to aid released prisoners but have had difficulty in convincing employment offices to serve their residents.

COMMUNITY INVOLVEMENT IN MANPOWER PROGRAMS

One possible approach to the difficulty of relating prison training to realistic employment opportunities would be to have training programs conducted by private companies and unions that can employ the offenders once they have been trained and after they have been released. In fact, several private companies, generally aided by government grants, have operated vocational training programs in federal and state prisons. Several such programs are operating currently in federal prisons, including a training program for electronic welders operated by Dictograph in

100. Pownall, "Employment Problems of Released Prisoners: Dimensions and Sociological Implications," in *University of Wisconsin Conference on Education and Training in Correctional Institutions* 63, 74 (1968).

Danbury, Connecticut, a program for aircraft sheet-metal workers operated by Lockheed in Lompoc, California, and a program for key-punch and data-processing operators in the women's prison at Alderson, West Virginia. Computer training programs are being given by private companies in at least three state prisons: by the Univac Division of Sperry-Rand Corporation in Pennsylvania, by IBM in Arizona and by the Honeywell Corporation in Massachusetts.

Although a pamphlet published by the AFL-CIO in 1955 suggested that local unions might participate in prison job-training programs, union officials consider that businesses are in a better position to train offenders than the unions. Thus they generally have done little in this area. However, unions have participated in a few isolated prison training programs. The International Ladies' Garment Workers has trained sewing-machine repairmen at the federal penitentiary in Danbury, Connecticut, and the Operative Plasterers and Cement Masons' International Association has joined with Portland Cement, a trade association, to design a pre-apprentice training program for Illinois prisoners that would lead to their acceptance upon release as regular union apprentices. And in what has been hailed as the first such agreement between a union and correctional personnel, the Appalachia Council AFL-CIO, financed by a federal grant, has contracted to train sixty prisoners working in the State Use Industries' print shop at the Maryland Penitentiary, to be followed by on-the-job training at two Baltimore printing firms when the trainees are paroled.

The recent use of privately operated training programs has left many of the problems of prison training unsolved. Although the privately run programs generally use more up-to-date production methods and equipment than institutionally operated programs, they occasionally train for specific jobs that have become obsolete by the time the training is completed. This has presented a particular problem in the aerospace and computer industries. In addition, private companies are no better able than correction departments to offer a variety of programs in any one institution. Programs continue to be subject to institutional and custodial constraints such as being physically removed from the outside world of work. Rigidities in sentencing and parole hinder participants from moving to on-the-job training when they are ready. Most serious, according to one perhaps self-serving federal official, the private contractors have done no better a job than prison industries in placing trained prisoners in jobs.

The chief advantage to privately operated job-training programs at present, according to an experienced correctional administrator, is that correctional officials can enforce high standards on the programs. When the quality of training is inferior, a contract can be canceled and instructors changed without hindrance by Civil Service regulations. In the future, if correction officials are able to offer sufficient financial incentives, contracts with private companies might be written to require placement of all trainees in jobs for which they have been trained.

Many of the problems associated with vocational training in institutions, such as the difficulty of offering a variety of programs and of tailoring training to available jobs, can be dealt with more easily when training programs are conducted in the community. As a recent report noted, "no matter how effective an employment and training program behind bars may be, one of equivalent quality in the community is bound to be more effective for most offenders."[101]

The Manpower Administration of the Labor Department has funded two programs to provide employment, job training and other services in the community for criminal defendants who have been arraigned but not yet tried. The Manhattan Court Employment Project, operated by the Vera Institute of Justice in New York, and Project Crossroads, by the National Committee for Children and Youth in Washington, D.C., recruit carefully selected defendants, primarily first offenders, from the courts to participate voluntarily in a ninety-day pre-trial program. Participants are placed in jobs or job-training programs, given counseling by project staff members (some of whom are ex-offenders) and referred to community social services. After ninety days the defendant appears in court with a member of the project staff. The project can recommend dismissal of charges, extension of time in the project or a return to court for trial.

Labor Department officials are particularly enthusiastic about these early diversion projects. The projects intervene early in an offender's criminal career and are considerably cheaper to operate than in-prison training (an average of $300 per offender in Project Crossroads compared to an average of $1,400 for each prisoner in a manpower-training program).[102]

A prime source of community-based vocational training is the JOBS Program. Since 1968 the Department of Labor, in conjunction with the National Alliance of Businessmen (NAB), has co-sponsored the JOBS

101. The President's Task Force on Prisoner Rehabilitation, *The Criminal Offender— What Should Be Done?* 12 (1970).
102. *See* Vera Institute of Justice, "Manhattan Court Employment Project" (1970); National Committee for Children and Youth, "Project Crossroads: Phase I" (1969), "Phase II" (1970).

(Job Opportunities in the Business Sector) Program to hire disadvantaged people, primarily members of minority groups, and give them the on-the-job training, counseling and other supportive services they need to be productive employees. The NAB enlists the support of private businesses and secures pledges of jobs. Employers pay the workers regular wages, and the Labor Department recruits applicants and pays the extra costs involved in training and special services for them. According to a Labor Department report, the program "is built on the premise that immediate placement in jobs at regular wages, followed by training and supportive services, provides superior motivation for disadvantaged individuals. This premise is supported by initial experience, although it is not yet fully tested."[103]

Preliminary evaluations have shown that the effectiveness of the JOBS Program varies widely from one plant to another. In addition, most projects have failed to develop effective links with educational, health and welfare services necessary to solve medical, domestic, legal and other problems that can interfere with the trainees' performance on the job.

Despite its problems, the JOBS Program continues to be a primary source of employment and job training for disadvantaged members of the work force, particularly in urban areas. Close to half a million employees have been hired and trained since the program began; more than half are still in the program. During the next few years the Department of Labor expects to increase the resources devoted to the program and to emphasize the upgrading of employees to more highly skilled jobs.

The JOBS Program is uniquely suited to providing vocational training and other job-related services to offenders in the community. Yet there have been no formal links between JOBS and the criminal justice system nor any organized efforts by the NAB to enroll offenders in JOBS projects. Although some people with criminal records may have been enrolled incidentally in JOBS as one of the "disadvantaged," the NAB has no statistics on the number of ex-offenders who have participated in the program. In addition, a ruling by the Solicitor of Labor that prisoners on work release do not fulfill the program's requirement that participants be "available for work" has eliminated work-release prisoners from participation in JOBS.

The Department of Labor recently made a start toward coordinating community manpower services with correctional supervision when it funded a special project to develop JOBS contracts with private employ-

103. *Manpower Report of the President* 62 (1970).

ers to hire and train parolees from the California Youth Authority. The project will investigate the availability of supportive services to the parolees and will compare the experience of the JOBS participants with that of a control group. According to a Labor Department official, the project also will

> increase the employers' capacities to work with ex-offenders by—among other techniques—using the parolees themselves to sensitize first-line supervisors. We must not presume that the required capacity already exists when it comes to working with ex-offenders. We hope to develop jobs for some of these men in personnel roles—where they can legitimately ease the way for the next man through the gate who has a record.[104]

The Law Enforcement Assistance Administration of the Department of Justice has a larger amount of funds to devote to innovative correctional programs than any other federal agency. However, under the Omnibus Crime Control and Safe Streets Act of 1968, the bulk of LEAA's funds are allocated through block grants to the states to be administered by state planning boards. In addition, LEAA has available some discretionary funds to be used to support experimental programs that have been underemphasized in state plans. One such area is the establishment of community-based programs for offenders, with particular emphasis on employment programs operated by private companies and projects that include the use of volunteers, paraprofessionals and ex-offenders.

Using discretionary funds, LEAA recently developed a Private Sector Correctional Program to involve private industry in hiring and training offenders and in coordinating the community services available to trainees. The objectives of this program make it the most comprehensive attempt so far to give offenders employment and supportive services in the community. The private-sector program has nine objectives. Although most of the twelve projects that have been funded so far do not contain all the components of the model program (the two projects dealing with juveniles vary substantially from the model), all the projects were designed with the model in mind.

Each private contractor is required to obtain commitments of specific jobs to be filled by offenders. Training programs then can be structured specifically for each job, rather than for jobs assumed to exist in the labor

104. Rosow, "Rehabilitation of Offenders," 75 *The Paper Book of the Delta Theta Phi Law Fraternity* 2, 5 (May 1970).

market. The commitment of jobs can come from the private contractor administering the program (so far no contractor has had the capacity to be the sole hirer), from a consortium of private companies, from existing JOBS or manpower programs. In North Carolina, where the State Employment Service reported that there were no more jobs to be found, contractors were able to locate 3,200 jobs in a three-month period.

Each job must contain possibilities for advancement (a "career ladder"). Trainees must be able to understand the performance required of them at each level, and each level must be designed as a realistic, obtainable goal. According to Donald A. Swicord, the labor expert who originated LEAA's Private Sector Program, "We are not playing a numbers game. We want only quality jobs, jobs with a future." In the North Carolina example mentioned above, the contractors used only 200 of the 3,200 jobs they discovered, since the others did not meet the requirement of quality jobs.

According to Swicord, training should include only what is necessary to perform the specific tasks required, and participants must be given the opportunity to practice what they have learned in an actual work situation in conjunction with the training. Any basic educational programs that accompany the training should be designed to teach only the material necessary to accomplish the specific job tasks. Although participants may request further educational programs, they are not considered essential to the program.

The program recognizes that the success or failure of the participant may very well be determined by the attitude of those around him and quite apart from his capability to perform the job. Consequently, project operators are required to develop programs designed to sensitize managers, supervisors and line foremen to the particular employment problems of offenders and to the long-range benefits to be expected from a successful program.

The programs will use paraprofessionals, some of them former offenders, as job coaches to offer continued support to the offenders in their adjustment to their jobs. They are expected to be available on a twenty-four-hour basis to intervene in any crisis situations to work under the supervision of professional counselors and to maintain contact with the probation and parole authorities responsible for the participating offenders.

Since the chances of offenders' adjustment to their jobs are maximized when proper attention is given to their health, legal and social needs, each private contractor is expected to marshal the services of community agencies to meet these potential needs. The services include counseling, directed toward the specific goals of making offenders stable employees in good jobs; legal services, both to aid offenders who have difficulty with law-enforcement agencies and to aid in solving such civil legal problems as leases, contracts, loans and domestic relations; health services; clothing and transportation; and family services.

Each project also is required to establish specific procedures with correctional agencies for referring offenders, who may be prisoners, probationers or parolees, to the project, as well as to coordinate project activities with those of the agencies legally responsible for supervising the offenders.

Since community support is considered vital to the success of this project, each project also must have an advisory committee representing all segments of the community, both public officials and private citizens.

Once a project has achieved its objectives, a goal that LEAA officials admit will take time and assistance, the private contractor should have established a system that can continue to operate without its intervention. According to LEAA, the major responsibility of the private contractors is "to develop a management system which coordinates all supportive services, develops community support and operates the program under specific agreements written in conjunction with, and in support of, local law-enforcement agencies. In effect, the private sector is responsible for using its management expertise to develop systems which, if effectively implemented, could be adapted and operated by police, courts, probation and parole, or institutions."

New Roles for Private Enterprise

The increasing use of private companies, as well as government agencies not usually involved in correction, to educate and train prisoners for employment raises an intriguing question: What other functions in the correctional system could be performed more efficiently and more realistically by contractors from outside the system? For example, departments of correction generally operate schools, hospitals, libraries, kitchens, laundries and other housekeeping services that duplicate facilities already existing in the community. In many cases it would be more efficient for correction departments to cease operating these duplicative services and instead contract with the private businesses or governmental agencies already operating them in the community to extend their services to prisons, jails and community correctional facilities. The private contract approach has several advantages, according to a recent study of the correctional services available in one California county:

> The . . . private business contract approach . . . provides a corrections–private business approach to the creative use of the jobs in the laundry, culinary, canteen and other service areas. Inmates hired by the private contractors for these services —and any contract should stipulate or provide incentives for the hiring of inmates—can learn employable skills, qualify for Social Security coverage, and earn money to help them in the often painful process of returning to the community and finding employment.[105]

The idea that correctional agencies should not operate their own food services, libraries, hospitals and the like but should purchase from or coordinate these services with outside sources and ensure their delivery to offenders, both in and out of institutions, could do much to bring various elements of the community into the correctional process and expand the number of institutions responsible for the rehabilitation of offenders. In addition, the approach might bring the world in which prisoners live a little closer to their communities.

NEW CAREERS

Ironically, there have been few efforts to employ offenders in the one field in which their past experience can be an asset rather than a liability. As in other areas of public employment, a criminal conviction generally has served as an automatic bar to employment by law-enforcement or correctional agencies. The New Careers program represents an organized attempt to create jobs in various agencies for some of the agencies' clients. In effect, it converts the consumers of the system from the problem into the solution. The limited results to date already have shown that the proper role of convicts and ex-convicts can be a powerful correctional resource.

The New Careers program was created in the mid-1960s as a possible solution to manpower problems. While labor statistics revealed that an

---

105. Institute for the Study of Crime and Delinquency, Model Community Correctional Program, Report II: *Community Organization for Correctional Services* 73 (1060).

increase in population, together with the spread of automation, had resulted in a lack of jobs for unskilled and semi-skilled workers, an increased demand for "human" (educational, social and health) services had created a shortage of trained professionals in those fields. Developed as an outgrowth of the war on poverty, New Careers was based on the idea that many of the functions ordinarily performed by professionals could be delegated to non-professionals (or "paraprofessionals," as they were called), thus creating new jobs and enabling the professionals to serve more people. According to several of the program's originators:

> In the New Careers system, the responsibilities of the professional are redefined so that he undertakes the direction, supervision and highly skilled technical tasks appropriate to his training and education, while nonprofessionals and subprofessional technicians undertake the simpler and more routine parts of the job requiring less skill, training and judgment. In this way, many new jobs for the semiskilled are created, the shortage of professionals is relieved, and the resources for services are increased.[106]

Correctional agencies have a head start in using their captive clients as manpower. There is nothing new about allowing imprisoned offenders to run the correctional system. Because of a shortage of paid employees and the need to give idle prisoners something to do, prisons have relied on inmates to do virtually all the maintenance work of the institution and sometimes (not only in the notorious Arkansas system) to guard other prisoners. In addition, prisoners frequently have been given jobs as clerks and as teachers of other inmates. Prisoners in California, Indiana and Michigan have worked as data processors on prison research projects.

There are two basic differences between the New Careers approach and these traditional practices: (1) the belief that because of their experiences offenders can make unique contributions to the rehabilitation of other offenders; and (2) the use of specialized training programs and job categories to make new careerists part of existing agency structures.

Self-help groups such as Synanon and Alcoholics Anonymous have demonstrated the truth of their premise that the most effective way to change a person's behavior is to make him a participant in the process of change, together with others who have similar problems. At the same

---

106. MacLennan, Klein, Pearl and Fishman, "Training for New Careers," 2 *Community Mental Health Journal* 135 (1966); *see generally* Pearl and Reissman, *New Careers for the Poor* (1965).

time, a growing disenchantment with the ability of middle-class professionals to work with clients who are poor and part of a foreign culture and life preference underlies the rationale for enlisting the services of people who themselves have experienced special problems in their own and their colleagues' reform. The recognition that offenders can make a unique contribution to correctional programs can cause their role to be viewed in a dignified rather than an exploitative way. Self-defensively, these programs may be viewed as a way to co-opt or neutralize one's antagonists by joining them rather than fighting them.

The success of New Careers programs in correction requires recognition by correctional professionals that they have failed and that there is truth in Pogo's line: "We have met the enemy and he is us." According to one of the first correctional administrators to employ offenders and former offenders in a correctional agency:

> . . . we want to make them part of our rehabilitation program efforts mainly because we need them and not because we feel sorry for them or want to help them. . . . Some ex-offenders can do important, sensitive, skillful things which professional staff cannot do. They understand some things better than staff do. They can have an impact upon other offenders which professionals have too often been unable to achieve. In other words, they're not to be considered cheap labor; they can be chief contributors.[107]

Attempts by correctional administrators to use offenders in the rehabilitation of other offenders as part of institutional programs include the group-work and therapeutic-community ideas that have been implemented in several institutions, the employment of inmate-students to assist other inmate-students in the use of self-instruction materials as part of new educational programs and the use of young offenders to supervise work crews in small, experimental institutions for juveniles.

Other efforts have been initiated by offenders themselves, generally operating outside of the official correction system, to involve themselves in preventing crime and drug addiction and offering their help to recently released prisoners. Prison inmates and former inmates have spoken to school and church groups, using their unique credentials to attempt to convince their audiences of the ultimate consequences of crime and drug

107. Luger, "Utilizing the Ex-Offender as a Staff Member: Community Attitudes and Acceptance," Joint Commission on Correctional Manpower and Training, *Offenders as a Correctional Manpower Resource* 50 (1968).

abuse. Groups such as the Fortune Society, the Seventh Step Foundation and Efforts From Ex-Convicts have evolved private "parole" organizations to provide employment, housing and other services they feel are not being provided by the agencies officially responsible for them.

Although the work done by ex-offender groups demonstrates the unique contribution that can be made by convicts and ex-convicts, they are not part of the organized New Careers program (however related to it they obviously are) because they do not necessarily involve preparation for permanent employment. Formal New Careers programs involve specialized training, generally of three to six months' duration, to permit workers with no other training or work experience (and generally with little formal education) to take jobs in established agencies; the restructuring of jobs so that they can be performed by people with minimal specialized training; relaxation of Civil Service regulations to permit offenders and other new careerists to begin employment at any stage for which their training and experience fits them; the creation of "career ladders" to provide for upward mobility for workers with the necessary interests and ability; and the availability of continuing education and training (for which time is allowed and paid for as part of the job) so that new careerists can be given the opportunity to advance to more responsible and sometimes traditional professional positions. In other words, the purpose of New Careers is to enable offenders to trade on their special knowledge in order to become part of the system.

The first program to train a group of offenders systematically for New Careers was launched in 1964 by J. Douglas Grant in the California Department of Correction's Medical Facility at Vacaville. Grant was one of the early experimenters with the therapeutic-community idea, which attempted to involve mental patients, and later offenders, in their own therapy. The New Careers concept was a natural extension of the therapeutic community. Grant's program was begun as a result of a conference on "The Use of the Products of a Social Problem in Coping with the Problem," organized by the National Institute of Mental Health in 1963. The conference brought together offenders, former offenders, correctional administrators and social scientists to discuss present and potential employment of offenders in programs ranging from correctional data processing to delinquency prevention. When it was over, one group of participants inaugurated the Center for Youth and Community Studies at Howard University, in Washington, D.C., to train high-school drop-outs from poverty backgrounds as day-care, recreation and research aides. The

Vacaville program, entitled the New Careers Development Project, applied the New Careers idea to offenders.

Eighteen participants were selected from prisoners who had experienced one of the group-living programs currently in operation in California prisons, on the basis of anonymous evaluations of each inmate obtained from other inmates in his group. The eighteen chosen were taken to Vacaville for four months' training. Participants organized into teams of trainees and staff members (part-time graduate students and professional consultants), which shared the administrative duties of operating the program and planning its content. By the end of the four months, most of the functions of the staff had been taken over by the trainees themselves.

Study groups were organized around five areas: interviewing skills; principles of group dynamics; organization-change strategies; research procedures; and current social trends and issues, such as poverty programs and the civil-rights movement.

In addition to participating in study groups, each team completed two special projects, including surveys of other inmates and prison staff members concerning their opinions of the use of non-professionals in programs for alcoholics, the mentally retarded, parolees and probationers; an exploration of the attitudes of inmates toward existing group-therapy and educational programs; and a detailed analysis of the participants' own training program. Training activities were supplemented by daily group meetings, which included role playing and other activities designed to develop an awareness of individual and group problems.

As soon as the institutional phase of the training had been completed and each participant obtained his parole, the trainees moved to various paid work assignments in the community. Calling themselves "program development assistants," the trainees performed tasks such as planning a project to use indigenous teaching assistants in an elementary-school summer program, conducting a survey to determine the possibilities of new careers in the state government and training community organizers for work with the poor. As long as funds were available, one member of the group worked full-time as a coordinator, helping other members in various parts of the state solve personal or employment problems.

Two years after the completion of the training program, sixteen of the eighteen participants remained in jobs connected with the development of new programs for social change. (Of the other two, one disappeared soon after his release from prison. The other was reimprisoned for a new crime and given a research job at San Quentin.) The type of jobs in which the participants were employed included community organizers under the sponsorship of federal and state economic opportunity offices; teacher-counselors in an experimental college program; directors of a neighborhood health center and an association for the mentally retarded; researcher for a job development demonstration program; and a staff member of the federally sponsored Joint Commission on Correctional Manpower and Training.

As a result of the apparent success of the project, various agencies, including the New York City Department of Human Resources, the state of Washington's Department of Institutions and the California Department of Correction, planned similar programs to train program developers for various roles in their agencies. State universities in California, Oregon, Washington and Massachusetts have instituted New Careers training programs. In Oregon, Arthur Pearl, one of the originators of the New Careers concept, aided by a grant from the Teacher Corps, has developed a program to prepare new careerists as high-school teachers. Some of the participants are still in prison; others are recent graduates of NewGate and Upward Bound programs.

The Social Action Research Center in Berkeley, California, supported by a grant from the U.S. Office of Education, is continuing the program that began at Vacaville and developing methods to train new careerists as program developers. Investigation of actual social problems is used as an introduction to formal academic study. This method is soon to be implemented at the University of California in Los Angeles to train probation and parole agents, along with offenders who are on probation and parole, to devise ways of involving clients and entire agency staffs in developing new programs and strategies for their agencies.

The New York Division for Youth has employed offenders and former offenders as staff members in its institutional and community programs for several years. The division's new careerists are drawn from three categories: youths still participating in rehabilitative programs, recent graduates from the division's programs and adults on parole from state prisons. The first group has had the most difficulty adjusting to staff positions, since neither the youths they were to counsel nor the professional staff members could easily view them as part of the staff. The other two groups have been successful as counselors in halfway houses and forestry camps. They have been particularly effective in the division's after-care offices, where they help youths recently released from correctional programs find employment and deal with other practical problems. In addition, new careerists have spent time developing community resources to aid recent graduates of the division's programs.

Some of the other correctional programs employing new careerists, discussed elsewhere in this book, include privately and governmentally operated halfway houses, which use ex-offenders as counselors and job developers; the California Youth Authority's student-aide program, which trains older Youth Authority wards as counselors to younger wards; and many of the growing number of drug-prevention and treatment programs, including the New York State Narcotics Addiction Program and the District of Columbia Narcotics Treatment Agency. The Vera Institute's Manhattan Court Employment Project assigns defendants who have been arrested but not yet convicted to former offenders, who assume primary responsibility for finding them jobs and giving them counseling and other assistance.

Police departments in Richmond and Los Angeles have hired former offenders to work in community-relations divisions, primarily in crime-prevention projects. The Los Angeles program, which began as a project for the hard-core unemployed, evolved into a program for offenders when it became clear that most applicants had police records.

One of the areas with the greatest potential for employing ex-offenders is in probation and parole departments where professionals long have complained of unmanageable caseloads and an overload of clerical and investigatory tasks. Currently the largest program for new careerists in probation or parole (or in any single agency, for that matter) is administered by the Los Angeles County Probation Department. Since 1965 the department has employed adult and youth aides through arrangements with federally funded antipoverty agencies. The aides perform functions ranging from transporting juveniles and their families to court to helping probation officers run group-counseling sessions. Although some of the new careerists are former offenders, others are "hard-core unemployed" from the geographical areas in which most of the offices' clients live.

After one year as an aide in the Los Angeles agency, a new careerist is eligible to take a Civil Service examination for a "community worker" position. These positions are permanent Civil Service jobs designed for people without the educational qualifications generally required of professional probation officers. Administrators hope that the use of new careerists in these roles will create a body of citizens in the community who know how to use the system. Many of the community workers have been used as part of probation teams in an experimental project, RODEO (Reduction of Delinquency Through Expansion of Opportunity), designed to provide community services to seriously delinquent youths and convicted adults who otherwise would be sent to institutions.

The California Department of Correction is using new careerists as aides in its parole centers and halfway houses (under current California law, offenders with felony records may serve on probation and parole staffs, but they may not become full-fledged agents). Various other probation and parole departments throughout the country have begun to experiment with the aide concept. New York State recently hired its first ex-offender (a college graduate) as a parole officer. The District of Columbia Department of Correction is experimenting with using former offenders without traditional professional training as parole officers. At the end of an experimental period, the success rates of parolees supervised by the new careerists will be compared with those of parolees supervised in traditional ways.

The few correctional agencies that have employed new careerists have used them primarily in community programs rather than as institutional staff members. The Los Angeles Probation Department and the New York Division for Youth have employed former offenders in forestry camps and found them particularly helpful in demonstrating to members of the surrounding communities the possibilities of successful rehabilitative programs. However, the Division for Youth found that new careerists, frequently members of minority groups and residents of urban areas, felt isolated and unhappy in rural areas and sometimes has had to transfer them to community programs. On the other hand, the Washington Department of Institutions intends to use new careerists (both men and women) as staff members in a new institution for women.

The most promising use of new careerists appears to be in developing community resources and in changing the environment from which offenders come. Such an approach frequently has been ignored or minimized by traditional social workers, who see their function in terms of treating their clients' individual problems or helping them to adjust to their environments. Studies have found that programs that enlist people from low-income backgrounds to change established institutions have resulted in changing the behavior and the outlook of the workers as well as of the institutions.

Federal funding for New Careers programs is available from several sources. Originally incorporated as an amendment to the Economic Opportunity Act in 1966, a New Careers program was transferred in 1967 from OEO to the Department of Labor, where it is now a part of the United States Training and Employment Service. Other legislation, such as the Vocational Rehabilitation Act, the Juvenile Delinquency Prevention and Control Act and the Omnibus Crime and Safe Streets Act, all provide specifically for federal grants to support New Careers programs. The Justice Department's Law Enforcement Assistance Administration recently announced eight grants totaling $600,000 for law-enforcement agencies to train 289 new and to upgrade 104 present new careerists (many former offenders).

Federal funds generally can be used to train and pay the full salaries of new careerists for their first year in a program. In the second year, federal support tapers off to 50 percent, and by the third year employing agencies are expected to pay the full wages of their new employees and to arrange for their continuing education. Although many projects have been begun, there has been a problem convincing agencies to continue employing new careerists after the initial two years so that the jobs do not disappear in the absence of federal support. (In California, however, both the Department of Correction and the Youth Authority, as well as the Los Angeles County Probation Department, have replaced federal support with state and local funds and retained former offenders in parole and probation departments when initial federal funds expired.)

Three significant problems have hampered the development of New Careers programs: state and local hiring restrictions, the attitudes of professional employees and the failure to develop permanent career ladders.

Employment of new careerists by government agencies remains impossible in most states and localities because of blanket restrictions against hiring ex-offenders. According to the findings of a survey reported by the Joint Commission on Correctional Manpower and Training, approximately forty states have statutory or administrative prohibitions against the employment of probationers or parolees by state agencies. In thirty-three states there are restrictions even on state employment of ex-offenders who have been released from supervision. Of 422 local probation and parole agencies surveyed by the commission, nearly three-fourths are prevented from hiring anyone with a felony record; the same proportion may not hire any offender on probation or parole.[108] In addition to these legal re-

108. Stubblefield and Dye, "Introduction," Joint Commission on Correctional Manpower and Training, *Offenders as a Correctional Manpower Resource* 1, 3 (1968).

strictions, administrative regulations prohibiting the association of parolees have prevented some agencies from hiring offenders who still are under parole supervision.

Legal restrictions can be removed if correctional agencies are committed to fighting for their elimination. A more substantial barrier to the employment of former offenders by law-enforcement agencies is the attitude of the personnel already in the agencies. The Joint Commission on Correctional Manpower and Training found that half of a national sample of correctional personnel felt that it would not be a good idea to hire ex-offenders in their agencies. A recent effort to remove the statutory prohibition against hiring people with felony records as law-enforcement agents in one state met resistance from the professional employees of the agencies involved. Law-enforcement and correctional personnel apparently believed that their own status would suffer if former offenders could be hired to fill their jobs.

Although many correctional employees have no specialized training, their philosophy frequently is set by those with advanced degrees in social work, who often consider social-work education essential for employees who work with offenders. Consequently, agencies that employ new careerists sometimes give them only routine investigatory and clerical functions to perform. The possibility that former offenders may have greater success in rehabilitating other offenders than experienced workers with specialized training cannot help but make some professionals anxious and defensive.

The professionals' emphasis on traditional training and methods may destroy the special ability of former offenders to relate to offenders under supervision. Milton Luger, former director of the New York Division for Youth, noted the fallacy of trying to make new careerists conform to traditional patterns set by professional staff members:

> Do we wish to encourage newer ex-offender staff members to become more like other employees in appearance and bearing in order to accelerate their acceptance by the general public and incumbent staff? In early Division for Youth experience, young new careerists strove for this acceptance by adopting all the trappings of respectability utilized by other staff. They soon were reporting for work with attaché cases and striped ties. Their written reports, replete with grammatical errors, reeked of psychological terms they had heard in their own treatment. It took a great deal of explanation to convince them that their acceptance

COMMUNITY CORRECTION / 663

by other offenders was being hindered by these affectations. Naturalness was one of their important assets, and it was being destroyed.[109]

According to J. Douglas Grant, the introduction of new careerists into existing agencies should prompt agencies to experiment with various roles for them and to revise their current staffing patterns.

The anxiety among professionals concerning their own status may be responsible for the third, and possibly most serious stumbling block to the development of the full potential of New Careers programs: the lack of opportunity for advancement. Even where entry-level jobs have been opened up to new careerists, little progress has been made in developing career ladders that permit the trainees to advance to positions of greater responsibility and prestige. A recent study of the employment of new careerists in New York City by the National Committee on the Employment of Youth found that due to their lack of college degrees, "opportunities for genuine career advancement for paraprofessionals are either severely limited or completely nonexistent." Although some agencies offered promotions for "equivalent experience" rather than college credits, the meaning of "equivalent" was never defined. The study concluded that "equal employment opportunity is meaningless unless there is also a guarantee of equal opportunity for advancement."

In probation and parole departments that have hired former offenders as case aides, no provision has been made to educate aides to become professional probation or parole officers. The differences in education and experience required for the two positions are virtually insurmountable. The subsidized education and training programs that were expected to move new careerists to professional positions in most cases have not materialized. Even the best known of the New Careers programs for offenders, such as those in the New York Division for Youth and the Los Angeles Probation Department, have not developed career ladders to enable offenders to achieve professional status. Some staff members have questioned the "morality of training persons in the area of social services, having them develop the personal dignity of a social-service worker, but then forcing them to seek employment elsewhere."

These examples point up a fundamental question about the viability of New Careers programs. Does the Establishment have a genuine com-

109. Luger, "Utilizing the Ex-Offender as a Staff Member: Community Attitudes and Acceptance," Joint Commission on Correctional Manpower and Training, *Offenders as a Correctional Manpower Resource* 55 (1968).

mitment to New Careers as more than a gimmick offering offenders only limited opportunities and responsibility? If so, the professionals in effect are confessing their inability to perform the task of rehabilitation unaided and confessing that they must look elsewhere for special expertise. This is in derogation of their own selfish interests however altruistic a confession it may be. It is unlikely to presume that this commitment exists.

The use of former offenders in rehabilitative roles calls into question the increased emphasis by correctional professionals on fulfillment of traditional academic requirements for employment in correction. If this training actually is necessary, some way must be found to enable former offenders to take advantage of it if they are not to be relegated to permanently subordinate positions. On the other hand, if former offenders really do have unique contributions to make, perhaps they should be giving the training instead of receiving it.

The difficulties offenders have experienced in becoming part of the formal correctional system while retaining their unique contribution, avoiding bureaucratic hindrances and earning increased responsibility, show that the New Careers approach cannot be the final goal of employment programs. Most new careerists cannot become professionals in the traditional sense; nor do we feel they should be. One answer lies in the private use of ex-offenders outside the established correctional system as an alternative to the formal system. While the New Careers concept originated as a way to make correctional clients a part of the law-enforcement establishment, its greatest contribution may be in allowing former offenders to operate a parallel, unofficial system that can take over part of the traditional correctional role.

The community is the appropriate place for a review of the American correction system to conclude. If only a very small part of the action is there now, certainly it is where the best talk leads and the successful, innovative programs are found. Radical a change as it would be to base correction essentially in the community, the notion is neither new nor outlandish.

We have concluded that the correction system today is very much a public-welfare system of correction for the poor which works parallel to and not nearly as well as the private, informal system-of-sorts which the affluent use for their own people to replace the official system. Consider two illustrative cases which strike us as telling examples of this point.

A black youngster (fifteen years old) from a poor section of Baltimore, Maryland, who had never been in trouble before, went with a gang of his friends to rob a store for spending money. In the course of the theft a resisting storekeeper was shot and killed by one of the youths who, without the subject's knowledge, had a gun. The boy was tried in the adult criminal court; he was convicted and sentenced to life imprisonment at the Maryland House of Correction. He was not eligible for parole until he had served fifteen years. While serving the last few years of that sentence he might have read the news accounts of the trial of a twenty-four-year-old gentleman tobacco farmer from rural Charles County in the same state. This son of a prominent businessman and former state official was tried for assault, resisting arrest and manslaughter arising out of a drunken episode at a fashionable society ball. After taunting a fifty-one-year-old hotel barmaid (mother of eleven) with racist insults, he struck her with a steel-topped cane because she was slow delivering him a drink. She collapsed and died. The judge sentenced him to six months in a county jail, but allowed him to remain free for a while in order to oversee the harvesting of his crops.

The first boy could be excused for getting the impression that two separate systems of justice were operating in these cases, or for wishing less that his fellow offender was subjected to Draconian measures than that he himself was afforded similar understanding and opportunity.

Perhaps the most succinct statement on the subject comes from Noah Pope, a little-known resident-client of the Maryland House of Correction in Jessup. Resigned, he told a recent crime and correction workshop: "The jail is for the poor; the street is for the rich."

That the poor lead less-advantaged lives than the rich is no revelation. Yet, class inequalities should be least tolerable in the system of dispensing justice. Recently, as specific episodes in our legal system have been revealed as unjust, we sometimes have been able to begin meaningful reforms involving, for example, such aspects of the system as bail and the right to counsel.

Less visible are the special ways in which the criminal justice system operates to prejudice the poor in its so-called "correction system." In fact, the simple but unpublished fact is that, to a remarkable extent, the correction process in America is composed of a double system of criminal justice, one public, the other private, each operating radically differently from the other.

A lone but unheeded voice in the correctional wilderness, that of criminologist Richard Korn, has criticized the hypocrisy of a system in which the rich get help and the poor get jail. He urged in one report that trends toward innovative and sympathetic community treatment of offenders should not be viewed as radical or even new. They are no more than the very same programs used "by the well-to-do on behalf of their deviant members": restitution, medical treatment, special schooling, training and other sensible alternatives to imprisonment. He went on to say:

> A wholly private and unofficial system of correctional treatment has long been available to the violent scions of the socially fortunate. In every middle-class community there are psychiatrists specializing in the treatment of the errant youth of the well-heeled, frequently with the full approval of the police and judicial authorities. Should private out-patient treatment prove inadequate, there is a nationwide network of relatively exclusive residential facilities outside the home community. Every Sunday *The New York Times* publishes two pages of detailed advertisements by private boarding schools catering to the needs of "exceptional youth" who are "unreachable" by means of "conventional educational methods."
>
> It would be wrong-headed and disingenuous to cite these facts as instances of dishonest official connivance with wealth or privilege. If anything, they reflect an honest recognition that the private, unofficial treatment of offenders is vastly superior to most available public programs. Keeping children out of reformatories is a widely approved and worthy objective, irrespective of whether the children are rich or poor. The scandal lies in the fact that such alternatives are denied to the poor, through nothing more deliberate than the incidental fact of their inferior economic position. The inequity of this situation provides one of the strongest moral grounds for overcoming it. Once it is recognized that the "new" approaches advocated for the correctional treatment of all are essentially similar to those already serving the well-to-do, the ethical argument for making these services universally available becomes virtually unassailable.[110]

The phenomenon, if it can be called that, which delivers poor offenders to an unnecessarily expensive and unfortunately ineffective prison system while reserving that course for only the exceptional affluent offender is especially destructive yet especially apparent with young

110. Korn, "Issues and Strategies of Implementation in the Use of Offenders in Resocializing Other Offenders," in Joint Commission on Correctional Manpower and Training, *Offenders as a Correctional Manpower Resource* 75 (1968).

offenders. The director of a home for delinquent boys recently advised us that his inmates from wealthy or middle-class families are referred there by private psychiatrists while those referred by the juvenile court are invariably poor children. While this may seem to reflect the equal treatment of rich and poor juvenile delinquents, it more pointedly demonstrates the differences these youngsters encounter in their contacts with officialdom. One group was referred privately by their parents; the other group went through the stressful police, detention and juvenile-court system before getting to this home. Most of these institutions are awful, and poor juvenile offenders not only have a harder time along the way to paying for their misconduct but they also end up more frequently in terrible public institutions which their wealthier counterparts ordinarily are able to avoid.

The 1967 President's Crime Commission reported that 90 percent of the youth in America have done something for which they could be committed by a juvenile court. Yet Sheldon and Eleanor Glueck have reported that only 5 percent of the children who are put in institutions for juvenile delinquency (that would be 20,000 of the 400,000 children in detention at the time of the last national crime-commission survey) come from families in "comfortable circumstances."

A recent study in Contra Costa County, California, graphically illustrated this phenomenon. According to this study, 46.3 percent of the nation's annual crop of arrested juveniles were released by the police after some informal handling and without charges being preferred. Many were simply reprimanded and released; in some cases the victim did not prefer charges or there was insufficient evidence for a charge or restitution was made. In California, 48.2 percent, slightly more than the nationwide average, were released in this fashion. But an analysis of practices in the upper-middle-class suburban community of Lafayette in Contra Costa County revealed that the percentage of juveniles released after arrest was 80.8 percent.

Correspondingly, of the total juveniles arrested, the nationwide average of those who were referred to a juvenile court for their offense was 47.8 percent. In California it was 46.5 percent, but in Lafayette it was only 17.9 percent. Of those who were institutionalized eventually, the nationwide average was 6 percent; the California average was 5.3 percent; in Lafayette County it was only 1.3 percent.

The report concludes: "These data clearly indicate that the . . . adjustment without benefit of the formal agencies of juvenile justice for middle-class suburban youth at the law enforcement level is considerably above the national and state averages." Furthermore, this process of disposing of delinquency in an informal fashion by law-enforcement agencies is a phenomenon which the report said "is also found at the probation department level, and within the juvenile court structure."[111]

A recent study of 30,000 court actions in one state, substantiated by studies in other states, disclosed that certain social categories of juveniles (racial minorities and lower economic classes) are treated differently by juvenile courts. These groups are especially liable to be apprehended, charged, referred, tried, adjudicated delinquents and committed. According to this report, the converse is true as well: "persons from higher socio-economic strata (but from similar sex, age, and offense categories) are more likely to receive probationary services than to be institutionalized and to receive clinical treatment services where these exist. . . ."[112]

While it is arguable that poor children commit more wrongs, the discrepancy in the disposition of criminal cases may be due more particularly to the fact that upper- and middle-class families are able to adjust their children's problems privately. Typical juvenile crimes like vandalism, truancy, illicit sexual relations are often repaired privately in the community by affluent families; the poor more frequently end up institutionalized. In fact, poor children sometimes are put in institutions for their own good regardless of the seriousness of their offense (for lack of a good home, for example), while children from prosperous backgrounds are usually released—also for their own good—even though they may have committed serious offenses.

It seems a common insight, if not a scientifically provable one, that all people transgress, but not all—in fact, very few—end up labeled and treated as criminals as a result. Former Supreme Court Justice Tom Clark has estimated that only 50 percent of all crime is reported. At recent Congressional hearings, unreported crime was estimated by another expert witness to be 90 percent of the total. One study of 6,000 offenses admitted by youths in one area found that only 1.5 percent were "brought to public attention by arrest or juvenile court hearing." Of that percentage of crime that is reported, only a very small fraction of the offenders are arrested, tried, convicted and go to prison. But it is clear that those in prison are of a rather homogeneous class, and the one general characteristic is that they are, for the most part, poor people.

111. Carter, *Middle-Class Delinquency—An Experiment in Community Control* (1968).
112. President's Commission on Law Enforcement and Administration of Justice 87 (1967). Vinter, "The Juvenile Court as an Institution," in Task Force Report: *Juvenile Delinquency and Youth Crime.*

One technique for appraising the validity of informal and admittedly logical impressions and of available official statistics which might indicate that crimes are committed more frequently by people in lower economic classes is the study of rates of voluntarily reported crimes by people in all classes. Social scientists have attempted to measure real delinquency rates through field observation, studying the files of social agencies, questionnaires and interviews, rather than relying on official, institutional records which indicate that delinquency seems to be related to socioeconomic status. These studies have shown that there is a marked difference between officially recorded crime rates of formal criminal-justice institutions like the police and the courts and the confidentially admitted criminal infractions of random groups. Studies rather uniformly reflect the conclusion that there is a traditional dichotomy between self-reported crime rates and institutional records of official crime statistics and that the latter are not accurate reflections of class differences. There is, in short, a considerable amount of unrecorded delinquency among teenagers from good homes and stable social backgrounds. Official criminal records are artificial in the sense that they mirror prejudices within the system and reflect the distortions of our law-enforcement habits and statistics. In fact, there are indications that the records of self-reported crime are more accurate than the official statistics. If this is so, it is evidence of the fact that poor people are *not* more inclined to commit crimes than wealthier people and that this theory is not a fair rationale to account for the fact that prisons hold disproportionate numbers of poor people.

Studies of "self-reported" crime have shown that while poor people end up in correctional institutions in disproportionate numbers, delinquent or criminal acts are committed by people at all levels of society. In one survey of 1,700 adults without criminal records, 99 percent of all those questioned admitted committing offenses for which they could have ended up in prison. The breakdown of these admitted but not punished offenses is interesting:

> Businessmen and lawyers were highest in perjury, falsification, fraud and tax evasion; teachers and social workers in malicious mischief; writers and artists in indecency, criminal libel and gambling; military and government employees in simple larceny; mechanics and technicians in disorderly conduct; farmers in illegal possession of weapons; laborers in grand larceny, burglary and robbery; students in auto misdemeanors.[113]

113. Wallerstein and Wyle, "Our Law-Abiding Law-Breakers," *Probation* (April 1947).

One sociologist, testing the thesis that the poor are institutionalized more because they commit more offenses, questioned a group of boys in a lower-class, high-delinquency, West Coast metropolis and compared their responses with appropriate court records. While all the white, Negro and Japanese students confidentially reported committing an equal number of offenses, the official records painted a remarkably different picture of juvenile delinquency by each group in that area. The official records of deviant behavior reflected class distinctions that did not correspond with the self-reported statistics, which showed similar amounts of crime in each of the three groups.[114]

There is a difference, it seems, between official records of delinquency and the true picture of the extent and sources of delinquent behavior. For a true picture, the last report suggested that the practices of official law-enforcement agencies and the basis of their crime reporting need study as well as the deviant persons with whom the agencies deal. This conclusion is supported by other experts, who have decided that there is no special relationship between delinquency and status.[115]

The Wallerstein–Wyle study in Fort Worth, Texas, compared delinquency rates of a group of college students with another group of known delinquents. While both groups committed similar crimes, the college group "enjoyed relative impunity." With careful understatement, this scholarly report concluded that the "socioeconomic status of the family" made an "undoubtedly important" difference in the way society treated the wrongs of these young men. Respectable people are lawless, the report concluded, but social status affected the amount of official punishment meted out for criminal behavior.

> Whether a man becomes a confirmed criminal may well depend less on what he does to society than on what society does to him. Pranks that cause a college student some uncomfortable moments in the Dean's office may send an East Side youth to the reformatory. Unlawful possession of a revolver may result in a warning to a suburban home owner, a prison sentence to a tenement dweller. Taking a sum of money as "honest graft" in business or public life is vastly different from taking the same amount from a cash register.
>   . . . It is perhaps less important to show that good citizens

114. Chambliss, "On the Validity of Official Statistics," *Journal of Research in Crime and Delinquency* (Jan. 1969).
115. Nye, Short, Olson, "Socioeconomic Status and Delinquent Behavior," in *Middle-Class Juvenile Delinquency* (1967).

are not always good than that these same citizens can commit crimes and still become eminent scientists, intelligent parents, leading teachers, artists and social workers, or prominent business executives.

A 1967 review of federal criminal statistics showed that defendants with assigned counsel found their cases dismissed less often and were acquitted less frequently than those comparable defendants who retained their own counsel.[116] Whether this difference is due to the poverty of the clients or of the talent of their lawyers—perhaps each is related—the fact remains that a poor class of defendants fare less well at the criminal-trial stage than their more affluent counterparts.

A similar result was found in another recent survey of crime and correction in San Joaquin County, California. Most crime is in the misdemeanor class. Misdemeanants usually do not have lawyers and, without counsel, go to jail more frequently and for longer terms. This conclusion corroborates the one we now know about the pre-trial stage of the criminal-justice process. Recent bail studies have proven that poor defendants who go to jail before trial subsequently get convicted and sentenced to prison more frequently than those who are able to afford bail and get released before trial.[117]

This evidence is not uniform. Some serious researchers have concluded that "among boys . . . social status is indeed inversely related to juvenile delinquency . . . more lower status youngsters commit delinquent acts more frequently than do higher status youngsters."[118] Others have calculated that poor boys have more of the problems that lead to delinquency and thus that criminal-justice resources are properly directed at lower-class offenders. The thesis has been advanced that the delinquency of poor, young offenders is more voluminous, more difficult to control, more concealed, more related to their acting out deeply ingrained roles of their cultures and altogether more socially costly. But this too is disputed.

One report that recently examined the applications of economic analysis to the social phenomenon of delinquency noted several indices for concluding that low income increases the tendency to commit crime.

116. Administrative Office of the U.S. Courts, Federal Offenders in the United States District Courts 1967, Table D-12 (1968).
117. Rankin, "The Effect of Pretrial Detention," 39 New York University Law Review 641 (1964).
118. Gold, "Undetected Delinquent Behavior," Journal of Research in Crime and Delinquency 37 (January 1966).

For example, low-income youths probably view their economic status as indicative of little chance for large payoffs through legitimate activity; the risks that result from losing time in jail are lower; they can rely on less family assistance and influence during early years when temptations are greatest and rewards for legitimate work are the lowest. There is, it is suggested, proof of a relationship between conditions of employment, youth crime and property crime with poverty. This report pointed out that since a rise of 1 percent in incomes in extremely delinquent areas can cause a 2.5 percent decline in delinquency rates, "the effect of income on delinquency is not a small one."[119] Another study suggested that the economic deprivation of the offender is a factor in accounting for differences in the rates of committing certain kinds of offenses. Apparently poorer people commit more victimizing crimes like robbery, and wealthier offenders are guilty of committing more nongainful offenses that stem from joy-riding and drinking. Nonetheless, it is difficult to avoid the conclusion stated in one recent volume dealing with this subject:

> Irrespective of social class, perhaps all boys break the law at one time or other. But official statistics seldom reflect this fact. We know that boys from the lower class are arrested more often relative to the frequency with which they commit offenses. Our research ought not to rely on these sources alone. . . .[120]

In fact, the available evidence seems to us to lend itself to a more expansive interpretation. Deviance, in an existential sense, seems to be common classless conduct; deviance as reflected by official correctional statistics and records of institutionalization appears to be related to social class.

Criminal correction then becomes a deadly cycle. The young and poor offender goes to juvenile and then to adult institutions more frequently and is anything but "corrected." While economic deprivation undoubtedly contributes to tendencies to commit crimes, the problem is compounded, not corrected, when arrested and convicted criminals are treated differently, with the poor faring worst.

Some experimental programs have been initiated recently to provide diversionary services early in the criminal justice process to poor youths and occasionally adults before they are convicted of crimes. Pre-

119. Fleisher, "The Effect of Income on Delinquency," *The American Economic Review* 134 (March 1966).
120. Chilton, "Middle-Class Delinquency and Specific Offense Analysis," in Vaz (ed.), *Middle-Class Juvenile Delinquency* 91 (1967).

trial diversion projects, such as Youth Service Bureaus that refer juveniles to community services without the intervention of the juvenile court, manpower-training programs that operate between the time of arrest and trial and community crisis centers to give help to offenders and their victims on a twenty-four hour basis, represent a sensible use of alternative community correctional resources. Hopefully, these efforts can begin to provide some of the help to poor offenders that traditionally has been available through private means to the well-to-do.

The differential treatment of rich and poor offenders might be rationalized if the public institutions that poor people are sent to were any good and accomplished for their wards what affluent families negotiate privately for theirs. But that is not the case. Most of these places are Dickensonian, bleak, evil; and our rising crime rates of young repeaters show that these institutions do not work.

The Gluecks and others have suggested that "powerful groups are often punished less frequently and severely than less powerful groups." There are few informative, let alone definitive, studies of criminal statistics, though most authorities agree that the poor comprise a disproportionate part of any prison population. Obviously, only the poor go to jail and have criminal records for failing to pay alimony, support, restitution or fines. Similarly, few wealthy people steal or commit crimes out of economic desperation. But in the classes of offenses that are committed by rich and poor equally, it is rarely the rich who end up in prison.

An increasingly volatile tangent of this phenomenon is the racial imbalance in American prisons. Negroes comprise one-third of all prisoners while only one-tenth of the population. Negroes have had higher rates of criminality and incarceration historically, assumedly due to their disproportionately low economic status. Recent studies based on arrest records, however, have shown that economic status alone does not account for high Negro crime rates (and that inborn racial traits were *not* a factor), but in fact that "psychological and cultural differences outweighed economic ones in fostering criminality."[121] In any event, there can be no doubt that the social factors which so markedly determine all crime rates affect Negroes most of all. This fact of life is apparent to anyone visiting American prisons, many of which leave an impression of being black institutions. It is corroborated by the messages of recent prison riots and by

121. Graham, "Black Crime: The Lawless Image," *Harper's* magazine, September 1970; Graham, *The Self-Inflicted Wound* (1970); Wolfgang and Cohen, *Crime and Race* (1970).

a growing black polemical literature emanating from the country's prisons.

What is of central importance is less the theoretical concern that our legal system in part discriminates between economic classes; rather, the question is whether this discrimination in the use of our correctional programs and resources is wise, economical and efficient. Some rational discrimination between rich and poor offenders might make sense. But the one we make—treating higher-class offenders one way for their and society's good while treating poor offenders another way to their and society's loss—seems by every standard to be wrong, wasteful and unfair. The public welfare correction system needs to be radically re-evaluated; and for the direction of this reform the public should look no further than themselves and their community.

Epilogue

Having made this critical, detailed analysis, we must conclude that the prison system not only does not work but works *against* every decent standard society should consider for its correction system. Imprisonment, with its progeny of accompanying procedures and practices, is a vicious and mean form of punishment that appeals to our baser, darker side and nothing more. In one important sense, the very discussion of the manifold amenities that could be added, the extremes that could be modified, the steps toward community-related reforms that could be taken presumes a commitment to the present system. It could thus be said that these reformative suggestions amount to a fatal concession.

We chose to spend as much time as we did talking about these reforms because we are well aware of the charge that it is easier to criticize than to make constructive suggestions, and because we are not so naïve as to fail to understand that political realities preclude—at least for the foreseeable future—the kind of broad, systemic reform that we would prefer. Nonetheless, we find it hard to conclude our work without expressing, at least briefly, our dream of a different, better system.

While we believe that this book supports a massive indictment of our corrective system, the system, however beleaguered, lumbers along. There is a current, hopeful air of reform, however, that has been spurred by public awareness of the need for fundamental changes and dramatized by recurring prison riots. Attica has become a searing symbol in prison history. There are two basic routes that this reform could take.

The first alternative—and it is here that most liberal reformers seem to find themselves—might be to clean up the system and improve it: hiring more probation and parole officers, providing lower caseloads, building new jails and prisons (which someone recently referred to as the correctional world's edifice complex and what some insiders call making "sweet joints"), sending guards to school and bringing schools to prisons, and taking other similar, worthwhile steps. We would not choose that route.

As we pointed out in Chapter II, the fundamental mistake we believe the correction system is about to make is taking just such steps, which we consider superficial and cosmetic. We prefer the more profound changes that we have suggested along the way in this book: diversion from the system altogether, creative exploitation of convicts and ex-convicts in the correctional process, pervasive victim-compensation programs and other related attempts at reconciliation between offenders and victims, contracting for services in the private sector wherever possible, a greater use of community resources, earned clemency, a totally open system always available to public scrutiny, and the drastic redesign of decent facilities for use in the small minority of cases where security is essential for community self-protection.

We agree with one writer who recently stated:

> The long history of "prison reform" is over. On the whole the prisons have played out their allotted role. They cannot be reformed and must be gradually torn down. But let us give up the comforting myth that the remaining facilities (and they will be prisons) can be changed into hospitals. Prisons will be small and humane; anything else is treason to the human spirit. We shall be cleansed of the foreign element of forced treatment with its totalitarian overtones. Officials will no longer be asked to do what they cannot do; they would be relieved of the temptation to do what should not be done: further utilize the iron pressure-chamber of prison life to change the offender.
>
> Crime arises from social causes and can be controlled and reduced (but not eliminated) through social action. *The myth of correctional treatment is now the main obstacle to progress; it has become the last line of defense of the prison system; it prevents the sound use of resources to balance public protection*

and inmate rights; and it diverts energy away from defending democracy through widening opportunity. It is time to awake from the dream.[1]

The walls—and all they lead to and represent—must come down, as John Bartlow Martin warned years ago. Our correctional philosophy must depart from its foundation in institutions. As we have shown in the last chapter, the idea of pursuing private community alternatives to prison institutions is not radical; it is what well-motivated people with good sense and some means usually do. To do otherwise in our public institutions is to give credence to claims that the correction system is hypocritically paternalistic, pseudomoralistic, racist, and classist.

We prefer the evolution of an alternative system that does not rely fundamentally on imprisonment and prison institutions. Until that mentality is accepted, we feel that all discussions about reform are topsy-turvy. Once we presume the existence and use of prisons and the consequent enslavement of men, then every amenity is a fight, every improvement a big deal: having women staff in men's institutions and men staff in women's institutions, allowing sexual cohabitation between prisoners and their wives, permitting freer access to mail and phone privileges—such simple basic things should be presumed, but in the context of a prison system they are considered presumptuous. Everything normal is a concession from the idea of imprisonment.

Calling the prison system with its appendages the correction system, and calling punishment treatment is illusory. The treatment rationale maximizes the intrusions on the people involved, with no proof, however, of its ability to modify behavior. Having passed through two centuries of a bad experiment attempting to use prisons to reform and rehabilitate, we would make a crucial error if our next change was to use prisons to alter psyches in a benign but unsure attempt to do good for unwilling subjects in the name of criminal justice.

The totality of the prison institution carries over to all of the processes that service it, including those that are carried out in the community and by non-correctional officials. Parole, probation, and clemency, for example, are administered in high-handed, aloof, closed, unresponsive, and undemocratic ways. Again, this is the way it is done because these processes are considered special dispensations to people who have once

1. Martinson, "The Paradox of Prison Reform," *New Republic*, April 29, 1972, at 23.

been labeled convicts, though there is no inherent reason why this must be so or why this must follow the decision to punish offenders.

The institutions themselves are run for the convenience of their administrators, not for their clients. The simplest kinds of deprivations—crude physical examinations, lineups for counts, the use of uniforms and numbers, denial of personal effects—are rationalized not as intentions but as necessities of the system. Responding to the administrator's claims that these and similar deprivations are necessary for what he termed "institutional survival," a federal judge recently abandoned the traditional judicial deference to the supposed requirements of prison society to declare that "if the functions of deterrence and rehabilitation cannot be performed in a prison without the imposition of a restrictive regime not reasonably related to those functions, it may well be that those functions can no longer be performed constitutionally in a prison setting."[2]

The system's errors and sins compound themselves and grind down human beings—both the keepers and the kept. While it is a correctional euphemism that men are sent to prison as punishment and not for punishment, in fact inmates are punished by the system's faults and not their own. Why wouldn't normal human beings react violently, cynically, hatefully to such a violent, cynical, hateful system? Perversely, the system responds to claims about its excesses by pointing to inmate failings as the reason why it operates as it does, and inmate successes as proof that it is working.

It is no part of any sentence that a man should be degraded, perverted, depersonalized in the process of serving his sentence; yet it happens all the time. The system creates an evil spiral. Once a man is involved in it, he has nothing—no privacy, no job, no social life, no opportunity. When he responds in natural if administratively unacceptable ways, then his few remaining shreds of contact with life are eliminated: his earned good time is taken away, his meager canteen privileges are canceled, he is thrown from a cell to a hole, all without due process of law.

The system disintegrates and with it the people that are in it. When the guard peers up the behind of the inmate, who is left with any human dignity? It is inevitable that the keeper and the kept should hate the society that created their situation and each other as the personifications of this hate.

2. *Morales v. Schmidt*, No. 71-C-29 (W.D. Wis., Apr. 6, 1972), at 14, 16.

For centuries all informed people have known this. We have evolved in reaction to these facts a rhetoric of reform: declarations of principles, blue-ribbon investigations, commission reports, a whole new nomenclature by which hacks become guards become correctional officers become treatment supervisors, although nothing that they do is fundamentally changed.

Even today, after Attica, Governor Nelson Rockefeller asks his legislature for $1,350,00 for a "special program facility . . . to house and provide a program for inmates requiring special treatment"—obfuscatory language out of *Alice in Wonderland* to describe a maximum-maximum prison to house those intrepid (politicized) inmates who revolted in the ordinary maximum-security prisons in New York.

Two centuries ago men had buckets in their cells instead of plumbing; later this was considered crude, and open toilets without seats were put in the small cells. Now more modern reformers recognize that this, too, is crude and inhumane and are developing air-conditioned cells with toilets that slide into the wall. No one has questioned the idea of caging men, only how to perfect the cage.

A federal judge in Wisconsin said in 1972 that after studying the local prison system he was persuaded the institution must end. It is, he urged, an intolerable institution "brutalizing to all involved . . . toxic to the social system . . . subversive of the brotherhood of man," more costly and less rational than even the system of slavery.[3] We agree.

3. *Id.* at 6.

Ronald L. Goldfarb
Linda R. Singer
1972

Selected Bibliography

Chapter I

The Attorney General's Survey of Release Procedures, Vol. V: *Prisons* (1940).

De Puy, "The Walnut Street Prison, Pennsylvania's First Penitentiary," 18 *Quarterly Journal of the Pennsylvania Historical Society* 130 (April 1951).

Galvin and Karacki, "Manpower and Training in Correctional Institutions," Staff Report of the Joint Commission on Correctional Manpower and Training, Ch. 3 (1969).

McKelvey, *American Prisons: A Study in American Social History Prior to 1915* (1936).

Teeters, *The Cradle of the Penitentiary: The Walnut Street Jail at Philadelphia, 1773–1835.* (Philadelphia Prison Society, 1955). An illustration of the Walnut Street Jail appears between pp. 84 and 85.

Chapter II

The Advisory Committee for Adult Detention, City and County of San Francisco, "San Francisco Adult Detention Facilities" (March 1968).

Alexander, *Jail Administration* (1957).

American Correctional Association, Directory of Correctional Institutions and Agencies (1970).

Amos and Manella, eds., *Delinquent Children in Juvenile Correctional Institutions* (1966).

Boslow and Kandel, "Psychiatric Aspects of Dangerous Behavior: The Retarded Offender," paper delivered at American Psychiatric Association Annual Meeting, New York City, May 4, 1965.

Boslow, Rosenthal, Kandel and Manne, "Methods and Experiences in Group Treatment of Defective Delinquents in Maryland," *Journal of Social Therapy*, Vol. 7, No. 2 (1961).

Bradley, Smith, Salstrom, *et al., Design for Change* (1968).

Breed, "Rehabilitation and Delinquency Prevention—The California Youth Authority in 1968," *American Journal of Correction* 24 (July–August 1968).

California Governor's Special Study Commission on Juvenile Justice, *A Study of the Administration of Juvenile Justice in California*, Part 2 (1960).

Cohen, "Educational Theory: The Design of Learning Environments," 3 *Research in Psychotherapy* 21 (1968).

——, Filipczak and Bis, *CASE I: An Initial Study of Contingencies Applicable to Special Education* (1967).

Cohn, "New Thinking for New Universities," *Architectural Association Journal* (London, 1964).

Coles, "Youthful Offenders," 161 *The New Republic* 12 (Oct. 4, 1969).

Dickerson, *et al.*, "Operational Guide for the James Marshall Treatment Program" (unpublished report, California Youth Authority, 1966).

Downey, "State Responsibility for Juvenile Detention Care" 1 (U.S. Department of Health, Education and Welfare, Youth Development and Delinquency Prevention Administration, 1970).

"Educational Therapy, The Design of Learning Environments," *Research in Psychotherapy*, Vol. 3 (1968).

Ferdinand, "Some Inherent Limitations in Rehabilitating Juvenile Delinquents in Training Schools," 31 *Federal Probation* 30, 32, December 1967.

Folks, *The Care of Dependent, Neglected and Delinquent Children* 9 (1902).

Forer, *No One Will Lissen: How Our Legal System Brutalizes the Youthful Poor* (1971).

——, Testimony Before the Senate Subcommittee to Investigate Juvenile Delinquency (91st Congress, 1st Session, 1969).

Galvin and Karacki, "Manpower and Training in Correctional Institutions," Staff Report of the Joint Commission on Correctional Manpower and Training 17 (1969).

Gerard, "Differential Treatment . . . A Way to Begin" (1969).

Hearings before the Subcommittee on Juvenile Delinquency of the Senate Committee on the Judiciary, 92nd Congress, 1st Session, May 3–5, 1971 (transcript).

House Select Committee on Crime, Juvenile Justice and Corrections, House Report No. 91-1806, 91st Congress, 2d Session (1971).

James, *Children in Trouble* (1970).

John Howard Association, Interim Report on the Cook County Jail (1967).

Knight, "The Marshall Program: Assessment of a Short-Term Institutional Treatment Program" (Part I, 1969).

Mattick and Aikman, "The Cloacal Region of American Corrections," 381 *Annals*, 109 (1969), 111.

Mattick and Sweet, *Illinois Jails—Challenge and Opportunity for the 1970's* (1969).

McCorkle, Elias, and Bixby, *The Highfields Story* (1958).

McCormick and Campos, "Introduce Yourself to Transactional Analysis" (1969).

McKelvey, *American Prisons: A Study in American Social History Prior to 1915* (1936).

"Minnesota State Training School—An Institution Reborn" (mimeographed, 1969).

Minnesota State Training School for Boys, "A Comprehensive Treatment Program for the Delinquent Adolescent" (1969).

National Conference of Superintendents of Training Schools and Reformatories, *Institutional Rehabilitation of Delinquent Youth* (1962).

National Council on Crime and Delinquency, *Correction in the United States* (1966).

Outerbridge, "The Tyranny of Treatment," *American Journal of Correction* 17 (April 1968).

Paulsen, "The Delinquency, Neglect, and Dependency Jurisdiction of the Juvenile Court," in Rosenheim, ed., *Justice for the Child* 44 (1962).

Platt, *The Child Savers* (1969).

Polsky, *Cottage Six* (1962).

Powers, *The Basic Structure of the Administration of Criminal Justice in Massachusetts* (Massachusetts Correctional Association, 5th ed., 1968).

Preliminary Report of the Governor's Special Committee on Criminal Offenders, State of New York, 202–06 (1968).

President's Commission on Law Enforcement and Administration of Justice, Task Force Report: *Corrections* 5, 75 (1967).

President's Commission on Law Enforcement and Administration of Justice, Task Force Report: *Juvenile Delinquency and Youth Crime* 3–9 (1967).

Report of the Advisory Panel Against Armed Violence to the Committee of the District of Columbia, United States Senate, 10 (91st Congress, 1st Session, 1969).

Report of the President's Commission on Crime in the District of Columbia 419, 706 (1966).

Rubin, "The Legal Character of Juvenile Delinquency, 261 *The Annals of the American Academy of Political and Social Science* 1 (1949).

Rubin and Smith, "The Future of the Juvenile Court: Implications for Correctional Manpower and Training," Consultant's paper for the Joint Commission on Correctional Manpower and Training (1968).

Saleebey, "Youth Correctional Centers: A New Approach to Treating Youthful Offenders" (1969).

Sherrill, *Military Justice Is to Justice as Military Music Is to Music* 191 (1970).

Smith, "California's Youthful Offender: Problems and Programs" 3 (paper prepared for the Prison Department, London, December 8, 1969).

Statement of Milton G. Rector, Executive Director of the National Council on Crime and Delinquency, before the Senate Subcommittee to Investigate Juvenile Delinquency of the Senate Committee on the Judiciary, 91st Congress, 1st Session, Pt. 20, at 5745 (1971).

Tappan, *Juvenile Delinquency* 3–13 (1949).

"Transactional Analysis for Youth Counsellors" (unpublished, California Youth Authority, 1969).

Vinter and Janowitz, "Effective Institutions for Juvenile Delinquents: A Research Statement," in *Prison Within Society* 180 (Hazelrigg, ed., 1968).

Vorrath, "Positive Peer Culture—Content, Structure and Process" (mimeographed, undated).

Warren, "Interpersonal Maturity Level Classification: Juvenile Diagnosis and Treatment of Low, Middle and High Maturity Delinquents" (1966).

Weeks, *Youthful Offenders at Highfields* (1958).

Chapter III

Administrative Office of the U.S. Courts, Division of Probation, The Presentence Investigation Report (1965).

Alexander, "A Hopeful View of the Sentencing Process, 3 *American Criminal Law Quarterly* 189 (1965).

Allenstein, "The Attorney-Probation Officer Relationship," 16 *Crime and Delinquency* 181 (1970).

American Bar Association Project on Minimum Standards for Criminal Justice, "Standards Relating to Appellate Review of Sentences" (approved draft 1968).

American Bar Association Project on Minimum Standards for Criminal Justice, "Standards Relating to Sentencing Alternatives and Procedures" (approved draft 1968).

"Appellate Review of Sentences," hearings on S.2722 before the Subcommittee on Improvements in Judicial Machinery of the Senate Committee on the Judiciary, 89th Congress, 2d Session (1966), p. 89 (statement of Professor Gerhard O. W. Mueller).

"Appellate Review of Sentences," a Symposium at the Judicial Conference of the United States Court of Appeals for the Second Circuit, 32 *Federal Rules Decisions* 249, 265 (1962) (remarks of Judge Soboloff).

Brewster, "Appellate Review of Sentences," 40 *Federal Rules Decisions* 79, 85–86 (1965).

Brown, "The Treatment of the Recidivist in the United States," 23 *Canadian Bar Review* 640 (1945).

California Board of Corrections, *Probation Study* (1964).

California State Assembly, *Parole Board Reform in California* (1970).

California State Assembly, "Preliminary Report on the Costs and Effects of the California Criminal Justice System and Recommendations for Legislation to Increase Support of Local Police and Correctional Programs" (staff report prepared for the Assembly Ways and Means Committee, 1969).

Cameron, "The New Zealand Criminal Compensation Act of 1963," 16 *University of Toronto Law Journal* 177 (1965).

Carter, "Variations in Presentence Report Recommendations and Court Dispositions," 2 Washington Department of Institutions Research Report 27 (November 1969).

Carter and Williams, "Some Facts in Sentencing Policy," in *Crime and Justice in Society* 396 (Quinney ed. 1969).

Chambliss, "The Deterrent Influence of Punishment," 12 *Crime and Delinquency* 70 (1966).

———, "Types of Deterrence and the Effectiveness of Legal Sanctions, 1967 *Wisconsin Law Review* 703.

Chappell, "Compensating Australian Victims of Violent Crime," 41 *Australian Law Journal* 3 (1967).

———, "The Criminal Compensation Act of 1967" 2 *Australian Bar Gazette* 7 (1968).

———, "The Emergence of Schemes to Compensate Victims of Crime," 43 *Southern California Law Review* 69, 78 (1970).

Childres, "Compensation for Criminally Inflicted Personal Injury," 50 *Minnesota Law Review* 271, 279–81 (1965).

Cohen, "The Integration of Restitution in the Probation Services," *Journal of Criminal Law, Criminology and Police Science* 315 (Jan.–Feb. 1944).

Cohen, "The Legal Challenge to Corrections: Implications for Manpower and Training" 64 (1969).

Conrad, "Decisions and Discretion: A Critique of the Indeterminate Sentence" (unpublished paper, 1970).

"Court Treatment of General Recidivist Statutes," 48 *Columbia Law Review* 238 (1948).

Dash, Medalie and Rhoden, "Demonstrating Rehabilitative Planning as a Defense Strategy," 54 *Cornell Law Review* 408 (1969).

Dawson, "Legal Norms and the Juvenile Correctional Process," in Cohen, *The Legal Challenge to Corrections* 88 (1969).

———, *Sentencing: The Decision as to Type, Length, and Conditions of Sentence* (1959).

Division of Probation, Administrative Office of the U. S. Courts, "The Presentence Report" (1965).

Doyle, "A Sentencing Council in Operation," 25 *Federal Probation* 28 (September 1961).

Driver and Miles, eds., *The Babylonian Laws* (1955).

Edwards, "Compensation to Victims of Crimes of Personal Violence," 30 *Federal Probation* 3, 7 (June 1966).

Enker, "Perspectives on Plea Bargaining," President's Commission on Law Enforcement and Administration of Justice, Task Force Report: *The Courts* 108 (1967).

Eremko, "Compensation of Criminal Injuries in Saskatchewan," 19 *University of Toronto Law Journal* 263 (1969).

Feres v. United States, 340 U.S. 135, 193–40 (1950).

Fry, *Arms of the Law* 126 (1951).

Gellhorn and Lauer, "Congressional Settlement of Tort Claims Against the United States," 55 *Columbia Law Review* 1 (1955).

George, "Comparative Sentencing Techniques," 27 *Federal Probation* (March 1959).

Goldberg, "Equality and Governmental Action," 39 *New York University Law Review* 205 (1964).

————, Preface, "Symposium on Governmental Compensation for Victims of Violence," 43 *Southern California Law Review* (1970).

Greenberg and Himmelstein, "Varieties of Attack on the Death Penalty," 15 *Crime and Delinquency* 112 (1969).

Hall, "Reduction of Criminal Sentences on Appeal," 37 *Columbia Law Review* 521 (1937).

Holbrook, "A Survey of Metropolitan Trial Courts—Los Angeles Area" 318 (report to the Section on Judicial Administration of the American Bar Association, 1956).

Hyde, "If Prisoners Could Talk to Judges," 51 *Judicature* 258 (1968).

Institute for the Study of Crime and Delinquency, Model Community Correctional Program, Report III: *Crime and Its Correction in San Joaquin County* 341–42 (1969).

James, "Tort Liability of Governmental Units and Their Officers," 22 *University of Chicago Law Review* 610 (1966).

Jeffrey, "The Development of Crime in Early English Society," 47 *Journal of Criminal Law, Criminology and Police Science* 647, 655 (1957).

Kadish, "The Advocate and the Expert—Counsel in the Peno-Correctional Process," 45 *Minnesota Law Review* (1961).

Kaufman, "Sentencing: The Judge's Problem," *Federal Probation* 3 (March 1960).

Kennedy, "Justice Is Found in the Hearts and Minds of Free Men," *Federal Probation* 3–4 (December 1961), 30 *Federal Rules Decisions* 401, 425 (1961).

Keve, *The Probation Officer Investigates* (1960).

Keve and Eglash, "Payments on a Debt to Society," *NPPA News,* September 1957.

Lamborn, "Remedies for the Victims of Crime," 43 *Southern California Law Review* 22 (1970).

Larsen, "A Prisoner Looks at Writ-Writing" 56 *California Law Review* 343 (1968).

"Law as an Agent of Delinquency Prevention," paper presented by Ted Rubin to the Delinquency Strategy Conference, California Council on Criminal Justice, Santa Barbara, California, February 18–20, 1970.

Lehrich, "The Use and Disclosure of Presentence Reports," 47 *Federal Rules Decisions* 225 (1968).

Linden, *The Report of the Osgoode Hall Study on Compensation for Victims of Crime* 27 (1968).

Lovald and Stub, "The Revolving Door: Reactions of Chronic Drunkenness

Offenders to Court Sanctions," 59 *Journal of Criminal Law, Criminology and Police Science* 525 (1968).

Low, "Comment on the Sentencing System: Part C," in Working Papers of the National Commission on Reform of Federal Criminal Laws 1335 (1970).

————, "Preliminary Memorandum on Sentencing Structure," in Working Papers of the National Commission on Reform of Federal Criminal Laws 1246–50 (1970).

Luger and Saltman, "The Youthful Offender," Appendix G to The President's Commission on Law Enforcement and Administration of Justice, Task Force Report: *Juvenile Delinquency and Youth Crime* 119 (1967).

Meador, "The Review of Criminal Sentences in England," in American Bar Association Project on Minimum Standards for Criminal Justice, Standards Relating to Appellate Review of Sentences (approved draft 1968), Appendix C.

McGee, "What's Past Is Prologue," 381 *Annals of the American Academy of Political and Social Science* 8 (1969).

Mitford, "Kind and Unusual Punishment in California," *The Atlantic*, March 1971.

Mueller, "Compensation for Victims of Crime: Thought Before Action," 55 *Minnesota Law Review* 213, 220–21 (1965).

National Committee for Children and Youth, Project Crossroads—Phase I and Phase II (1970).

Note, "Appellate Review of Primary Sentencing Decisions: A Connecticut Case Study," 69 *Yale Law Journal* 1453 (1960).

Note, "The Equal Protection Clause and Imprisonment of the Indigent for Nonpayment of Fines," 64 *Michigan Law Review* 938 (1968).

Note, "Fines and Fining—An Evaluation," 101 *University of Pennsylvania Law Review* 1013, 1021–22 (1953).

Note, "The Ghetto Disorders: A Reconsideration of Post-Riot Remedies," 21 *University of Florida Law Review* 84, 88–89 (1968).

Note, "The Influence of the Defendant's Plea on Judicial Determination of Sentence," 66 *Yale Law Journal* 204 (1956).

Note, "Jury Sentencing in Virginia," 53 *Virginia Law Review* 968, 969 n.2 (1967).

Note, "Riot Insurance," 77 *Yale Law Journal* 541, 547–52 (1968).

Note, "Use of Restitution in the Criminal Process," 16 *UCLA Law Review* 456 (1969).

Packer, *The Limits of the Criminal Sanction* (1968).

Parsons, "The Present Investigation Report Must Be Preserved as a Confidential Document," *Federal Probation* 3 (March 1964).

The President's Commission on Law Enforcement and Administration of Justice, Task Force Report: *The Courts* (1967).

"Procedural Due Process at Judicial Sentencing for Felony," 81 *Harvard Law Review* 821 (1968).

Proposed New York Penal Law, Study Bill, Senate Int. 3918, Assembly Int. 5376 (1964).

Rettig, "Ethical Risk Sensitivity in Male Prisoners" 4 *British Journal of Criminology* 582 (1964).

"Riots and Municipal Liability," 14 *New York Law Forum* 824, 832–33, 835 (1968).

Rubin, "Allocation of Authority in the Sentencing-Correction Decision," 45 *Texas Law Review* 455 (1967).

———, *The Law of Criminal Correction* (1963).

———, "The Supreme Court, Cruel and Unusual Punishment, and the Death Penalty," 15 *Crime and Delinquency* 121, 126 (1969).

Savitz, "A Study in Capital Punishment," 49 *Journal of Criminal Law, Criminology and Police Science* 338 (1958).

Schafer, "Victim Compensation and Responsibility," 43 *Southern California Law Review* 55 (1970).

———, *The Victim and His Criminal: A Study in Functional Responsibility* (1968).

Schuessler, "The Deterrent Influence of the Death Penalty," 284 *Annals of the American Academy of Political Science* 54 (1952).

Sengstock, "Mob Action: Who Shall Pay the Price?", 44 *University of Detroit Journal of Urban Law* 407, 423–26 (1967).

Schultz, "The Violated: A Proposal to Compensate Victims of Violent Crime," 10 *St. Louis Law Review* 247 (1965).

Shank, "Aid to Victims of Violent Crimes in California," 43 *Southern California Law Review* 85 (1970).

Silverstein, *Defense of the Poor* 123 (1965).

Smith, "The Youthful Offender in America" (mimeographed, California Youth Authority, 1969).

Spincks, "In Opposition to Rule 34(c) (2), Proposed Federal Rules of Criminal Procedure," *Federal Probation* 7 (October–December 1944).

Starrs, "A Modest Proposal to Insure Justice for Victims of Crime," 55 *Minnesota Law Review* 285 (1965).

Steele, "Counsel Can Count in Federal Sentencing," 56 *American Bar Association Journal* 37 (1970).

Stein, "Imprisonment for Nonpayment of Fines and Costs: A New Look at the Law and the Constitution," 22 *Vanderbilt Law Review* 611 (1969).

Subin, *Criminal Justice in a Metropolitan Court* 105 (1966).

Tappan, *Crime, Justice and Correction* (1960).

———, "Habitual Offender Laws and Sentencing Practices in Relation to Organized Crime," in Ploscowe, ed., *Organized Crime and Law Enforcement* (1952).

Vera Institute of Justice, Bronx Sentencing Project (mimeographed, 1970).

———, "The Manhattan Court Employment Project—Phase I and Phase II" (1970).

Wald, "Poverty and Criminal Justice," The President's Commission on Law Enforcement and Administration of Justice, Task Force Report: *The Courts* 142, Appendix C (1967).

Weeks, "The New Zealand Criminal Injuries Compensation Scheme," 43 *Southern California Law Review* 107 (1970).

Wilson, "A New Arena Is Emerging to Test the Confidentiality of Presentence Reports," 25 *Federal Probation* 6 (December 1961).

Wolfgang, "Victim Compensation in Crimes of Personal Violence," 50 *Minnesota Law Review* 223 (1965).

Youngdahl, "Development and Accomplishments of Sentencing Institute in the Federal Judicial System," 45 *Nebraska Law Review* 513 (1966).

Chapter IV

American Correctional Association, *The Organization and Effectiveness of the Correctional Agencies* (1966).

Attorney General's Survey, *Attorney General's Survey of Release Procedures*, Vol. 2: *Probation* (Washington, 1939).

Beless and Pilcher, "Progress Report of the Probation Officer—Case Aide Project" (unpublished, University of Wisconsin, Center for Studies in Criminal Justice, 1969).

Benjamin, Freedman and Lynton, *Pros and Cons: New Roles for Nonprofessionals in Corrections* (1966).

Burnett, "The Volunteer Probation Counselor," 52 *Judicature* 285 (1969).

California Department of the Youth Authority, "Probation Subsidy Program" (unpublished report, August 1968).

California State Assembly, Preliminary Report on the Costs and Effects of the California Criminal Justice System and Recommendations for Legislation to Increase Support of Local Police and Corrections Program (staff report prepared for the Assembly Ways and Means Committee, March 1969).

Cocks, "From 'WHISP' to 'RODEO,'" 21 *California Youth Authority Quarterly* 7 (Winter 1968).

Cohen, "The Legal Challenge to Corrections: Implications for Manpower and Training" 64 (1969).

Davis, "A Study of Adult Probation Violation Rates by Means of the Cohort Approach," 55 *Journal of Criminal Law, Criminology and Police Science* (1964).

DiCerbo, "When Should Probation Be Revoked?," 30 *Federal Probation* (June 1966).

Dressler, *Practice and Theory of Probation and Parole* (1959).

Elton-Mayo, "Probation and After-Care in Certain European Countries" (report to Council of Europe, European Committee on Crime Problems, 1964).

Fish, "The Status of the Federal Probation System," 12 *Crime and Delinquency* (1966).

Gronerwold, "Supervisory Practices in the Federal Probation System," 28 *Federal Probation* 19 (September 1964).

Heijder, "Some Characteristics of the Dutch Probation System," 11 *International Journal of Offender Therapy* (1967).

Hunsicker, "Probation: Los Angeles County's Progressive Ventures in Treatment," Department of Health, Education and Welfare, *Delinquency Prevention Reporter,* 3, 5–6 (January 1971).

Institute for the Study of Crime and Delinquency, Model Community Correctional Project, Report III: "Crime and Its Correction in San Joaquin County" (1969).

Institute for the Study of Crime and Delinquency, Model Community Correctional Project, Appendix Report: "The Model Community Misdemeanant Probation Program" (1969).

Jacks, "An Experiment in Criminal Correction," 33 *Texas Bar Journal* 25 (1970).

Joint Commission on Correctional Manpower and Training, *The Use of Ex-Offenders as a Manpower Resource* (1968).

Keve, *Imaginative Programming in Probation and Parole* (1967).

————, Report to the Ford Foundation on Probation in the United States (unpublished, March 1967).

Michigan Crime and Delinquency Council, The Saginaw Probation Project (1963).

Miles, "The Reality of the Probation Officer's Dilemma," *Federal Probation* 18 (March 1965).

Nan, "A Day in the Life of a Federal Probation Officer," *Federal Probation* 17 (March 1967).

National Commission on Reform of Federal Criminal Laws, Sentencing Chapters (draft, October 11, 1968) § 302.03(d).

Newman, *Sourcebook on Probation, Parole and Pardons* (2nd ed. 1964).

Note, "Judicial Review of Probation Conditions," 67 *Columbia Law Review* (1967).

The President's Commission on Law Enforcement and Administration of Justice, Task Force Report: *Corrections* (1967).

Prins, "Training for Probation Work in England and Wales," 28 *Federal Probation* (December 1964).

Reed and King, "Factors in the Decision-Making of North Carolina Probation Officers," 3 *Journal of Research in Crime and Delinquency* 120 (1966).

Report of the President's Commission on Crime in the District of Columbia (1966).

Royal Oak Municipal Court Probation Department, *Concerned Citizens and a City Criminal Court* (1968).

Rubin, *The Law of Criminal Correction* (1963).

Scheier, Preface to U.S. Department of Health, Education and Welfare, Office of Juvenile Delinquency and Youth Development, Volunteer Programs in Courts (1969).

Scheier and Goter, "Using Volunteers in Court Settings," Office of Juvenile Delinquency and Youth Development (1968).

Scudder, *Prisoners Are People* (1952).

Smith, Berlin and Bassin, "Group Therapy with Adult Probationers," *Federal Probation* 3 (September 1969).

Tappan, *Crime, Justice and Correction* (1960).

Taylor and McEachern, "Needs and Directions in Probation Training," *Federal Probation* 18 (March 1966).

Treger, "Reluctance of the Social Agency to Work with the Offender," *Federal Probation* 23 (March 1965).

Underwood, "Games in Probation and Parole" (unpublished paper, California Youth Authority, Division of Delinquency Prevention, 1969).

"Volunteer Programs in Courts," (Office of Juvenile Delinquency and Youth Development, 1969).

Wahl, "Federal Probation Belongs with the Courts," 12 *Crime and Delinquency* (1966).

Wald, "Poverty and Criminal Justice," The President's Commission on Law Enforcement and Administration of Justice, Task Force Report: *The Courts* (1967).

Wallace, "A Fresh Look at Old Probation Standards," 10 *Crime and Delinquency* (April 1964).

Warren, "The Case for Differential Treatment of Delinquents," 381 *Annals* 47 (1969).

Chapter V

Attorney General's Survey of Release Procedures, Vol. IV, *Parole* 25–27 (1939).

Bixby, "A New Role for Parole Boards," *Federal Probation* 24 (June 1970).

Boller, "Preparing Prisoners for Their Return to the Community," *Federal Probation* 43 (June 1966).

Bruce, Burgess and Harno, *The Working of the Indeterminate Sentence Law and the Parole System in Illinois* (1928).

Bureau of Rehabilitation of the National Capital Area, *Services to Expiration of Sentence Releases* (1963).

Burkhart, *Parole in California* 2–3.

California Department of Corrections, Special Intensive Parole Unit Reports, Phases I-IV (1953–64).

———, Report to the Legislature on Parole Unit Work Program (1968).

———, The Parole Work Unit Program: an Evaluative Report (unpublished, 1967).

Catalino, "A Prerelease Program for Juveniles in a Medium-Security Institution," *Federal Probation* 41 (December 1967).

Chappel, "The Lawyer's Role in the Administration of Probation and Parole," 48 *American Bar Association Journal* 742 (1962).

Clark, "The Texas Prerelease Program," *Federal Probation* 53 (December 1966).

Cohen, *The Legal Challenge to Corrections* 43–44, 50–52 (1969).

Conrad, *Decisions and Discretion—A Critique of the Indeterminate Sentence* (unpublished, 1970).

Davis, *Discretionary Justice* (1969).

District of Columbia Department of Corrections, *The Youth Services Division* (unpublished, 1970).

Dill, "History of Parole System in California," paper presented at the Parole Action Study Staff Meeting, Center for the Study of Law and Society, University of California, Berkeley, California, September 1, 1967.

Dressler, *Practice and Theory of Probation and Parole* (1959).

Federal Probation Officers Association, A Compilation of State and Federal Statutes Relating to Civil Rights of Persons Convicted of Crime (1960).

Glaser, *The Effectiveness of a Prison and Parole System* (1964).

———, "The Efficacy of Alternative Approaches to Parole Prediction," 20 *American Sociological Review* 283 (1955).

———, "Prediction Tables as Accounting Devices for Judges and Parole Boards" 8 *Crime and Delinquency* 239 (1962).

Glueck and Glueck, *500 Criminal Careers* (1930).

Gottfredson, "Assessment and Prediction Methods in Crime and Delinquency," The President's Commission on Law Enforcement and Administration of Justice, Task Force Report: *Juvenile Delinquency and Youth Crime* (1967).

———, "A Shorthand Formula for Base Expectancies" (California Department of Corrections, Research Report No. 5, reissued November 1, 1965).

———, "Comparing and Combining Subjective and Objective Parole Predictions" (California Department of Corrections, Research Newsletter, September–December 1961).

Gottfredson & Ballard, Jr., "Offender Classification and Parole Prediction" (Institute for the Study of Crime and Delinquency, December 1966).

Gottfredson, Ballard, Jr. and Bonds, "Base Expectancy at California Institution for Women" (California Department of Corrections, Research Report No. 15, September 1962).

Griffiths, "The Role of Research," in Amos and Manella, eds., *Delinquent Children in Juvenile Correctional Institutions* 36 (1966).

Hakeem, "Prediction of Parole Outcome from Summaries of Case Histories," 52 *Journal of Criminal Law, Criminology and Police Science* 145 (1961).

50 *Harvard Law Record*, April 30, 1970.

Johnson, "The 'Failure' of a Parole Research Project," 18 *California Youth Authority Quarterly* 35 (Fall 1965).

Keve, *Imaginative Programming in Probation and Parole* (1967).

Kingsnorth, "Decision-Making in a Parole Bureaucracy," 6 *Journal of Research in Crime and Delinquency* 210 (1969).

Korn and McCorkle, *Criminology and Penology* (1959).

Luane, *Predicting Criminality* (1936).

Mannheim and Wilkins, *Prediction Methods in Relation to Borstal Training* (1955).

Memorandum from Walter Dunbar, former Chairman of the U.S. Parole Board, to the National Commission on Reform of Federal Criminal Laws re:

"Suggested Modifications of the Paroling Authority" (unpublished, February 7, 1969).

New York Division for Youth, "Duties and Responsibilities of Aftercare Service Bureau" (unpublished memorandum, 1969).

New York State Division of Parole, "Manual for Parole Officers" (1953) (lecture by George Combs, 1839).

Note, "*Anthropotelemetry*: Dr. Schwitzgebel's Machine," 80 *Harvard Law Review* 403 (1966).

Ohlin, *Selection for Parole* (1951).

"Perspectives on Correctional Manpower and Training," staff report to the Joint Commission on Correctional Manpower and Training (1969).

Preliminary Report of the Governor's Special Committee on Criminal Offenders (New York, 1968).

The President's Commission on Law Enforcement and the Administration of Justice, Task Force Report: *Corrections* (1967).

Public Systems, Inc., "A Study of the Characteristics and Recidivism Experience of California Prisoners," in California Assembly, report of the Select Committee on the Administration of Justice, Parole Board Reform in California, Appendix I (1970).

Report of the President's Commission on Crime in the District of Columbia (1966).

Robison, Robison, Kingsnorth and Inman, *By the Standard of His Rehabilitation* (1970).

Robison and Takagi, "Case Decisions in a State Parole System" (research report. No. 31, Research Division, California Department of Corrections, November 1968).

Rubin, "Needed—New Legislation in the Correctional Field" (paper presented to the Oregon Corrections Association Annual Conference, October 15, 1969).

Savides, "A Parole Success Prediction Study" (California Department of Corrections, Research Newsletter September–December 1961).

Schwitzgebel, "A Program of Research in Behavioral Electronics," 9 *Behavioral Science* 233 (1964).

Stanton, "Is It Safe to Parole Inmates Without Jobs?" 12 *Crime and Delinquency* 147 (April 1966).

Underwood, "The Department of the Youth Authority" (unpublished memorandum, 1968).

Vold, *Prediction Methods and Parole* (1931).

Chapter VI

American Correctional Association, *Manual of Correctional Standards* (3d ed. 1966).

Attorney General's Survey of Release Procedures, Vol. III, *Pardon* (1939).

Bacon, *A New Abridgement of the Law; An Essay on Crimes and Punishments* 152 (Albany, 1872).

Cozart, "The Benefit of Executive Clemency," 32 *Federal Probation* 33 (June 1968).

England, "Pardon, Commutation and Their Improvement," 39 *Prison Journal* 23 (1959).

Federal Probation Officers Association, A Compilation of State and Federal Statutes Relating to Civil Rights of Persons Convicted of Crime (1960).

Gough, "The Expungement of Adjudication Records of Juvenile and Adult Offenders: A Problem of Status," *Washington University Law Quarterly* (1966).

Grupp, "Some Historical Aspects of the Pardon in England," *American Journal of Legal History* (1963).

Hartland, *Primitive Law* (1924).

Lavinsky, "Executive Clemency: Study of a Decisional Problem Arising in the Terminal Stages of the Criminal Process," 42 *Chicago-Kent Law Review* 13 (1965).

McCarthy, "Sort of a Free World," *The New Republic* 16 (February 8, 1969).

McPherson, *The Political History of the United States of America During the Period of Reconstruction* (1871).

Note, "The Effect of a Pardon on License Revocation and Reinstatement," 15 *Hastings Law Review* 355 (1964).

Note, "Executive Clemency in Capital Cases," 39 *New York University Law Review* 136 (1964).

Nussbaum, *First Offenders—A Second Chance* (1956).

Orfield, *Criminal Appeals in America*, Ch. 1 (1939).

Powers, *The Basic Structure of the Administration of Criminal Justice in Massachusetts* (5th ed., 1968).

President's Commission on Law Enforcement and Administration of Justice, Task Force Report: *Corrections* (1967).

Riley, *Memorials of London and London Life* 563 (1868).

Rubin, "The Supreme Court, Cruel and Unusual Punishment, and the Death Penalty," 15 *Crime and Delinquency* 121 (1969).

Stephen, 4 *New Commentaries on the Laws of England* 422 (1903).

Thorpe, *Ancient Laws and Institutions of England, The Commissioners on the Public Records of King William IV*, Vol. I (1840).

Weihofen, "Pardon and Other Forms of Clemency," in Rubin, *The Law of Criminal Correction* (1963).

Williams, "The New Exodus: Go North, Young Man," *The New Republic* 15 (May 16, 1970).

Yager, "Executive Clemency," 33 *Journal of the State Bar of California* 221 (1958).

Chapter VII

Advisory Commission for Adult Detention Facilities for the City and County of San Francisco, Annual Report (1968).

American Correctional Association, *Manual of Correctional Standards* 270–271 (3d ed. 1966).

Amsterdam, "Criminal Prosecutions Affecting Federally Guaranteed Civil Rights: Federal Removal and Habeas Corpus Jurisdiction to Abort State Court Trial," 113 *University of Pennsylvania Law Review* 793, 884–96 (1965).

Anderson, *Ombudsman Papers: American Experience and Proposals* (1969).

Ardrey, *The Territorial Imperative* (1966).

Barkin, "Impact of Changing Law Upon Prison Policy," 48 *Prison Journal* 3 (1968).

Brown, "Black Muslim Prisoners and Religious Discrimination: The Developing Criteria for Judicial Review," 32 *George Washington Law Review* 1124 (1964).

California Legislature, Assembly Office of Research, Report on the Economic Status and Rehabilitative Value of California Correctional Industries (1969).

Cherry, "A Look at Prisoner Self-Representation," 48 *Prison Journal* 28 (1968).

Cohen, "The Legal Challenge to Corrections: Implications for Manpower and Training" 64 (1969).

Cohen, "Reading Law in Prison" 48 *Prison Journal* 21 (1968).

Comment, "Administrative Fairness in Corrections," *Wisconsin Law Review* 587 (1969).

Comment, "Federal Injunctions Against State Actions," 35 *George Washington Law Review* 744, 804–806 (1967).

Comment, "Legal Services for Prison Inmates" *Wisconsin Law Review* 514 (1967).

Comment, "Prisoner Restrictions—Prisoner Rights," 59 *Journal of Criminal Law, Crime and Police Science* 386, 389–92 (1968).

Comment, "Resolving Civil Problems of Correctional Inmates," *Wisconsin Law Review* 574 (1969).

Conrad, "Violence in Prison," 364 *Annals* 113 (1966).

Davidson, "The Worst Jail I've Ever Seen," *Saturday Evening Post*, July 13, 1968, at 17.

Davis, *Administrative Law Text 28.01* (1959).

Davis, "Sexual Assaults in the Philadelphia Prison System and Sheriff's Vans," *Transaction*, December 1968, at 8.

"Discipline by 'Rape' at U. S. Prison," *National Catholic Reporter*, April 23, 1969, at 1.

Federal Rules of Civil Procedure, Rule 23 (Advisory Committee Notes).

Fitzharris, "The Desirability of a Correctional Ombudsman" (report to the California Assembly Committee on Criminal Procedure, 1971).

Frankino, "Manacles and the Messenger: A Short Study in Religious Freedom in the Prison Community," 14 *Catholic University Law Review* 30 (1965).

Friedenthal, "New Limitations on Federal Jurisdiction," 11 *Stanford Law Review* 213, 216–18 (1959).

Goldberg and Dershowitz, "Declaring the Death Penalty Unconstitutional," 83 *Harvard Law Review* 1773 (1970).

Goldfarb, *The Contempt Power* (1963).

Greenwald, "Disposition of the Insane Defendant After 'Acquittal'—The Long Road from Commitment to Release," 59 *Journal of Criminal Law, Crime and Police Science* 583 (1968).

Hall, *The Hidden Dimension* (1966).

Hearings Before the Senate Subcommittee to Investigate Juvenile Delinquency of the Senate Committee on the Judiciary, 91st Congress, 1st Session (1969).

Hirschkop and Millemann, "The Unconstitutionality of Prison Life," 55 *Virginia Law Review* 795 (1969).

Jackson, "Our Prisons Are Criminal," New York *Times*, September 22, 1968, at 62 (magazine).

Jacob, "Prison Discipline and Inmate Rights," 5 *Harvard Civil Rights—Civil Liberties Law Review* 227 (1970).

Jacob and Sharma, "Justice After Trial: Prisoners' Need for Legal Services in the Criminal-Correctional Process," 18 *Kansas Law Review* 493 (1970).

Jaffee, *Judicial Control of Administrative Action* 595 (1965).

James, *Civil Procedure* 494–95 (1965).

Jiudice, "State Prisons and the 'Free Community,'" 41 *New York State Bar Journal* 672, 675–76 (1969).

Kimball and Newman, "Judicial Intervention in Correctional Decisions: Threat and Response," 14 *Crime and Delinquency* 1, 4 (1968).

Larsen, "A Prisoner Looks at Writ-Writing," 56 *California Law Review* 343 (1968).

Leopold, "What Is Wrong with the Prison System?," 45 *Nebraska Law Review* 33, 50 (1966).

Lorenz, *On Aggression* (1966).

Minton and Rice, "Using Racism at San Quentin," *Ramparts*, January 1970.

Monachesi, "The Italian Surveillance Judge," 26 *Journal of Criminal Law, Crime and Police Science* 811 (1936).

Monthly Labor Review, January 1969, at 3.

Mueller, "Punishment, Corrections and the Law," 45 *Nebraska Law Review* 58, 83–87 (1966).

Muraskin, "Censorship of Mail: The Prisoner's Right to Communicate by Mail with the Outside World," 48 *Prison Journal* 33, 34–38 (1968).

Murton and Hyams, *Accomplices to the Crime* (1969).

Myers, "Sensory Deprivation (Sleep Saturation?) and Performance," research report No. 2, Naval Medical Research Institute, October 1968.

Myers, Johnson and Smith, "Subjective Stress and Affect States as a Function of Sensory Deprivation," in *Proceedings*, 76th Annual Convention, American Psychological Association 623–24 (1968).

Note, "Beyond the Ken of the Courts: A Critique of Judicial Refusal to Review the Complaints of Convicts," 72 *Yale Law Journal* 506 (1963).

Note, "Civil Restraint, Mental Illness and the Right to Treatment," 77 *Yale Law Journal* 87 (1967).

Note, "Constitutional Rights of Prisoners," 110 *University of Pennsylvania Law Review* (1962).

Note, "The Cruel and Unusual Punishment Clause and the Substantive Criminal Law," 79 *Harvard Law Review* 636–37 (1966).

Note, "Detainers and the Correctional Process," 1966 *Washington University Law Quarterly* 417.

Note, "Effective Guaranty of a Speedy Trial for Convicts in Other Jurisdictions," 77 *Yale Law Journal* 767 (1968).

Note, "Federal-Question Abstention: Justice Frankfurter's Doctrine in an Activist Era," 80 *Harvard Law Review* 604 (1967).

Note, "Habeas Corpus—Effect of Supreme Court Change in Law on Exhaustion of State Remedies Requisite to Federal Habeas Corpus," 113 *University of Pennsylvania Law Review* 1303 (1965).

Note, "Multiparty Federal Habeas Corpus," 81 *Harvard Law Review* 1482, 1483–85 (1968).

Note, "The Detainer: A Problem in Interstate Criminal Administration," 48 *Columbia Law Review* 1190 (1948).

Note, "Legal Service for Prison Inmates," *Wisconsin Law Review* 514, 520–22 (1967).

Note, "The Nascent Right to Treatment," 53 *Virginia Law Review* 1134 (1967).

Note, "Prisoner Assistance on Federal Habeas Corpus Petitions," 19 *Stanford Law Review* 887 (1967).

Note, "Prison 'No-Assistance' Regulations and the Jailhouse Lawyer," 1968 *Duke Law Journal* 343.

Note, "Prison Restrictions—Prisoner Rights," 59 *Journal of Criminal Law, Crime and Police Science* 386 (1968).

Note, "The Right of Expression in Prison," 40 *Southern California Law Review* 407 (1967).

Note, "Student-Employees and Collective Bargaining Under the National Labor Relations Act: An Alternative to Violence on American College Campuses," 38 *George Washington Law Review* 1026 (1970).

Note, "Suits by Black Muslim Prisoners to Enforce Religious Rights— Obstacles to a Hearing on the Merits," 20 *Rutgers Law Review* 528 (1966).

Oaks, "Habeas Corpus in the States—1776–1865," 32 *University of Chicago Law Review* 243 (1965).

Packer, "Making the Punishment Fit the Crime," 77 *Harvard Law Review* 1071 (1964).

Report of the Arkansas Penitentiary Commission (1968).

"Report of the Committee on Habeas Corpus," 33 *Federal Rules Decisions* 367, 384 (1963).

Report of the Task Force on Law and Law Enforcement to the National Commission on the Causes and Prevention of Violence, Law and Order Reconsidered 579 (1969).

Ross, "Industrial Jurisprudence and the Campus," in *Arbitration and Social Change, Proceedings of 22nd Annual Meeting of National Academy of Arbitrators* 43 (Somers ed. 1970).

Rothschild, "Arbitration and the National Labor Relations Board: An Examination of Preferences and Prejudices and Their Relevance, 28 *Ohio State Law Journal* 195, 210–11 (1967).

Rubin, *The Law of Criminal Correction* 286–87, 291–94 (1963).

———, "The Law Schools and the Law of Sentencing and Correctional Treatment," 43 *Texas Law Review* 332 (1965).

———, "Needed—New Legislation in the Correctional Field" (paper presented to the Oregon Corrections Association Annual Conference, October 15, 1969).

———, "The Supreme Court, Cruel and Unusual Punishment, and the Death Penalty," 15 *Crime and Delinquency* 121 (1969).

Selye, *The Stress of Life* (1956).

Sensory Deprivation: Fifteen Years of Research (Zubek ed. 1969).

Seewald, "The Italian Surveillance Judge," 45 *Nebraska Law Review* 96 (1966).

Smith, Merrifield and Rothschild, *Collective Bargaining and Labor Arbitration*, Ch. II (1970).

Sneidman, "Prisoners and Medical Treatment: Their Rights and Remedies," 4 *Criminal Law Bulletin* 450 (1968).

Southern Regional Council, Special Report—"The Delta Prisons: Punishment for Profit" (1968).

"Special Project—The Collateral Consequences of a Criminal Conviction," 23 *Vanderbilt Law Review* 929 (1970).

Spector, "A Prison Librarian Looks at Writ-Writing," 56 *California Law Review* 365 (1968).

State of California, Youth and Adult Corrections Agency, *The Organization of State Correctional Services in the Control and Treatment of Crime and Delinquency*, Ch. VI (1967).

Sykes, *The Society of Captives* 70–72, 95–99 (1958).

Symposium, "The Ombudsman or Citizens' Defender: A Modern Institution," 377 *Annals* 1 (1966).

"Symposium: The Right to Treatment," 57 *Georgia Law Journal* 673 (1969).

"Symposium—The Right to Treatment," 36 *University of Chicago Law Review* 742 (1969).

Turner, "Establishing the Rule of Law in Prisons: A Manual for Prisoners' Rights Litigation," 23 *Stanford Law Review* 473 (1971).

University of Minnesota, "A Proposal to Establish an Experimental Ombudsman for the Minnesota Department of Corrections" (1971).

"The Use of Fact-Finding in Public Employee Disputes Settlement," in *Proceedings* of 22nd Annual Meeting of National Academy of Arbitrators, Ch. V (Somers ed. 1970).

Van Alstyne, "The Demise of the Right-Privilege Distinction in Constitutional Law," 81 *Harvard Law Review* 1439, 1462 (1968).

Wechsler, "Federal Jurisdiction and the Revision of the Judicial Code," 13 *Law and Contemporary Problems* 216, 225 (1948).

Weinstein, "Revision of Procedure: Some Problems in Class Actions," 9 *Buffalo Law Review* 433 (1960).

Wilson, "Legal Assistance Project at Leavenworth," 24 *Briefcase* 254 (1966).

Wright, "Class Actions," 47 *Federal Rules Decisions* 169 (1969).

———, *Federal Courts* 169–77 (1963).

Wright, "The Need for Education in the Law of Criminal Correction," 2 *Valparaiso Law Review* 84 (1967).

Chapter VIII

Adams, *The San Quentin Prison College Project: Final Report, Phase I* 62 (1968).

AFL-CIO Community Service Activities, *The Man Who Lived Again* (1955).

Aller, "Lessons Learned from Vocational Training Programs Given in a Prison Setting," in University of Wisconsin, *Conference on Education and Training in Correctional Institutions* (1968).

Alston Wilkes Society, Executive Director's 1969 Annual Report, Columbia, South Carolina.

———, "Older Adult Offender Project—First Year Progress Report" (1968).

American Correctional Association, *Manual of Correctional Standards* (3d ed. 1966).

Anderson, "Work Release Sentencing," 28 *Federal Probation* 7 (December 1964).

Asbell, *New Directions in Vocational Education* (U.S. Department of Health, Education and Welfare, Office of Education, 1967).

Attorney General's Survey of Release Procedures, *Prisons* (1939).

Ayer, "Work-Release Programs in the United States: Some Difficulties Encountered," 34 *Federal Probation* 53 (March 1970).

Benjamin, Friedman and Lynton, *Pros and Cons: New Roles for Nonprofessionals in Corrections* (1966).

Bennett, *I Chose Prison* (1970).

Blacker and Kantor, "Halfway Houses for Problem Drinkers," 24 *Federal Probation* 18 (June 1960).

Blauner and Shaffer, *New Careers and the Person* (1967).

Breed, "Rehabilitation and Delinquency Prevention—The California Youth Authority in 1968," *American Journal of Correction* (July–Aug. 1968).

Bresslin and Crosswhite, "Residential Aftercare: An Intermediate Step in the Correctional Process," 27 *Federal Probation* 37 (March 1963).

Brown, *Manchild in the Promised Land* (1965).

Bureau of Prisons, *New Bridges to the Community: A Collection of Studies on the First Year's Experience with the Work Release Program* (1967).

California Youth Authority, *Foster Grandparent Program* (1969).

Carter, "Middle-Class Delinquency—An Experiment in Community Control" (a report to the President's Commission on Juvenile Delinquency and Youth Development, 1968).

Carter, Dightman and Holliday, "A Progress Report on the Work Release and Training Release Programs in the Division of Adult Corrections." 2 *Washington Department of Institutions Research Report* 5 (1969).

Case, "'Doing Time' in the Community," *Federal Probation* 9 (March 1957).

Chambliss, "On the Validity of Official Statistics," *National Council on Crime and Delinquency Journal* 71 (January 1969).

Citizens' Council on Delinquency and Crime, Position Statement on Work Placement for Youthful and Adult Offenders (1966).

Clark & Wenninger, "Socio-Economic Class and Area as Correlates of Illegal Behavior Among Juveniles," 27 *American Sociological Review* 826 (December 1962).

Cleaver, *Soul on Ice* (1968).

Collins and Weisberg, "Training Needs in Correctional Institutions," Department of Labor, Manpower Research Bulletin No. 8 (April 1966).

Committee on Youth and Correction, Community Service Society of New York, A Study of Four Voluntary Treatment and Rehabilitation Programs for New York City's Narcotic Addicts (1967).

Conrad, *Crime and Its Correction* 274–77 (1967).

"Correctional Rehabilitation," U.S. Department of Health, Education and Welfare, Social and Rehabilitation Service, Rehabilitation Services Administration, Washington (1969).

Correctional Research Associates, *Community Work—An Alternative to Imprisonment* (1967).

Cressey, "Changing Criminals: The Application of the Theory of Differential Association," 61 *American Journal of Sociology* 116 (September 1955).

Cromie, "A Chance to Go Straight," *Saturday Evening Post* (April 30, 1960).

Dentler and Monroe, "Social Correlates of Early Adolescent Theft," 26 *American Sociological Review* 733 (October 1961).

Dorsey, Anderson, Hecht and Montilla, "Community Correctional Centers of the D.C. Department of Corrections" (draft, October 1970).

"Education and Training in Correctional Institutions—Proceedings of a Conference" 95–105 (University of Wisconsin, 1968).

Egerton, "Where They Try to Make Winners Out of Men Who Have Always Lost," *Southern Education Report* (May–June 1966).

England, "A Theory of Middle Class Juvenile Delinquency," 50 *Journal of Criminal Law, Criminology and Police Science* 353 (1960).

Erwin, "Cook County Jail's Short-Term Education Program," *American Journal of Correction* 14 (March–April 1970).

Fleisher, *The Economics of Delinquency* (1966).

———, "The Effect of Unemployment on Delinquent Behavior," 71 *Journal of Political Economics* 543 (1963).

Fortune News.

Glaser, "Crime, Age and Unemployment," 24 *American Sociological Review* 679 (1959).

———, *The Effectiveness of a Prison and Parole System,* Chs. 11, 12 and 14 (1964).

Gold, "Undetected Delinquent Behavior," 3 *Journal of Research in Crime and Delinquency* 27 (January 1966).

Grant, "The Offender as a Correctional Manpower Resource," paper presented to the First National Symposium on Law Enforcement, Science and Technology, Chicago, Illinois, March 9, 1967.

Grant and Grant, *New Careers Development Project: Final Report* (1967).

Grupp, "Work Release in the United States," 54 *Journal of Criminal Law, Criminology and Police Science* 267 (1963).

———, "Work Release—The Sheriff's Viewpoint," 13 *Crime and Delinquency* 513 (1967).

Gwyn, *Work, Earn and Save* (1963).

Hall, Milazzo and Posner, *A Descriptive and Comparative Study of Recidivism in Prerelease Guidance Center Releasees* (1966).

Halvorson, "Work Release in Norway," 44 *Prison Journal* 26 (1964).

Hartung, "A Critique of the Sociological Approach to Crime and Correction," 23 *Law and Contemporary Problems* 703 (Autumn 1958).

Hecht, Effects of Halfway Houses on Neighborhood Crime Rates and Property Values: A Preliminary Survey (D.C. Dept. of Corr., Research Rept. No. 37, 1970).

Holmes, "The Volunteer Returns to the Court," 18 *Juvenile Court Judges Journal* 133 (1968).

J. F. Ingram State Vocational School, Progress Report in Vocational Training and Adult Basic Education, unpublished July 31, 1970.

International Halfway House Association, Directory (2nd edition 1969).

"It's Almost Just Like Home," 13 *Perspectives* 23 (Washington Department of Institutions, 1969).

Jewish Committee for Personal Service, Los Angeles, California, Self-Study (1967).

Johnson, "Report on an Innovation—State Work Release Program," 16 *Crime and Delinquency* 417 (1970).

———, "Work-Release—A Study of Correctional Reform," 13 *Crime and Delinquency* 521 (1967).

Joint Commission on Correctional Manpower and Training, *The Offender as a Correctional Manpower Resource* (1968).

Kehrberg, "Half-Way Houses: Good or Bad?," *American Journal of Correction* 22 (January–February 1968).

Keller and Alper, *Halfway Houses: Community Centered Corrections and Treatment* (1970).

Kirby, "Crofton House: An Experiment with a County Halfway House," 33 *Federal Probation* (March 1969).

Korn, "Correctional Innovation and the Dilemma of Change from Within," 10 *The Canadian Journal of Corrections* 449 (July 1968).

Krasner, "Hoodlum Priest and Respectable Convicts," *Harper's* magazine 57 (February 19, 1961).

Kuehn, "The Concept of Self-Help Groups Among Criminals," *Criminologica* 20 (May 1969).

Kvaraceus and Miller, *Delinquent Behavior: Culture and the Individual* (1959).

Law Enforcement Assistance Administration, First Annual Report (1969), Second Annual Report (1970).

MacPherson, "The Role of New Careerists," 23 *California Youth Authority Quarterly* (Fall 1970).

"Making Prison Training Work," 3 *Manpower Magazine* (January 1971).

Manpower Report of the President (1970).

McCollum, "Education and Training of Youthful Offenders," in *The Transition from School to Work, Manpower Symposium* 108 (Princeton University, May 9–10, 1968).

McMillan, "Work Furlough for the Jailed Prisoners," 29 *Federal Probation* 33 (March 1965).

Meiners, "A Halfway House for Parolees," 29 *Federal Probation* 47 (June 1965).

"*Michael Nicolson, et al. v. The Connecticut Halfway House, Inc.*," 27 *Connecticut Law Journal* (March 2, 1966).

Minton and Rice, "Using Racism at San Quentin," *Ramparts*, January 1970.

Monger, "Probation Hostels in Great Britain," 33 *Federal Probation* (September 1967).

Nishinaka, "A Part-Way Home Program," 19 *California Youth Authority Quarterly* 13 (Fall 1966).

Nye, *Family Relationship and Delinquent Behavior* (1958).

Nye, Short and Olson, "Socioeconomic Status and Delinquent Behavior," in *Middle-Class Juvenile Delinquency* 80 (1967).

Ohlin, *The Development of Opportunities for Youth* (1960).

Palmer, Community Treatment Project, Seventh Progress Report, Part 2: *Recent Research Findings and Long-Range Developments at the Community Treatment Project* 60–61 (CTP Research Report No. 9, Part 2, October 1968).

Pennsylvania Prison Society—Annual Report, 1969.

Pleck, Simon and Riley, *The Effectiveness of a Correctional Halfway House* (1969).

Powers, "Half-Way Houses: A Historical Perspective," *American Journal of Correction* 20 (July–August 1959).

Royal Oak Municipal Court Probation Department, *Concerned Citizens and a City Criminal Court* (1968).

Ryan and Silvern, eds., *Goals of Adult Basic Education in Corrections* (1970).

Sagarin, *Odd Man In* (1969).

Sands, *The Seventh Step* (1967).

Sard, "A Chance on the Outside," in 2 *American Education* (Department of Health, Education and Welfare 27, 1966).

Scherer, Ivan, *et al.*, "Probationer Diagnosis without Money—The Use of Professional and Non-Professional Volunteers in a Court Testing Program," Boulder County Juvenile Court, Boulder, Colorado, September 1968.

Shanley, Lefever and Rice, "The Aggressive Middle Class Delinquent," 57 *Journal of Criminal Law, Criminology and Police Science* 145 (1966).

Sigurdson, "Expanding the Role of the Nonprofessional," 15 *Crime and Delinquency* 420 (1969).

Southeastern Correctional and Criminological Research Center, Description of North Carolina Work Release Program and Pre-Release Program (1970).

Spivack, Allen and Plair, "A Comparison of Performance in the Community: Youth Center vs. Community Treatment Center Releasees" (District of Columbia Department of Corrections Research Report No. 29, November 1970).

Sternberg, "Synanon House—A Consideration of Its Implications for American Corrections," 54 *Journal of Criminal Law, Criminology and Police Science* 447 (1964).

Sultan and Ehmann, *The Employment of Persons with Arrest Records and the Ex-Offender* (1971).

"Symposium: Making Prison Training Work," 3 *Manpower* magazine, January 1971.

Tappan, *Crime, Justice and Correction* (1960).

Testimony before Subcommittee No. 3 of the House Committee on the Judiciary on H.R. 2175, 91st Congress, 2d Session, June 25, 1970.

Texas Department of Corrections, *Overview, Windham School District Program* (1970).

The Bureau of Rehabilitation of the National Capital Area, Report on Shaw Residence (1968).

"The Road Back," 1 *Manpower Magazine* (June 1969).

The San Francisco Rehabilitation Project for Offenders, Northern California Service League, San Francisco, California.

"Training in Prison" (U.S. Department of Labor Program Report No. 9, 1968).

United Nations, "The Role and Potential Value of Volunteers in Social Defense," *International Review of Criminal Policy*, No. 24 (1966).

U.S. Bureau of Prisons, *The Residential Center: Corrections in the Community* 11 (1968).

Vasoli and Fahey, "Halfway House for Reformatory Releasees," 16 *Crime and Delinquency* 292 (1970).

Vera Institute of Justice, The Manhattan Court Employment Project (1969).

Verin, "Work Release in France," 44 *Prison Journal* 28 (1964).

"Vocational Rehabilitation Services in a State Penitentiary System," Oklahoma Rehabilitation Service and Oklahoma State Penitentiary, 1967.

Waaben, "Work Release in Denmark," 44 *Prison Journal* 38 (1964).

Wallerstein and Wyle, "Our Law-Abiding Law-Breakers," *Probation* (April 1947).

Welty, *Look Up and Hope—The Life of Maud Ballington Booth* (1961).

Wiklund, "Work Release in Sweden," 44 *Prison Journal* 35 (1964).

Wisconsin Department of Public Welfare, Division of Corrections, Foster Home Report (1966).

Wright, "Poverty, Minorities and Respect for the Law," *Duke Law Journal* 425 (1970).

Yoder, "Wisconsin Throws Them Out of Jail," *Saturday Evening Post*, 25, February 4, 1956.

Index

[Page number in italics refer to footnotes.]

Williams v. Steele, 463
Williams v. United States Department
   of Justice, 428
Williams v. Wilkins, 380
Willis v. White, 372, 446
Willits, John M., 213–14
Wilson v. Girard, 84
Wilson v. Kelley, 368, 399, 507
   censorship of mail and, 408, 420,
      509, 510
   class actions and, 479, 483, 487
   forced labor and, 394, 395, 500
   racial discrimination and, 411, 412,
      413
Wilson v. State, 308
Wilwording v. Swenson, 454, 467, 471
Wines, Enoch, 40–41
Winston v. United States, 438
Wiretapping, 149
Wisconsin, 216, 493, 679
   Correctional Service of, 599
   Division of Correction of, 537
   halfway houses in, 566, 567, 586
   Juvenile Review Board of, 586
   parole services in, 264, 267
   State Board of Charities and Reform
      of, 528
   work release programs in, 528–29,
      537–38, 539
Witherspoon v. Illinois, 142
Women, 93, 553, 623, 647
   halfway houses for, 595
   prisons for, 47, 49–50, 589–90, 596,
      647
   sentencing of, 171, 172
   work release programs and, 528
Women's Prison Association (N.Y.),
   597
Work Release Act (District of Columbia), 568
Work release programs, 527–52, 566,
   588

administration of, 532–33, 536–37,
   541–43, 549
costs of, 541–42
earnings under, 541–42
federal system and, 533, 538, 539,
   543–44, 546–47, 549–50
furloughs and, 548–52
parole and, 527, 532, 549
Workhouses, 20
Workman v. Commonwealth, 197
World War I, 355
Wormwood Scrubs borstal center
   (London), 94–95
Wren v. Smith, 480
Wright v. McMann, 381–82, 425, 430,
   494, 505
   access to court and, 427, 436, 450
   Civil Rights Act and, 368, 423, 445,
      451
   court actions by prisoners and,
      454–56, 465, 469, 483
   cruel and unusual punishment and,
      380, 385, 386, 390, 449, 509,
      524
Wyatt v. Ropke, 153

YMCA, 564, 570, 577, 578
Yokefellow Prison Ministry, 598
York v. Story, 446
Young adults, 51, 93
Young v. Ragon, 169
Younger v. Gilmore, 369, 432
Youth Crime Control Project, 72, 569,
   579
Youth Development and Delinquency
   Prevention Administration, 57
Youth Services Bureau, 673
Yuma, Ariz., Marine facility, 81

Zink v. Lear, 327
Zwickler v. Koota, 454